Public Finance

ALDINE TREATISES IN MODERN ECONOMICS

edited by Harry G. Johnson
University of Chicago and
London School of Economics

Public Finance

CARL S. SHOUP

Columbia University

ALDINE PUBLISHING COMPANY
Chicago

First published 1969 by
Aldine Publishing Company
529 South Wabash Avenue
Chicago, Illinois 60605

Library of Congress Catalog Card Number 69–11227
Designed by Chestnut House
Printed in the United States of America

To the memory of
Robert Murray Haig
and
Edwin Robert Anderson Seligman

ACKNOWLEDGMENTS

I am indebted to many colleagues and students for their comments on earlier drafts of the present work, but particularly to John G. Head, Harry G. Johnson, and William S. Vickrey, whose careful and extensive examination of the manuscript resulted in substantial structural changes and alterations in analysis. A number of the chapters were discussed in two public finance seminars, at Columbia University and the Australian National University, by Marion Hamilton Gillim, C. Lowell Harriss, W. R. C. Jay, Russell Matthews, and G. Max Neutze, and by student members of these seminars. Responses to inquiries in particular areas were given generously by Douglas Dosser, Clive Edwards, Staffan B. Linder, Kelvin Lancaster, and Richard E. Slitor.

It remains to express my greatest indebtedness, which is to Robert Murray Haig and Edwin Robert Anderson Seligman. Professors Haig and Seligman introduced me to the field of public finance and supplied the stimulation and the standards that are the prerequisites to any endeavor of this kind.

Foreword

THE PURPOSE of the Aldine Treatises in Modern Economics is to enable authorities in a particular field of economics to make their knowledge available to others in the form they find easiest and most convenient. Our intention is to free them from an insistence on complete coverage of a conventionally defined subject, which deters many leading economists from writing a book instead of a series of articles or induces them to suppress originality for the sake of orthodoxy, and from an obligation to produce a standard number of pages, which encourages the submergence of judgment of relevance in a pudding of irrelevant detail. The Aldine Treatises seek to encourage good economists to say what they want to say to their fellow economists, in as little or as much space as they consider necessary to the purpose.

The present volume treats of the economics of public finance. Its author, Carl S. Shoup, can be justly described as the dean of contemporary public finance experts; his breadth of knowledge and practical experience is unparalleled in a field in which these are the hallmarks of professional competence. Professor Shoup has served as a consultant in public finance problems at various levels of government in the United States and to a number of other countries' governments as well. Probably his most influential post was as director of the Shoup Tax Mission to Japan in 1949-50—a mission whose findings are still a standard source of information on Japanese public finance—but his influence in practical affairs has also been manifest in many other contexts. In addition to his contributions through public service, Professor Shoup has exercised a major influence on the development of academic public finance, through his own writings and through the students he has guided in his seminar at Columbia University.

This book ranges over the whole field of public finance and reflects the author's practical experience in developed and developing countries alike. In the hands of some, so much variety of problems and levels of analysis could well prove impossible to marshal within a coherent and comprehensible framework of exposition. But Professor Shoup has succeeded in imposing a logical structure on his material, a structure derived from his own conception of the scope and content of the field and his deep understanding of the social criteria commonly applied in evaluating problems of governmental expenditure and the taxation required to finance it. As a result, he is able to lead the reader into detailed analysis—for example, of the optimal allocation of expenditures on police protection—without losing sight of the principles that should govern grander problems such as the desirable distribution of disposable income.

One of the many features of this treatise that has intrigued me, as an editor not himself a specialist in this field, is indeed the emphasis that Professor Shoup has given to the analysis of government outlays and the criteria that should be applied to them, in contrast to the analysis of taxes—usually of more direct interest to the non-specialist and the citizen at large—and of the macro-economic aspects of public finance. Another is the extent to which, in his treatment of taxation, he has been able to draw on his knowledge of European tax systems to broaden his analysis both in theoretical and in practical terms. Still another is his illuminating treatment of the problems posed for macro public finance by the existence of different levels of government, and the resulting difficulty of coordinating their fiscal policies.

This treatise, which brings together the fruits of Professor Shoup's lifetime of academic and consulting work, represents despite its bulk a severe distillation of the vast knowledge of its author. It will be useful as a guide for students interested in grasping the outlines of the field of public finance, as a cross-section of economic analysis as a whole. In addition it will especially be useful as a reference volume for academics and officials concerned with the contemporary state of knowledge with respect to public expenditure, taxation, and the use of fiscal measures in the pursuit of macro-economic policy objectives.

HARRY G. JOHNSON

Contents

List of Figures

List of Tables

BOOK ONE
Public Finance Analysis

CHAPTER ONE

Public Finance: Scope and Effects

A. NATURE AND SCOPE OF PUBLIC FINANCE

1. Public Finance and Market Finance

THE DISCIPLINE OF public finance describes and analyzes government services, subsidies, and welfare payments, and the methods by which the expenditures to these ends are covered through taxation, borrowing, foreign aid, and the creation of new money.

Public finance deals with a resource-allocating system that makes little use of the pricing mechanism, though considerable use of money. But not even money is employed in one branch of public finance: the free supply of government services (police protection, for example, or public health). And money, but no pricing, is involved in the distribution of subsidies and welfare payments. The government covers the cost of these activities chiefly by exactions (taxes) the severity of which for any one household or business firm generally depends little if at all on the amount of service, subsidy, or welfare payment that the household or firm receives. Consequently, users and recipients cannot signal their preference for a service by bidding up its price and the rationing of a certain total amount of the service among potential users has to be accomplished by some means other than pricing. On the other hand, both money and pricing are utilized when the government engages labor or other factor services or purchases goods and services produced by firms.

The governmental services rendered to households and firms influence their economic activity, and may be appraised by the same criteria of equity, efficiency, and the like that have been so intensively applied to revenue measures. The present work includes some description and analysis of these aspects of government expenditure, since, in the view taken here, the flow of government services is as much a part of public finance as are the revenue measures or the purchase of goods and services by means of which the governmental services are rendered.[1]

1. Perhaps the term public finance should be replaced by public economics (cf. Leif Johansen, *Public Economics* [Chicago: Rand McNally, 1965]), but the simpler course is to retain the familiar name with the understanding that it goes beyond finance proper.

The government is not the only body that operates with money yet without appeal to market prices (except in purchasing factor services and goods). The family and the nonprofit institution are the other chief examples. It is instructive to inquire how the government's non-price–allocating system differs from that of the family or of the church, charitable organization, or foundation.

The government's system operates with the aid of a legal power of compulsion. But in many countries one or more members of a family or of a religious or charitable organization have possessed or still do possess legal powers of compulsion over other members. The chief difference between the government's allocating system and that of the family, church, or other nonprofit institution lies in the degree of impersonality of the rules under which the government distributes its services and allocates the burden of covering the costs. Impersonality means that (1) a given set of rules, for example, a tax law, is decreed to be equally applicable to everyone in a specified subgroup, usually a large subgroup, all firms selling at retail, for example, and (2) the rules are backed by sanctions, usually fines or prison sentences, equally applicable to all violators of the law, whoever they may be. In contrast to this regime, the family distributes among its members the goods consumed in the household by informal and often fluctuating criteria, and ordinarily does not formalize its sanctions in impersonal terms. The nonprofit institution, also, does not usually operate by impersonal rules, whether in obtaining its funds or in distributing them. The degree of impersonality governing relations among adults or near-adults varies directly with the degree of difficulty that the individual faces in withdrawing from the group. Fluctuating favoritism and vague criteria may be bearable if one can always detach himself, sooner or later, from the group.

In its use of impersonal rules the government resembles the market more than it does the family or nonprofit institution. But since the government does not make use of the market's kind of impersonal rules, that is, prices, it must devise its own rules. Formulation of these rules assumes overwhelming importance in public finance. In taxation, the rules may reflect at one extreme certain concepts of distributive equity widely held in the community and at the other extreme, the political power of a minority to coerce the rest of the community.

Governments do sell some goods and services at prices set more or less to cover cost. They do so sometimes as an alternative to direct control of a natural monopoly in the hands of private enterprise, in order to assure that output is expanded beyond the level reached under the private profit motive. Sometimes they do so because the industry, monopolized or not, creates nonmarketable services, that is, services that the market cannot price. A postal system may tend to unify a nation by increasing the level of a shared, common culture, and may improve the cultural milieu by reducing illiteracy. The government, owning the enterprise, can then set selling prices that take into account these externalities. For the sale of goods and services at a price, public finance, as distinct from economics in general, has little to offer except through its analysis of nonmarketable goods in general. If a subsidy to private firms, instead of government ownership, is the tool employed to remedy the market imperfection, the public finance student has additional expertise to bring to bear, through his acquaintance with subsidy techniques in general. Or, the government may impose a tax that will induce either reduction or elimination of a private activity that produces a negative externality, a disservice, and that may also finance compensation to the injured parties. In any event, the presence of negative externalities will influence the choice by the government among alternative tax measures for general finance.

In still another instance the government creates a monopoly to obtain a large profit, in place of leaving the industry in competitive private hands and taxing it. Here, too, the reasoning that informs tax policy becomes relevant, and the government's action is an appropriate subject for public finance.

A nation's public finance is thus distinguishable from its market finance. This is so, even in a socialist economy, as in the Soviet Union, where the government produces and distributes most of the economy's output. In a socialist state the consumer pays a price for food but receives fire protection free of charge. The price of food may contain a tax element, through being set purposely well above cost, or it may reflect a subsidy. Yet in either instance, a core of cost pricing exists. The fire protection service, on the contrary, carries no element of pricing whatsoever.

We have seen that the government normally obtains the goods and factor services it uses by purchase in the market. Here, too, the government is engaging in market finance, and the discipline of public finance has little to say about this aspect of its activity. Even in a socialist economy the government purchases labor in the market. The store clerk and the fireman are both paid wages, although the clerk produces services that are sold by the socialist state for a price, while the firefighter's service is distributed free of charge. Exceptions to purchase of labor occur when the government requisitions it or accepts volunteers for the armed forces, jury duty, road work, school boards, civil defense, fire departments, and hospitals. These unpaid services have their family counterpart in home activities and, in nonprofit organizations, in services of volunteers.

In a private enterprise economy the government not only hires factor services but also purchases goods from private firms. On well-organized competitive markets such purchases offer nothing distinctive for the student of public finance. Often, however, the government is the sole purchaser, as in military procurement, or it deals with a monopolist, and the terms of the contract may be analogous in some respects to taxation. Renegotiation of a government contract after performance may assure elimination of excess profit; this procedure has been explicitly employed as a substitute for excess profits taxation.[2]

2. The distinctions drawn in this section are chiefly in economic terms. For differences between public and private groups based primarily on relative importance of wants satisfied, geographic universalism, and compulsion (or indissolubility), see E. R. A. Seligman, "The Social Theory of Fiscal Science," *Political Science Quarterly*, March and June, 1926, especially June, 1926, pp. 358 ff. See also Gerhard Colm, "Why Public Finance?" *National Tax Journal*, September, 1948, reprinted in his *Essays in Public Finance* (New York: Oxford University Press, 1955).

2. Public Finance and Resource Release

In buying products and labor the public finance sector competes with both private-sector buyers and government-owned enterprises. It must restrain demand from those sources if it is to obtain what it needs at going prices. It does so by taxing, or borrowing from, those rivals in demand, or it may spend newly created money, either freshly printed currency or new deposits that it causes the central bank to create by selling it government obligations, and in this way pull resources away from households, firms, and government enterprises by outbidding them at higher prices or inhibiting their spending through price controls and rationing.

Taxation, borrowing, and inflationary new-money finance are therefore designed to discourage consumption spending or investment spending, or both (in the socialist states, the group to be inhibited may in large part consist of government enterprises that buy on the market.) The commonly voiced objection to taxes, that they discourage investment or consumption, is thus misplaced. Any tax must deter spending on consumption or investment goods if it is to be a useful alternative to borrowing or new-money finance.

If a tax also impairs the supply of resources, that is another matter. A tax that induces persons to reduce their working hours compels the government to restrict by that much more the private sector's use of manpower, if the government's needs are to be met.

The market sector of the economy provides a convenient channel through which the taxing government can extract money. Taxes can be attached to some market operation, being stated as a percentage of sales, or purchases, of either goods or factors, or as so much per physical unit of the thing bought or sold. The particular form of statement employed fixes the pattern in which deprivation of resource use is spread over income groups, geographical groups, and other groups in the market sector. It is this deprivation that is the real sacrifice made by the private sector.

In new-money finance, where limitation on resource use by the private sector is accomplished by a continual rise in prices, the pattern of deprivation is more difficult to discern. This fact, we shall see, is one of the reasons why new-money finance is employed.

Borrowing usually induces a somewhat smaller decrease of private spending than does taxation. If it induces none at all, directly or indirectly, it forces no release of resources unless it causes an increase in prices and so is akin to new-money finance.

To deprive the market sector of resources and to obtain cash with which to buy factor services and goods, the government might combine direct control of resource use with creation of money. No rise in prices need result, in principle. Analysis of direct controls, however, lies outside the field of public finance as defined for the present work.

B. EFFECTS OF A PUBLIC FINANCE MEASURE

To state the effect of a public finance measure is to make a comparison between what is and what would have been if the measure had not been in force. Alternatively, it is a comparison between what is, without the public finance measure, and what would have been if the measure had been in force. Or, if some future period is specified, the comparison is between two forecasts. In any event, the comparison involves at least one hypothetical state of affairs that, being hypothetical, cannot be observed. No operational definitions can be used, although econometric techniques can sometimes extract information that is close to what might be observed if an experiment could be performed, all other things being truly kept unchanged. These formidable analytical difficulties are accompanied by a conceptual problem, that of stating precisely the question that is to be answered, including, especially, a specification of just what other things are presumed to be held constant, or what alternative measures are used as the basis of comparison.

1. Taxes

A. QUANTITATIVE ESTIMATES

The problem is most difficult when the answer is to be cast in quantitative terms rather than as a statement of tendencies or direction of change. A common quantitative question is: To what extent is a certain tax shifted, if at all, forward in product prices or backward in reduction of factor payments?

If the tax is limited to a particular commodity, say cigarettes, the answer is usually given in terms only of (1) the change in the price of the taxed commodity, (2) the movement along the schedule of marginal cost, ex-tax, of producing and marketing the commodity, and (3) the change in the number of units of the commodity sold. Under three conditions to be specified below, this information, which can be obtained by partial equilibrium analysis, is sufficient to gain a useful answer to the question, Who bears the tax?

(1) Broad-based Taxes

If the tax is a broad-based one, a general sales tax or an income tax, for example, those conditions are not met. Let us consider the introduction of a value-added tax. Since this tax is imposed on a quantity (value added) that the business firms are not attempting to maximize, they must increase selling prices or reduce factor prices, or, in an atomistically competitive environment, plan to go out of business. Some of them will be stopped short of this, or will reenter the industry, when product prices rise or factor prices decline as production is cut back. But by how much do product prices rise, and by how much do factor payments fall, and for which products, and which factors? At this point the analysis collapses. The demand and cost functions employed in partial equilibrium analysis are of no use here. They are specified on the assumption that either prices in all other sectors or cost functions in all other sectors are unchanged. But there is little point to studying price changes under a tax in Sector A, say the wholesale wheat market, on the assumption that all other prices or cost functions are unchanged, then studying price changes under the same tax in Section B, say the retail shoe market, on the same assumptions, and so on, and then adding the results.

It might be thought that shifting and incidence analysis for an increase in the rate of a large tax could be carried at least one or two steps under an assumption that the revenue was being accumulated in the government's cash balance at the central bank, thus allowing a first round of deflation to occur.[3] This analytical fragment would then be placed on the shelf, together with others of like nature (decrease of income tax, increase in police service, and so on), so that the policymaker could take any two or more fragments of analysis that gave offsetting income effects and fit them together to get a real-life answer to real-life shifting and incidence. This procedure seems, however, quite impracticable. The stopping place for the one analysis cannot be specified clearly enough for later mating with a similar fragment having the opposite income effect, in a quantitative type of conjecture. And if it could be, there are still no income or price elasticities to guide the analysis other than the partial equilibrium elasticities, which are useless in appraising a broad economic change.

If only one of the price effects of a tax is the subject of study, instead of the entire bundle, it is sometimes possible to obtain a real-life answer even for a broad-based, substantial-rate tax while abstracting from the use made of the tax revenue, and all other price effects. If a profits tax is levied on one large sector of the economy and not on the other, and if the two sectors differ only in this respect, the price of capital, hitherto uniform over the entire economy, will henceforth differ between the two sectors (cum tax) by exactly the amount of the tax, whatever the use made of the revenue short of reducing some other tax on profits. Mobility of capital between sectors is, of course, assumed.[4] If the only question posed is, what will be the difference in rate of profits before subtracting tax, and if the question does not touch on whether the price of capital in the untaxed area rises or falls, nothing need be said about the use made of the tax revenue.

---

3. Something like this seems to be implied in Bent Hansen's statement of "what it means to let isolated parameter changes serve as a starting point for incidence theory. . . ." See his *The Economic Theory of Fiscal Policy*, trans. by P. E. Burke (London: Allen and Unwin, 1958), pp. 99–100.

4. See Arnold C. Harberger, "The Incidence of the Corporation Income Tax," *Journal of Political Economy* (June, 1962), 70: 218.

(2) Narrowly Based Taxes

With respect to a narrowly based commodity tax, the three conditions that must be satisfied if the incidence of such a tax is to be ascertained are as follows.

1. The consequent increase in factor supply to untaxed industries must not be large enough to depress appreciably the factor supply schedules in those industries. The increase will reflect migration of factors from the taxed industry owing to the substitution effect of the tax, and, possibly, an increase in total factor supply caused by the reduction in factor income.

2. Demand schedules for products of non-taxed industries must not be altered appreciably by the substitution and income effects on consumers exerted by the change in the price of the taxed industry's product. The substitution effect shifts those demand schedules up (or down, if the non-taxed commodity is complementary in consumption), and the income effect depresses them.

3. The tax revenue must be used in a manner that does not appreciably affect the supply or demand schedules for the product of the taxed industry, or of any untaxed industry that is closely rival or complementary in supply or demand.

The first of these conditions implies some mixture of the following: a low tax · rate and either (a) no substantial second-best specialization of these factors to any untaxed industry that would make the supply of the factors to the taxed industry very elastic so that a large proportion of them would migrate when factor rewards in that industry declined slightly, or (b) a low ratio of resources used in the taxed industry to resources used in the untaxed areas to which the factors could repair.

The second condition implies a low tax rate, and either (a) no single or small number of untaxed substitutes to which demand will be diverted, or (b) a small proportion of the household budget devoted to the taxed commodity.

The third condition implies both a small amount of tax revenue relative to national income and an absence of earmarking of a kind that affects demand or supply schedules of the taxed industry.

Under these conditions the analysis can be confined to the taxed commodity without yielding results appreciably incomplete or incorrect. If conditions 1 or 2 fail with respect to only one or a few untaxed industries, partial equilibrium analysis can be preserved by extending it to take into account prices and quantities in those industries. If they fail with respect to a wide range of industries, only general equilibrium analysis, or some rough approximation to it, will give a meaningful answer. If condition 3 fails because the revenue is earmarked in a way that affects supply or demand functions of the taxed industry, partial equilibrium analysis can be extended to take account of the use made of the revenue; it is still partial equilibrium analysis, since it remains concentrated on one or a few sectors of the economy. If condition 3 fails because the tax revenue is so large relative to the aggregate output of the economy that no conceivable use of it can avoid affecting substantially the demand and supply schedules of the taxed commodity, conditions 1 and 2 probably fail also. In either event, general equilibrium analysis is required.

A low-rate cigarette tax, or a small change in the rate of the tax, meets all three conditions. A heavy tax on retail tobacco outlets may fail to meet condition 1 because factors in the taxed sector, particularly land and existing buildings, migrate to other uses where they depress product prices, while consumers continue to obtain cigarettes by, say, mail order. A heavy tax on manufacture of cigarettes may fail to meet condition 2 because of the substantial income effect on smokers that may induce them so to reduce the household's consumption of, say, milk that the price or amount of milk is seriously affected.[5] A tax on cigarettes earmarked for use in a health campaign against cigarettes fails to meet condition 3, since use of the tax proceeds raises the demand schedules for cigars and smoking tobacco and lowers those for cigarettes. An unearmarked general sales tax fails, for any one commodity, on all three counts, and for commodities in the aggregate it fails to meet condition 3, at least in a closed economy. In an open economy, partial equilibrium analysis may be employed even for a general sales tax or other broad-based tax in ascertaining the incidence on domestic as against foreign factors and consumers, since the rest of the world is assumed not subject to the particular tax change. Under these circumstances, a nation-wide general sales tax becomes a selective sales tax viewed from the world as a whole. But this incidence analysis cannot divide the domestic income groups as finely as can partial equilibrium analysis for a small tax in a closed economy. The only distinctions that can be drawn among domestic factors, and consumers, refer to their employment in, or consumption of products of, the export industries, the import-competing industries, and the remaining domestic industries.

A small change in the rate of a broad-based tax is not amenable to partial equilibrium analysis, just because it affects so large a part of the economy. A decrease of a value-added tax rate from, say, 20 per cent to 19 per cent is a slight change in percentage, but analysis of its effects cannot utilize the elasticities defined for partial equilibrium analysis.

On the other hand, the instantaneous rate of change in certain economic variables per unit change in the rate of a broad-based tax is meaningful in many instances. The value-added tax is neutral with respect to integration of business firms, in the sense that the rate of change in degree of vertical integration that is induced per unit change in the rate of the value-added tax is zero. The cascade type of turnover tax is unneutral in this respect; the rate of change in degree of vertical integration is positive (see page 222 below). Again, the rate at which selling price must be increased per unit increase in a corporation income tax rate to recoup the tax increment in higher profits is higher, the higher is the initial income tax rate (since an already high tax rate consumes most of the additional pre-tax profit gained by raising selling price). Such a statement is technically useful even though it says nothing about whether prices can in fact be increased and hence nothing about the degree of forward shifting, a quantity that can be ascertained only under general equilibrium analysis. Rates of change need not be misleading in this context if they are not used to multiply an increment of some variable to obtain an increment in another variable, under invalid *ceteris paribus* assumptions.

5. For example, the British tobacco tax, which yields more than the British purchase tax (see Chapter 10).

(3) Tax Burden Tables

Tabulations purporting to show the distribution of the burden of a total tax system by income classes, under certain assumptions about shifting and incidence, are useful only as two or more such tabulations are compared, to show changes in the distribution of the burden when taxes are changed. Only the changes in burden distribution can be conjectured. The distribution of total burden under any one tax system is an invalid concept; it assumes what is either untrue or meaningless, namely, that the existing distribution of income-before-tax would remain unaltered if the tax system did not exist. Fortunately, this restriction on the use of such tabulations is not serious for policy-makers, since they are usually interested only in the existing distribution of income-after-tax, that is, distribution of disposable income, and how it may be changed by changes in the tax system.

These points need emphasis in view of widespread implications or assertions that a single one of these "tax-burden" tables supplies information about distribution of the tax burden. As an illustration, let us consider a simple case in which the only tax in the economy is a uniform general sales tax. Let the total supply of each factor be perfectly inelastic (the point to be made is strengthened if total supplies are not perfectly inelastic). Let each household's saving be zero and net investment in each industry zero (again, the point is strengthened by the opposite assumption). A table is drawn up by assuming that the tax is shifted forward to consumers (the same objections, to be given below, would hold for a more complex assumption, say half of the tax shifted backward, half forward).

(1) Income class	(2) Aggregate income	(3) Aggregate consumption at market prices	(4) Aggregate tax on consumption	(5) Aggregate expenditure after tax	(6) Tax as percentage of income
$0 to $10,000	$1,000,000	$1,000,000	$100,000	$ 900,000	10%
Above $10,000	$3,000,000	$3,000,000	$300,000	$2,700,000	10%

What this kind of table does show is distribution of expenditure after tax, by income class, that is, distribution of real disposable income (ignoring the value of government services). What it does not show is what would happen if the sales tax were repealed, or what would be happening if the sales tax had never been imposed. That it does show this is nevertheless implied by the percentages in the last column, which appear to say that in the absence of the sales tax each income class would gain an equal percentage increment in disposable income. In fact, both repeal of the tax and the measure taken to reach a new equilibrium (e.g., reduction in government spending or increase in another tax) would cause shifts in demand functions throughout the economy that would only by coincidence result in $1,000,000 of aggregate income accruing to those who would now be in the $0 to $10,000 income class, and $3,000,000 of income accruing to those who would now be in the above $10,000 income class, to say nothing of the shifts of individuals among these classes. The difficulty lies in the facts that columns (2) and (3) depend in part on

(4) and that the new equilibrium cannot be specified without stipulating what is done to meet the revenue loss occasioned by repeal of the tax.[6]

B. QUALITATIVE ESTIMATES

If total-economy quantities are not sought, however, conjectures on the tendencies or direction of the effects of broad-based taxes are valid without specifying the other changes in the public finance system (see page 8 above). An example is an answer to the question, Does an income tax tend to increase or decrease risk-taking? To be sure, the other simultaneous changes in the public finance system (reduction of another tax, increase in government expenditure, reduction of government debt, or increase in government's cash balance) will probably affect risk-taking, and if a quantitative estimate is required of change in risk-taking in the entire economy, those other changes must be specified. But they may be abstracted from, if the question is limited to the effects of the income tax on the probability distribution of possible outcomes of a venture.

Similarly, most of the other effects of taxation that are relevant to the criteria for choice to be discussed in Chapter 2 can be analyzed in nonquantitative terms or as rates of change without specifying the other simultaneous alterations in the public finance system. But the effect on distribution of income and wealth, being inherently an economy-wide quantitative effect, cannot be so estimated. The only effect that can be described quantitatively is the total, net effect of all the simultaneous changes: the change of principal interest, say an increase in the corporation income tax rate, and the accompanying changes in the way of decreases in other tax rates, increases in government spending, decrease in government debt, or change in government's cash balance.

C. SPECIFICATION OF ACCOMPANYING CHANGES

Specification of these other, simultaneous changes is therefore an integral part of the analysis. Such specification may be at any one of three levels. First, stipulations are made as to what is done with the revenue raised by the tax increase, or how the revenue loss from a tax decrease is made good.

The tax revenue may be assumed to be spent on the same commodities and services that would have been purchased by the private sector if the tax had not

6. The meaning of these tax burden tables has been analyzed critically by Professor A. R. Prest, in his "Statistical Calculations of Tax Burdens," *Economica* (August, 1955), 22: 234–45. The conclusions expressed here differ from Prest's chiefly in emphasizing the possibility of comparing two alternative after-tax distributions (at least one of them hypothetical, of course) as of the same point in time and in casting doubt on the validity of even marginal-change comparisons for broad-based taxes. See especially *ibid.*, pp. 244–45. See also the observations by Bent Hansen, *op. cit.*, pp. 99–100, and A. R. Prest, *Public Finance in Theory and Practice*, 3d ed. (London: Weidenfeld and Nicolson, 1967), pp. 120–21. See also Chapter 23 below, page 577.

been levied.[7] This pattern of purchases will of course vary with the kind of tax imposed. If the use made of the purchases is ignored, that is, if the free government service rendered is not taken into account, the effects obtained are those of a tax and its associated pattern of government spending. The effects are not those of a particular tax alone, but of a particular tax and a particular pattern of expenditure of the tax money. In Musgrave's terminology the resulting change in distribution of disposable income is an instance of budget incidence. If the value of the free government service is to be included in households' disposable incomes in computing this distribution, the new distribution is the result of taxation, government expenditure, and free government service: a budget-and-service incidence.

The tax revenue may be assumed, instead, to be a replacement for an equal amount of revenue from some other tax. The resulting change in distribution of disposable income may be said to describe the "money differential incidence" of the tax substitution. But equal money yields from alternative taxes do not necessarily force the private sector to give up the same amount of resources, in the same pattern, and as a consequence this equal-yield stipulation may involve a change in the amount and pattern of resources used by the government.[8]

Second, it may be stipulated that the government continues to use the same amount and pattern of resources; the relevant changes in the rates of the two taxes are no longer equal-yield changes. The effect of the resource-equivalent changes on the distribution of real disposable income may be termed simply "differential incidence."[9] No techniques have been suggested, however, short of general equilibrium analysis, for ascertaining the increase in the rate of one tax, say a value-added tax, that will be the resource-equivalent of a stated decrease in the rate of some other tax, say a personal income tax.

At a third level of specification, it must be noted that the pattern and the total of resources used by the government cannot be kept unchanged when one tax is decreased and another increased, without affecting employment, and if employment is already at the level stipulated in the policy program, a third tax, and perhaps more, will have to be changed simultaneously. What, now, is the consequent change in the distribution of real disposable income a result of? It does not represent the differential incidence of the first two taxes, since three or more taxes have had to be changed. To illustrate, let us suppose that there are two factors, labor and capital, initially employed in certain amounts, by the private and the government sector, and that it is stipulated that no change in these initial levels of employment of the two factors is to occur as a consequence of changes in taxation. It is further stipulated that the government's use of the two factors is to remain unchanged. It follows that the private sector's use of each factor remains unchanged. The policy question at

---

7. See A. G. Harberger, *loc. cit.*, p. 218. This assumption is particularly convenient when it is further assumed, as by Harberger, that consumers always spend half their disposable income on product X and half on product Y. For demand functions of this type, see Friedman, *Price Theory* (Chicago: Aldine Publishing Company, 1962), pp. 39–43.

8. See R. A. Musgrave, *The Theory of Public Finance* (New York: McGraw-Hill, 1959), pp. 211–12.

9. As it is by Musgrave (*ibid.*).

issue is a change in the distribution of real disposable income. In order to make that distribution less unequal, a personal income tax is to be increased and a general sales tax is to be decreased. But, except in the unusual case where both taxes affect employment of the two factors in the same pattern, no new set of rates of these two taxes can reproduce the initial pattern of employment. A given increase in the personal income tax can be matched with a certain decrease in the sales tax that will keep labor employed as it was initially, but then the employment level of capital will change. In an interdependent system consisting of two goals, a certain level of employment of labor and a certain level of utilization of capital equipment, and only two tax instruments that can be changed in value, here a personal income tax and a sales tax, there is normally but one, unique, set of values, that is, one unique set of rates for the two taxes that will achieve both goals. If these goals were being achieved initially, the then existing set of tax rates is that unique set. To change the distribution of disposable income, which now enters as a third goal, while maintaining the initial values for the other two goals, requires a change, also, normally, in a third tax rate, say the corporation income tax rate. But the resulting change in disposable income is then clearly the result of a change in three tax rates, not two. Differential incidence becomes a many-dimensioned concept, when more than two goals are to be attained, or maintained. In this example, there can be no differential incidence of the personal income tax and the sales tax under the standard of unchanged resources used by government, unless a change in level of use of at least one of the resources in the private sector is to be permitted.

These matters will be discussed in some detail in Chapter 19. The point to be made here is that the inadequacy of the equal-yield standard for the differential-incidence concept is not remedied by resort to an equal-resource-absorption standard. They both suffer from abstracting from certain other goals that, in a general equilibrium system, cannot be abstracted from, without denying them status as goals. Only if there is but one goal to be attained, say level of employment of a single factor, or of all resources considered as composed of a homogeneous factor, can the values of two instruments only be varied (for some other purpose) while maintaining that goal. But so narrow a point of view, which is only a little less narrow than the point of view implied by the equal-yield standard, will usually not be of much interest.

To take a more complex case, if there are eight goals to be achieved, by the public finance system, eight public finance instruments will normally be required, with a unique set of eight rates or values. If the value for one of these goals is to be changed, as when the distribution of disposable income is to be made less unequal, while the values of each of the other seven goals are to be unchanged, the values of all eight of the public finance instruments must normally be changed. All eight are changed, just to alter one of the goal values (and to keep the other goal values unchanged). The new distribution of disposable income is necessarily the "incidence" of changes in eight public finance instruments.[10]

10. Bent Hansen (*op. cit.*, especially pp. 93–98) emphasizes the further difficulty that there will be an indefinite number of sets of instruments ("many different combinations of parameter changes," p. 94) available, so that the "incidence" concept is undefined until a par-

If this conceptual problem of the effects of "a" public finance instrument is so formidable, under this third level of specification, how has policy been able to go forward, and how has the analytical tradition of conjecturing the effects of "a" measure been accepted so widely for so long a time?

A possible answer is that the changes caused in the other goal values are usually negligible. If an increase in the income tax and a decrease in the sales tax (two instruments), intended to make the distribution of disposable real income less unequal while retaining the existing level of resource use by the government (two goals), had only a negligible effect on employment, price level, balance of payments, and rate of economic growth, it could be assumed that no other changes in the public finance system would be called for, and the differential incidence of these two taxes would be defined, approximately. This possibility is not to be ruled out, but neither can it be taken for granted as a certainty, with respect to all changes in broad-based taxes, expenditures, or other public finance instruments. The history of public finance analysis has been one of disregarding the other changes, but probably not so much on this kind of assumption as on a lack of understanding of the inter-dependence of the system of public finance instruments and goals. The habit of partial equilibrium analysis, strongly and validly entrenched in most of public finance analysis after J. S. Mill and before Keynes, that is, in the era of micro public finance, has been carried over all too easily but invalidly to describe and analyze a change that requires a state of mind, if not the actual engine, of general equilibrium analysis.

Still, it would seem very restrictive to eschew all attempt at conjecturing the distributive results of substituting one broad-based tax for another until the entire model had been worked out in each case. No harm is done if differential incidence is estimated in the usual way, provided the answer obtained is recognized as only a tentative answer, almost sure to be changed appreciably when other instrument values are changed in order to keep other goal values constant.[11]

2. Government Transfer Payments and Services

Subsidies and welfare payments, in contrast to taxes, can almost always be treated by partial equilibrium analysis with respect to their shifting and incidence. There are no broad-based subsidies, analogous to a general sales tax or an income tax; any one subsidy usually fulfills the three conditions laid down on pages 9 and 10 above. So too, usually, does any one type of welfare payment. The shifting and incidence of a broad-based negative income tax (see Chapter 6), however, cannot be analyzed as such, for the reasons just given with respect to broad-based (positive) taxes.

ticular set is selected. Hansen's interest at this point in his analysis is how to keep unchanged all the other "budget items which are endogenous variables in the model" (p. 94) rather than, as in the text above, how to keep all other goal values unchanged, but the problem is the same in the two cases. Subsequently, Hansen considers the case where an income tax is increased "while . . . other specified fiscal policy parameters are altered in such a way that both the budget-balance and employment [two goals] are kept unchanged" (*op. cit.*, p. 97).

11. See Appendix to this chapter.

Distribution of the benefits from free government services, taking account of possible relinquishing of benefits to others through market forces (see Chapter 4) can be estimated by partial equilibrium analysis if the question concerns only increments of decrements of the service. Some of these services, police or fire protection for example, use a total of resources so small relative to the economy's income that partial equilibrium analysis is useful even in establishing the incidence of the entire service rather than increments or decrements. Such an estimate is usually of little interest, however. Unlike a particular kind of tax which a society can dispense with altogether, a particular kind of free service can usually not be reduced to zero if the economy is to continue to function; police and fire protection are examples. The several free services are not good substitutes for each other to the degree that taxes are; a nation may preserve its general character without any general sales tax at all, but not without any police force at all.

The reference here is to free services supplied by government, not to government expenditures as such. Government expenditure of money for the purchase of factor services and of products from the private sector does not (with some important exceptions) differ in its effects from similar expenditures by the private sector. The amount of the expenditure must be specified, of course, if a large tax is being introduced; the net result of the tax and expenditure on the price level, employment, and so on, is then studied. But it is of limited interest to the public finance student whether the expenditure is on cement, string, bulldozers, or clothing. The nature of the service rendered as a result of these expenditures is indeed important, i.e., whether the cement, string, bulldozers or clothing are used to provide highway services or to collect garbage. Only when the government is a monopsonist, or when it concentrates its expenditure on a small sector or geographical area of the economy, does the public finance student have a particular interest in it.

Payments of social security benefits, assistance payments, and other expenditures not on goods and services must, on the contrary, be specified as to both amount and type. The expenditure itself is now the analogue of the free service that is dispensed following the purchase of goods and services by the government.

3. Summary

In summary: partial equilibrium analysis, which abstracts from the use made of the revenue, or similar immediate counterparts, and which abstracts also from the need to change the values of other instruments if other goal values are to be kept unchanged, is useful in estimating almost any of the effects of free distribution of a service, or of a subsidy or welfare payment, and is useful also in analyzing effects of revenue measures, except that quantitative estimates of shifting and incidence are not possible even conceptually unless certain conditions are met. These conditions are never satisfied by broad-based taxes. For them, a general equilibrium approach is the only valid one. The partial equilibrium analyses are given in Book Two below under the heading Micro Public Finance. This label of Book Two is not completely accurate, since the substitution of one large tax for another will also be studied, a measure that implies general equilibrium analysis, and conjectures will be offered on tentative differential incidence. But the contrast of the contents of Book Two with those of Book Three is consistent enough to justify the use of Micro Public Finance for the first and Macro Public Finance for the second.

APPENDIX TO CHAPTER ONE

Professor Musgrave, in his *Theory of Public Finance*, specifies either partial equilibrium analysis (chs. 11–14) or general equilibrium analysis (chs. 15 and 16). For the latter, he studies differential incidence. Those two chapters carefully avoid reference to the effects of "a" tax (except in passing, as on page 353, where Musgrave remarks that "A general proportional income tax may—and most likely will—result in a change in relative factor prices, depending upon differences in the elasticity of supply for various factors . . ."); they deal only in terms of substitution of one tax for another. "We must now examine what happens to the relative position of various groups in the economy as one tax is replaced by another of equal yield. In order to have a standard of comparison, let us assume that each of the alternative taxes is introduced as a replacement for a general and proportional income tax" (pp. 374–75). In Musgrave's preceding chapter an unnecessary step is inserted where it is said that "Since this is the first tax to be considered, . . . [a] point of reference must first be established, against which the differential incidence of other taxes can be measured. For this purpose, we shall examine the budget incidence that results if the government increases goods and services expenditures, financed by a general income tax" (p. 355). The difficulty of using any part of the partial equilibrium analysis in the general equilibrium setting is shown by the small amount of carryover of the conclusions from Chapters 11–14 to Chapters 15–16. The chief value of the analysis in Chapters 11–14 lies clearly in its application to policy measures that meet the three conditions given on page 9 above.

Professor Prest employs the differential approach even when dealing with non-quantitative statements of direction, but obtains information for a tax as a whole, rather than merely with respect to its difference from another tax, by comparing it with a hypothetical tax that is assumed to exert a zero amount of the effect under consideration. Thus, when discussing the effects of a certain tax on allocation of resources, he uses "a dummy tax which is conceived to be a tax of equal yield to that under consideration but without any effects on the allocation of resources." He points out that "This is an artificial standard of reference, as it is in principle impossible to test any actual tax scheme to see whether it fulfills these criteria" (*Public Finance in Theory and Practice*, 3d ed., 1967, p. 33; see also *ibid.*, pp. 81–82). Thus a diagram shows the effects of a direct tax on allocation of resources using three price lines: one that exists in the absence of a price-distorting tax, and the two that exist under a tax on one of the commodities and a tax on both (i.e., a tax on income) (*ibid.*, p. 35). The first of these lines seems not essential to the analysis. The optimal character of the general tax is demonstrable merely by noting that as its rate changes there is no change in the marginal rate of substitution of one of the commodities for the other (that is, the partial derivative of the marginal rate of substitution with respect to the rate of tax is zero). Or, as does Prest, we may compare a no-tax situation with one in which a tax is rebated to the payor in lump-sum fashion (*ibid.*, pp. 74–75). As to effect on distribution, Prest again compares the results under any one tax with those under "a distributionally neutral . . . tax" (*op. cit.*, p. 120), that is "another tax . . . which of itself does nothing to alter the size distribution of income [from what it would be if———?] within the private sector of the economy" (*idem*). He notes: "As with our previous reference standards, there is by definition no method of empirical investigation [or even introspection, it would appear] to find out what sort of tax would have the necessary properties, for it would be impossible to vary such a tax whilst holding all other Government transactions constant" (*idem*). He concludes, however, that, although "The concept of an equal-yield distributionally neutral tax is therefore fraught with difficulty" (*ibid.*, p. 121), the alternatives are "less satisfactory," that is, tracing the joint effects of an increase in tax and a change elsewhere in the system; in particular, "the alternative of simply exploring the *net* effects of raising one tax and lowering another [is not] as fruitful in this part of public finance as it is at other points" (*idem*). Prest continues, however, to the point where, "We are now able to make a straight comparison between direct and indirect taxes instead of relating them separately to a reference standard" (*ibid.*, p. 125). Prest's approach does not yield a statement of both the allocation effects and distributional effects of, say, an income tax. For allocation effects, the income tax is compared with a lump-sum tax. For distributional effects it is compared with a distributionally neutral tax. Perhaps the latter can be one of the infinite number of possible lump-sum taxes.

Prest has emphasized, in another connection, the invalidity of speaking of the effects of "taxation" when the substitution of one tax for another alters total yield and, consequently, the volume of cash or national debt ("The 'Economic Efficiency' of Taxation: A Note," *Economic Journal* [June, 1960] 70: 415–19). And his "The Budget and Interpersonal Distribution," in Institut International de Finances Publiques, *Congrès de Prague*, Sept., 1967 (Saarbrücken: Institut International de Finances Publiques, 1968), pp. 80–98, presents a rigorous and comprehensive analysis of the logical problems involved (including comments on R. A. Musgrave, "Estimating the Distribution of the Tax Burdens," in Colin Clark and G. Stuvel (Eds.), *Income Redistribution and the Statistical Foundations of Economic Policy* [London: Bowes & Bowes, 1964] and on recent United Kingdom investigations); this paper covers both tax and expenditure changes.

For a review of incidence concepts advanced by H. G. Brown, Due, Jenkins, Musgrave, Parravicini, and Rolph, see James M. Buchanan, "The Methodology of Incidence Theory," in his *Fiscal Theory and Political Economy* (Chapel Hill: University of North Carolina Press, 1960); Buchanan remarks on the use and misuse of the ceteris paribus technique:

We may legitimately throw into *ceteris paribus* those variables which are either entirely unaffected by the movement of the variable upon which our analysis acts, or if affected, vary to such slight degree that the assumption of constancy does not invalidate our conclusions. But it is illegitimate to assume as constant things which, by the very nature of our analytical operation, must vary. . . . One may select the other-tax reduction route. . . . Or the balanced-budget method may be used. Or, if one chooses, he may impose a tax change, change neither government expenditures nor other taxes, and trace through the full effects of the monetary deflation which results (pp. 142, 143).

The analysis in the present text follows Buchanan up to this point, but not in his statement: "There seems to be widespread agreement that the Brown–Rolph conclusions concerning the incidence of a completely general excise tax are correct . . . [since] resource owners are . . . made worse off relative to non-resource owners . . ." (p. 139). For reasons just given, there can be no incidence of "a" completely general excise tax (and nothing else).

There remains the problem, what to make of the econometric studies of a period of years in which corporate tax rates have changed. The view taken in the text of the present work clearly implies that if these studies reveal the effect of anything, it cannot be of the corporate tax rate changes alone. The corporate tax increases involved so much change in revenue, relative to gross national product, that there must have been appreciable effects on corporate sales and profits from the use made of the money, yet neither the Krzyzaniak–Musgrave study (Marian Krzyzaniak and Richard A. Musgrave, *The Shifting of the Corporation Income Tax* [Baltimore: Johns Hopkins Press, 1963]) nor the recent study by Robert J. Gordon ("The Incidence of the Corporation Income Tax in U.S. Manufacturing, 1925–62," *American Economic Review* [September, 1967], 57: 731–58) seem to have made adequate allowance for this problem. Under the view taken here, that the very concept of the incidence of a corporation income tax (or other broad-based tax) as such is invalid, these econometric studies necessarily reveal nothing about this nonexistent phenomenon. For a discussion and critique, especially of the econometric technique, of the Krzyzaniak–Musgrave study, see Richard E. Slitor, "Corporation Tax Incidence: Economic Adjustments to Differentials under a Two-Tier Tax Structure," and Richard Goode, "Rates of Return, Income Shares, and Corporate Tax Incidence," in Marian Krzyzaniak (Ed.), *Effects of Corporation Income Tax* (Detroit: Wayne State University Press, 1966). A brief but incisive critique is given by Alan Williams in his review of the Krzyzaniak–Musgrave volume in *Economica* (February, 1965), 32: 97–98. John G. Cragg, Arnold C. Harberger, and Peter Mieszkowski (in "Empirical Evidence of the Incidence of the Corporation Income Tax," *Journal of Political Economy* [December, 1967], 75: 811–21) find that when the Krzyzaniak–Musgrave procedure is corrected for what they consider obvious biases, it indicates that capital bears approximately 100 per cent of the burden of this tax; and they doubt that this procedure, even when thus corrected, can yield a valid inference concerning the incidence of the tax.[1]

1. The most comprehensive recent work on tax incidence is that by Horst Claus Recktenwald, *Steuerüberwalzungslehre*, 2d ed. (Berlin: Duncker & Humblot, 1966), which also supplies numerous references to the literature.

CHAPTER TWO

Criteria

CERTAIN CRITERIA are commonly appealed to in choosing among countless alternatives a particular pattern of government services and the means of financing. To be sure, policymakers do not balance all these criteria nicely and create an entire system by a single set of decisions. The process of choosing is historical and incremental; an existing pattern of taxes and government services will have been determined bit by bit over a long period of time. But the accretion is not haphazard; it is guided by general standards.

The present chapter describes the criteria currently appealed to in private-enterprise economies, as distinguished from socialist economies, e.g., the Soviet Union. Some of these criteria were formulated centuries ago.[1] Criteria that were once important but that are now held irrelevant are not covered here.[2]

Most of these criteria become macro-economic goals, in Book Three below. The remaining criteria, notably those having to do with some aspects of equity, are viewed rather as attributes that the community desires all public finance instruments to possess, rather than as goals to be achieved by the use of these instruments, along with non-public finance instruments, as the case may be.[3] Whether they are later viewed as goals or attributes, they are criteria, by which any particular public finance instrument, considered in isolation, may be appraised.

On some criteria the community will be found united, once the question at hand

1. A comparison of Adam Smith's canons of taxation (as given in *The Wealth of Nations*, not as commonly abridged) with the public finance criteria given in the present chapter will reveal both the enduring nature of the former and their incompleteness, even for taxation alone, in the light of modern conditions.

2. For example, a degree of personal application of the tax that allows it to be used to purchase political allegiance. To Louis XIV the *taille*, as a tax on personal wealth or income, seems to have met this criterion, but the salt tax (*gabelle*) could not. This may have been the reason why the monarch was willing to farm the salt tax to a syndicate of financiers, but did not farm the *taille*; discrimination by personal status (e.g., nobility, clergy) probably required close control by the king's own bureaucracy. Some tax criteria that were almost universally accepted but a few decades ago are now largely discarded, at least for national governments: stability of yield and neutrality, for example. For a listing and appraisal of such criteria, see Fritz Neumark, *Grundsätze der Besteuerung in Vergangenheit und Gegenwart* (Wiesbaden: Steiner, 1965), pp. 9–12.

3. See Chapter 19, Section A.

is well understood. These criteria raise no conflict-of-interest issues; they may be termed consensus criteria. Examples are reduction of uncertainty in taxation, and, considered by itself, achievement of full employment. Others generate sharp differences of opinion, since they call for making some persons worse off in order to benefit others; they are conflict-of-interests criteria. A conflict criterion therefore supplies a standard, a guide to policy, but one which is imposed against the wishes or judgment of some members of the community. Examples are a certain degree of progression in taxation and stability of the price level.[4]

Each set of criteria breaks down into two subgroups. One is concerned with equity, the other with allocation of resources ("efficiency," when no difference of opinion is involved).

An equity criterion might at first seem out of place in a consensus group, since equity in public finance has commonly been discussed in terms of distribution of burdens or benefits by income or wealth, a matter that obviously involves conflicts of interest. There are some criteria of equity, however, that command universal agreement, as will be demonstrated shortly.

The object of the present analysis is not to determine what should be done but to understand what is being done. Of course, recommendations will be offered where specified goals are being pursued with obviously inefficient or inequitable instruments.[5]

It will be found that several of the criteria are of more significance for understanding tax policy and new money finance than for understanding expenditure policy and that they need to be supplemented, and some of them suppressed, to understand borrowing policy. As already noted in Chapter 1, the several major sources of revenue are more or less good substitutes for one another with respect to the chief task involved, namely, raising money and reducing private-sector aggregate demand, while the several types of government service are not usually good substitutes for one another. Hence the choice among alternatives is a more sharply defined problem with respect to taxes, and other revenue measures, and the criteria now to be listed are correspondingly more important for taxes. This distinction should not be exaggerated, however. We shall see that within a particular government service alternative modes of supplying the service are to be judged by some of these criteria.

4. Criteria of a type that have been arrived at only after resolution of, or compromise over, sharp conflicts of interest seem to have been somewhat underemphasized in much of public finance literature, where it appears to be a common assumption that a certain course of action is inherently just, or at least is approved by the community in some general sense, e.g. progressivity in taxation. Among the exceptions, where some explicit analysis of conflicts of interest are to be found, are Roy Blough, *The Federal Taxing Process* (New York: Prentice-Hall, 1952), pp. 4–11, and Cesare Cosciani, *Istituzioni di scienza delle finanze* (3d ed.; Turin: Unione Tipografico—Editrice Torinese, 1961), chapter 3, "L'Economia finanziaria quale studio degli assetti coercitivi," which explores the compulsory aspects of public finance, comparing them with the contractual aspects (see also James M. Buchanan, *Fiscal Theory and Political Economy* [Chapel Hill: University of North Carolina Press, 1960], pp. 64–68, and *Public Finance in Democratic Process* [Chapel Hill: University of North Carolina Press, 1967], pp. 128–31). Recent studies in the theory of voting for taxes and expenditures, by Downs, and Buchanan and Tullock—a subject that is not covered in the present work—explicitly seek to understand conflicts of interest.

5. See Appendix to this chapter.

A. CONSENSUS CRITERIA

1. Equity Criteria

There is a generally accepted standard of equity, or fairness, with respect to public finance measures: equal treatment of those equally circumstanced. It is "a principle predominantly founded in analogy with equal treatment before the law."[6] A corollary is: almost equal treatment of those almost equally circumstanced. Only relevant circumstances are to be considered, of course, relevant by community consensus. If there is a conflict of opinion about the relevance of a particular circumstance, the issue falls in the group of conflict criteria to be discussed in Section B below.

It happens, however, that this consensus criterion is often not observed. Circumstances that are generally agreed to be irrelevant are allowed by law or regulations to affect the amount of tax due, or subsidy or welfare payment or free service received. Persons who are, it is generally agreed, equally circumstanced may then be treated unequally, and persons almost equally circumstanced may be treated quite differently.

How can this be, when a community consensus on the relevance of the circumstances is postulated? The answer lies partly in the fact that equal treatment of equals has several aspects, and they are not fully compatible; an attempt to provide equal treatment in one respect may lead to unequal treatment in another. It lies partly, too, in the fact that the community is not willing to devote as much effort to the drafting and administration of the public finance laws as would be necessary to achieve equal treatment under all these aspects. Finally, given a certain amount of money to spend, the fiscal administrator will commonly seek to maximize his performance in terms of revenue collected, or subsidy or welfare payment distributed, or free service rendered. This aim can conflict seriously with equal treatment of equals (see items 5 and 6 below).

A. THE SIX ASPECTS OF EQUAL TREATMENT

Equal treatment of those equally circumstanced, and almost equal treatment of those almost equally circumstanced, has six aspects: relevance, certainty, impersonality, continuity, uniformity of mispayment, and uniformity of cost of compliance.

1. There is the basic aspect, implicit in the consensus idea, that the circumstances selected, in ascertaining whether certain persons are equally circumstanced, must include only those that accord with the community's ideas on relevance. Due deliberation by the community is assumed. An example is supplied by the income tax treatment of imputed net rent of owner-occupied dwellings. Such rent is almost

---

6. Douglas Dosser, "Economic Analysis of Tax Harmonization," in Carl S. Shoup (Ed.), *Fiscal Harmonization in Common Markets* (New York: Columbia University Press, 1967), vol. 1, p. 20.

everywhere exempt from income taxation. Is the explanation for the exemption to be found in the fact merely that no money or other consideration changes hands during the year? If the community were asked to accept this fact as universally relevant for deciding that one person should be taxable and another exempt, under the income tax, it would not do so, and indeed has not done so.[7] Receipt of money or other consideration from another person is therefore not considered a general test for ascertaining whether two persons are equally circumstanced for purposes of liability to income tax. The widespread exemption of imputed net rent must evidently reflect some aim other than equal treatment, perhaps a subsidizing of home ownership, or equality of mispayment of tax (see Section 5 following).

2. The relevant circumstances must be defined broadly enough so that impersonality is preserved (see Chapter 1, Section A.1). This aspect of equal treatment is violated when the "group," the members of which are treated impersonally, reduces to one or a few persons or business firms. Impersonality is lost if laws and regulations are highly individualized. Although any one taxpayer will welcome favorable treatment in the law, he will still appreciate the value of impersonality as a general standard.

3. On the other hand, the relevant circumstances must be defined closely enough so that one knows in advance what will be the consequences with respect to the tax he will owe, or the subsidy, welfare payment or government service he will receive if he undertakes a specific course of action. This is Adam Smith's canon of certainty, and its economic and social importance can scarcely be overemphasized. Certainty is an aspect of equal treatment because it assures the individual that he will be treated equally in successive periods if the same bundle of relevant circumstances recurs. But if the law or regulations are not quite specific, disputes will arise as to whether the "same" bundle has recurred.

4. A small change in the relevant circumstances, quantitatively or qualitatively, must not lead to a large change in tax due, or subsidy, welfare payment or government service received.[8] There must be no gaps, jumps, or, in general, no discontinuities in the tax or other function. The second aspect of equal treatment, impersonality, implies this fourth aspect, which, however, deserves separate statement because it affects groups both large and small. Failure to observe this rule of continuity can, by the same token, be distinguished from adherence to the rule of certainty (the third aspect). Two examples of qualitative discontinuities under a sales tax will illustrate this point. If a sales tax law exempts the sale of processed foods, some dividing lines will have to be specified, in law or regulations, between what is deemed processing and what non-processing; handling, packaging, and transporting may, for example, be considered non-processing. But the lines, however drawn, will separate actions that common sense will view as being almost alike. Yet there may be no lack of certainty (third aspect), and the groups of persons involved may be large and the treatment impersonal (second aspect). A sales tax

---

7. Compare the homeowner with the owner of a shop who consumes some of the merchandise (Chapter 11, page 305).

8. See C. Lowell Harriss, "Sources of Injustice in Death Taxation," *National Tax Journal* (December, 1954), 7: 291.

imposed on the sale of tangible personal property can be avoided by substituting for a sale a contract of rental that comes to virtually the same thing but that is quite distinct legally, so that there is no uncertainty as to the tax consequences of a given course of action. Again, no specific individual or small group of individuals is given special treatment. Quantitative discontinuities, similarly, can occur without impairment of the second and third aspects of the equal-treatment criterion, as when small firms, say firms with a sales volume below a specified figure, are completely exempt from a sales tax, while larger firms are taxed in full on their total sales. A quantitative discontinuity is often easier to avoid than a qualitative discontinuity. In place of the type of exemption just noted, which may be termed a "disappearing" exemption because it disappears abruptly once a given point is reached (here, given level of sales), a "dwindling" exemption may be provided, that is, one that decreases gradually to zero over a range.

5. The degree of error in payment, whether the payment is to the government (taxes) or from it (welfare payment, subsidy) must in principle be the same for everyone making (or receiving) the payment. Granted that some degree of underpayment of tax, for example, is bound to occur, this criterion requires that everyone be underpaying his tax by the same percentage. Then, no one taxpayer is being treated unjustly relative to the other taxpayers (as to taxpayers as a group, relative to non-taxpayers, see page 26 below). If recipients of subsidies or of welfare payments are being overpaid, this criterion requires that all be overpaid by the same percentage. Underpayment of tax results not only from evasion, as when the taxpayer submits a falsified return or bribes the tax assessor or tax collector, but also from unintentional failure to observe the law because of ignorance, and from ineptness on the part of the tax official, as when he undervalues a parcel of real estate, without any pressure from the taxpayer. Underpayment, as understood here, does not include tax avoidance (these terms are defined in Chapter 17, Section B).

This criterion of equal percentages of underpayment of tax is intuitively most appealing with respect to a proportional tax. Under a progressive income tax, in contrast, it is not clear that everyone would agree that equal treatment was being dispensed if the taxpayer in the high surtax brackets and the taxpayer in the first bracket both underpaid by, say, 10 per cent; the very idea of progressivity might imply that the percentage of error should also be progressive, for equality of treatment. But as a rough formulation of the criterion, equal percentage of error seems useful. Certainly it has more appeal intuitively than equal absolute amount of underpayment. And some such criterion is needed in an imperfect world where general underpayment is in some countries, for some taxes, a commonplace.

This criterion might even be expanded to cover receipt of free government services, police protection for example, were it not that standards for what is the correct amount to be distributed to a certain subgroup under a given law are difficult to formulate (see Chapter 4).

The goal of an equal percentage of underpayment of tax among all taxpayers can usually be achieved only at the fiscal cost of failing to collect as much revenue from the tax as could otherwise be obtained, given the amount of administrative resources available. In practice, therefore, this criterion is rarely observed, even though in itself it probably qualifies as a consensus criterion.[9]

The official may collect more tax than is due, owing to misunderstanding, misguided zeal, gross carelessness, or perhaps more reprehensible attributes. This overpayment of taxes by some may be compared algebraically with underpayment by others, to measure degree of differential treatment. If A is taxed $200 more than he should be, and B $100 less than he should be, the absolute degree of inequality of treatment is the same as if B had been undertaxed by $300. The term "erroneous tax payment," or, briefly, "tax mispayment," may be used to include both underpayment and overpayment.

If all taxpayers under a certain tax pay exactly, say, 40 per cent less than the law clearly says they should pay, it might be argued that there is unequal treatment as between these taxpayers as a group and between all other citizens or residents as recipients of government services or as payers of other taxes (not thus uniformly evaded). This conclusion is of doubtful significance. It is by no means certain that, because one group, that is, all those subject to a certain tax, pay less than the law says they should, any other group has to pay more, or receive less in government services, than if the law were strictly enforced on the first group. If it were so enforced, the only result might be a proportionate lowering of the tax rate by legislative action. Uniform underassessment of properties by real estate tax assessors, in clear defiance of the law, is an illustration. In contrast, if an income tax law is widely evaded, the fact that it happens to be about equally evaded by all, say by 40 per cent, does not imply that the legislators would reduce the rates proportionately if the evasion were reduced to, say, a uniform 10 per cent. And if a subsidy to a certain industry is uniformly overpaid to all, in clear violation of law, a rectification of this error would not usually be followed by any increase in the rate of subsidy. Each case must be considered in the light of the community's attitude, but certainly in at least some instances evasion, even if uniform in degree, must be termed a failure to treat all members of the community equally in a very broad sense.

6. The cost to which the taxpayer is put in complying with the tax or other fiscal law must ideally be equal for all. Here, intuition suggests defining equal cost to mean an equal percentage of the tax itself. The same criterion applies to the cost to which a recipient is put in obtaining the welfare payment or the subsidy that is due him. This criterion seems never to be closely observed, however, even in a tax law or regulations, perhaps because of lack of data on the degree of inequality.

B. Measuring the Degree of Unequal Treatment

Choice among alternative public finance measures will be facilitated if they can be measured, or ranked, according to the degree to which they depart from the criterion of equal treatment of those equally circumstanced. Such a measure can be obtained by an adding of differences, or some similar calculation, in either of two dimensions: people, and money. Let there be three groups of persons, Group A, Group B, and

9. See Chapter 17.

Group C, all of whom are in fact equally circumstanced but are distinguished by the fact that all those in any one group are treated differently from all those in any one of the other groups. All those in A, however, are treated alike, all those in B alike, and all those in C alike. Let a change in the tax law, or in technique of tax administration, decrease the difference in amount of tax collected from each member of Group B compared with each member of Group A, but at the cost of widening the difference in tax between each member of Group B compared with each member of C. The principle that seems to be intuitively acceptable is that first explicitly formalized by Johnson and Mayer and later developed independently in somewhat different form by the Whites, namely, that a change in degree of inequity between two large groups of dollars or persons outweighs an opposite change between one of these large groups and a small group, or to say much the same thing in more technical terms, inequity is lessened if the relative degree of dispersion of differential treatment, weighted by the numbers and by the distances or the squares of the distances from a central value, is decreased.[10] The dispersion of course includes both underpayment and overpayment, as defined by some legal or normative criterion.

2. Economic Efficiency Criteria

The economic efficiency criteria that give rise to virtually no difference of opinion as to their desirability are full employment and a Pareto-optimum allocation of resources. Opinions will differ on the degree to which still other criteria are to be sacrificed, if need be, to achieve a given degree of approach to these two goals, but the goals themselves are generally accepted. Indeed, involuntary unemployment is itself a species of a Pareto non-optimal situation, but convenience in analysis suggests that it be treated separately.

A. Full Employment

Full employment is defined as a state of affairs in which each member of the labor force is being afforded employment, or self-employment, in an amount such that he is not willing to increase his hours of work at the prevailing real wage.

A complementary goal is full utilization of plant and equipment, defined as utilization up to the point where a further increase in output, through an increment in complementary factors, is obtainable only at an increase in average total cost. It is assumed here that, whatever opinions may be held as to the advisability of operating at a higher level of output, there will be no objection to operating up to this level.

10. See Shirley B. Johnson and Thomas Mayer, "An Extension of Sidgwick's Equity Principle," *Quarterly Journal of Economics* (August, 1962), 76: 454–63, and Melvin White and Anne White, "Horizontal Inequity in the Federal Income Tax Treatment of Homeowners and Tenants," *National Tax Journal* (September, 1965), 18: 225–39. For a summary of some aspects of the Johnson–Mayer techniques in terms of the Whites' illustrative case, and further comments on these articles, see Appendix to this chapter.

Utilization in the region of increasing total average cost is discussed in connection with price stability in Chapter 24.

The fact that full employment and full utilization cannot always, if indeed ever, be attained simultaneously will be taken into account in Chapter 22, in the context of a changing equilibrium level.

Full employment is a goal that commands almost universal support. Some employers, to be sure, prefer a certain amount of unemployment in the name of what they term labor discipline, but for most practical purposes involuntary unemployment is unanimously agreed to be undesirable.

Price stabilization, on the other hand, is primarily a distributional criterion (see Section B.2.D. below). Achievement of full employment and price stability are commonly lumped together in the discussion of fiscal policy objectives. This consolidation is convenient for many analytical problems, but it has the disadvantage of blurring the important social distinction between a consensus criterion (full employment) and a conflict criterion (price stability). Certain groups in the community gain by inflation while others lose. The difference between the two criteria becomes sharply evident when employment is so high that a further approach to full employment through fiscal policy is seen to be obtainable only by allowing prices to rise.[11] In that event, those who are firmly employed, with interests in pension funds that are being invested in fixed-income securities, are likely to oppose further efforts to reduce unemployment through fiscal policy.

A government service is especially suited to implement a full employment policy if (1) the level of output can be varied to accord with the state of the labor market, without appreciable inconvenience to the users of the service, or (2) the level of inputs can be varied without simultaneously varying the level of output. Education is not suitable under point (1), but it may be partly suitable under point (2), if construction of schools can be timed in part to take up slack in the construction industry without disturbing the planned flow of the service, education. That flow is a function of the rate of use of school buildings once constructed, not of the construction itself. In practice, it will be seen (Chapters 5 and 22) that the community's demand for a regular flow of output makes even procedure (2) difficult.

The suitability of a tax for a full employment policy depends largely on the reaction of taxpayers to anticipated changes in rates and to the efficiency of the tax's built-in flexibility. (Chapters 8–16 and 22). Transfer payments differ among themselves, from this point of view, chiefly in their built-in flexibility, which indeed is for some, perverse (subsidies, as against welfare payments). (Chapters 7 and 22).

B. ABSENCE OF EXCESS BURDEN

(1) Taxes and Subsidies

If a tax system or a subsidy system can be altered in a manner such that the same amount of revenue can be received, or dispensed, while making some persons

---

11. Given certain constraints on the public finance instruments (see Chapter 19).

better off without making anyone worse off, an excess burden exists, which can be removed or reduced by such an alteration. It is an excess burden because the total burden on the taxpayers exceeds the amount of the tax revenue, or because, for a subsidy, the benefit conferred is exceeded by the cost.

Excess burden arises when a tax or subsidy creates a divergence among rates of substitution, either in production or consumption, or between production and consumption.[12] The producer, or consumer, is pressured by the substitution effects of the tax into using what are for him inferior production techniques or inferior patterns of consumption (out of a given disposable income), merely in an attempt to minimize his tax bill. A lump sum tax, a poll tax for example, that offers no chance for tax minimization will create no excess burden, no burden in excess of the tax revenue itself. A perfectly general income tax at a proportional rate that taxed leisure as well as money income would also offer no chance to the taxpayer to reduce his tax bill by changing his production or consumption patterns. Of course, the taxpayers do not succeed in minimizing their aggregate tax bill after all, under the taxes that cause excess burden; the government simply sets the tax rates high enough to yield the desired revenue, given the estimated attempts at minimization.

Policy makers have given little attention to excess burden. This indifference is due partly to unfamiliarity with the concept, but it also reflects the evident technical difficulty of designing a public finance system that will avoid tax-minimizing pressures at the margin of activity, while achieving all the other aims, especially the aims concerning distribution of disposable income and wealth. It is these pressures at the margin that create excess burden.

Moreover, reduction of tax-minimizing pressure at some one point in a generally imperfect economic system may so worsen the allocation of resources elsewhere in the system that the net result is a loss in welfare.[13] In practice, any economic system exhibits many divergences between price and marginal social cost, most of them not traceable to the public finance system. Reduction of a tax on Commodity A may expand its output closer to an optimum at the expense of drawing factors of production away from another commodity, B, that is still further from its optimum (perhaps because of a heavy tax on it), with the possible net result that the decrease in welfare from the reduction in output of B will exceed the increase in welfare

12. For a comprehensive statement of the types of tax that are compatible with each of successively more rigorous conditions for utopian efficiency (conditions for optimum trade, maximization of production, optimization of production, and optimization of effort), see J. E. Meade, *Trade and Welfare* (London: Oxford University Press, 1955), Chapter 4. For a diagrammatical analysis in terms of rates of substitution, and for references to the literature on excess burden, see Richard A. Musgrave, *The Theory of Public Finance* (*op. cit.*), pp. 140–54. For an analysis in terms of consumer surplus and producer surplus, see Harold Hotelling, "The General Welfare in Relation to Problems of Taxation and of Railway and Utility Rates," *Econometrica* (July, 1938), 6: 242–69, reprinted in Richard A. Musgrave and Carl S. Shoup (Eds.), *Readings in the Economics of Taxation* (Homewood, Ill.: Irwin, 1959), pp. 139–70.

13. See Earl R. Rolph and George F. Break, "The Welfare Aspects of Excise Taxes," *Journal of Political Economy* (February, 1949), 57: 46–54, reprinted in Richard A. Musgrave and Carl S. Shoup (Eds.), *Readings in the Economics of Taxation* (Homewood, Ill.: Irwin, 1959), pp. 110–22; Meade, *Trade and Welfare* (*op. cit.*), p. 8, and Chapter 7 ("The Marginal Conditions for the Second Best"); and Richard G. Lipsey and Kelvin Lancaster, "The General Theory of the Second Best," *Review of Economic Studies* (1956), 24 (1): 11–32.

from the increase in output of A.[14] In these circumstances, however, the chance of increasing welfare by reducing the tax, if any, on B and increasing the tax on A might appear great enough to warrant action, despite all the uncertainties in a second-best situation; an attitude of complete ignorance is perhaps not justified. Alternatively, a subsidy might be paid to the producers of B (if they were not taxed to begin with), perhaps financed with a tax on A, so that a small subsidy together with this tax would be enough to induce the desired reallocation of resources. If for other reasons (say, to stimulate employment) a large net subsidy element were desired, the subsidy to B could be made larger and the tax on A, smaller.[15]

Changes that are likely to reduce the excess burden more in one sector than they increase it in other sectors may be found among small-yield taxes that bear heavily on allocation of resources and that can be replaced by slight additions to broad-based taxes. An example might be a heavy tax on real estate transfers that could be replaced by a slight percentage increase in a general income tax. In addition, the structure of each broad-based tax commonly harbors a number of special provisions that amount to small discriminatory taxes or subsidies on one or another allocation of resources, and which can be reduced or eliminated without seriously impairing the observance of other criteria, and without much fear of adding to excess burdens elsewhere even in a second-best world. The percentage depletion provision in the United States federal income tax illustrates this point, in the eyes of those who find it unjustified on other grounds. But when a large-scale change in the public finance system is under consideration, computation of net gain or loss on excess burden account becomes more difficult.[16]

An excess burden arises when a tax induces a worker to accept a smaller amount of disposable real income than he would under a tax of equal amount that has no substitution effect. The discussion of this case is here merged with that presented

14. See Harry G. Johnson, "The Economic Theory of Customs Unions," *Pakistan Economic Journal* (March, 1960), reprinted in his *Money, Trade, and Economic Growth* (Cambridge, Mass.: Harvard University Press, 1962), pp. 49–52, for an analysis of the effects of replacing a tax on a particular commodity by a lump sum tax when other commodities remain taxed and the government is assumed either "to maintain tax rates unchanged, or to adjust the amount of lump sum taxation so as to maintain an unchanged total revenue" (*ibid.*, p. 49), and when the other commodities may be either substitutional or complementary to the one that is being untaxed.

15. See William J. Baumol, *Welfare Economics and the Theory of the State* (London: Bell and Sons, 1965), pp. 103–4. The suggestion in Alfred Marshall, *Principles of Economics* (8th ed.; London: Macmillan, 1920), pp. 467–70, that industries of decreasing return be taxed to subsidize industries of increasing return (both industries apparently assumed competitive) is now generally accepted to be an incorrect illustration of taxes and subsidies for externalities. What should be subsidized (second-best worries apart) is a competitive industry showing positive externalities, whether the industry's marginal cost, after allowing for these externalities, is increasing or decreasing; and a non-competitive decreasing-cost industry is a good candidate for a subsidy simply because it is likely to be monopolized. See Paul A. Samuelson, "The Monopolistic Competition Revolution," in Robert E. Kuenne (Ed.), *Monopolistic Competition Theory* (New York: Wiley, 1967), pp. 112–13.

16. But an approximation may still be feasible. See Arnold C. Harberger, "Taxation, Resource Allocation, and Welfare," in *The Role of Direct and Indirect Taxes in the Federal Revenue System*, Conference Report of the National Bureau of Economic Research and the Brookings Institution (Princeton, N.J.: Princeton University Press, 1964), pp. 25–75, and comments by E. Cary Brown and William Fellner, pp. 70–80.

below, under the conflict criteria, regarding the amount of labor to be supplied. The effect on supply of labor is probably small for any but a broad-based tax, say an income tax or a general sales tax, and for taxes such as these, only a differential analysis is valid. As with the problem of incidence, so too here, when a quantitative answer is required, differential results alone are meaningful. Since all of these broad-based taxes exert substantial substitution effects, the choice is one between second-best measures. In these circumstances the decision is likely to be guided by what the policy-maker considers to be the more desirable amount of labor, from the viewpoint of economic growth. On this issue, opinions will surely differ, if only because under one of these taxes certain persons will be induced to work more, and under the other tax, certain other persons.

But it may prove useful, for small taxes, to analyze the effects on the supply of labor in partial equilibrium terms, comparing the results under the tax with those under no tax. Or it may prove useful to move to the macro level in a rather unreal setting by comparing the results under the tax in question with those under a hypothetical, if quite impracticable, poll tax (see Chapter 11, Section B.3.B and Chapter 12, Section B.4.B).

The excess burden as discussed up to this point is reflected in a change in the consumption of a commodity or the use of a factor, owing to the substitution effect of the public finance measure, say a tax, as distinct from its income effect. The wedge between rates of substitution can be observed, with respect to the units of the good, or factor, that are still being consumed, or used, despite the tax. But when the tax is so high that it eliminates use completely, the excess burden may attract little attention, since no transactions remain in which the tax wedge can be observed.[17] This extreme case rarely occurs under taxation of commodities but is not uncommon under taxes on factors, or, more specifically, on methods of doing business or methods of production or marketing, or financing. Methods that are more costly apart from the tax are adopted, and no tax at all is paid. A striking illustration is the extra amount of vertical integration induced by a turnover tax, explained in Chapter 8 below. With respect to this extra amount, turnover tax disappears completely. Another example is the virtual disappearance of corporate financing by ordinary (not convertible) preferred stock, in a country where bond interest can be deducted in computing taxable corporate income, but dividends paid cannot be (see pages 312, 314 below).

A welfare payment creates no excess burden, aside from its influence on the supply of labor through its substitution effect, for reasons inherent in the definition of a welfare payment, as given on page 145 below.

(2) Government Services

Distribution of a service free of charge by the government depresses the rate of substitution in consumption below that of the rate of transformation in production, as does a subsidy. The free service is the extreme case where the rate of substitution in consumption is zero; the consumer of the service gives up nothing at all to obtain

17. For the special case of corner solutions under an excise tax, see Chapter 10, Appendix.

it. This statement abstracts from the tax or other measures used to finance the service, but even if they were considered, the statement would remain true from the viewpoint of the household or firm, for it receives the service whether or not it pays tax.[18] A free government service therefore involves excess burden; if the household receiving the service were given instead an equivalent sum of money, it would not normally spend all the money on that service. It would prefer a mixed incremental pattern of consumption: only a little of that free service and a little more of each of many other goods and services. This preference is inhibited; hence the excess burden.

This conclusion is of much less importance than the similar conclusion with respect to taxes, for two reasons. First, the equivalent cash grant to the household would not enable it to buy any of the service at all, not even the smaller amount it would prefer (while buying a bit more of many other things), if the service is of the nonmarketable type that is not sold: the services of the military establishment, for example, or the disease-prevention services of the public health service. The household does not have a choice between (1) a certain amount of free service S and (2) a sum of money with which it can buy a smaller amount of S and a little bit more of good A, good B, and so on. If the household is to obtain any of service S at all it must join with other households in agreeing on the amount of S to be supplied and the distribution of the bill (taxes) among themselves. This agreement is accomplished through the political process and can in principle be so patterned that no excess burden arises. This qualification to the excess burden argument is weakened in so far as the service will be supplied, although in a more costly manner, by the market if the government does not supply it (see the definition of a group-consumption good in Chapter 4). And it virtually disappears if the service could be marketed at about the same level of cost, as may be true, for example, of education, or refuse removal.

Second, a free service is commonly given because it benefits not only the direct recipient but also others, who benefit from his consumption of the service. This external effect, this positive externality, when added to the consumer's own direct benefit, may be deemed to create a package of benefit that is at least as large as would be the benefit accruing to the direct recipient alone if he were given a cash grant that he spent, as he presumably would, without regard for external effects on others. This second qualification to the excess burden argument is really but another version of the first, since the external effect is a type of service that, like military service or prevention of disease, cannot be marketed to individual purchasers.

A free service to a firm normally creates an excess burden in the technical sense; the factor-mix becomes different from that which the firm would utilize, for reasons of efficiency, if it were given the lump-sum equivalent of the cost of supplying the service and if it could purchase as much of the service, or as little, as it desired. Again, since in practice the service is commonly not marketable except at a higher cost, and often gives rise to externalities, the remarks above apply here also.

18. User taxes aside; see Chapter 21.

c. Conflicts Among the Consensus Criteria

The fact that the criteria just described are commonly accepted by everyone does not imply an absence of conflict, for, although there is no conflict among persons over the criteria, there may be conflict among the criteria themselves, in the sense that achievement of one may impede or prevent achievement of another, if the public finance instruments are too few in number, or are constrained.[19] A general sales tax may include an exemption for small shopkeepers (not small consumers) in order to obviate gross inequalities in compliance costs (criterion 1.A.6 above), although the exemption itself is recognized to be unjustified under the rationale of the tax. Violation of one of the consensus criteria through an attempt to observe another one more closely reflects the fact that the community is faced with a trade-off problem, and commonly sacrifices a bit of each of the consensus criteria in order to achieve an optimum combination.

B. CONFLICT CRITERIA

1. Equity Criteria

Five of the conflict-of-interests criteria are distributive criteria. They specify certain kinds of distribution of benefits or burdens among income classes or other groupings. These distributive criteria are assembled here under the subheading Equity, in deference to established usage, although it is equity of a kind that involves conflicts of interest.

Another seven conflict criteria stipulate certain types of resource reallocation that make some persons worse off. Those who are made worse off are not compensated, either because total product decreases, or, more generally, because the very purpose of the resource reallocation is to improve the lot of some persons in the aggregate by more than the increase, if any, in total product. Conflicts of interest are obviously involved.

The five distributive criteria that explain much of existing public finance systems are:

(*a*) Distribution of burdens progressively, and of benefits regressively, by income and wealth. For free government services, however, almost no criterion at all has been formulated by the community or even by public finance analysts (see Chapter 5).

(*b*) Distribution of these benefits and burdens among households of like income or wealth to take account of type of income, size and composition of family, including age and occupation (e.g., clergy) of members, and use of income.

(*c*) Distribution of burdens and benefits by geographic area, principally to export

19. See Chapter 19.

burdens to other countries to the degree feasible, and, within the country, to favor depressed regions.

(*d*) Distribution of benefits or burdens in a manner that does not discriminate against ethnic, color, or status groups. This criterion is commonly taken for granted, but deserves explicit statement in view of the extent to which such discrimination is practiced, at least covertly, in some communities.

(*e*) Distribution of tax burdens by methods that promote widespread tax consciousness (in some nations the negative of this criterion is the accepted one).

If any one of these five criteria is followed, a substantial minority will object; their criterion will be just the opposite. Each of these criteria reflects therefore but one side of an issue that generates conflicts of interests, sometimes an intense conflict.

The distribution that the equity criteria are concerned with is of benefits and burdens, not use or impact. If a household using a city park nearby must pay more rent for its house or apartment just because it is near the park, the benefit of the service yielded by the park accrues to the landlord while use of the service remains with the household-tenant. Distributive equity standards look to the beneficiary, whether that be the immediate user or someone else. Similarly, the benefits from subsidies and welfare payments must be traced if the equity criteria are to be useful. A tax burden may rest on others than those who feel the initial impact, through shifting of the tax. The concepts of shifting a burden, or passing-on of a benefit, and methods of measuring the degree of shifting or of passing-on are discussed in the several chapters dealing with free government services, unrequited government payments (subsidies and welfare payments), and taxes, including inflation (see also Chapter 1, Section B.2).

A. Distribution of Burdens Progressively, and of Benefits Regressively, by Income or Wealth

If the level of a free government service given to a household were proportional to the household's income, the rich would receive more of the service than the poor; if it were progressive with income, the rich would get still more.

A regressive distribution of the free service, which is the most favorable mode for the poor, would give to the rich a lower level, the same level, or a higher level of service per household than it would give to the poor, but in the third instance the difference in the level of service to the rich would be less than in proportion to the difference in incomes.

In fact, no general pattern for distribution of free services can be discerned, as the following chapters will indicate. Some services, certain types of medical care, for example, in certain countries, are distributed regressively, that is, in favor of the poor; others, fire protection being perhaps the best illustration, may be distributed proportionally or even progressively by income or wealth.

Each service differs markedly from the others in the type of want it satisfies. Since consumer tastes differ, regressive distribution of any particular government service has not been as forcefully insisted on as a progressive distribution of a tax. The lack of any immediate money tag that will indicate what the distribution really is no doubt accounts for part of this contrast with tax analysis. A contributing factor has been the tendency to emphasize the polar case of the completely indivisible service, national defense, for example, for which the question of distribution cannot arise.

Equal distribution of a service per head or per household, a criterion that is generally rejected for a tax, is implicitly accepted for some government services, and even this modest aim may be overruled by one of the conflict efficiency criteria to be described below, as in the distribution of police protection throughout a city (see Chapter 5, Section B.7).

Subsidies and welfare payments to households are commonly regressive with income or wealth, so much so in some instances as to impair incentives notably. The analogy with taxation is fairly close, but there is little in public finance literature dealing directly with this issue in general terms.

Free services as well as subsidies and welfare payments, when given to business firms, cannot be characterized in these terms until some conjectures are formed on the incidence of the benefits from the services and payments, just as with taxation (see Chapter 4, Section E).

A large body of analysis accumulated over the years describes and evaluates criteria for distribution of taxation by income or wealth classes. The conflict of interests among taxpayers is here direct, obvious, and seemingly measurable. Mediators have appeared from time to time in the persons of academic authorities who have attempted to supply distribution formulae that would satisfy themselves if not all the parties to the conflict. The most notable of these formulae are those of equal sacrifice, equal proportional sacrifice, and least aggregate sacrifice, each of them viewed in the light of their effects on incentives.[20]

As might have been expected, however, for an arena of conflict, none of these doctrines, or any other readily summarizable formula, has ever been accepted by policymakers. In any one instance, the degree of progression in a tax on income, or on wealth, or on transfer at death or by gift is only a compromise that reflects other features of the environment. The top marginal rates of 80 or 90 per cent that characterized income taxes in the major countries for many years were war-born measures that arose partly as a counterbalance to wage freezes, and excess profits taxes on corporations. But the compromise is likely to be more durable, the more the discussion has been informed by abstract analysis.

Even if everyone agreed that, say, equal proportional sacrifice were the proper rule, no guide to policy for progression for any one tax would result, since the rule applies to the tax system as a whole, excepting those taxes levied deliberately as quasi-prices to cover costs, as in highway finance. The degree of progressivity of an entire tax system, however, like that of a single broad-based tax, is conceptually

20. For an elegant analysis of these now familiar concepts, see F. Y. Edgeworth, "The Pure Theory of Taxation," in his *Papers Relating to Political Economy* (London: Macmillan, 1925, 3 vols.), Vol. 2, pp. 100–22, reprinted in R. A. Musgrave and A. T. Peacock (Eds.), *Classics in the Theory of Public Finance* (London: Macmillan, 1958), pp. 119–36 (Edgeworth's essay originally appeared in *Economic Journal*, 1897). (See also Chapter 25 below, page 627.)

valid only in a differential sense; one tax system is merely more or less progressive than another.

Inflationary finance, defined here as a pattern of government finance that is accompanied by a rise in prices, results in a distribution of real disposable income, by income and wealth classes, different from that that would obtain under enough additional taxation to stabilize the price level. We abstract here from those instances in which wage-price and similar spirals make it impossible to stabilize the price level because an increase in taxation is made the occasion for a further rise in pre-tax money incomes.

B. DISTRIBUTION THAT TAKES ACCOUNT OF TYPE OF INCOME, SIZE AND COMPOSITION OF FAMILY, AND USE OF INCOME

Taxes and subsidies, and also welfare payments, if not government services, are purposefully varied among households of equal income or wealth to take account of type of income, size and composition of family, and use made of income. Generalizations respecting this "horizontal equity" problem are so few and limited in scope that the issue is deferred to the analyses in Chapters 6–16 below.

C. GEOGRAPHICAL DISTRIBUTION IN FAVOR OF DEPRESSED AREAS OR THE HOME COUNTRY

One nation may succeed in exporting part of its domestically imposed taxes or of the burden of inflationary new-money finance to other nations, or may be forced by the market to bear part of another nation's taxes or inflation. The possibility of such transnational tax or inflation shifting is coming to be of more importance with the removal of internal barriers to trade within common markets, and as low-income countries seek more revenue for development, partly through inflation, multiple-exchange rates, and export and import taxes. Similarly, services rendered free to a country's nationals may spill over in benefit to other countries, as with certain military and public health outlays. The same issues arise for states or local units as against the rest of the nation of which they form a part.

Within a nation, or a state or locality, the tax-subsidy-service pattern will often differ by location. Sometimes the differences reflect merely a localization of a particular tax-service combination, as with mosquito eradication districts or school districts, but often the differences are not so supported, and may even be inadvertent: for example, a personal exemption uniform in dollars under a national income tax will be of more benefit in low cost-of-living areas.

D. DISTRIBUTION DISCRIMINATION AGAINST CERTAIN ETHNIC, COLOR, OR STATUS GROUPS

Ostensibly, race, ethnic group, or status are not made the basis for differential treatment in public finance; there are few instances of laws that have made such distinctions explicitly. The criterion here is that the government service or the transfer payment or the tax should not be readily usable for discrimination of this kind. In practice, many fiscal instruments lend themselves all too easily to such discrimination, as will be shown in Chapter 5 and following.

E. EXPLICIT DISTRIBUTION, CONCEALED DISTRIBUTION, ILLUSORY DISTRIBUTION

A conflict of interests arises in choice between methods of taxation that do, and those that do not, stimulate widespread tax consciousness, accurate or erroneous. Retail merchants have on occasion insisted that a retail sales tax be stated separately on sales slips in the hope that consumer awareness of the tax would inhibit the legislator from raising the rate and might even induce him to repeal the tax. Legislators who seek relief from consumer pressure on this score will vote for prohibiting separate statement of the tax. They will be sympathetic to proposals for government enterprises, say tobacco factories, retail liquor stores, or lotteries, the profits from which reflect a tax, not even the rate of which is made explicit (see Chapter 16).

Those who benefit from the expenditures of earmarked taxes, the users of highways, for example, may insist on separate statement of the tax at the retail level in the hope that this visibility will deter anyone from suggesting diversion of the tax revenue to general purposes of government.

Those who view an informed electorate as a valuable community resource will favor tax consciousness, but those who believe the electorate mistakenly opts for too few public goods may extol tax anesthesia. And those who prefer a concealed distribution include some who prefer that it be concealed from them too; a case in point is the legislator who votes for inflationary finance because neither he nor any one else (he supposes) can say where its burden rests (see Chapter 18).

Domestic borrowing by the government creates the so-called debt illusion, which is really a tax illusion, that is, a failure to appreciate that the present value of future taxes to service the debt is as large as would be a current tax levied in lieu of borrowing (see Chapter 18). Extinction of a domestically held debt gives rise to the illusion of a tax burden.

Distribution of benefits must usually be in an easily recognizable pattern, to enlist support, not distributed so that no one is aware of them, or in a manner generally unascertainable.

As the debt redemption case illustrates, tax awareness may itself be illusory, either because no true net burden exists, since the tax merely replaces some other potential tax, or because the person who is believed to bear the tax does not do so. Similarly, with respect to subsidies, welfare payments, or free services, there may be illusion as to distribution of the benefits (see Chapter 4). Fiscal illusion thus consists either in failure to realize that a burden or benefit does (or does not) exist, or in evident misapprehension as to its incidence.[21]

21. For an exhaustive treatment of fiscal illusion, see Amilcare Puviani, *Die Illusionen in der öffentlichen Finanzwirtschaft* (Berlin: Duncker and Humblot, 1960), translated by Marianne

2. Reallocation Criteria

Seven criteria commonly have to do with reallocation of resources, either within the private sector, as with the first six criteria below, or within the public sector, as with the last one. These reallocations of resources are intended to achieve certain economic objectives other than redistribution of disposable income, but, like redistribution, they reflect conflicts of economic interests, not a unanimously agreed upon movement to a Pareto optimum. They concern (a) rate of economic growth, (b) supply of labor, (c) degree of risk-taking, (d) price stability, (e) maintenance of an exchange rate, (f) public-purpose outlays by the private sector, and (g) intergovernmental and intragovernmental coordination

Although conflict among criteria is not inherent, in practice trade-offs must be accepted because of constraints on public finance instruments, or inadequate information on the working of the economic system.[22] The intricate dilemmas posed by these interlocking paths toward diverse goals explain much of what at first sight appears inconsistent or even downright absurd in public finance policy. An enthusiastic advocate of economic growth may also want his tax proposal to favor the poor and to avoid all excess burden; he ends with a compromise that is inexplicable by any one of these goals alone. To be sure, conflicts among criteria occasionally afford a solace: a public finance measure judged harshly by one of the criteria may be partly redeemed in terms of another. An illustration is the percentage depletion provision for natural-resource industries in the income tax law of the United States. This provision may displease its critics mightily because of its gross distributive injustice or because it creates a grave excess burden by inducing substantial misallocation of resources, but the more it can be condemned on the one score the less it can be condemned on the other. The greater the volume of resources drawn into, say, the petroleum industry by the depletion provisions, the lower is the price of petroleum and the fewer are the fortunes attributable to those provisions. A tobacco tax supplies another illustration. The lower the marginal rate of substitution of tobacco for other things, the more heavily does the income effect of the tax bear on a particular group in a pattern difficult to justify under any of the generally accepted distributive criteria, yet the smaller is the excess burden of the tax: its incidence may be deplorable but its allocative distortion (substitution effect) is then minor.[23]

A. Rate of Economic Growth

The rate at which income per head will grow under full employment can be increased by public finance measures that restrain certain types of consumption, thus

Hartmann and Felix Rexhausen from the Italian, *Teoria dell'illusione finanziaria* (Milan: Sandron, 1903). See also the summary of Puviani's book, and references to others, especially Günter Schmölders, in James Buchanan, *Public Finance in Democratic Process* (Chapel Hill, N.C.: University of North Carolina Press, 1967), Chapter 10.

22. See Chapter 19.   23. See Chapter 10.

freeing resources for investment in the broadest sense, including education, medical care, and improvements in the pattern and level of nutrition for children and working-age adults that increase their productive capacity, present or future, by more than the cost of these improvements (all discounted to a given date). Some of those whose consumption is restricted for this purpose will object, not agreeing that the present sacrifice is worth the gain, present and future, even if that gain materializes in time to be enjoyed by them rather than only by a future generation. No consensus can be reached on the rate of growth to be achieved by government action; hence the issue is one of conflict of interests among members of the present generation.

Certain individuals may be willing to save more, provided everyone else saves more, so that a civic pride in a growing country or altruism on behalf of a future generation can be satisfied. And if the risk factor for the individual is larger than for the nation as a whole, each individual again may be willing to participate if everyone else does.[24] But these forces making for consensus on a greater rate of growth than the market will provide are probably weak in most instances.

Even those who are favored, relatively, by the measures taken for economic growth may yet oppose it. To the very wealthy families in underdeveloped countries an increase in per capita income may be unwelcome even if the increment is distributed disproportionately in their favor. They have little use for more money except as counters in a game, and any increase whatever, however small, in the economic power of the poor whose services they buy diminishes the social power of the wealthy. If, further, the increment goes disproportionately to the poor, the wealthy may become appreciably inconvenienced through a shortage of household servants, as the supply becomes extremely inelastic when far more attractive kinds of work develop.[25]

B. Amount of Labor Supplied

The number of persons in the labor force, including in labor force those whose work yields imputed income (chiefly housewives), and the number of hours and the intensity of work are affected by the pattern and size of the public finance system. Since an economy without any public finance system at all is not feasible on any substantial scale, the amount of labor supplied under a given public finance system cannot be compared with the amount that would be supplied under no such system. But the question may arise whether the community wishes to raise or lower, or leave unchanged, the amount of labor that is forthcoming under the existing public finance system. No consensus can be expected on this issue; whatever may be the

---

24. On these points, see Baumol, *Welfare Economics and the Theory of the State*, pp. 131–33.

25. ". . . the highest income groups in low-income countries can already command most of the material goods of developed nations plus the readily available personal services of a low-income society. Such groups have little to gain from a dynamic process of economic development. . . . The higher income people may even lose ground as development raises wages in the personal services sector without compensating increases in productivity in the sector" (John W. Mellor, *The Economics of Agricultural Development* [Ithaca, N.Y.: Cornell University Press, 1966], p. 6).

decision, including decision by default, it represents a compromise among conflicting interests or opinions. This issue is closely connected with that of economic
growth.

C. INCREASE IN AMOUNT OF SOCIAL RISK-TAKING

Investment spending in any economy is allocated in a certain pattern among ventures that differ both in their expected returns (the mean value of the possible outcomes of the venture, each outcome being weighted by the probability of its occur-
ence) and in the risk they present, that is, in the degree of dispersion of the possible
outcomes of a venture around its expected return, as measured by the variance or
its square root, the standard deviation. The greater this degree of dispersion of
possible outcomes, the greater is the risk, by the definition of risk now commonly
employed in such analysis. Thus the degree of dispersion measures the degree of
risk.

A change in the public finance system may alter both the mean return and the
risk of a given venture in either of two ways. First, it may change these quantities
as they appear to the individual investor, without changing them at all in real terms;
it does so by taxes or subsidies that alter the investor's disposable income, as distinct
from the real income, before tax or subsidy, associated with any of the possible outcomes of the venture. Secondly, it may alter the cost schedules and demand schedules relevant to the production and purchase of the product so that even the mean
return and the degree of dispersion as computed before tax or subsidy are altered.

The change in pattern of investment spending that follows either of these changes
in mean returns and degrees of dispersion will depend, *inter alia*, on the pattern of
the indifference curves of individual investors with respect to mean return and
degree of risk. It can be shown[26] that under certain plausible assumptions about that
pattern, a tax measure that reduces both the mean return and the degree of risk in
the same proportion for all ventures will induce investors to reallocate their investment funds in a manner such that the degree of risk to them as computed before
subtracting tax or adding subsidy exceeds the degree of risk they were facing before
the tax and subsidy were enacted. Note that that earlier degree of risk may still be
greater than the risk they now face after subtracting tax or adding subsidy, and to
them this latter degree of risk is the significant one. But to the economy as a whole,
it is the degree of risk as computed before subtracting the tax or adding the subsidy
that is the significant figure, for without increasing this degree of risk the economy
cannot be said to engage in a greater degree of real risk taking.

This goal, a greater degree of real risk taking, may however not be achieved even
if investors are persuaded to increase the degree of pre-tax, pre-subsidy risk that
they accept, for they can do this simply by a reshuffling of their portfolio holdings
among themselves, without embarking on ventures that carry a greater real risk.
This reshuffling takes the form of de-diversification. Just as diversification of one's
investment holdings normally decreases the risk attached to the entire portfolio of

26. See Chapter 12, Section 4.b.

the particular investor, so does concentration of one's holding increase that (pre-tax, pre-subsidy) degree of risk. For example, given two equal-size investors and two identical but independent risky ventures, let each investor take half of each venture initially. If subsequently the portfolio holdings are reshuffled so that each investor holds the entire ownership interest in just one of the ventures, each investor will be faced with a greater probability-weighted degree of dispersion of possible outcomes, that is, with a greater risk, although social risk-taking will not have changed: the two ventures are as before. (The mean return, in this instance, will be unchanged). Thus a tax or subsidy measure that induces investors to accept what are to them larger pre-tax, pre-subsidy risks than before may or may not induce them to accept ventures with greater risk than before; it will not, if it induces them merely to re-shuffle their portfolio holdings among themselves. Perhaps something of both re-actions is to be normally expected, at least if the constellation of real ventures does offer some ventures, not hitherto undertaken, that combine a larger risk with a larger mean return in appropriate ratios (on a pre-tax pre-subsidy basis).

A satisfactory theory of effect of public finance measures on degree of social risk taken evidently requires the use of a general equilibrium model, to take account of the changes in real investment, by specifying varying degrees of risk and mean return of alternative real ventures. Thus far, apparently only one model in general equi-librium terms has been developed, to show the effect of taxation on risk-taking.[27] This model uses Cobb-Douglas production functions in a three-industry economy, composed of two equally risky industries and one non-risky industry. In this model a general sales tax, coupled with the government's spending the tax money just as the taxpayers would have spent it, results in a shift of some capital and labor from the non-risky industry to the risky industries. The somewhat unexpected nature of this conclusion suggests the danger of relying on intuition or partial equilibrium analysis in this field.

In the chapters below, partial equilibrium analysis will however be employed, on occasion, to indicate possible tendencies, but without claiming to indicate the final result. Where appropriate, conjectures will be offered with respect to differential effects on risk-taking, as when an income tax is substituted for a sales tax. In the present state of analysis on this subject, however, these conjectures must be con-sidered very tentative indeed.

The degree of social risk that is to be aimed at is a problem in conflict of interests; there can be no consensus, as with elimination of unemployment. On the one hand, the risk-averting investor may be viewed as undertaking too little risk from a social point of view, because from that point of view there is a pooling of risks that is un-available to the usual investor, who cannot diversify completely. On the other hand there seems no basis for urging that public finance systems be changed to induce an increase in social risk-taking without limit. At any rate, if some Pareto optimum level of risk-taking can be formulated and achieved, on the grounds of pooling of

27. Aiko N. Shibata, *Effects of Taxation on Risk-Taking: A General Equilibrium Analysis.* Unpublished doctoral dissertation, Columbia University, 1968. Presented as invited dissertation at the American Economic Association, December, 1968, Chicago. The tax in this model is non-cumulative, and is implicitly restricted to consumer goods.

risks, a still greater increase in risk-taking can be conceived, and that part, at least, becomes a subject of conflict of interests.

As with the question of the amount of labor supplied, the issue of amount of risk to be undertaken is closely connected with the criterion of increasing the rate of economic growth.

D. PRICE STABILITY

A choice between price stability and a rise in prices, and among varying degrees of rise in prices is made in public finance when counter-cycle programs are pursued (see Chapter 22) and when inflationary finance as a means of resource reallocation is contemplated (see Chapter 18). In principle, a decline in prices might be considered for either purpose, but in practice almost any community will be found united against such a policy. Even those who would stand to gain from a decline in prices are too fearful of the resultant strain on the social fabric to give it their support.

The conflict of interests between those who desire price stability and those who want more or less price inflation is settled in various patterns in different countries. For convenience in exposition, the criterion is here worded as price stability, but with the understanding that this criterion, if it does prevail, is the outcome of a clash of opinions, arrived at by majority vote, or by the power of an oligarchy or whatever other group is able to dominate the scene. This point needs emphasis the more, as it is traditional in public finance to assume that price stability is an obvious standard to which all sensible men will repair. This assumption seems to imply that price stability is advisable on Pareto-optimum terms; at least some persons can be made better off, and no one need be made worse off, if prices are stable than if they are rising. If total real output is greater under the stable price level, this result follows, provided that the optimum is defined without regard to whether compensation is in fact paid to those who are disadvantaged. If total real output is greater under a slightly rising price level, as when an economy is moving up along a Phillips curve under high employment, the distributive effects of the rise in prices could in principle be countered, if all those who gained thereby could be taxed to compensate those who lost. In practice, it appears that the most that could be done would be to pay enough compensation to render the combination of rise in prices and rise in output attractive to all but a modest minority.[28]

Under deliberately inflationary finance, in contrast, the object is to make some persons better off at the expense of making some others worse off than they would be if government resources were obtained more by tax finance or ordinary borrowing; no compensation to those who are disadvantaged is possible even in principle. Compensation is applicable to the full employment instance, but in practice bondholders and other holders of fixed money claims know that no effort will be made to compensate them for their loss of real purchasing power by allocating to them a part of the increase in real output made possible by the policy that also generated the rise in prices.

28. On this point, see Abba P. Lerner, "Employment Theory and Employment Policy," *American Economic Review* (May, 1967), 57: 1–18.

E. Maintenance of a Given Exchange Rate

A criterion occasionally applied in the choice of a tax or a transfer payment but only rarely in choice of a free service to be rendered (although frequently in the choice of input mix) is its power to reduce external disequilibrium, that is, to reduce a continuing and substantial deficit or surplus in the balance of payments. This type of disequilibrium would not exist if the exchange rate were free to fluctuate. Since most countries peg the exchange rate within narrow limits, this criterion amounts to maintenance of a given exchange rate.

To reduce a deficit, the tax system may be made to fall more heavily on those who purchase either imported goods or home goods that could be exported ("exportables"), and more lightly on those whose tastes or investment spending needs run to domestically produced goods that are not exportables. The resulting income effects may be complemented by substitution effects induced by subsidies on exports and special duties on imports.

These changes make some persons worse off than if the disequilibrium were allowed to persist, with eventual devaluation or revaluation of the currency. The criterion therefore represents an outcome of a conflict of interests.

A tax, an unrequited payment by the government, or a government service may be under consideration for reasons having nothing to do with maintenance of a given exchange rate, but its probable effect on that score will normally be counted for or against it.

F. Promotion of Public-Purpose Outlays by Private Sector

Certain private-sector outlays are deemed so laden with a public purpose that they are stimulated by tax laws or subsidies; philanthropic and religious outlays are examples. Public moneys are thus spent at private direction. The governmental budget process is bypassed when the stimulation is achieved by tax-law provisions. It is largely bypassed when it is achieved through subsidies. This avoidance of the budget process is often quite deliberate, reflecting a belief either that the decisions on precisely how to spend the money advantageously require more expertise than the government can provide, or that dangerous social tensions would be built up by the legislative process. A tax credit for investment spending illustrates the first of these reasons (see Chapter 12) and deductibility of contributions to religious, charitable, and similar organizations illustrates the second, and perhaps the first, also. The definition of a tax-incentive type of subsidy and the task of measuring the amount are considered on page 54 below, under Subsidies (pages 150–51), and in the taxation chapters, Chapters 8–16.

G. Intergovernmental and Intragovernmental Coordination

Since a public finance measure of any one governmental unit will almost always affect the public or private sectors of other political areas, policies of taxation, subsidies, welfare payments, and even free governmental services are commonly adopted with an eye to those effects. Sometimes, it must be confessed, the action reflects a desire to gain forcibly an immediate advantage, but since more than one can play this game, most of the provisions are in fact coordinative rather than exploitative. They fall into two groups: horizontal coordination between states of roughly equal independence, and vertical coordination between a superior unit of government and its subordinate political units, especially in a federal state.

Intragovernmental coordination refers to coordination of a given public finance instrument, say a general sales tax, with other activities of the levying state. Typical questions in taxation are: does the existence of this tax affect the computation of other taxes (e.g., is the sales tax deductible in computing income subject to income tax?), and, are goods or factor services sold to the government or property owned by the government, or government enterprises, subject to the sales tax, or income tax or property tax?

C. INCIDENCE AND THE CRITERIA

The incidence of a tax must be determined before the tax can be tested by the criteria suggested above. The same is true with respect to a subsidy or welfare payment or free service. Accordingly, in analyzing the several services, subsidies, welfare payments, and taxes in the following chapters, something is said on the incidence of the benefit or the burden before analyzing the public finance measure in the light of these criteria.

D. INTRA-SYSTEM REACTIONS OF EXPENDITURES AND REVENUES

The components of a public finance system are so interrelated that a policy change in the amount of one of them is likely to induce automatically a change in the amounts of several others. An increase in the police force, for example, will probably reduce the number of fires and so reduce the amount spent by the fire department. The interrelations are even stronger among the revenue elements. An increase in new-money finance will automatically induce an increase in tax revenues. An increase in real estate tax rates will reduce the yield of an income tax, if real estate taxes are deductible in computing taxable income. An increase in the government's debt, and hence its annual interest charge, will represent a somewhat smaller net drain on its finances if the interest on government bonds is subject to income tax, provided that such taxation is not fully offset by the creditors' demand for a higher coupon rate. These intra-system relations will be noted in each of the following chapters wherever they appear to be appreciable.

APPENDIX TO CHAPTER TWO

The two dimensions in which inequities can be ranked are: money and people. We first consider money. If imputed net rental cannot be taxed under the income tax for one reason or another, would repeal of the deductibility of interest on mortgages on owner-occupied homes increase or decrease the inequity of the existing situation? It would (A) increase inequity (on grounds of irrelevance) as between (1) a homeowner with a mortgage and (2) one without; it would (B) decrease inequity as between (3) a tenant living in a mortgage-free dwelling and (1) a homeowner with a mortgage; and it would (C) leave unaffected the inequity as between (2) a homeowner without a mortgage and (3) a tenant living in a mortgage-free dwelling.[1]

We consider first the two homeowner groups and seek some quantitative expression of the amount by which dollar inequity is increased if deduction of mortgage interest is denied.

By disallowing deduction of mortgage interest there is created an inequity in income tax base equal to (a) the dollars of imputed net rental, that is, net of depreciation, in the mortgaged group, times the fraction that the mortgage interest is of that rental, (b) multiplied by the number of dollars of rental times that same fraction, in the non-mortgaged group. Let

r_m = imputed net rental in mortgaged group
m = fraction of r_m taken in mortgage interest
r = imputed net rental in non-mortgaged group

Then the inequity created by disallowing deduction of mortgage interest is

$$I = (mr_m)(mr) = m^2 r_m r$$

and

$$\frac{dI}{dm} = 2mr_m r$$

$$\frac{dI}{dr_m} = m^2 r$$

$$\frac{dI}{dr} = m^2 r_m$$

$$m \leqslant 1$$

Let $r < r_m$

1. For simplicity we abstract from the fourth case, tenants living in mortgaged dwellings.

At one extreme, if $m = 1$, that is, if mortgage interest takes all the net imputed rental, then, if deduction of mortgage interest is disallowed, a dollar more of mortgaged imputed rental increases inequity by r dollars. The new mortgaged dollar, matched against each of the r non-mortgaged dollars, creates r dollar-units of inequity. But an increase of one dollar in r, given the change to non-deductibility, increases inequity by r_m dollars; the new r dollar is matched against each of the large number of r_m dollars. Inequity in dollars is increased more by the addition of one dollar to the small group than by addition of it to the large group. Transfer of one dollar from the large group to the small group decreases inequity in the large group by less than it increases inequity in the small group.

We turn now to the decrease in inequity as between (3) a tenant living in a mortgage-free dwelling, and (1) a homeowner with a mortgage, when deduction of mortgage interest is disallowed. This decrease can be computed by a formula similar to the one above, and compared with the increase in equity between (1) and (2) as found above; the net result of disallowing mortgage interest as a deduction for income tax is then either positive or negative. If, in money terms, Group (2), non-mortgaged owner-occupied homes, is very small relative to Group (1), mortgaged owner-occupied homes, and relative to Group (3), non-mortgaged rented houses, the gain in equity from treating (1) and (3), the large groups, more nearly alike will be seen to outweigh the loss in equity from treating large Group (1) and small Group (2) more unlike than initially. This intuitive conclusion can be understood by supposing that the size of small Group (2) shrinks until it approaches closely to zero. If it were in fact zero, that is, if all owner-occupied houses were mortgaged, and all to the same degree, disallowance of interest as a deduction would increase equity as between homeowners, and tenants living in mortgage-free dwellings, without decreasing equity as between any other two groups.

Use of the second dimension, number of persons, can be illustrated in a contrasting manner by supposing that the tenant group, (3), is small relative to the homeowners with mortgages (1), who in turn are the same in number as the homeowners without mortgages (2). Let the total amount of inequity be the number of individual inequities. Now, by parity of reasoning with the money-units computation, counting each dwelling unit instead of each dollar as one, it will be seen that disallowing deduction of interest, since such action will increase inequity between two large groups, that is, the two homeowner groups, while decreasing inequity only as between a large group (mortgaged homes) and a small group (tenants), will on balance increase inequity.

The analysis above has utilized the approach originated by Johnson and Mayer, in which relative amounts of inequity, or indexes of inequity, are built up from sums of absolute differences between paired items. The approach originated by Melvin White and Anne White compares coefficients of variation (standard deviation divided by mean). The "Coefficient of Variation is . . . sensitive and mathematically tractable and facilitates combining and comparing groups at different income levels." This method gives more weight to extreme variations, a result that in the Whites' view helps justify the use of that method from an ethical point of view. They comment favorably, however, on the Johnson–Mayer technique: "As an alternative to measures based on deviations from the mean, the use of paired differences, perhaps in some quadratic function, may provide a measure that corresponds even more closely to the notion of fairness" (*op. cit.*, p. 227). The chief ethical issue seems to be whether extreme deviations should be given extra weight, and this is a problem either in personal value judgment or in appraisal of community reaction.

BOOK TWO
Micro Public Finance
Part I: Government Outlays

CHAPTER THREE

Types of Outlay and Receipt; Expenditure Administration

A. TYPES OF GOVERNMENT OUTLAY[1]

1. Explicit Government Outlays

GOVERNMENT OUTLAYS are either explicit or imputed. Explicit government outlays are either transfer payments or payments for goods and services. Transfer payments, in turn, are either unrequited transfer payments, involving no quid pro quo, or are payments for property, representing asset transactions. Unrequited transfer payments are chiefly donative, consisting of welfare payments, subsidies, and aid to other governments, foreign or domestic, but are sometimes compulsory, notably as reparations.

Property payments may be divided into purchases of existing real assets, chiefly land and buildings, and purchases of financial instruments, as in open-market operations where the government or its agent, the central bank, buys its own obligations from the private sector, or buys private-sector obligations, commercial bills for example.

The line between property payments for existing real assets and purchases of goods and services is drawn by including in payments for goods and services only those payments that commonly stimulate current production directly. Computers or pencils bought new by the government may have been produced before the government decided to buy them, but if the government is the first purchaser, that is, if the goods are not second-hand, it may be assumed that the government's order, or anticipation of it, stimulated current production, either of these items or of those that replace them in stock.[2]

---

1. The outlays and receipts are given in tabular form on page 489.

2. The criterion might be employed that the factor payments induced by the purchase have not appeared in the national income accounts of a preceding year, were it not that part of the price of the computer, or pencils, goes to cover depreciation of the machines that helped make the computer or pencils; this part of the purchase price reflects factor activity of an earlier year when the machinery itself was produced.

Purchase of an old building does not directly stimulate current factor activity, however much it may indirectly stimulate, such activity by improving the tone of the real estate market. In contrast, purchase of a new building is a purchase of goods and services for the reasons given above with respect to new computers or pencils.

The government's outlay for a building is an investment expenditure. The government invests, in the national-income sense, and the seller of the building disinvests. When the building was constructed, it represented an investment by the one at whose order it was built. A formal rule to implement the distinction drawn in the paragraph immediately preceding is the following: If the disinvestment that is the other side of the coin to the government's investment occurs in a year subsequent to the year in which the building was constructed, the government's investment is not to be counted as a purchase of goods and services; the government is buying a "used" or "old" building. The purchase of goods and services, that is, the stimulation of factor activity, is to be attributed to the party who ordered the building constructed in that earlier year; the date of attribution is the year of construction. But if the government's purchase of the building occurs in the same year as that in which the building was constructed, the government's purchase may be assumed to be the event the anticipation of which stimulated the factor activity that went into creation of the building, even if the building changes hands several times during that year before the government buys it. The government is purchasing a "new" building. The purchase of goods and services may be attributed to the government rather than to the other party, if any, at whose order the building was constructed.

Government purchase of land is not a purchase of goods and services except to the extent that the purchase price covers the cost of new grading, drainage, and the like; the rest of the purchase price does not directly stimulate factor activity. In general, little land is new land, and so, as with secondhand buildings, computers, or pencils, purchase of it is, with the exception noted above, a property payment.

When the government rents a building, machine, or other asset, part of the rental goes to cover depreciation (excepting land), part to cover maintenance costs incurred by the owner, and the rest as interest and profit. The latter two parts are payment for current factor activity, or approximately so, but the part of the rental that goes to cover depreciation is payment for an existing real asset. The depreciation part of the rental payments is a substitute for an outright purchase price. The rule suggested above for an outright purchase price of a building may be applied here. If the building was new when the government leased it, the entire rental payment may be regarded as one that directly stimulated the factor activity of creating the building, and the later factor activity of maintaining it. Over a long-term lease the activity so stimulated recedes into the past; it is not current factor activity. It would be preferable, for the aim of measuring the impact of the government on current economic activity, to capitalize the lease payments into a single sum in the initial year of the lease, and include this sum, rather than the subsequent rental payments, as a purchase of goods and services. In the absence of such an accounting procedure, inclusion of the rental payments is a second-best alternative, better than omitting the entire rental, or omitting that part of it that reflects depreciation.

If the building is already a used one when the government leases it, inclusion of the rentals in purchase of goods and services is tantamount to including the purchase price of a used building. The capital value of the building has already entered the national income accounts in the earlier year when the present private owner, or some predecessor, purchased it from the one who built it, or had it constructed at his order. Inclusion of that part of the rental that covers depreciation in purchase of goods and services would be double counting.

Interest paid by the government on its obligations is not an outlay for purchase of an existing asset, real or financial. It must therefore be a purchase of services of some kind. The service that it purchases is the yielding up of liquidity, that is, fore-going the certainty that the asset can be a substitute for money because it can be sold at a predetermined price at any given time. On occasion, however, the service purchased is evidently something other than the yielding up of liquidity.

The aggregate of property payments by government is typically small, with respect to real assets, but large with respect to financial assets. Central banks commonly purchase substantial amounts of financial instruments on the open market, with a view to stabilizing the economy or influencing its rate of growth.

2. Imputed Government Outlays

An imputed government outlay is an expense that does not give rise to a money transfer. Either (1) it is an accounting substitute for recording a money outlay of an earlier year, for example, an annual depreciation charge for a building owned and used by the government, the cost of this building not having been recorded as an expense in the year of purchase, or (2) it occurs simultaneously with a twin item of imputed income, the two offsetting each other. An example of such an offset is the imputed interest yielded by a government-owned and government-used build-ing, offset by an imputed outlay because this imputed interest is deemed spent at once in producing the governmental service that the building is instrumental in supplying. An imputed outlay to cover risk-bearing may also be presumed; the contribution made by the use of the building is deemed valuable enough to cover such a charge, that is, the building earns an imputed income large enough to pay a fee for risk-bearing.[3]

The sum of depreciation, imputed interest, and the imputed charge for risk-bearing is the imputed rental of the government-owned building. But if the pur-chase price of the building has been included as an expense in the year of purchase, only the imputed interest and the imputed charge for risk-bearing can be entered as outlays in the subsequent years' accounts without double counting. And de-preciation, unlike imputed interest expense and imputed risk-bearing expense, is not linked simultaneously with an equal item of imputed income. Depreciation in a given year does not itself reflect factor activity in that year; it merely represents the gradual transformation of a durable asset into another good.

3. For further discussion of depreciation, imputed interest, and imputed charge for risk-bearing, see pages 492–93 below.

Another example of imputed outlay that is offset by imputed income is the extra money compensation that the government would have to pay a military conscript to induce him to volunteer. By conscripting him at a much lower wage the government acts as if it paid him that higher wage and simultaneously taxed the difference away from him. The imputed outlay is matched by an equal imputed tax revenue.

Again, if the government allows a taxpayer in, say, a 40 per cent income tax bracket to deduct a $100 contribution to a charity, or if it gives him a 7 per cent credit against tax for a $100,000 investment in machinery, it is as if the government allowed no such deduction or credit (hence took $40 more in tax, or $7,000 more) and then itself gave $40 to the charity or supplied $7,000 toward purchase by the private firm of the machine. Imputed tax revenue is exactly offset by imputed outlay.[4]

Volunteer services to government may be regarded as a combination of imputed income, received as a gift from the volunteer, which is spent at once, imputedly, on hiring him.

Other offset imputations are those arising from compulsory loans to the government, loans by the government that involve some risk of default, loans by the government at low interest rates, and government guarantee of private loans.

A compulsory loan contains, for those who would not subscribe to the loan voluntarily, a tax element. The government receives imputed tax revenue from the compelled lender, in the form of part of what he pays for the government bond. The government also incurs an imputed interest charge. This is in addition to the actual interest it pays. This imputed interest charge is what the government would have to pay to the compelled lender to induce him to lend the money freely, if he were also subject to an explicit tax equal to the implicit tax that is hidden in the compulsory loan (see Chapter 16, pages 425–26).

Governments commonly make "soft" loans, that is, loans of a type that on the average will almost surely not be repaid in full, and some of which are so expected to be entirely uncollectible that they are virtually subsidies or welfare payments. On the dates when the government fails to receive the stipulated interest, that fact will be attested to by the simple absence of a cash receipt. The government's surplus will be smaller that year, or its deficit larger, than if the interest had been paid. The default shows up in the government's accounts as a "negative receipt"; receipts are smaller than they would have been if no default had occurred. This method of accounting for defaults understates the government's outlay, if the loan itself was not treated as an outlay when it was made.

As an extreme case, let us consider a loan made by the government in perpetuity (no maturity date) against the payment of a market rate of interest perpetually. If the loan itself is not counted as an outlay, and if the debtor defaults at once and never pays any interest on the loan, receipts are perpetually smaller than they would have been if the borrower had not defaulted, instead of outlays being larger.

The reverse treatment—larger outlay total in case of default, receipts total un-

4. The United Kingdom, by substituting a cash subsidy to investment spending for excess and accelerated depreciation, has increased the apparent size of the government sector by far more than it has increased (if at all) the real size.

changed by default—calls for either (*a*) inclusion, in outlay, in the year the loan is made, of an imputed payment to a reserve for bad debt losses, with a credit to receipts account and a debit to the loss-reserve account in the year when the default occurs; or (*b*) in the year when default occurs, inclusion in outlays for that year of an imputed outlay, the amount defaulted, with a corresponding entry for imputed receipts (as if the interest had been paid to the government and turned back by it to the debtor). Choice between the two methods depends on the relative importance attached to smoothing out this outlay item over a series of years and to avoidance of temporary inaccuracy that any reserve accounting necessarily entails.

If the government makes a loan at an interest rate lower than it could have obtained on the market, the cost represented by the interest foregone affects only the receipts total, not the outlay total, unless extra accounting entries are made, as follows. There are two methods of making such entries.

This kind of loan is in part an outright grant, and in part a true loan of an amount such that the interest stipulated on the total "loan" plus the excess of the redemption value over this true-loan part is enough to represent a market rate of interest on that part. The grant element can therefore be written off as an expenditure in the year that the "loan" is made. The receipts side for later years will include not only the interest actually paid but also the "capital gain" on the loan, the amount by which the redemption value exceeds the true loan segment of the "loan." Alternatively, the outlay total, for each year of the life of the loan, can be increased by an imputed expense representing the difference between the stipulated interest and the market rate, and this imputed expense will be matched by an entry for imputed interest received.

Governments commonly guarantee loans made by certain types of lenders to certain types of borrowers, especially in the mortgage field. If the debtor defaults, government outlays increase explicitly, as the government makes good on its guarantee. The alternative, inclusion in outlays in year of guarantee of a payment to a reserve for anticipated outlays to make good the guarantees, may be preferred, to average the outlays over the years, and to record at once the conditional obligation that is assumed by taxpayers, present and future.

3. Free or Subsidized Government Services as "Outlays"

The goods and services and the property purchased by the government, other than financial assets, are used by it in rendering services that are either dispensed free of charge or sold at a price. The "outlay" of the government might be defined to consist of the services it dispenses free of direct charge and the loss it incurs in selling at prices below cost, plus only that part of outlay on goods and services and real assets that it recovers through sale of the services. The emphasis placed in this chapter and in Chapter 4 on the economic effects of the free dispensing of services could justify such a classification, but to avoid too sharp a break with established usage, government "outlay" will here include all government expenditure on goods and services and on property purchases, and will not include the services dispensed free of charge.

B. TYPES OF GOVERNMENT RECEIPT

1. Explicit Government Receipts

Explicit government receipts are either transfer receipts or receipts from the sale or rental of goods and services. Transfer receipts are (*a*) unrequited receipts, involving no *quid pro quo* from the government; or (*b*) receipts from the sale of property, representing asset transactions ("property sales receipts"); or (*c*) receipts in the form of new money created within the government sector.

Unrequited transfer receipts are either compulsory (taxes, including the tax element in compulsory loans, and certain fees) or donative (usually aid from other governments, foreign or domestic).

Property sales receipts are either from the sale of real assets, the production of which was not stimulated directly by the sale, as when government stockpiles are reduced or old buildings are disposed of, or from the sale of financial instruments. These instruments may be either the government's own obligations or equity interests, newly issued or not, or obligations or equity interests of others that the government has been holding. Open-market sales of government obligations by the central bank give rise to property sales receipts when government is defined in the widest sense to include the central bank. Sale by the treasury of newly issued securities of course gives rise to a property sale receipt.

Money created within the government sector reflects exercise of the sovereign power of the state. The government may obtain such money by a transaction that in a formal sense seems to be an asset transaction, when it turns over to its agent, the central bank, a government obligation in exchange for a newly created deposit in the central bank. But all this occurs within the government sector, unless the central bank is truly owned and operated by the private sector. The government exchanges its own I.O.U. with itself for a deposit in its bank. This is for most purposes equivalent to printing currency or issuing coins with a metal content smaller than the market value of the coins. Currency is sometimes termed non-interest-bearing debt of the government carrying no maturity date (consols without interest), but this description is not helpful for analysis of the kinds of problem with which the present work is concerned. Creation of new money by privately owned commercial banks when they purchase from the government its own obligations or other financial assets it holds reflects, in contrast, an asset transaction; the government receipts are property receipts from the sale of financial assets. It will prove useful, however, to distinguish between (1) property receipts coming from sale by the government of its obligations to the non-money creating part of the private sector on the one hand, and (2) property receipts from sale by government of financial instruments to private-sector money-creating purchasers (typically commercial banks), and (3) receipts reflecting money created within the government sector (see Chapter 18).

Receipts from the sale of goods and services include all receipts where the production of those goods and services was directly stimulated by the sale. Post office receipts are a common example. The dividing line between receipts from the sale of goods and services and property sales receipts is thus the same as that given in Section A above for government purchases. The remarks there on rental, interest, and depreciation may be applied here, with appropriate modification to allow for the government as recipient rather than spender.

2. Imputed Government Receipts

Imputed receipts have already been noted above, as counterparts of imputed outlays.

C. EXPENDITURE ADMINISTRATION

In a large business firm, authority to make decisions can be safely delegated on a broad scale to subordinate officials more or less to the degree that their performance can be appraised in terms of its effect on the goal of the firm, which is primarily profit. But in a large organization that does not sell its output and does not have to compete in the capital market for equity funds, extensive delegation of authority is more hazardous, since there is no single measure resembling profits by which performance may be appraised. Accordingly, in the government and in certain non-profit private organizations the translation of policy goals into specific implementing measures can be left to the operating personnel only if the policy-makers repose a high degree of confidence in them. This is so even under the most favorable circumstances, when the unit of output can be measured and its cost ascertained, for there is still no direct competition with other organizations to exert continual pressure for efficiency. The operating personnel do not stand to lose their jobs because their organization cannot survive beyond a certain degree of inefficiency. In the more common case, the unit of output is not defined; no count can be made of units of output; efficiency of the operating department cannot be evaluated by observing how much is accomplished with a given amount of input. The operating personnel then stand even less chance of being exposed for inefficiency.[5]

5. A private firm may become less efficient beyond a certain size, owing to "control-loss features of hierarchical organization" (Oliver E. Williamson, "Hierarchical Control and Optimum Firm Size," *Journal of Political Economy* [April, 1967], 75: 123–38). Accordingly, a small governmental unit may be more efficient than a large firm, but for a given size the circumstances noted above tend to make achievement of efficiency, if it can be measured at all, more difficult for the non-market organization.

1. Degree of Delegation of Authority over Input Mix

The lack of profits as a measure of performance and the difficulty of defining and costing output lead policy-makers to formulate their goals in terms of inputs. What they delegate to the implementing personnel, insofar as they delegate anything, is authority to purchase and use specified types of inputs, without holding that personnel responsible for meeting output or efficiency goals. When the policy-makers check on the implementers' performance, it is to ascertain whether the specified inputs have in fact been obtained, and, as the case may be, used in the manner specified.

The policy-makers are the legislators and the executive (president, prime minister, cabinet, junta, dictator).[6] At the planning stage they depend on their budget bureau, planning board, treasury department,[7] or similar extension of their policy power to present to them a budget for the coming year or biennium. It is a budget of inputs, not outputs. In turn, the budget bureau will have depended on the operating departments to supply an initial draft of this budget of inputs.

If the budget bureau officials, and the policy-makers they serve, have little faith in the ability or integrity of the operating departments' personnel, the initial draft of the budget of inputs will be requested from them in great detail. The resulting line-item budget will specify for, say, a police department so many typewriters, so many patrolmen of one or another grade, so many patrol cars of a specified type, perhaps even so many pencils and pens. If the department believes that it can increase its efficiency by substituting some patrol cars for some patrolmen, it must convince the budget bureau's representative. Thus the policy formulators participate in management decisions through their deputies, the budget bureau examiners. Initiative, originality, and morale in the operating departments are correspondingly restricted. This result is desirable if the departments are staffed with mediocre personnel, which indeed they are apt to be if management functions rest largely in the budget bureau.

The foregoing paragraphs sketch the technique of expenditure administration in the budgetary stage that has been common, in both national and subordinate governmental units in nonsocialist countries.[8] In recent years some governments have moved a considerable distance toward the other extreme. At that extreme the budget of inputs would state only, with respect to any one operating department, or perhaps for each program within a department, a lump sum, to be devoted to specified ends. More commonly, the department will ask not for a lump sum but for

6. For a discussion of the alternative types of budget agency—executive, administrative, legislative—see, e.g., William J. Shultz and C. Lowell Harriss, *American Public Finance* (8th ed.; Englewood Cliffs, N.J.: Prentice-Hall, 1965), pp. 100–101.

7. As, for example, in the United Kingdom.

8. Presumably the same problems are encountered and much the same solutions are adopted in socialist countries, since the distinction between marketed and non-marketed goods obtains there also (see Chapter 1 above, Section A.1). The marketed goods are sold, however, under conditions far less competitive than those of a private enterprise economy.

a series of more or less lump sums divided into object accounts: so much for personal services, so much for contractual supplies and services, and so on. The personal services account may be subdivided, for example, into personnel compensation, personnel benefits, and benefits to former personnel; contractual supplies and services may be subdivided into travel, transportation of things, rent, and so on. The finer the subdivision into these object accounts, the more the technique retreats toward that of the old line-item budget. And even the broad divisions of funds, that between personnel and contractual services, for example, cannot be rigidly fixed if the operating department is to have flexibility in selecting the most efficient input mix without first having to persuade the budget bureau.

The ends, the output goals, of the various programs within a department are not usually stated in units of product. The operating department merely describes its output goals in general terms: making the city reasonably safe from criminals, and preventing traffic mishaps (by a police department), not holding the crime rate and the automobile accident rates down to specified levels. A department thus sketches what it hopes to do and asks for a considerable degree of freedom to choose among input mixes for each of its programs, without being required to persuade a budget bureau official of the wisdom of each input mix.

In this sense the department submits a "performance budget,"[9] even when units of output cannot be defined, and hence performance in terms of cost per unit of output cannot be defined. When output can be defined and per unit costs computed, the term "performance budget" is still more appropriate.

This performance budget procedure requires faith in the integrity and ability of the operating personnel. Indeed, it was largely to check fraudulent purchases of inputs at unconscionable prices that the line-item budget was instituted at a time when only haphazard budgeting procedures existed.

2. Grouping of Inputs by Type of Output

The general absence of defined units of output in the performance budget, at its present stage of development, must be emphasized. In this respect the performance budget is still very much of a compromise, still largely a documentation of inputs insofar as it contains any detail. Its chief differences from the line-item budget are that it delegates to the operating department more of the decisions regarding input mix, and groups inputs according to the several types of output the department is producing.[10] This grouping yields "activity schedules," each activity being a type of output. But still the performance budget is essentially a budget of inputs, save in the

9. See Jesse Burkhead, *Government Budgeting* (New York: Wiley, 1956), chapter 6.

10. The term "performance budget" is sometimes used to indicate a statement of successive levels of inputs: for example, fuel and labor are related to building space. The second level of input (here, building space) gives a little more indication of what the output will be than does the first level (fuel, labor). Counting of number of forms processed per employee allows comparisons of employee efficiencies, but the two inputs, forms and labor, still yield only an intermediate product, processed forms.

few instances where outputs can be easily quantified and marginal cost ascertained: water supply or refuse removal, for example.

This nonquantified grouping of inputs according to type of output can be extended to cut across operating-department lines, for a description of programs in the large. In that event, a "program budget"[11] sometimes termed a "functional budget," emerges. The policy group sets up a list of "programs"—for example, defense, foreign aid, public health—and presents to the public a statement of total expenditures proposed under each program. Foreign aid may involve some part of the budget of the state department or ministry of foreign affairs, some part of the military budget, and so on. But the "program budget" is still a budget of inputs, unless the programs specify goals in quantitative terms.

When a single program is fragmented among two or more departments, traditional budgeting by department makes difficult a comparison of different kinds of inputs, some of which inputs are used only by one department, some used only by another. Since each department's budget is examined separately at the planning and appropriating stages, by the budget bureau or legislative committees, special effort is required to compare such inputs as possible substitutes for each other. Yet the comparison is essential to determine whether the total program might be carried out more cheaply by using somewhat less of one of the inputs and somewhat more of another.

For example, let a military output be administered by three departments, army, navy, and air, and consider the three programs of deterring a potential missile-armed enemy, limiting damage in case that enemy strikes, and fighting a conventional ground war. The first program requires, *inter alia*, submarine-based missiles (navy), intercontinental missiles (air force); the second requires air defense aircraft (air force) and anti-missile missiles (army and air force); the third requires, among other things, a marine corps (navy), armored divisions (army), and tactical aircraft (air force). Departmental budgets submitted separately, with no cross-department comparison of component inputs, provide no single listing of all the various inputs for any one program. Submarine-based missiles will be in one budget, intercontinental missiles in another. There will be no occasion for the budgetary process automatically to inquire whether the same degree of deterrence could be purchased by reducing the input of submarine-based missiles by some money amount and increasing the input of intercontinental missiles by a smaller amount.

A comparison of one program with another program is also hindered when the budgets are formulated in terms of departments. Program budgeting promotes a complete comparison among programs, raising questions much beyond the traditional consideration only of incremental additions to or subtractions from last year's budget, department by department. Perhaps huge trade-offs will now be stimulated: cut one program by a quarter and increase another by a third, without spending any more or less in the aggregate. In such a case it is even conceivable, though perhaps not likely, that, because programs commonly cut across departments, each department involved in the trade-off will, after it, be administering the same total of funds as before.

11. See Appendix to this chapter.

In any event, comparison among programs is something that can be done only at top decision levels, and it calls for more centralized decisions than does the traditional incremental, department-by-department formulation of a budget for a given year.

Legislative appropriation or authorization to spend may still be made in the traditional manner by acts each of which consists of appropriation of money to, or authorization to spend by, a specified department or departments. Program budgeting can still be effective, for the amounts alloted to each department will have been determined in the light of a comparison of programs, and, for any one program, a comparison of instruments. With the aid of program budgeting the policy-makers are better able to compare competitive inputs and also competitive outputs; that the final authorization is in terms of departments does not matter. The task is simplified, of course, if a particular type of input is associated only with a particular department (long-range bombers, air force) and if the amount of the department's total budget that is to be devoted to each program is specified (an air force budget would be subdivided, among other tasks, between deterrence, damage limitation, and conventional war).

The fact that a single input may contribute to two or more outputs, two or more programs, does not in principle hinder the use of the program concept to arrive at totals for programs and to break each of these totals down by operating departments for administrative purposes. In principle, input itself is to be counted only once in the budgeting process, and each of the two outputs is only counted once. In practice, as long as output is measured in units of money input, there is a difficulty: how to divide the input amount, administered by some one department, between the two outputs, which are parts of two distinct programs, one of which programs is at least in part the responsibility of another department? Some arbitrary decision must be made, but it has to be arbitrary, not because the concept of program budgeting is faulty, but because outputs are being measured in terms of inputs.

3. Pre-Audit and Post-Audit Control over Inputs

The second stage of expenditure administration occurs after the budget of inputs has been approved by the executive and legislature and is returned to the operating departments for implementation. Safeguards are erected to assure that the money is spent as directed. In their extreme form these safeguards permit no contract to be signed, and no payment to be made, until some official outside the operating department has verified that the proposed contract or payment corresponds with the budget as adopted. This official may be in the budget bureau or in a bureau primarily concerned with financial inspection and control, perhaps the controller's office. But no one in or outside the operating department has the responsibility to verify that a given output level has been achieved or that cost per unit of output does not exceed a stated target; no one is accountable for holding the crime rate to a predetermined level, for example, or for seeing that the marginal cost of crime prevention does not exceed a certain amount.

The third and final stage of expenditure control occurs after the event; it is post-audit. Commonly the post-audit comes too late to accomplish more than punish the guilty to serve as a deterrent. Often a parliamentary body appoints its own post-audit body[12] as an assertion of independence of and supervision over the entire executive arm of government.

Even the most extreme form of performance budgeting must retain some degree of checking on input purchase and use of inputs. Line-item accounting is always necessary to some extent. But line-item budgeting in the sense that someone outside the operating department must approve the input-mix is another matter.

4. Output Budgeting

Because of the many different senses in which the term "performance budget" is commonly taken, it is preferable to use the term "output budget" to designate those plans and records of accomplishment that are cast in terms of quantities of defined units of output. If these units cannot be sold at a price, because they are group-consumption goods,[13] the department is not exposed to competition, and the policy formulators may therefore wish to supervise somewhat the department's decisions on patterns of inputs, to insure efficiency. But since cost per unit can be computed, inspection of this figure may be a substitute for participating in the management function directly.

The activities of government that can be planned and controlled by output budgeting are those that yield a bundle of products that are more or less homogeneous in quality. Tons of garbage collected are more homogeneous than number of children educated. Not every mosquito is as dangerous as every other, but a decrease in number of mosquitoes is a more homogeneous marginal concept than decrease in number of crimes. Group consumption is not the determining feature here; education is harder to measure than destruction of mosquitoes.

An intermediate product is easily mistaken for an end product, as the mosquito illustration suggests. If mosquitoes are being destroyed not because they are a nuisance but because they spread malaria, mosquito destruction is an intermediate product, hence itself an input. Decline in rate of malaria infection is then the product to be measured, the output.

The fact that a product is an intermediate good does not bar a statement of it in terms of an output budget. If the decrease in number of malaria mosquitoes is known, this figure can be stated in an output sub-budget of the budget for malaria control.

12. For example, the Controller-General, in the United States.
13. See Chapter 4 below, pages 66–74.

APPENDIX TO CHAPTER THREE

As with the term "performance budget," so too with "program budgeting," terminology has not yet become standardized. A program budget is sometimes what has been described above as an activity schedule, distinguishing different activities carried on within a single department. Sometimes the term is employed to connote an expenditure estimate that covers several years rather than the one or two years customary for budget periods. And to some a program budget is chiefly an assurance that alternative methods of achieving a given objective are to be explored adequately, to obtain a least-cost estimate.

For varieties of meanings that have become attached to the term "program budgeting" see Roland N. McKean and Melvin Anshen, "Limitations, Risks, and Problems," in David Novick (Ed.), *Program Budgeting* (Cambridge, Mass: Harvard University Press, 1965), pp. 286–87, and Arthur Smithies, "Conceptual Framework for the Program Budget," in Novick, *op cit.*, pp. 34–36. The recent United States literature on PPBS, "planning programming budgeting system," insofar as it deals with outputs, usually stops with descriptions of "objectives," e.g., "Personal Safety," including "Law Enforcement," "Traffic Safety," and others, "Law Enforcement," for example, being broken down into 'Crime Prevention," "Crime Investigation," and so on, without, however, defining the units of output. See, for example, Harry P. Hatry and John F. Colton, *Program Planning for State, County, City* (Washington, D.C.: State-Local Finances Project, George Washington University, 1967). Another example may be taken from the "functional allocation" of appropriations for the Internal Revenue Service, referred to by Shultz and Harriss, *op. cit.*, p. 105: rulings, planning, collection, audit of tax returns, tax fraud and special investigations, legal services, and taxpayers' conferences and appeals. In the view taken here, these are categories of inputs, not outputs.

The PPBS was first used in the United States in the Department of Defense under Secretary McNamara in the early 1960's, and in 1965 President Johnson directed that all federal agencies convert to this system as soon as practicable. As of the end of 1967, progress had been necessarily uneven. The Justice Department had been given a temporary reprieve, and the Department of State had abandoned its initial program structure as having been unsatisfactory; work on a new structure had been stopped pending development of an interagency foreign affairs programming system.[1]

According to a Congressional report:

To avoid reshuffling [of funds within agency budgets], some agencies have applied PPBS only to new programs and have ignored older, and usually, more costly, programs. . . . Since programs are not presently structured on a broad, cross-agency basis, a

[1] John P. Crecin, "PPB and the Federal Budget" (unpublished memorandum prepared for Robert M. Trueblood, member of the President's Commission on Budget Concepts, August 18, 1967), p. 29. In general, "agencies are still groping and searching for appropriate program definitions and categories, developing PPB staff, and educating agency officials on procedures. PPBS in non-defense agencies is still at a very primitive stage" (*ibid.*, p. 42).

program designed to achieve a given objective in one agency may have high priority, while a program to achieve the same objective in another agency may have low priority. This creates the danger of program conflict and duplication.[2]

This report emphasizes the output orientation of PPBS, but this aim must be taken with some reserve as long as units of output remain as generally undefined as they are at present. The subcommittee, however, is emphatic:

PPBS focuses on the output of programs whereas traditional budgetary approaches tend more or less inevitably to emphasize expenditure inputs. It assesses as fully as possible the total costs and benefits, both current and future, of various alternatives. It endeavors to determine rates of return for programs, as well as the rate of return that may have to be foregone when one program is chosen over another.

PPBS is a refinement of existing procedures rather than a completely new approach. Among its advantages is that of focusing attention on programs rather than on agencies. Through evaluating program costs, PPBS can put both old and new programs to a test of their worth.[3]

2. Joint Economic Committee, Congress of the United States, "The Planning-Programing-Budget System: Progress and Potentials," Report of the Subcommittee on Economy in Government, December, 1967 (Washington, D.C.: Government Printing Office, 1967), pp. 3–4.

3. *Ibid.*, p. 1.

CHAPTER FOUR

Government Services in General

IN ADDITION TO THE criteria for public finance measures listed in Chapter 3, there are certain issues peculiar to the rendering of free services that can be discussed in general terms.

A. REASONS FOR FREE DISTRIBUTION

Certain types of service are commonly distributed by the government free of charge. These include some services that could instead be sold on the market. Tangible goods, on the other hand, are rarely distributed free of charge. They are sold for a price by either government or private firms, partly because the recipient of free tangible goods can often resell them instead of consuming them. Few if any services can be resold.

Goods or services sold by the government at a loss will be discussed in Chapter 6, under Subsidies. Those sold for a profit, for revenue gain, will be covered in Chapter 10, where the gain is treated as a form of taxation if it exceeds a normal return on capital.

The reasons why the government distributes certain services free of direct charge may be grouped under four main heads:

1. Preservation of the nation-state
2. Group consumption
3. Redistribution in kind
4. Miscellaneous
   a. Difficulty of measuring output
   b. Uninsurable costs
   c. Group identity
   d. Exploitation

Each of these reasons is discussed separately in the present chapter; each government service is discussed separately in Chapter 5.

1. Preservation of the Nation-State

Certain government services are rendered to maintain the identity of the nation-state against the threat of aggression from abroad or of secession or insurrection at home. The individual, however he may feel about these matters, is not left free to consume the services or not as he wishes. Rather than force him to purchase a certain minimum amount on the market, assuming that he could do so, the government finds it more convenient to produce the service itself and distribute it free of direct charge (but see Section F below). In this way it can more surely control the quality and character of the service.

This service of maintaining the political status quo is supplied by the military forces (army, navy, air force) and by internal security forces. It is to be distinguished from the police service, which affords protection against lawbreakers operating singly or in small groups. But the two services are complementary in production. If each individual were left to purchase on the market his own protection against criminals, secession or insurrection would have more chance of success, and even conquest from the outside would be more likely.

Another service that helps maintain the identity of the nation-state is enforcement of contracts. This service is supplied by the police and the courts. The property law of a nation reflects a certain national unity, even when it differs somewhat among subordinate jurisdictions (for example, states in the United States). To leave all disputes to be settled by arbitration purchased on the market would be expensive and inimical to that unity.

The notion of a minimum with respect to the level of the service must be emphasized. Above that minimum there is a real option between, say, privately purchased arbitration and extension of the public courts. There is similarly a real choice available with respect to additional expenditures on defense against conquest and expenditures on other goods or services, when defense expenditures have been carried so far that it has become a matter, not of preserving the nation-state (this aim is now assured), but only of preserving it with less than a certain minimum "acceptable" amount of damage if the worst should come to pass, or of varying the geographical distribution of the damage (see Chapter 5, pages 102–104 below). And military expenditure for conquest is obviously optional, unless conquest is somehow necessary to survival. In some countries, military expenditure is in large part simple exploitation. In all countries it contains an element of conspicuous public consumption, with its pagentry and trappings.

2. Group-Consumption Goods

A group-consumption good, almost always a service rather than a tangible commodity, is a good that can be supplied in a given amount to a given group of households or firms in a given area more efficiently under a non-marketing technique of production and distribution, that is, a technique whereby the good must be supplied simultaneously to all members of the group, no particular one of which can be excluded from enjoying the service. "Efficiently" is a concept that involves both demand and cost conditions, but for simplicity, efficiently will be taken here to mean simply, at lower cost per capita.[1]

A few services apparently could not be rendered in the marketing mode at any cost; for example, some of the services supplied by the military, and the benefits from the exploration of space. For most services, however, it is a matter of relative cost of alternative techniques: (1) the marketing technique, whereby any particular would-be consumer is excluded if he will not pay a price for the service or if he is not granted a ration of the service under a rationing plan for a service supplied free of charge, and (2) the non-marketing technique, that is, the non-exclusion technique, here termed the group-consumption technique. A service is therefore defined here as a group-consumption good if that form of producing and distributing it is the cheaper, and as a marketable good if the excludable form is the cheaper.

The terms "public good" and "private good" may be used in place of group-consumption good and marketable good, respectively, but they are not employed here for two reasons. First, confusion has arisen from a tendency to use "public good" to include all collective-consumption goods, even though some collective-consumption goods are marketed. A collective consumption good is one that, if supplied to one person, can be supplied to additional persons at zero incremental cost.[2] Second, some group-consumption goods are in fact supplied privately rather than by government, because they are byproducts, in the form of externalities, of goods that are marketable.[3]

The cost of supplying the service by the marketing technique includes the resources used in operating the price mechanism or the rationing machinery.[4] The cost of supplying it in the group-consumption mode includes the cost of tax administration and the excess burden caused by taxation.

As a somewhat fanciful illustration, we may suppose that mosquitoes afflicting a certain group of households can be destroyed by draining pools and swamps, or alternatively by stationing men with sprayers and swatters in and around each of the households that would pay for this service. In this case, the per capita cost of the service, elimination of mosquitoes, is almost certain to be lower under the group-consumption, non-marketing technique, unless the group of households is very small, say two or three; the group-consumption technique might be the cheaper even then.

This cost-based distinction between group-consumption and marketable goods is most serviceable in incremental terms: cost of obtaining an increment in the level of service, per capita, rather than total cost of that level of service per capita. Starting

1. See Appendix A to this chapter.
2. See page 68.
3. See the illustration on page 72.
4. This "cost of prices," as Linder terms it, may be considerable. See Staffan B. Linder, "The Cost of Prices," (article forthcoming). The value of time lost and patience strained at congested toll gates, theater ticket offices, supermarket check-out points, and the like may be much larger than is generally appreciated.

from one level of a given service, an increase in the level of the service may be achieved at lower cost under a non-marketing technique, while at another level of the same service the marketing technique may afford the cheaper increment. Once a police force has been built up to a certain level, the next increment of the output, protection against theft, may be obtainable more cheaply by installing burglar alarms than by increasing the police force further. But the alarms are of no use without some police force. Layers of the marketing mode may thus be sandwiched in between layers of the group-consumption mode, on a least-cost basis. The service is then definable only in incremental terms.

Almost all tangible commodities are marketable goods; to supply these goods in a manner such that no particular individual in the group can be excluded is almost always the more expensive way, if indeed it is possible.

A certain service may in fact be rendered, at a given time and place, in the less efficient mode. This fact does not alter the definitions given above. If a certain service is being sold at a price when it could be rendered more cheaply in the non-marketing mode, it is a "marketed" service, but not, by the definition employed here, a "marketable" service.

An entirely different distinction between type of good depends on whether the total cost of supplying a given level of the service to each individual remains unchanged as the size of the consuming group increases. If it does remain unchanged, as does, for example, the total cost of forecasting the weather for a given area, the service is a collective-consumption good. The service with this cost characteristic may be either a marketable service or a group-consumption service, depending on efficiency conditions. A theatrical performance, up to the capacity limit of the theater, is probably in most instances a marketable, collective-consumption good; certainly it is commonly marketed. Weather forecasting and, except possibly for a very small group of consumers, the elimination of mosquitoes through destruction of their breeding grounds are nonmarketable (i.e., group-consumption) goods that are also collective-consumption goods. As long as total cost does not increase as numbers served increase, which may be anywhere from the dozens of persons to the millions of persons, the service is a collective-consumption good, whether it is a group-consumption service or a marketable service. Given the total input, the addition of one more household or firm to the consuming group does not impair the level of consumption of that service by any of those who are already consuming it. The size of the group beyond which total cost rises as the group grows still larger is the collective-consumption limiting size.

The rise in total cost beyond this limiting size, as number of consumers in the group increases, may be abrupt, because of lumpiness of factors. It may then be zero for another large addition to the numbers of the group until this new lumpy factor is fully engaged. Alternatively, the total cost may rise gradually and steadily with numbers in the group, once the collective-consumption limiting size is passed.

When total cost does rise abruptly as one more household or firm is served, and then remains unchanged for a further increase in size of the group, the service is a collective-consumption good with respect to increments in size of group up to, and beyond, the increment that caused the abrupt increase in total cost. It is a non-collective-consumption good with respect to that particular increment in size of group. If total cost is at first unchanged as numbers increase and then starts to increase gradually and continuously as numbers increase further, the good is a collective-consumption good only up to the size of group where total cost starts to increase.

It must be emphasized that the remarks in the two preceding paragraphs apply alike to group-consumption goods and marketable goods.

In all that has been said up to this point, the area within which the households and firms receive the service is assumed to be defined and held constant. This assumption is central to cost analysis of a group-consumption good. The technique employed to distribute a good in this manner, rather than in a marketable form, is ordinarily one whereby the service is broadcast over a given area from a point of input. Under this nonmarketable technique, everyone within the area can enjoy the service if he wishes, and indeed for some services no one in the area can abstain from receiving it; the service is non-rejectable. This central aspect of the group-consumption technique of production and distribution holds, whether the addition of one or more consuming unit in the area does or does not increase total cost of rendering the service at the stipulated level, that is, whether the good is not, or is respectively (for the given initial size of group) a collective-consumption good.

The level of service that is broadcast from a point of input may or may not be uniform throughout the area in question. Outside the area it is zero; but within the area the service level commonly tapers off as the recipient is located farther and farther from the point of input. A single police patrol car, which is an input, renders a higher level of the service, protection against crime, to those within a short distance of it than to those located farther away. The patrol car illustrates the further proposition that the point of input need not be geographically fixed; it may be mobile. It also illustrates the idea that other similar points of input may be operating under the same authority at the same time, so that an area is blanketed by the cones of service rendered, one cone rendered by each patrol car. The forest of overlapping cones of service may assure an almost uniform level of the service, protection against crime, to all within the area. Finally, the patrol car illustrates a third point, that the area of service covered by a single input may extend beyond the geographical jurisdiction of the authority that directs that input. As the patrol car moves on or near the periphery of the city whose officials direct its course, the cone of protection that it provides extends over into a contiguous city or district. There is a geographical spill-over of the service.

Evidently, when the input units are mobile, an authority that controls such a unit, or more than one of them, can discriminate to some degree in the level of service that it renders to various sub-areas within the total area of its jurisdiction. The patrol cars may be grouped so heavily in one part of the city, relative to the tendency to crime there, that the crime rate is much lower in that part of the city than in others. But mobility is not essential to this kind of sub-area discrimination in level of service. It is enough if there is more than one input unit and if, technically, not all the input units have to be located together. Thus the locations of the firehouses of a city fire department will help determine the relative degrees of fire protection afforded to various geographic sub-areas within the city. We may say that the households and firms thus differentially affected are "subgroups" within the group to whom the authority in question is responsible for rendering the service. Sometimes it is feasible technically to discriminate, as to level of the service afforded under the group-consumption technique, among subgroups on other than a sub-area basis. Thus in communities afflicted by ethnic bias, where individuals of a certain skin color are given a lower level of protection than others, the precise location of the input centers is not determinative; a community that gives a lower level of protection against crime to blacks than to whites is able to do so, technically speaking, almost regardless of the particular sub-area in which the black happens to be when occasion for the service arises. But in general it remains true that different levels of service can be given to subgroups only on a geographical, sub-area, basis. This fact contributes to the social and economic importance of geographical segregation.

The group may be defined in engineering terms rather than in jurisdictional terms; this alternative is discussed on page 74 below.

Not all instances of uneven levels of service among the members of a group reflect deliberate discrimination. The unevenness may be random, or at least not controllable by those who render the service. Accordingly, spatial discrimination among subgroups, as defined here, includes only those cases where the sub-areas containing these subgroups can be carved out at will for application of lower levels of the service. The level of police protection offered by a city may be much lower in a sub-area consisting of a particular police district, or even only of a few particular blocks. If the boundaries of such a sub-area can be shifted at will, the service is here said to be one for which intra-group discrimination is feasible, that is, different levels of service can be offered to spatial subgroups at will.

Total cost of offering the service to a given size of group in a given area presumably changes with changes in the pattern of discrimination among subgroups with respect to level of service offered in each subgroup. If an average level of service for the group as a whole can be defined, and maintained, there is probably one pattern of discrimination among subgroups that will minimize total cost. This problem, which is analogous to, but by no means precisely the same as, the problem of distinguishing between marketable and nonmarketable goods on the grounds of efficiency, is exemplified in the decision on how to distribute a police force of a given size (see Chapter 6, page 117).

In contrast to the sub-area boundaries that can be set at will are the boundaries fixed by nature, leading to involuntary discrimination. For example, let there be two mosquito-breeding ponds, one north of the city, the other south of it, each supplying mosquitoes only to its nearest half of the city. Although the city authorities can practice intra-group discrimination as between these two halves of the city, by destroying one breeding ground but not the other, it cannot eliminate mosquitoes from, say, wealthy districts that lie along the northern and southern peripheries of the city while allowing mosquitoes to plague the poorer districts in the city's core. Accordingly, mosquito abatement is for this city to be classified as a service for which intra-group discrimination is not feasible. The reason for so classifying the services where the pattern of feasible intra-group discrimination for spatial areas is set by nature is that in practice there will be little such discrimination, because the patterns allowed by nature rarely fit the discrimination patterns desired by those in power, or by the electorate at large. In any event, discrimination along area patterns set by nature tends to lead to disintegration into smaller political units, each with control over an area in which no spatial discrimination at all will be feasible.

As already noted, a community will not necessarily select that technique, group-consumption technique or marketing technique, that allows the service to be supplied most efficiently, or, more loosely, at the lowest per capita cost. Other considerations will always influence the decisions of which technique to use. Distribution of real disposable income is one of them. A service that is marketable, under the least-cost definition employed here, may be rendered in fact under a non-excludable technique (group-consumption technique). The community may not desire to ration the use of the service by price, or indeed by any technique whereby a particular household or firm can be excluded from the service, or can be limited in its use of it, relative to others in the group. Conversely, the community may choose to employ a marketing technique even when the cost per capita is higher than under an alternative, group-consumption technique. But these community decisions cannot be the basis for definitions formulated in the present analysis. If the definitions of the two types of goods were grounded on which technique the community in fact uses, they would be influenced by too many variables to be helpful in analysis. It will prove more convenient to use the definitions based on test of per capita cost (more precisely, efficiency), remembering that any given type of service may be in incremental terms a group-consumption good at one level of the service and a marketable good at another level.

The term "marketing technique" has a wider connotation than pricing, as suggested by the reference in the preceding paragraph to rationing. Rationing may be by direct control rather than by pricing. Education, for example, is commonly supplied in schoolhouses, entrance to which might be denied to any particular child, either on a price basis or on some other rationing basis, including ethnic bias. And the number of hours of education given to each child is in fact rationed directly. Alternatively, education may be broadcast by radio or television, from which no one can be excluded. The recipient must have a radio or television set, to be sure, but the fact that this complementary consumption good must be purchased on the private-sector market does not invalidate the distinction between the two techniques of rendering education. The government may tax the radio or television set, and thus in practice use the pricing mechanism to exclude would-be recipients of education, but again the efficiency distinction of the two ways of distributing the performance of the teacher remains unaffected. In the discussion to follow, use of the term, "maketing technique," as opposed to group-consumption (i.e., "nonmarketing") technique will be continued, on the understanding that the marketing technique may include some rationing device other than or additional to pricing. From this point of view, public education, at least with respect to the service rendered by the teacher in the schoolroom, is commonly given under a marketing technique, not under a group-consumption technique. This is so, even though admission to the schoolroom is not priced. Admission is rationed; the technique used is such that any particular child can be excluded, or given a lower level of service (shorter teaching period). The fact that all children are commonly treated alike by class group in a given school does not negate the fact that the technique used is a marketing technique, as contrasted, say, with education over a loudspeaker in the town square. The essence of the group-consumption technique—the loudspeaker technique, in this illustration—is that, if it is employed, no particular person in the group that is receiving the service can be entirely excluded from enjoyment of the service. Subgroups, usually sub-area groups, can, we have seen, be limited to a lower level of the service and in rare instances can be entirely excluded from the service, but discrimination, including exclusion, is still by a subgroup, not by particular individual.

The definitions adopted in this section are chosen because they appear to be the most useful set for dealing with the issues that the present work is concerned with. Experience in analyzing these issues may well suggest changes in those definitions. But in any event the definitions commonly used heretofore seem inadequate, at least for economic analysis, because they abstract from cost considerations, and focus too much on the physical characteristics of the service.

It was suggested on page 67 that for a few services the physical characteristics of the service are indeed decisive; regardless of the level of service, the size of the group, or the area covered, they cannot be distributed by a marketing technique (individual-rationing technique) no matter how much one might be willing to spend to put them on this basis. One notable example is exploration of space, at least in its present stage (see pages 107–108). Another example is the improved cultural milieu that the community enjoys from the education of members of that community. This improved milieu is a product distinct from the education itself, and it cannot be rationed or priced in a manner to exclude any particular individual in the group. Similar externalities[5] that arise from improved housing and from improved medical care (to be distinguished from public health measures) cannot be provided by a marketing technique. But protection against crime and protection against fire can be supplied by a marketing technique, although less efficiently (with exceptions) than by the group-consumption technique.

Figure 1 illustrates the distinction between group-consumption goods and collective consumption goods, showing how one service may fall in both categories. It also distinguishes between those group-consumption goods for which discrimination in level of service among subgroups is feasible and those for which it is not. The area outside the circles is occupied by marketable goods that are not collective-consumption goods. The examples given in Figure 1 are in physical terms alone ("theatre performance," "mosquito abatement," etc.) for convenience in exposition, but must be accepted with the reservations necessary due to the definitions in terms of efficiency, or, loosely, in terms of per capita costs of alternative techniques.

It is difficult to find illustrations for certain of the sub-sets generated by Figure 1. A group-consumption good of the collective-consumption type (area CJBEDK in Figure 1) usually does not lend itself well to discrimination among subgroups. A mosquito abatement program implemented by destroying certain breeding grounds can scarcely be so handled that any selected subgroup of individuals or firms can be

5. See Appendix B to this chapter.

supplied at a lower level of this service than others (see area HJBEDK). A few instances can be found: a television program can be blacked out for certain nearby areas, and so falls in the segment CJHK in Figure 1).

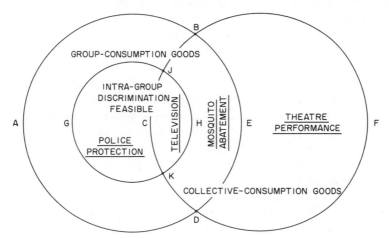

FIGURE 1. Group-Consumption Goods (with and without Intra-Group Discrimination) and Collective-Consumption Goods

a The concepts of "jointness" and "external economies" employed by John G. Head and the concepts of "ownership externalities," "technical externalities," and "public good externalities" employed by Francis M. Bator can be placed in the areas of Figure 1. See Head, "Public Goods and Public Policy," *Public Finance* (1962), 17(3): 197–219, and Bator, "The Anatomy of Market Failure," *Quarterly Journal of Economics* (August, 1958), 72: 351–79.

There seems to be no service commonly supplied free of charge by governments that is a group-consumption good, but not a collective-consumption good, for which it is not feasible to discriminate among geographic subgroups as to level of the service (set ABJGKD). Illustrations can be found outside the governmental field, however. One is Meade's apple blossoms on which other farmers' bees feed.[6] If one more bee-keeper enters the industry, his bees' consumption of the fixed supply of apple blossoms reduces consumption by the other bees; consumption is not collective. Yet any one apple farmer can neither exclude any selected bee-keeper's bees from feeding on the blossoms of his trees nor discriminate against any subgroup of bee-keepers. This bees-apples case falls in Meade's category of external economies or dis-economies due to unpaid factors. Another example appears to be Head's oil field that, once discovered, can be tapped by wells drilled from outside the boundary of the land to which the discoverer holds title. The group consumption is of the oil field owner's exploration and discovery activity, which, along with the oil itself, is consumed by those who drill from outside. The unfortunate owner of the oil field cannot "discriminate" among subgroups.[7] Meade's other type of externality, the creation of atmosphere, illustrates what is here termed a combination of collective

6. *Trade and Welfare*, pp. 39–41.
7. J. G. Head, "Public Goods and Public Policy," *Public Finance* (1962), 17(3): 210.

consumption and group consumption, no intra-group discrimination being feasible (HJBEDK). In Meade's illustration, any wheat farmer can increase his use of rain by growing more wheat without depriving any other wheat farmer of rain.

The group-consumption (nonmarketing) mode in most instances, but not in all, causes the service to be non-rejectable; the service not only must be made available to all in the group, but everyone must consume it. For the most part, non-rejectability does not decrease anyone's welfare as he sees it, but there are striking instances to the contrary: fluoridation of drinking water, for example. A weather broadcast, on the other hand, may be rejected (not listened to), and a fireworks display may be left unseen. In these instances the individual possesses the technical means of rationing himself out of the "service"—to him a negative service—although the mode in which it is supplied prevents the supplier from pricing out or otherwise rationing out any particular individual in the group.

A "group," as already noted on page 70, may be defined either in engineering terms or in political terms. In engineering terms a group is a collection of household and firms, usually the exclusive occupants of a given geographic area, that are affected by the input component that is the most geographically comprehensive one in a bundle of complementary input components. One input component is thus more comprehensive than another if it simultaneously affects more households and firms than does a complementary component. A police information broadcasting system is a more comprehensive input component than any single police patrol car. The group, then, is defined in terms of that input component that in practice, as it is employed with other inputs, is the most comprehensive of all the associated inputs. No single household or firm in such a group can be excluded from the benefits from this input component and hence cannot be entirely excluded from the service rendered by the bundle of inputs. Within this group various levels of service can be rendered to various subgroups, by altering the location of the less comprehensive input components, here, the patrol cars. And if the most comprehensive component is modified physically, as by installing a broadcasting system of more power, together with a rearrangement of the less comprehensive components that allows use of this now-extended comprehensive component, the size of the group, as defined in engineering terms, is changed.

Politically, a group, for present purposes, is a collection of households and firms that have a voice, directly or indirectly, in determining the level of the service to be rendered and the area over which it shall extend (or the non-area discrimination that is to be practiced, as by color or race). Such a group usually has control over more than one bundle of inputs at a time, each bundle consisting of complementary units of input (one of which is the most comprehensive). The geographical location of members of the political group may include areas not reached by the service over which it has control, or influence, as where residents of rural areas are permitted to vote on a proposal to allow a city in the same state to issue bonds that will be serviced entirely by its own inhabitants for purposes not affecting the rural area. And the political group may be smaller than the group to which the service is rendered, as suggested above by the spill-over examples.

3. Redistribution in Kind

Public education (as distinct from the improved milieu it creates) is, as we have seen, rendered in a marketing mode, discrimination down to the level of any selected individual being feasible. But no price is usually charged; the service is rationed directly. Free medical care is also given in the marketing mode, but rationed directly, or indirectly by queuing. Demand for the externalities yielded by these services seems not to have been the sole explanation for the growth of free education and free medical care, especially the latter. Free distribution of these services by the government reflects in part a demand from low-income direct beneficiaries for redistribution of income in kind, financed largely by taxes resting on households of higher income levels.

Redistribution in kind rather than a cash grant has several advantages from the household's point of view. Within the family, the members who most desire the service can be sure it will be available. No such assurance accompanies a cash grant; the member of the family who receives the money may spend it on liquor or tobacco, or travel, or clothing, or lose it by gambling.[8]

Redistribution in kind is easier to achieve, politically, than cash redistribution. First, the service is usually offered to all. The well-to-do household, though it may not avail itself of the service, does not view the offer as quite the useless round-trip that would be evident if it were taxed heavily and received an equivalent cash grant. Second, the sympathies of the well-to-do are more readily invoked by an appeal to repair the lack of a particular consumption good than by an appeal for money, especially for gainful-consumption goods (see pages 592–93), or for services that obviate an appeal for a larger public expenditure later: free medical care may forestall heavy relief costs. Third, they are assured, as are certain members of the low-income family, that the aid cannot be turned into cash and diverted to other ends; the low-income recipients of education and medical care cannot, as the high-income recipients can, substitute these free services for similar services they were purchasing on the market and thus in effect transform the income in kind into income in cash.[9] Redistribution in kind also occurs when certain services are sold at a price well below cost. This topic will be treated in Chapters 6 and 7.

4. Miscellaneous

A few other forces making for free distribution of certain services by the government can be distinguished, as follows.

8. See Michael Young, "Distribution of Income within the Family," *British Journal of Sociology* (1952), 3: 305–321.

9. See page 94 and Appendix C to this chapter.

A. DIFFICULTY OF MEASURING OUTPUT

If the unit of product is difficult to define, the market's pricing mechanism cannot operate well, for it depends on counting or measuring what is sold. Sales price per unit must be stipulated, and the consumer must be assured that he can count or measure what he gets, at least in some rough fashion. The producer must consequently be able to compute cost per unit. Counting or measuring is difficult if the product is a preventive service (see page 78). When a patrolman is added to the police force, the number of crimes may decrease, but the cause-and-effect relationship is less clear than when a worker is added to a textile mill and the output of cloth increases. The crime rate might have decreased anyway; no one doubts that the output of cloth would not have increased.

Thus the dispenser of a preventive type of service, if he is to demonstrate that he is supplying something, must point to a time series (so much crime then, less crime now), or compare with other communities. Many preventive services are sold on the market, usually in the form of tangible intermediate goods—seat belts, vitamin pills—but massive, highly expensive services of the preventive type are generally not marketable (e.g., civil defense shelters). Insurance is of course not a case in point, being compensative rather than preventive. These issues are developed further in pages 78–79 below, where suggestions are offered on how to measure the output of preventive services.

B. UNINSURABLE COSTS

Heavy peaking of consumer costs against which the market mechanism offers inadequate methods of insuring gives rise to demand for free distribution by the government, financed by a quasi-insurance type of tax, if not general taxation. Major medical outlays by low-income consumers, especially elderly persons, is an illustration. Automobile insurance for low-income drivers may prove to be another.

C. GROUP IDENTITY

One of the great consumption goods is the feeling of identity, either with a group or with the achievement of a representative of the group. This feeling becomes intense not only in time of war but also in pursuit of some exciting, large-scale project that can be undertaken only through collective action. In a wealthy society of today exploration of space yields this kind of consumer satisfaction.

D. EXPLOITATION

Exploitation of one group by another is a sufficient explanation for much of government's activity in many times and places. The activity may then be viewed, analytically, as a sort of intermediate product that assists a special group to enjoy its private-sector goods, or, alternatively, as a consumers good supplied only to the privileged group. It is a group-consumption good; the benefits accruing to a high-income ruling group from expenditure on a military force to control a mass of destitute workers cannot usually be monopsonized by some of the favored group.

B. DEFINITION OF UNIT OF OUTPUT

The concept of a physical unit of output of a government service is necessary for study of production functions, cost functions, and measures of efficiency, that is, ratios of output to input.[10] It is necessary also for study of the pattern in which a service, say police service, is distributed among the subgroups (spatial groups, usually) of a community.

Physical-unit demand functions and cost functions are necessary if a distinction is to be drawn between producers' and consumers' surpluses, and if elasticities of demand and of supply are to be defined. Moreover, the physical-unit functions are convenient, if not indispensable, in a study of the analogue of tax shifting and incidence, namely, benefit transfer and incidence (Section E below).

In view of the importance of physical-unit concepts with respect to government services, it may appear strange that virtually no such concepts have been formulated.

10. In cost-benefit analysis much of what might at first be taken for units of output are seen to be units of input (see Chapter 3 above, page 59). Although productivity cannot be computed without a measure of output, since it is to be expressed as the ratio of output to input, the direction of change in productivity over time, i.e., whether up or down, may be conjectured by an intuitive weighing of changes that tend to decrease productivity, e.g., decline in hours worked per week (if "input" is measured not in man-hours but in man-weeks) and those that tend to increase productivity, e.g., apparently favorable changes in administrative methods, and use of new mechanical techniques. On this basis Fabricant (Solomon Fabricant, *The Trend of Government Activity in the United States since 1900* [New York: National Bureau of Economic Research, 1952]) concludes that for the period 1900–1940, "The net result probably has been a decline in input relative to output" (p. 101). He does not attempt to measure output, or to suggest a conceptual basis for measuring it.

Peacock and Wiseman (Alan T. Peacock and Jack Wiseman, assisted by Jindrich Veverka, *The Growth of Public Expenditure in the United Kingdom*, National Bureau of Economic Research [Princeton, N.J.: Princeton University Press, 1961]) are concerned with the changes over time in the ratio of government input plus transfer payments to geographic community output (gross national product at factor cost), this aggregate being defined, as is customary, to include total government input (they use the term expenditures, not input) (pp. 4, 7). They assume "fixed and constant technical coefficients, so that doubling the amount of a service provided implies doubling the amount of labor, material, and so forth, purchased" (p. 139). They touch on the problem of measuring output: "Maintaining the same standard of service should really be discussed in terms of maintaining the health of the community as reflected in such things as mortality and morbidity rates" (p. 139).

Recent interest in urban problems, especially with respect to efficiency, including problems of externalities, has stimulated attempts to define units of output. See especially Werner Z. Hirsch, "Quality of Government Services," in Howard G. Schaller (Ed.), *Public Expenditure Decisions in the Urban Community*, Conference sponsored by Resources for the Future (Baltimore: Johns Hopkins Press, 1963), and G. M. Neutze, *Economic Policy and the Size of Cities* (Canberra: Australian National University, 1965), especially Chapter 5, and sources cited therein.

But it may be recalled that no physical-unit concept of output has been devised for a large proportion of the private sector, particularly trade and the professions. Quality differences in products as they leave the factory pose the same question. Housing is another illustration. One output measure remains for the private sector: the amount of money the service will sell for. Input is then also measured only in money, and if an increment of money input is smaller than the resulting increment of money output, expansion of the service will of course increase profits. While equilibrium analysis is therefore still feasible, in the absence of physical units of product,[11] much other analysis, as indicated in the preceding paragraph, must be forgone. For example: as the spread between increment of money receipts over increment of money expenditures becomes smaller, as the total spent increases, it is not possible to say to what extent this narrowing of the spread is due to relative inelasticity of demand and what part to relative inelasticity of supply.

The physical unit of output of a group-consumption service, if such a unit can be defined, is measured in two dimensions (besides time):[12] (1) number of households or firms served, and (2) level or intensity of service; for example: three units of service per week (this is the level of service) to each of ten households is expressible as thirty household-weeks of units of service. Ten units of service per week to each of three households is also thirty household-weeks of units of service.

1. Preventive Services

In measuring physical units of level of service, preventive services may be contrasted with creative services. A creative service is itself agreeable to consume, or, if rendered to a business firm, creates a new product, intermediate or final. A preventive service is here defined as a service that is not in itself agreeable to consume or receive, but that is valued nevertheless, because it prevents, or is deemed to prevent, something even more disagreeable from happening. If rendered to a business firm, it reduces costs of producing an existing product.

The larger part of services supplied by the government are preventive services: reducing the amount of crime, limiting fire damage, restricting the spread of disease, for example. Deterring real or fancied would-be aggressors is in most countries the preventive service that absorbs the most resources.

The quantitative level of a preventive service must be measured indirectly by ascertaining what the service fails to prevent. Crime prevention affords a good example. No one knows how many crimes a given police force prevents; only the crimes it does not prevent can be counted. Moreover, to conjecture how many crimes will be committed if there is no police force can serve no purpose. Some

11. See, e.g., James Heilbrun, *Real Estate Taxes and Urban Housing* (New York: Columbia University Press, 1966), Chapter 2, "The House-Operating Firm."

12. A third characteristic, geographic area covered, must be considered in constructing a total cost function for the service (see Section C below), but it is regarded not as a dimension of output but as part of the environment, like the weather, that influences the ratio of output to input.

minimum of police service is essential to the existence of the community. In contrast, some minimum of a free creative service is usually not essential to existence of the community, however deplorable entire absence of the service might be. Examples are: a recreation facility, broadcasting, and even free education, viewed solely, for the moment, as a consumer service.

Consequently, analysis of most of the preventive services cannot deal in terms of the total amount (total level) of service rendered. Total input can of course be measured, but to take input for output is to beg the question. Analysis must be in terms of decrements, from an unknown total: one more crime eliminated, from an unknown total of crimes that would be committed if the service were not rendered at all. Moreover, the decrements cannot usefully be assumed to progress indefinitely until prevention is complete. No government is going to spend enough money to prevent all crimes, or to prevent or extinguish without appreciable loss all fires.

2. Creative Services

A creative service is difficult to measure for reasons somewhat different from those applying to preventive services. The state of affairs resulting from a creative service, for example enjoyment of a park, is commonly not as easily quantified in physical terms as are the events remaining to be prevented, e.g., crimes, by a preventive service. Still, some physical measure can sometimes be found: square feet of park space, for example, standardized in some rough manner. But it must be confessed that there are instances where no physical unit seems even conceptually possible; in that event we are correspondingly restricted in the analysis, as explained at the start of this section.[13]

C. COST FUNCTIONS OF GROUP-CONSUMPTION GOODS

As noted in Section A.2 above, the total cost of supplying a group-consumption good varies with level of service, but it may or may not vary with change in numbers served and with geographical area covered. Little is known about most of these cost functions; the considerable amount of data available on variation of per capita expenditure with numbers served, or with density of population, does not usually indicate the nature of the cost functions because the unit of output is not specified.[14] A formal framework for analyzing these cost functions is a necessary prelude to empirical studies. The beginnings of such a framework are presented below.

13. See note 10 above.
14. See the references to other studies in the relevant parts of the next chapter.

1. Marginal, Total, and Average Costs with Respect
to Level of Service and Number Served (Area Constant)

To obtain marginal, total, and average cost curves with respect to level of service, that is, with respect to number of units of service rendered, the separate marginal, total, or average cost curves of serving each member of the group must be added vertically (not horizontally), if the good is a group-consumption good. From the definition of a group-consumption good, that is, a nonmarketable good, it follows that each physical unit of the good must be supplied to each member of the group. The quantity axis, the x-axis in conventional diagrams, must be labeled, not simply "number of units," but "number of units supplied to each member of the group." The y-axis measures "aggregate marginal cost," "aggregate total cost," or "aggregate average cost," the word "aggregate" referring to the multiplicity of persons in the group.

There thus exist for a group-consumption good certain aggregate marginal, average, and total costs, both with respect to level of service (number of physical units) and with respect to number of recipients (households and firms) supplied with a given level of service. For the time being, geographical area covered by the service is assumed fixed.

The second of these groups of cost, the one that varies with number of recipients, is not under the control of the governmental unit that renders the service, since it cannot control the number of households or firms that are to exist in the given area over which the service is to be supplied. Migration and births and deaths cannot be wholly controlled. Indeed, if the number who are receiving the service could be fixed at the desire of the government, it could exclude any who would not pay a price, and, if this was not costly to do, the service rendered would not be one of group-consumption. The variation in size of group occurs at the volition of those who join or leave the group, though of course national governments, particularly, can exercise some control through immigration (or emigration) laws.

For analytical purposes the group may simply be postulated to vary in size as the analyst wishes. Thus the area that is cleared of mosquitoes by drainage of ponds may be thought of as accommodating a varying number of households or firms over time, or by comparative statics analysis it may be postulated to accommodate varying numbers at one point in time, but there is nothing in the nature of the technique of rendering the service that allows the dispenser of it to determine the number who shall receive the service.

A single household or firm, by entering or leaving an area, may therefore raise or lower the average per capita cost of a given level of service to all the others in the area. The migrant thus creates an externality, just as does a motorist who enters or leaves a congested highway. The consequences of this kind of externality will be explored in Chapter 21.

The cost of supplying an incremental household with 1 unit, or 2 units, or 3 units, or more, of the service, as the case may be, is shown in Figure 2 by the vertical distance between the curves in that figure. More generally, the cost of supplying a given number of units of the service to an i'th household is the vertical distance from the aggregate marginal cost curve that includes the i'th household (but no more) to the aggregate marginal cost curve that includes the $(i-1)$th household (but no more).

In Figure 2, but not in the subsequent figures (for simplicity), there is added a supplementary quantity axis, labeled x', to designate the total number of units of service supplied. Thus if 2 units of service are being supplied to an area containing one household, the total number of units supplied is 2; if there are two households in the area, total number of units supplied is 2×2, or 4; if there are three households, $2 \times 3 = 6$ units are supplied. This supplementary x-axis is applicable to all subsequent figures, though in the pure collective-consumption case, to which we now turn, it loses some significance, at least with respect to cost.

Figure 3 illustrates the marginal cost condition for a collective consumption good (whether a group-consumption good or a marketable good). This condition is but the limiting case of what was illustrated in Figure 2. For a collective-consumption good the marginal cost of supplying a second or third household with a given number of units of the service is zero. The marginal cost curves with respect to each household are still added vertically, but the amount so added, beyond the First Household, is zero; each i'th aggregate marginal cost curve beyond the curve for the First Household coincides with the First Household curve.

Returning to Figure 2, we see that the curves there have been drawn to illustrate the possibilities that the marginal cost of serving one more household a given number of units of the service may be either decreasing (compare the vertical distance from 1 to A with that from A to D) or increasing (AD is less than DG). Of course it may be constant; and in the collective-consumption case it is constant at zero, once the First Household is served. Figure 2 also illustrates constant aggregate marginal cost and increasing aggregate marginal cost with respect to level of service: the distance from 1 to G is the same as that from 2 to H, but is less than that from 3 to J.

For simplicity, in Figure 2, the vertical distances between the curves are in the same proportion to the distance from the x-axis to the First-Household curve, at 1, at 2, and at 3 units, but there is no a priori reason why they need to be.

Total-cost curves for the Figure 2 case are drawn in Figure 4. The vertical distance represents of course the area underneath the respective marginal curve in Figure 2.

Average per-unit cost is shown in Figure 5; the totals in Figure 4 have been divided by 1, 2, and 3 respectively.

A quite different concept, average cost per household, is shown in Figure 6; the totals in Figure 4 have been divided by 3, 3, and 3.

In each of these figures, the distance along the x-axis can be chosen by the supplier of the service, but, as already indicated, he cannot choose the distance up the y-axis. That distance depends (except in the limiting case of Figure 3) upon how many households decide to live in the area.

With respect to increments in the level of a service supplied to a fixed number of

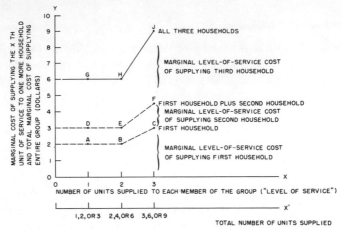

FIGURE 2. Marginal Cost of Group-Consumption Good for Level of Service and Number in Group (Non-Collective-Consumption Good)

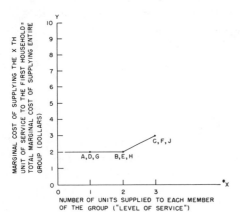

FIGURE 3. Marginal Cost of Group-Consumption, Collective-Consumption Good, for Level of Service and Number in Group

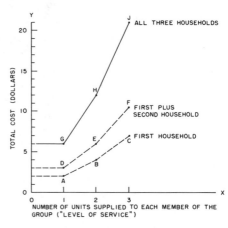

FIGURE 4. Total Cost of Group-Consumption Good, for Level of Service and Number in Group (Non-Collective-Consumption Good)

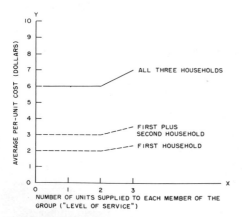

FIGURE 5. Average Per-Unit Cost of Group-Consumption Good, for Level of Service and Number in Group (Non-Collective-Consumption Good)

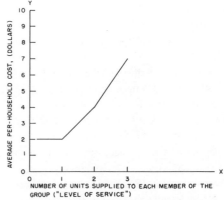

FIGURE 6. Average Per-Household Cost of Group-Consumption Good, for Level of Service (Non-Collective-Consumption Good)

recipients in a given area, we have seen that marginal cost is always positive; total cost always increases. Eventually total cost will increase more than in proportion to the increase in level of service. Initially, however, the increase may be less than in proportion; marginal cost is declining, or, if rising, it follows an initial large investment (overhead cost), which itself may be smaller per capita as more are served.[15] If the level of service can be varied among subgroups within the area, initially decreasing marginal costs may tend to prevent gross discrimination in the geographical pattern of service. The wealthy sub-areas will be the more willing to help finance for the poorer sub-areas a higher level of the service than those sub-areas would otherwise be given. And apart from this aspect, it may be easier, as Chapter 21 will indicate, to reach agreement on financing increments of service if the community attempts to move to a Pareto optimum in accordance with the Wicksell unanimity rule that is explained in that chapter.

With respect to an increase in the number of recipients of a given level of a service (non-collective–consumption goods), the rise in total cost may be either abrupt or gradual. If gradual, the rise will almost surely be such that per capita average cost will continue to decline for some time as the size of the group increases. The rate of decline will of course be lower than when total cost does not increase at all with group size (collective-consumption good).

Incremental per capita cost will sooner or later increase with size of consuming group. Eventually, therefore, average per capita cost will rise. The size of the group at which average per capita cost starts to rise is here termed the minimum-cost group (minimum per capita cost). As just noted, the marginal cost, the increment of cost required to serve one more user, will have been rising before the minimum-cost group size is reached, except where the additional factor that is brought into use at the collective-consumption limit is very lumpy.

Up to the size of the minimum-cost group, it is to the advantage of those in any area to attract households and firms from other areas, to reduce the per capita cost, and is to the disadvantage of those in any area to lose households and firms. Fiscal relations among these gaining jurisdictions and losing jurisdictions will be affected, the losing jurisdictions perhaps demanding grants in aid from the gaining jurisdictions.[16] Within any one jurisdiction there is continual dispute over the pattern in which the service is distributed throughout the jurisdiction's area, a dispute that concerns both efficient allocation in the Pareto-optimum sense and the distribution of real disposable income including free government services.

If the service is a collective-consumption good, average per capita cost falls in proportion to the increase in numbers served, since the marginal cost with respect to numbers served is zero. For some types of collective-consumption goods, the number of recipients in a given area can increase indefinitely without adding to the total cost of rendering the service; there is no collective-consumption limiting size.

---

15. For a discussion of change in per capita cost of a service as numbers increase, especially change due to economies or diseconomies of scale, see G. M. Neutze, *Economic Policy and the Size of Cities* (Canberra: Australian National University, 1965), especially pp. 21–24, and Chapters 5 and 6.

16. See Chapters 21 and 25.

A radio or television broadcast is an example. Eradication of mosquitoes from a swamp whence they have been plaguing a given area is another (see also page 103).

For other types of collective consumption, total cost remains constant only up to a capacity point, as with a city park. If more than a certain number attempt to enjoy the service, it can be maintained at the same level of quality only by an increase in total cost, to enlarge the park or to create another park. A municipal auditorium is a similar example. If the park or auditorium can be planned in any one of a continuous series of sizes, the service is not one of collective consumption at all, in the planning stage; to plan to serve one more user, a slightly greater total cost must be accepted. Once the structure or space has been constructed or laid out, consumption is collective within the capacity limits of that structure or area.

To distinguish this type of collective consumption from that exemplified by the radio or television broadcast, or mosquito eradication, it may be termed short-run collective consumption. Short-run collective-consumption services are typically marketable services, not group-consumption goods.[17] The fact that the size of the structure or the area can be varied in the planning stage seems to be an indirect technical hint that, when the facility is in operation, exclusion of any individual will be practicable. Those services for which no capacity limit exists are commonly both collective-consumption goods and group-consumption goods simultaneously.[18]

2. Marginal, Total, and Average Costs with Respect to Area Served (Level of Service and Number Served Constant)

We have seen that the total cost of rendering a service under a group-consumption technique varies in certain ways, or remains constant, as numbers in the group change, given the level or levels of the service, and given the geographical area within which the group receives the service. Also, the total cost of rendering such a service varies, almost always directly, with the level of service, or levels, given to a group of fixed size within a given area. We now inquire how total cost varies if the level of service and the size of the group are both fixed, but the area within which this fixed-numbers group receives the service expands or contracts. Size of group, level of service, and area covered are the three chief determinants of total cost of rendering a service under a group-consumption technique.

The answer varies according to the service. The possibilities will be illustrated in Chapter 5, where the major services offered by governments are examined separately. Sometimes total cost will rise, then fall, or fall, then rise, as area increases, and whether it first rises or falls will depend on the size of the area with which the analysis starts. Indeed, the cost function by area is even more complex. Any given service, say protection against crime, usually employs many technically different types of input: for example, patrol cars, and a receiving-sending system that allows the patrol cars to communicate with the central station and with each other. If a given population disperses over a wider area, the total cost of affording a given level

17. Area EBFD in Figure 1.   18. Area CJBEDK in Figure 1.

of protection rises as far as the patrol cars are concerned, but remains unchanged—within a wide area—with respect to the internal communications system. And it is conceivable that the total cost for patrol cars, instead of increasing with area, will decrease as congestion and consequent delays in answering calls or pursuing criminals decreases. Finally, among rival techniques for supplying the service in a group-consumption manner, one technique may increase in total cost, while another will decrease, as area expands (and therefore the reverse, if area contracts), while behaving differently, too, with regard to changes in size of group and level of service. The authority may therefore substitute one group-consumption technique of supplying the service for another as numbers served, level of service, or area covered change.

For a truly collective-consumption service, total cost remains unchanged, as the number of persons served increases, only if the geographical area over which the recipients are spread remains unchanged. The total cost of the radio or television broadcast referred to above will increase if the fixed number of recipients spreads out over a wider area, necessitating a more powerful transmitter. Mosquito eradication for a fixed number of households will eventually require attention to more swamps, as the fixed population disperses.

For such a service, an increase in density of population (number of inhabitants per square mile) does not change the total cost if it occurs through an increase of population in a given area. Average cost per inhabitant falls proportionately to the increase in density. But if density increases through a contraction of area, the population remaining constant, total cost falls and average cost per inhabitant falls, although not necessarily in proportion to the increase in density; for example, if a broadcasting station with enough power to cover 1,000 square miles at a total cost of k dollars serves initially a population of 1,000, and later, a population of 2,000, average cost per recipient falls from $k/1,000$ to $k/2,000$, that is, by one-half, while density is decreasing by one-half. If, instead, the initial 1,000 inhabitants move closer together, without changing in number, so that they occupy only 500 square miles, the total cost of a broadcasting station will no doubt be less than k dollars, but not necessarily just $k/2$ dollars.

Thus a change in density will affect per capita cost of a collective-consumption good differently depending on how the change in density comes about. There is no unique relation between density and per capita cost, for a collective-consumption good. Of two metropolitan areas with the same density (evenly spread), one covering twice the area of the other (hence possessing twice the population of the other), the larger will incur a greater total cost for a given level of a collective-consumption good, but per capita cost may be higher, lower, or the same.

There may be instances of collective-consumption goods that do not vary in total cost with size of area covered, but none comes to mind.

For a group-consumption good that is not a collective-consumption good, total cost for supplying a fixed number of persons with a given level of service does not inevitably increase as that fixed number becomes dispersed, over a larger geographical area. Traffic control, for example, probably decreases in total cost. But total cost of fire protection increases, or, if initially the concentration is very high, first decreases, then increases.

Moreover, since total cost now increases with the number served in a given area, the per capita cost in such an instance may vary in a number of ways, instead of varying inversely and proportionately, as with a true collective-consumption good.

Accordingly, the relation of per capita cost to density, and of incremental per capita cost to an increment in density may be increasing, decreasing, or constant, according to circumstances.

These variations in total cost with area served, population and level of service constant, tend to induce concentration or dispersion, with consequent implications for intergovernmental relations. If other forces, gregariousness for example, tend to induce ever-increasing concentration, and if costs of government service rise with concentration, the optimum allocation of resources between private and public funds is altered.

3. Complementary Relationship

Many services may well be complementary in production. The higher the level of education, the less costly it may be to reduce the crime rate from a given level of crime. In a three-commodity world, the increase in the share of the community's resources going to education leaves a smaller total of resources for crime prevention and for market products, and the end result of an increase in education may therefore be a higher, not a lower, crime rate. Yet the marginal cost of crime prevention at a given level of crime, that is, the cost of preventing one more crime, given a certain level of crime, is lower, the larger the amount of resources that is devoted to education. This complementary relationship is particularly marked between certain services and certain welfare payments or subsidies.

D. VALUE OF SERVICE TO RECIPIENT

A free government service exerts a positive income effect on the recipients, or on those to whom the recipients relinquish the benefits, and the size of the income effects depends of course partly on the value attributed to the service by the recipient or other beneficiary. The income effect tends to increase the beneficiary's purchase of marketed goods and services (see Chapter 22 below, pages 540-41), and is to be taken into account in computing the distribution of real disposable income (see Chapter 23 below, page 586). These considerations raise the question how the initial benefit to the recipient is to be measured. If a physical unit of the service has been defined (Section B above), and if a value can be assigned to each unit, the total benefit can be computed. Where the physical unit cannot be defined, a value may perhaps be assigned to the service en bloc.

The service received may be an externality, that is, a joint product with a marketable service. The improvement in milieu due to the educating of others is thus a service posing all the problems of measurement and the like that the services of public health, defense, and similar activities raise. The problem of measuring benefit is a familiar one in the field of project evaluation, that is, cost-benefit analysis (see pages 520–22), but it is posed here in its most acute form, to include group-consumption services that have no close substitutes on the market.

As in usual demand analysis, two measures of total value to the recipient household may be considered. One is the value that the household places on the marginal unit of service, multiplied by the number of units it receives. The result is the total it would have to pay if the service could be purchased by it on a competitive market. The other is the all-or-none computation: what is the most the household would pay if its only alternative were to forego, not just a marginal unit, but the entire amount of the service?[19] In choosing between these two computations, the following point is relevant.

The market forces that may compel the household or firm to relinquish benefits from government services operate usually with respect to locational differences in levels of the service, and these differences in level of service are commonly a small proportion of the amount of the service available at the least favored location: somewhat more police protection in one district of the city than in another (not zero protection in that other district), somewhat easier access to a city park than in another district (not zero access to any city park in that other district). Accordingly, it will be more fruitful, usually, to operate in modest incremental terms, asking, what is the value to the recipient of the increment in government service, and how much of this value do market forces compel him to relinquish?

In any event it must be specified whether the value being reckoned is a net value, that is, after subtracting what the recipient will have to pay in tax toward covering the cost of the service, or whether it is a gross value in the sense either that the recipient's consequent tax is abstracted from, or that he is supposed not to be subject to any increment of tax, at least at or near the margin of the service rendered. In the analysis to follow, unless otherwise specified, the gross value concept will be employed, consistent with the partial equilibrium analysis generally used in this Book Two.

In a few instances the value of the free service to the household is easy to estimate because the service saves a certain market expense and is not prized for its own sake (the service is a preventive service). If free collection of household refuse replaces purchased collection, the value of the free service to the household is at least the amount of expense saved. Sometimes the free service both saves expense and gives something more. A higher level of fire protection may not only decrease the premium payable for fire insurance but also reduce fear and the chance of inconvenience and other disutilities not coverable by insurance.

The benefits of a free government service are not necessarily, or even usually, distributed equally among the members of a household. The initial impact may be only on the husband, the wife, or the children. And the initial beneficiary may be compelled by customs of the household to relinquish the benefit to some other member. A city park may benefit chiefly the wife and children; a municipal golf

19. See Milton Friedman, *Price Theory*, p. 15.

course, the husband. These facts suggest that, in order to value the service, the household must be disaggregated. It then becomes difficult to ascertain just how much the wife—not to mention the children—would pay for the park service if it were available only at a price, since the answer depends partly on the intra-family disposal of the household's income. In general, then, it seems preferable to keep the analysis at the level of the household, although this course will be seen to be unfruitful for much of the unrequited-payments discussion (Chapter 7).

A business firm values a free government service either at what it saves the firm in expense or at what it gains the firm in gross receipts.

E. RELINQUISHING BENEFITS FROM
FREE SERVICES (INCIDENCE OF SERVICE BENEFITS)

It will be recalled from Chapter 2 that a free government service cannot be tested against the criteria listed there until its incidence and its rival or complementary effects are known or conjectured. The findings on incidence reveal the location of the income effect of the free government service and so take one step toward knowledge of how that service affects allocation of resources in the private sector, as well as providing the information needed for application of the distributive tests. The findings on rival or complementary relationships with the private sector provide the second and final step for knowledge of the allocation effects.

The income effect of the free service will be exerted on someone other than the household or firm that directly absorbs the service when the incidence of the service differs from its impact. An illustration is supplied by a city park that is used by nearby apartment house dwellers who are forced by competition among themselves to pay a higher rent to the building owner, to enjoy this free good. The residents thus lose part of the benefit while continuing to make use of (enjoy) the service. Another illustration is special police protection that spares a firm from having to hire its own guards but that does not increase its profits, because competition from firms receiving the same free service forces it to lower its selling prices; the incidence of the free service to the firm is on the consumers of the product produced by it and on factors other than the firm's ownership capital.

When the user of the service loses part or all of the benefit, the benefit will be said to be "relinquished" to others. The user might be said to "shift" the benefit, were it not for the connotation, acquired from the use of "shifting" in tax analysis, that one is gladly ridding oneself of a burden, instead of, as here, being compelled to lose a benefit.

Some firms may incur a loss because they or their customers are excluded from the service. In the park example, owners of property located so far from the park that residents do not benefit from it, but near enough so that a residence close to the park is in other respects a good substitute, will experience a decline in property values.

The test for whether the benefit from the government service has been relinquished by the initial recipient is a comparison, at a given point in time, between the existing economic condition of the household or firm and the condition it would have been experiencing at that time if the service had not been rendered.

Since the second half of this comparison is a description of a hypothetical state of affairs, the definition just given is not itself an operational one; the hypothesis that a relinquishing of the benefit has occurred cannot be tested directly. Sometimes a rough sort of testing can be carried out by analyzing a time series, either through techniques that are presumed to eliminate the influence of other factors, leaving as a residue the result of the government's action, or by selecting a short period during which the public finance measure is apparently so overwhelmingly the major influence that a post-hoc-ergo-propter-hoc assumption seems reasonably safe. The latter approach is used in "common-sense" appraisals of many tax changes, as when a cigarette tax is raised by a cent or two a package and the price of cigarettes rises correspondingly.

A statement of the distribution of benefits and losses from a free government service must therefore specify the point or period of time for which that description is valid. As time passes, those who are reaping the benefits from the service may change. In the example above, those already resident near the park may benefit initially; as leases expire, the benefit may pass to the building owners; as still more time elapses, owners of building sites may obtain the benefits. Eventually, an equilibrium may be reached: the particular households or firms benefited may no longer change. But this outcome is not certain. The benefits, as well as the losses, may continue moving through groups of households and firms indefinitely.

A free government service is not usually attached to a market transaction, as are many taxes and subsidies. The amount of the free service given to a household or firm does not vary directly with the amount or value of some marketable product that it buys or sells, or some factor payment that it makes or receives.[20]

Accordingly, the amount of the free government service cannot usefully be expressed as a certain percentage of the price of some marketable good, or as so much per physical unit of a good.[21] Hence the extent to which the benefit of this service is relinquished by the initial recipient cannot be expressed by comparing the value of a unit of the service with a change in price of some marketable good or service. Instead, the value of the free service, quantified as suggested above, is to be compared with the loss of real market income that the service recipient suffers from a consequent decline in price or quantity of things he sells, or rise in price or quantity of things he buys. Changes in totals rather than changes in per unit quantities are compared. The decline or rise in the service recipient's real market income must be directly attributable to his receipt of the free service; it is a decline or rise that would not have occurred if he were not receiving the free service. If the two values just offset one another, the benefit of the free service has been completely relinquished to others.

20. In this respect the free government service is the analogue of a death or gift tax and contrasts with excise taxes and income taxes.

21. Again, like a death or gift tax.

1. Consumer Services

Relinquishing the benefit from a free consumer service is most likely to occur if that service is locational, that is, if enjoyment of it is conditioned strictly upon the consumer's location in space, as with the city park. The process by which the benefit is transferred from the consumer to the landlord, and ultimately to the site owner, is as follows. When the park is constructed, households compete for the favored site, and push up rentals. Land some distance from the park, as noted, will fall in value as households move to the newly prized area. Over the long run, land near the park will be more intensively built on than if the park had not come into existence, and less intensive use will be made of dwelling land distant from the park. Relative intensive margins of building on land will thus alter.

Intensity here is measured in terms of total cost of construction of dwelling space per unit area of land. As more and more building is put on a given area of land, increasing costs are encountered; it costs more to add a certain amount of dwelling accommodation of a specified quality as the buildings go higher and higher. At the new long-run equilibrium, so much more building will have been put on the land near the park that the last unit of building will only just pay for itself, despite the high rentals that can be charged because of the park's presence. The previous units, the intra-marginal units, of added building will more than pay for themselves; the excess, together with the added rentals paid for dwelling space that existed before the park was open, constitute the higher land rent. A similar process, in reverse, proceeds on land distant from the park.

Some services to households may or may not be locational, depending on circumstances. Strengthening the police detail in a certain residential area will raise rents in that area (abstracting from the taxes imposed to finance the service). But strengthening the police detail in all residential areas of a certain type within the city will raise rents only in so far as households move from similar dwelling areas in other cities to bid for like accommodations in this one. Since this reaction may well be slow and moderate, the benefit of an increment of police protection that is widely and uniformly distributed is more likely to stay with the household.

Residential areas of strikingly different types that house different ethnic or income groups are not good substitutes for each other. Widespread increments of police protection can therefore give rise to increased rents if each increment is concentrated in a small part of the area of a given residential type.

2. Producer Services

Government services that are supplied free of charge to business firms are here termed producer services. They include some creative services, a common example being research findings of a government bureau that has been organized to help a particular industry produce a new product.

Education that enhances productive power is a creative service to the individual. If the wage-earner or salaried employee is viewed as a firm selling his labor,[22] such education is a producer service. It will simultaneously be a consumer service if the individual values the education apart from its productive aspects, but we are concerned here only with its productive aspects.

A preventive service may increase productivity generally. Police protection in a residential area enhances the productivity of all the area's residents. They will normally be employed in so many different sectors of industry and trade that this enhancement effect is unlikely to influence allocation of resources among those sectors. The service is not likely, therefore, to benefit firms in particular industries or consumers of particular products.

On the other hand, a preventive service may instead be concentrated on one or a few industries: for example extra police protection in a jewelry trading district or government research that discovers a new method of extracting oil from shale economically. Usually the preventive service to the producers must be analyzed in terms of increments, not totals, for reasons already given, but in the present examples the producer service is so restricted that the result under a certain amount of the service can be compared with the hypothetical result under zero service.

An increment of free service to business firms in a particular industry lowers the average per unit cost of production for all firms in that industry. It may also lower marginal cost. If it lowers marginal cost by a uniform amount regardless of how many units are being produced, we may employ, in reverse, the familiar theorems of excise-tax incidence in the short run, that is, over the period during which the number of firms in the industry remains unchanged.

Under competition and increasing marginal cost to the firm, the firm will seize the opportunity to make profits by increasing its output along its new low marginal cost curve until marginal cost again equals price, which for the moment is unchanged. But as all firms act this way, industry output increases and price falls. Moreover the temporary excess of price over average cost, before the price declines, attracts new firms to the industry. A new equilibrium will be reached at a lower market price. If the industry can expand at a constant cost to the industry, by adding new firms, price will fall by the full amount of the value of the service to the firm. The benefit will have been entirely relinquished to consumers of the product. The physical quantity of factors employed directly by the industry will tend to decrease to the extent that a smaller quantity of factors is needed to produce a unit of output, owing to the free government service. The factors dispensed with for this reason will at least in part be engaged by the government to produce the service now given free of charge to firms or to meet the increased demand for the product.

Under increasing costs to the industry, product price will fall, but by less than the benefit, the cost-reduction, per unit of product. Only a part of the benefit will have been diverted to purchasers. The rest of the benefit will accrue to at least some of those factors that have not been displaced by the free service, and to factors drawn

22. In principle, there should also be included those services that increase the output of an imputed product in the home, cooking and housecleaning, for example.

freshly into the industry, since the increasing-cost assumption implies an increase in wage to at least one factor.

Under monopoly, the familiar tax theorems regarding a fixed tax per unit would similarly apply in reverse. A little reflection indicates, however, how unreal is the assumption of constant marginal benefit per unit of product from a free government service to business firms. A government subsidy (to be treated in Chapter 6) is another matter; as with many taxes, it is commonly a constant amount per unit of output. But a free government service, such as special fire protection to a certain industry, is more likely to reduce each firm's short-run fixed costs than its variable costs. Fire insurance premiums paid are a typical short-run fixed cost that will be reduced, though outlay on insured inputs may almost immediately increase. If the benefit does reduce variable costs, it is unlikely to reduce them uniformly over all ranges of output.

When the benefit affects only the level of a firm's fixed costs, it can operate on prices and quantities of product only through an increase in the number of firms in the industry.

3. Hypothetical Examples

Some hypothetical examples may serve to fix the ideas suggested in the pages above:

1. An extra detail of police is supplied by the city free of charge to an amusement park, at a cost to the city of $100. If this protection had not been supplied, the amusement enterprise would have engaged private policemen at a cost of $150. In either case the firm's other expenses and its gross receipts would have been unchanged. The benefit to the firm is $150, no part of which is relinquished to others.

2. Competing shopowners in a certain district are supplied with additional free fire protection by the city at a cost to it of $5,000 a year: more fire engines are located closer to the district. As a result, insurance companies serving these firms lower the premiums on fire insurance policies by $10,000. The firms, which together sell 10,000 units of a product to the public, lower their selling prices by $1. Abstracting for the moment from the possible consequent increase in number of units demanded by the public at the lower price, the benefit from the free producer service is $10,000, all of which is relinquished to consumers.[23]

3. An individual, A, receives a certain amount of vocational education free of charge from the government that enables him to increase his lifetime earnings, net of increased costs accompanying these earnings, by a present value of $10,000. He does not enjoy the vocational training. The price of the service that A will sell is not depressed by the training which is given to A alone. He has received a producer benefit of $10,000, no part of which is relinquished. He is here considered a business firm, in his capacity as a vendor of labor.

4. The vocational training of No. 3 is supplied, not only to A, but also to 99

---

23. To the degree that this district competes with other districts for trade, some part of the benefit will accrue to building owners and landowners.

others, with the result that the selling price of their skill is somewhat depressed, through competition among them, from the level that would have obtained if none of them had been trained. Each of the trainees, including A, possesses a present-value increment of $4,000 in lifetime net earnings, a total of $400,000. If the selling price of their skill had remained unaffected by the increment in supply of 100 skilled persons, the vocational training would have yielded a present-value increment in lifetime earnings of $1,000,000. Consequently, the producer benefit to A and his fellows is $1,000,000, of which $600,000 is relinquished to consumers.

5. In No. 4, each individual so enjoys the vocational training itself that he would pay $1,000 rather than go without it, even if it did not affect his future earnings. The benefit to the trainees now amounts to $1,100,000 of which $1,000,000 is a producer benefit (since the training does in fact increase future earnings) and $100,000 a consumer benefit. Of the $1,000,000 producer benefit, $600,000, as explained above, is relinquished.

We recall that the foregoing definitions and examples are all constructed on a micro basis; no account is taken of how the government obtains the money required to cover the cost of supplying the service.

A society in which a large part of the national income must be spent on preventive services is not as well off as a society of equal resources that experiences no higher crime rate, disease rate, and fire rate while devoting less of its resources to preventive efforts and more to free supplies of recreation, travel, or other creative services. It is not as well off, in the sense that, given a choice between living in the one or the other society, individuals would prefer to live in the latter. These differences have implications for economic growth. A society whose members respect the rule of law, are thoughtful of the rights of others, and cautious in guarding against natural disasters or human proclivity to accident can release that much more resources for creative services, whether public or private.

F. REJECTABLE SERVICES

The household or firm may wish to reject the free service. Whether it can, and if so, whether the government is concerned by the rejection, depends on the nature of the service. The government is concerned over possible rejection if the service carries externalities: education for example. In contrast, if members of a household have no desire to listen to the broadcast of a weather report, presumably no one cares. If the marginal cost of offering the service to the rejecting household is positive, the government will be concerned over the waste of resources.

A free service can be rejected, in whole or in part, in two ways: directly and indirectly. The direct way is simply to refuse to accept the service; the household does not turn on the radio for the weather broadcast. But direct rejection is not always feasible. Technical features may make direct rejection impossible, as when a city's drinking water is fluoridated, or when the government uses force, as through truant officers.

Indirect rejection of the free service occurs when the household reduces its purchases of a good that is a close substitute for the free service, perhaps indeed the very same good. Education is an example. Suppose that household A is both purchasing education, say private music lessons, and accepting free education of other types from the public school. If the public school now requires every pupil to take music lessons, partly because of the advantage that everyone gains by having musically educated fellow citizens, it will probably fail to induce Household A to increase its total consumption of music education by the amount of the free music education, since that household can reduce the music education it has been purchasing on the market.

The same problem for the government exists if the household reduces its purchases of some good that, although not identical to the free service, is a very close substitute for it in the eyes of both the government and the household. In an attempt to reduce the number of fires, the government may increase its outlay on the fire department, but households may partly negate this effort by purchasing fewer fire extinguishers just because the government is giving better fire protection.

When the free service is a perfect substitute for a good the household is already purchasing, the effect of the service on the household is the same as a cash grant large enough to purchase an amount of the rival, marketed good that gives the same satisfaction to the household as the amount of the free service it receives. A cash grant with no conditions attached has an income effect but no substitution effect. The income effect will induce the household to take a little more of each superior good, including saving and leisure. Hence the household will consume a little more music education than before, in the example above, while purchasing less music education than before. In effect, a part of the free service, music education, has been indirectly rejected.[24]

APPENDIX A[1] TO CHAPTER FOUR

In a world of two persons, A and B, consuming two goods, Good 1 is assumed always to be dispensed in the marketing mode, but Good 2 is dispensed either in the marketing mode or in the group-consumption mode (i.e., no excludability). If Good 2 is dispensed in the latter mode, a Samuelsonian utility frontier[2] is depicted on a diagram that ranks Person A's utility on the horizontal axis and Person B's utility on the vertical axis. In Figure 7 this utility frontier is shown by the line GG'. It is labeled GG' (group-consumption good) to indicate that Good 2 is being dispensed in a manner such that no particular person can be excluded from enjoyment of the good if it is dispensed to any one person in the group.

24. See Appendix C to this chapter.

1. See John G. Head and Carl S. Shoup, "Public Goods, Private Goods, and Ambiguous Goods" (article forthcoming in *Economic Journal*).

2. Paul A. Samuelson, "Diagrammatic Exposition of a Theory of Public Expenditure," *Review of Economics and Statistics* (November, 1955), 37: 350–56, p. 352, chart 4.

If Good 2 is instead dispensed in the marketing mode, another, alternative utility frontier arises, shown in Figure 7 by MM'. The service is, say, a lighthouse beacon, which may be scrambled and can then be detected only by ships equipped with an unscrambling device, which must be purchased.

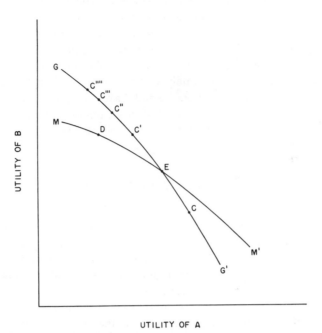

FIGURE 7. Utility Frontiers for Group-Consumption Mode and Marketing Mode of an Ambiguous Good

In Figure 7 these alternative utility frontiers, GG' and MM', intersect. Because they do intersect, it is not possible to say that the service, the warning beacon of the lighthouse, is unambiguously a marketable good (private good) or unambiguously a group-consumption good (public good), under the test of economic efficiency. It is an ambiguous good. The efficiency test calls for operating somewhere on the envelope curve formed by the GE segment of the GG' curve and the EM' segment of the MM' curve. Compared with any point on that envelope curve there is no point on the ME segment of the MM' curve or on the EG' segment of the GG' curve that will make both A and B at least as well off as they are at the point on the GEM' envelope curve. Thus at point D on the ME segment, both A and B are worse off than they would be within the range C''' to C' on the GE segment; A is worse off at D than he would be at any point on GE to the left of C''' (say, at C''''); B is worse off than he would be at any point in the range C'E. Similar comparisons may be made starting with a point such as C on the EG' segment of the GG' curve.

If the GG' curve were to lie outside (i.e., further from the origin than) the MM' curve at all points, this Good 2 would be unambiguously a group-consumption good.

Starting from any point whatsoever on GG' it would be impossible to obtain on the marketing curve MM' any point that would make both A and B at least as well off as they were at the point on GG'.

Persons A and B land on a particular point on the GG' curve (or on the MM' curve if the good is dispensed in the marketing mode) because of a number of influences, the most important in the present context being (1) the cost schedules of the good under the mode chosen, (2) the distribution of factor ownership, which helps determine A's and B's demands for the two goods, and (3) the pattern in which there are shared the infra-marginal costs of goods that are marketed in the group-consumption mode (here, only Good 2, and only if it is marketed in that mode), since this pattern, too, affects A's and B's demands for the two goods.

The construction of Figure 7 does not of course limit the discussion to two goods, and the analysis is valid in principle for any number of persons.

APPENDIX B TO CHAPTER FOUR

The term "externality" is here limited to designate a group-consumption good that is a joint product with a marketable good. This kind of group-consumption good happens also to be always a collective-consumption good. The term externality is not here applied to a group-consumption good that is a joint product with another group-consumption good. If an additional patrolman not only reduces crime but also increases the level of fire protection through the reduction of crime, neither of these services is said to be an externality of the other; they are simply jointly produced group-consumption goods.

The externality may be negative; a marketable good may give rise to disservices to individuals or firms that these unfortunate recipients cannot buy away from, because it is not feasible for the factory that emits smoke, for example, to spare a selected household or firm from the smoke upon payment of a price. Group action is required (see Chapter 21).

Products that are merely complementary in production bear a weaker relation to one another than do joint products. More of one complementary product can be produced without producing more of the other. Joint products, as that term is used here, are fixed in their proportions of output. The complementary relation, in contrast, says only that the more of one that is being produced, the lower is the marginal cost of producing the other, at a given level of production of that other. Apple blossoms are a joint product with apples.

Buchanan prefers to extend the term externality to include the consumption of what is here termed a group-consumption good by individuals when that good is deliberately supplied by or to a given individual (see his review of Musgrave's *Theory of Public Finance*, in *Southern Economic Journal* [January, 1960], 26: 234–38). An even wider scope for the term is advocated by Head to include the multiplier and real balance effects ("Public Goods and Public Policy," *Public Finance* [1962], 3: 217); Baumol (*Welfare Economics and the Theory of the State*, p. 29) expresses a similar view. Broad definitions are called for when one is engaged in throwing light on hitherto unappreciated similarities; narrow definitions, when the emphasis is on discovering differences. The latter is the immediate goal in the text above.

An externality as defined in the present analysis possesses the characteristics posited by Baumol (*op. cit.*, pp. 26–27) of (1) interdependence *at the margin* in a manner such that a further slight increase in the marketed service increases the utility of the recipient negligibly, because of the manner in which the function varies in the neighborhood of the recipient's own maximum of utility, while the utility of the recipient of the externality is still increasing appreciably, his utility not being at or near a maximum (on this point, see also Buchanan and Stubblebine, "Externality," *Economica* [November, 1962], 29: 371–84, cited by Baumol), and (2) lack of accompanying compensation.

A geographical spill-over of a service or disservice (see page 69) is an externality in the broad sense in which the word externality is commonly used. In the present analysis, however, externality is given a narrower definition, for reasons noted above, and is distinguished from a spill-over, which is a geographical concept involving only one service at a time, a service—or disservice—rendered over an area only part of which is within the boundaries of a political group, that is, within the boundaries of the governmental unit that decides upon and dispenses the service.

There is no spill-over of intra-group discrimination. City A cannot raise and lower as it wishes, the level of service supplied by it to some subgroup within its boundaries relative to the level that it supplies, through spill-over, to some subgroup in City B. The level of the spill-over is fixed by, though it is not the same as, the level of the service rendered within the dispensing government's boundaries. Spill-overs resemble externalities in being strictly joint products with the primary product.

A merit want, as it is defined by Musgrave (*Theory of Public Finance*, p. 13) is met by a service that, although subject to the exclusion principle (that is, is a marketable good), is purchased in an amount smaller than that for a social optimum, at least in part because the purchasers underestimate the benefits they will receive. Externalities are not involved in the definition of a merit want. Neither are economies of scale, or imperfections of competition. Education is given as an illustration, but the improved social milieu that results from it is apparently not what makes education a service that satisfies a merit want. The recipients of a merit-want service are required or induced to accept more of it than they would freely purchase, either because it is offered free of charge or at a subsidized price, or because acceptance is enforced by police power in view of the fact that "situations arise, within the context of a democratic community, where an informed group is justified in imposing its decision upon others" (*op. cit.*, p. 14). Apparently the decision must be made by majority vote. A clear definition of merit wants seems not to emerge from Musgrave's discussion, and it may be simpler to say that the majority receives a benefit in the nature of an externality either (1) from the satisfaction it obtains from requiring others to accept something that it is sure they will appreciate later, or (2) from the improved social milieu. For a more sympathetic view of the merit-want concept, see John G. Head, "On Merit Goods," *Finanzarchiv* (March, 1966), 25: 1–29; for the view that this concept "has no place in a normative theory of the public household based on individual preferences," see Charles E. McLure, Jr., "Merit Wants: A Normatively Empty Box," *Finanzarchiv* (June, 1968), 27: 474–83.

On occasion it may be useful to broaden the scope of the term externality so that it may include group-consumption goods that are complementary in production to marketable goods rather than joint in production, especially when analyzing negative externalities. In many instances the level at which the group-consumption disservice is being produced can be reduced by altering, at a certain cost, the technique of producing the marketable good. Air or water pollution exemplify this kind of disservice. Positive externalities seem to supply fewer cases of this variable-ratio possibility.

An externality normally cannot be distributed in a discriminatory manner among subgroups. It falls in the subset HJBEDK in Figure 1. That subset could therefore be divided into those services that are joint products with marketable services (improved milieu from education) and those that are not (mosquito abatement, for example). To avoid complicating Figure 1 unduly, no such distinction is made in the area HJBEDK.

APPENDIX C TO CHAPTER FOUR

The manner in which a free government service may be used indirectly as if it were a cash grant, even though the service itself cannot be resold, is illustrated in Figure 8.[1]

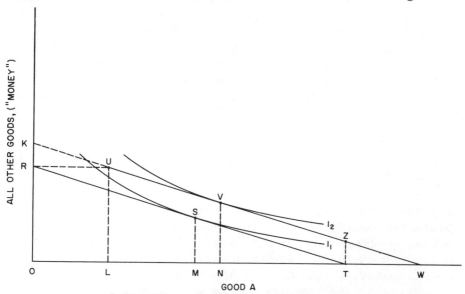

FIGURE 8. Use of Government Service as if It Were a Cash Grant

Let the amount of the purchased good in question, Good *A*, be measured along the *x*-axis, and all other goods on the *y*-axis. Before the free service is rendered, the

1. For the case where the good or service is distributed not free but at a subsidized price and can be resold, see Chapter 6, pages 158–60.

household, facing the price line *RST*, purchases *OM* of Good *A* and *MS* of all other commodities, which are designated "money" for convenience. The government now gives the household *OL = TW* of Good *A*, or gives it a perfect rival to Good *A* that is equivalent to *TW* of Good *A*. The household cannot resell *TW*. The possibility line now facing the household is *UVW*, which is parallel to the former price line, but does not intersect the *y*-axis because now the household cannot have zero of *A*; if the household spends no money on *A*, it has (*a*) *OL* of *A* (= *TW*) and (*b*) the amount of money it would have had previously had it then spent nothing on *A*. This amount of money is *LU = OR*. The household's new equilibrium point is at *V*, where it buys only *LN* of Good *A*, less than it bought before, which was *OM*; this amount *LN* together with the free receipt of *OL* yields it *ON* of Good *A*. The household then has *NV* of money. The indifference curves could be drawn so that *V* would be to the left of *S*.

A money grant to the household in the amount *TZ* would yield a new possibility line identical with *UW* except that it would extend to cut the *y*-axis at *K*. This extension does not change the equilibrium point unless *A* is so inferior a good that the money grant would lead the household to reduce its use of *A* below *OL*. In that event the free amount of *A*(= *OL*) is not as beneficial to the household as the money grant *TZ*. The household is compelled to use *OL* of Good *A*, since it cannot resell it.

Since the free supply of *OL* of Good *A* has the same effect as a cash grant, save in the exceptional instance just noted, it exercises an income effect on the household but not a rival effect. In this respect it resembles a poll tax, in the reverse direction.

If, for example, every household has been purchasing six hours of education a day, receiving no education free, and if now the government supplies two hours of education a day free, each household, released from spending money on two hours of education, will, we assume, use this money to purchase a little more of every marketable good, including education; at its new equilibrium, a certain household may purchase five hours of education, thus consuming seven hours of education instead of six. Let us assume constant costs, so that prices facing the household do not change. By the theorem for maximizing a household's welfare, the household's marginal rate of substitution of the good for money must equal the price. The price is unchanged. Hence the household's marginal rate of substitution of Good *A* for money must remain unchanged, in the face of free receipt of two hours of *A*; it is kept unchanged by a move northeast in Figure 8 to a point where both more of *A* and more of money are consumed, provided *A* is a superior good. Accordingly, less money is spent on *A*, though more *A* is consumed than before.

The non-resalable free service may be something the household cannot purchase on the market; it is then both non-purchasable and non-resalable: an "*NPNS*" good. Income is now the sum of Good *A*, "money," and the *NPNS* good.[2] The possibility line of Figure 8 remains in the same position that it occupied before the *NPNS* service was available; it remains *RT*. But the *NPNS* free service does of

---

2. More simply, income is the *NPNS* good plus all other goods, including money; but Good *A* is kept distinct at this point in preparation for the discussion in the second paragraph below.

course have an effect on the diagram: it changes the indifference map. The household is better off than before. In what respects is the indifference map changed?

One possible, but unlikely, outcome is that the household will continue to consume the same amounts of Good A and "money" as it did before the $NPNS$ free service was available. Then the indifference map for Good A and money is altered only in that any given curve now represents a higher level of welfare than before. Any given curve in the new map denotes the same welfare level as some one other curve, in the old map, that was to the north and east of the equilibrium point. For example, in Figure 8, the initial equilibrium point being at S, on I_1 and the free service now being introduced, let the former curve I_1 now be denoted by I_2, and similar upward valuations be put on the other curves, while all else on the diagram remains unchanged. This state of affairs reflects a free service that in a special sense is neither a rival for nor a complement to, in any degree, either Good A or any of the other goods ("money"). The special sense refers to the fact that there is assumed here no change in price of any good that can be priced, only a peculiar kind of change in income, the free receipt of a non-purchasable non-resalable consumer good.

Another possible outcome is that upon receipt of the $NPNS$ free service the household will divert some of its money purchases from A to other market goods, but not to the extent that it would do if the free service were just the same as (perfect rival to) Good A. What happens to Figure 8 in this instance? Again, the possibility line remains RT, and again each indifference curve now has a new, higher, label; but in addition the shapes of curves are altered by the $NPNS$ service in a manner such that RT becomes tangent to an indifference curve at a point northwest of S, reflecting the fact that the household consumes less of Good A and more of "money." An increase in the city's fire-fighting equipment, for example, may lead the household to purchase fewer fire extinguishers.

Moving to the new equilibrium point along RT, on a new high-label, new-pattern indifference map, is equivalent to moving up from RT and then to the left on the old indifference map. The change from the old to the new equilibrium may therefore be decomposed into a straight-up movement on the old indifference map, an income effect, and a movement northwest, along an old-label, old-shape indifference curve, a substitution ("rival") effect. But this rival effect does not, of course, reflect any change in prices that face the household; there is no direct change. And the household still cannot alter the amount of the service it is receiving, by any action it may take.

Finally, receipt of the $NPNS$ good may so alter the indifference map that the household comes to rest along RT on the high-label map at a point southeast of S, so that it consumes more of Good A.

The $NPNS$ free service itself never gets on to the indifference map unless it is a perfect rival to Good A. It cannot ever be a perfect rival to "money," i.e., the collection of all goods other than A and the free service, since it is but one special good, and cannot be resold.

CHAPTER FIVE

Particular Government Services

EACH OF THE CHIEF services commonly supplied by governments free of direct charge will now be analyzed in turn, in the light of the discussion in Chapter 4 of cost functions and other aspects, and the criteria listed in Chapter 2. The twelve direct services covered in this chapter are grouped in four categories, in ascending order of possibility of discrimination, first among subgroups, then among individuals.

The first category comprises four direct services that are group-consumption goods; to produce them in marketable form would be too costly or technically impossible. They are also goods for which virtually no intra-group discrimination is feasible; within a group there can be no subgroups, as those terms are defined in Chapter 4, with respect to the service in question. To these four direct services may be added externalities, as narrowly defined in Chapter 4; only three are considered here, those from education, housing, and medical care. All of the goods in this first category happen to be collective-consumption goods,[1] at the levels at which they are customarily supplied; some exceptions, however, will be noted.

The four direct services are (1) the several services rendered by the military, (2) public health, (3) exploration of space, and (4) contract enforcement and other civil rights enforcement. The externalities just listed are discussed under (5).

The second category also consists of four direct services: (6) fire protection, (7) crime prevention, (8) highway and street construction and maintenance, and (9) flood control and drainage. All four of these are group-consumption goods, at least for the minimum levels of service demanded in most communities, but they are of a type that allows discrimination among sub-groups as to the level of service afforded. They happen all to be non-collective-consumption goods.[2]

Exclusion of any particular household or firm is feasible, without incurring appreciably higher costs, with respect to the next two services, (10) education and (11) waste removal, and also for the next two, (12) medical care and (13) services from cultural and recreational facilities.[3] The household or firm is in law or in fact compelled to consume the first two of these four services.[4]

1. In Figure 1, they lie in the set CJBEDK.

2. In Figure 1, they lie in the set GJCK.   3. Set EBFD in Figure 1.

4. This distinction is not made in Figure 1. The set CJHK is not covered in the present chapter, because of its relative unimportance.

A. SERVICES FOR WHICH NO PLANNED DISCRIMINATION AMONG SUBGROUPS IS FEASIBLE

1. Military Outputs

The outputs of the military establishment consist of deterrence, damage limitation in the event of war, simple conquest, and internal control for a privileged group. Deterrence and damage limitation are means of preserving the nation-state. Conquest has sometimes been used to heighten group identity, as well as to gain supposed material advantage by force. In any event, these four outputs are group-consumption goods, not marketable goods.

Definition of level of service is difficult, in the absence of any countable units of output or indexes of output. The military's output exemplifies strikingly the problem of distinguishing between means and ends, input and output, intermediate good and final good. Deterrence affords a good illustration.

Deterrence of a potential enemy is a final product; it is prized for its own sake. This product, to be sure, it but a means to a number of other ends, including preservation of a way of life, but what the government asks of the military is as much deterrence as the means available allow. The crew at a missile site are a means, not an end. For a given level of deterrence, and all other things equal, the less manpower at the site, the better. The missile itself is a means. The community may count its missiles and feel better off if it has more of them, but only because it equates more missiles with a higher level of deterrence. Not even the units of a given "force structure" (number of bomber wings, number of missile squadrons, and so on) can be counted as end-product, except in sub-optimization techniques.

A clue for distinguishing input from output is this: If the service is not marketable, because discrimination down to the level of the single household or firm is not feasible, anything that is marketable is not a unit of output. A bomber could conceivably be put up for auction. Even a flight by bombers could be sold for the exclusive use of a single purchaser. But deterrence itself, achieved through the existence of bombers and through practice flights, is not marketable. The bomber of the flight of bombers must be rejected as a unit in which to measure output.

Levels of deterrence can be ranked ordinally, if not measured cardinally; one combination of means can be said to deter a given nation more than another combination of means costing the same amount. Still, simple ranking will not quite do, in attempting to decide how much to spend on the military establishment. A sort of probabilistic quantification seems to be required: by spending a certain amount additional, the likelihood of an attack is reduced from 1 in 5 to, say, 1 in 100. In the budget process this kind of quantification may not appear explicitly, but major decisions by the executive, its budget bureau, and the legislative body seem to be dictated by it.

The marginal cost of deterring another nation from using nuclear weapons, given the population and the area of the deterring nation, is initially a step function, then steadily decreases and then at some point begins to increase. Below some minimum level of expenditure on deterrence, an increment of expenditure does not deter at all; the potential enemy concludes he would still be safe from effective retaliation once he had dispatched his missiles. Above that minimum level of expenditure successive equal increments of expenditure produce increasing increments of odds against an attack. For example, an initial $10 billion a year leaves unaltered at, say, 0.5 the no-expenditure probability that the potential enemy will not employ nuclear weapons, but another $1 billion increases that probability to 0.51, the next $1 billion to 0.53, and the next $1 billion to 0.56 (from 0.5 upward the function is assumed to be continuous). At some point, however, increasing marginal cost will appear, if only because the probability can never reach 1.0. As it approaches that level, immense absolute increments in military expenditure by the deterring country can increase the probability of no attack but slightly. Indeed, beyond some point, an increase in expenditure may actually reduce deterrence by tending to provoke a preventive attack.

Nuclear deterrence will therefore account for none of the military expenditure of a small country, since it cannot rise above the threshold of the step function. A large country that has crossed the threshold is likely to purchase increments of probability that the potential enemy will be deterred up to, and perhaps beyond, the point where the incremental costs increase.

Deterrence from the use of conventional weapons, especially deterrence from a small war, or a guerrilla activity, is perhaps an increasing-cost activity throughout, after some initial but small step in the function. Damage limitation, in contrast, is an increasing-cost operation from the start. An increment of funds will probably achieve proportionately less.

An increase in the population of the deterring country has no effect on the total cost of deterring another country to a given degree, since deterrence is dependent, not on what general damage the potential enemy can inflict, but on what can be visited upon him. Deterrence is thus a true collective-consumption good, decreasing in per capita cost proportionately with the increase in population (given the level of deterrence and the area of the deterring country). As area increases, population and level of service remaining the same, total cost of deterrence may decrease, as the potential enemy faces a larger area within which the retaliatory force can be dispersed. But against nuclear weapons the decrease is slight.

Total cost of damage limitation probably increases more than in proportion to the increase in the percentage of the population or percentage of wealth saved from destruction. For a given percentage, it may increase less than in proportion to population (area fixed) but surely more than in proportion to area (population fixed), owing to the cost of additional anti-missile sites.

For internal control by a privileged group, total cost increases more than in proportion to the level of such control achieved, for the reasons given above with respect to deterrence, and also probably more than in proportion to population.

The value of military output to the individual is reflected in the community demand for deterrence and damage limitation.

No household will be forced to relinquish to others any of the benefit of the services of the military, by increases in prices of the things it buys or decreases in its factor rewards, except as rentals rise slightly in the areas more directly protected by unevenly dispersed anti-missile sites.

Military output observes the consensus criterion of equity, since no intra-group discrimination is feasible (with the exception just noted, of anti-missile sites). The service creates no excess burden in the technical economics sense.

Military output is not a very promising instrument of counter-cycle policy in most countries, owing to the urgency with which current objectives of deterrence and the like are viewed. But military input is more promising, insofar as it can be varied without varying appreciably the current level of military output, as when much of the expenditure is on capital goods or when heavy inventories are typical.

The distributive criteria are significant only geographically: location of anti-missile sites, and the fact that much of the service of deterrence is exported to other nations, free of direct charge (but not, of course, damage limitation).

Economic growth is stimulated by absence of fear of conquest or destruction and indeed may be negative if fear increases beyond a certain level, so that capital is steadily exported.

The country's exchange rate will be under pressure if military inputs must be imported or purchased abroad for use abroad. On the other hand, a military build-up leads to exports of arms produced domestically. On balance, for a large country not engaged in wars abroad, the net pressure on the exchange rate is likely to be small. Military output is an extreme example of the tendency, noted in Chapter 2, for government services to be less amenable to appraisal by the criteria given there than are taxes or welfare payments.

2. Public Health

"Public health" is limited here to reduction of contagious or infectious diseases. It excludes medical care, which is designed to aid a particular individual, and sewer systems, water supply, and street cleaning, which are required even in the absence of contagion and infection. Examples of public health measures are malaria mosquito eradication, research on cause and cure of disease, and compulsory vaccination.

Public health measures redistribute income in kind, by reducing the health gap between rich and poor (abstracting from methods of financing the service). The rich can purchase substitutes, however imperfect, for public health: for example, a private source of uncontaminated water, insect sprays (and manpower to apply them), and a location distant from infected areas. The poor cannot buy most of these substitutes at all, largely because the substitutes are lumpy, that is, cannot be purchased in small amounts.

Since public health services are preventive, they must be measured in terms of the job yet to be done, the amount of the anti-good not yet suppressed. What the malaria rate would be if no public health measures at all were taken is unknown, but reductions in the existing rate of infection or contagion can be observed. Of course public health reduces the rates of many different diseases, and no common physical unit of measurement can be employed to measure the total service. Cost functions, standards for distribution, and the like must be defined separately for each disease. The following observations are restricted to those that hold for all the diseases.

For a given population and area, if the disease is attacked by destroying some insect carrier, as by spreading oil on mosquito-breeding ponds and by spreading DDT on walls of dwellings, marginal cost declines until a considerable proportion of the insects are destroyed, and thereafter increases. This conjecture is based on observations at extremes. Killing one malaria mosquito will reduce the malaria rate not at all. Not killing the last malaria mosquito is unlikely to allow the rate to rise from zero. In between these two zero points, therefore, the decrease in prospective malaria rate per mosquito killed will first rise from zero, then fall to zero. To be sure, the marginal cost of killing a mosquito may not remain constant, but it seems hardly likely to change in a manner that will negate the conjecture above about marginal cost of reducing the malaria rate.

The cost functions for suppressing the several diseases are in some cases complementary. The substance that kills the malaria mosquito is also inimical to certain other forms of insect life that carry other diseases. The cost function of public health is peculiar in this, that more input is usually required to reach a given level of performance than to maintain it afterward. It took more input to reduce the yellow fever rate in the United States to zero than is required to maintain that zero rate. For almost all other services, police or fire protection, for instance, input must be kept at a high level if a given level of output is to be maintained, and in one case, refuse removal, the longer the given level of service has been in effect, the more costly it is to maintain (see Section 11, this chapter). Even in public health, unless the insect carrier is totally exterminated, input may have to be kept at a high level indefinitely, as resistant strains develop.

If level of service and area are held constant, an increase in population will usually increase total cost of public health little if at all; public health is therefore almost a collective-consumption good. The potentially increased chance of contagion or infection from an increase in population density does not materialize if the disease is completely under control (malaria, for example, in a large city that is growing in population). But some aspects of public health do increase in total cost as numbers increase: compulsory vaccination and inspection of food handlers, for example. Public health is therefore not completely a collective-consumption good. But per capita cost probably falls as population in a given area increases.

For a given level of public health service, dispersion of a given population over a larger area increases the expense of applying preventive measures but reduces the chance of contagion or infection. On balance dispersion probably reduces total cost of a given level of public health service.

The household's benefit from a public health measure can be stated in money terms, in part, as in the reduction of bills for medical care or medical insurance, and in increase in earning power arising from absence of illness.[5]

5. For a detailed study of costs and benefits of public health measures directed against

The business firm, too, obtains monetary gains as its production costs are lowered through reduction of absenteeism due to illness and increased working ability of those remaining on the job.

The monetary gains of public health are not relinquished by the individual through increases in prices of the things he buys or reductions in his factor prices. The health-service benefits are not highly locational, unless workers have been induced by extra wages to accept employment in areas where the disease is prevalent. The health service that wipes out the disease then also wipes out the differential in wages. The business firm, on the other hand, commonly loses to consumers or factors the benefits of the public health services that initially increase its profits by lowering its labor costs. The services are so widespread, affecting all firms in so much the same manner, that competition will usually prevent firms from obtaining added profits for more than a short period.

Public health services are not directly rejectable. The wealthy reject them indirectly to a small degree by reducing their expenditures on services that are imperfect substitutes. But most of these privately purchased services are so attractive anyway that the rich continue to consume them in nearly unchanged amounts even when benefiting from an intensive public health program.

Since public health services are almost all collective consumption goods, they generally meet the consensus criterion of equity, as explained in Section 1 above for military output. A small amount of excess burden appears because there exist some substitutes, however imperfect, for public health services.

The output of public health cannot readily be varied to help maintain full employment, except as research and development can be speeded up, perhaps only slightly. Nor does public health possess the attribute of military output of allowing considerable swings in input without disrupting the flow of output. Most of public health inputs are labor rather than capital equipment, and such inventories as are carried cannot be altered substantially in size without impairing the service.

With respect to the conflict-of-interests criteria, distribution of benefits regressively by income or wealth probably occurs under most health services, in the restricted sense given on page 34. As to geographical distribution, some of the benefits of any country's health services are exported, just as that country imports benefits from the health services of others. The net distribution the world over seems clearly in favor of poorer countries, where disease is more prevalent.

Public health services promote economic growth, but not because they induce restriction of consumption, for they do not. They improve productivity by reducing illness and early death, and some part of the resulting increase in income will be spent on investment goods. Even risk-taking may be increased; entrepreneurs who are healthy and vigorous may well be more daring.

This increase in productivity per worker has the same implications for the balance of payments as does an invention.[6] Cost of production falls, the terms of trade turn

tuberculosis, cancer, and poliomyelitis, see Burton A. Weisbrod, *Economics of Public Health* (Philadelphia: University of Pennsylvania Press, 1961).

6. See James Meade, *The Balance of Payments* (London: Oxford University Press, 1951), pp. 82–84.

against the country, and exports increase in physical volume. If, as is likely, exports also increase in domestic-money volume, imports will increase. In the normal case, where the sum of the elasticities of demand for imports is greater than one, if wages are constant, the increase in productivity brought about by the public health measure will improve the balance of payments and thus exert pressure for an increase in wages or an appreciation of the currency.

The income effect of the increase in real income that the now healthier worker is able to obtain from a given amount of labor time tends to decrease the amount of labor time offered. But the substitution effect of public health is to increase the real income obtainable by an extra hour of work. As with an income tax, where the two effects operate in just the reverse fashion on supply of labor, the balance may go either way; the supply of labor may increase or decrease. Better health makes leisure more enjoyable but also reduces the onerousness of labor; again, the net inducement may be for more or for less work.

3. Exploration of Space

Exploration of space refers here to exploration on a larger scale and with more general objectives than those of atmospheric sounding rockets, communications satellites, and military manned orbiting laboratories.

The services rendered by exploration of space are more nonmarketable than those of any other government activity, not excluding that of the military. They consist chiefly of the excitement of exploring the unknown and the tension created by the risks assumed by identifiable individuals (the astronauts). Expectation of marketable benefits to come is another, but unimportant, factor. Enhancement of group identity is also involved.

The amount of space exploration in physical terms must be defined separately for each of the few huge objectives that are set: landing men on the moon or landing instruments on Mars. A level of output prior to achievement of the goal may be expressed in terms of the probability that has been achieved that the goal will be reached within a specified time. Even for this concept of output, cost functions are difficult to define, to say nothing of estimating them. In any event, total cost of a given level of output does not change appreciably with population or area of the space-exploring country. The benefits of the service accrue to all households. The value placed by the household on this benefit varies widely; for some the value may be nil or even, to the apprehensive, negative.

Lead times are so long and the several sectors of a space effort are so intricately interdependent that the program cannot be accelerated or decelerated to accord with recessions, recoveries, and booms. The services, except perhaps that of the heightening of group identity, are distributed world wide without charge. Disservice may be distributed too, if success invokes envy or disappointment elsewhere.

The effects of the space program on economic growth are doubtful, but some technological advances may be anticipated that will increase productivity. The immediate products are the consumer services of excitement, tension, and group identity. In general, exploration of space is the least readily appraised by the criteria of Chapter 2 of any of the major government activities. This fact is not a coincidence, for these criteria have been formulated under pressure of social, political, and economic forces over a long period of time, and space exploration was not even thought of during all but the last few years of that period.

4. Contract Enforcement and Other Civil Rights

Enforcement of contracts and other civil rights are supplied by a system of courts that stand ready to hear disputes and a system of sanctions to enforce the decisions. It is the presence of this system that is the group-consumption good. The hearing of any particular case is of course a marketable good; court fees are commonly charged. And those who make use of the courts must often purchase a privately marketed good, the services of an attorney. These marketable services, which are not even collective-consumption goods, are complementary to the use made of the system when it falls short of its optimum performance, that is, when the system does not, by its mere presence, deter the cheats and the frauds, and does not inhibit carelessness. At its optimum level of performance, the system of courts and sanctions induces everyone to honor his word and to avoid ambiguous contracts.

Potentially, the system permits of intra-group discrimination, through discriminatory treatment in or out of the courtroom. The discrimination is against subgroups, not usually against a particular individual or firm, except as court fees are charged. These subgroups are ordinarily identified not by geographical location, as in so many other services (see the discussion of fire protection and police protection, below), but by race, color, or status, or sometimes by level of income. Still, the basic element in the system, the mere presence of it, tends to protect everyone, so that the service can be classified chiefly as one that does not allow intra-group discrimination.

Government-dispensed justice is supplemented by market-purchased arbitration, but the latter depends for its efficacy on the existence of a system of courts to which either complainant can resort if need be. Justice is central to the existence of the nation-state; a distinctive, common, and well-enforced system of property and personal rights is what marks a nation-state off from an alliance of states. When the government supplies free of charge the services of a lawyer, it does so partly to assure the credibility of the system, which would be impaired if it were known in advance that those too poor to engage their own attorney would be fatally handicapped in court. Partly also the free service is supplied as a deliberate method of redistributing income in kind.

The effectiveness of the system can be impaired by overuse. If access to it is too easy, the system will be kept busy with cases that would have been settled fairly promptly out of court with less net loss to each party than occurs when litigation is resorted to. A moderate degree of clogging of court calendars is therefore generally accepted as desirable. The actual delay often surpasses that standard, to the cost especially of those not wealthy enough to stand the financial strain imposed by the passage of time. Such congestion impairs the quality of the service. But the amount of impairment is impossible to measure cardinally.

The product of the system of courts and enforcement officers cannot be broken down into units except in terms of hours spent by the plaintiff or defendant in court and similar measures of direct use, which is only a part of the product. As suggested above, the most valuable part of the system's product is that received by those who, because it does exist, do not have to make direct use of it. At the same time, a reduction in the number of appearances in court does not necessarily indicate an increase in the level at which the service is being rendered. Still, given no change in the rest of the community atmosphere, such a reduction can be interpreted as an improvement in level of service. And although units of this service cannot be defined, different levels can be ranked ordinally. A higher level requires greater total input, population and area being fixed, perhaps more than in proportion.

For a given level of contract enforcement and other civil rights, an increase in population in a given area probably does not increase total cost appreciably, at least if the level is already high. If the system is working so well that it has unused capacity, based on some technological lumpiness for a certain minimum level of service, an increase in population does not increase total cost. If the system is working on so low a level that the courts are clogged even beyond the point remarked on above, an increase in population will no doubt increase total cost of that low level of service appreciably. But the basic element in the system, noted above, is its mere existence, more than the actual utilization of it, and this existence is itself a collective-consumption good.

As area increases, with population and level of service constant, total cost, both of constructing the system and of utilizing it, may well remain almost constant. In this respect contract enforcement resembles space exploration and conquest. No value can be put on an increment or decrement of justice for any given household or firm except in the restricted sense of what they would not have recovered in damages and the like if they had not been allowed to sue. This method of reckoning benefits cannot be generalized; what the plaintiff wins, the defendant loses. Suits that are foregone because of a prospective delay of years, owing to unduly congested court calendars, likewise represent as much loss to one as gain to another. The true social cost of long delay is in transactions not consummated, ventures not undertaken, or even deceit practiced, just because it is known that no case can be brought to trial without undue delay.

The mere presence of the system satisfies the test of equal treatment of equals, but if a dispute reaches the courts, the sub-criteria of impersonalization of administration and equality of costs of compliance are likely not to be met.

No excess burden is created, but the contribution to a counter-cycle full employment program is negligible. The level of service can scarcely be varied contracyclically without complaints from the recipients of capricious and unfair treatment, and the inputs are mostly personnel, not capital goods or inventories. Perhaps there is a slight degree of built-in flexibility, as recessions generate business failures and consequent litigation.

The service of the courts is distributed adversely to the poor in some jurisdictions, or adversely to groups that lack political power. Of the reallocation-of-resources criteria, that concerning economic growth is significant here. No undertaking, the fruits of which will not mature until some time has passed, will seem attractive in an environment where contracts cannot be enforced. And those projects that are nevertheless attempted will bear the penalty of high rates of interest demanded by skeptical creditors. A major handicap to economic development in many low-income countries is the lack of a credible system for enforcing contracts. Risk-taking, too, is probably discouraged.

As to the supply of labor, there may be some indirect effect. If saving now for consumption later is made difficult through lack of a contract-enforcement system, one of the incentives to give up leisure for work is removed.

5. Publicly Produced Externalities[7]

The present chapter discusses only publicly produced externalities, defined as externalities that arise from services that are rendered (or financed) free or at a subsidized price by the government. Privately produced externalities which are associated with goods that are fully priced (aside from these externalities) are noted in Chapter 21.

The improved environment, or milieu, produced jointly with free or subsidized education is an illustration of a publicly produced externality. So also is the reduction in danger of infection or contagion to others that is achieved by medical care to a particular individual (this is to be distinguished from a public health measure). Another example of improved environment is that which results from eradication of slum housing. There are many other externalities, but the present Section 5 will be restricted to these three, as they are probably the most important cases.

"Joint production" is taken here, as on page 96 above, in the strict sense that the amount of the externality produced with a unit of the primary good is not capable of variation in any planned way. The primary, marketable goods are discussed in Sections C and D below, and (housing) in Chapter 7. The reason for limiting externality to a joint product with a marketable good is that the joint production of this nonmarketable good helps explain why the marketable good is in fact not limited to distribution on a fully priced basis, though technically it could be.

If two nonmarketable goods, that is, two group-consumption goods, are produced jointly, one might be termed an externality of the other. This terminology might be useful if one of them was a collective-consumption good and the other not. On balance, however, it seems more useful here to restrict the term externality to a non-marketable good that arises when a marketable good is produced.

These publicly produced externalities (improved milieu, etc.) are extreme instances of group-consumption goods for which no intra-group discrimination at all is possible. Given the level and geographic distribution of the marketable service,

7. For the definition of externality used in the present work, see Appendix B to Chapter 4.

the education, the medical care, or the housing, it is not possible to alter the pattern of the externalities. And even if the marketable-service distribution pattern were to be altered just to affect the distribution pattern of the externalities (a most unlikely measure), the results would be quite uncertain.

The externalities are true joint products with education, housing, and medical care. Hence neither total cost nor marginal cost can be allocated between any one of these marketable products and its associated externalities. A derived supply price exists, in principle, both for the marketable good and for its externality. This supply price is derived by subtracting from the total cost for a given level of output of the joint products (e.g., the total cost of a given level of education with its associated given level of milieu) the demand for that level of one of the joint products (e.g., the demand for that level of education). The manner in which this derived supply price varies with level of service, with numbers served, and with area therefore depends in part on how the cost varies of producing the package of the marketable good plus its externality. This point will be considered in the sections below on education, medical care and (Chapter 7) housing. In any event, the per capita cost of supplying any given level of the package decreases as the numbers of those enjoying the externality increase, since the externality is a true collective consumption good and so can be supplied to more consumers, within capacity limits, at zero cost. The marketable services of education, medical care and housing, on the other hand, increase in total cost as the numbers to be served increase.

These externalities satisfy the consensus criteria, except that they have no relation to counter-cycle policy for full employment. Their geographic distribution usually extends well beyond the area within which the marketable services themselves are enjoyed. If the political group (see page 74) consists only of those who enjoy the marketable good, a geographical spill-over results in the form of the externalities, which of course cannot be distributed unevenly, in any planned pattern, on grounds of the color, race, or status of the recipient.

B. SERVICES FOR WHICH PLANNED DISCRIMINATION AMONG SUBGROUPS IS FEASIBLE

The four major group-consumption services for which discrimination in level of service is feasible among subgroups of the policy-formulating and financing groups are fire protection, crime prevention, street construction and maintenance, and flood control and drainage.

6. Fire Protection

In a city where the government supplied no fire protection, a subscriber to a marketed fire service would of course obtain more protection than a non-subscriber. But he would regret the presence of non-subscribers. As long as a considerable proportion of the city consisted of non-subscribers, the protection sold to subscribers would exhibit sharply increasing marginal cost of level of protection, if this level of protection were expressed in terms of the mean and variance of a probability distribution of various degrees of fire damage. This would be so because of the conflagration hazard. Moreover, for any given level of protection, this marginal cost would fall as the number of subscribers increased. Thus an increase in subscribers would both lower the marginal cost curve and make it less steep. Meanwhile, non-subscribers, including probably some outside the area of subscription (spill-over), would be receiving at least some protection. Thus a market in fire protection, though it could exist to a limited degree, would leave the level of service far below that which would be purchased through political action, unanimously.

The service of fire protection consists chiefly of limiting the damage once a fire has started, but it includes reduction in the number and severity of fires through education of households and firms in fire prevention. The service of fire protection as here defined does not include enforcement of governmental regulations on the use of fire-resistant building materials, maximum number of persons allowed in public places, and the like. Such regulations do cause resources to be devoted to reducing the fire hazard, but they do not reflect a direct distribution of service by the government free of charge.

The degree of fire hazard is to be measured, in principle, by the expected (mean) damage from fire for a stated period, and, for a more refined measure, also by its variance. The computation of possible injury or death by fire in terms of money raises questions that will not be pursued here. It is assumed that some money measure of combined damage consisting of injury and fatalities for property and persons can be constructed, to measure the output of the fire protection service, in incremental terms: an increment of fire protection service reduces the prospective loss by so much.

The output of the fire department can be measured only in increments, not in totals or averages, because the service is a preventive one, and there is no way of knowing (and no need to know) how much fire damage would occur if the government offered no fire protection service at all. What can be observed is the reduction in rate of fire damage when an increment of fire protection is added. A clue to the amount of such reduction is the decrease in fire insurance premiums that occurs when an increment of fire protection service is added. In principle, the expected loss from fire involves multiplying each possible level of loss, including zero loss, by its probability. Since an infinite number of such levels exist, the computation in principle must be of a density function for a continuous distribution. In practice it will be only a rough approximation achieved by using ranges of damage and some representative value within each range.

As the level of free fire protection for a given area and population is increased, total cost certainly rises, and so also, probably, does marginal cost. There appear to be no great indivisibilities and no low-reward inputs that must be made before certain high-reward inputs become feasible. In this sense, fire protection operates under increasing cost. Ultimately, input may reach a level such that outbreaks of fire will have been reduced to chance occurrences, each one the result of a combination of innumerable forces that cannot be controlled or foreseen. At this level, a heavy incremental input will bring little, if any, increase in level of service.

An increase in the number of households and firms within a given area will increase the total cost of a fixed level of fire protection. But the increase may be less than in proportion (decreasing marginal costs), at least up to some large number of recipients. As the recipients in an area increase beyond this point, buildings rise so high that incremental cost per recipient starts to rise.

A decrease in area covered, while level of service and number of recipients re-remain unchanged, will at first decrease total cost, if the initial situation was one of a population very thinly spread. Cost per capita, of a given level of service, thus decreases for a while as density of population increases by inward migration of a fixed number of persons. As implied in the paragraph immediately preceding, if density increases through an increase in the population in the initial, broad area, cost per capita may, or may not, decrease, and if it does decrease, it will not do so, except by coincidence, at the same rate as when density increases by constriction of an area occupied by a given population.

So, as with the collective-consumption services, no unique relation is defined for this non-collective–consumption service between change in density and change in per capita cost. As the area covered by the fixed population constricts further, total cost of a given level of service starts to rise, and will eventually rise more than proportionately, as fire protection must be extended to high-rise buildings.

Benefits from an increment of fire protection will tend to be relinquished through increases in rental if the increment is distributed unevenly by geographic subgroups. Ordinarily, marked differences in the level of protection exist not so much among cities as among sub-areas within a city: slum as against rich neighborhoods.

Fire protection can be rejected in part, indirectly. A city that attempts to reduce fire damage by increasing its fire stations, personnel, and equipment may be partly frustrated by householders who thereupon purchase fewer fire extinguishers and by firms that install fewer sprinkler systems or become more careless with trash.

When intra-group discrimination is possible, as it is with fire protection, the consensus criterion of equal treatment of equals may be violated. With respect to fire protection, the discrimination in level of service is usually among subgroups that differ in what they cost the government to attain a certain level of service. That level, measured for example in terms of expected (mean) number of fires per household, is usually lower (the expected number of fires is higher) in those areas where the cost of achieving a given level of service is higher.

Expenditures on fire protection must usually rise in times of prosperity, since additional stations and equipment are needed as new housing subdivisions are opened and as business districts grow. Fire protection expenditures are therefore unsuitable for counter-cycle policy. The excess-burden issue is of little weight here for reasons given in Chapter 2.

The disparities in level of fire protection within a city work against the poor, at least if the level is measured either as above (expected number of fires) or by expected injury and loss of life from fire. But if the measure of incremental output is instead the expected damage to property, fire protection may well be distributed fairly evenly. There are fewer fires per household in the rich district, but each fire is more costly in money terms, since the rich have more property. If injury and loss of life were quantified as the present value of loss of future money earnings, fire protection again might be found to be distributed fairly evenly, but few would accept such a distribution as an ethical norm.

Evidently, regressive distribution of fire protection by income or wealth, which would tend to make distribution more nearly equal in terms of expected number of fires per household and expected injury and loss of life, is not the criterion accepted in practice. Indeed, the issue has scarcely been raised. As matters stand, no distributive principle at all is enunciated in the law or elsewhere, though some principle or principles must be followed implicitly. Probably the standard followed is.connected loosely with household income or wealth.

A level of fire protection lower, as judged by any of the measures noted above, is given to certain ethnic, color, or status groups in some communities. This type of discrimination is feasible only because the members of the disadvantaged racial or other groups are clustered geographically. If the households of a certain ethnic or color group were scattered randomly throughout the city, subgroup discrimination by race or color would be technically unfeasible.

Economic growth is of course facilitated by fire protection. Here, economic growth is scarcely a conflict-of-interests criterion; capital does not need to be preserved at the expense of consumption. Fire damage is always to capital goods, whether consumers' durables or producers' goods.

Risk, in the sense of relative dispersion of possible outcomes of a venture, is reduced for almost any venture by an increment to fire protection service. At the same time, the expected value of the venture is improved in real terms and will be improved in money terms too except as competition reduces that value. All in all, fire protection is clearly one of the most important stimuli to economic growth.

There now becomes relevant the criterion of maximizing output of the service, given the total amount of input for the service decided on by the city or other financing body. The city's goal may be, for example, to reduce the total number of fires in the city to a minimum, given the total amount of money to be spent on the fire department, or, as an alternative but similar goal, to minimize total money value of damage to property in the city. To achieve such goals, fire stations, equipment, and personnel must be so distributed throughout the city that an incremental transfer of those resources from one part of the city to another would reduce the number of fires or the money value of damage in the one area by just the amount it would allow them to increase in the area from which they were transferred. Cost at the margin would then be equal throughout the city. But this kind of geographical distribution of fire-fighting resources would only by coincidence also satisfy any one of the distributional standards suggested by the equity criteria above: equal protection of all individuals from becoming victims of fire, or equal protection of a dollar's worth of property. City-wide maximization of output will normally not permit equality of protection against fire, among subgroups. It is not known whether the actual distribution of fire protection within a city typically approaches more closely the one or the other type of goal.

An increment of fire protection automatically reduces money spent on medical services to those injured by fire, and where such services are supplied free by the same government, the money it spends on the increment to fire protection is a gross amount to be netted out by subtraction of the decrease in hospital and allied expenditures. The connection is, of course, a loose one. Welfare expenditures are no doubt also reduced automatically by an increment of fire protection to a poor neighborhood.

7. Prevention of Crime

The output of a police force is here taken to be crime prevention, that is, protection of households and firms from illegal aggression by individuals or small groups, as opposed to aggression by groups so large that insurrection or secession is the prospect, or aggression from other nations. The functions of a police force other than reduction of crime are treated elsewhere, e.g., traffic control, or are not covered in this work, e.g., assistance to persons in distress. A minimum amount of protection against crime is necessary to the continued existence of the nation-state.

Supplementary purchase of protection against crime is common, in the form of safe deposit boxes, burglar alarms connecting with private detective agencies, heavy-duty locks for doors and windows, and burglar insurance. If police forces of modern cities were reduced, these expenditures would increase markedly except among the low-income groups. Accordingly, redistribution in kind may well be the most powerful single reason for the existence of modern police protection at the levels now typical of large cities.

Police service is primarily a preventive service; patrol is obviously so, and apprehension of the criminal is itself primarily aimed at preventing further crime. The physical output of the service is the number of undesirable events, suitably weighted, that are being prevented. This output can be measured only indirectly and incrementally. The number of crimes, suitably weighted, that a given police force prevents in a given time period cannot be known. The number of crimes not prevented is known, or rather is known to a high degree for some crimes, e.g., burglary, but to a low degree for others because the victim is reluctant to report, e.g., confidence games. Changes in the crime rate over time or from one similar district to another can be observed as police and equipment are added to or subtracted from the total force,[8] though the many other influences acting simultaneously on the crime rate make interpretation of the data difficult. The crime rate per hundred inhabitants, or other number, is a rough measure of the exposure of the individual to crime. Reduction of that exposure is the end product of the police function, the final consumers' good. Increments in level of police protection for a given area and population are

8. Experiments of this type are currently being carried on in the United Kingdom by operations-research personnel.

achieved only at increasing marginal cost. Almost by definition, those crimes most easily prevented are those prevented first.

As the population in a given area increases, total cost of a given level of police protection obviously rises. It probably rises in a greater proportion than population. Crime prevention thus resembles internal control by the military, in the increase in marginal cost of maintaining a given level of the product (control or prevention) as population in a given area increases.

A decrease in area, population and level of service remaining constant, almost surely decreases total cost, at least up to a point, as patrol distances are decreased. This fact is only partly offset by a tendency for crowding to breed crime, owing to irritation, discomfort, and the like, and the ease with which interaction between two persons can occur. Hence an increase in density of population that occurs by a compression of a given number of persons into a smaller area exerts, up to a point, an effect on total cost just the opposite of that caused by an increase in density that occurs through an increase of population in a given area.

The value to the recipient of an increment of free police service is the sum of (1) the amount by which he will reduce his purchases of crime prevention including burglar alarms and the like, (2) what he saves in burglary insurance, and (3) the increment he is willing to pay in higher house rent or land price to enjoy the increment of free police service. Evidently, the benefit from the free distribution of police service will be relinquished in part to landowners, if there are consistent geographic differences in level of service in competing areas.

Crime prevention service offered by the government is rejected directly to a minor degree, by failure to make the most of the service available. More important is indirect rejection through reduction in purchase of private patrol services, burglar alarms, special door and window locks, and the like. Total expense devoted to crime prevention no doubt increases, but by less than the increase in the government's expense.

It is much more difficult for the police to maintain a high standard of administrative impersonalization than for the firemen. Discrimination against or favoritism for certain individuals or firms is in some jurisdictions a commonplace. Equal treatment of those equally circumstanced is to this degree not achieved.

Crime prevention service cannot be varied counter-cyclically; the reverse, if anything, seems called for. But the input pattern may possibly be varied counter-cyclically over time, with respect to capital-goods inputs. Even this much is difficult to achieve; a new police station or a fleet of patrol cars can hardly be postponed until the next recession.

Levels of protection against crime are commonly lower in poor areas of a city than in wealthy areas, although the standards followed have not been made explicit. There seems to be a tendency to distribute the police force more in proportion to the total value of property in an area than in proportion to the number of inhabitants or, for business districts, daytime population. But here it is easy to confuse output with input, and it is distribution of output that is at issue. For this, some measure of exposure to crime must be devised: e.g., the probability of loss, through crime, of a dollar's worth of property over a given span of time in a given sector of the city.

This probability can be computed largely by the use of the crime rate the sector has been experiencing.

Equal work load for patrolmen is an explicit standard in one large city. This calls for patrolmen to be so distributed that each patrolman has roughly an equal number of crimes to report during his eight-hour shift. Solving the crime is another matter, the province of the detective force. Equal protection per person would call for a distribution such that, no matter in what part of the city he lived, the individual would be faced with the same probability of being the victim of a crime, and the same variance. For this standard particularly, different types of crime must be given different weights. This equal protection standard clearly is not followed in any large city.

Maximum prevention of crimes suitably weighted, for the city as a whole, is still another standard, and it almost certainly conflicts with the equal protection standard. A police force is spatially distributed for maximum total output when the marginal cost of crime prevention (crimes being suitably weighted) is the same in all districts. Observation suggests that this goal would require that in some areas that are notably the source or scene of crimes, (*a*) the input of police would be heavier per capita than in other districts, while (*b*) the crime rate remained higher in these more intensively policed districts than in others, in order that (*c*) the marginal cost of crime prevention might be not extremely unequal from one district to another.[9]

This conflict among objectives is latent; it seems never to have been examined in detail. Indeed, discussion of these issues has been discouraged by refusal to reveal data on crime rates broken down by areas within a large city, in some metropolitan areas.[10] But the problem of how much weight to give to the conflicting standards of equal protection, minimization of crime for the city as a whole, equality of work load, and perhaps still other standards for distributing the police force spatially and temporally, is being resolved implicitly, one way or another, by every police commissioner every day.

An increment to the police force reduces risk in certain types of business more than it does in others. It thereby promotes a reallocation of resources. Again, conflicts among standards for distribution arise. Should the police force be so allocated spatially and temporally that the risk of loss by theft or other crime is the same for all

9. See Carl S. Shoup, "Standards for Distributing a Free Governmental Service: Crime Prevention," *Public Finance* (1964), 19: 383–92, and Douglas Dosser, "Notes on Carl S. Shoup's 'Standards for Distributing a Free Governmental Service: Crime Prevention,'" *Public Finance* (1964), 19: 395–401. For an analysis of optimality conditions that give normative answers to the question, "how many resources and how much punishment *should* be used to enforce different kinds of legislation," see Gary S. Becker, "Crime and Punishment: an Economic Approach," *Journal of Political Economy* (March/April, 1968), 76: 169–217. In contrast, the analysis in the text above assumes a given total of outlay and poses questions of distribution of the service among subgroups, abstracting from the problem of financing the service.

10. Police Commissioner Howard R. Leary will make available to the public for the first time a tabulation of number of crimes distributed by precincts in New York City, starting with calendar 1968 data. "The Police Department has not published the reported crime statistics of the city's 80 precincts on the grounds that it has been concerned about alarming people by pinpointing the areas with the most crimes," according to the *New York Times* (January 29, 1968). The *Times* obtained, and published, data for the first ten months of 1967 (*ibid.*).

types of business? If so, is the risk to be equal per dollar of capital engaged, or per dollar of sales, or per person employed?

A lower level of crime prevention service to certain color, ethnic, or status groups is a criterion followed in some communities, but it is scarcely ever explicit in laws or regulations.[11]

Crime prevention increases the net product of the economy, partly by inducing some individuals to produce rather than steal, partly by supplanting inefficient private-sector methods of preventing crime, and partly by reducing fear. This increment of product may or may not be proportionately more in the form of investment goods than is the rest of the economy's output; no information is available on this point, hence it is not known whether crime prevention stimulates growth in a relative sense, though it doubtless increases investment (as well as consumption) in absolute amount. The greatest reallocation effect of crime prevention is to induce acceptance of ventures that would be too risky without police protection or that would require insurance premiums too high to allow an attractive mean yield. An increment of expenditure on crime prevention automatically lowers expenditures on fire protection, hospital services, and court costs.

8. Highway and Street Construction and Maintenance

A highway and a street differ in the cost incurred in excluding any particular individual; the highway is usually the more marketable good. But for both services it has so far been deemed too costly to institute a marketing system on a broad scale, supposing one were desirable. Toll roads are still the exception even in the few countries where they exist; tolls for street use are virtually unknown. Rapid advances in the art of toll collection with the aid of electronic devices may, however, soon render feasible a widespread network of tolls, perhaps especially for congested areas of cities.

A price of sorts is already being charged for motor vehicle use of highways and streets, through the user taxes on motor fuel and motor vehicles. The fact that such taxes are practicable does not, however, justify placing these services in the same category as education and waste removal, where any given individual can be excluded from the service at little or no cost, against payment of a price that can be adjusted to the amount of service rendered.

First, discrimination among individuals by means of vehicle and fuel taxes is crude. Those who use costly highways that allow greater speeds with less driving strain pay the same rate of motor fuel and motor vehicle tax as those who use inferior roads. Thus some parts of a highway network cost much more than the revenue they generate, and others, costing much less, yield a true tax.

11. "Crime rates [in the ghetto], consistently higher than in other areas, create a pronounced sense of insecurity. For example, in one city one low-income Negro district had 35 times as many serious crimes against persons [presumably, per resident] as a high-income white district." National Advisory Commission on Civil Disorders, *Report* (New York: Dutton & Co., 1968), p. 14. See also *ibid.*, pp. 266–69 and 307–309.

Second, many countries with a heavy and growing motor vehicle population collect considerably more in motor fuel and motor vehicle tax than they spend on highways and streets. The price resembles what a private monopoly would charge in being higher than the marginal cost of the service.

Third, countries that do earmark these revenues for highways and streets do not uniformly cover all highway and street costs in this manner. Again the connection between price and incremental cost is loose.

Fourth, if users of the roads want more service, they still have to act through the political mechanism. It is quite unlikely that a road network could ever be supplied through the market mechanism, for reasons to be given presently, though an occasional toll road or bridge of course can be.

Still, highways and streets pose a case different from that of fire protection and crime prevention, for in those cases there is still less possibility, if any at all, of establishing a connection between incremental tax charge to the user of the service and the incremental cost he causes or benefit he receives. The difference will be kept prominently in view in the paragraphs to follow, while recalling that discrimination down to the level of the individual user is not yet as feasible as it is for education, or waste removal (see Section C below), or medical care, or cultural and recreational facilities (see Section D below).

A. HIGHWAYS

Two kinds of government-supplied transportation service may be distinguished. To enjoy the one, the user must add a market-purchased input to be used jointly with the government-supplied facility. To use the other, he need purchase nothing on the market. The motorist or trucker contributes a privately purchased vehicle and motor fuel. The rapid-transit rider contributes nothing but his time, which for present purposes is not significant. The pedestrian on city streets contributes only time and his own effort.

The need for a market-purchased input allows the dispenser of the free facility to employ a close substitute for marketing, by imposing a charge on the purchase of the complementary market-purchased input. A private concern can operate a toll gate, but it cannot in practice administer a charge on the purchase of complementary inputs, the vehicle and motor fuel. Highway service could be supplied by a nation-wide, regulated private monopoly, much as a nationwide telephone service is supplied in the United States, only if the monopoly's revenue could be obtained from tolls. A private monopolist of highways would certainly not be given a tax collector's power to investigate and penalize automobile manufacturers and motor fuel producers and distributors.

As a network of intersecting highways expands, the number of toll gates needed per mile of highway may increase, at least in some range, more than in proportion to the number of roads. Expense to the toll collector and inconvenience to the motorist thus grow so rapidly that a universal toll-gate technique for highways is impracticable. The electronic or other devices noted above that register the extent to which a given vehicle uses a given road, combined with periodic billing of the user, eliminate the inconvenience. Military considerations and regional political forces are further explanations of why governments, not private enterprise, supply the services of highways.

The service provided by the government is the possibility, which may or may not be taken advantage of, that within a given period of time a certain number of trips can be made over a given distance, between the points the user desires to leave and reach. The number of trips possible, that is, the capacity of the highway, depends on the number of lanes, the speed at which the cars travel, the distance between cars at any given speed, and the length of life of the highway, its durability. The number of points served depends on length and spatial pattern of highway.

The combination of speed and leeway that allows the maximum number of trips is dependent on such features as lack of curvature and grade. But technical considerations dictate certain minima for these and similar features, including minimum load bearing and clearances. Above these minima there is a more or less continuous function relating increase in total cost to increase in any one of these aspects of level of service over a given area offered to a fixed population. Presumably, the total cost for any one of these aspects increases by more than in proportion to the increase in level of service (increasing marginal cost). The time taken to construct the highway is another source of increasing marginal cost; the more rapidly the highway is constructed, at least after a point, the more it will cost. All of these increasing marginal costs occur without reference to congestion, that is, without reference to an increase in cost imposed on other motorists when one more vehicle comes on the highway, this cost taking the form of time lost and perhaps also higher money operating costs.

An increase in number of households and firms, given the level of service and the area, increases total cost, and probably at a more than proportional rate (increasing marginal cost), as land that is increasingly valuable for other uses needs to be allocated to highways. There are, however, powerful economies of scale at work, and until land costs rise substantially, an increase in the number of persons served may be accommodated under decreasing average costs.[12]

An increase in density caused by containing a given population in a smaller area probably increases total cost of a given level of service, perhaps also more than in proportion to the decrease in area. The decrease in area decreases the need for transportation, that is, the demand for transportation, but that fact is to be distinguished from the change in the per capita cost of supplying a unit of transportation.

The initial benefit to the recipient of the highway service, before any of it is relinquished to others, is for business firms the saving in cost plus the net return on those sales that it could not have made at all if the highway had not been available. These amounts, so far as they exceed the return on the additional capital employed, are relinquished in part to consumers of highway-transported goods, in part to specialized factors in the highway-using industries, including additional factors

12. See William S. Vickrey, *Microstatics* (New York: Harcourt, Brace and World, 1964), pp. 250–51.

engaged because of the expanded demand for the highway-transported products as their prices fall.

Benefits to households using the highway for non-business purposes are measured by what the household would be willing to pay if it had to, to use the increment of highway (increment of width, or length, etc.). The service is locational enough to imply some relinquishing of that benefit to owners of sites on or near the highway, if the benefit is not absorbed directly by highway tolls. Landowners elsewhere lose, more or less correspondingly. As the network is expanded, reverse movements in site prices occur, and eventually land rents should everywhere be about as before, if not lower. In general, over a long enough period of time, the household would probably be able to retain most, perhaps all, of the gross benefit it would have received from highways.

Rejection of highway service is easy and is encouraged by the presence of substitutes in the form of other types of transportation or a change in location, and by the complementary costs of owning and operating a motor vehicle. And highway use to some extent reflects rejection of competing forms of transportation, some of them owned by the same government that supplies the highways;[13] there is thus an indirect rejection of the service, transportation. But such rejection commonly troubles the policy-makers less that does indirect rejection of an increment of fire protection or police protection. There are fewer interdependencies associated with use of highways. Moreover, policy decisions concerning close substitutes in transportation are often made by different authorities, with little or no coordination of policy. A highway department shows little concern over a decline in use of rail facilities, although the social worth of an increment of highway is offset by a decrease in use of rail or other facilities that were not already congested.

Highway service conforms to the consensus type of equity criteria better than any other government service, by its nature. The only possible exception is the favoritism or extortion that can be practiced by a corrupt highway-patrol force, whose activities, however, might better be cataloged under the police function.

Among all services rendered by government, highways are the most promising with respect to a contracyclical policy of full employment. The planned growth in the level of this service can be varied without causing so strong a reaction from the users as will occur for police and fire protection, education, or public health. Variation in degree of maintenance of highways is also feasible. And the inputs can be varied, over time, without correspondingly immediate variations in level of service, if large stretches of highway are not to be opened in any case until the entire segment is finished. Since the input is almost entirely a capital good, wide swings in private spending in the construction industry can be partly offset. But there remain serious problems of timing, as with all public works projects of considerable magnitude, whatever the service they render.

Excess burden may easily be greater in highway service than in police or fire

---

13. An illustration is supplied by the plans announced in 1967 by Great Britain and Germany to tax or otherwise force off the highways some of the heavy trucks that transport steel and other materials that the government-owned railroads are equipped to handle, allegedly more economically.

protection because of the influence highways exert on modes of production and marketing. A free highway that is located inefficiently, owing to ignorance or carelessness in planning, will divert transportation of goods and persons from what would have been a socially more efficient mode, when account is taken of the cost of constructing the highway or the alternative mode. Inadequate compensation, if any, is commonly given for destruction of neighborhood values by large freeways.

The equity conflict criteria are quite relevant to a system of free highways, viewed in abstraction from methods of financing. Disputes over priorities, for example, farm-to-market roads as against arterial highways, have revealed the importance that various social and income classes attach to the "distribution," spatially, of highways. The struggle here has been between factors of production in one industry and another, and also between factors generally and those who desire a highway as a consumers' good. Viewed as a consumers' good, a highway network can be used by the very poor to a limited extent if at all. An increment of highway spending is more likely to benefit the well-to-do relative to the poor than an increment of most other government services, except as it is a producers' good that lowers the cost of products important in the budgets of the poor. Depressed areas can be notably aided by highways placed with a view to their problems.

Judged by the several reallocation criteria, the advantages of highways are not clear. A highway itself is of course a capital good, hence reflects economic growth, but there is no assurance that the use made of it will be such that, apart from construction of the highway itself, the share of investment in national income will increase. On the saving side, households are subjected to conflicting pressures from the availability of a free highway system. The income effect of that availability will normally be to induce the household to increase its saving out of a given money income, but since this particular consumer good, the highway, is complementary in consumption with items that must be purchased on the market, it may induce more spending out of a given money income. The lower prices of goods transported on the free highway should lead to some increase in household saving. External equilibrium is not directly affected, since highways, except as they are used by foreign tourists, are not exported, and they facilitate both imports and exports.

Leisure may either increase or decrease under a free highway system. On the one hand, leisure is made more attractive by this added method of using it, that is, pleasure driving; but that use is conditioned on possession of the complementary goods—vehicle, motor fuel, and so on—that will in principle be obtained in part by increasing one's earnings.

B. STREETS

Streets, unlike highways, are used by both vehicles and pedestrians. For pedestrians no toll charge is feasible, and for vehicles a toll is difficult to administer, with the possible exception of electronic tolls in congested areas. Special taxation of adjacent real property to recoup the cost of constructing streets that have increased the value of such property has had only limited success.

On the other hand, more streets than highways have been produced and sold by private firms. In some countries entire towns, or sections of towns, have been created by private developers, complete with streets. The cost of street construction has been covered by prices charged by these developers for houses, store buildings, and vacant lots, with which the streets are complementary in consumption. In contrast, private enterprises that sell gasoline and motor vehicles do not find it worth while to throw in highways and recoup the cost in the products they sell. No one producer has the exclusive right to sell gasoline or vehicles for use in a given area. Similarly, when houses are erected in a new town by a number of competing builders, the streets are not provided by the builders. In general, therefore, streets are group-consumption goods, even though they may be paid for in the price of a lot.

The service provided by streets is measurable in the same terms suggested above for highways. An increment of width to a street increases the number of possible simultaneous users; an increment of distance makes new points accessible; an increment of durability reduces maintenance and replacement costs. Reduction of curvatures, grades, and crossings to increase speed are less important, as are also alternative lengths of time taken for construction.

The cost functions for the several units of street service are much like those for highways, with this notable difference, that an increase in width of street causes an increase in distance that must be traveled, either horizontally or vertically. The wider the street, the higher must the buildings rise, for a city of a given population and given area, with consequent increase in expense of construction of a cubic foot of usable space at the intensive margin of building. These cost aspects of an increment to street width will, however, evidence themselves just as they do, for other reasons, with highways, that is, by the opportunity cost of the land acquired for the increment of width. Once a city has been constructed, an increment of street width costs even more because of the expenses of demolition and rebuilding.

As the population increases, a given level of street service within a given area becomes more expensive in much the way described above for an increase in level of highway service, and perhaps without the initial tendency to decreasing average costs. If the area within which a given number of households and firms are located is constricted, total cost for a given level of street service may actually decrease, at least up to a point, as it does for police service. Admittedly, the problem of defining a given level of street service becomes even more difficult, when area alone is changed.

The initial recipients of the benefits from streets are the households that use them and the firms that can thereby receive goods and accommodate customers. Some minimum of street availability is essential to any use at all of dwelling or business structure; the benefit from that minimum amount cannot be separated from that of the dwelling or business structure itself; it is like the benefit from the use of one shoe.

The benefit from an increment of street accommodation above the minimum is probably in part relinquished to site owners. Much depends on whether we are considering increments made in the planning stage. Given the cities as they now are, the immediate question is, rather, what would happen to site values and rents if the streets in only a certain part of the city were graded, or paved, or widened, or better maintained—and what would happen if these improvements were made simultaneously throughout the city? At the extreme, improvement of a single street would bring to it households from other parts of the city who would bid up site values there appreciably, while site values would decline imperceptibly over other larger areas of the city. The benefits of the improvements to the single street would be relinquished by residents of that street to landowners. At the other extreme, if the condition of all of the streets in all the residential areas of the city were raised to that of what had hitherto been the best streets, there would be no increased demand from residents desiring to move from other poorer street areas, since there would be no such areas. Nearby suburbanites might move into the city; attracted by the better streets, residents of other cities might do the same; some of those who might have left the city would stay. Over a long period all the residents, rich and poor, might find themselves paying higher site rents; some of the benefits would have been relinquished to landowners. In that event some of the very poor might leave the city to find lower living costs in other cities with poorer streets. But if all cities distributed street service evenly, at the same level, site values could rise only if the service induced migration from rural areas. Site values express differentials in site environment. In business areas, improved street service also goes to site rents in much the way indicated above.

An increment of street service will not alter appreciably the pattern or level of spending of the households living on the street except perhaps as it serves as an example of what more neatness, better lighting, etc., can do. In this sense the street service is not rejectable even indirectly by a reduction in purchase of marketable substitutes. In practice it is not rejectable directly either, in the ordinary course of life.

The service rendered by streets satisfies well, almost automatically, the consensus type of equity criteria, and not at all the consensus criteria of no excess burden and responsiveness to unemployment. The excess burden arises from the fact that an increment of free street service, just because it is free, will induce an expansion of street width and length that increases notably certain costs that must be covered by market prices. Wider streets in a business district induce business firms to use methods of production and marketing that are suitable for structures that rise more and spread less, methods that carry an increasing cost that must be offset against the benefits of the increment of width of streets. But in practice, the decision whether to widen a street, in the planning stage or thereafter, is made not by the individual user each time he uses a street, but by policy groups that are faced simultaneously with the financing problem. Because of this, the amount of excess burden in fact created is far less than it is under, say, free medical service, where the amount of such service consumed depends on decisions made every day by each of the large number of potential consumers.

For a counter-cycle full employment policy, street construction and repair are virtually useless. Indeed, they will tend normally to accentuate cycles. The contrast with highways is striking. The cause is of course the strongly complementary relationship that street service bears to the marketed services of housing and retailing and to a lesser degree, of wholesaling and manufacturing. In a business boom streets must be built, if these marketed services are to be availed of; in a recession, streets that lead nowhere are a much more conspicuous example of temporary waste than, say, an underutilized courthouse.

With respect to the conflict criteria, distribution of street service is the subject of intense, if often repressed, disagreement, especially since residential street service is commonly distributed unequally among districts within a city. The distribution is usually proportional or even progressive with respect to income and wealth. The dwellings reflecting the highest income and wealth of households are given the best street service: wider streets, better lighting, better maintenance. The street is deemed to be so much an extension of the dwelling that a certain equality of level of dwelling and street is accepted by the policy-maker, if not by the residents of the poorer areas who must consume a far lower level of street service. The minimum street is narrow, unpaved, perhaps even ungraded, and poorly maintained. Such streets are common in slum areas, especially racially exploited areas through which other residents of the city do not usually have to pass. More tax revenue per square foot of street surface is commonly collected in high-income areas; in slum areas in certain cities,[14] no tax at all is collected. To what degree the tax differentials may account for unequal street service is a subject for further enquiry.

Street service in one area of a city affords residents in any other area, and indeed nonresidents, local access in the first area. This access is a service significant for some other-area residents or nonresidents, but for many it is of little importance. Residents of high-income areas of a city exhibit little concern over the level of street service in the poor areas of the same city compared with their concern over the level of education afforded the poor.

The reallocation criteria may or may not be satisfied by an increment to street service; all depends on the location and type of street service, and no generalization seems possible, except with regard to maximization of service, as follows:

In some poor areas, heavy use per square foot of street, and vandalism, especially with the lighting system, may mean that more money per square foot of street area must be spent to maintain a given physical level of service than in high-income areas. To the degree that this is so—and it is not so, in many poor areas, especially in the smaller cities—a conflict arises between equal distribution of the service and maximum service over the city as a whole. If a unit of service costs, at the margin, more in one area of the city than in another, a unit of input to the service transferred from the high-cost area to the low-cost area will add more service to the latter than it will subtract from the former, by definition of high and low marginal cost. A larger total of service will be supplied. But if the high-marginal-cost area is a poor area, and the low-cost area a rich one, a service will be taken from the poor and given to the rich. When the service has been redistributed so that marginal costs are equal everywhere in the city, equal amounts of the service will not be offered everywhere in the city except by a rare coincidence. This conflict between equality of service and maximum service is the same as that noted above in discussing police and fire protection.

14. Notably in some countries in Latin America.

Distribution of street service among different business areas in a city varies directly with its usefulness to the type of business. Any gross discrepancy against a type of business, say the shopping center, creates pressures from the business community that are heeded; any gross discrepancy in the other direction invites attention from those in the city administration who wish to enlarge spending elsewhere.

9. Flood Control and Drainage

Flood control and drainage are supplied free by government not only because they would cost far more to produce in a marketable form, if indeed that is possible, but also sometimes because they represent a way to redistribute income in kind in favor of certain specifically distinguishable low-income groups, notably low-income farmers and residents of unprotected areas bordering rivers, especially in underdeveloped countries. Redistribution may not occur when the cost of these projects is recovered by charges on the benefited group, but these instances account for only a minor fraction of these two services in most countries, even when cost-benefit studies are common. A rule that the benefit must at least equal the cost if the project is to be undertaken does not say that those who obtain the benefit must defray the cost.

Reclamation and irrigation, in contrast, are not included here because they are not commonly free services to the individual user at his margin of use; the more he uses, the more he usually pays. They are government-operated enterprises, rendering services that can be varied in amount down to the level of any selected household or firm. If the services are sold below cost, the reasons for that policy are to be analyzed under subsidies (Chapters 6 and 7), not under free services.

The unit of output of flood control is largely the increase in property values, notably land values, in the areas benefited, less the decrease of values in competing areas that do not benefit. To these increments in money value of property most observers will want to add another type of output unit: number of lives saved, amount of destruction avoided. To say that these are already embodied in the property value differentials is in this view to take the existing distribution of income too much for granted and to assume too much foresight on the part of those directly affected.

Drainage, in contrast, can be measured as to output entirely in terms of increase in property values, net after decrease of value of competing properties, adding, of course, any public health aspects of drainage.

Both flood control and drainage probably show decreasing marginal cost for level of service, owing to lumpiness within a considerable range, followed by increasing cost. But for an increasing population, total cost may not increase at all, and for a decreasing area (population and level of service constant), total cost may actually decrease.

Benefits to initial recipients are measured by what they would pay if they had to, and this may be much less than what other more wealthy households or other firms would pay; in that event the initial recipients must move elsewhere. The benefits will have been relinquished to the landowners and would have been so even in the absence of migration. Indeed, the analysis may be simplified with no loss of content by assuming that the services of flood control and drainage are directed to the owners of the land initially. Some part of the benefits reach consumers of crops grown on these lands as production increases. These services are not rejectable directly. They do tend to reduce expenditures on substitutes, and to this degree the government's increment of the kind of service they render is to some degree rejected.

Flood control and drainage are distributed to subgroups so large and the benefits are so indivisible within the subgroup that the consensus criteria of equity are fairly well satisfied. Excess burden may, however, be considerable insofar as these services, being free, induce individuals to reside or to farm in places that are costly in terms of total resources used, including those used in providing these services.

For a counter-cycle public works policy, flood control and drainage offer more possibilities than any other of the services covered in the present chapter with the possible exception of highways and certain parts of military output. The timing of the service itself must be postponed, or advanced, since once the capital investment is made the service is automatically available or almost so; as with highways, however, it may on occasion be possible to meet a given date for availability while varying the time pattern of input. Variation in the timing of the service itself is often feasible, since each flood control or drainage project often stands by itself and is not in a complementary position vis à vis other ongoing services. And a project typically represents a net addition, not a renewal of a facility that is wearing out. But if the project is a large one, the slow build-up to on-site peak employment and the gradual decline may not fit in well with the current cycle, not to mention the induced off-site activity.

The conflict criteria are heavily involved, but the facts remain obscure, at least with respect to distribution by income or wealth of residents, firms, or landowners. The geographical pattern of distribution is of course easily discernible.

Economic growth is represented by the facilities themselves, but as with fire and police protection, it is not possible to say whether the increment in production they make possible is more or less of consumers' goods than the existing average for the economy. Risks are reduced, especially by flood control.

C. DISCRIMINATION AMONG INDIVIDUALS FEASIBLE (MARKETABLE GOODS): COMPULSORY CONSUMPTION

The two free services now to be discussed, education and waste removal, are commonly supplied by governments in the marketing mode, not in the group-consumption mode, and this is so, even though no price is usually charged by the government (see page 71). Instead, these services are severely rationed to each household or firm. Few recipients obtain as much of these services as they would like at the zero price. This is true also of nonmarketable goods, public health for example, but the distinctive feature of the rationing of education or waste removal is the necessity of rationing each individual separately. Rationing is the more necessary, in that each service soon reaches a region of increasing marginal costs as the level of the service is increased.

An exception to these statements is sewerage, which under certain conditions is supplied in the group-consumption mode.

10. Education

The amount of elementary education per child that is supplied free of charge differs widely from country to country. Within any one country it usually differs markedly by region or district. Within a region or district it may differ greatly by social status, race, color, or even creed, of recipient. These differences suggest that several forces, differing in relative strength from time to time and place to place, account for the free distribution of elementary education. Three of the most important of these forces are the following.

1. A demand by the poor for an income-creating instrument that they can purchase only in small amounts if at all, because of their poverty. In many countries the poor have enough political power to require the wealthy to supply them with some of this human capital. The process is one of redistribution of percentage shares of income. Total income over the long run may increase in the process if the resources employed in education have not been used for investment elsewhere, or even if they have. These remarks assume that the taxes employed to finance education will take more money from the well-to-do household than from the poor household receiving the same amount of education. Obviously, this is the state of affairs, nominally; all it calls for is a tax system less regressive than a poll tax, and perhaps not even that. Incidentally, a capital asset in the form of education is one that cannot be taken away once it is given, if those in power have a change of heart, or if they refuse to supply the poor with adequate police protection.

2. A demand by the poor, especially the illiterate poor, for a consumer's good. Whether or not it adds at all to the recipient's earning power, the ability to communicate and receive by reading and writing is valued for the dignity and enhancement of personal relations that it affords the learner. In this category belongs the increase in political power that literacy brings, again regardless of its effect on ability to earn. The observation made above about the tax system applies here also.

Other consumer goods, clothing, food, and shelter, for example, are usually not provided free of charge to the poor. The reason seems to be that these tangible, separable goods can be resold. In contrast, the recipient of education does not face the temptation to resell it in order to finance a more immediate need. Moreover, no struggle arises within the family over who shall receive this free good. Wives in poor households may for this reason demand free education more vigorously than they demand free food, free clothing, or cash grants.

3. A demand by most of the community for the externalities (improved milieu).

The beneficiaries, however wealthy, cannot make their demand for these externalities felt through the market mechanism.

In certain societies, where a dominant few exploit the many for their own ends, the first two demands for free education cannot assert themselves, and the third demand does not exist. Indeed, education of the masses becomes a discommodity to the rulers, as it imperils their political control.

The unit of direct service in education can be defined either as the amount by which the individual is educated,[15] or as the amount of opportunity the individual is afforded to become educated. If a teacher of specified capability devotes a certain number of hours of uniform teaching effort to educating a bright pupil B and the same number of hours to educating a dull pupil D, the outputs, in terms of B's and D's abilities to read, write, and do arithmetic will differ. Whether output is more usefully measured in terms of the equal number of hours of teaching or the unequal abilities that result depends on what the demand is deemed to exist for: results, or opportunity offered. For the simplest kind of elementary education, reading, writing, and arithmetic at a level that, while low, provides release from illiteracy, it is the resulting abilities that are uppermost in the minds of the recipients both of the direct service and of the externalities. Extra teaching for the slow learner will be expected and provided. It is assumed, reasonably, that almost everyone will learn to read and write if enough effort is applied. But at the higher levels even of elementary education, and certainly at all levels of secondary and college or university training, there is no community pressure anywhere to devote more time to the dull than to the bright, in order that all recipients may achieve a uniform capability. It is not assumed that almost everyone can achieve such a level, if enough teaching effort is applied. Accordingly, at the simple elementary level the teaching effort is only an input needed to achieve a required output; at higher levels of education, the teaching effort is itself acceptable as a measure of output. The illiterate's demand is a demand to be taught to read and write; the student at higher levels asks simply to be given the opportunity, that is, to be given the teaching. The demand by those who benefit from the externalities is similarly asymmetrical: at the lowest level of education, the demand is for externalities from literacy, which is a reasonable goal. At the higher levels of education the externalities are sought not in terms of everyone's reaching a specified level of skills but rather in terms of some proportion of the total doing so. This proportion depends on inherent capacity of the learner more than on total hours of teaching devoted to the recipients in the aggregate: to keep all students in college eight years instead of four would not change appreciably the proportion of students that reached some specified minimum level of skill.

The cost functions appear to be of about the same kind, whichever of the two measures of education is adopted, with some exceptions to be noted below. If the number educated is held constant, it seems likely that successive increments in level

15. For dimensions in which this amount might be measured, see J. A. Kershaw and R. N. McKean, *Systems Analysis and Education* (Santa Monica, California: RAND Corporation, 1959), pp. 8–9, cited and appraised by Werner Z. Hirsch, "Quality of Government Services," in Howard G. Schaller (Ed.), *Public Expenditure Decisions in the Urban Community* (Baltimore: Johns Hopkins Press, 1963), pp. 173–78.

of education can be obtained only at increasing cost, insofar as those increments can be measured or compared: for example, incremental vocabulary.

As the number to be educated increases, level of education and area constant, the total cost of producing a certain minimum ability to read, write, and figure will increase. The manner in which it will increase depends on whether the brightest are taken first. If they are, severely increasing marginal costs are encountered when education is measured in results, merely by definition of brightness. This fact will not influence much the number to whom such education is given in a wealthy society, but in a poor society the high incremental cost of achieving a certain minimum level of reading, writing, and arithmetic for the dullest, say, one-tenth, of the youth may lead, not perhaps to an outright refusal to admit such children to the school, but to a tolerance of virtual illiteracy for them, that is, a refusal to supply enough remedial extra teaching to them to assure that they reach the minimum level. And if the slowest learners are defined to include not only those who are not very bright but also those who, although intelligent, are handicapped by home or other cultural conditions, even wealthy cities have shown themselves unwilling to spend the money required to assure a minimum level of attainment at the elementary school level.

When the children are of uniform grade and background, marginal cost of achieving for all of them a certain minimum level of achievement will first decrease, if the number of pupils is very small, because of indivisibilities of factors, then increase as the number educated increases further. Some of the additional teachers will be drawn from occupations where they could earn more than from the hitherto prevailing teachers' salaries. Some of them will be inefficient; more hours will need to be spent by them to achieve the minimum results. When those circumstances are combined with differences in learning ability, the incremental cost of assuring a certain level of achievement by the dullest, or least motivated, or most culturally handicapped children can be substantial.

For a given number of pupils and a given level of achievement, total cost increases with dispersion, because of indivisibilities of factors (schoolhouses, equipment, even teachers when the pupils are spread thinly over a wide area), coupled with transport costs. The increase is probably more than in proportion to the increase in area. These facts alone are enough to explain much of the difference in educational levels achieved in agricultural countries and in industrialized, urbanized countries. It follows that total cost can be reduced by concentrating the given number of pupils in a smaller area. Since the number of pupils is held constant, the circumstances making for increasing marginal cost mentioned in the second paragraph above do not arise.

The direct benefits of the service of education are of course readily locatable: the children educated or their households. The externalities of education, in contrast, are distributed among the entire populace, in a pattern that, if differential, cannot be discerned.

Universal, simple elementary education yields a benefit to the direct recipient that, in a general manner of speaking, he does not have to give up through market prices. By making those educated more productive, such education permits them to receive more. Education enhances the marginal productivity both of a given labor force and of the given amount of capital with which they are working. If only a part of the labor force has been allowed education, an extension of education will probably lower the marginal productivity of the hitherto privileged group. But even this outcome is not certain, because of the complementary nature of certain different units of labor.

An increment of free education is indirectly rejectable, by households already purchasing education from private schools, correspondence schools, or tutors; they can reduce the one while absorbing the other. In practice, this possibility is not very important. Some of the education purchased is regarded as better than or complementary to the free education offered, and some of it supplies other consumer goods as joint products: entertainment on television or radio, for example.

Since each child in the classroom can be the object of personal attention or neglect, the equity criterion of administrative impersonalization is not in practice always satisfied. Impersonalization means in this context only that no special favors or penalties are meted out by the administration, here the teacher, that are inconsistent with the professed goals of the service. Lack of such impersonalization in the education law, as distinguished from administration of the law, is rarely if ever found.

Participation costs are far from equal in many instances. The low-income farming family sacrifices more in money terms, and much more psychically if interpersonal comparisons are allowed, than the well-off urban family who lose no immediate source of income by their children's absence from the home. In some underdeveloped countries the resistance aroused by heavy participation costs for rural families is a formidable barrier to truly universal education. Since there is no close substitute for education, and since the amount of purchased education is in all countries moderate or small, the excess-burden problem is of little importance.

Of all the major government services, education offers the least opportunity for counter-cycle variation. This fact is self-evident with respect to level of service. As to level of input, the important capital items are buildings and equipment, and their construction or purchase must be closely timed to growth in numbers of pupils and students. The community is not likely to tolerate overcrowding in prosperity merely to help a public works program in a recession of uncertain future date. It may be willing to speed up a building program in a recession, especially since construction commonly lags behind needs in any event, but if it builds too far in advance of needs, it runs the risk of errors in location and size of structure, and is unable to take advantage of the latest technology.

Since education is rationed, and in most countries at a level far below what would be demanded at a zero price, the pattern in which this service is distributed is an object of contention. In few countries, if any, is the distribution of free education equal, using as measures of product those suggested above. The differences are chiefly by region, by race or color, and by religion. Groups within a community who are deprived of power to vote or otherwise influence selection of the executive or legislators are likely to be found receiving little or no simple elementary education. This fact suggests that the demand for such education comes only to a limited degree from those who would in a democratic society benefit from its externalities, either because they are not aware of the possibilities or because they live in a non-democratic society where their privileged status makes the externalities disadvantageous to them, threatening their position of superiority.

Even the power to vote will not bring equality in education for a cluster of low-income households who form a political unit responsible for the level of education; they have not the resources. The prevalence of such regions or districts in even the wealthiest countries suggests again that the externalities are weaker, or less favorable, or at least less appreciated, than might at first be thought. In some instances, to be sure, the milieu of only the immediate region would be improved by education, but the more typical case is the poor region with a high birth rate and a high rate of emigration of young persons of working age to other regions. These other regions get free of charge what abilities are embodied in the immigrants, their education, such as it is, having been paid for by the district of emigration. Perhaps no one region of immigration thinks it worth while to finance education in any one region of emigration, since the emigrants scatter to many areas.

In general, then, it appears that, taking a nation as a whole, more education is distributed to high-income households than to low-income households,[16] but not enough more to make the distribution proportional to income. And in small, rich school districts the greater amount of education is more or less matched by the higher school-tax bills. Taking the world as a whole, one gains the same impression: more education per household in the richer countries.

Education is a form of human capital that in many countries, especially in poor countries, carries a rate of return well above that available on the kind of investment that is included in national income data. It easily satisfies the criterion of economic growth. The resources devoted to education, including the student's own time, would doubtless have been used at least in part to produce consumers' goods, hence the growth is obtained at the expense of immediate consumption. The high rate of time preference at the margin characteristic of households with very low incomes explains in part the low level of education in underdeveloped countries.

Education probably lays the ground work for acceptance of greater risks by the coming generation of entrepreneurs, in the sense that it probably makes individuals somewhat more willing to accept an increment in dispersion of possible outcomes in return for a given increase in mean yield. It does so largely by enabling them to assess the future more accurately and so be less subject to vague apprehensions, taboos, and superstition. But by the same token education reduces a blind willingness to challenge uncertainty with hunches. On balance, education may decrease the amount of true risk assumed while at the same time increasing the mean return. Ventures hitherto overlooked which carry less risk and a higher expected return are substituted by the educated entrepreneur for ventures worse on both counts that are accepted by the ignorant.

16. This statement refers to output (creation of abilities to read, write, etc.). "In the critical skills—verbal and reading ability—Negro students are falling further behind whites with each year of school completed." National Advisory Commission on Civil Disorders, *Report*, p. 25. And in many instances educational input also is less, per child, in the poor districts, or in districts inhabited chiefly by certain ethnic or color groups.

External equilibrium of poor areas is affected only indirectly, yet in the long run substantially, by the loss to more prosperous areas through emigration of the young men and women they have trained to a certain level. Often the loss would not occur if a high quality of education could be supplied by the poor region up through the college or graduate level, to the able and ambitious student who in the absence of local facilities must emigrate to obtain such education and, once having emigrated, becomes reluctant to leave the other advantages he has found.

Education may or may not increase the hours of labor offered, given the wage rate or salary. Education allows the recipient to make more use of his leisure time; what might otherwise be a period of boredom becomes one in which his mental and physical capacities can be enjoyably exercised. But meanwhile his awareness of consumption opportunities has been enhanced, opportunities that can be taken advantage of without any increase in leisure, indeed even if leisure decreases somewhat, but that do require more money. Still other consumption possibilities, to be sure, require more leisure for implementation. Introspection and observation suggest that these opposing forces, though strong, are not far from balancing each other.

Maximization of education with given resources requires that it be so distributed that moving an increment of input from one school district, school, grade, or indeed individual child to another would not change the total output. This maximization standard is almost sure to conflict with the standard of equal distribution, as it does in police and fire protection. The conflict between maximization and equal distribution is particularly important in poor areas. The loss of total education from spreading severely constrained resources in an equal-distribution pattern will be greater, in percentage terms, than in richer areas.

An increment of education reduces government expenditures on crime prevention on balance, though it may increase certain types of crime, embezzlement, for example. It also reduces government outlay on fire protection, public health, and medical care. Education induces an increase in expenditures on highways and streets, and cultural and recreational facilities. It increases tax revenue automatically, after a considerable lapse of time, by increasing productivity and hence, to some degree at least, national income.

11. Sewerage, and Garbage and Refuse Disposal

In rural areas, waste removal is commonly purchased on the market or is supplied by the household's or firm's own efforts. In large cities garbage and refuse disposal commonly, and sewage disposal always, are furnished only by the government. In towns, villages, and small cities, the pattern is varied.

In sewerage, group-consumption techniques and marketing techniques coexist, though not usually in any one area: for example, common sewerage and individual septic tanks. Much depends on the density of settlement. For sparsely settled areas common sewerage facilities are too expensive relative to septic tanks or simple holes in the ground, and the danger of contagion from improper disposal is less than in densely settled areas.

The common sewerage system does not permit of discrimination, save on an all-or-none basis; a geographic sub-area either has adequate or nearly adequate common sewage disposal or, as in some slum areas or areas segregated by race or color, has none at all. Accordingly, common sewage disposal is never sold on the market by a private firm. The occasional sewage disposal fees charged by the government are compulsory; they do not give the user an option to decrease his level of consumption of the service.

Garbage and refuse removal is supplied in the marketing mode, either privately for a price, or by the government, usually under direct rationing of the service (see page 72). It is a marketable service even in built-up areas, since discrimination can be carried down to the level of the household or firm, and since these recipients are allowed by the authorities to vary their demand for that service within a considerable range. But since disposal one way or another, if only by indefinite storage of inorganic material on the premises, is compulsory, again because of externalities, the government commonly supplies most or all of the service, occasionally charging a fee (compulsory price).

The disposal service is creative rather than preventive; hence the quantity of it supplied can be measured more readily than that of police or fire protection. Physical units of sewage flow or of garbage or refuse removal can be defined.

The cost of supplying varying levels of sewage disposal to a fixed population in a given area in some respects resembles that for bridge and highway traffic, since sewerage is transportation. But transportation is here succeeded by storage or destruction. As time passes the cheap forms of storage, usually dumping in bays or rivers, become used up and expensive treatment plants must be built. The current cost per unit of of sewerage is thus a function of both the level of current service and the level and time period of past service.

The current cost of garbage and refuse disposal is even more a function of the cumulative volume of service rendered in the past. Swamps and other areas set aside for landfill must be succeeded after a time by incinerators, which themselves become more expensive to construct as their increasing number requires incorporation of "scrubbing" devices and other anti-pollution techniques if the surrounding area is not to become uninhabitable or at least very unpleasant.

For these reasons the annual cost of sewerage and of garbage and refuse disposal for a given population and a given area can be expected to rise steadily, over time. Moreover, the per capita tonnage of garbage and refuse rises as per capita incomes increase.[17] As population in a given area increases, total cost of a given level of

---

17. Household refuse in the United States is increasing at a rate of 4 per cent a year, that is, appreciably more than the rate of population increase. More is being spent on its disposal (more than $3 billion a year) than on any other public services except schools and roads (*Report by Committee on Pollution* [Dr. Athelstan Spilhaus, chairman] of National Academy of Sciences, to Federal Council for Science and Technology in the executive office of the President [*New York Times*, April 1, 1966]. A Suffolk County, N.Y., supervisor states that "garbage disposal is the most difficult long-range problem of a purely mechanical nature that local government has to face" (*New York Times*, October 9, 1966). For dimensions in which

sewerage or of garbage and refuse removal rises faster than in proportion, as more and more valuable space must be allotted to these tasks, even apart from the cumulative factor just noted.

Concentration of a given population into a smaller area tends to reduce total cost by shortening pipelines, distances traveled by dump trucks, and the like, but tends to increase total cost by demanding increments of more and more valuable land or more and more costly underground work. In addition, high-rise buildings are more costly to service.[18] If the dumping sites are included in the area posited, concentration causes a more rapid rise in the increment of total cost that is due to the cumulative factor. On balance, dispersion of a given population probably reduces total cost initially, then increases it.

Since the household or firm must in any event have its sewage, garbage, and refuse disposed of, the benefit of the free public service is at least as much as what the recipient would pay to get the market to do the job. This yardstick, to be sure, is not available with respect to sewerage in a large city, but no yardstick is needed for that. A service that is compulsory on the recipient and is uniform throughout the area raises no problem of differential benefits.

In small cities, villages, and towns that provide free disposal service the direct recipient of it must yield most or all of the benefit to building owners and ultimately landowners, unless the city competes not at all with other cities for residents and firms. If the free service is financed by real estate taxes (see Chapter 15), there may be no net discernible monetary benefit to anyone, except as public disposal proves more efficient than private disposal. In large cities a similar question may arise for garbage and refuse collection, but not, as we have seen, for sewage disposal. Within a city that supplies disposal service free, those areas that are discriminated against by being excluded from the sewerage service or by being given a lower level, including perhaps a zero level, of garbage and refuse removal will be characterized by land prices slightly lower than if such services were provided: slightly, for these are commonly areas segregated by poverty, race, or color, whose inhabitants have little chance to move out and into which few others wish to move. An increment of garbage and refuse removal is indirectly rejectable by those who are already purchasing this service. In practice, such rejection as occurs is not sufficient to concern the government.

The consensus type of equity criteria are all satisfied by government-supplied sewage disposal, and are normally so by garbage and refuse disposal, except where

residential refuse collection may be measured, and some empirical findings on cost functions, see Werner Z. Hirsch, *op. cit.*, pp. 171–73.

18. If a ten-foot length of one-inch pipe will service the first story of a building, the pipe cost per story will be constant only if a second story requires merely lengthening the one-inch pipe by another ten feet. But since on occasion the waste from the second story will have to be carried through the lower ten feet at the same moment as the waste from the first story, addition of the second story requires an increment to the diameter of the pipe for the first story as well as the small-diameter ten-foot length for the second story; or, alternatively, the first-story pipe is left at one inch and twenty feet of one-inch pipe are obtained for the second story. More precisely, the pipe diameter would not have to increase proportionally, since the carrying capacity increases faster than the diameter; but the essential point remains, namely, that the addition of the second length of pipe requires some increase in the size of the first length.

service proves faulty in minor ways unless the household or firm is willing to tip the men.

Excess burden is not significant. With respect to counter-cycle policy for full employment, sewerage is likely to be as perverse in its timing as is the supplying of streets. Boom periods in residential construction necessitate concurrent expansion of sewers. Postponement is impossible. Advance construction is expensive in terms of interest, and as with school buildings it involves heavy risk of errors in location. Sewage treatment works may present some flexibility in timing, but not much. Garbage and refuse disposal plants, landfill, and the like can be planned ahead with less chance of error in location or in forecasting degree of need. Still, the counter-cycle possibilities for this type of public works seem quite limited.

The conflict type of equity criteria are important, at least for garbage and refuse removal. Equal distribution of the service would be intolerable. The household with the smallest amount of refuse and garbage would see it all hauled away, and every other household would be left with its excess over that amount.

Unequal distribution of the service may be preserved from favoritism by a rule that all refuse and garbage of each household will be carted away; the service is offered without limit. This formula would prove too costly, since free service is explicable here only by externalities, which do not extend to cover all possible refuse a household would develop under an unrationed service. Rationing is therefore commonly enforced, in three ways. First, objects over a certain size or of certain types are not taken. Second, the refuse must be placed in garbage cans or refuse containers. Third, the cans or containers are allowed to pile up on the curb until households are deterred from adding to the load. This third method calls for a more precisely expressed standard of rationing, such as allotting so many men and trucks per unit of area, usually per standard city block, a method which is commonly used. Since there are more households per block in the poor areas of a city, the city's input of the service per household is generally lower the poorer the household. But a poor family generates less garbage and less refuse than a rich family, except as oil, gas, or electricity replaces the ash-creating fuels in the higher-income households. On balance, these three methods of rationing the disposal service result in removing about all the refuse and garbage a rich family creates (except for the size-of-object limitation), while allowing refuse and garbage to pile up on streets and in alleyways of the poorer districts.[19]

In the slums of some cities, particularly in some Latin American countries, no garbage or refuse disposal service at all is offered. The households are so desperately poor that almost none accumulates, but the ostensible reason for no service is that no local tax is imposed on the land or shacks in these areas.

The reallocation criteria have little application to these disposal services. Much more important are the intra-system reactions, especially with public health. A city with faulty disposal service, at least for sewage and garbage, will find demands on its public health services multiplied.

19. Compare National Advisory Commission on Civil Disorders, *Report*, p. 14. See also *ibid.*, p. 273, for "the peculiarly intense needs of ghetto areas for sanitation services."

D. DISCRIMINATION
AMONG INDIVIDUALS FEASIBLE
(MARKETABLE GOODS): VOLUNTARY CONSUMPTION

12. Medical Care, including Hospitals

Free medical care is distinguished from public health by its marketability. In this respect medical care resembles education and contrasts with the services rendered by the military. But medical care provides only limited externalities in contrast to education and public health.

The demand for free medical care, like that for education, is a demand for redistribution of income through a service that cannot be resold by the recipient. The service is primarily a consumers' good but only in part a gainful or even productive consumers' good, since much of it goes to the aged who are in retirement. In countries where per capita income is low, medical care may prevent a sizeable decrease in production when it is rendered to members of the household who are, or who will grow up to be, in the labor force. Another source of demand for government supply of the service, not found in education, is the unpredictability of large, lumped expenditures.

A feature of the demand for free medical care is the great percentage difference between the amount of input that will be demanded at zero price compared with the amount demanded when a price is charged, based more or less on cost. The difference is great in the sense of being markedly larger than for education or other marketable services that the government supplies free of charge. This difference in amounts of input demanded would persist, we may conjecture, even in a society where money income was evenly distributed. Demand for medical care probably becomes highly inelastic at a price slightly above zero. In this respect it simply follows the general rule.

Medical care is both a preventive and a creative service. The output is to be measured in principle partly by success in maintaining good health. Success of this type is extremely difficult to measure in physical units. As with crime prevention, measurement must be in increments of reduction in what is being fought, here reduction in rates of diseases. In part, however, medical care can be measured in terms of improvement of health or ability once a disease or an accident has struck. The physical units employed to measure the amount of care will be many and diverse: number of teeth filled, number of broken limbs treated, number of appendectomies, and so on.

A correspondingly large number of cost functions must be defined, and a no priori generalization seems possible as to the nature of the marginal costs at increased levels of service (population and area being fixed) except the obvious one that they probably increase as less skilled and less talented personnel are drawn into the profession as demand increases. Even that outcome is not certain; an increase in demand that is allowed to express itself in higher factor rewards may divert talent from other fields. In the short run, a great expansion of medical care will produce rapidly rising costs because of the short run inelasticity of supply of personnel and facilities, unless the government, as an almost monopolist, fixes the prices of inputs, a reaction that seems likely.

The cost issue is the more important for medical care because this free service cannot easily be rationed in total amount by the donor, the government. Consumption of medical service, even when free, will differ enormously from one person to another, depending largely on state of health. To impose some general maximum per person, say fifty hours of medical service a year, seems inconsistent with the reasons why such service is being offered free, hence the state, if it offers medical care at zero price, is under pressure to offer all the service that anyone wants at that price. It may dampen the demand a little by forcing patients to queue, or wait weeks or months for postponable care or remedy. In contrast, education is commonly rationed more or less uniformly, at least as to input.

As population in a given area increases, the total cost of a stated level of medical service no doubt increases, but it may well increase less than in proportion, owing to indivisibility of factors, until less skilled personnel must be attracted to the medical profession. Concentration of a given population into a smaller area almost surely decreases total cost of a given level of medical care, if the initial dispersion has been great, since the average cost of transporting patient to doctor or hospital decreases, and lumpy factors, for example a hospital, are used more efficiently. Eventually, of course, those savings will be outweighed by the costs due to crowding, as concentration increases, and total cost will rise. The direct beneficiaries of the service are, as in education, easy to identify. In addition, in contrast to education, there is no important group of recipients of large externalities.

The small part of free medical care that increases productivity as distinguished from the part that is a pure consumers' good probably does not depress the wages of those treated, by increasing the available supply of labor. But if this type of medical care were massive and extensive, and if in an underdeveloped country it increased the man-hours of labor by, say, 50 per cent, wages per hour would decline except as one hour of labor now was more productive than before, when enfeeblement or illness caused many labor hours to be of low quality. But even if the wage rate fell, the household would normally be better off, as total hours worked increased, unless indeed the capital equipment was so slowly malleable and so difficult to increase that labor's marginal productivity dropped precipitately.

The consumer good, medical care, is not locational enough to siphon off benefits to landlords or site owners. The household is not likely to lose the benefits through market changes. Within the family, however, free medical care may cause a substantial change in redistribution of real income. Money that had gone to meet medical bills is now available for other things. (We still abstract from taxes needed to finance medical care.) The redistribution is probably in favor of the chief breadwinner, in the sense that the medical bills will have been met, not out of the housewife's allowance, if any, but from reserves controlled by the husband, or from a debt incurred by him for this purpose and serviced by him at the expense of non-necessities. Intra-family redistribution will also be in favor of the younger working generation as they are freed from paying medical bills for aged parents.

Medical care is easily rejectable directly, more easily than any other free government service. Ignorance, superstition, and inertia may hold consumption of this free service far below levels sought by policy-makers. Compulsory acceptance of medical care is politically and socially feasible only for certain kinds of care that the public can be convinced creates great externalities, vaccination being the prime example. Indirect rejection of an increment of medical care through a decrease in purchased care is less serious, since it will be limited to income groups that are already receiving what the policy-makers regard as adequate care, and that are not demanding free care as a form of redistribution of income. Low-income households will spend less on ineffective and dangerous nostrums, a nominal rejection that is really an acceptance of true medical care.

Free medical care is apt to violate the consensus type of equity criteria, since the government, in an attempt to reduce the cost from what it would be if no rationing at all were in force, may include arbitrary cut-off lines, in terms of type of care (dental care may be excluded), types of input (a charge may be made for prescriptions), and length of care (beyond a certain period the patient may have to pay part of the cost). Personalization, in the form of discrimination against or favoritism for individual patients, is unlikely to be found in the law, but may easily occur in practice.

A counter-cycle policy for full employment may be implemented, if at all, by timing of hospital construction. Usually, the timing of this construction is dominated by the current or immediately prospective need for medical care. The service of medical care itself cannot of course be varied contra-cyclically without gross infraction of the equity criterion of equal treatment of equals. The fact that a person becomes ill in a boom is scarcely a cause for denying him the care he would get in a recession.

Distribution of medical-care input by income classes is highly regressive in those countries where the standard of care varies little if at all with the recipient's income, and where treatment is freely accorded to all. Living conditions, working conditions, and relative ignorance of hygiene of the poor lead to a disproportionate number of illnesses and accidents among them. Wealthy families may continue to purchase medical care, if they are allowed to. The poor in such countries thus probably receive more input of free medical care per household than the rich. Of the poor, those with large families receive the most.

Three standards for distribution are found in the countries that supply any free medical care. Uniform availability to all, subject only to queuing or time delays, with some possibility of buying one's way out of the system and back into the market is one standard that is found, in Britain for example. In some countries free medical service is distributed only to those with incomes below a certain level. In still others the reverse rule applies: Free medical service is not supplied to those below a certain level of income. This standard is perhaps never advertised as such, but when free medical service in an undeveloped country is in fact restricted largely to urban inhabitants, the rural poor, who are poorer than the urban poor, are in fact excluded.

Discrimination in level of free medical service by color, race, or social status is common in areas where general discrimination on these bases is the custom. The ease of discriminating among individuals, that is, the essential marketability of medical care, offers an exceptional opportunity for this government service to conform to the aims of the dominant group in such communities.

Economic growth is enhanced by free medical care only insofar as growth increases with the increase in real income resulting from the increase in labor productivity per hour spent on the job and the increase in number of hours worked in a lifetime that comes with improvement in health and acceleration of recovery from injuries and illness. This increase accompanies most medical care to children, as future members of the labor force, and the active adult population, including housewives if imputed income represented by work around the house is counted in national income.[20] A large part of free medical care, however, as already noted, is dispensed to persons beyond working age. In any event, nothing can be said a priori as to what proportion of this increased productivity goes to creating capital goods. If human capital is included in wealth, the present value of the increase in the worker's future earnings that results from medical care makes this service a notable instrument of capital formation.

To the extent that free medical care allows the recipient to reduce his expenses or substitute marketable goods and services, it induces him to consume a little more of a great many things, including leisure. Hours of scheduled work may therefore decline. But actual hours of work will tend to rise as absenteeism is reduced through improved health, and output per hour will tend to increase. Free medical care, by increasing productivity, reduces the welfare load and increases the yield of the tax system, including the social security taxes. It also tends to increase the total of old-age pensions paid.

13. Cultural and Recreational Facilities

The fact that government-supplied recreational and cultural facilities are usually offered either free of charge or at a price that does not cover cost indicates that redistribution in kind is the chief explanation for this governmental activity. An externality in the form of an improved cultural and social milieu is also involved.

An increase in level of park and other recreational service, and probably also of cultural facilities, eventually encounters rising marginal cost per unit of service as more valuable space must be taken. If amount or level of service is held constant but the number served increases, the same considerations indicate eventually rising

20. "It was a matter of daily experience to observe the obvious signs of malnutrition in the appearance of wives of unemployed men with families. They obviously did without things for the sake of their husbands and children, and it was by no means certain that they keep for their own use the 'extra nourishment' provided expressly for them in a large number of cases by the Unemployment Assistance Board." Pilgrim Trust, *Men Without Work* (London: Macmillan, 1902), quoted by Michael Young, "Distribution of Income within the Family," *British Journal of Sociology* (1952), 3: 306.

marginal cost per person served. Concentration of a given number of users in a smaller area of residence will at first decrease total cost, if cost of transportation to and from the facility is included in total cost, but ultimately total cost rises, and eventually more than in proportion to the decrease in area, owing to overcrowding. If these transport and dwelling costs are excluded from the calculation, the size of the area in which the users of the facility reside appears to have no influence on total cost.

Counter-cycle policy for full employment may be implemented better than with most government services, by varying the timing of large capital inputs without altering appreciably the time pattern of output over the long period. The construction of parks and mountain trails, for example, can be advanced or deferred in a manner that is not practicable with school buildings or streets. Even the level of output can be varied somewhat, counter-cyclically, by manning the facilities more amply in a period of depression.

In a city, at least, recreational facilities, especially parks, and perhaps also some of the cultural facilities, are so locational in their benefits that rents for nearby dwellings may rise somewhat. Redistribution in kind is thus impaired, as it is also by the expenses of travel noted above and other outlays that are complementary to use of the facilities. Perhaps the most important of these complementary expenses, at least for recreational facilities devoted to boating, camping, fishing, hunting, and the like, is leisure, insofar as an increment of leisure denotes earnings foregone. In those countries where a two-week to a month's vacation is guaranteed to, and required of, every worker, these free recreational facilities are distributed much more regressively with income than in others. Discrimination by color or race or social status is technically feasible, and is intensively practiced, often without legal sanction, in communities thus biased.[21]

Of the reallocation criteria, only that of work versus leisure is significant here. In themselves, these free recreational facilities tend to reduce the supply of labor, but the money charges for complementary services may more than redress the balance.

E. SUMMARY OF COST FUNCTIONS

The conjectures above with respect to cost functions of the major governmental services are summarized in Table 1, where "Up" means "increasing" and "Down" means "decreasing" (but positive, unless otherwise noted). An increase in level of service, population and area constant, is accompanied by a decreasing average

21. "Poor recreational facilities" (e.g., lack of swimming pools) ranked fourth–fifth (tied with "Inadequate education"), in the "weighted comparison of grievance categories" among Negro communities in certain cities of the United States, compiled by the National Advisory Commission on Civil Disorders, in its *Report*, p. 149. The three higher-ranked grievance categories were "police practice," "unemployment and underemployment," and "inadequate housing." In York, Alabama, according to a Negro minister, Negroes cannot get a card at the "public" library. *Wall Street Journal*, Aug. 14, 1968, p. 1.

cost per unit of service for several services, up to a point; eventually, average cost rises for all services. But in the range where average cost is decreasing, the level of service agreed upon by the community, or at the other extreme by a dictator or oligarchy, may be in the far end of that range. In this range, tax rates that are set to cover total cost, although rising as the level of service rises, need rise less than in proportion.

If the community paid closer attention to marginal cost and the marginal increase in tax rate necessary to cover marginal cost, as Wicksell's principle implies (see Chapter 21), the level of service agreed on would be somewhat lower than that reached under the average cost reckoning, since, when marginal cost starts to rise, average cost continues to decline for a while. The services where average cost falls for some time with an increase in level of service are: deterrence of a potential enemy, public health, externalities from medical care, and flood control and drainage (average cost is undefined for space exploration, for externalities from education and housing, and is unknown for conquest and medical care).

Empirical studies may be able to reject or leave unrejected the conjecture made above, that the level of service offered will more often be at a level not far from where average cost ceases to decline.

For the other services, where average and marginal costs rise continuously as the level of service increases, the question again arises whether the community is guided by average cost rather than by marginal cost. Although both rise continuously, average cost is always below marginal cost for any given level of service. The community may be devoting more resources to the service than it would care to do if it compared marginal cost with marginal tax effort (see page 519).

As more and more persons occupy a given area, per capita cost of supplying a given level of service falls for many services, notably deterrence and conquest; public health; space exploration; contract enforcement and civil rights; externalities from education, housing, and medical care; fire protection (up to a point); flood control and drainage; education (up to a point); and medical care itself. Persons in low-population countries can obtain these services at an acceptably low per capita cost only by migrating to high-population countries, and as they do, the per capita cost falls still lower in the country of immigration and rises still higher in the country of emigration. These remarks abstract from the demand side; a country so small as to be neither a threat to a nuclear power nor a prize worth conquest will need little or none of the service, deterrence. But demand for some of the other services does not thus decrease with population, and the cost functions exert some pressure to make the less populous countries smaller. This pressure is somewhat less intense with respect to those services, namely public health, contract enforcement and civil rights, and medical care, which show a positive rather than a zero marginal cost, that is, where total cost increases somewhat as population increases, instead of remaining virtually unchanged, as it does for deterrence, conquest, space exploration, the externalities, and flood control and drainage. Fire protection and education are in prosperous countries usually carried to levels where per capita cost is increasing and so do not attract immigrants in those countries on a per capita basis.

Emigration from sparsely settled rural areas and towns to densely populated

Table 1 Presumed Cost Functions of Government Services[a]

	INCREASE IN LEVEL OF SERVICE			INCREASE IN POPULATION			INCREASE IN AREA		
	Total cost	Average cost	Marginal cost	Total cost	Cost per capita	Marginal cost	Total cost	Cost per capita (also, Av. cost per unit)	Marginal cost per unit of area
Military									
Deterrence, nuclear	Up	Discontinuous, then down, then up	Discontinuous, then down, then up	Unch.	Down	Zero	Down slightly	Down slightly	Negative and unch.
Deterrence, conventional	Up	Discontinuous, then down, then up	Discontinuous, then down, then up	Unch.	Down	Zero	Down	Down	Negative and unch.
Damage limitation (%)	Up	Up	Up	Up	Unch.	Positive and unch.	Up	Up	Up
Conquest	?	?	?	Unch.	Down	Zero	Unch.	Unch.	Zero
Internal control	Up	Up	Up	Up	Up	Up	Up or down (?)	Up or down	?
Public health	Up	Down, then up	Down, then up	Up slightly	Down	Slightly positive and unch.	Down (?)	Down (?)	Negative and unch.(?)
Space exploration	Up	Not defined	Up	Unch.	Down	Zero	Unch.	Unch.	Zero
Contract enforcement, civil rights	Up	Up	Up	Up slightly	Down	Slightly positive and unch.	Unch.	Unch.	Zero
Externalities									
From education	Up	Not defined	Not defined	Unch.	Down	Zero	Unch.	Unch.	Zero
From housing	Up	Not defined	Not defined	Unch.	Down	Zero	Unch.	Unch.	Zero
From medical care	Up	Down, then up	Down, then up	Unch. (but see text)	Down	Zero	Down	Down	Negative (and unch.?)
Fire protection	Up	Down, then up	Up	Up	Down, then up	Down, then up	Down, then up	Down, then up	Negative, then positive
Police protection	Up	Up	Up	Up	Up	Up	Up	Up	Up
Highways	Up	Up	Up	Up	Up	Up	Down	Down	Negative
Streets	Unch., then up	Down, then up	Zero, then up	Up	Up	Up	Up	Up	Up
Flood control, drainage	Up	Up	Up	Unch.	Down	Zero	Up	Up	Up
Education	Up	Up	Up	Unch., then up	Down, then up	Zero, then up	Up	Up	Up
Sewerage, and garbage and refuse disposal[b]	Up	Up	Up	Up	Down	Up	Down, then up	Down, then up	Negative, then positive
Medical care	Up	?	?	Up	Down	Positive and unch.	Down, then up	Down, then up	Negative, then positive
Recreation, cultural facilities	Up	Up	Up	Up	Up	Up	Down, then up	Down, then up	Negative, then positive

a "Unch." means "unchanged".
b Marginal cost also rises as cumulative service over time rises.

cities is promoted, as is emigration between countries, by the decrease in average cost of these services, excepting those services that for political and social reasons are undertaken always by national governments (deterrence and conquest) and those for which the minimum expenditure that must be made before any unit of service at all can be supplied is very high (space exploration).

As geographical area served increases, population and level of service remaining constant, total cost and therefore also cost per capita and per unit of service decline for a number of services: nuclear deterrence (slightly), conventional deterrence, perhaps internal control, perhaps public health, externalities from medical care, highway service (but the demand for highway service increases as area increases), and, up to a point, beyond which total cost increases, fire protection, sewerage and garbage and refuse disposal, medical care, and recreation and cultural facilities. In contrast, dispersion increases the total cost of damage limitation from nuclear war (owing to the cost of anti-missile missile sites), police protection, street service, flood control and drainage, and education.

The practical significance of this set of conjectures is somewhat less than for the others above, because a given size group does not commonly have the option of spreading out over a larger area, without changing the total number of persons involved, or of crowding into a smaller area, again without changing the number of persons in the group. These options do exist, however, in the planning of new towns, and in decisions whether a city that is going to grow in population anyway shall grow "up," with high-rise apartments, or "out," if land is available, with one- and two-family dwellings.

For those services that are commonly offered by cities rather than by states or by national governments, the score is a mixed one: A somewhat dispersed city gets its fire protection, sewerage, garbage and refuse disposal, medical care, and recreation more cheaply, up to a point, but with further dispersion it finds that costs are rising. Public health cost may decrease steadily with dispersion, and so too the externalities' costs from medical care. But the cost of police protection rises continuously with dispersion, and so too the cost of streets and education. These conjectures imply some minimum-cost size of area to be covered by a given population, for a given level of each of the services.

CHAPTER SIX

Unrequited Payments in General

A. TYPES OF UNREQUITED PAYMENT

PAYMENTS NOT MADE for a consideration are unrequited payments. When paid by the government to the private sector, they are subsidies or welfare payments. A subsidy is conditioned on a particular economic performance: growing sugar-beets, for example, or reducing wheat acreage, or buying milk. A subsidy is therefore almost a payment for a consideration, but legally it is not a purchase, and so is included here in unrequited payments. A welfare payment, in contrast, say a relief payment to a needy family, or an old-age social security benefit, is not conditioned on any current performance, and it is not solely a return of savings with interest. It, too, then, is an unrequited payment, at least in part, and often entirely so.

Taxes are unrequited payments by the private sector to the government. But, as the heading of this chapter indicates, the term unrequited payments will be reserved for subsidies and welfare payments. The concept of a tax, nevertheless, is important in distinguishing one type of subsidy (or welfare payment) from another, as will appear presently; and certain kinds of tax have a subsidy element in them by the encouragement they give, at the margin, to an increase in private sector activity: for example, a tax on idle land. The point in all such distinctions is the difference, if any, between the direction of total flow and the direction of change at the margin. A few examples will illustrate this point.

Consider a relief payment to a needy family, the amount of which is conditioned on the level of the family's own income. In total, this is a positive flow from the government to the private sector. But at the margin it is a negative flow if the private sector increases its economic activity, just as is an ordinary income tax. If a member of the household on relief brings in a little money from a part-time job, the relief payment decreases. In contrast, consider a subsidy to a sugar-beet producer. This too is a positive flow from the government to the private sector. And it is a positive flow at the margin also, when the private sector increases its economic activity; if the farmer grows more beets, he gets a larger total subsidy. Accordingly, the relief payment tends to discourage economic activity in the private sector, while a subsidy tends to encourage such activity. The family on relief is subjected to an implicit tax at the margin of the family's economic activity. It is a tax-type of unrequited payment from government to private sector, but, with respect to the total flow, it is a negative tax. We may use the word "tax" to refer to the effect at the margin, and the word "negative" to indicate that the total flow is in the opposite direction to that of a tax, and, combining the two words, call the relief payment a "negative tax," or, more precisely, a negative-tax type of unrequited payment from government to private sector. The sugar-beet subsidy, in contrast, is not a negative-tax type of unrequited payment. It has no tax element in it at all.

The same kind of distinction may be observed among different types of tax. Practically all taxes, to be sure, are pure taxes, in that both the total flow and the marginal effect of private economic activity are payments from the private sector to the government. But there are exceptions. The tax on idle land, mentioned above, illustrates this point. It is clearly a tax in its total flow, which is from the private sector to government. But as the landowner becomes active economically, and makes use of his land, this flow diminishes, and finally vanishes, when he makes enough use of the land to become fully exempt from the tax. The tax on idle land has a subsidy aspect, in that it encourages private-sector economic activity at the margin. But it is a negative subsidy in its total-flow aspect, since, if any money flows at all, it flows from private sector to government. For short, we may term the tax on idle land a negative subsidy, just as the relief payment may be termed a negative tax.

Unrequited payments by government to private sector therefore fall into two groups:

1. One group consists of those that are welfare payments or subsidies with respect both to (a) total flow and (b) direction of change in total flow as private-sector economic activity increases. All such payments are simply "welfare payments," or "subsidies," with no modifier. In practice few if any welfare payments are of this type.

2. The other group consists of those that are likewise welfare payments or subsidies with respect to (a) total flow, but that resemble taxes in their marginal aspect, that is, in (b) direction of change in total flow as private-sector activity increases. The total flow from government decreases as that activity increases. These are negative-tax subsidies, or negative-tax welfare payments. A negative-tax welfare payment has been illustrated above (relief to a needy family). An example of a negative-tax subsidy is payment to a farmer for reducing acreage in use. This payment is designed to repress production.

The negative-tax welfare payment or subsidy may be characterized by its base. If a welfare payment decreases as the household increases its income, it is a negative income tax. If the welfare payment decreases as the household increases its wealth, it is a negative wealth tax. The payment to a farmer that increases as he decreases his acreage is a negative land tax.

The two groups of unrequited payment from government to private sector are indicated in Figures 9 and 10. Group 1, the pure welfare payment or subsidy, is represented by the upper portion of the curve in Figure 9. Group 2, the negative-tax type of welfare payment or subsidy, say relief to a needy family, or payment for reducing farm acreage, is represented by the lower portion of the curve in Figure 10.

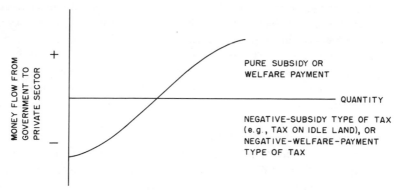

FIGURE 9. Pure Subsidy or Welfare Payment and Negative Subsidy or Negative Welfare Payment

[a] The slopes of these curves have been exaggerated, for emphasis. No part of the slope should exceed 45 degrees, which represents a marginal rate of 100 per cent.

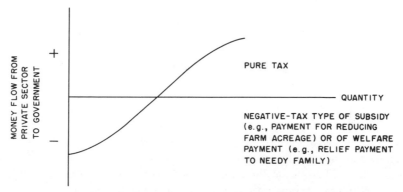

FIGURE 10. Pure Tax and Negative Tax

[a] The slopes of these curves have been exaggerated, for emphasis. No part of the slope should exceed 45 degrees, which represents a marginal rate of 100 per cent.

The remaining portions of the two curves represent the two kinds of tax: the negative-subsidy[1] type of tax, the tax on idle land, for example, in the lower portion of the curve in Figure 9, and the pure tax, say an income tax, in the upper portion of the curve in Figure 10. As the continuity of each curve suggests, the pure type of subsidy or welfare payment shades off into the impure type of tax (Figure 9) and the pure type of tax shades off into the impure type of subsidy or welfare payment.

These distinctions have nothing to do with a change in the rate of tax, or rate of subsidy. The consequences of a change in rate give rise to quite a different classification. An increase in the rate of a tax may either increase or decrease the total flow

1. A negative-welfare-payment type of tax is conceivable and doubtless exists somewhere. A tax on leisure would be an example.

from private sector to government; that is, the marginal effect of a positive change in tax rate may be either positive or negative. If it is negative the tax is not on that account a negative-subsidy type of tax, as is a tax on idle land. The fact that an increase in tax rate decreases the total revenue from the tax is important but is not relevant for distinguishing between pure taxes and negative-subsidy types of tax. Similarly, an increase in the rate of a subsidy of, say, so many cents a pound, might conceivably induce a relaxation of private effort, owing to the income effect of the increase in rate. Then the total subsidy would decrease, but it would not on that account be a negative-tax type of subsidy.

Save for the social security programs, the analysis to follow is in partial-equilibrium terms; the sources of the moneys paid out are abstracted from. The question posed is how the recipient of the unrequited payment, and other relevant households and firms, act in the presence of the payments compared with how they would act if the payments were not made but, sometimes unrealistically, if their other relations with the government and the private sector were unaltered. Transfer payments in the form of property payments will be considered under the same assumptions, but briefly, since they are essentially market transactions, and, as such, of no special interest to public finance.

B. WELFARE PAYMENTS

Private charity has been found an inadequate source of welfare payments for much the same reason that group-consumption services are not marketable. At least this is so insofar as the aim of private charity is more than aid just to a particular person or family and includes the reduction of want in general, for humanitarian reasons and also to avoid strain on the social fabric. These ends are to each single donor group-consumption goods; if they are to be attained by (supplied to) any one donor, they must be attained by (supplied to) all donors in the group simultaneously. The donors must organize their giving by a contract among themselves; the government is the agent.

Aside from this point, welfare payments do not lend themselves to generalizations as readily as do subsidies. Further consideration of welfare payments is therefore deferred to the analyses of the several major types given in Chapter 7.

C. SUBSIDIES

1. Considerations Peculiar to Subsidies

A. REASONS FOR GOVERNMENT ACTION

(1) Types of Subsidy

The economic performance upon which payment of a subsidy is conditioned may be of almost any type, but common examples are production or consumption of a certain good or service, increase in use of a factor of production, and penetration of a particular market, notably the export market. Subsidies are consumer subsidies, factor subsidies, or special-purpose subsidies. A consumer subsidy is designed to benefit low-income consumers by enabling them to increase their consumption of a particular commodity or service without an offsetting decrease in their other consumption. A factor subsidy is intended to benefit factors specialized to an industry by raising rates of compensation or decreasing unemployment. Special-purpose subsidies, not designed to benefit either consumers or factors as such, may be aimed at any of the goals suggested by the criteria in Chapter 2; common goals are economic growth, maintenance of a fixed exchange rate, and an increase in output of goods that carry positive externalities.

A competitive market has no means of implementing a subsidy, quite apart from the conflicts of interest that arise in financing it. If everyone agreed that a subsidy on sugar was desirable, perhaps to avert shortage in time of war, competition among sellers would prevent civic-minded consumers from effecting such a subsidy.

A subsidy may consist of an actual flow of money or only an imputed flow. The two chief forms of imputed subsidy are the loan guarantee and tax reduction, both to be discussed presently.

The subsidies noted up to this point include all pure subsidies. They also include negative-tax types of subsidy, and negative-subsidy types of tax. The negative-tax subsidy is highly specialized; a major example will be described in Chapter 7, Section C.2 (agricultural subsidies). This kind of subsidy is usually designed to raise factor prices. The negative-subsidy type of tax, notably the tax on idle land, is levied for the benefit of consumers.

(A) LOAN GUARANTEES

Under a loan guarantee the government assures the creditor that the loan he has made will be serviced and repaid, if necessary by the government itself. Although no money may in fact need to be paid by the government, it has nevertheless granted a subsidy. The cost of the subsidy is the amount that taxpayers would be willing to give to be relieved of the obligation. As to the benefit from the guarantee, the consequent reduction in interest rate is not a good measure, since some part of the benefit would normally accrue to the lenders, just as would some part of a direct subsidy per unit of borrowing. In principle the benefit is the sum of the increase in lenders' surplus and the increase in borrowers' surplus, this sum being analogous to the sum of increases in producers' and consumers' surpluses, under a commodity subsidy.

The actual payments, if any, made under a guarantee program say little about the cost or the benefit of the program, since the government is not a business firm operating with capital freely subscribed by risk-takers in a competitive market.

The firms obtaining this guarantee are usually financial intermediaries, especially purchasers of home mortgages. The stimulus of the subsidy is chiefly to the industries supported by the borrowing. Government guarantee of home mortgages stimulates financial intermediaries, but even more so the building industry. Guarantees direct to manufacturing and marketing firms are sometimes made when their customers are firms or households in certain foreign countries.

Imputed subsidies in the form of guarantees are to be distinguished from insurance that is fully financed by premiums collected from the affected parties. The government may engage in such insurance because it is able to average risks over numbers larger than can be covered by any one builder, bank, finance company, or sometimes even private insurance company. Government insurance of investment abroad against loss from expropriation, devaluation, and non-transferability may contain a subsidy element, depending on the premiums charged.

(B) TAX-REDUCTION SUBSIDIES

Imputed subsidies in the form of tax reduction allow the household or business firm to reduce its tax liability by some fraction, usually far less than 100 per cent, of the amount of the stipulated type of economic activity: contribution to a charitable or religious organization, outlay for capital equipment, or increase in export sales, for example. That fraction is stipulated in the law when the tax reduction takes the form of a credit directly against the tax otherwise due. It is determined by the marginal tax rate of the particular taxpayer when the tax reduction takes the form of a deduction of the amount spent, of sales gained, or whatever, for computation of the net tax base subject to the tax. Both credit and deduction are commonly subject to ceilings of some sort. The tax in which the credit or reduction is embodied is to this extent a negative-subsidy type of tax.

An imputed, tax-reduction subsidy resembles in some respects a tax exemption or a restricted definition of a tax base. A government desiring to encourage investment spending may either (1) offer a cash subsidy to any firm equal to some fraction of its investment outlay, (2) allow a deduction, in computing taxable income, of the firm's investment outlays, or (3) replace the income tax by an expenditure tax, that is, a tax levied solely on consumer goods (see Chapter 13). In general, the results will be much the same under these three alternatives, at least under a proportional rate income or expenditure tax and a cash subsidy at the same rate.[2] And the revenue loss

2. For an indication of why these three methods give about the same results, see the explanation in Chapter 11 (income tax) of the effects of 100 per cent accelerated depreciation, which provides still another way of effectively exempting income from investment spending. For a critical resumé of tax-reduction subsidies in the United States, see Stanley S. Surrey, "The

(strictly, loss of command over allocation of total resources) must be made up by heavier taxation elsewhere; in this sense all three methods involve a roughly equal cost to the Treasury, that is, to the rest of the community. But if policy 3 were implemented, that is, if an expenditure tax at the same rate replaced an income tax, no one would suggest that there be entered in the budget an imputed subsidy equal to the tax revenue lost by moving to the expenditure-tax base and, correspondingly, an imputed revenue item of the same amount. On the other hand, a cash subsidy (policy 1) must, all would agree, be entered in the budget as a government expenditure. No imputed revenue item is needed in this case. Present practice for the in-between case, the tax-reduction type of subsidy (policy 2) is not to enter an imputed-subsidy item in expenditures and the corresponding imputed revenue item.

The argument for including the policy 2 figures in the budget but not those of policy 3 is not one of cost to the community: as just indicated, the cost is essentially the same in all three instances. The argument rests rather on the fact that under policies 1 and 2, cash subsidy and tax reduction, each business firm decides for itself whether the government shall pay it the subsidy, and so, whether other tax-payers shall shoulder a corresponding burden, while, under policy 3, expenditure tax in place of income tax, this option is not open to the individual firm: it receives the subsidy, in a manner of speaking, no matter what it does. The distinction is more formal than real. A firm that will reject a certain venture when neither policies 1, 2, or 3 are in force but that will engage in the venture when the cash subsidy is offered (policy 1) will also engage in it when either policy 2 or policy 3 is in force.

In macro analysis it is common practice to lump taxes and unrequited transfer payments together, as plus and minus items respectively, and to use only the net figure. The remarks above suggest that for broad types of subsidy somewhat the same practice may be useful. Still, the cash subsidy and the tax-reduction techniques do involve the private sector directly with the government budget, in a manner not found with respect to the "missing" part of the tax base when an expenditure tax replaces an income tax. The individual firm's option to draw, or not to draw, money from the Treasury under policies 1 and 2 makes the case for recording the subsidy payments explicitly. Under the same reasoning, personal exemptions granted by income tax law, for example if the first $500 of every single person's income is deducted in computing taxable income, are not here considered as imputed welfare payments. In the discussion to follow, the word subsidy when used alone will mean a cash subsidy. Implicit subsidy refers either to a government guarantee or to a tax reduction.

(2) Consumer Subsidies and Factor Subsidies

Since a consumer subsidy is virtually always less than 100 per cent of the unsubsidized price, the price system still performs the rationing function. In contrast, free distribution of a marketable service, say education, requires some form of non-price

United States Income Tax System—the Need for a Full Accounting" (Washington, D.C.: United States Treasury, Nov. 15, 1967).

rationing. The choice between subsidy and rationed distribution of this service is thus partly a choice among rationing methods. In rare cases the government supplies all of the service that consumers want at zero price, as under some programs of free medical care, but rations by queuing or other delay. A comparable subsidy is one that is 100 per cent of the unsubsidized price. Choice between these two methods depends in large part on whether the government can anticipate and supply the pattern of the service that the market could supply. If the good cannot be marketed, because it is too costly to exclude any particular consumer (see Chapter 4), it cannot be subsidized; free distribution is the only feasible method.

Consumer subsidies are employed to redistribute disposable income in a society that is not willing to accord the recipients the freedom of choice that accompanies a cash grant. Sometimes the society desires to stimulate the type of consumption described in Chapter 23 as gainful, or at least productive. Items included in a cost of living index are subsidized in order to restrain escalation of money wages.

Cash subsidies are sometimes substitutes for tax exemption. In place of exempting food under a retail sales tax, for example, it may be easier administratively to grant a subsidy to food producers that is assumed to be passed on to consumers.[3] Thus a subsidy on food is financed by a tax on food, and the net effect is no subsidy, no tax. In terms of the discussion above, the government employs a positive policy 1 and a negative policy 3.

The in-between policy, imputed subsidy through tax reduction, is rarely used for the purpose of aiding consumers as such. Where consumption of a highly specialized type is encouraged by tax reduction, charitable giving or college tuition outlay, for example, the argument for the implicit subsidy is based largely on externalities. This type of consumption is expected to benefit the community [see Section (3) below]. Low-income consumers do not pay enough direct taxes to gain much from a tax-reduction subsidy based on those taxes.

Factor subsidies are commonly granted to once prosperous industries that have fallen into decay and that employ specialized factors. Factor subsidies are rarely in the imputed form of tax reduction, since the factor owners are often too poor to be paying much tax.

A factor subsidy will in principle apply to exports but not to imports; it will be imposed on the origin basis (see Chapter 8, page 209). A consumer subsidy will normally apply to imports but not to exports (destination basis).

The distinction drawn here between a consumer subsidy and a factor subsidy is in terms of purposes, not results. A subsidy intended to increase consumption of a good may in reality expend most of its force in raising factor rewards in the producing industry, and vice versa (see Section c below). But this type of error is probably infrequent. Whether the government pays the subsidy direct to the consumer or direct to the producer is a technical distinction. It has no economic significance, aside from market friction, or illusion.[4] A consumer subsidy may therefore be paid to producers, and a factor subsidy may be paid to consumers.

3. As in Norway; see Chapter 9, page 247.
4. See pages 153, 273.

(3) Special-purpose Subsidies

The consumer and factor subsidies are to be appraised primarily under whatever criteria are adopted for distribution of disposable income. Special-purpose subsidies are designed chiefly to meet one or more of the other criteria, notably maintenance of a given exchange rate (see Chapter 24), attainment of a stipulated rate of economic growth (see Chapter 23), and movement toward a Pareto optimum of resource allocation by capturing certain positive externalities (as defined in Chapter 21).

B. Shifting and Incidence

(1) Closed Economy

Since no subsidy is ever applicable to all goods alike, there is no subsidy analogous to a general sales tax. No subsidies are computed as a percentage of total income; hence there are no subsidies analogous to an income tax. Subsidies, explicit or implicit, are therefore in practice the analogue of either excise taxes, ad valorem or specific, or of a tax on a particular factor, a tax on interest, for example. Accordingly, a subsidy usually covers only a small part of the economy and its effects can be analyzed in partial equilibrium terms, that is, without taking into account how the revenue was obtained to finance it. Some subsidies are so large, relative to the economy's total income, that they can be analyzed as to incidence only through a differential approach, as explained in Chapter 1. This kind of subsidy is so infrequent that it will not be considered further in this chapter.

In a competitive industry or trade, a per-unit subsidy on a product simultaneously increases output, raises price to the seller, and lowers price to the buyer, except in four extreme cases now to be noted. "Price to the buyer" is market price, less the subsidy if the subsidy is paid to the buyer. "Price to the seller" includes the subsidy if it is paid to him.

The effect of the subsidy is the same, whether it is paid to the seller or to the buyer, unless institutional rigidities or other frictions inhibit the free working of the market. At the new equilibrium, price to the seller, if the subsidy is paid to him, is larger than what the price to the buyer would be if the subsidy were paid to him, by exactly the amount of the subsidy, and the quantity sold is the same in both instances.[5]

The four extreme cases (decreasing cost to the industry is discussed on page 154) are: (1) perfectly inelastic supply and (2) perfectly elastic demand, both of which cause the price to the seller to rise by the full amount of the subsidy, while the price to the buyer remains unchanged, so that the benefit of the subsidy rests entirely with

5. For the theorem that it makes no difference which side of the market a tax is levied on or, by inference, to which side of the market a subsidy is given, see, e.g., F. Y. Edgeworth, "The Pure Theory of Taxation," in *Papers Relating to Political Economy* (London: Macmillan, 1925), reprinted in Musgrave and Shoup (Eds.), *Readings in the Economics of Taxation* (Homewood, Ill.: Irwin, 1959), p. 263, note 24.

the seller; (3) perfectly elastic supply and (4) perfectly inelastic demand, both of which cause the price to the buyer to fall by the full amount of the subsidy, while the price to the seller remains unchanged, so that the incidence of the subsidy accrues entirely to the buyers.

In the more usual, in-between cases, under competition, the incidence of the subsidy is divided between buyer and seller (consumer and producer) in the ratio of the elasticity of supply to the elasticity of demand. If, for example, the elasticity of supply is very great while the demand is almost perfectly inelastic, that ratio will be large and almost all of the subsidy will go to reduce price to the buyer; price to the seller will rise by only a small proportion of the subsidy.[6]

In the short run, the per-unit subsidy on a product induces the competitive firm to expand output to the point where price to the buyers, which is initially unchanged, equals marginal cost less the subsidy. As all firms in the industry take the same action, industry output increases and price to the buyers falls. Each firm then retraces its steps, part way, until the new, lower, short-run equilibrium price to the buyers plus subsidy equals marginal cost. Each firm is now producing more than initially, but less than immediately after announcement of the subsidy, and is making excess profits. New firms enter the industry, depressing further the price to buyers, until long-run equilibrium is reached, at a price to buyers lower than initially, but, under increasing cost to the industry, not lower by the full amount of the subsidy.

The analysis up to this point has abstracted from the possibility that the supply curve of the industry will be negatively sloped, as a result of increasing returns to the industry that can arise from improved milieu (not from a lowering of prices of factors purchased by the industry) as the industry grows larger. Each firm's costs, old and new firms together, become lower for any given output per firm, as the industry expands appreciably. Yet, since no one new firm is large enough to expand the industry appreciably, by entry, and no one old firm is large enough to accomplish that goal by itself expanding, the cost lowering does not occur until an external stimulus, as by a subsidy, is given. Under these conditions, the short-run, long-run analysis above must be modified as follows. As all firms react to the subsidy by expanding output along what looks to each firm like an increasing marginal cost curve, each firm finds to its surprise that, while price falls, the firm's average cost and marginal cost curves fall also. Each firm then retraces its steps by less than in the analysis given above, or may even expand its output further, despite the decline in price. The entry of new firms attracted by the excess profits causes a further fall in all firms' cost curves, along with a further fall in price. The new equilibrium of the industry may be such that marginal cost plus subsidy is less than marginal cost alone at the pre-subsidy equilibrium. Price to the seller has then fallen, and price to the buyer has fallen by more than the amount of the subsidy. The incidence of the subsidy is more than 100 per cent on the buyer.

Even if marginal cost has been reduced only slightly by expansion of the industry, that reduction will be counted as a partial offset to the cost of the subsidy, in macro analysis.

Results contrary to the generalizations above will obtain if allowance is made for

6. The analysis in terms of slopes, on pages 273–74, can also be applied to subsidies.

strongly rival or complementary relationships between subsidized and unsubsidized commodities. By applying in reverse the Edgeworth paradox for an excise tax under competition,[7] it can be shown that if one commodity is rival both in production and in consumption to another commodity, a subsidy paid to the producers of one of the commodities may cause the price to the buyers of both commodities to rise (not fall). It is not known whether the particular kinds of supply and demand conditions necessary for this paradox are fairly common or quite rare.

For an ad valorem subsidy on a product the conclusions stated up to this point hold, but not in precisely the same terms, since such a subsidy, expressed as a percentage of the price to the buyer, is the equivalent of a per-unit subsidy that decreases in rate as output increases and price to buyers decreases. Whether an ad valorem subsidy decreases price to buyers by more or less than an equivalent per-unit subsidy depends on the sense given to "equivalent," which may be any one of the following: (*a*) the ad valorem rate is equal to the per-unit rate at the pre-subsidy equilibrium price; (*b*) the two subsidies are of equal rate at the new equilibrium price reached under the subsidy; (*c*) the two subsidies, at their respective and presumably different equilibria are the same in aggregate amount.

If the ad valorem subsidy is a percentage of the price to the seller, it increases per unit as output increases, since the price to the seller rises as he produces more, unless he is not operating under increasing costs, or, more generally, unless the industry is not so operating.

A subsidy to a non-monopolized factor of production of so much per unit of the factor, and granted no matter in what industry the factor is engaged, is in the usual case divided between the buyers of the factor, now always business firms in the various industries, and the sellers of the factor services (workers, landlords, capitalists, in the broadest grouping). The price to the factor sellers rises; the price to the buyer-firms falls. Extreme cases aside, the ratio of the rise in price of the factor to the decrease in the price the firms pay for the factor is equal to the ratio of the elasticity of demand for the subsidized factor (demand by industry and commerce in general) to the elasticity of supply of the factor.

In an extreme case, if the supply of the factor is perfectly inelastic, as it is for land, price to the factor owner rises by the full amount of the subsidy and the buyer gains none of the subsidy. The same result occurs if the economy's demand for the factor is perfectly elastic for quantities larger than that used at initial equilibrium. This state of affairs is virtually impossible. It implies that the subsidized factor is a perfect substitute for other factors (and they for it) in all fields in which it is used. No such factor seems likely to exist in the real world.

If, on the other hand, the supply of the factor is perfectly elastic to the economy as a whole, for quantities greater than that at the initial equilibrium, price to the buyer falls by the full amount of the subsidy. But this case, too, seems quite an unlikely one. The same result occurs if the demand for the factor is perfectly inelastic, in all sectors of industry and commerce, a condition that may obtain for a few types of highly specialized labor or highly specialized land or certain exotic natural resources.

7. See Chapter 10, pages 277–78.

A subsidy is in practice sometimes restricted to a particular factor engaged in a particular industry: capital employed in the merchant marine, for example. The analysis above for a product subsidy and a factor subsidy must then be combined. The conclusions can be stated in terms of a factor subsidy, but the elasticities of demand for the factor and of its supply are now elasticities to the industry in question, not to the economy as a whole. All of the elasticities will usually now be greater, or the inelasticities less. Those two of the extreme cases that seem quite unlikely if the factor subsidy applies generally now become at least possible. Demand for the factor may possibly be perfectly elastic, at least for a modest increase in the quantity of the factor beyond the initial equilibrium use, since the factor may be, in that one industry, a perfect substitute for other factors, within this range. And supply of the factor to this one industry may be perfectly elastic, even though it is not so for the economy as a whole. The other two extreme cases which are possible under a factor subsidy not limited to one industry seem if anything less likely when the subsidy is given only for employment in a certain industry. Supply of a factor to the economy in general may be perfectly inelastic, but scarcely so to any one industry, in view of the possibility that units of the factor can move from one industry to another. Demand for a factor by the economy as a whole may, in rare cases, be perfectly inelastic, but scarcely so with respect to a particular industry, since consumers of that industry's product can substitute other products.

Ad valorem rather than unit subsidies to factors give results similar to those above, adjusted for the fact that, viewed as a subsidy per unit, the subsidy decreases automatically as more of the factor is used, if it is expressed as a percentage of the price to the buyer of the factor, and increases if it is expressed as a percentage of the price (including subsidy) to the factor owner.

If a subsidy of so much per unit of product is paid to a single firm, which is rarely the case, that firm will of course be engaged in imperfect competition, facing a demand curve of less than perfect elasticity, and it will not usually be a member of an oligopoly or of a monopolistic competition group, large or small. Consequently, the excise tax analysis for the monopoly case can be applied, in reverse, to a subsidy. But since the single-firm case is more frequently encountered under excise taxation than under subsidies, detailed analysis of that case is deferred to Chapter 10, and the conclusions, rephrased to fit a per-unit product subsidy rather than a similar tax, are summarized here:[8]

1. The four extreme cases noted above do not apply to a monopoly.

2. Under any cost conditions, the monopolist's output will increase and price to the buyer will fall.

3. If the monopoly operates under constant cost, price to the buyer falls by only a fraction of the subsidy, even though factor rewards do not increase. The balance of the subsidy goes to increase the monopolist's profit, which is not a factor reward.

4. If marginal cost to the monopolist is increasing, a per-unit product subsidy may cause the price to the buyer to fall by an amount larger than the subsidy, an outcome not possible under competition.

8. The four conclusions valid only for a small tax (Chapter 10, page 277) are not reproduced here in subsidy terms.

5. If both the demand function and the total cost function are linear, price to the buyer will fall by just half the subsidy.

6. If supply is physically limited short of the output the monopolist would sell if he could, under no subsidy, the subsidy does not lower the price to the buyer. The monopolist retains the full benefit of the subsidy.

A subsidy paid to a monopolized factor is so rarely encountered in practice that its incidence will not be analyzed here.

A subsidy to an industry characterized by monopolistic competition can be analyzed by the techniques developed by Due for excise taxes on such an industry;[9] this extension of subsidy incidence is not pursued here.

(2) Open Economy

In an open economy, a subsidy on a product that is exported will encounter a perfectly elastic demand if the country's supply is but a small part of total supply on the world market, as with a small country exporting coffee, for example. The subsidy under these conditions is retained entirely by the domestic industry, which thereupon expands its output; it presumably operates under increasing costs. The subsidy benefits, as it is no doubt intended to benefit, factors specialized to that industry and factors newly brought into the industry. If there is some domestic consumption, domestic consumers do not benefit, since price to them does not fall, as long as the world market will take all the additional output stimulated by the subsidy, without weakening. But if the country is so large a supplier of the world market that demand for the product is less than perfectly elastic, a subsidy will go in part to the foreign consumer and, as the case may be, to the domestic consumer.

If an imported commodity is in perfectly elastic supply to the country in question, because that country is so small a consumer on the world market, and if there is no domestic production, a subsidy on the product, which here amounts to a subsidy on imports of it, goes entirely to the domestic consumer. A small country desiring to lower the cost of certain foodstuffs to its inhabitants, foodstuffs not grown domestically, can do so readily by subsidizing imports. If there is initially some domestic production, and the subsidy is paid to imports and domestic production alike, no impetus to expansion is given to domestic production, since the perfectly elastic import supply guarantees that the price to the domestic consumer will fall by the full amount of the subsidy. But if the subsidy is paid only to domestic production, that production expands and imports shrink until the price to the consumer is again the world (unsubsidized) price. The subsidy benefits only the domestic producers of the subsidized good, not at all the consumers. Thus in the presence of a perfectly elastic import supply the government can benefit either consumers only or domestic producers only.

9. See John F. Due, "Monopolistic Competition and the Incidence of Special Sales Taxes," from his *The Theory of Incidence of Sales Taxation*, reprinted in Musgrave and Shoup (Eds.), *Readings in the Economics of Taxation*, pp. 340–76.

If the import supply is less than perfectly elastic and there is no domestic production, a subsidy on the imported good will go partly to the foreign producer, partly to the domestic consumer, as price ex-subsidy rises with the expansion of imports. If domestic production exists or is created by a subsidy to imports and domestic production alike, that production does expand as the price ex-subsidy rises. If the subsidy is limited to domestic production, imports being unsubsidized, the consequent decrease in imports will be accompanied by a fall in price of the imported good. Domestic production therefore will not expand as far as it would if import supply were perfectly elastic. Consumers do then gain somewhat from the subsidy.

Thus the presence of less than perfect elasticity of import supply prevents the government from benefiting only consumers, or only domestic producers, and makes it certain that a part of the subsidy will go to foreign producers, unless imports remain unsubsidized.

Subsidies to goods that are supplied wholly by domestic production, either because imports are prohibited or because they would not be imported anyway (for example, most retail services), can be analyzed as above, under a closed economy. Since factors, too, are likely not to be regularly imported or exported, there is not much to add to the analysis already given above for a closed economy if the subsidy is to a factor rather than to a commodity. An exception may be necessary in some instances for capital.

c. Effectiveness of Subsidy

(1) Increasing Consumption[10]

A subsidy intended to increase consumption of a particular good will dissipate much of its force if the price elasticity of either demand or supply is small. A large part of the subsidy then goes to financing increased purchases of unsubsidized goods, or increased saving, or, if supply is not very elastic, it goes to increase producers' surplus.

Consider first the results for a competitive industry when the supply side, that is, supply of the subsidized commodity, is perfectly elastic (constant cost), so that none of the subsidy goes to increase producers' surplus. A demand curve of unit elasticity over the range from unsubsidized price to subsidized price will allow the percentage increase in number of units of the subsidized article purchased to equal the percentage that the subsidy per unit is of the subsidized price. Thus, if the unsubsidized price (producers' price) is $1.00 and the subsidy is 40 cents a unit, and if 100 units were being purchased at $1.00, $166\frac{2}{3}$ units will be purchased at 60 cents. The percentage that the subsidy (40 cents) is of the subsidized price (60 cents), namely, $66\frac{2}{3}$, is the same as the percentage increase in units purchased.[11] None of the subsidy goes

10. Parts of this analysis are based on James Heilbrun's "Concerning the Margin between Public and Private Spending" (unpublished manuscript).

11. Or, for small increments, a given percentage subsidy computed on the original price gives rise to an almost equal percentage increase in units purchased.

to increase spending on other goods, or to increase saving, and the consumers' spending on the subsidized article also remains unchanged. Total spending on the subsidized good by consumers and government together increases by just the amount of the subsidy paid.

But if demand is of less than unit elasticity over the relevant price range, the percentage increase in units purchased will fall short of the percentage that the subsidy is of the subsidized price. Consumers spend less on the subsidized good than they did when it was unsubsidized, and more on other goods, or save more. Total spending on the subsidized good increases by less than the amount of the subsidy. In effect, part of the subsidy is dissipated in the purchase of other goods and in saving. This result is to be anticipated for any good, eventually, if the subsidy is made larger and larger, for, although an individual's demand may be of unit elasticity, or more, in the price range covered by a small subsidy, it is sure to become of less than unit elasticity at some lower price. Demand in the aggregate may continue elastic if additional individuals are drawn into the market as the price decreases, but eventually market demand, like individual demand, must become of less than unit elasticity. In general, then, less of a small subsidy per unit will be dissipated in other purchases and in saving than of a large subsidy per unit.

If, instead, the elasticity of demand is greater than unity over the price range covered by the subsidy, the consumer decreases his spending on other goods and his saving, to increase his spending on the subsidized good. The percentage increase in units of that good purchased exceeds the percentage that the subsidy is of the subsidized price. This result may not be a welcome one. The decrease in spending on other goods and in saving may partly negate the aim of the subsidy, since a high elasticity of demand implies that good substitutes are available. Not much progress toward the social or other aims implied by the subsidy may be achieved if expansion of the subsidized good is obtained only at the cost of reducing consumption of goods that serve much the same purpose. Of course, what is a good substitute in the consumer's eyes may not be so to the policy-maker. A milk subsidy may reduce children's consumption of soft drinks or in some countries even coffee or alcohol rather than their consumption of bread.

All the conclusions up to this point remain valid if the supply side of a competitive industry reflects increasing costs, but they are less important, since the increase in number of units purchased will be less for any given demand curve, the more costs increase. At the extreme, where supply is perfectly inelastic, there is of course no point to a subsidy intended to increase consumption of the good, any more than when demand is perfectly inelastic.

If costs decrease as output expands, the conclusions above concerning different types of demand schedules become more important, since the increase in the number of units purchased will be greater than under constant costs.

Conceivably, a subsidy can decrease the number of units consumed of the subsidized good. This will occur if the thing subsidized is a Giffen good within the price range covered by the subsidy, that is, if both (1) the income elasticity of demand is negative and (2) the income effect of the subsidy outweighs its substitution effect. On the other hand, while we have seen that a subsidy on one good may cause the prices of both goods to rise, these circumstances do not imply that the number of units purchased of the subsidized good will decrease.[12] The rise in both prices may occur if the two goods are rival both in production and in consumption, and certain not unreasonable types of demand and supply functions obtain.[12]

If the subsidized good can be resold by the consumer at the unsubsidized price, his income is increased by the subsidy but the cost of the good to him is not really reduced. The cost to him is what he must forego if he consumes the article, and in this instance what he foregoes is the unsubsidized price. The consumer will now operate as a firm taking at the subsidized price as much as the government will sell him, and reselling it at the higher price. The continued existence of the initial unsubsidized price implies that the subsidy is granted only to a very small group of consumers in a limited amount; otherwise, their offerings would drive the price down. These consumers will probably consume more of the subsidized good than before, but only because of the income effect of the subsidy. The subsidy exerts no substitution effect if resale at a constant unsubsidized price is possible.

Even the small group receiving a limited supply may be unable to resell at the unsubsidized price, because, say, they cannot supply certain marketing services that are covered by that price. If in this case they can sell at something above the subsidized price, the difference between the unsubsidized price and what they can resell for reflects a grant of marketing service to them by the government, a service they cannot resell. This grant of marketing service exerts a substitution effect and induces an increase in consumption of the subsidized good by the consumer receiving the subsidy. The size of this nontransferable subsidy (the marketing element, in this example) depends not on the size of the formal subsidy per unit but on the excess of the unsubsidized price over the price realizable by the consumer upon resale. An increase in the subsidy would not stimulate consumption through the substitution effect if that excess remained unchanged, as it probably would.

In practice, governments subsidize services rather than tangible goods, if the aim is to increase consumption of that good by a particular class of consumers, since services cannot usually be resold. Services given off by a consumer durable, a house for example, can be resold, but prohibition of resale can be enforced to a degree that is not possible for clothing and food. This is one reason why it is common to have housing subsidies or subsidized medical care restricted to a particular class of consumers, while subsidies on clothing and food are usually available, if at all, to everyone.[13] When purchase by everyone is subsidized, resale at the unsubsidized price is impossible.

Subsidies to exported goods of a type that lower the price to foreign households are no less subsidies because they benefit foreigners.[14] Consumers' choice working through the market mechanism is still allowed to affect the pattern of consumption.

12. See page 155 above, and Chapter 10, pages 277–78, below.

13. Under the United States food stamp program and school lunch program, precautions are taken to see that the food is not resold.

14. Pigou, dividing government outlays only into transfer payments and non-transfer payments, decided to place subsidies on exports in the latter category (A. C. Pigou, *A Study in Public Finance* [3d rev. ed.; London: Macmillan, 1949], p. 20).

If the government purchases the exported goods and sends them abroad gratis, the act is a free distribution of government product, not an unrequited payment. By subsidizing exports, instead, the government leaves the foreign purchaser free to decide whether he shall increase, and to what extent, his receipt of these particular goods.

(2) Increasing Factor Rewards

A subsidy intended to increase factor rewards in a certain industry, enacted because the industry is depressed or enjoys unusual political influence, will be the more effective, the less the industry responds to the subsidy by increasing output. The achievement of this aim therefore requires supply conditions the opposite of those that help meet the aim of increasing consumption of a certain product.

The required inelasticity of the supply curve need exist only for output in excess of the amount being produced before the subsidy was granted. But this condition is the more likely to be fulfilled, the more inelastic is the supply immediately below the initial output, since no a priori reason exists for a sudden change in slope just at that point. The subsidy will therefore be most useful in an industry that employs specialized factors that cannot be easily increased in number when demand rises owing to the subsidy. Even such an industry will employ certain kinds of factors that are in fairly elastic supply to the industry; they will not gain appreciably by the subsidy.

If the industry's supply curve is very elastic in a free market, the subsidy can be made helpful for factors (and not helpful to consumers) by government control of output. The supply curve beyond the initial, no-subsidy equilibrium point can thus be made artificially inelastic. Farm programs commonly employ this technique. The remarks above hold true regardless of the demand conditions, but they are the more significant, the more elastic is the demand for amounts beyond the initial no-subsidy output.

2. Criteria

The degree to which subsidies observe the several criteria given in Chapter 2 varies so markedly with product or factor subsidized that details are postponed to Chapter 7.

CHAPTER SEVEN

Particular Unrequited Payments

A. WELFARE PAYMENTS

WELFARE PAYMENTS are determined either by formulae given in the law or, within wide limits, at the discretion of a government official. An old-age insurance beneficiary can know, from a study of the law and regulations, what he will receive; a needy family on relief can never be certain what the case worker will recommend or allow. The formula type of welfare payment meets the test of impersonality (Chapter 1).

Welfare payments are analyzed in this chapter without reference to the financing measures, with the exception of social-security insurance benefits.

1. Formula Type of Welfare Payments

In most of the countries with established social security systems, the following welfare payments are of the formula type: old age and survivors insurance benefits; unemployment compensation; family allowances; resource-conditioned benefits; and maternity grants. The first four of these will be analyzed here.[1]

The discretionary type of welfare payment is exemplified chiefly by public assistance programs and foreign aid.

Each welfare payment will first be examined with respect to the reasons why the government undertakes it and whether the benefit is transferred to others by the initial recipient. The relevant criteria of Chapter 2 will then be applied.

---

1. Veterans' benefits paid without regard to current income or current need of the recipient are in effect retroactive increases in compensation. They reflect second thoughts on the part of the government and are also a retroactive substitute for higher military pay in wartime, when wage freezes and other restrictions were in force and military pay was not allowed to exceed or even equal civilian pay. Market forces are not likely to deprive the veterans of even a part of the benefit from the payments.

A. OLD-AGE AND SURVIVORS BENEFIT ("INSURANCE") PROGRAMS

The old-age benefit system to be analyzed here is one that is representative of most of those now in effect, in that it (1) is financed by a tax that can be identified with a particular individual, say a flat tax per worker, or a payroll tax (a personal income tax and an expenditure tax collected from consumers fall in the same category), (2) pays in benefits to certain members of the retired generation an aggregate amount equal, roughly, to the proceeds of the tax that is being collected currently from certain industry categories of workers, (3) distributes this aggregate among the older individuals largely but not entirely according to the relative amounts of tax paid by each of them or his employer in his earlier, working, years, and (4) pays no benefits to those who spent their working years in certain occupations not covered by the system.

If the labor force in covered occupations increases in numbers while the tax rate remains unchanged, aggregate benefits paid will exceed the aggregate of hypothetical annuities based on what each recipient and his employer paid in tax in the working years. To the degree that an increase in productivity in the covered occupations is not reflected in the rate of discount used in computing the hypothetical actuarial annuity, current benefits are in the aggregate still larger than the aggregate of the annuities. Finally, if the price level rises, and the tax yield increases on this account, the aggregate of money benefits exceeds that of the hypothetical actuarial annuities by still more.

If the system were financed by a general sales tax, or a value-added tax, or a series of excises or import or export taxes, the aged could not be logically divided into those covered and those not covered by the system according as they had or had not helped finance it. And if everyone were covered, there would remain the problem posed by the fact that the system could not pattern the distribution of benefits by the relative earnings or income or expenditure during the recipient's active years. That part of the redistributional element in the system, i.e., the part that moves disposable income from the more well-to-do of the older generation to the less well-to-do of the same generation, would then necessarily be much stronger than under the systems commonly in use, especially those that rely on payroll taxes.

Governments engage in old-age and survivors insurance programs partly because of a demand by the younger generation that they be freed from the risk of having to contribute unpredictably large sums to aged parents or other relatives, especially at a time when they are struggling to raise their own families. It may be assumed that the younger generation are on the whole risk-averters, not risk-seekers, and that they prefer the impersonality of the public finance system to direct pressures from aged relatives.

The prospective aged desire a government-financed system, in order that they may be assured against privation caused by a fall in the value of money or by lack of relatives willing and able to provide support, especially in hard times. A currently financed benefit system indirectly rebates or reduces an inflation "tax" by which many members of a retired generation are otherwise thrust into poverty. Even under a stable price level the real incomes of many households are so low in their active years as to preclude saving for a subsistence level of consumption in old age, except by so reducing consumption in their active years that their productivity declines or the indubitable current sacrifice seems too great relative to the probability of penury in an old age that may never come.

These considerations, apart from that based on inflation, would be less important if low-earning families received substantial transfer payments during their active years through, say, a negative income tax. They might then be expected to save enough to finance their old-age consumption through private pension and insurance plans. Although the negative-income tax proposals do not usually call for payments large enough to make such saving easy, or even possible, there is an element of this transfer-payment-for-saving in many of the existing systems. The payroll tax, for example, commonly does not exempt even the lowest-income employee, or his employer. If his take-home pay is insufficient he may be given relief assistance or some other form of discretionary type of transfer payment. In effect, part or all of the transfer payments to him during his active but low-paid years helps him pay the tax that is financing old-age benefits to the current older generation.

Even if private saving were made feasible by a large negative income tax, there would remain some demand for a government-operated old-age benefit system because of the cost of administering a private system involving large numbers of small payments on a voluntary, contractual basis. For example, no private insurance company could induce all business firms to withhold premiums on the scale that the tax system can enforce.

In addition the demand for a government-financed old-age benefit system reflects a demand for redistribution of income downward; most of the non-actuarial elements in existing programs are weighted that way.

Demand for such a system also comes from some households that are not threatened by a poverty level of consumption in old age. These households wish to reduce the otherwise sharp decline in income from active years to retirement years. But if the price level could be counted on to remain stable, it may be doubted that many of them would demand a government-financed system. For them, a privately financed system would be practicable. The decline in income upon retirement is often a reflection of the abnormal height to which income rises in the latter years of an active and successful man's career. For such a person old age can be a time of planned dissaving. The common practice of comparing post-retirement investment income with pre-retirement income overstates the gap to be covered by a pension system, since there need be no presumption that the aged person must never consume any part of his capital. For him, the size of a life annuity that he can purchase is a figure to be taken into account.

Many problems remain for the private saver, but by far the larger part of the demand for a government-financed non-funded old-age system seems to be due either to fear of inflation or to fear of poverty in old age that can be averted if at all only by severe demands on younger members of the family if worst comes to worst.

The aged person will relinquish the benefit of his pension to the extent that his children or other relatives reduce their financial assistance. At the extreme, the older generation would finance its own benefit program; the current taxes paid by the younger generation would be offset exactly by the reduction in intra-family transfers. Normally, however, the recipient retains some of the benefit, if not all of it. Still another beneficiary is the philanthropist, who can now divert his resources to other good works.

If the pension recipients tend to gather in certain areas especially suitable for older persons, their aggregate demand will benefit landowners and merchants there, somewhat to the detriment of those elsewhere.

Old-age insurance programs generally observe the equity criteria in the consensus group, except that the individual's status often changes abruptly when his earnings reach a certain level. In some systems the aged person loses a period's benefits completely if he earns more than a stipulated amount in that period; in effect, a marginal implicit tax of far more than 100 per cent is placed on his earned income at that point. If, to qualify for the old-age pension, he must have worked a certain amount of time or for a certain number of periods before retirement, or if his cumulated earnings must have reached a certain amount, potential recipients who fall just short of these qualifying tests, owing perhaps to illness or involuntary un-employment, are treated very differently from those who have had only slightly better earnings records. The aged person's benefit could instead be reduced by some increasing percentage of his current earnings, and the qualifying tests could admit the potential pensioner into the system gradually.

Old-age benefits increase automatically during business recessions as aged workers are discharged and so resume receipt of their pensions under provisions of the type just mentioned, but the percentage change in the total is small.

Since the pensions never rise above a maximum that is modest, judged by the country's income distribution; since they increase, if at all, less than in proportion to the recipient's lifetime earning experience; and since they decrease, if indeed they do not vanish abruptly, as current earned income increases, they are a sharply regressive benefit, analogous to a progressive tax. But they are not regressive with total current income; the aged recipient may receive any amount of investment income without reduction of his pension. This fact reflects the quasi-"insurance" philosophy of the system, which implies that the recipient has purchased his own retirement pension, at least in part, through payroll tax deductions. If the pension were varied inversely with income from private sources in old age, the insurance or self-financing rationale would in effect be replaced by a means test.

Geographical discrimination occurs only indirectly, as workers who spend their lives in depressed areas earn so little in a lifetime that the old-age benefit is appreciably lower, except under programs that pay uniform benefits to all. Differences in living costs from one region to another are not taken into account. This fact is particularly important with respect to those who work in one country and retire to another. They do not usually on that account lose their benefits, and, since typically the paying country is richer and is more costly to live in than the country of retirement, the international distribution of income by country of recipient is made somewhat less unequal, and the trans-national worker gets a larger real income for a given amount of work than his fellow worker who retires where he works, or his compatriot who has stayed at home to work. The trans-national worker also has a type of guarantee against hardship from inflation if, as is usual, it is the poorer country that is more likely to devalue its currency.

With respect to the amount and allocation of resources, under a government-financed old-age system compared with no such system, saving may increase over a period of decades and hence, if total input is the same in either case, investment rises and consumption falls. But there are so many forces at work that no generalization seems feasible. The reduction in uncertainty as to what old age will bring with it may make saving by the prospective recipient appear either more worth while or less necessary. In the absence of the system intense intra-family demands on the younger generation may force them to reduce consumption by more than would a tax to finance a government system. On the other hand, the government system might reduce saving appreciably if it extended to investment income in old age the rule applied in some countries with respect to earned income in old age, so that the pension decreased or disappeared as one's investment income in old age increased. Both saving during active years and saving in old age might be discouraged (or dissaving encouraged).

The effect of the system on the supply of labor is likewise conjectural. That supply is reduced slightly by a provision that reduces benefits when income is earned in old age. For those in the pre-retirement years, the effects of the tax are largely offset by the reduction in demands made on them for intra-family transfers to aged relatives. Perhaps the substitution effect of the impersonal tax is stronger than that of the intra-family payment; if so, the reduction in the supply of labor is correspondingly greater, or the increase (if the income effect of the intra-family transfers is more powerful than that of the tax) correspondingly less. A peculiar element in those systems that rely on the payroll tax is that this tax determines, not the absolute amount that one receives in the later years of old age (under a system that each year pays out as much as it takes in), but the amount that he receives relative to others of his generation. The more he has earned during his lifetime (within limits) under this system, the larger is his slice of the total paid in the later year. This result is not of course apparent in the formula, but is inherent in a policy that increases benefits to match increases in current revenues. Hence the individual worker is given an incentive to work longer or harder, up to the taxable limit, than do his fellow workers of the same generation. If everyone reacts this way, no one gains, but that fact will not influence the individual worker's reaction.

Acceptance of a birth-control program by the poorer households in a less developed country is likely to be increased by a government-financed old-age system, as it reduces a given generation's need for many children to supply potential sources of support in old age.

An increase in old-age benefits decreases the government's expense for old-age assistance (means-test payments), if the increase occurs by bringing into the system those who would otherwise be in difficulties, or by raising a level of old-age benefits that is quite inadequate. Otherwise there is little offset to an increase in old-age pensions. Few countries subject old-age benefits to income taxation.

B. Unemployment Compensation

No private enterprise firms have ever written unemployment compensation insurance, largely because of the "conflagration" hazard, but also partly because of the moral hazard; only the government has the degree of authority needed to require proof that the unemployment is involuntary, that is, that no suitable job is available. And, if this handicap could be overcome, a private company would have to formulate a schedule of premiums so complex and so differentiated, among industries and localities, that it would be engaged in endless disputes with clients and regulating authorities. Finally, a private firm would face the same difficulty as in old-age insurance with respect to the demand that the insurance be made compulsory, a demand from relatives who will otherwise be burdened by supporting the unemployed and from those who want to be forced to save for periods of unemployment. Compulsory insurance is not incompatible with private-sector supply of the insurance, but the government would have to subsidize insurance for the particularly poor risks, who would be quite unable to pay the especially high premiums their discouraging prospects would make necessary.

An unemployment compensation system financed by a uniform rate of tax on all labor income reduces reluctance of workers to enter industries with records of cyclical unemployment. Wages in these industries relative to wages elsewhere thereby tend to fall. To this extent the unemployment compensation system benefits consumers of goods produced by, and factors specialized in, those industries, and disadvantages consumers and specialized factors of other industries. These remarks apply with much less force to periods of massive unemployment. They probably apply with a good deal of force to industries where seasonal unemployment is substantial and well anticipated. Even there, labor mobility among industries may be so small that the loss of benefit through lower relative wages is not significant.

Part of the benefit is diverted to relatives, friends, and donors to charitable organizations who would otherwise contribute to the support of the unemployed.

Unemployment compensation systems satisfy the consensus type of equity criteria except on two counts. First, as with old-age payments, awkward dividing lines create injustice among workers almost similarly circumstanced. A worker may be denied entry into the system if he is self-employed or the employee of a very small firm. If his unemployment extends beyond a given period the rate of benefit drops abruptly to zero, though this treatment may be considered something like that given under a "dwindling" technique (see page 219), since for the first few days beyond that period he is, viewed from the start of unemployment, only a little worse off than one who succeeded in resuming employment just before the end of the period. The injustice is in any event somewhat less than under the old-age pension program, since the worker can to a greater degree than the old-age benefit recipient manipulate the circumstances that set these abrupt dividing lines; he can change his type of unemployment, but the elderly person cannot change his age (though he can change, while still young, his working record).

Second, the means test is replaced by the available-work test, and the decision whether an unemployed worker is in fact rejecting a job opportunity that is appropriate in the light of his work history and skills is a personal decision made by the administrator, with only general guidance from the law and regulations. Administrative personalization, in the unfavorable sense, may therefore impair the equity of the program.

An unemployment compensation program ranks highest among all welfare payments in its reaction to business depressions, save for the common tendency to stop benefits after a certain period of unemployment has elapsed, and to impose a substantial waiting period before benefits begin. The first of these provisions tends to convert a moderate recession into a deep depression, once the moderate recession has reached a certain degree of intensity.

Some excess burden is created by the diversion of resources into unemployment-prone industries;[1] the social rate of transformation is made different from the rate of substitution faced by the consumer, with respect to the products of those industries vis-à-vis the products of other industries.

Under the conflict criteria, the payments themselves, abstracting from methods of financing them, are doubtless regressive with current income, since one who has been involuntarily separated even from a high-paying job now has a zero wage, which is less even than the most unskilled employed worker is earning. On the other hand, he may be receiving supplementary payments from a company fund and may have investment income of his own. But it is income over a longer period that is of more interest in this case. Although the level of benefits commonly varies directly with the rate of pay received, the relation is regressive, partly owing to cut-off points, and this feature alone guarantees some regressivity of benefits with respect to income over a period of years.

The compensation can be made to vary with composition of the family.

Geographical distribution of unemployment benefits may not favor depressed areas, if the unemployment there is of long standing for those who are unemployed, while those who remain working have fairly steady jobs even though the area is stagnant as a whole. Unemployment benefits will usually have been supplanted, in those circumstances, by means-test relief payments.

Migrating workers pose a more difficult equity question here than they do under old-age pensions. If they leave the home country temporarily because of unemployment there, is the host country obligated to support them when it develops unemployment also? It may argue that it has little or no responsibility and in fact will provide little aid under laws that require long-continued work before appreciable compensation rights are built up.

Risky enterprises are favored by an unemployment compensation system. The wide dispersion of possible outcomes that defines high risk includes outcomes that will result in discharge of many workers, and those taking jobs in these industries may well settle for a lower wage scale than if no unemployment compensation plan were in force. This argument is an extension of the benefit-diversion analysis at the beginning of this section.

---

1. Unless merit rating is fully operative, so that the tax rate for any one industry declines if the unemployment record of that industry improves.

A compensation program is likely to impair slightly the balance of payments of an advanced, industrialized country, if it undertakes to transfer compensation payments into the currency of the country whence its foreign workers came and to which they have returned, and if the workers' own repatriated savings do not fall by an equal or larger amount.

In a highly exposed, low-income country, unemployment compensation on an impersonal basis that is without any means test may be more than the country will want to afford. Fluctuations in demand for such a country's exports may throw so much of the labor force out of work so often that they and the rest of the community will not desire to be forced to save enough, in good times, to pay formula benefits in poor times. Little if any of the cost of such benefits can be passed onto the world consumers, if the country's production is a small part of the world total. Correspondingly, labor will not be reallocated much among industries by the absence of unemployment compensation.

The potentially important allocation effect, quantitatively, is that between work and leisure. If the work-availability test is thoroughly enforced, the promise of payments should induce no voluntary "involuntary" unemployment. Even if it is not thoroughly enforced, the circumstances of employment may be a safeguard against abuse of the system. In an industrialized economy where hours of labor per day cannot be varied easily by every worker (even after allowance for "moonlighting"), and where intensive work under piece rates is frowned upon by one's fellow workers, "fully employed" workers may be working less than they would prefer to at the current wage. That wage could therefore be reduced, and the worker would not reduce his supply of work, since the income effect would not point in that direction, and the substitution effect will not have been fully operative under the assumptions mentioned. If, under these circumstances, the wage is now implicitly reduced[2] by a promise that the worker will receive something if unemployed, even if the unemployment is voluntary, the supply of labor will still not be reduced. In fact, however, the available-work clause is enforced to some degree. In general, then, unemployment compensation presumably has little effect on the total amount of labor supplied, although it may encourage insistence on the worker's habitual or preferred category of employment, reducing the supply of labor in less-favored jobs.

An increase in unemployment compensation payments will not reduce means-test payments for the many families that, owing to supplementary benefit payments from the employer, or to investment income, would not fall to the level required for means-test payments. Nor will it, of course, reduce such payments when the economy is so poor, or so socially fragmented, that no means-test payments of any scope exist. Thus the offset will be small in high-income industrialized economies and, hypothetically, in very low-income underdeveloped countries: hypothetically, because such countries will presumably have no unemployment compensation system.

2. Unemployment compensation is therefore a negative-earned-income-tax welfare payment. The negative tax is only on earned income, in contrast to means-test payments or resource-conditioned payments, which are negative taxes on income in general.

c. FAMILY ALLOWANCES

In their simplest form, family allowances are cash payments to the family, usually monthly, of so much per child during the child's minority. Usually the payments schedule is more complex; the first child may not count, and successive children may count for different amounts.

Family allowances are either subsidies, given to induce population growth through a rise in the birth rate and a decline in the death rate of children, or welfare payments, given on broad social grounds. But in contrast to maternity benefits, they do not discriminate between families according as the mother works outside the home or in the home, and they are of course far larger per family, over the family's lifetime. Competitive private-enterprise firms cannot pay higher wages to fathers or mothers with large families unless they are allowed to discharge such employees first when business falls off and engage them last in booms. For the same reason, a family allowance paid by the government does not set in motion market forces that make the recipient family lose part of the benefits by reductions in rates of factor payment or increases in prices of the things it buys.

Within the family, however, a struggle over the benefit is common and must be appreciated if certain provisions of the laws are to be understood. The chief issue is whether the check for the monthly allowance shall be made out to the father or to the mother.[3] If to the mother, more of the allowance is likely to be spent on food and clothing for the children and less on liquor, tobacco, and gambling, even if the husband decreases the proportion of his take-home pay that he turns over to his wife, or, in an improving economy, fails to increase it as much as he otherwise would.

The family allowance is explicitly stated, contains no discontinuities, is impersonally formulated in the law and regulations and administered without discrimination or favoritism, and entails no participation costs unless the child is deliberately conceived as a means of making money from the allowance. It has no more connection with full employment than does the maternity allowance, but it puts no pressure on the housekeeping wife to become a wage-earner.

The family allowance is regressive with income, for two reasons. First, the amount paid per child is either the same regardless of the level of family income or increases not more than in proportion to the family income (compare the several types of income tax allowances for children, page 329). Second, low-income families commonly have more children than high-income families. Of course, to the extent that the allowance induces an increase in the number of children, per capita incomes of the low-income families are not increased by as much as might at first appear. Of all welfare payments, this one takes most into account the size and composition of families, though not completely, since it provides nothing for elderly relatives living with the family. The family allowance ultimately benefits somewhat those foreign

---

3. As in the United Kingdom, where the government's proposal was amended on the floor of the House to pay the allowance to the mother. On these aspects of the family allowance, see Michael Young, "Distribution of Income within the Family," *British Journal of Sociology* (1952), 3: 311–12.

countries to which the young men and women emigrate, to the extent that the allowance improves their capital, human and other.

Economic growth will be promoted only if the children, if any, that are conceived because of the allowance are afforded adequate nutrition and education. These children also are the cause of a change in pattern of work, inducing more work in the home and, depending on the size of the allowance, more or less work outside the home (for the household as a group). Leisure decreases. But if the allowance induces no increase in the number of children, it serves as a simple addition to income; more leisure is taken, and less work outside the home, while work in the home remains about the same as if no allowance were granted. Evidently the economic consequences of the family allowance will vary according as it turns out to be a subsidy or a welfare payment.

D. RESOURCE-CONDITIONED PAYMENTS (NEGATIVE-TAX WELFARE PAYMENTS)

A resource-conditioned welfare payment is so called because it is conditioned on the household's shortage of own resources. It is therefore in principle a means-test payment, but in practice it differs from the usual means-test assistance payments to the needy in several respects (see Section E below), notably the degree of discretion left to the government official to determine the amount of the payment. A good deal of discretionary power is given to the case worker under the means-test assistance program; the resource-conditioned welfare payment, on the other hand, is determined more impersonally, by the wording of the law.

Few countries grant resource-conditioned payments, and none of these few operate a comprehensive system. All major industrialized countries operate means-test assistance programs. Some of these programs, to be sure, approach the degree of impersonality that characterizes a resource-conditioned payment program, especially the "categorical" aids to certain categories of needy: the blind, the aged, dependent children, and the disabled. But even under these programs the case worker, more than the wording of the law, determines the amount to be paid in each instance. These categorical payments therefore fall within the public assistance group of payments discussed in Section E below.

A resource-conditioned payment takes into account not only the household's earnings and investment income, and perhaps net worth, but also its receipts from welfare payments under categorical and similar narrowly defined programs, for example, unemployment compensation and sickness or disability benefits paid to compensate for loss of earnings. It does not need to take into account means-test assistance payments, since presumably no household would be receiving both general assistance payments and resource-conditioned payments.

The resource-conditioned welfare payment differs in principle from the quasi-insurance benefit payment, which is determined in part by reference to past income, through the record of past contributions.

The resource-conditioned payment is a negative-tax welfare payment (see

Chapter 6, pages 146–48). It is a welfare payment, because the money flow is from government to private sector. But it is a tax at the margin; the greater the household's earnings or investment income, the smaller is the flow of government money to it. The tax is a negative tax as long as the money flow continues to be from government to the private sector. If the only resource of the household that is taken into account in determining the size of the payment is the household's own income, the welfare payment is a negative-income-tax welfare payment. The term currently employed to describe it, namely, "negative income tax," therefore accords with the terminology suggested here, if the addition of "welfare payment" to the phrase is understood, and if income, or rather the shortage of it, is the only resource on which the payment is conditioned.

Some assistance programs require that close relatives who are deemed able to help support the needy household do so. These programs levy an implicit income tax not only on the needy household itself but also on relatives, including some who are perhaps barely able to support themselves; if their earnings increase, a part of the increment must go to the support of the needy person. A resource-conditioned welfare payment is unlikely to take into account the incomes or other resources of close relatives, if only because of the difficulty of spelling out in the law the precise manner in which the negative tax would apply to them. For them, indeed, the tax would not be a negative one, since they would be receiving nothing directly. It would be a pure tax; they would be required to relinquish part if not all of an additional dollar they earned, as long as their relative remained needy. This peculiar form of pure taxation is practicable on an ad hoc basis under an assistance program, which may even include a provision that requires the needy person to sue his relatives if they refuse to cooperate with the assistance administrators. Such a provision would be difficult to implement and enforce under an impersonal law for a resource-conditioned payment program.

The negative-tax welfare payment brings out into the open, through the schedule of rates in the law, the marginal tax rate that is only implicit in the assistance program. That program commonly employs a marginal rate of implicit tax of 100 per cent, since it commonly reduces the welfare payment dollar for dollar as the household's own income increases (see Section E below). A 100 per cent marginal rate of tax will not be tolerated when it is made explicit in a negative-tax law. But since most societies do not consider themselves wealthy enough to impose a marginal tax rate of less than 100 per cent on relief recipients, for reasons that are given below, they are reluctant to move to a system that would require explicit statement of the marginal rates.

A negative-tax welfare payment system that would be considered generous even by standards of wealthy countries must still impose marginal tax rates that appear very high compared with the marginal rates of positive taxes on the higher-income groups. These high marginal rates are necessary for two reasons.

First, there is some very low level of income below which the government will not allow the household to fall ("the minimum"), when the household's own income decreases. As the household's own income falls below that level, the government makes up the entire difference. Then, if the household's own income later rises, after having fallen into this range, the government must take the entire increment of own-income by reducing the welfare payment correspondingly.

The government imposes a 100 per cent marginal rate of tax on own-income in this range. The 100 per cent rate can be avoided only if the government keeps the household above the minimum as own-income decreases until own-income has fallen to zero (abstracting from the possibility of negative own-income). Thus if the minimum is $2,000 a year, the government might pay the household $2,000 if own-

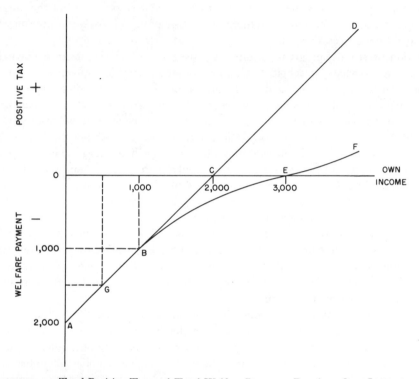

FIGURE 11. Total Positive Tax and Total Welfare Payment, Based on Own Income

ncome was zero, $1,995 if own-income was $10, and in this manner avoid a 100 per cent marginal tax rate, but at the cost, to be sure, of sustaining a much larger total of welfare payments.

Second, even if the household's own income exceeds the minimum, the marginal rate of tax must remain high, though less than 100 per cent, for a considerable further range of own-income, unless indeed the level of own-income at which the welfare payment ceases is itself to be quite high. A low marginal rate of negative tax implies a low marginal rate of decline in the welfare payment as own-income increases. Consequently, the welfare payment will not disappear until the household's own income has reached a high level.

These points are illustrated in Figure 11, which is of the same type as Figure 10 in Chapter 6.[4] The household's total income is the sum of its own income (measured on the x-axis) and the negative-tax welfare payment made to it by the government, or the difference between its own income and the positive tax that it pays to the government. The negative-tax payment is shown by the distance on the negative segment of the y-axis; the positive tax, by the distance on the positive segment of that axis.

The 45-degree line ABCD is an extreme case; it represents support of the household's disposable income at the $2,000 level whenever the household's own income is below $2,000, and repression of its disposable income to the $2,000 level whenever own-income exceeds $2,000. The marginal tax rate, shown by the slope of this line, is 100 per cent throughout. If the positive tax is not to begin until own-income is $3,000, a curve like ABE represents total welfare payment or, when it rises above the x-axis, total positive tax. The slope of this curve is again the marginal rate of tax, and it decreases steadily from 100 per cent at own-income of $1,000 to, say, 20 per cent at own-income of $3,000.

In the range of own-income where the positive tax applies, that is, above $3,000 in Figure 11, the marginal rate must increase as own-income increases, if the positive tax is to be progressive. Hence there will have to be a point of inflection in the total curve, as shown by Figure 11, where the welfare payment changes into a positive tax. The marginal rate has decreased from 100 per cent to 20 per cent as own-income has risen from $1,000 to $3,000, and it then increases from 20 per cent to, say, 60 or 70 per cent as own-income rises above $3,000.

In practice, the marginal rate would decrease and then increase by slight jumps, and the total curve would consist of a number of straight lines and slight corners, but the general outline would be as in Figure 11.

If the repressive effects on willingness to work that are exerted by the high marginal tax rates in the negative-tax range are deemed inappropriate, the slope of the segment BE can be made to decrease more rapidly, but then the positive tax will come into effect only at a level of own-income higher than $3,000.

The marginal rate can be set at zero for the lowest levels of own-income by paying a fixed amount to anyone whose own income does not exceed a certain amount.[5] In terms of Figure 11, let this fixed amount be $1,500 for everyone whose own income does not exceed $500. A horizontal line drawn from the $1,500 point on OA to intersect the AB line at G replaces the AG segment of the AB line. The zero marginal rate of tax on own income up to $500 is then succeeded by a 100 per cent marginal rate up to B, and a decreasing marginal rate from B to E.

Alternatively, the marginal rate of the negative tax can be made positive but fairly

4. The same type of diagram is used by Christopher Green, in his *Negative Taxes and the Poverty Problem* (Washington, D.C.: Brookings Institution, 1967), *passim*. For a diagram with the ordinate measuring net income instead of tax, see A. T. Peacock, *The Economics of National Insurance* (London: Hodge, 1952), pp. 110–11.

5. This is the type of income-conditioned payment adopted in New Zealand. As of 1950, "the standard social security benefit was £130 a year, for which any resident was eligible if his income did not exceed £78. For every £1 of income in excess of this amount, his social security benefit was reduced by £1" (Eveline M. Burns, *Social Security and Public Policy* [New York: McGraw-Hill, 1956], p. 23).

low at the lowest income levels. It might be, say, only 10 per cent as own income rises slightly above a zero level, where the negative-tax payment is, say, $2,000. The marginal rate could then increase steadily throughout the welfare-payment range, as shown in Figure 12 by the line AH, and also through the positive-tax range.

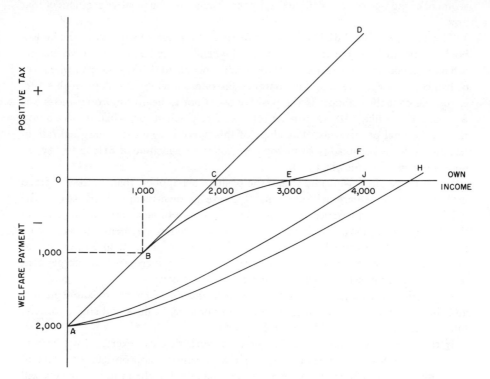

FIGURE 12. Total Positive Tax and Total Welfare Payment, Based on Own Income: Figure 11 Programs Compared with Increasing-Marginal-Rate Plan

No point of inflection would be needed. But this technique requires a very expensive welfare program unless the marginal rate in the initial bracket of positive tax is to be very high, that is, unless the slope of the curve AH in Figure 12 is to be very steep as it crosses the x-axis, so that the positive tax will begin at some level not too far above $3,000. The technique is therefore impracticable for all but a wealthy society.

If, to make it practicable, this system were grafted onto one that imposed a marginal rate of 100 per cent on the lowest incomes, as it would if the curve segment BE were convex to the x-axis rather than concave as it is in Figures 11 and 12, the transition would be abrupt indeed, from a 100 per cent marginal rate to one of 5 or 10 per cent.

The welfare payment curve can be kept concave to the x-axis, as is the curve AH, yet be made to intersect that axis not very far to the right, by employing a high marginal rate of implicit tax at the beginning, that is, as the household's own income increases from zero, and making that marginal rate higher still as the curve approaches the *x*-axis. Then the curve must corner at the point of intersection with the *x*-axis, to reduce the marginal tax rate to a level acceptable with a positive tax. In Figure 12 the curve AJ illustrates this combination;[6] it calls for the marginal tax rate to rise from 60 to 70 to 80 to 90 per cent as own-income rises above $0, $1,000, $2,000, and $3,000 respectively, or in finer gradations if desired. At $4,000 the marginal rate either (1) drops to zero per cent until the positive tax begins, at some own-income level above $4,000, or (2) drops to, say, 10 per cent or 20 per cent if the positive tax starts at $4,000.

If high marginal rates are deemed inevitable in the welfare-payment region (the lower half of the present diagram) because of constraints on total cost of program, and if the deterrent effect of those rates on labor is considered inadvisable, the resource-conditioned welfare payment can be modified by injection of an effort-conditioned element: anyone who is both employable and unemployed, and will not accept suitable employment, is denied the welfare payment. This system is a two-part program: an unemployment compensation program for employables, a resource-conditioned program for all others. The marginal rate of implicit tax on prospective earned income of an unemployed employable is always zero per cent; if he works, he gets his wage; if he does not work he gets nothing.

The final step in this direction is to drop the resource condition and pay a flat grant to everyone, except to employables who are unemployed and will not accept suitable employment; this is the payment part of the social-contract proposal put forward by Lady Rhys-Williams. It, too, is a dual system: unemployment compensation for unemployed employables and an unconditional grant for all others. Figure 13 shows the unconditional-grant part of the Rhys-Williams program as the line AK, which extends indefinitely to the right, at a zero slope. If the positive income tax begins at $3,000 of own-income, the combined system of negative tax and positive tax is represented by the two lines AK and EF. If E'F' is drawn with the same slope as EF, the vertical distance from E'F' to the *x*-axis represents the net welfare payment (unconditional grant less positive tax). In this program the marginal rate of tax on prospective earned income that is lower than the income level where the positive tax begins is actually negative; if the unemployed person who is offered a suitable job refuses it, he gets nothing, while if he accepts it he gets both his wage and the unconditional payment.

6. This type of negative income tax is approximately that discussed by Edward E. Schwartz in "An End to the Means Test," in Robert Theobold (Ed.), *The Guaranteed Income* (New York: Doubleday, 1966). See also Milton Friedman, *Capitalism and Freedom* (Chicago: University of Chicago Press, 1962). James Tobin has suggested that a family with no other income receive a basic allowance scaled to the number of persons in the family and that the allowance be reduced by a certain fraction, say one-third, of other income received; this schedule would give way to the existing positive income tax schedule at the point where the two tax schedules produce the same tax liability ("Improving the Economic Status of the Negro," *Daedalus* [Fall, 1965], 94: 889–95). A detailed examination of "some of the sticky technical problems" posed by the negative income tax is presented by James Tobin, Joseph A. Pechman, and Peter M. Mieszowski, in "Is a Negative Income Tax Practical?," *Yale Law Journal* (November, 1967), 77: 1–27, the answer being in the affirmative. For a comprehensive analysis, see Christopher Green, *Negative Taxes and the Poverty Problem* (Washington: Brookings Institution, 1967).

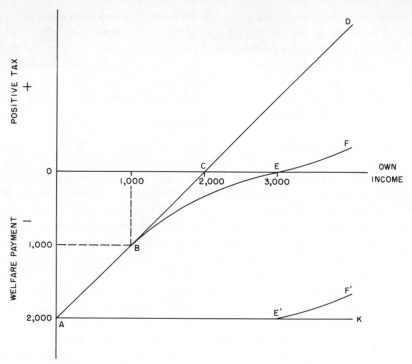

FIGURE 13. Total Positive Tax and Total Welfare Payment, Based on Own Income: Figure 11
Programs Compared with Rhys-Williams Program

The question may arise whether a positive spending tax can be satisfactorily linked
with a negative income tax. If the household is not spending exactly all its income,
there are two possibilities. If this household is dissaving, that is, spending more
than its own income, and if the welfare payment begins when income falls below a
certain transition level, and if the positive spending tax stops when spending falls
below that same figure as a transition level (say, $3,000 income and $3,000 spending
respectively), a household could be both receiving a welfare payment and paying a
spending tax. This state of affairs would obtain for all households with an income
below $3,000 that were spending more than $3,000.

If on the contrary the household were saving part of its income, it could be in a
position of neither receiving a welfare payment nor paying a spending tax. This
would be the condition of all households with an income over $3,000 but spending
less than $3,000. Neither the cross-hauling of revenue nor the absence of flow either
way necessarily condemns the program.

The dissaving household would be under marginal pressure to decrease its spending and simultaneously not to increase its income. If its members nevertheless
wanted to earn income, but were unable to do so, that is, if the marginal pressure to
decrease income were not strongly effective, the net result might satisfy the community's aims. Those households with fairly low income would be induced to save

part of the welfare payments they were receiving. This saving might even be a major aim of the welfare program.

An absence of flow of money in either direction for the saving households in this range is still more likely to be considered acceptable. If the household is able to save, despite its low income—its own income is, say, $3,200 and its spending, $2,900—no need for positive or negative taxation may be considered to exist. The household would of course be under no marginal pressure to decrease either its earned income or its spending. In general, no insuperable problems arise in joining a positive spending tax with a negative income tax.

A negative-tax welfare payment conditioned on resources meets the consensus type of equity criteria unless application of the basic principle is restricted by ceilings, floors, alternative methods of computation, and the like, or unless, as is probably common, there are unequal degrees of error in payment, either through overpayment to those who falsify the relevant data or through underpayment, including no payment at all, to those who are not fully aware of their rights. These payments help check recessions, and would do so more promptly in that the reaction would be automatic as incomes declined. The benefit would be distributed regressively and could take into account family status. Residence rather than citizenship would presumably be the basis for eligibility.

Some part of the welfare payment would be saved by some recipients, including those who would dissave less because of the payment, so that some part of the welfare payment would be to this degree an aid to growth. The fairly intense substitution effect against work arising from the high marginal rate of tax would be, above the minimum level, less than that under most assistance programs, where the implicit tax rate is 100 per cent.

The resource-conditioned welfare payment would not act to reduce directly the other welfare payments that would remain in the system, namely, the categorical assistance payments. But of course that welfare payment would itself decline with every increase in these categorical means-test payments. Alternatively, the means-test payments could be excluded in computing "resources" to set the resource-conditioned welfare payment and then be adjusted in the light of the level of that payment.

2. Discretionary Types of Welfare Payment

E. PUBLIC ASSISTANCE PAYMENTS

Means-test payments under a public assistance program and resource-conditioned welfare payments (negative income taxes) differ, as we have seen in Section D above, more in practice than in principle, since means and resources are essentially the same. These differences in practice, noted briefly in Section D above, will now be described in more detail.

First, the negative income tax is administered by tax officials, while the public assistance program is administered by case workers. The tax administrators will follow closely the statutory language of the negative income tax and the rules given in published regulations that interpret the statute, if they act as they do under a positive income tax. The case worker exercises more discretion in determining the amount of the payment, since the public assistance law commonly contains no rate schedule or only the skeleton of one.

Second, the assistance program usually contains a needs-test element, to be distinguished from a means-test element. The case-by-case approach makes it possible to obtain, at a low incremental cost of administration, information on the household's needs as reflected not only by number and ages of children but also by ethnic and other consumption patterns. These circumstances, apart from the number of children, presumably will not be taken into account by the negative-income-tax law. Unfortunately, the case-by-case approach also makes it easy to enforce community bias against color, ethnic, religious or other non-economic groups by denying or reducing welfare payments to households in those groups. The case worker may even argue that the members of the group have less need because they are accustomed to a low standard of living even when employed. Locational differences in welfare payment levels are easily implemented also, particularly urban against rural. Under the negative income tax these distinctions according to color, race, or religion will almost surely not be tolerated, and geographical distinctions will be difficult to allow for.

Third, the usual assistance program lacks machinery for appeal to the courts from the decision of the case worker or his superior.[7] If a negative-income tax statute followed that of a positive income tax, a right of appeal to the courts would be guaranteed.

Fourth, the proponents of the statutory negative income tax advocate a marginal rate of tax short of the 100 per cent that is characteristic of the existing systems of assistance to the needy. They can do so because they do not propose to legislate a fixed sum to be distributed among the needy, as is the common practice (but by no means universal practice) under assistance programs. The assistance administrator, working with a fixed total to be distributed among a constantly fluctuating amount of needy families, must resort to a sub-optimizing procedure. If there are, say, 100 households under his jurisdiction, and if all are at the same relief level, adjusted of course for differences in household composition and needs, a dollar more earned by one household will call for reallocation of a dollar of the fixed relief appropriation equally among all the households, so that this family's assistance payment is reduced by 99 cents and each of the others' is increased by 1 cent.

Fifth, the amount paid under the usual assistance program depends on potential income. If a deserting father returns to his family, the relief payment will cease, or decline, in some jurisdictions, whether or not he finds work, on the grounds that the family now has a source of support that should and can be used. If close relatives are able to support the family in whole or in part, the assistance payment may be

7. See Eveline Burns, *The American Social Security System* (New York: Houghton Mifflin. 1949), pp. 33–34.

reduced accordingly, whether or not the relatives are in fact contributing. A negative income tax will presumably not be based at all on potential income.

Sixth, the assistance program is commonly a mixture of negative income tax, negative wealth tax, and negative excise tax. A household with income low enough to make it eligible for assistance, but possessing property, will usually be required to liquidate the property and use up the proceeds, with certain exceptions, before assistance payments will be made. A family on relief that spends its money on items that the case worker deems non-essential may find its relief payment reduced. The property element, to be sure, if not the excise tax element, might conceivably be embodied in a negative tax statute, which would then be a negative income and property tax law.

Seventh, in certain times and places a work requirement has been coupled with the means test for assistance payments; the negative income tax carries no such requirement. Work relief programs that simply offer jobs at standard pay for work that is provided partly to maintain morale do not quite belong in this category, since the individual has the option of going on to a lower-income assistance level without working.

In general, the chief difference between the two regimes (negative income tax and assistance payments) lies in the degree of impersonality with which they are formulated in statutory language and administered by the field force. But these differences can easily be overestimated. Under the statutory negative income tax the tax official, here presumably an auditor, must be given power to verify the statement to be submitted by the recipient household detailing its earnings and income from other sources. Probably most of that income, if there is any of it at all, comes from part-time jobs where there is no withholding of tax by the employer for the positive tax. The tax administrator will therefore not have as good a means of verifying the family's statement as he has under the positive income tax in general. This fact places more responsibility on the tax official to study each household as a distinct case. And the precise extent to which the official shall make use of his powers of investigation cannot very well be specified closely in the law or regulations.

Recipients of means-test assistance payments will not lose their benefits through changes in market prices of what they buy or what (if anything) they sell, excepting possibly rentals in slum areas, which rise as poor households become able to pay more for space. But then relief payments will rise too, at least in some jurisdictions (but negative income tax payments will not rise, or will rise more slowly). In the end the household on relief still has a place to live, but some part of the assistance expenditure will have accrued indirectly to landlords. The households with negative income tax may be in more danger from competition with each other for dwelling space than households on relief.

Means-test assistance scores poorly on all but one of the consensus type of equity criteria. Even when the law's statement of conditions appears on the surface to be quite explicit, it is really ambiguous, since the conditions are in terms of concepts, for example, "income," below a certain level, that in turn are difficult to define (see Chapter 11 on income taxation), or are expressed vaguely by "subsistence," "poverty," and similar terms.

Severe discontinuities are common in the categorical type of aid, since definite lines must be drawn to divide what is really a spectrum into yes-no compartments. Even non-categorical assistance payments draw arbitrary lines, as in listing the relatives who must contribute before assistance will be given by the government: brothers as distinguished from half-brothers, for example, or uncles from cousins. If assistance is not granted to transients, an arbitrary time definition is the only substitute for vagueness. Unequal degrees of erroneous payment are common (see page 25 above).

The payments themselves create no excess burden, except possibly through control by the case worker over the household's expenditure pattern, or through distribution of relief in kind. Assistance payments are not given to persons who, becoming unemployed, move to other regions or countries, whereas unemployment compensation, as we have seen, may continue. And those who, having become unemployed elsewhere, move into the country, or state, are usually cared for under relief (if they are not receiving enough in unemployment compensation from their jurisdiction of former residence) but not, by this jurisdiction, under one of the quasi-insurance programs. Borrowing from income tax terminology (see page 292), we may say that the means-test payments, in common with family allowances, are on a residence basis while the quasi-insurance programs are on a source basis.

Residence, however, may be defined to require a certain minimum amount of time spent in the jurisdiction, as do income tax laws. Habitually floating households are excluded, with the effect that some households that would otherwise be stable geographically are forced into floating, and in their enforced mobility in search of aid may use up more real resources in travel and related expenses than they produce for the economy by finding a job, if they do.

In many countries means-test assistance payments are made by governments of very open economies, namely, local units, in many countries: cities, towns, villages. A disparity of levels of relief among local units within the mobility range of the recipient induces migration that tends to reduce the disparities. If the disparities are due largely to differing local abilities to finance means-test assistance, migration tends to place a greater burden on well-to-do taxpayers and to reduce the burden on lower-income taxpayers. But the chief contributors to the migrating household may be those already receiving assistance in the wealthier locality, if that locality, insofar as it operates with a fixed total appropriation for assistance, reduces the standard of living deemed essential as the assistance load increases. By the same reasoning, the households that did not migrate may benefit a little, since the locality of emigration may decide that it can now afford a somewhat higher standard for the minimum. Thus the minimum residence requirements will be in the interest of means-test recipients who are already established in well-to-do districts, and detrimental to those established in the poorer localities.

Saving is increased, and dissaving is decreased, little if at all by the assistance payments themselves, in contrast to unemployment compensation; hence the economic growth criterion is not met and is perhaps irrelevant here. The relief payments are made steadily, over a period of some length, to meet daily necessaries rather than an emergency, and are often given only when not only the household but close relatives have exhausted or drawn down to a certain minimum their net worth. Accordingly, in the absence of assistance payments, and abstracting from the methods used to finance them, little further dissaving would occur, if only because little would be possible.

In a less conventional sense of saving, however, means-test assistance payments may accomplish a good deal, for they may build up human capital by replacing enfeeblement with vigor, and this investment may be reflected fairly soon in increased aggregate product. Any analysis of economic effects of payments to the very poor is of little consequence if it omits the effect on human capital, physical and intellectual.[8]

Assistance payments are for the most part spent on domestically produced goods and services, if "domestic" means the same country, chiefly shelter, food, and clothing of a low quality. The few countries in which such purchases would be largely of imports are usually so poor that a formal system of means-test assistance payments exists on a modest level if at all. Little pressure is put on the exchange rate. But if "domestic" means the same local jurisdiction, that is, the same city, province, or state, much of the assistance payment may go to increasing imports from the rest of the country, with consequent loss of currency or bank deposits to those areas.

Unquestionably the most important reallocation effect is that between paid work and either housework or leisure. There seems no doubt, even in the absence of empirical studies,[9] that the customary implicit tax rate of 100 per cent or slightly less reduces appreciably an amount of job-seeking that would have resulted in paid work, some of which would be additional work, not merely displacement of someone already on a job. Indeed, the cost may exceed 100 per cent of the wage, when to reduction of relief payments there is added fare to and from work and other occupational outlays, or if the relief payment is reduced by one dollar for every dollar of contractual wage, not take-home pay.

The supply of paid labor, we have seen, is not appreciably reduced by means-test assistance payments insofar as those payments go to the incapacitated (blind, mentally deficient, psychotic, or otherwise disabled). Moreover, since a limited amount of work is preferred by most persons to complete idleness, even a more-than-100-per-cent charge at the margin will not discourage work completely by those who are not incapacitated. But paid work may be discouraged completely if useful work around one's own home offers enough activity for activity's sake, and this is clearly so for one large group of relief recipients, mothers of children in broken homes ("dependent children").

Since the 100 per cent implicit tax drops to zero when the earned income reaches a level at which means-test assistance drops to zero, a full-time job paying substantially more than means-test relief can be attractive despite the initial range of 100 per cent implicit tax.

8. See Carl S. Shoup, "Production from Consumption," *Public Finance* (1965) 20(2): 173–202.

9. See, however, C. T. Brehm and T. R. Saving, "The Demand for General Assistance Payments," *American Economic Review* (December, 1964), 54: 1002–18.

An increase in means-test assistance payments has little effect on other governmental outlays or revenue, save perhaps some automatic reduction of government expenditures on health care; but even that case is artificial, since a government that dispenses medical care free is no doubt already operating an assistance program at about as high a level as it is disposed to do under any circumstances.

F. FOREIGN AID

Foreign aid is here defined to be "the value of the subsidy implicit in the total flow of resources,"[10] that is, exclusive of transfers for a direct consideration, notably loans at free-market rates of interest. For "subsidy" in this definition "unrequited payment" must be substituted for conformity with the terminology that was adopted in Chapters 3 and 6. A further restriction of the term "aid" is adopted for analytical purposes here, to exclude those payments that, while unrequited in a direct, immediate sense, are nevertheless understood by both donor and donee country to be given in exchange for something, in a sense that domestic assistance payments are not given.

First, a large part of foreign "aid" is a purchase, by the government of the donor country, of services from a foreign government, for present or potential future delivery, in order that the donor government may render certain services to its own people, notably military protection. This part of foreign "aid," being the purchase of an input, must be analyzed under the type of output that it provides. For present purposes, the home government's purchase of military aircraft from a domestic firm and the purchase of military support, or a promise of it, from a foreign country, are on the same footing, and both are included implicitly in the discussion in Chapter 5, Section A.1.

Second, much aid is given on condition or on the assumption that the recipient country will maintain a government committed to a political, social, or business ideology satisfactory to the donor country. This purchase of political and social commitment is the nonmilitary aspect of protection from potential enemy nations and again is a subject for Chapter 5.

Both of these types of "aid" expenditure are laden with externalities in the form of disadvantages for other countries that are bidding, in rivalry, for the donee country's support. The more one country gives, the more the other has to give to achieve a certain level of commitment.

Thirdly, a substantial part of foreign aid is designed to subsidize certain domestic exporting industries and is discussed in the following section of this chapter, Subsidies. Agriculture is a notable example of such an industry.

The remainder of foreign "aid" is a welfare payment, aid proper. It is more or less a means-test type of program, resembling domestic assistance programs in that the use the donee country makes of the aid is intended to be somewhat supervised, although in practice the supervision or specification may turn out to be ineffective.

10. I. M. D. Little and J. M. Clifford, *International Aid* (Chicago: Aldine Publishing Company, 1965), p. 13, and Chapter 3, "The Principles of Aid Giving."

This true aid is given usually because of altruistic distress on the part of inhabitants of the donor country because of current misery of others. The altruism is sometimes diluted by a fear that current misery will cumulate in time to a desperation that will endanger the world.

This welfare-payment type of foreign aid has at times been supplied in large amounts by the private sector, through charitable and religious organizations, and indeed it is for this aspect of aid to other countries, not the military protection or ideological commitment or subsidy aspects, that the private sector is best suited to complement the government's efforts. This fact explains in large part why most government "aid" is instead a purchase of something from the donee government. The welfare motive cannot, however, be adequately supplied by the private sector in terms of technical welfare economics, for reasons given in Chapter 6.[11]

True aid from government to government is more common from a rich donor to a hitherto rich but currently poor donee country, rather than to chronically poor countries.[12] The inhabitants of the rich donor country can more easily identify themselves with essentially rich neighbors fallen on hard times than they can with those living in societies whose cultures, having been long adapted to poverty (and wealth for a very few) are strange.

Foreign aid, in the restricted sense that it is understood here, does not conform closely to the consensus equity criteria. The need for it to do so is the less in that the recipient governments are few and so can be given welfare grants tailored to each country's particular needs. Accordingly, a formula approach, applicable to all potential donees alike, is found only in foreign aid channeled through international organizations, where the need for a formula reflects not so much a desire to be impersonal toward donees as a desire by donors to be assured that they are indeed in agreement. And the criteria for eligibility are stated only in broad terms.

In the relative absence of formulae for granting aid, the issue of breaks, gaps, or discontinuities becomes a minor one. The chief problem with respect to the consensus type of equity criteria becomes that of personalization. When so few donees (countries) are involved, the impersonalization that is said in Chapter 1 to be a hallmark of accepted public finance policy cannot exist, at least not in law and administration simultaneously. Either the law specifies just how much shall go to each country or the administrators of the program exercise wide discretion. In sum, the consensus type of equity criteria are chiefly designed for the large-numbers case: hundreds, or thousands, of individuals or firms that are recipients of assistance or subsidies, or are taxpayers, not a dozen or so nations.

A change in the level of foreign aid is not an appropriate counter-cycle instrument for the donor country except as it is reflected back in a like change in exports, which

11. International commodity agreements for minimum prices (coffee, for example) are in principle a form of aid, financed by consumers located chiefly in certain countries to the advantage of factors of production located chiefly in other countries. If these plans are to be workable, the governments of both types of country must be at least tacitly involved. For still other types of aid, see Little and Clifford, *op. cit.*, pp. 51–52.

12. Compare the volume of Marshall Aid by the U.S.A. with its later aid to historically poor countries, even after making allowance for the parts of those aids that were in return for something (Little and Clifford, *op. cit.*, p. 24).

will be small, since foreign aid as here defined excludes strictly tied aid (see the section below on Subsidies).

Welfare payment aid is in general distributed regressively to income or wealth, among the particular group of donee countries that happen to be holding the attention of the donor country at the time. This latter qualification is significant. No donor country recognizes a permanent geographically bounded group of potential recipient countries as its responsibility with regard to welfare aid, in contrast to a nation or a city vis-à-vis its residents. But within the group that the donor nation happens to be concerned with, implicit interpersonal comparisons of utility are carried over from households, as within a city, to nations. The poorer is the nation currently, in terms of average per-person income, the more it will likely receive in foreign aid of the welfare type, per person. Little effort is made by the donor country to go below the simple average figures, hence most of the equity criteria of the conflict type are not considered relevant.

The recipient country is often urged to make use of the welfare type of foreign aid in investment projects, especially infrastructure, even when the economic growth of the recipient country would be speeded up by investing food, medical care, and education in the people, especially the current labor force and the young. In any case, an implied promise by the donee to so increase domestic output within a forseeable future that aid can then be decreased is a feature of all welfare foreign aid programs. That this is so can be appreciated by asking whether a request for aid would be met if the donee admitted to the somber view that the grant would merely alleviate misery as long as it continued and if repealed would be followed by the same deep level of misery that prevailed initially.

The current external equilibrium of the donor country is directly affected by this welfare type of foreign aid, as noted earlier. A country, no matter how rich, cannot give aid to another country (true aid), however poor, without experiencing at least a slight pressure for devaluation, once it has encroached notably on its foreign reserves. The devaluation would be a simple acknowledgment of the fact that giving makes the donor poorer, materially. But a proposal to devalue, or to take alternative measures that would maintain the initial value of the currency, stirs conflicts of interest even among those who are in principle united in their willingness to sacrifice personal wealth to aid the inhabitants of a poor country.

The income effect of welfare foreign aid will reduce the labor supply in the recipient countries by much less, if it reduces that supply at all, than the increase that can be brought about through energy increases as a result of more food, better shelter, and more medical care.

B. SUBSIDIES

1. Housing Subsidies

Subsidies to housing are designed to increase the consumption of housing by certain groups of consumers, notably, low-income households or veterans, rather than to increase the rate of factor rewards in the building industry or in the real estate sector. Housing subsidies are therefore consumer subsidies.

Housing subsidies appear as (*a*) cash subsidies to privately owned rental housing, with or without controls on the amount of profit the landlord can earn, or (*b*) the excess of market rental over actual rental charged to tenants of government-owned housing, or (*c*) government-guarantee of mortgages taken out by either homeowners or landlords that goes beyond a guarantee that can be justified actuarially by the insurance premium, if any, that the government charges. The subsidy is almost never offered as a cash grant to an owner-occupier to help him defray the cost of constructing his house. It never appears as a guarantee of performance under a rental contract as distinguished from a mortgage contract, because long-term leases to households are uncommon or unknown in most countries; dealings in leases of occupancy units rather than ownership rights of those units, while frequent for business real estate, are the exception in housing.

The frequency of subsidies of housing for the poor, and the rarity of subsidies for clothing or food for the poor, as distinguished from subsidies that apply to all consumers of whatever income level, are explicable partly by the fact that housing cannot be resold as readily as food or clothing, but chiefly by the inelasticity of supply of housing for the poor, on the competitive market, coupled with a rapid rate of increase in the absolute number of the poor in urban centers owing to migration from rural areas and a general increase in population. The result of inelasticity of supply and upward shift in the aggregate demand curve for housing by the poor is to create a degree of crowding that the community comes to regard as intolerable, largely because of the negative externalities it imposes on all, through increases in rates of crime, disease, mental illness, and similar consequences of high density. These externalities are no worse than those that would result if a growing population of the poor were restricted to an almost fixed total of food, or of clothing, to be divided among them, but the supply of food and clothing for the poor is so elastic that the addition to demand made by an increasing absolute population of the poor (assuming no proportionate decline in per-person income) results in little if any rise in price in most countries. And mere movement of the poor from rural areas to cities does not increase the aggregate demand of the poor for food and clothing to the same degree that it increases their demand for urban dwelling accommodation.

Inelasticity of supply of housing for the poor in an already built-up urban area results from (*a*) the high cost of demolition to make way for a greater amount of dwelling accommodation on a given site, (*b*) technical inability to construct new "old" housing, and (*c*) the length of time it takes for an increase in demand only for old housing to be reflected in an increase in demand for new housing and a consequent increase in amount of new housing which would allow all existing housing to move down one grade in the market, and so increase the supply of old housing that the poor could afford. This last consideration, (*c*), is important just because of consideration (*b*); dilapidated housing, which the well-to-do are willing to leave for the poor, can be produced only by first building new housing for the well-to-do. No such curious supply condition exists for clothing or food. To be sure, new housing can be constructed to sell to the poor at the prices they have been paying for dilapidated housing, but only if the dwelling space thus offered to each poor household is so small that the consequent overcrowding leaves the household worse off even than it was in its dilapidated, less crowded, housing.

Inelasticity of supply of housing for the poor has been demonstrated by waves of immigration into cities that have pushed up prices of dilapidated housing substantially without increasing the supply of such housing. In countries damaged by war, where much dilapidated housing has been destroyed, a free-market process of waiting for new housing to become dilapidated would have led to intolerable crowding, hence the rationing of new housing, coupled with subsidies.

A housing program limited to subsidizing the low-income household by the government's paying a portion of the rent or of mortgage installments would increase housing consumption by the poor only if it were large enough to enable the poor to bid housing away from the income classes immediately above them. To allow the free market to reallocate housing in this manner would enrich, at least in the short run, existing owners of housing. The alternative of rationing the existing supply of housing infringes on the market expectations of those who are not poor. Accordingly, housing subsidies are usually restricted to newly created housing, rationed to the poor at rentals below cost; direct rental or ownership subsidies to the poor to enable them to compete in the open market for housing are rare. The guarantee programs referred to above are usually not much more than pure insurance programs.

Only a small part, if any, of the subsidy of newly erected housing for the poor goes to increase factor rewards in the building industry; the supply of factors to the building industry is far less price-inelastic than is the supply of used houses for the poor. Site owners will capture part of the subsidy unless condemnation (compulsory sale at a price set by judicial authority) is a part of the subsidy program. Given adequate condemnation procedures, little of the housing subsidy is diverted from the tenants, provided, it must be emphasized, that the subsidy is not simply one designed to help the poor bid more vigorously against the income classes above them for the supply of housing afforded by the free market at a competitive price. To be sure, even this latter procedure would in time create increased housing for the poor by increasing total housing, but the time lag and the permanently higher site rentals, reflecting the increasing-cost nature of housing designed to enable persons to work in a certain area,[13] seem to have been, so far, effective arguments against this simple subsidy method.

Accordingly, the criteria of Chapter 2 will be applied in the paragraphs to follow only to housing subsidies that are coupled with either (a) construction of new housing that is rationed to the poor at below-cost rentals or sales prices, or (b) redistribution of the existing stock of housing by rationing.

Effectiveness of a housing subsidy, particularly with regard to its goal of reducing negative externalities, could in principle be impaired by a highly inelastic demand on

13. To increase the supply of housing for persons who work in a given area, housing must either be applied more intensively on any given site, with increasing costs of construction at the margin, or be extended outward geographically, with increasing costs of travel (commuting).

the part of the poor. In that somewhat unlikely event, reverse rationing would be required, in the sense that the poor household would be required to purchase a certain minimum amount of the new housing; the rental would be set at a level that would leave what the policy-makers would decide was adequate for other consumption and saving.

Rent ceilings coupled with tenant's right of continued occupancy comprise a system of rationing with subsidy. The subsidy is paid by those who happen to be the owners of the housing at the time the program is imposed. The distributive consequences are haphazard, except as landlords are optimistically viewed as a homogeneous group of well-to-do persons, and the allocational consequences are to reduce the supply of housing by removing inducement to maintain the existing supply. Although rent-ceiling programs have been common, especially in postwar periods when social and political disorientation has deterred governments from taxing or inflating to supply housing subsidies from the public fisc, or from introducing a government-formulated rationing system, they will not be analyzed further here, since they are so obviously unable to attain the goals of a housing subsidy consistently over a long period of time.

Housing subsidies do not score highly under the consensus type of equity criteria. The subsidy law can be explicit in its statement of conditions for receiving the subsidy only at the expense of introducing discontinuities through sharp definitions, as when households are eligible for a subsidy if, but only if, the household income is below a specified level. Aside from this income specification the standards for qualification for the subsidy tend to be so vaguely expressed in the law that, as with means-test assistance payments, the administrative personnel exercise considerable discretion. The effectiveness of this discretion is enhanced by the frequently long waiting lists from which tenants are chosen and the power to expel tenants who are deemed not to observe the rules of behavior that are part of the price paid for the privileged status. Nor is it clear that the costs to the potential tenants of participating in the program are more or less equal to all. On the other hand, the subsidy law is free of the implicit "one-person" clauses, those that favor in fact, though not ostensibly, a particular individual, and which are found in laws of income tax and death and gift taxes.

Construction of subsidized housing cannot well be synchronized with slack periods in the construction industry, or in business in general, because of the long lead time needed for acquiring land and closing construction contracts. Even construction itself takes so long and peaks so pronouncedly during this period on any one project that counter-cycle timing becomes quite difficult.

If externalities are disregarded, the housing subsidy creates some excess burden, but, since it is the externalities that are largely responsible for the subsidy, the community must be regarded as seeking to move toward a Pareto optimum rather than away from it, by this subsidy.

Since most of the housing subsidy goes to consumers, not producers, the subsidy is distributed regressively with income, at least as between those eligible for subsidized housing and those not eligible. Within the subsidized group the result is not known, since not all of those eligible do obtain the housing; conceivably, a larger proportion of those with higher incomes than of those with lower incomes, in this eligible group, happen to be selected to occupy the limited amount of housing. Add to this the fact that eligibility is not solely on an income basis, and the pattern of distribution becomes still less clear. But in any event the size and composition of the family are usually taken into account, the larger families receiving the larger subsidy per household if not per person.

The geographical distribution of housing subsidies is striking in almost all countries. Rural housing is subsidized hardly at all, except on farms, where home, office, and factory headquarters are often in one building. There, a subsidy to farming is in part a subsidy of farm housing. Housing laws rarely mention color, race, or status, but the ability to discriminate in administration of the law makes these attributes potential bases for distribution of the subsidy.

Economic growth is represented by the dwelling itself, but the financing method may have reduced investment elsewhere. Families benefiting from the housing subsidies are not likely to save more than they would have saved, since the aim commonly is not to reduce the amount that the poor have been spending on housing but to give them more for the same expenditure. The degree of private risk is reduced by those housing programs that subsidize rentals of newly constructed dwelling units but that in exchange set certain limits on profits; the hope evidently is that the expected profit will be increased, relative to the dispersion of possible outcomes.

The income effect of a housing subsidy will by traditional reasoning tend to decrease the amount of labor supplied by the household, but against this is to be placed an expected increase in efficiency as the working members of the household enjoy better health, obtain more rest, and find their consumption goals rising, under the improved housing. Government expenditures on crime prevention, medical care, and fire protection will be expected to decrease. And consumer expenditure per unit of marketable good purchased (of a given quality) will probably decline as health improves.

2. Agricultural Subsidies[14]

Agricultural subsidies increase rates of reward to agricultural factors; food subsidies reduce food prices to consumers, particularly to low-income consumers.

A subsidy unaccompanied by output restriction will normally both increase price to producers and reduce price to consumers. Agricultural subsidies are therefore commonly accompanied by restrictions on output, either directly or by restriction of one or more types of input, especially farm land. To the extent that techniques for inducing restriction of output or input take the form of finance measures, they are included in the present discussion.

Restrictions are not imposed when a country that is a heavy importer of food-

14. This section is based on an unpublished paper of mine presented at the Columbia University Economics Research Center in 1963, which states the sources drawn upon for the factual background (information on sources will be supplied on request).

stuffs wishes to keep prices low to consumers, and pays the farmer the difference between the unsupported market price and a price agreed upon in advance as one that the farmers should receive.[15]

The subsidies have arisen in response to several conditions peculiar to agriculture.[16] One is an elasticity of less than unity that apparently characterizes demand for many farm products within a broad range of prices, coupled with the family farm's inclination to increase its labor input when its gross revenue declines owing to an increase in total output. These factors are the more important as weather, disease, and other natural forces make it impossible to predict output from a given input, and as the farmer in export agriculture finds prediction of prices for the coming year especially difficult. The increased work and misery that must be undergone before gross incomes rise again in response to weather or discouragement has been deemed too high a price to pay to obtain the advantages of a free market in farm products. If the family farm is replaced by large, more capital-intensive farm factories for certain crops (wheat, for example, but not coffee, in contrast) the response of production to a decline in gross income, to say nothing of a decline in profits, may come to resemble more that of producers in industry. Agricultural subsidies may correspondingly diminish.

A second condition peculiar to agriculture in all the countries that subsidize farmers is the large internal migration from rural areas to cities that has been induced by the rapid rise in output per worker in agriculture, resulting from great advances in technology.[17] Whether so intended or not, farm subsidies have made it easier for the migrating younger generation to take with them a bit of capital with which to start their lives in the cities. In this sense farm subsidies have been partial substitutes for urban subsidies.

A third condition is the expansion of agricultural acreage induced by many governments in World War II, to counter wartime shortages of farm labor and agricultural imports. The losses incurred during subsequent peacetime contraction of acreage were considered in part the responsibility of government.

Livestock (cattle, calves, hogs), poultry, and vegetables have one or another in some countries been left unsubsidized, presumably because those who raised or produced them experienced these three conditions less intensely. Some farm commodities have been subsidized without restriction on production[18] in an effort to replace imports in part with increased domestic output. But the aggregate market value of all these non-subsidized or non-restricted agricultural commodities is in most countries with price-support programs, perhaps in all of them, much less than that of the subsidized, restricted products. And in at least one country (United

15. As under the United Kingdom farm program.

16. An explanation based on the presumed political power of farmers implies that this concentration of power is much the same in all countries of the Western world, since agricultural subsidies are common to virtually all of them.

17. From 1936 to about 1960, a net of over 20 million persons left agriculture in the United States (L. E. Fouraker, discussant, "Wheat: a Permanent Need for a Farm Program?", *American Economic Review* [May, 1961], 51: 373).

18. In the United States, wool and, for a time, soybeans.

States) three farm sectors have accounted for the bulk of the farm-program costs: hard red winter wheat produced on the high plains, feed grains, notably corn and grain sorghums, and dairy products.

Price-support and market-price subsidy are the chief financial measures that implement farm programs. Under price support, the government buys a farmer's produce, or makes him a no-recourse loan on it, that is, the farmer is not held responsible if the government cannot sell the collateral for enough to cover the loan. The government then resells the produce on the market or destroys it or exports it at a loss.

Under market price subsidy, as noted above, the government does not intervene directly in the market; it allows the produce to find its price level and pays the farmer the difference between this and a price deemed fair or efficacious for the aims of the farm program. A third technique, open-market operations, is noted briefly below.

Either price support or market-price subsidy may be coupled with direct restrictions on input or output, or with fiscal inducements to reduce output or input in the form of negative tax subsidies. The price-support technique may be preferred if output is to be restricted, because that technique provides a way to police observance of the restriction measures. Under price support the government deals with individual farmers, one at a time; it knows their names and addresses, and can condition the price-support payment upon verification that the input or output restrictions have been observed. The price-support technique also allows the government readily to hold the product off the market, to destroy it, or to export it to an isolated market; under market-price subsidy, the government does not come into possession of the product.

The market-price subsidy technique, because it lacks these methods of policing restriction measures or of withholding output from the domestic market, normally results in a lower price to that market than does a price-support program. If no restrictions at all are placed on output, so that it expands under the stimulus of the subsidy, price to the farmer rises, as increased output encounters rising marginal cost, and price to the consumer declines, though by something less than the subsidy per unit.

The general taxpayer finances the subsidy program to a greater degree than he does the price-support program, which is carried largely by the consumers of the product. In effect, an implicit tax on the consumers of the particular commodities is imposed by a price-support program, a tax that is registered nowhere in the government's accounts, and is not isolated in the national-income accounts.

Under a price-support program, the market price can be lower than the support price as long as the government is accumulating stocks, or is reselling at once at a loss. In the latter instance, however, the difference from the market-price subsidy program is only in the policing aspect just noted.

The government may both accumulate stocks and sell enough on the market to assure that the market price stays well below the support price. The spread in price induces farmers to enter the price-support program, selling their produce to the government rather than on the market; yet prices to users are lower than they would be under a higher price-support program. Since some users are themselves pro-ducers, as when feed grains are sold to poultry raisers, intra-agricultural conflict may thus be lessened.

Price to the consumer will normally fluctuate less from year to year under price supports than under a market-price subsidy, since the government accumulates and decumulates stockpiles of the product purchased from farmers.

The subsidy technique is more effective than price support for an agricultural output that is an input on the same farm for a commodity that is itself outside the farm program. Corn, for example, fed to hogs raised on the same farm, corn being covered and hogs not covered by the farm program, illustrates this point in the United States. Since the government itself cannot buy that corn, and does not buy hogs, it cannot help this farmer by the price-support method, unless there is a large enough market in corn provided by non-integrated farms and the government adopts the technique just mentioned of keeping the market price below the support price. The integrated corn-hog farm can then sell its corn at the support price and purchase at the lower market price. But this procedure may be at least inconvenient. Instead, the government can pay the farmer a corn subsidy of so much a unit. But now the government must take measures to be assured that the farmer's declaration of amount of own corn used is not an overstatement. In general, the vertically integrated farm is likely to be at some disadvantage under a farm program that applies to his intermediate products but not to his end products.

Open market operations in a farm product by the government have some charac-teristics of each of the two chief techniques just discussed. The farmer-by-farmer approach of the price-support program is lacking, but by keeping the market price above the level it would otherwise fall to, open-market operations imply an accumu-lation of stocks by the government, and eventual sale abroad, destruction, or sale at a much later time at a loss.

Fiscal techniques to induce input restriction are usually directed at but one factor, land. Administratively, reduction of input of land is easier to verify than reduction of input of labor, fertilizer, machinery, and the like. It is also easier to measure. Technological progress is said to be discouraged less under land restric-tion, but this argument should apply almost equally to labor reduction if that were feasible.

Reduction is commonly measured from a base period, and, like a base-period excess-profits tax, the base-period type of "excess input negative tax" raises difficult problems of fairness and economic distortion. A farmer whose land produced no corn in the base period because he was practicing crop rotation cannot "reduce" his current-year planting of corn, to receive the subsidy, the negative tax. The proper length of the base period is debatable: Shall it be a two-year period? One of five years? To prevent the farmer from withdrawing only the least fertile land, an imputed yield must be attributed to each parcel of land, calculated from the yield it actually gave in the base period. If the subsidy is ad valorem, a price must be attributed to the hypothetical yield.

The question arises whether the subsidy shall be graduated. The greater the reduction in acres used, or hypothetical yield foregone, the higher, in absolute terms, could be the marginal rate of subsidy. This would be a regressive negative-tax subsidy. As the farm's input, and hence its output and revenue, increase from a highly restricted level, its marginal financial relation with the government becomes less favorable just as under an ordinary tax, but at a decreasing rate, just as under an ordinary regressive tax. This is the type of graduation likely to be adopted; the increase in flow of money from government to enterprise accelerates as input decreases, a feature that is necessary if inputs are to be decreased at minimum cost to the government, since the first decreases of input are presumably the easiest ones to induce. Moreover, a decrease of input to a certain level may be made a prerequisite to participation in a price-support program. Beyond that point, reliance is on the subsidy alone, and a higher rate of subsidy is needed.

A progressive marginal rate of a negative tax subsidy would be awkward; the marginal rate would suddenly decline from a high level to zero at the base period level of input, where the subsidy is no longer paid. Regressive graduation of marginal rate of a negative-tax subsidy may be coupled with something analogous to a dwindling personal exemption for income taxation (see pages 219, 329). Farmers with less than a certain amount of acreage may be paid for retiring all their base-period acreage rather than only for a reduction up to a certain percentage of the farm's base-period acreage. On the other hand, the fiscal inducement to input reduction may consist simply in eligibility to participate in the price support or subsidy program. The negative-tax subsidy is then only a threshold negative tax, itself yielding no revenue to the farmer, but taking away all his revenue from price support or subsidy if he fails to make the threshold reduction.

Finally, the analogue of a lump-sum tax is found in some farm programs: mandatory reduction of input of a factor, coupled with a payment to the farmer. This is a negative-tax subsidy, conditioned on the existence of a state of affairs that the negative tax itself in no way induces. To be sure, at a level of decision higher than that of the single farmer, the payment may be considered an incentive offered to producers as a group for accepting a mandatory input-reduction program. Still, there will always be some who are opposed to the regime, but must live with it; to them the negative-tax subsidy is a pure lump-sum negative tax.

The input of one factor, credit, is commonly subsidized by the government to farms. Other instances of subsidized factor input occur occasionally.[19]

Fiscal techniques to induce output restriction, in contrast to input restriction, are rare because a fixed degree of effective output restriction is not usually feasible under any technique. The weather, for one thing, can thwart a low-output goal. Harvesting restrictions and, above all, marketing restrictions are feasible. They are normally accomplished by direct controls and so will not be examined here in detail. A fiscal device, a positive tax for example, would not be effective once the crop had been produced, except as costs of marketing the already produced crop were significant relative to the costs of holding for later sale. Otherwise, the already produced crop would be in perfectly inelastic supply and would be marketed for what it would bring,

---

19. For example, a 1961 proposal in the United States that the Commodity Credit Corporation sell feed at 75 per cent of the support price to cattle grazers, as contrasted with cattle feeders, who had been damaged by the drought.

provided that that amount exceeded the tax. Only a prohibitive tax, which is in effect a direct-control measure, would have any effect.

The direct controls that are not covered here, because they involve no public finance measures, no flows of funds to or from the government , include controls on acreage (acreage allotments), marketing quotas, restrictions on entry, and price controls that prohibit sale at less than a stipulated minimum price.[20]

Most, perhaps virtually all, of the benefits from a program of price-support payments and negative taxes on inputs tend to go to the individual who owned the farm, or the allotment attached to the farm, when the program of payments or negative taxes was introduced, or the rates raised. The prospective stream of payments was capitalized in the price of the farm land. Subsequent purchasers of the land therefore tended to benefit little if at all. The tenant farmer or sharecropper receives none of the payment. Factors producing complementary producers' goods, especially fertilizer and farm machinery, benefit from the change in factor-mix induced by these programs, but this is not a benefit that has been diverted from the owners of the land.

The benefits of a market-price subsidy will be divided between producer and consumer, as indicated above, directly with relative elasticities of demand and supply, respectively, unless the subsidy is accompanied by input restriction.

Agricultural programs rank fairly high in the explicitness with which the law states the conditions for receiving the subsidy, and in the impersonality of those conditions. The criterion of continuity of the subsidy function, or negative-tax function, is fairly well observed even under price-support programs; this criterion is easier to follow under market-price subsidies. Administrative equity criteria are often violated, partly because of the technical complexity of some of the price-support subsidies. There is room for interpretation of the law by administrators, and compliance with the subsidy rules probably costs more, in percentage of crop revenue, for the small farmer.

The subsidies, price-support or otherwise, tend to increase in periods of recession because of slightly reduced demand for farm products, but this tendency can easily be more than offset by variations in weather and foreign demand. Except for the few instances of lump-sum subsidies, excess burden is created; the rate of substitution between the subsidized product and an unsubsidized product is for consumers made to differ from the rate of transformation in the production of those commodities. Price supports turn domestic consumers to other commodities or to foreign sources; subsidies turn domestic consumers toward the subsidized product and away from imports. When a subsidy is granted for reducing input of one factor, commonly land, an increasingly intensive margin of cultivation for the product grown on the land is encouraged, leading to a higher marginal cost, ex-subsidy. Price support for

20. Thus, under "market orders" in the United States, regional groups of producers can agree, with the approval of the Secretary of Agriculture, that their product shall be sold only at certain prices, or higher, or that the total quantity sold shall be fixed. Milk is a prominent example of a product subject to market orders. Some part of the resulting price of milk to consumers might be thought of as a tax levied by the producers on consumers with the aid of the government, but that view is not taken here; market orders are not regarded as public finance instruments.

a commodity that is used as an input at subsequent stages likewise induces an inefficient factor mix.

Distribution of farm subsidies and price-support payments by income class have presumably been regressive, analogous to progressive taxation, if the income classes taken are those that existed before the farm programs were enacted. The farm owners in that period of distress were probably disproportionately in the low-income classes of the entire population in those countries that adopted farm programs. Within the farm owning group, however, the subsidies and payments have probably always been progressive by income. At the present time, a measurement of regressivity or progressivity has limited meaning, insofar as present farm owners have had to pay for the farm benefits in the price of the land they have purchased.[21]

The financing of the subsidy, as distinct from the subsidy itself, is another matter. Under a price-support program the financing is almost surely regressive with consumer income (see the remarks above on the implicit tax), but under a market-price subsidy all depends on the type of tax used to finance the program.

The reallocation criteria most involved are those of risk-taking and work versus leisure. The farm programs reduce the dispersion of probability-weighted outcomes and so reduce the amount of risk available to be taken. And they increase the amount of leisure taken by preventing drastic declines in gross revenue that, through the income effect, drive farm families to more work.

The effect of farm-program payments on tax revenues and other fiscal sectors of the paying government (intra-system reactions) must be important, but they are difficult to discern. Part of the cost of farm subsidies is no doubt recouped automatically through income taxation of large farmers, but farms pay so little income tax in the aggregate that the percentage thus recovered is probably modest. Certain government expenditures, notably those for relief, are presumably lower than they would be, at least in some years, if farm production were unregulated and unsubsidized.

Some part of the increase in farm income is saved, but the significance of this fact for economic growth is limited in this partial-equilibirum approach that abstracts from the taxes levied to finance the program. If consumers' elasticity of demand for the affected products is less than unity, they will spend less than under no program if the market-price subsidy system is used, but more than under no program if the price-support crop-restriction system is used. Only in the former case is some consumer income released for possible saving.

The structure of foreign trade has been historically an important factor in the choice between the market-price subsidy program and the price-support program. A country that is a large importer of foodstuffs will tend to choose the market-price subsidy method, to avoid political repercussions from consumers, who must pay a sizable increment, most of which will accrue to the government as protective duties rather than to the domestic farmer.[22] A country that exports a large part of its

21. For an analysis of the distributive effects of the United States farm program, see John E. Floyd, "The Effects of Farm Price Supports on the Returns to Land and Labor in Agriculture," *Journal of Political Economy* (April, 1965), 73: 148–58.

22. If the importing country obtains its food supplies largely from affiliated countries against which it is reluctant to impose protective tariffs, it has almost no choice but to use the market-

agricultural output will be more willing to raise domestic prices of its farm products keeping the export price below the domestic level.

3. Food Subsidies

Food subsidies, contrasted with agricultural subsidies, are designed to reduce food prices to consumers rather than increase factor rewards to purchasers. Any farm program that uses the market-price subsidy technique will accomplish both aims to a degree. But the extreme case of a food subsidy is that where the total supply of food is more or less fixed for the period in question, as under a blockade. If the price system were allowed to operate freely in the face of unequal distribution of money income and wealth, the resulting distress of the poor would prove socially and politically unacceptable. More generally, even when the food in question is being produced freely up to marginal costs, some poor households will buy so little of it that again social and political considerations will dictate increasing their consumption of it. These households are then offered the food at a subsidized price. A means test is implied, but rationing is not, other than by the subsidized price.

A mixed program of agricultural aid and food subsidies develops when the government buys up part of a crop at a support price and then seeks to dispose of its stockpile to households who would not have purchased it in the first place. The government will then sell the food to these consumers at well below market price, or distribute it free, on a means-test basis and with some policing to prevent resale. A food subsidy may be a substitute for an exemption of foodstuffs under a general sales tax.[23]

4. Transportation Subsidies

No country subsidizes transportation in general. Instead, certain modes are subsidized for reasons peculiar to those modes. A non-toll highway, or other infrastructure supplied at zero price is technically not a subsidy, as that term is used here, though of course it as well as any other free government service to the transport industry must be included in any comparison of treatment of the several forms of transportation. If the government sells the use of the infrastructure at prices that do not cover costs, it is granting a subsidy, not supplying a free government service.

In two major modes of transportation, walking and travel by motor vehicle, the user supplies his own means of locomotion; the private airplane and private boat exemplify minor modes of this type. The user is thereby in a position to create

price subsidy method. This fact, and the other differences just referred to in international trade patterns, probably explain why the United Kingdom employs the market-price subsidy method and the United States the price-support method.

23. See Chapter 9, page 247, note 6.

congestion, defined as a state of affairs in which the subtraction of one vehicle or pedestrian would decrease the costs incurred by all others who are using the infrastructure at the same time. Congestion occurs also when the user does not supply his own means of locomotion, as in mass transit. No one mass transit rider by himself, however, can cause the congestion without the consent of the owner of the vehicle. Ownership of the vehicle gives power to exclude any particular individual from consuming this mode of transportation at any particular time over any specified route. In contrast, the government, as owner of the highway system or of the street system, has not yet developed an acceptable method of excluding any person it wants to at any chosen time from using any specified part of the infrastructure. Until engineers develop such a method it is more realistic to view the users of most highways and streets as being free to create congestion costs as they wish. Since congestion is a cost, it reflects a subsidy to consumption when it is not matched by a price to cover the cost; it is then free congestion. The subsidy is unwillingly or even inadvertently paid by the users of the highway or street to each other. The congestion may be so intense that one additional user of the highway gains no more for himself than the total of what he subtracts from others, or it may be even more intense, so that one more user causes more cost to others than the benefit he receives.

Certain transportation subsidies are a product of inflation, and in this sense are inadvertent, not having been planned or even anticipated by anyone. A private monopoly of some mode of transportation, being commonly subject to regulation, can be prevented from raising the fare to match a general increase in prices and costs, while being compelled to continue service as long as its working capital holds out, perhaps for many years. Such a restriction is the more likely to be imposed if users of the service have no close substitutes for it and find the service essential to earning a living without changing either job or residence. When replacement or maintenance can no longer be deferred, the owners of the system sell it or abandon it to the government, which then must inject massive subsidies if it is not to raise the price of transport.

If the government itself owns the infrastructure and vehicles, resistance to a rise in fare will be expressed directly at the polls, especially by low-income mass transit riders. Even an increase in the motor fuel tax will provoke political disturbances in a country where the low-income workers ride buses. The poor do not like the price system, because they are poor and do not intend to allow it to remove from them a redistribution of real income in their favor that has been effected by an inflation-caused lag of prices behind cost of replacement and maintenance. Transportation subsidies to rail and bus lines, especially in certain of the less developed countries, would have been much lower in real terms if no general rise in prices had occurred.

Merchant marine subsidies have commonly been given to maintain a fleet of ships and crews to man them that would be needed in time of war. Ship construction has been subsidized on condition that the ships be readily convertible to troop transport. Railroad networks have been designed in large part for troop movements to frontiers. The cost of all these subsidies could logically appear in the military budget.

Certain airline subsidies are inputs to a government service best described as national prestige.

Mass transit subsidies are chiefly subsidies to the expense of earning an income. These or other passenger transportation subsidies are sometimes offered only to users who pass means tests or who travel at times and in modes that imply a low income. The aim then is to increase the real income of the poor or to increase incentive to work by reducing one cost of working, commuting. To achieve these ends the service must be rendered in a form that makes it non-resaleable; tickets or tokens, for instance, must be non-transferable.

Whether highways, which are used largely as a consumers' good, are subsidized by governments in advanced industrial countries is a disputed question of fact. Free congestion, we have seen, reflects a subsidy, but not one provided by the government. The revenue from motor fuel taxes and motor vehicle taxes in most of these countries is of the same order of magnitude as expenditures on highways and streets. But these quasi-prices are only loosely related to the costs of particular segments of the system. The cost of constructing urban motor expressways, millions of dollars a mile, is probably nowhere nearly covered by the tax revenue from motor fuel used on these segments plus revenues from motor vehicle taxes even if allocated entirely to such segments. On the other hand, some highways may increase values of certain properties more than they decrease values of others, so that a part of the expense may in principle be covered by a tax on increments in real estate values, provided that decreases in values give rise to tax relief.

Subsidization of transportation for use as a consumers' good is supported on the grounds that lumpiness of infrastructure and, in the supersonic age, even of the vehicle, results in so low a marginal cost of carrying one more passenger or parcel of freight, within a wide capacity range, that a price based on that marginal cost will leave uncovered a very large part of total costs. In principle, this problem could be met by a differential pricing schedule announced to prospective users and based on some one of many possible ways of allocating disposable consumers' surplus, before construction of the infrastructure or the vehicle is started. If the prospective consumers' responsiveness indicated that total costs could be covered, no subsidy would be required; if the responses indicated that total costs could not be covered, lumpiness itself would offer no grounds for proceeding. But in practice no such predetermined differential pricing is practicable. The argument then runs that, rather than do nothing, it is preferable to construct the supersonic plane, or the bridge, then set the fare to cover operating costs (exclusive of depreciation and interest) and congestion costs, and finance the rest of the total cost, if it is not covered by the congestion fee, by some tax that hopefully does not disturb margins of economic activity. The difficulty of finding such taxes weakens this argument, and if they can be found, questions of equity arise; why should one man's economic rent help finance another man's consumer good?

Excepting elevator service, transportation subsidies rarely reach 100 per cent, where transportation would be a free government service distributed without rationing. Transportation is a consumer good that is enjoyable in itself, or is a cost-reducing intermediate good, far more than is, say, medical care, and the demand for it at prices approaching zero is correspondingly more elastic, leading to great outlay by a government that supplies it at zero price.

Implicit or explicit interest and depreciation charges on infrastructure or equipment owned by the government or donated by it to private concerns are rarely listed in the public accounts as transportation expenses. The subsidy to transport is correspondingly understated.

The subsidy, more often than not, is a subsidy of long-run costs. If long-run marginal costs for a transportation industry are decreasing, the subsidy reduces fares or freight charges by more than the subsidy. If those costs are increasing, the fares or freight charges fall by less than the subsidy, which is therefore captured in part by the specialized factors retained in, and called into, the industry, or not expelled from it, as the industry sells more units of service than it would at an unsubsidized price. The division of the subsidy benefit between users and factors depends on relative elasticities of supply and demand. Elasticity of demand is probably rather small for a mass transit system service, given all other conditions, including the rate of technological improvement in competing modes of transport. If competitive pricing is followed, the fare will therefore decrease by almost the amount of the subsidy. The increasing-cost element will have little effect on output, since demand will not expand appreciably in any event.

If demand is more elastic, price to users declines by less. The amount of benefit varies as between the units of use that would occur under no subsidy (basic units of use) and the units of use attracted to the industry by the subsidized price. The phrase "units of use" is employed, since any one person will normally account both for some of the basic units and some of the newly attracted units of use. The newly attracted units receive less benefit than the basic units, and there is of course almost no benefit to those units of use that are only just attracted to the system by the subsidized price.

The subsidy may, but in practice rarely does, include only transportation that is limited to geographical areas that are close substitutes for other areas served by unsubsidized transportation. In this event, some of the subsidy benefit will be relinquished to landowners in the favored areas, through higher rents. Another version of this case may occur when a transit system has been varying its fare according to distance. If a subsidy is then introduced that makes the net fare vary less with distance, the commuter will increase his demand for the more remote location. If the commuter has the option of living within walking distance of his work, a subsidy to transportation will increase his demand for the remote site, raising rents there and lowering them in the walk-to-work area. This option usually does not exist for more than a small proportion of the working force.

The opposite case, where the subsidy has little or no influence on dwelling site rents, is exemplified by a large urban mass transit system that will in any event be charging a flat fare regardless of distance.[24] A lowering of such a fare through a subsidy will not disturb the relative attractiveness or more and less distant sites. The subsidy will go entirely to increase the real income of the commuters, at least if it reduces long-run costs that are fairly constant. (This analysis abstracts from measures

24. The New York City subway system, for example.

of financing the subsidy.) This kind of mass transit subsidy will therefore not encourage decentralization of dwelling accommodation.

A business-firm user of subsidized transportation will pass all of it on to its vendees, and the subsidy will accrue in its entirety, ultimately, to consumers of the products thus transported, if the industry to which these firms belong is a competitive one of constant cost. Factors in increasing-cost industries will retain part of the subsidy (see Chapter 6).

Subsidized transportation is largely an intermediate product, and one, moreover, that commonly facilitates production of free government services. The consonance of transportation subsidies with the criteria of Chapter 2 can therefore be ascertained in part by reference to the appraisal of those free services in Chapter 5.

The equity criteria of the consensus type are less applicable to transportation subsidies than to almost any other measure of public finance. Each subsidy is usually paid to one or a few large business concerns, and impersonalization is correspondingly limited. But it is observed in the sense that the business firm receiving the subsidy is not allowed to discriminate on a personal basis among the users of the service who benefit from the subsidy. If discrimination is practiced, it is at the command of the subsidizing government, designed again to serve certain government ends: education, for example, if reduced fares on transit systems are granted to schoolchildren. The terms of some of the subsidies are complex, those for the merchant marine construction program, for instance, with corresponding dangers of discontinuities and even lapses of explicitness of conditions for receiving the subsidy. These matters of detail are not covered here.

A full employment policy over a potential business cycle is hindered by subsidies of current operating costs, since the amounts paid decline with decline in business. The built-in flexibility is perverse. Subsidies for the construction of infrastructure can only in rare cases be timed to check a recession or promote recovery. The lead time needed for planning is too great and the period of construction is too long for the bulk of the projects.

The subsidies are not usually of the lump-sum type, but they remove, rather than create, an excess burden, if they enable price to be closer to marginal cost in both the long run and the short run. Moreover, the subsidies are usually designed to capture certain other positive externalities.

As to the conflict equity criteria, no generalization seems feasible for the transportation subsidies, because of the wide variety of ends the subsidies serve. Quite probably these subsidies on the whole tend to yield benefits that are distributed regressively by income or wealth, but with a number of exceptions. The geographical pattern of the benefits is designedly very uneven.

Among the reallocation criteria, that of economic growth is relevant, since these subsidies result in large additions to the economy's capital equipment, gross. Whether the increase is also net depends on the source of financing. And there is no assurance that the increased transportation service will itself be used to promote capital investment.

External equilibrium is commonly a reason given for transport subsidies: availability of domestic shipping and airlines reduces the need for foreign exchange;

exports can be increased by subsidizing outbound rail traffic. Under some circumstances, a generalized subsidy to freight can improve the balance of payments. To take a polar case, let us suppose that all domestic production for export is located in the center of a large country and virtually all consumers live along the periphery. Subsidized freight rates then stimulate exports but not imports; the subsidy is something like a devaluation, for current trade purposes, of the country's currency. This extreme case is approached in certain underdeveloped countries that export extractive materials from the interior but import chiefly consumer goods for a populace living near the ports.

5. Postal Service

Postal deficits are the rule in most countries, for several reasons.

Literacy in less developed countries is increased if newly educated adults and children are given incentives to read and write. A subsidized postal service provides such an incentive, at a cost that is relatively low. Even completely free postal service for household mailing of letters and postcards could be justified on these grounds, as well as reduced or free postage for journals and newspapers, at least to consumers in remote parts of the country.

In countries that have experienced inflation much of the postal subsidy is of the inadvertent type. The level of service is correspondingly low, as postal administrators seek to reduce the deficit by holding down costs.

In highly industrialized countries first-class mail usually pays its way. The postal deficit reflects the social importance attached to wide circulation of journals and to a low-cost parcel service, especially between rural areas and the cities.

Parcel transport (but never first-class mail) is in some countries supplied by private firms, which are protected from government competition by size and weight limits on parcel post. Conceivably, a private firm might be granted a monopoly of the postal service, under rate regulation, but its incentives for efficient operation and adequate extension of the service might be impaired if it were required to operate at a deficit to be covered by government subsidy. The benefits of subsidized postal service to households are divided between sender and recipient in unknown ratios. Firms presumably relinquish the benefits of postal subsidies owing to competition, and consumers benefit unequally, depending on their consumption patterns.

The classification commonly employed by policy-makers in determining size of subsidy is that of letter mail, journal mail, circular mail, and parcel post. With ingenuity, however, the postal subsidy could be restricted to household-to-household mail, perhaps through distinctive letter forms and labels supplied by the government.

The postal subsidy ranks high under the consensus type of equity criteria. The conditions of use of the subsidized service are stated explicitly, no jumps or gaps occur in the subsidy function, and little or no personalization is found in the postal-service laws. Even at the administrative level, while inefficiencies may abound, there seems to be little personal discrimination by the postal officials or employees against particular households or firms. The two efficiency criteria, on the other hand, are not observed, except as a deficit may be viewed as an attempt to capture externalities.

With respect to the goal of full employment, the postal service might be utilized somewhat more than it has been in most countries. The large numbers of temporary mail carriers that are successfully used in periods of peak loads, to handle Christmas mail for example, suggest that in a recession some of the unemployed could be hired and the number of deliveries per day increased. Advance planning of postal facilities might allow some speeding up or postponement of construction of post offices, to accord with the state of employment.

The benefits of postal subsidies are on the whole quite regressive with respect to income and wealth, except over the lowest ranges of income, since the very poor make little use of subsidized postal service unless the subsidy is 100 per cent. The postal subsidy takes no account of differences in family status, though here again some ingenuity might prove fruitful. The geographical impact of the subsidies is often highly differential, often intentionally so, as the subsidy may be tailored to raise the level of communication with remote parts of the country.

6. Medical Care

Subsidized medical care lies between free medical care, analyzed in Chapter 5, and sale at a competitive price. Direct rationing of medical care, it will be recalled from Chapter 5, is difficult, yet unrationed free medical care may cost more than the community is willing to pay. The objectives can be achieved for the most part at a far lower cost if the government defrays only some part of the medical bill, or itself supplies medical care at a price well below cost. Price is then the rationing instrument, except possibly with respect to those so poor that they are allowed free medical care under a means test.

The percentage of the medical bill covered by the government can be made steeply progressive, reaching 100 per cent above some level, for each illness or accident. This formula protects households against uninsurable money drains of large size.

7. Export and Import Subsidies

An export subsidy is not usually applied to all exports, except in hidden form, as when freight rates are tailored to this purpose (see Section 4 above), or through multiple exchange rates (pages 424–25). Insofar as all exports are subsidized equally, the action is tantamount to a devaluation of the currency for trade purposes that is incomplete unless a corresponding tax is placed on imports. A general subsidy of exports is usually motivated by balance-of-payment considerations rather than by concern for any particular industry or group of factors. Whether the aim is achieved depends largely on the elasticity of demand for exports.

Exemption of exports from sales taxation and refund of sales taxes embodied in the exported good's price from earlier stages are discussed in Chapter 8.

A subsidy to exports of a particular product that accounts for only a part of total exports is usually designed to increase the rewards of domestic factors engaged in the industry and has little connection with balance-of-payments difficulties. The degree of success of such a measure depends on the elasticity of foreign demand for the subsidized good. At one extreme, if demand is perfectly inelastic (an unlikely case) the money value of export sales plus subsidy is the same as that of export sales before the subsidy was in force, and the factors gain nothing, unless the subsidy is exempt from income tax. All the benefit of the subsidy goes to foreign consumers. At the other extreme, if foreign demand is perfectly elastic, a likely case for a small country in a world market, the subsidy will increase producers' surplus in the industry by an amount equal to the aggregate subsidy less, approximately, one-half of the following amount: the increase in unit sales times the per unit rate of subsidy. A small country exporting staple raw materials to the world market can therefore usually redirect a part of the national income to the factors in one or more of its exporting industries. The factors so benefited will be those most specialized to the industry, notably certain types of land and specialized labor.

The built-in flexibility of export subsidies is usually perverse. In a recession, especially one due partly to a fall in the demand for exports, the aggregate subsidy paid declines. An unchanging lump-sum subsidy to the exporting industries would be preferable for the goal of full employment, but almost surely not for any of the main aims of the subsidy. These remarks apply also to import subsidies in the sense that a decline of activity brings with it a decline in subsidy payment.

A subsidy of a certain type of import is usually but part of a wider subsidy scheme, as when subsidized exports carry some import content, or when the supply of a consumer necessity, certain foodstuffs for example, has declined drastically and a temporary expansion of imports is sought as a means of averting price increases that would severely affect low-income households.[25]

25. For subsidies to monopolies, see Chapter 21; for tax exemptions viewed as subsidies, see pages 54 and 150–51.

BOOK TWO
Micro Public Finance
Part II: Government Receipts

CHAPTER EIGHT

General Sales Taxes: Turnover
Tax and Intermediate Single-Stage Taxes

IN THE ORDER OF their appearance historically, the general sales taxes are the turnover tax, the manufacturers' sales tax, the wholesale sales tax, the retail sales tax, and the value-added tax. It happens that each of these taxes discriminates less than its immediate predecessor among types of business and methods of doing business. Analytically it might therefore be more convenient to start with the value-added tax, which exerts a uniform impact, and appraise the others as deviants from this archetype. But the historical order is followed here, to emphasize the social and economic pressures for uniformity of treatment that have shaped the development of general sales taxation over some five decades.

An expenditure tax collected from households, although its aggregate base is the same as that of a true retail sales tax, is discussed in Chapter 13, as an alternative to the income tax. It affords the same opportunity as does the income tax to vary the tax bill according to family size and composition and to apply a progressive rate scale.

A. TURNOVER TAX

The modern turnover tax,[1] dating from the last years of World War I, represented an attempt to collect large amounts of revenue with tax administrative machines that had been crippled by war, in countries struggling with inflation. The basic premises of those who introduced the tax were two. First, in these circumstances

1. Of the 24 countries to adopt a turnover tax up to 1968, 12 had abandoned it by that year, and three more plan to do so by 1970. The tax will then be found only in Austria, Mexico, certain states in India, and the socialist economies of eastern Europe, Russia, and China. See note 47. The only conversions to a turnover tax from another general sales tax were in the Netherlands, under the German occupation (from a manufacturers' sales tax) and in Italy, which moved from its retail sales tax of 1919–20 to a turnover tax excluding retail sales (finally included in 1940). Japan repealed its turnover tax of 1948 in 1950, not replacing it with any general sales tax. See Due, *Sales Taxation, passim,* for details on turnover taxes other than those of the socialist countries.

rates of evasion could be restricted, and perhaps made nearly equal (see Chapter 2), and costs of compliance could be made nearly equal, only under a tax collectible from business firms, not households, and imposed at a rate low enough so that few firms would find it worth while to risk incurring the penalties of evasion. Second, only an ad valorem tax without specific money-stated exemptions, brackets, and the like would maintain the real revenue yield during an inflation, without severe damage to the structure of the tax.

Events were to prove the first of these premises false, in several of the countries that tried the tax; they came to prefer a higher rate of tax on something less than the entire volume of business transactions. The second premise, in contrast, proved sound. The ad valorem tax, freed from all specific money-stated amounts, did not decline in real yield as prices rose, as would a specific excise tax, based on a physical quantity, and the simple internal structure of the tax was not damaged, in contrast with the distortion of the progressive income tax (see Chapter 12).

1. Conceptual Basis of Turnover Tax

In its basic form the turnover tax strikes all transfers for a consideration in the production and distribution of goods and services. By excluding transfers within a single business firm, the government avoids difficult problems of valuation. A transfer between parties adverse in interest, a buyer and a seller independent of one another, each desiring a price advantage, usually generates memoranda, documents, invoices, and other papers bearing on value.

By excluding transfers not directly part of the production-distribution process, the government purports to remove grounds for complaint by taxpayers, since they are assumed able to incorporate the tax in selling price. The weakness of this assumption is revealed in the numerous departures from the basic concept of the turnover tax, the exemption of farmers for example, that will be described below.

With respect to foreign trade, any sales tax disposes of several alternative methods of treatment. The full list of seven possibilities is given in Table 2. For this purpose a commodity or service is classed as being either (1) produced at home (H) and consumed at home (h), (2) produced at home (H) and consumed abroad (a), or (3) produced abroad (A) and consumed at home (h). Each class of goods may be either taxable or exempt, hence the seven combinations in Table 2, plus the no-tax combination.

Some of these seven combinations are rarely encountered: the universal type, which taxes imports, exports, and goods produced for home use (No. 1 in the table);[2] the domestic-only type, which exempts both exports and imports (No. 4);[3] and the

2. France taxed exports for a brief period, in 1926–27, under the turnover tax (Carl S. Shoup, *The Sales Tax in France* [New York: Columbia University Press, 1930], pp. 43–44, 87–88).

3. A local unit with constitutionally limited taxing powers may have to use a combination that approaches the domestic-only tax. Under New York City's general business and financial tax, a form of turnover tax, gross receipts from interstate transactions had to be apportioned;

export-import type, which exempts goods produced for home use (No. 5). The origin-principle sales tax (No. 2), which exempts only imports, is employed chiefly by subordinate units of government that possess no power at all to tax imports from the rest of the country. Exports can be taxed by a local unit without endangering the exchange value of the currency, although the local unit may of course suffer from emigration of factors. The origin principle is being considered for eventual use at the national level in economic unions with respect to trade among members, so that border controls within the union can be dispensed with. In passing, we note that the origin principle is the prevailing form for income taxation.

Thus the combinations characteristic of sales taxes are the remaining three: the destination-principle type (No. 3), which exempts exports but taxes imports;[4] the export tax (No. 6); and the import tax (No. 7), usually a protective tariff. Neither the export tax nor the import tax is commonly a general tax, on all exports, or all imports; they will therefore be discussed in Chapters 10 (Excises) and 16 (Export Taxes, Import Taxes). The choice for a turnover tax is therefore between the destination principle and the origin principle.

Table 2   Types of Sales Taxes with Respect to International Trade

Type	Hh^a	Ha^b	Ah^c	Designation
1	T	T	T	Universal Sales Tax
2	T	T	E	Origin-Principle Sales Tax
3	T	E	T	Destination-Principle Sales Tax
4	T	E	E	Domestic-Only Sales Tax (Pro-international-trade)
5	E	T	T	Export-Import Sales Tax (Anti-international-trade)
6	E	T	E	Export Tax
7	E	E	T	Import Tax
8	E	E	E	No Tax

KEY: T = Taxable   h = Consumed at home
        E = Exempt   A = Produced abroad
        H = Produced at home   a = Consumed abroad

[a] Non-trade-goods, import-competing goods, and exportables consumed domestically.
[b] Exported goods.
[c] Imported goods.

If exchange rates were flexible and if there were no flows of capital, return on capital, or unrequited payments between countries, a change from the destination principle to the origin principle would have no economic consequences aside from division of the tax revenue among the taxing countries.[5] The currency of the country that substituted the origin principle for the destination principle would de-

the tax could be imposed only on the part allocable to the city. For details, see Robert M. Haig and Carl S. Shoup, *The Financial Problem of the City of New York* (New York, privately printed, June, 1952), pp. 214–15.

4. In practice, imports of certain kinds of service are difficult or impossible to reach: travel abroad, for example.

5. Carl S. Shoup, "Taxation Aspects of International Economic Integration," in Institut International de Finances Publiques, *Aspects financiers et fiscaux de l'intégration economique internationale* (The Hague: van Stockum, 1954), pp. 91–93, and references there cited, especially the Tinbergen Committee Report of 1953.

preciate, to restore external equilibrium with no change in allocation of resources except those that the transition period might induce temporarily. But since the conditions for economic equivalence of the two principles are not normally present in the real world, it seems advisable to contrast their initial pressures on imports and exports of two countries under an unchanged exchange rate.

In any event, the distinction between the destination principle and origin principle for the turnover tax is somewhat less important than might be thought at first, owing to the cumulative feature of that tax. An origin-principle tax is applied to exports but not of course to transactions in another country. An exporting country that substitutes the origin principle for the destination principle still taxes only a fraction of the total cumulated tax base of the exported commodity, since it cannot tax the marketing transfers that occur in the consuming country at the wholesale and retail stages. Only the consuming country can impose a turnover tax on the marketing stages, whether the destination or origin principle is used. And it follows that the consuming country is likely to get the larger share of the total turnover tax on a commodity that moves in international trade, even under the origin principle, since the early-stage values added in the producing country are repeated in the tax base when the wholesaler and retailer are taxed in the consuming country. Accordingly, a difference in tax rate between the producing country and the consuming country puts less pressure on consumer demand to move from one country's manufactures to another's than the tax-rate difference might at first seem to indicate.[6]

6. A numerical example may help to fix this idea. A commodity is produced in Country A and is exported to Country B. An origin-principle turnover tax is imposed, at a rate of 10 per cent of the price, including the tax. The first tax in A is upon sale of, say $10 worth of raw materials to a manufacturer in A. The turnover tax is collected again upon sale of the finished good, say for $50, by the manufacturer in A to a wholesaler in B. The commodity is sold by the wholesaler in B to a retailer in B for $60, and is resold by the retailer for $100. The cumulated turnover tax revenue at the 10 per cent rate for both countries will be divided between the governments of A and B, under the origin principle, and alternatively under the destination principle, as follows:

	Origin Principle		Destination Principle	
	A	B	A	B
Upon sale by: raw materials producer	1	–	0	–
manufacturer	5	–	0	–
Upon importation	–	0	–	6
Upon sale by: wholesaler	–	6	–	6
retailer	–	10	–	10
Totals	6	16	0	22

If A and B start each with the destination principle and both change to the origin principle, only 6/22 of the cumulated tax on this commodity is shifted over to the treasury of A, the producing country. Let A now decide to increase the rate of its origin-principle tax to 30 per cent, while the consuming country B keeps its rate at 10 per cent. A's manufacturers are not as severely burdened, in competing with B's manufacturers for the market in B, as might at first appear. The difference in tax rates, 20 percentage points, applies to only a small part of the retail value, including tax. In the example above the cumulated tax on the commodity produced in A and exported to B would be 34 per cent. If domestic production in B has the same stages as does production in A, a competing domestically produced good in B pays a cumulated tax of 22 per cent of retail price. The tripling of A's turnover tax rate from 10 per cent to 30 per cent increases the tax load on its product from 22 per cent to 34 per cent, that is, only about one-half instead of twice.

Under a single-stage sales tax, for example, the manufacturers' sales tax to be examined in Section B below, a nominal difference between rates represents a similar real difference. The distinction between the origin and the destination principles is far more important for international trade under a manufacturers' sales tax than under a turnover tax.

If the origin principle were in use, conceivably the country of origin, A, might agree to pay to the country of destination, B, the amount of tax that it, A, collected on goods exported to and consumed in B, in return for a similar understanding for goods exported from B to A. The division of tax revenue would be the same as under the destination principle, if the two countries imposed the same tax rate. It would be the same, even if the ostensible rates differed, provided certain technical features obtained, to be noted in Chapter 9 below on the value-added tax (use of the tax-credit method). At the same time, certain administrative advantages would be gained, since it is simpler not to exempt exports and not to tax imports than to exempt and tax.

This combination of origin-principle tax base and destination-principle division of revenues is sometimes termed the "consumption type" of origin-principle taxation, as it is the consumer country that gets all the revenue, but this terminology conflicts with use of the term "consumption type" of value-added tax to denote a tax that excludes capital goods completely from its base, as explained in Chapter 9 below. A combination of origin-principle tax base and destination-principle allocation of revenue is therefore here termed a "consumer-country" type of sales tax.

Since it is impossible to ascertain just how much turnover tax has become embedded in any given export good, even under the unrealistic assumption that forward shifting of the tax has been complete, the turnover tax law or regulations (destination principle) commonly stipulates a few alternative tax rates for computing the export refund. Each rate is applied to a specified class of goods in the hope that this will serve adequately, though of course not precisely, to adjust burdens among competing industries. The tax refund will in principle include any import compensating tax embedded in a commodity made partly from imported materials. The tax paid by a firm that sold directly to an export trader can be easily ascertained, and the precise amount can be refunded to the trader, but computation of tax embedded from earlier stages can never be exact.[7] And the shifting must be estimated in the differential sense, e.g., compared with selling prices under a corporation income tax.

The base of the import compensating tax, or "turnover equalization tax,"[8] is

---

7. In Germany, there is refund of the 4 per cent tax on the sale that the manufacturer made to the export trader; this refund is 4 per cent of 92 per cent of the export trader's sale price, on the assumption that he obtains an 8 per cent profit margin. Rebate for prior turnover tax "is computed on a sliding scale (between 0.5% and 3%), depending on the nature of the exported product. . . ." The estimated import compensating tax that was paid on material entering into the export good is also taken into account (Henry J. Gumpel and Carl Boettcher [correspondent], *Taxation in the Federal Republic of Germany*, World Tax Series, Law School of Harvard University [Chicago: Commerce Clearing House, 1963], p. 826. Germany replaced the turnover tax by a value-added tax effective January 1, 1968.

8. "Umsatz-Ausgleichsteuer" in Germany (*ibid.*, p. 827).

usually the customs value, including customs duty and excise taxes if any. It is not possible to compute exactly the cumulated turnover tax that any particular good would have paid had it been produced within the taxing country, if only because that amount would depend on what particular firms had produced it. The degree to which the domestic tax would have been absorbed by factors rather than raising the relative price (compared, e.g., with results under a corporation income tax) is also unknown.

If, in the face of these uncertainties, the importing country contents itself with imposing only the rate of tax that applies on a single transfer,[9] that country will in most instances fall short of imposing a truly compensating tax. To tax an imported good only at the statutory rate applicable to each single transfer is to imply that the good, had it been produced domestically, would have been taxed but once, that is, it would have been produced by a vertically integrated firm. An offsetting factor, in addition to the possibility just mentioned that part of the tax would have been absorbed by factors of production, is that importation may not be accompanied by a sale; hence the imported good may experience an extra tax, compared with a domestically produced good, in the differential sense.

If the importing country attempts to make the import tax truly compensating, a series of rates must be set up, for various classes of goods,[10] as a rough approximation to take account of the varying number of taxable transfers each class of goods would have experienced had they been produced at home.

2. Incidence in an Open Economy

In a closed economy the question what is the incidence of a general turnover tax is a meaningless one, for reasons given in Chapter 1, and repeated briefly here. First, the tax is but one part, one side, of a public finance event. The other part, the counterpart of the tax—increase in government expenditure, repeal of another tax, retirement of debt, decrease in private-sector money stock if the tax receipts are held idle in treasury balances (see Chapter 19)—cannot help but influence, by about the same order of magnitude as does the tax itself, the demand and cost functions of the taxed goods and any untaxed substitutes or complements in production or consumption. Second, abstracting from the counterpart of the tax, the general turnover tax is universal in scope and therefore affects the cost conditions of every commodity and service.

These two circumstances make useless the customary partial equilibrium analysis, which constructs demand and cost functions for a particular commodity on the assumption either that the prices of all other things are fixed (Marshall) or that the

---

9. As does Germany (*ibid.*, pp. 830–32).

10. As Italy has done since 1954, when the export refund, as distinguished from, and in addition to, exemption of the export sale itself, was introduced (Charles K. Cobb, Jr., and Francisco Forte [correspondent], *Taxation in Italy*, World Tax Series, Law School of Harvard University [Chicago: Commerce Clearing House, 1964], pp. 749–53).

conditions of supply (in the sense of cost) of all other commodities are fixed (Pigou, Joan Robinson).

To ask who bears the burden of the general sales tax is something like asking who bears the burden of the wages bill. In contrast, the question of what is the incidence of the tax can be answered, in principle, with a useful degree of accuracy if the tax leaves free a large area to which taxed factors or consumers may repair and if the tax revenue is so small relative to the income of the entire economy that the effects of the counterpart measure will be spread thinly enough over the taxed and untaxed sectors that they may be neglected. The existence of a large tax-free area makes it feasible to construct opportunity cost schedules for factors in the taxed sector, schedules that are not appreciably disturbed by the use, whatever it may be, of the tax revenue. Of course, if the use is specified to be concentrated in the same field that is taxed (highway taxes supply an example), or in a field of close substitutes or complements, a statement of incidence is still meaningless if the counterpart is not included in the computations.

In an open economy, the incidence of a general sales tax becomes ascertainable to a degree, because the "general" sales tax is no longer truly general: it does not apply to the rest of the world, which now constitutes a large tax-free area. The use made of the general sales tax revenue will be concentrated in the taxing country and so will no doubt influence appreciably the demand and cost schedules of virtually all goods in that country. This fact, as we shall see below, limits severely what can be said about the incidence of a general sales tax in an open economy, without specifying the counterpart measure, just as a statement of incidence of a motor fuel tax dedicated to highway construction does not mean much without taking into account the influence of highway use. But the existence of the rest of the world as a tax-free area to which consumers in the taxing country, if not always factors, can resort makes possible the construction of supply and demand schedules for certain goods under assumptions of perfect elasticity of demand for exports and supply of imports. To some extent, then, the "general" sales tax in an open economy can be analyzed in much the same fashion as an excise tax in a closed economy.

These points will now be illustrated by analysis of what happens when a general turnover tax is levied in an open economy on the destination principle and the exchange rate is fixed.[11]

If export demand and import supply are perfectly elastic, a condition approximated in countries that account for a small part of the world trade in the commodities they export and import, two groups of domestic factors will escape the incidence of the turnover tax.

Since exports are exempt under the destination-principle turnover tax, domestic manufacturing factors that produce exportables will divert output from domestic

11. See Hirofumi Shibata, "The Theory of Economic Unions: A Comparative Analysis of Customs Unions, Free Trade Areas, and Tax Unions," in Carl S. Shoup (Ed.), *Fiscal Harmonization in Common Markets* (New York: Columbia University Press, 1967), vol. I, *Theory*, pp. 145–264; and Charles E. McLure, Jr., "Commodity Tax Incidence in Open Economies," *National Tax Journal* (June 1964) 17: 187–204, and *An Analysis of Regional Tax Incidence, with Estimation of Inter-State Incidence of State and Local Taxes* (Unpublished Ph.D. dissertation, Princeton University, 1965).

consumption to the foreign market until the home demand will support a price that reimburses the manufacturers completely for the tax imposed at the manufacturing stage. Factors in the wholesale and retail trades that distribute exportables to home consumers cannot turn to the export trade without some loss of efficiency. These factors therefore cannot escape the burden of the tax, in contrast to manufacturing factors in the export industries and factors in the still earlier stages.

Since imports are in perfectly elastic supply, they must command a price equal to the old domestic price plus tax if they are to continue. If, at the new equilibrium, some imports do continue, their price, and consequently the price of import-competing goods, must have risen by the full amount of the tax. Domestic manufacturers of import-competing goods will not have reduced their physical volume of sales, since perfect elasticity of supply can scarcely be assumed for them in any event. They will be passing on to consumers the full amount of the tax on their sales. But it is different with the wholesaling and retailing factors.

Imports are normally imports of tangible commodities. These commodities proceed through domestic wholesale and retail channels to the domestic consumer. The value of the commodity as it reaches the consumer consists in large part of value created by the wholesale and retail trades, which are not import-competing industries. The perfectly elastic foreign supply is therefore usually a supply of commodities only up to, but not beyond, the wholesale stage. The domestic competitors of those who provide that perfectly elastic supply are manufacturers and raw-materials producers; they do not include wholesalers and retailers.

The demand for services of wholesalers and retailers declines as imports decline. Under these circumstances the turnover tax on imported and import-competing goods puts pressure on domestic consumers and on factors in the wholesaling and retailing of those goods,[12] but no pressure at all on factors engaged in manufacturing import-competing goods. Indeed, there will be no pressure against these factors even if the manufacturing firms that hire them are not vertically integrated, and this despite the bias of the turnover tax against such firms.[13] This bias is retained in the compensating import tax, and it is this fact that protects the domestic non-integrated firms. The rates of the compensating import tax will, in principle, at least, be heavier for the products that, if produced at home, would be produced in non-vertically integrated industries, whatever may be the case in the foreign country of manufacture. The turnover tax will therefore increase the price of these particular imported products relative to the prices of other imports. Some shift of demand to the integrated industries' products will thereupon take place. But this shift will affect only imports, not domestic manufacturers of the import-competing goods, assuming that imports do not fall to zero for any of these products. The reallocation of demand away from products that are "non-integrated" in the sense connoted above will occur entirely among imports. The domestically non-integrated manufacturers are perfectly protected by the combination of a compensating import tax

---

12. Even marketers handling only import-competing goods will feel the pressure of the tax, since tax can be reduced by reducing the amount of marketing value that is added to the import-competing good's manufactured value.

13. See pages 221–23.

that takes degree of integration into account and a perfectly elastic foreign supply.

If part of an industry's output, before the tax is introduced, comes from integrated firms and part from non-integrated firms, the import tax cannot of course compensate precisely for the domestic tax in both sectors. If the import tax rate on this particular product compensates for the cumulative turnover tax on domestically non-integrated manufacturing, it becomes in part a protective duty for the integrated sector of that industry, which then expands relatively, reducing imports still more. If the import tax rate is set at a level that takes no account of the extra cumulated tax on non-integrated manufacturers, those manufacturers must reduce their output, to the benefit of importers and integrated domestic producers.

Except for the rare case of a product made and marketed by a firm that is completely integrated vertically, the turnover tax rests more heavily on value that is added at an early stage, in the production of raw materials or manufacturing, than on value added at a later stage by the activities of wholesaling and retailing.[14] This heavier taxation of early-stage value added probably reduces the demand for imports relative to the demand for domestic factor activity. Wholesaling and retailing are supplied primarily by domestic factors. Cumulated tax can be reduced, and price after tax lowered, by changing the mix of value added at the manufacturing stage and prior stages and value added by marketing. A less durable or less finely manufactured version of a commodity, supported by more advertising and other marketing expense, will tend to replace the original version and, in so doing, will reduce imports and expand demand for domestic factors.

Commodities that in any event contain a high proportion of marketing value added will attract less tax than commodities most of the value added of which is from raw materials and manufacturing. This fact, however, does not inevitably imply a reduction in imports.

If the decline in manufactured imports under the impact of the turnover tax goes so far that one or more of the imported goods is no longer imported at all, conditions of supply for manufacturers of import-competing goods become important. At this point, analysis of the turnover tax alone becomes invalid, for reasons given on page 213 and in Chapter 1. But it may at least be said that consumers of the commodity the importation of which has ceased will bear less of the cumulated tax than they would if imports of the good were continuing, under the tax.

If demand for the taxing country's exports is not perfectly elastic, the producers of exportables, upon diverting some of their output from the taxed domestic market to the tax-free foreign market, will find that export prices fall. Factor rewards in the export industries are no longer protected from the pressure of the turnover tax. Foreign purchasers now stand to gain from the domestic turnover tax.

If the supply of imports is not perfectly elastic, the destination-principle tax reduces imports less than under the perfect-elasticity assumption. The foreign factors that continue to send goods to the taxing country are willing to accept, ex-tax, something less than the price under no tax. Thus part of the tax is shifted to them. The import price cum-tax rises, but by something less than the tax. Factors in

14. Because the early-stage values added are repeated in the sales at later stages. See pages 223–24.

the import-competing manufacturing industries are no longer fully sheltered while imports continue. The tax therefore forces some decrease in manufacturing factor rewards in the import-competing industries.

In general, the incidence of the turnover tax is spread more widely than when export demand and import supply are perfectly elastic. Three parties that were unharmed by the tax under the perfect-elasticities assumption now share in the burden. They are the manufacturing factors in the export trade, those in the import-competing trades, at least as long as imports continue, and foreign factors.

The conclusions drawn up to this point are of limited usefulness. They assume an unaltered foreign exchange rate, despite the incremental surplus in balance of trade that is implied, in the perfect-elasticities case, by an increase in physical volume of exports at unchanged prices and some decrease in imports. If the currency has to be revalued upward to attain external equilibrium, the factors producing for export will have to accept lower rewards in order to stay in business, and so too will the factors producing import-competing goods, as imports would tend to increase. Ultimately, then, it seems unlikely that any substantial group of factor suppliers will escape pressure from the destination-principle turnover tax and its consequences, insofar as those can be meaningfully conjectured without taking into account the use made of the tax revenue.

If the turnover tax is imposed on the origin principle, factors in the export industries bear part of the tax on exports under a perfectly elastic foreign demand. If the exportables-goods industries are to continue to export, they must reduce production to a level where the marginal cost of production, ex-tax, is lower than initially, by the amount of the tax. They need not reduce production, and hence costs ex-tax, to this level if domestic consumption of their exportables so increases, as price cum-tax is reduced in this sector, but not for other domestically produced goods, that a new (partial) equilibrium is reached with exports having ceased. But this outcome seems unlikely. If it does occur, part of the incidence of the tax on exportables is on domestic consumers of exportables.

Since imports are not taxed, while import-competing manufactures are taxed, and and since the domestic price of imported goods cannot rise, under the assumptions of perfectly elastic supply of imports and an unchanged exchange rate, factors producing import-competing goods must, if they are to continue to compete with imports, reduce their output until marginal cost ex-tax has fallen by the amount of the tax. The incidence of the tax is on these factors, not on consumers of import-competing manufactures so far as the manufactured value is concerned (wholesale and retail trade services, not usually being imported, must be analyzed as non-traded "products").

The incidence of the origin-principle turnover tax, under the assumption of perfect elasticities for foreign trade, will therefore be divided between all domestic factors and that part of domestic consumer spending that does not consist of imported values. None of the tax is shifted abroad.

If export demand is less than perfectly elastic, some part of the tax on exports will rest on the foreign buyers instead of on the factors in the export industry or possibly domestic consumers of exportables. And if import supply is not perfectly elastic, the tax-free imports will expand only if domestic prices rise somewhat (and therefore foreign prices of these imports too). Part of the tax on import-competing manufactures will thus be passed on to domestic consumers. Foreign factors will bear none of the tax.

The remarks made on page 213 concerning the limited usefulness of the conclusions reached under the destination-principle assumption apply equally of course to this analysis under the origin principle.

3. Differential Incidence: Turnover Tax and Value-Added Tax

Although macro public finance analysis is in general postponed to Book Three, it will be employed in these chapters on broad-based taxes (Chapters 8, 9, 11–16) to estimate differential incidence, since incidence of any one of those taxes alone is analytically a meaningless concept save for certain short-run aspects of foreign trade.

For the other half of the differential comparison a value-added tax will be assumed, imposed at an equal-yield uniform rate, with complete exemption of capital goods ("consumption type").[15] The uniform impact of such a tax will aid in analyzing the discriminating features of the other taxes, except the pure type of retail sales tax, which is the analytical equivalent of the value-added tax.

Even for differential incidence, with the value-added tax as the reference tax, only a few general remarks can be offered, owing to lack of relevant data. One such remark is that the turnover tax produces a heavier impact on factors who produce and on consumers who purchase goods that are heavily weighted with early-stage value added, if the degree of vertical integration is not much greater for those goods than for goods embodying chiefly late-stage value added. Upon substitution of a turnover tax for a value-added tax, prices of early-stage goods will rise relative to prices of other goods, and factor rewards of those who produce or market early-stage goods will tend to fall relative to other factor rewards. But no data are available to support even a conjecture as to whether the effect would be chiefly a change in product prices or chiefly a change in factor rewards. And if the answer to this were at hand, the distribution of the incidence of the tax change by income classes would still not be known. Let us suppose that under this change in tax structure the factors producing and marketing the early-stage goods could find employment elsewhere at little reduction in rates of pay and that consumer demand for these early-stage goods proved fairly insensitive to the relative rise in price (these two assumptions are somewhat contradictory if early- and late-stage goods between them make up, in about equal shares, the economy's entire output). Are these consumers more likely to be rich, or poor? In general, those households whose budgets are allocated largely to early-stage goods are probably poor; they spend little if anything for goods that embody expensive marketing services: prestige retail locations, status advertising, delivery service, continued credit, and long-distance transportation of perishable products. They buy at supermarkets, or at tiny shops. And they spend

15. See page 253.

little on domestic service, or foreign travel. There must be so many exceptions to this generalization that until empirical studies ascertain how important the exceptions are, the conjecture must remain highly uncertain. But these are the kinds of assumptions that must be made if the turnover tax is to be considered harsher for the poor than a value-added tax.

4. Criteria

A. CONSENSUS CRITERIA

The turnover tax scores well on some of the six aspects of the consensus criterion of equal treatment of equals (Chapter 2, pages 23–27), but falls far short on others.

The circumstances relevant to equal treatment are few and relatively simple, since the "equals" are only business firms and the circumstances are chiefly volume of sales. The circumstances can be defined broadly enough to guarantee impersonality; there are few counterparts in the turnover tax to the one-taxpayer clauses that mar the income tax and the death and gift taxes. At the same time the circumstances can be defined closely enough to assure a reasonable degree of certainty.

Where the turnover tax fails is in respect to discontinuities and lack of equality in mispayment of tax and in cost of compliance. Let us consider these three aspects in turn.

Intra-firm transfers are not taxable, but any definition of "intra-firm" involves a quantitative discontinuity when one firm is owned wholly or partly by another and sole reliance is not placed on legal form of organization. If a business firm decides to incorporate its sales division separately while retaining 100 per cent ownership of that division, transfer of product from parent firm to the selling subsidiary may be held nontaxable by the law because the subsidiary is 100 per cent owned. But what if the parent company owns only 99 per cent of the subsidiary? 75 per cent? Some quantitative dividing line must be drawn. If, in contrast, sale to the subsidiary is taxable in all cases, on the ground that the subsidiary is an independent legal entity even if 100 per cent owned by the parent, a qualitative discontinuity exists where a branch or division becomes a corporation.

Another discontinuity, qualitative, is that between (1) an isolated sale by an individual not in a business, the sale not being made with intent (a) to repeat this kind of sale, or (b) to realize gross receipts or profits, and (2) all other sales. The former type of sale, or some variant of it, is usually not subject to turnover tax, primarily for administrative convenience.[16] Other definitional discontinuities are those arising from distinctions between employee and independent entrepreneur, and between resale by the vendee to his vendor and simple cancellation of the initial sale, when delivery on the initial sale has already been made,[17] and from definitions

16. For Germany, see "The Concept of the Entrepreneur" and "Characteristics of the Entrepreneur" in Gumpel and Boettcher, *op. cit.*, pp. 784–88.

17. *Ibid.*, p. 797.

of time and place of transfer, or sale, or delivery,[18] and definition of wholesale sale, real property, and similar concepts.

Any tax that applies to large numbers of small business firms will be marked by mispayment of tax, most of which will be deliberate underpayment. The small firm will typically evade a larger percentage of its tax bill than the large firm. To reduce the average level of evasion by the small firm to that of the larger firms and to assure a more uniform degree of evasion among the small firms would require that the given amount of tax-enforcement resources be allocated in a manner that would reduce total revenue from the tax substantially.

But it is the small firm that is disadvantaged with respect to cost of compliance. The cost is high to the small firm because the tax requires a marked change from virtually no bookkeeping to at least a rudimentary sort of bookkeeping. This is not easy for the often semi-literate shopkeeper.

These two administrative inequities can be avoided by accepting a departure from the basic concept of the turnover tax, namely, exemption of small firms.[19] This can be accomplished by exempting a certain amount of sales volume per firm, per year or month. The exemption can be (*a*) granted to all firms, large and small, or (*b*) made to vanish gradually above a certain level of sales ("dwindling exemption"), or (*c*) made to disappear suddenly once a certain level of sales is reached ("disappearing exemption"). Under the dwindling exemption the actual marginal tax rate on sales is higher than the statutory rate for some distance above the complete exemption level, and there is a discontinuity in the marginal rate under the disappearing exemption.[20] Any exemption whatever tends to induce a small firm to cease growing before it reaches the taxable level, and induces a large firm to spin off small, wholly owned subsidiaries,[21] if smallness is defined in terms of direct, not indirect, ownership.

A cruder solution to the numbers problem is to exempt all firms belonging to a sector in which tiny enterprises are numerous, and exempt no firms, not even the smallest, in the remaining sectors. Thus all retailers and all farmers, in certain

18. *Ibid.*, pp. 797, 803, 822–30.

19. France has differed from Germany in this respect. The French turnover tax of the 1920's and 1930's allowed no exemption to small firms as such (but see the remarks on farmers, below, and the *forfait* regime, footnote 22, below). French insistence on attempting to tax all retailers and small producers, including even the smallest shops and workplaces, was a major factor in increasing the unpopularity of the turnover tax to the point where it was replaced by single-stage taxation at the manufacturing level (see Section B below). In France, in 1922, 48 per cent of the taxpayers could have been exempted with a loss of only 2 per cent of the turnover tax revenue (Carl S. Shoup, *The Sales Tax in France*, p. 105). In 1924, a total of 1,484,379 retailers with an annual turnover of not more than 300,000 francs (approximately $24,300) paid an average annual tax of 428 francs (about $35). *Ibid.*, p. 109.

20. The German turnover tax exemption dwindles to zero between DM 120,000 ($30,000) a year and DM 132,000 ($33,000) a year turnover (from DM 120,000 to DM 140,000 for entrepreneurs whose receipts are derived exclusively from professional services or from services as commercial agents or brokers) (Gumpel and Boettcher, *op. cit.*, pp. 812–15). In dwindling over the range from DM 120,000 to DM 132,000 the exemption causes the marginal turnover tax rate in this range of sales to be 8 per cent rather than the statutory rate of 4 per cent.

21. See, with respect to Finland, John F. Due, *Sales Taxation* (London: Routledge & Kegan Paul, 1957), p. 169.

countries, can be exempted. A quasi-solution, also rather crude, is to require the tax administrator to estimate gross receipts of the very small firms, and hence estimate the tax due, by external indicia: number of employees, size of shop or store, and the like.[22]

Transfers for which no money value is stipulated give rise to inequities of administration because of the difficulty of setting taxable values. Examples are withdrawals of goods by an entrepreneur, typically a shopkeeper, for his personal use, and barter. A withdrawal is usually held a taxable act, and barter, a doubly taxable act.

The turnover tax has certain advantages with respect to counter-cycle changes in tax rates for a full employment policy. The base of the tax is broad enough to exert substantial leverage on the economy. The rate structure is usually so simple that there will be little dispute over the pattern in which rates shall be reduced, a problem that hinders counter-cycle use of a progressive income tax. The legislature will be correspondingly less reluctant to delegate authority to the executive to change the rate for counter-cycle purposes.

Once the turnover tax rate has been lowered, consumers are on notice that they will do well to purchase as much as possible before a business recovery makes advisable a restoration of the higher tax rate. On the other hand, anticipatory postponement of buying at a time just before the rate is to be reduced will temporarily increase unemployment. These matters are explored further in Chapter 22, where the sales tax and income tax are compared with respect to the anticipatory reactions to the income and substitution effects of tax rate changes.

Changes in the turnover tax rate cannot readily, if at all, exclude very low-income households from the impacts of a counter-cycle policy, and this may be a serious disadvantage, for reasons given in Chapter 22. Changes in turnover tax rates disturb competitive relationships between vertically integrated firms and their competitors.

The built-in flexibility of a destination-principle turnover tax, that is, the sensitivity of its yield, under a given tax rate, to a decline in national income depends on whether that decline originates with a decrease in demand for exports. If it does, national income falls initially without any decrease in the tax bill, since exports are exempt; sensitivity on this first round is zero. Only when the depression spreads to domestic spending through multiplier and accelerator effects will the turnover tax yield fall. Part of that fall will reflect a decrease in imports, with a consequent decline of the tax yield not associated with a simultaneous decrease in national income; and this fall in tax yield will do a good deal to check the recession in domestic spending[23] if the supply of imports is perfectly elastic, for in that event all of the decline in tax revenue from imports represents that much less tax taken from domestic households and firms: foreign suppliers will have been bearing none of the tax. If the supply of imports is less than perfectly elastic, some of the decrease in

22. In French terminology, this reliance on estimated sales is called the *forfait* regime. It was introduced in 1924 (Shoup, *op. cit.*, pp. 71–81, 250–53).

23. In the sense that the recession will be less than it would have been if, in place of the tax on imports, the government employed a completely insensitive tax, say a poll tax, and if government spending were the same under either tax.

the tax bill will benefit foreign suppliers; to that extent, the sensitivity of the tax provides no stimulus to domestic output, except through the presumably modest and delayed foreign repercussion of that benefit on domestic exports. Thus a small, very open economy gets little immediate stimulus from built-in flexibility as exports decline but a great deal as imports decline. But the stimulus, rather than relieving domestic unemployment, may serve chiefly to reduce the decline in imports.

In any economy, open or closed, the turnover tax will exhibit less built-in flexibility than the income tax if households try to maintain their spending levels by saving less, or by dissaving more, as their incomes fall.

Since the turnover tax strikes all consumer goods but only that portion of investment goods not made by the user, and since investment spending declines faster than consumer spending in the initial stages of a depression, the sensitivity of the turnover tax will tend to be somewhat less than unity, that is, the yield of the tax will tend to decline by a smaller percentage than the national income. Working in the other direction is the fact that a greater percentage decline is apt to occur in manufacturing and raw materials production than in wholesaling and retailing, that is, for early-stage, heavily taxed value added more than for the late-stage value added. This is so, partly because entrepreneurs find it more difficult to lay off workers in the marketing sector, to match the decline in business.

The efficiency of any given degree of sensitivity, that is, the ratio of the increase in private-sector spending[24] to the decrease in the tax bill, is higher for the turnover tax than for the value-added tax if, which is by no means certain, more of the turnover tax is a burden on low-income consumers and low-income factors.

If the turnover tax is based on the origin principle, its sensitivity will provide no stimulus against a recession that starts domestically insofar as the domestic decline in buying is centered on imports, which are tax-free. But a decline in exports is accompanied simultaneously by a decline in the tax bill, a bill that has been coming out of the pockets of domestic factors, if the demand for exports is perfectly elastic.

Excess burden is created by the destination-principle turnover tax with respect to consumers at home compared with consumers abroad, for, no matter where the good is produced, the tax is discriminatory, since it applies only, but always, if the good is consumed at home. An origin-principle tax creates excess burden in the opposite way, that is, with respect to production at home compared with production abroad. Under macro analysis, however, when use made of the tax revenue is taken into account, it will be found that no excess burden need exist if the destination-principle tax revenues are spent for the benefit of home consumers and if the origin-principle tax revenues are spent for the benefit of home producers.

The turnover tax reduces the price of leisure; the consequences of this fact are discussed under the Conflict Criteria, below.

The heavier burden placed on non-vertically integrated firms is another aspect of excess burden; so too is the discrimination against early stages of production (unless vertical integration is complete) and against capital-intensive methods of production. The following paragraphs describe and analyze each of these three tax differentials and their consequences.

24. Relative to what it would have been under a completely insensitive tax.

Vertical integration of business firms induced by the turnover tax[25] reduces efficiency by reducing specialization. The specialization thus lost may be in the manufacturing of components that are assembled into a finished good, as with an automobile. It may be in an entire stage of the distributive process, as when wholesalers are replaced by commission merchants or brokers, with consequent assumption of most of the wholesaling function by the manufacturing (vendor) or retailing (vendee) firms. The retail stage will usually remain formally distinct, but may come under the ownership of producers, or retailers themselves may integrate backward.

In industries where a considerable amount of non-integration remains despite the turnover tax, there will nevertheless be a relative shrinkage of the non-integrated sector. Before the turnover tax was introduced, production in the industry was in principle extended in its non-integrated sector and in its integrated sector to levels such that the marginal cost of the finished good to the consumer was the same for the two sectors. If both sectors operate under decreasing returns to outlay, the turnover tax penalty on non-integration forces production in the non-integrated sector to contract and induces that in the integrated sector to expand at least relatively, until marginal costs, now including turnover tax, are again equal.

This tax differential against non-integration has been reduced in some countries by amending the law, not because the legislator is worried over excess burden, malallocation of resources, and higher costs of production and distribution, but because he is sensitive to complaints arising from disturbance of long-established competitive relations. Hardship posed by transition to a new business status is a powerful political argument. On these grounds, wholesalers are commonly exempted or given a low rate of tax, to avoid forcing them to become commission merchants or brokers, hence taxable only on their commissions. This favored treatment must be narrowly defined if it is not to be extended by clever taxpayers to activities that are essentially manufacturing. Thus the law may require that the wholesaler, to gain the exemption or low rate, must not have processed, improved, or converted the material or commodity in any way.[26]

Alternatively, commission merchants and brokers could be taxed on the value of their dealings instead of on the amount of their commissions. But now the tax would

25. A sale from one commonly owned firm to another, as in Germany, is sometimes referred to as a sale under "horizontal" integration, but the integration need not be of the horizontal type; indeed, the benefits by way of exemption of the transaction from the turnover tax occur chiefly when the integration is vertical. Exemption of a sale between commonly owned firms, that is, when a third firm owns both of the transacting firms, is known as application of the *Unternehmereinheit* principle, to be distinguished from application of the *Organschaft* principle, which allows parent-daughter transactions to be ignored.

26. Always, it appears, exceptions to this rule must be made. In Germany, the "permissible types of processing or improvement" that allow the reduced rate (1 per cent) still to apply "cover mainly certain treatments of agricultural products and equipment, and the addition of accessories to automobiles and trucks" (Gumpel and Boettcher, *op. cit.*, p. 817). Complete exemption is granted to wholesale delivery "of certain essential raw materials, semi-finished products, and foodstuffs" (*ibid.*, p. 805), and the list of permissible processing or improvement here is not the same as for the 1 per cent tax (*ibid.*, p. 817). "There is a large body of case law dealing with tax-exempt wholesale deliveries . . ." (*ibid.*, pp. 805–806). "The feeding of cattle is not an act of processing, but the fattening of the animals is. . . . The weighing, cutting, or measuring and ordinary packaging of merchandise" does not cause loss of the tax exemption (*ibid.*, p. 808).

induce direct dealing between manufacturer and retailer or ultimate consumer.[27] Independent manufacturers are induced by the turnover tax to become processors of materials owned by others. To tax all such processors on an imputed-sales basis would be harsh treatment of those who had been processors before the tax existed.[28] Immediately following importation certain transfers may occur that, if taxed, will be eliminated, to the disturbance of a geographical network of importation.[29]

Tax-induced vertical integration can be lessened by taxation of intra-firm transfers or movement of goods. This action is so drastic a departure from the basic concept of the turnover tax that it has rarely been attempted. The most striking examples are in textile manufacturing and producer-retailer integration.[30]

Vertical integration of factor relationships is to be distinguished from vertical integration of production or distribution. Independent agents may assume the status of employees of the client firm in order to avoid the turnover tax. The members of an advertising agency, for example, taxable on its gross receipts, may be induced by a high-rate turnover tax to dissolve the agency and find positions as employees in expanded advertising departments of the former client firms.

Under an origin-principle turnover tax, pressure for vertical integration will be greater on import-competing industries than under the destination-principle tax, since firms in these industries will now meet tax-free competition from abroad.

The pressures toward vertical integration and allied actions just discussed are intensified if the turnover tax is pyramided, in the sense that the pre-tax percentage margins of profit on sales are somehow maintained in the later vertical stages even though the percentage is now computed on a base swollen by the turnover tax applied at earlier stages. Success in maintaining pre-tax percentage margins in this manner implies, however, an increase in percentage return on capital engaged in the business, and it is not evident why this is to be expected even in an imperfectly competitive industry.

A different issue is the question whether imposition of the tax at an early stage in the economic process somehow imposes an excess burden in the form of an interest charge on the tax that is advanced to the government at so early a stage. In principle, the answer is no; this issue is discussed below, under single-stage taxes (page 238).

The extra burden placed by the turnover tax on early-stage value added has gone virtually unnoticed, perhaps because that burden exists only if vertical integration is not complete, and increases with vertical disintegration. Thus the tax penalty against non-integration tends to monopolize attention. Yet the two tax penalties are

27. For the grain trade, in France in the 1920's, "where dealers continually attempted to appear to the tax agents as mere commission agents," the solution adopted was to tax all classes of dealers in grain at a special low rate (Shoup, *op. cit.*, p. 54).

28. French flour millers became processors for others, in the 1920's, milling without taking legal title to the grain. This proved to be one of the most difficult problems under the turnover tax, and was a chief reason why a special single-stage replacement tax was enacted for this industry (Shoup, *op. cit.*, pp. 53–54, 263).

29. For Germany, see Gumpel and Boettcher, *op. cit.*, pp. 828–30.

30. Transfer of yarn from the spinning department to the weaving department of an integrated textile mill is subject to the full tax (4 per cent) in Germany (*ibid.*, p. 798). Germany also attempted to tax at 3 per cent deliveries made by manufacturers to wholly owned subsidiaries that were retail outlets, but the measure was declared unconstitutional (*idem.*).

quite distinct. Of two industries with precisely the same lack of vertical integration, that is, with the same number of transfers at the same stages, one industry may be producing an article in the value of which wholesale and retail services play an important role while the other industry's product consists mainly of value added at early stages.

No turnover tax law, it appears, incorporates provisions designed to lessen this type of discrimination, and few students of public finance have even mentioned it. Perhaps this tax penalty against early-stage types of consumer products has had little effect, but this result would be surprising, in view of the opportunities to reduce the cumulative impact of the turnover tax by transforming a commodity so that it is manufactured less thoroughly or less finely or less carefully and promoted more heavily by expenditure on advertising, retail location, and the like. Such transformation as has occurred has perhaps been so gradual as to escape notice, or has been readily attributable to other causes. Insofar as transformation has not proved practicable, the resultant shift of consumption toward lightly taxed articles that are somewhat rival has no doubt also been gradual and attributed to other forces.

With respect to capital-intensive methods of production, the turnover tax creates an excess burden in two ways.

First it makes the rate of substitution of future goods for present goods as seen by the producer (ex-tax) differ from that faced by the supplier of funds. Second, it varies the amount of this divergence between the two rates of substitution erratically, taking only those capital goods or those components of a capital good that are not produced within the using firm.

In practice, almost any capital good will attract some turnover tax, but the amount of tax will vary considerably from good to good and firm to firm. Inventory-intensive methods of doing business are to be included in capital-intensive methods.

B. CONFLICT CRITERIA

The criterion of progressivity by income or wealth is commonly but erroneously applied in judging the turnover tax alone, without comparison with some other tax. The error arises from assuming that the incidence of a broad-based tax can be defined meaningfully in isolation, as can the incidence of a small excise tax (see Chapter 2).[31] The only legitimate questions are of the following kind: Is the turnover tax progressive relative to, say, an equal-yield value-added tax? Is a destination-principle turnover tax progressive relative to an origin-principle turnover tax? Does exemption of foodstuffs coupled with a correspondingly higher rate on the remaining taxable goods produce a tax that is more progressive than the one without the food exemption? What of exemption of farmers? Of small retailers? Since almost no research has been done on these questions, only a few conjectures are offered here.

31. For an estimate (meaningless, in the view expressed here) of the distribution of the burden of the German *Umsatzsteuer* by income class, for 1952, see the study by the IFO-Institut für Wirtschaftsforschung, *Untersuchungen zur grossen Steuerreform* (Munich, 1953), pp. 150–51, cited by Due, *Sales Taxation*, p. 59. Apparently, although this point is not covered explicitly by Due, this study assumes complete forward shifting of the tax.

A turnover tax is regressive compared with a value-added tax insofar as the extra tax on early-stage value added is an extra tax on low-income consumers, as may well be the case, for reasons given in Section 3 above. The penalty that the turnover tax places on non-integration may work either way.[32] The turnover tax burden on capital goods relative to the lack of any direct burden on them under a consumption type of value-added tax reduces the national income by inducing relatively inefficient labor-intensive methods of production. A smaller proportion of that smaller total income may then go to lower income groups, as the relatively larger amount of labor applied to capital causes a reduction in the marginal productivity of labor. This conclusion implies some elasticity in the supply of capital, chiefly because of opportunities for investment abroad. But if the supply of capital is quite inelastic, the turnover tax burden on capital goods relative to that under the consumption type of value-added tax may simply reduce capital's share of a largely unchanged national income.

All in all, a tentative conclusion seems justified that the turnover tax is probably somewhat regressive compared with the consumption type of value-added tax.

As between a turnover tax without exemption of food,[33] and a turnover tax of equal yield that exempts food, the latter is probably progressive relative to the former; only "probably," because (1) some of the tax relief from exemption of food may be captured by factors specialized in the food industry, including farm land, and (2) the correspondingly higher tax rate on all other goods, including clothing and other non-food necessaries, is itself a regressive change. Exemption of farmers is probably regressive, even though they lose part of the benefit in lower relative prices of their products, and even though many farmers have little capital.

Dwelling rental, and imputed rental of homeowners, are commonly exempt from the turnover tax. If these rentals were taxed, allowing a lower tax rate on all other goods, the change would probably be regressive, though much depends on the extent to which taxability of rentals would reduce incomes of factors in the building and real estate industries. As to a destination-principle turnover tax compared with an origin-principle turnover tax, no implications concerning progressivity seem evident.

Families with the same family income often differ in family size while spending about the same per family. Income and expenditure per person are then lower in the larger families. The turnover tax can make little or no allowance for this fact, and insofar as it does, the effect may not be that desired. Exemption of food may move part of the turnover tax burden from the poorer persons to the less poor persons, that is, from large families to small families of the same family income and expendi-

32. These differentials are presumably the cause of the striking differences in estimated accumulated turnover tax as among different finished products found in studies cited by Due, in his *Sales Taxation,* for Germany (p. 60) and Austria (p. 79). But unless the differences are read as differences from a uniform rate of burden that could be reached under, say, a value-added tax, they, like the incidence estimates, lack meaning.

33. For Germany, see Gumpel and Boettcher, *op. cit.,* p. 810; for France (1920's) see Shoup, *The Sales Tax in France,* index, Foodstuffs. Items commonly favored are grains, flour, bread and other non-luxury bakery products; milk; sugar; edible fats. In some instances these exemptions have been intended to check inflation when wages were tied to a cost-of-living index.

ture, but the outcome is uncertain for the reasons just given in discussing the exemption of food. A credit against income tax for turnover tax assumed to be paid by households would be of no use to those living in families with family income so low relative to size of family that they pay no income tax because of the personal exemptions, yet it is members of these households that need relief the most. Apparently no turnover taxing jurisdiction allows such a credit (for the credit under some retail sales taxes, see page 247).

Geographical discrimination within the taxing jurisdiction, say in favor of a depressed area, can be implemented to an uncertain degree, by exempting sales within the area, sales for export from the area, and sales for import into the area. Exemption of imports and exports are difficult to administer, since the destination of shipments must be verified, without the aid of a border control system of the kind that makes export exemption practicable in international trade.

Exemption of imports is more important to households in the depressed area in general than is exemption of exports from the area. The benefit of the import exemption will accrue largely to households in the area, and only in small part to factors outside the area, since it is a large area (the rest of the country) that is competing to supply a small area (the depressed area); the supply of imports to the depressed area will be almost perfectly elastic, just as in the small-country case discussed in Section A.2 above, and the subsidy to imports will correspondingly be reflected in selling prices. Demand for the region's exports will similarly be almost perfectly elastic, and remission of tax on such exports will increase output without causing a decline in prices. But most of the added income earned by the increase in export volume at unchanged prices may go to factors whose owners are not at all depressed and who may indeed be living elsewhere: landowners, stockholders, creditors. No doubt some of the increase in earnings will appear as higher wages and a larger volume of employment in the depressed area, but the proportion will differ widely from one area to another.

In summary, the aid granted by exempting imports to the depressed area is more likely to be concentrated on those households that are in need than is the aid granted by exemption of exports, but the latter type of aid, though more of it is wasted on factor-owners not requiring help, is less self-perpetuating, since it on the one hand lifts incomes of some families by creating more jobs and raising wages, while continuing the pressure on those not thus benefited to leave the area.

The full force of these import and export exemptions for a depressed area cannot be exerted under a turnover tax unless exports give rise to a refund of turnover tax paid at earlier stages and unless a similar refund is given to firms sending goods into the depressed area. But this intensification of the turnover tax relief to the depressed area would induce efforts at evasion, through falsification of documents of destination, besides being difficult to compute.

Discrimination by ethnic, color, or status groups is almost impossible under the turnover tax, just because it is so impersonal, so unadaptable to individual differences. Those who favor fiscal illusion and a concealed distribution of the tax burden possess a powerful instrument in the turnover tax. This tax is never stated separately to consumers from the purchase price.

Capital-intensive methods of production are made relatively more costly by the turnover tax, as explained earlier, unless the capital equipment is produced entirely by the firm that uses it. The turnover tax therefore tends to check economic growth more than does the value-added tax of the consumption type, or the true retail sales tax, unless the supply of capital (rate of saving) is perfectly price-inelastic.[34]

A still more important check to growth, especially in under-developed countries, may be a restriction of gainful consumption caused by the turnover tax, at least compared with income taxes that exempt low-income consumers. Even though not much is known about the relative incidence of these two taxes, it seems likely that very poor consumers fare worse under the turnover tax, or indeed any general sales tax. Gainful consumption, it will be recalled, is consumption that more than pays for itself in increased output. Much of this consumption must occur in childhood, hence may be counted as investment in human capital.[35]

With respect to risk-taking under a turnover tax, the results of a general equilibrium model employing a flat-rate non-cumulative general sales tax on consumer goods are relevant. In that model, as already noted in Chapter 2 above (Section B.2.c), it is shown that under such a tax, used to finance government expenditures which duplicate those that the taxpayers themselves would have made, investors possessing a certain plausible attitude toward risk and mean return will move some capital and labor from the non-risky sector in this model to the two risky sectors, provided that the income effect of the services rendered by the government by means of the tax-financed purchases of goods and services are disregarded. Such a sales tax, and use of revenue therefrom, reduces both private mean return and private standard deviation of outcomes of risky ventures, that is, mean return and standard deviation in terms of incomes after tax.

The problem alters when differential tax analysis is employed, as when a turnover tax is compared with the tax of reference in the present work for incidence analysis, namely, the value-added tax, consumption type. That tax indirectly exempts the return from capital goods, by exempting the purchase of such goods from tax, in a manner explained in Chapter 9, Section B.1.A(3)(B) below. The turnover tax strikes capital goods, both when sold in intermediate form and when sold in final form (but not when produced by the user, except as the user purchases materials to construct them). The turnover tax of course applies regardless of what the subsequent experience with the capital good turns out to be, whether a profit or a loss. The turnover tax seems relatively unfavorable to risk-taking.

The price effects of the introduction of a destination-principle turnover tax (abstracting from the use made of the tax revenue) tend to improve the balance of trade, particularly if export demand is perfectly elastic, for then export prices do not decline under the increase in physical export volume that occurs as the tax exemption allowed to exports draws more domestic resources into the export sector.

---

34. On this point see page 332.

35. For the definition of gainful consumption, see Chapter 23. See also Carl S. Shoup, "Taxes and Economic Development," *Finanzarchiv* (1966), 25: 385–97, and "Production from Consumption," *Public Finance* (1965), 20(1–2): 173–202.

The physical volume of imports meanwhile decreases as imports become more costly. The use made of the tax revenue may of course counter these tendencies.

The tax therefore exerts the same tendency as devaluation of the currency, but it differs appreciably from devaluation. It at once increases the real cost of production of import-competing goods and non-traded goods. It does not make exports cheaper to the foreigner in his own currency. And it increases the cost of different imports by different percentages, to allow for varying degrees of vertical integration.

The increase in price of imports in the taxing country's currency does not accrue to the foreign supplier, as it does under devaluation, but the significance of this difference to the foreign seller is nil, since under the tax he does not need correspondingly more of the home country's currency to keep unchanged the proceeds of his sales in his own currency.

If export demand is not perfectly elastic, export prices will fall as factors move into this tax-free area, and the balance of trade will tend to improve on this account only if foreign demand is sufficiently elastic (disregarding foreign repercussions); it will otherwise worsen. If import supply is not perfectly elastic, import prices ex-tax will fall, and physical volume will decline (though less than under perfectly elastic import supply), thus improving the balance of trade on this account, compared with no tax. Under these less than perfect elasticities, terms of trade will improve or worsen, depending on how far export prices fall relative to import prices. The net result of imposing the destination-principle turnover tax, under these elasticities, will be an improvement in the balance of trade unless foreign elasticity conditions are so unfavorable that the consequent decline in the money value of exports outweighs the decline in money paid to foreigners for imports. The result thus tends to be in the same direction as under perfect elasticities, but not surely so, and in any event to a smaller degree. Again, these tendencies may be countered by the use made of the tax revenue.

Under an origin-principle turnover tax, the balance of trade tends to worsen, at least if the elasticities are perfect, even though the terms of trade remain unchanged (the money from the tax on exports is kept within the country). Imported goods, which are now tax-free in competition with taxed import-competing goods, rise in physical volume, compared with no tax. Exports are taxed but their price including tax remains unchanged, and in physical volume exports therefore do not rise and probably decline. Unlike upward revaluation of the currency, introduction of an origin-principle turnover tax directly raises costs of all domestic producers and does not directly lower the cost of imported goods in domestic currency. Again, these tendencies may be countered by the use made of the revenue.

If the elasticities are less than perfect, export prices will rise, and even though they rise by less than the tax, the taxing country gains on terms of trade in the export sector, since it keeps the tax revenue. Imports, although not taxed, will rise in price, as they increase somewhat in competition with the taxed import-competing goods. The likely outcome, for the origin-principle tax under elasticities less than perfect, is still an incremental deficit in the balance of trade, since there is certain to be an incremental deficit in imports, and there will be an incremental export surplus only if demand for exports is of less than unit elasticity.

The turnover tax has no immediate effect on short-term capital movements. Inflow of long-term capital will be discouraged and outflow of domestic long-term capital encouraged, as the tax decreases the net return from domestic investments relative to that obtainable from investments abroad (abstracting from the use made of the tax revenue).

If an already established turnover tax, imposed at a certain rate, say 10 per cent, is changed from the destination principle to the origin principle, the result is essentially the same as an upward revaluation of the currency by the same percentage (10 per cent), except that revaluation also affects capital flows, interest and dividend flows, and gifts, all of which are left unaffected by the tax change.

Under revaluation, domestic tax revenue is not directly affected. Under a tax change from destination to origin principle the tax revenue is of course directly affected, but on balance it remains more or less unchanged, since revenue is gained on exports but is lost on imports. The two measures, revaluation and tax change, are therefore roughly similar in this respect also.

A change from the one principle to the other under the turnover tax thus offers an alternative to a change in the exchange rate as a means of maintaining or re-establishing external equilibrium. In practice, since all turnover taxes, indeed all general sales taxes, use the destination principle, a change in principles is currently available only to counter a surplus in the balance of payments, not a deficit. The countering may be too strong or too weak, depending on the height of the tax rate. Only a partial shift from destination to origin principle might be called for, to maintain external equilibrium. Thus a 10 per cent destination-principle tax might be changed to one that taxed imports only 9 per cent while continuing to exempt exports or, alternatively, taxed imports at 10 per cent and exports at 1 per cent. Or conditions might be such as to call for a tax on imports at 8 per cent while exempting exports, under a 10 per cent tax, and so on, in an endless number of possible combinations. In effect, two taxes would be in force, one on a destination-principle basis, the other on an origin basis. If they were of the same rate, each at 5 per cent in this example, the system would consist of one universal sales tax and one domestic-only sales tax, at equal rates (see Table 2 above). Accordingly, given a sales tax rate sufficiently high, an external surplus can in principle be precisely removed by a certain narrowing of the difference between the tax rate on imports and that on exports. By the same reasoning, the size of that difference is of no significance if the exchange rate is flexible (abstracting from other than trade flows, see Section A.1 above). In practice, no consideration seems to have been given to a policy that lies in between the destination principle and the origin principle.

There is still another price aspect to consider. We have seen that the turnover tax bears heavily on early-stage value added (unless vertical integration is complete). Imports consist chiefly of early-stage value added, since wholesale and retail services are usually produced at home. A turnover tax may on this account bear heavily on imports. But this argument is not conclusive. Imports may be just the kind of commodities that have a large amount of late-stage, domestically produced value added attached to them after importation, by advertising and retail services. Domestically produced articles may be of a kind that contain chiefly early-stage value added. Then, even if all imports were of early-stage value added, a turnover tax would impose a heavier cumulative burden on domestically produced articles and would encourage imports, relative, say, to a value-added tax. It is assumed here that both imports and domestically produced articles are marketed by use of domestic factors. At any rate, it can be said that only by coincidence will the discrimination against early-stage value added under the turnover tax leave the competitive position of foreign and domestically produced articles (both being domestically marketed) the same as under a tax that does not so discriminate. The turnover tax will almost surely on this account either encourage or discourage imports, relative to such other tax.

One of the income effects of the introduction of a turnover tax is a reduction in expenditure on imports and exportables (as well as on non-traded goods). The tax therefore tends to reduce a deficit on current account, but whether by more or less than other equivalent broad-based taxes is not known. If as conjectured above (pages 224–25), the turnover tax bears more heavily on the poor than does the value-added tax, and if imports and exportables are chiefly for the rich, the turnover tax does not improve the balance of trade as much as does the value-added tax. Again, this discussion abstracts from foreign repercussions.

The turnover tax probably induces members of low-income households to work more than they would under an equivalent value-added tax (consumption type). The effect on members of high-income households seems less definite. The conjecture regarding low-income households assumes that necessities of life are largely early-stage goods, hence heavily taxed under the turnover tax, and that a considerable part of this differential burden rests on consumers. The statutory rate of the turnover tax is lower than that of an equal-yield value-added tax because the total base is higher. For the moment let us assume that "equivalent" means equal-yield.[36] The low-income worker is then subject to an average turnover tax rate considerably higher than he would pay under an equal-yield value-added tax. But the marginal rate is considerably lower than that he would pay under a value-added tax, if he has just reached a point where his marginal purchases are chiefly of the semi-luxury, late-stage type of product, which is lightly taxed under the turnover tax. If he earns more money by working overtime, or by speeding up under piece rate payment, he will spend this extra income chiefly on lightly taxed goods, to the extent that he does not save it. A worker or salaried man or executive, at a higher income level, will be paying turnover tax at average and marginal rates both lower than he would be paying under an equal-yield value-added tax (recall that the statutory rate of the turnover tax is the lower) if most of his purchases are of late-stage goods.

The traditional comparison in public finance analysis is between amount of work under the tax in question and under no tax. Then the income effect of the tax, which induces more work, is compared with the marginal effect (substitution effect), which induces less work. This approach is useful when the tax is coupled with a government outlay to supply services free of charge. Then, there are four distinct effects, acting simultaneously, to be evaluated: the income effects of the tax

36. See page 13.

and of the free service, and the substitution effects of both. Each pair of income and substitution effects can be studied separately.

As a step toward this kind of analysis, we may ask whether the turnover tax increases or decreases work in the partial-equilibrium sense of comparison with a no-tax situation, without specifying what is done with the tax revenue. But the problem seems virtually insoluble by a priori reasoning, or rather, the answer is that it all depends. Choosing among sets of equally plausible assumptions about rates of change in elasticity of supply of labor as the take-home pay changes under a tax that is presumed not to affect the wage gross of tax, the analyst can reach either a more-work or a less-work conclusion. Since the various possibilities are most easily grasped in terms of income taxation, the details of that analysis are deferred to Chapters 11 and 12 below, pages 311, 335.

By its nature, the turnover tax does not strike transfers that are gifts. It therefore creates a tax differential in favor of giving, whether to friends and relatives or to religious, charitable, educational, and other institutions, compared with spending for consumption. Giving must compete equally with saving, however, since neither use of one's funds attracts turnover tax directly. Indirectly, we have seen, the turnover tax reduces the real return, as opposed to the money return, that can be obtained from saving; but indirectly, too, the return from the gift is reduced to the extent that the donee cannot purchase as much as if there were no turnover tax. The net effect of the turnover tax on giving is probably positive, but slight, unless the turnover tax law exempts sales to the charitable and other institutions.

Other public-purpose private outlays can be stimulated by granting low rates or exemption from the turnover tax, but few instances are found in turnover tax laws, unless purchases of farm products, foods, and the like are viewed as public-purpose outlays.

Intergovernmental coordination under the turnover tax is concerned chiefly with (1) taxability of sales to, or by, subordinate or superior units of government, and (2) allowance to be made for other types of tax imposed by those units on transfers that would normally be struck by the turnover tax.

If the taxing jurisdiction, say the national government, exempts from its turnover tax all sales by private firms to provincial, state, or local units of government, it makes an indirect grant of funds to them. The amounts could be substantial if the exemption included refund of turnover tax paid at earlier stages in the private sector, as with sales for export.

Purchases by foreign governments usually raise no special problem under the destination-principle turnover tax, since exports are exempt. Sales by other units of government concern chiefly government enterprises, particularly those supplying water, gas, electricity, and heat.[37]

Certain taxes levied by subordinate units may be deemed to have preempted some of the field that otherwise might be covered by a very general turnover tax. This is in part the reason why real property rentals or imputed income from real property

---

37. Exemption is granted to those sales made by enterprises of subordinate units of government in Germany. Gumpel and Boettcher, *op. cit.*, p. 809. The national government's postal, telephone, and telegraph enterprises do not pay turnover tax (*ibid.*, p. 211).

are commonly exempt from the turnover tax. Subordinate units impose, in one country or another, taxes on real property,[38] transportation,[39] financial transfers,[40] transfers of real property,[41] and insurance contracts,[42] to name only the chief examples. Unlike the excises on tobacco, alcohol, jewelry, and luxuries in general, these particular taxes have resembled the turnover tax itself in possessing little rationale for existence except that of administrative ease. To impose on such transactions the turnover tax too would be to lean too much on expediency. Moreover, some of them, notably certain financial transfers, seem to have little to do directly with the productive process (this does not mean they are nonproductive), a test that is not made explicit in turnover tax laws but that seems to be the only explanation for certain common provisions, for example, exemption or a low rate upon the sale of an entire business.[43]

Intragovernmental coordination suggests that sales to the taxing government should be exempt from the turnover tax, to enable the government to make its purchase on the basis of real social cost. Exemption of sales by enterprises of the taxing government is another matter. Any such exemption probably tends to favor certain groups of consumers in a manner difficult to justify.

To estimate the net yield of a turnover tax introduced in a system that already includes an income tax, some allowance must be made for the fact that the turnover tax is deductible in computing the base for the income tax. If money prices rise by the amount of the turnover tax, money yield of the income tax is not reduced (unless physical volume falls), but in real terms the yield declines.

Changes in the level of other taxes do not affect in real terms the yield, per percentage point of tax rate, of the turnover tax. If an income tax is introduced, to allow the rate of the turnover tax to decline, no reduction in the real yield of the turnover tax occurs, aside from that due to the reduction in rate of tax, since the income tax is not deductible in computing the base of the turnover tax. If an excise is introduced, to lower the rate of the turnover tax, it may increase the money yield per percentage point of turnover tax rate, since the turnover tax will usually be based on the sales price inclusive of excise tax, but in real terms, after deflation by an index of product prices, there is no increase in the turnover tax yield.

---

38. As in Germany (Gumpel and Boettcher, *op. cit.*, p. 810). Exemption from the turnover tax involves "subtle technical distinctions, for example, the rental of a separate garage or individually marked storage space for an automobile is considered a lease of real property and exempt, unless the lessor also undertakes to service the car. Conversely, the storage of an automobile in a large garage with no definite place assigned to it is in the nature of a bailment . . . and therefore is taxable."

39. In Germany (Due, *op. cit.*, p. 53).

40. In Germany (Gumpel and Boettcher, *op. cit.*, p. 809).

41. In Germany (*idem.*).

42. In Germany (*idem.*).

43. In Germany, a 1 per cent rate applies to sale of an entire business or of an independent division of a firm. Certain exempt assets are deducted (e.g., cash) and certain intra-family transfers are exempt (*ibid.*, p. 819). In Italy, all sales of entire businesses are exempt (Cobb and Forte, *op. cit.*, p. 723).

B. MANUFACTURERS' SALES TAX

Most of the countries that became dissatisfied with the turnover tax before 1967 moved, with but one exception,[44] to a single-stage tax on sales by manufacturers. But in a few of these countries this transition was piecemeal and incomplete; the single-stage tax was substituted only in one or another sector when an administrative advantage was foreseen because the number of taxable firms would thereby be reduced appreciably. In some countries this step-by-step movement did not go very far; in others, it flowered into a massive system of differential rates, as in Austria (*Phasenpauschalierung*) and Italy (*una tantum*). The formidable task of setting a single-stage tax rate for a given commodity so that it would closely approximate the cumulative burden of a turnover tax at a specified rate has been termed useless, in view of the essential arbitrariness of that cumulative feature.[45] But since these single-stage replacement taxes were introduced commodity by commodity over a considerable period of time, the revenue-conscious finance ministers demanded that each replacement tax rate yield revenue equivalent to the turnover tax foregone.[46] Moreover, since end products compete with one another for the consumer's dollar, it was important for those industries that remained under the turnover tax that each single-stage rate be no lower than the former cumulative turnover tax rate. In this manner the inter-industry competitive equilibrium that had been reached under the arbitrary economics of the turnover tax was preserved. Still, to extend the replacement-tax system to some 400 commodities, while attempting to equate each single-stage tax to the turnover tax it replaced (Austria) does seem to reflect a loss of perspective.

The other countries that abandoned the turnover tax broke completely with the old pattern and employed a uniform-rate manufacturers' sales tax, the subject of the present Section B.[47] In this way they eliminated most of the unevenness of impact upon differing patterns of industrial organization and marketing. The manufacturers' sales tax is not neutral as among products, as we shall see shortly, but this kind of discrimination is considered a minor defect by most legislators. They are commonly much less concerned over discrimination among products than over discrimination among competitive methods of doing business.

44. Norway, in 1940, moved to a retail sales tax (see Chapter 9, Section A.1). For developments since 1966, see Chapter 9, Section B.1.

45. Due, *Sales Taxation*, pp. 74–76.

46. See the history of the replacement taxes in France in the 1920's, in Shoup, *The Sales Tax in France*, Chapters 5 and 12.

47. With only two exceptions (Chile and Greece), every one of the eleven countries employing in 1957 a single-stage manufacturers" sales tax came to it after an unhappy experience with a turnover tax (dates are introduction of turnover tax and manufacturers' sales tax, respectively: Argentina, 1931, 1935; Brazil, 1924, 1934; Canada, 1920, 1923; Cuba, 1922, 1946; Ecuador, 1925, 1941; France, 1917–19, 1936; Indonesia, 1950, 1951; Uruguay, 1928 (only 0.3 per cent), 1941; Yugoslavia, 1921, 1931. The only countries to have abandoned the manufacturers' sales tax are the Netherlands (see footnote 1) and Finland (see footnote 53). (Due, *Sales Taxation, passim.*).

1. Conceptual Basis of Manufacturers' Sales Tax

The conceptual base for the great majority of manufacturers' sales taxes is the value of the commodity as it leaves the last manufacturing firm to process it. In a few countries, the tax base is the value added by each firm in the manufacturing sector. The mechanics of value-added taxation are explained on pages 253–55. Aside from certain administrative considerations, the analysis to follow applies equally to either form of manufacturers' sales tax.

The stage at which the commodity becomes taxable is commonly defined in terms of business firm rather than in terms of function: manufacturing firm rather than the process of manufacturing. If a manufacturer integrates vertically forward by assuming some wholesaling and retailing functions, yet remains primarily a manufacturing firm, the concept imposes the tax on a value of the commodity that includes certain wholesaling and retailing costs. The tax is heavier; in this sense the manufacturers' sales tax discriminates against vertical integration forward by a manufacturer. Correspondingly, the tax encourages a modest degree of vertical integration backward by a retail or wholesale firm, which, by taking over storage, handling, transportation, and perhaps other functions ancillary to manufacturing can buy at a lower price, hence with a smaller sales tax loading. But if the marketing firm integrates too far backward, the taxable price of what it buys may be ruled to be higher than the actual price (see Section 4.A below).

It may be argued that the basic concept is that of a manufacturing tax, not a manufacturers' tax. The view taken here to the contrary is based on the grounds that, as with the turnover tax, an essential element of the concept is limitation of the tax to transfers for a consideration (see Section A.1 above). This limitation means that the firm, not the function, is, at least within limits, the defined boundary for taxation.

The manufacturers' sales tax introduces an idea not found in the turnover tax, that of a tax-suspension area. A certain sector of the business community is marked out, "manufacturers," in this instance, and every firm within this group is "licensed." Commodities that never enter this group never incur tax; an illustration is fruit that a farmer takes to market to sell to consumers. Commodities that enter this group of licensed firms pay no tax upon entry and may be transferred tax-free within the group; the buyer within the group quotes his license number to his vendor and takes the commodity free of tax. Upon egress from the group, including withdrawal from the firm for the owner's personal use, tax falls due, typically when a manufacturer sells to a wholesaler or retailer, that is, when a licensed firm sells to an unlicensed firm. Thus wheat may be sold by the farmer (unlicensed) to the miller (licensed) without tax; the miller sells flour to the bakery company (licensed) tax-free, but upon sale of the bread to a wholesaler or retailer (unlicensed) the tax is levied.

The definition of the area covered by the term "manufacturing" is determinative of the scope of the tax. Products can always escape the tax altogether if they can escape entry into the manufacturing sector.

This tax-suspension area is sometimes called a "free area." This is not an apt designation, since the true free area is that part of the business world that lies outside the manufacturing sector: the area embracing farmer and consumer, in the illustration above. The tax-suspension area is a necessary device when the tax is placed athwart the channels of commerce rather than right at the end of each channel, as under the retail sales tax, or rather than being imposed bit by bit on every firm, manufacturer or not, as it adds value to the commodities it handles (value-added tax). The tax-suspension idea is irrelevant for the turnover tax, which makes no attempt to tax every final product only once.

If every final product is to be taxed no more than once, suspension of tax on the entire sales value while the commodity moves around within the zone is essential, in the complex industrial world where semi-finished products in various stages of completion shuttle between factories, and where manufacturing consumables, fuel for example, enter the zone and are destroyed in use but add a value that will be taxed when the final product emerges from the zone.

Some commodities, in the normal course, emerge from the zone and then re-enter it, as when oil produced in the manufacturing zone is sold by wholesalers to other manufacturers. Methods must be devised for averting duplicate taxation that will occur if the ordinary rules are followed. For this and similar reasons wholesalers are sometimes allowed to be licensed, under a manufacturers' sales tax, just as if they were manufacturers. They can purchase tax-free on the understanding that they will pay tax on such of their sales as are not made to other licensed taxpayers. This device has been extensively used at times in some countries;[48] in effect, the manufacturers' sales tax is then converted partly into a wholesalers' tax.

International trade is taxed under the destination principle; the origin principle has been used only by subordinate levels of government. The distinction between the two principles is of more importance to the treasuries of the exporting and importing countries under a single-stage tax than under a turnover tax. The entire tax on any product is captured by one country or the other (see Section A.1 above). An administrative advantage over the turnover tax is that only one rate need be stipulated for export exemption or refund or compensating import tax.

A few countries have employed the "universal" type of manufacturers' sales tax, taxing both imports and exports, usually in conjunction with the value-added technique.

Sales of capital goods are not usually exempt under the manufacturers' sales tax, partly for administrative reasons given in Section 4.A below. If all capital goods are to be taxed, those produced by the user must be taxed on an imputed transfer.

Exemption of capital goods is also feasible under the value-added type of manufacturers' sales tax, in a manner to be explained in Chapter 9, Section B.2.A below; the tax on value added at each stage is computed by first reckoning a tentative tax on the firm's entire gross receipts, then crediting against that tax the amount of tax shown on purchase invoices. Upon sale of the final product, that is, the capital good, the entire tax paid up to that point will be evident from the purchase invoices at the last stage;[49] this amount is then refunded.

48. For Canada, see Due, *Sales Taxation*, pp. 150–51.

49. This statement does not hold if one or more earlier stages have been exempted.

2. Incidence in an Open Economy

The conclusions reached on incidence in an open economy for a turnover tax apply
also to a manufacturers' sales tax. When export demand and import supply are
perfectly elastic, the factory prices of exportables and of import-competing goods
(if imports do not fall to zero) do not decrease. Foreign consumers and foreign
factors are not harmed by the tax. If the elasticities are less than perfect, the incidence of the tax is more widely spread, as described in Section A.2, above.

The manufacturers' sales tax exerts no special pressure against non-integrated
industries, but (for an equal-yield tax) it does apply even more pressure than the
turnover tax against early-stage value added, for it exempts completely instead of
taxing lightly all value added below the manufacturing stage. The statutory rate of
tax will be much higher, for an equal yield, than that of the turnover tax; the discrimination between value added at the manufacturing and earlier stages and value
added at wholesaling, retailing, and other post-manufacturing stages is intense.
Imports may well decline as methods are devised to alter the value texture of a final
product by putting less into manufacturing it and more into marketing it. Even
without this induced change in value texture, imports will be discouraged unless
they happen to be of goods that are already markedly late-stage goods. If they are not
of this type, the manufacturers' sales tax will be more repressive of imports than the
turnover tax will be, because of the greater tax differential it imposes on early-stage
value added.

3. Differential Incidence:
Manufacturers' Sales Tax and Value-Added Tax

Compared with a value-added tax (consumption type) a manufacturers' sales tax is
likely to be an even greater burden on low-income consumers than is the turnover
tax (though we recall that the comparative amount of the tax that rests on factors
rather than consumers is not known). This is so because of the greater discrimination, just noted, against early-stage value added. Not only is the rate differential
between early- and late-stage values added greater than under the turnover tax, but
now the existence of the differential does not depend on absence of complete vertical
integration. Even a product produced and marketed by a firm vertically integrated
from raw materials through the retail stage will attract a lower tax charge, the larger
is the proportion of late-stage value added.

Otherwise, the differential incidence of the manufacturers' sales tax against the
value-added tax is almost nil.

4. Criteria

A. Consensus Criteria

The manufacturers' sales tax, just because it seeks to avoid multiple taxation of value added at any one stage, encounters a definitional problem not present under the turnover tax. The problem is that of defining a finished good and distinguishing it from an intermediate good.

An administrative consideration intensifies the definitional problem and leads to severe qualitative, or definitional, discontinuities, for the following reasons. Among the goods and services that a manufacturer purchases there will be certain tangible goods that will be used up in the process of manufacturing and so will not become physically incorporated in the manufacturer's product; they are "producers' consumables." Many of them can be used, without further processing, by households, or by firms outside the licensed area, notably wholesalers and retailers. Examples are fuel and certain chemicals. A temptation to make money at the expense of the fisc is now present. The manufacturer, although professing to purchase these goods for use in manufacture, and so obtaining them tax-free, may resell them, without charging tax, to households or nontaxable business firms, or may divert them to use within his own household. The fuel or the chemicals thus illegally diverted escape taxation entirely. Accordingly, tax administrators everywhere are reluctant to allow the producer of a finished yet potentially intermediate good, say fuel, an exemption on sale of it to manufacturers as a truly intermediate good, for fear of illegal diversion. The definition of a purchase for resale (purchase of an intermediate good) is therefore commonly made a very narrow one, and the definition of a finished good is correspondingly broadened, so that a good is deemed purchased for resale (commonly after processing) only if it appears physically in the product sold by the manufacturer-purchaser. This physical appearance in the taxable product affords a method of checking, to make sure that the manufacturer has not diverted his purchase to a nontaxable user.

Taxation of producers' consumables is a departure from the basic concept of a manufacturers' sales tax, justifiable only on administrative grounds.

Capital goods, too, are not physically embodied in the finished product. The common refusal to allow manufacturers to buy capital goods tax-free is based chiefly on this same administrative consideration. Where exemption is granted, it is usually restricted to capital goods that cannot be readily used by non-taxable firms, or households: machinery, for example, as against office furniture and motor vehicles.[50]

There is no occasion to attempt to tax intra-firm transfers (unless all capital goods are to be taxed), since the manufacturers' sales tax does not vary with vertical integration, save for limited integration between manufacturing and marketing sectors.

Exemption of small firms loses a smaller proportion of the tax base than under the

50. Due, *Sales Taxation*, pp. 153 and pp. 370–373.

turnover tax, since manufacturing is usually more concentrated in large firms than is business activity in general.

A reduction in the rate of the manufacturers' sales tax to maintain or regain full employment has the advantages and shortcomings of the turnover tax (see Section A.4.A above), with two exceptions. First, competitive conditions between integrated firms and others are not disturbed by changes in the tax rate. Second, anticipatory postponement of buying when a recession begins, or anticipatory buying when full employment is approached, is apt to be even more severe than under a turnover tax. The manufacturers' tax is collected only on sales to business firms (with rare exceptions), while much of the turnover tax revenue comes from tax on sales to households. Business firms are usually more able to engage in anticipatory buying or anticipatory postponement than are households and are under competitive pressure to do so.

The built-in flexibility of a manufacturers' sales tax is even greater than that of the turnover tax, because of the fact that raw materials and manufacturing value added will commonly decline faster than value added in marketing. The efficiency of any given degree of sensitivity is greater, too, if, as conjectured above, early-stage value added is a larger percentage of low-income budgets.

The manufacturers' sales tax creates far less excess burden than the turnover tax with respect to vertical integration and far more with respect to early-stage taxation, for reasons already given. It resembles the turnover tax in its discrimination against capital goods, in practice.

Vertical integration upward by powerful retailers who buy direct from manufacturers that are virtually captive firms gives them a competitive advantage unless countered by "uplift" provisions, which require the manufacturer to value his sales, for tax purposes, at more than the actual price received. But the establishment and policing of such an uplifted sales price, with its imputed element, is difficult.[51] If competition for independents develops instead from large manufacturers who take over wholesalers' functions and sometimes own retail outlets, the manufacturers' sales tax reduces that competition instead of intensifying it, unless the tax is imposed on a hypothetical price reached by a process the reverse of "uplift."

It has been alleged that a tax collected at an early stage imposes an extra burden in the form of an interest charge that could be avoided if the government would tax only the final stage, retail sale. The interest charge in question is that on the tax paid. The manufacturer must recoup this interest, even in a perfectly competitive economy. The issue is distinct from that of pyramiding, discussed above, which implies abnormal profit. The burden is said to be extra because, although the consumer must pay the interest charge in the price of the goods, the government does not receive the interest.

This argument, despite its distinguished sponsorship,[52] is faulty. If the govern-

---

51. So much so that even in Canada, where protests from independents have been vigorous, this uplift has not yet been attempted. See *ibid.*, p. 162.

52. A. Cournot, *Researches into the Mathematical Principles of the Theory of Wealth*, trans. by Nathaniel T. Bacon (New York: Macmillan, 1929), p. 70; W. Frend, *Principles of Taxation* (London: Mawman, 1804), p. 43; and, according to Ricardo, Say, and Sismondi (see David Ricardo, *Principles of Political Economy and Taxation*, Piero Sraffa, Ed. [Cambridge: Cambridge

ment introduces a retail sales tax instead of a manufacturers' sales tax, and introduces it at the same date, the consumers must pay tax, starting at once, instead of having a few weeks or months of tax-free purchases until the manufacturers' tax, with interest superimposed, works its way down into retail prices. The extra amount thus paid by consumers for the first few weeks or months could have been loaned out perpetually to earn enough interest to compensate for the interest-on-tax element reaching the consumer through a manufacturers' sales tax. If it takes a year (for simplicity) for the manufactured good to reach the consumer after it leaves the factory, and if he pays $100 at retail without tax but $110 under a 10 per cent retail tax, and if (abstracting from wholesale and retail margins, for simplicity) a 10 per cent tax is imposed on manufacturers rather than on retailers, then, with interest at 10 per cent a year, the consumer under the manufacturers' sales tax buys the article at retail for

$100   the first year
 111   the second year and thereafter ($100 cost + $10 tax + $1 interest on tax),

while under the retail sales tax he buys for

$110   the first year and thereafter.

The $10 he saves in tax the first year under the manufacturers' sales tax compared with the retail sales tax can be loaned out at $1 a year interest forever, to supply him with the extra $1 he pays in the second and succeeding years under the manufacturers' sales tax. The fact that the typical consumer cannot in practice loan out the few pennies he saves the first year under the retail sales tax is a frictional element that helps form his preferences between present and future consumption; it does not support the faulty argument cited above.

The taxation of certain intermediate goods—producers' consumables and capital goods—creates an excess burden by encouraging methods of production that, although inherently less efficient, save tax by using more inputs of a kind that appear physically in the product.

B. CONFLICT CRITERIA

The manufacturers' sales tax is probably even more regressive with income relative to the value-added tax than is the turnover tax, because of the greater discrimination against early-stage value added. Otherwise, with exceptions to be noted in the paragraphs immediately following, the appraisal of the turnover tax with respect to regressivity, family composition, status, area discrimination, economic growth, risk-taking, external equilibrium, labor supply, public-purpose outlays, and inter- and intra-governmental coordination applies to the manufacturers' sales tax, with due allowance, where appropriate, for the heavier burden on early-stage value added.

University Press, 1951–55], p. 379). Ricardo pointed out the flaw in this argument (*ibid.*, p. 380). For further comment see Carl S. Shoup, *Ricardo on Taxation* (New York: Columbia University Press, 1960), pp. 198–200.

The manufacturers' sales tax is better suited than other general sales taxes for exempting food, housing, and clothing in an attempt to reduce the burden on low-income groups. Many foods are not processed, and others are commonly the sole products of the particular manufacturer. Exemption is then easier administratively than at the wholesale or retail stage where one firm commonly handles both taxable commodities and exempt foods, and so must keep separate records for exempt and taxable sales. A housing exemption can be implemented in part by following a natural inclination to regard on-site assembly as a non-manufacturing activity. At earlier stages, however, it is often impossible to know whether the building materials will end up in housing or in other construction. In countries where prefabricated housing and shell housing are important for low-income families, that manufacturing activity can be specifically exempted. Clothing can be completely exempted at the factory, but home-sewn or other homemade clothing will bear the tax on the cloth and other materials.

These exemptions can scarcely be accorded without granting benefit to households in middle- and upper-income groups, but this is a technical shortcoming of all general sales taxes.

The manufacturers' sales tax encourages the keeping in use of old machinery by intensive servicing and repair. These activities, commonly taxed under the turnover tax, are exempt under the manufacturers' sales tax.

Prices of imported products to the domestic consumer are raised by varying percentages, depending now, not on degree of vertical integration but on the relative importance of wholesale, transportation, retail, and other post-manufacture costs.

The origin-principle manufacturers' sales tax, because of its higher rate, induces an even greater shift in demand from value added in import-competing manufacturing and earlier-stage sectors to foreign value added. Under the turnover tax much of the taxable value is added at the wholesale and retail stages where little or no competition is felt from foreign factors. Similarly, taxation of exports puts more pressure on factors manufacturing exports than does an equal-yield origin-principle turnover tax.

C. WHOLESALERS' SALES TAX

1. Conceptual Basis

A wholesalers' sales tax is a modified manufacturers' sales tax and can be analyzed briefly by noting the respects in which it differs from the latter. We have seen that

53. No country has substituted a wholesalers' sales tax for another type of sales tax, and only Denmark and (by the definitions used here) Eire have abandoned a wholesalers' sales tax. The six countries now imposing only a wholesalers' sales tax (with dates of adoption) are Australia (1930), New Zealand (1933), Pakistan (1948), Portugal (1966), Switzerland (1941), and the United Kingdom (1940). Finland employs what is in effect a value-added tax: wholesale sales tax together with a tax on value added at retail (Alan Tait and John F. Due, "Sales Taxation in Eire, Denmark and Finland," *National Tax Journal* [September, 1965], 18: 286–96). The Eire wholesale sales tax, which exempts food, medicines, clothing, and fuel, is now coupled with a retail sales tax, to comprise an incomplete form of turnover tax.

in principle all manufacturers but no wholesalers are liable for a manufacturers' sales tax. Under a wholesalers' sales tax, on the other hand, liability attaches not only to all wholesalers, but also to those manufacturers who sell directly to retailers or consumers. A manufacturer can bypass a wholesaler; a wholesaler, imports aside, cannot bypass a manufacturer. This distinction has been somewhat blurred in practice by the fact that under a manufacturers' sales tax it has proved convenient (see Section B.1 above) to license some wholesalers, allow them accordingly to buy tax-free, and tax them on their sales. Still, the distinction in principle remains, and a substantial part of the revenue from a wholesalers' sales tax will normally be collected from manufacturers. This proportion will be largest in an industrialized economy where large retailers stock private brands made to their order by manufacturers, and where large manufacturers undertake wholesaling functions and sometimes own retail outlets.[54]

The fact that the area within which incomplete goods may circulate tax-free is a little larger under the wholesalers' sales tax is an administrative advantage. An incomplete good is an intermediate good that has some processing or assembling or the like yet to be done. The same remark applies to producers' consumables. Fewer tax refunds are needed, since fewer goods leave and then return to the licensed sector.

Exemption of small wholesalers costs less revenue than exemption of small manufacturers. Large manufacturers do not normally sell through small wholesalers; they sell either direct or through large wholesale houses. This part of the tax base is not lost by exempting small wholesalers. And small manufacturers sell only in part through small wholesalers. Because of the greater percentage of wholesale firms that are small, the tax authorities may prefer to operate at the manufacturing stage, if no exemption is to be granted to small firms.[55]

The further down the line the single-stage tax is levied, the easier it becomes to implement the destination principle. On this score, the wholesale tax is to be preferred to the manufacturers' tax. A larger proportion of imports will have entered the country's commercial stream before the taxing stage is reached and so may be allowed into the country free of compensating import tax. These imports will be caught automatically as they pass through the later, domestic, taxing stage. A larger proportion of exports will have left the country before passing through the domestic taxing stage and so will require no refund of tax.

Under the origin principle, on the other hand, the wholesale tax standing by itself is inadequate; a special export tax must be levied on manufacturers who export directly instead of through wholesalers, or they must be treated as are manufacturers selling directly to retailers.

54. Due, *Sales Taxation*, p. 174.
55. This appears to have been the case in Canada. See Due, *Sales Taxation*, p. 151.

2. Incidence and Criteria

The remarks above on the differential incidence of the manufacturers' sales tax hold also, in general, for the wholesalers' sales tax.

An administrative advantage of the wholesalers' sales tax that is relevant for equal treatment is that manufacturers who sell direct to retailers do not need to be taxed on a hypothetical price that is less than the actual price, to be able to compete with manufacturers selling to independent wholesalers. If in fact the manufacturers' sales tax allows no such hypothetical price, the advantage of the wholesalers' sales tax is an allocative one; it exerts less tax pressure against downward integration.

Giant retailers who reach upstream and take on some wholesaling and manufacturing functions must be more closely watched under a wholesalers' tax. They will commonly pay their manufacturers a lower price than will the small retailer even if he buys direct from the factory. If the value added by wholesaling functions is to be consistently included in the tax base the lower price paid by the large retailers must be "uplifted" even more than under a manufacturers' sales tax[56] if they are not to gain a tax advantage over the non-integrated producer-wholesaler-retailer system of marketing, or over the small retailer dealing direct with the manufacturer. The tax inducement to some upward integration is stronger than under the manufacturers' sales tax.

The low price to the big retailer may, on the other hand, represent not his taking on some of the wholesaling or manufacturing functions, but true elimination of some of those functions, at least some of the wholesaling functions. To uplift the actual price, for tax purposes, as if such services did exist is to create an artificial tax base that will be difficult to maintain in the face of protests it will evoke.[57] The practical problem is to distinguish these cases from those where the low price paid by the retailer reflects assumption by him of some wholesaling functions. Discounts for quantity purchases may reflect either elimination or assumption, or some of both.

The discrimination in favor of goods with a large service element in their retail value that is accorded by the manufacturers' sales tax is somewhat reduced by the wholesalers' sales tax, for it draws into the tax base the value added by the service of wholesaling. The change is small, however. Retail services are usually a greater element in final value than are wholesale services. Other services—transportation, electricity supply, professional and other personal services—remain exempt insofar as they attach to the commodity after it leaves the taxable stage. If they are sold direct to consumers the tax base is usually the same under a wholesale tax as under a manufacturers' sales tax.

---

56. See page 238 above.

57. The "uplift" required by the British purchase tax authorities prior to 1955 was probably in large part of this type. To be sure, the mere absence of wholesale firms in some line of trade is not proof that wholesaling functions do not exist, but when 90 per cent of all sales are made by manufacturers to retailers, as in the furniture industry, in Britain (see Due, *Sales Taxation*, p. 215), much of the ordinary kind of wholesaling functions is probably not being performed, because it is not needed.

CHAPTER NINE

General Sales Taxes:
Retail Sales Tax, Value-Added Tax

A. RETAIL SALES TAX

1. Conceptual Basis

A RETAIL SALES TAX in its pure form is the equivalent of a comprehensive consumption type of tax on value added (see Section B below) except that it does not offer an option between the destination principle and the origin principle. An origin-principle retail sales tax is a contradiction in terms with respect to exports, and poses insuperable administrative problems for imports. A separate tax would be needed on exports, and it would have to be based on a supposed retail value that the exports would command abroad. Imports would have to retain their identity through the retail stage in order to benefit from the exemption the origin principle would offer them. The following analysis of the retail sales tax will therefore not include an origin-principle variant, in contrast to the analyses of all other types of sales taxation.

The retail sales tax is well suited to the destination principle, which it can implement with little or no border control. All imports other than by the ultimate user can be allowed to enter free of any import compensating tax; the imported goods will be fully taxed as they pass from the domestic retailer to the domestic user. This fact makes the retail sales tax especially suitable for subordinate units of government that have no border controls already established for customs: states, provinces, counties, cities.[1]

The retail sales tax possesses the breadth of the turnover tax without its discrimination against early-stage value added and non-integration. Since almost the

---

1. Central governments imposing, as of 1968, a general sales tax limited to the retail level include Honduras (1964), Costa Rica, Iceland (1960), Norway (1940), Rhodesia, and Sweden (1960, thirteen years after repealing a similar tax of World War II). For Honduras, see Section 4 below. None of these retail taxes, except Norway's, replaced an existing tax. Provinces in Canada, most of the states and some of the local governments in the United States, and some states in India use the retail sales tax.

entire tax is collected from retailers, it is difficult to enforce at a high rate in view of the existence of a large number of tiny firms that keep inadequate books if any, yet in many countries account for a substantial part of total retail sales.

A low-rate retail sales tax can be used as a constituent part of a low-rate high-yield general turnover tax, or some other general indirect tax system, or as a separate tax at a low rate to help meet the more modest revenue needs of state, provincial, or local units. The retail revolution, originating in the United States and now spreading widely, concentrates retail sales in department stores, chains, supermarkets, and large specialty shops, and is thereby creating the milieu necessary for a high-rate retail tax that can contribute significantly to a national government's budget. In federalized countries, however, states and localities are not likely to give up their claims, based on prior possession, to a sales tax that can function without border control.

The retail sales tax, like the turnover tax and the general value-added tax, permits the inclusion of all services, in contrast to taxes on manufacturers or wholesalers.

The analysis here is devoted first to a retail sales tax that covers all consumer purchases of goods and services, and not, in principle at least, any business-firm purchases. It then moves to a retail sales tax that exempts most consumers' services, which is in fact the prevailing type of retail tax.

Since the retail sales tax is especially suitable for administration by a subordinate unit of government, owing to its relative lack of need for border control, it will be analyzed here chiefly on the assumption that it is being imposed by a city or other large local unit.

2. Goods and Services Consumer Retail Sales Tax

A. Incidence in an Open Economy

In an open economy, the extreme case of a perfectly elastic export demand and import supply does not much exaggerate the circumstances for a city, or even sometimes for a province or state. Producers in a retail-sales taxing city who can sell part or all of their output outside the city will divert it to this external, tax-free market until the price within the city rises by enough to let them recoup the entire tax. City producers of import-competing goods will also recoup the tax in higher prices if out-of-city suppliers reduce their shipments into the city until the price rises by the amount of the tax. For a city, if not for a nation, this outcome seems likely.

Since producers within the city of non-traded goods, that is, goods not imported into or exported from the city, and not competing directly with imports, are not protected from the tax, they will have to bear part or all of it. Many services are largely non-traded. The retail sales tax will therefore disadvantage the city's sellers of services, including the service of retailing, more than its manufacturers of tangible commodities.

Border control must in principle be imposed with respect to goods purchased outside the city by city residents. In practice, states and local units do not usually enforce control at the border. They bill the user directly for the tax when they can easily ascertain that he has imported an article of some value. Their source of information may be a motor vehicle license bureau or an out-of-city retailer who has agreed to notify the city authorities of orders from city residents. When such information is not obtainable, the tax will be evaded to some degree on consumer durables and on other commodities of large unit value, expensive clothing for example. Services supplied outside the city, notably professional and mechanical services, are in effect imported by the city resident who buys them. So too is travel outside the city. The strictest border control could scarcely detect all imports of this kind, embodied as they are in the user himself or in his possessions. Even for tangible commodities of small unit value, consumers will find that the time and effort needed are modest enough to make evasion seem worth while, if they live near that part of the city's periphery that is close to another city's non-taxed shopping center or service center. These illegal operations depress the sales volume of wholesalers, retailers, and sellers of services, professional or otherwise, located in the peripheral areas of the city.

B. DIFFERENTIAL INCIDENCE: RETAIL SALES TAX AND VALUE-ADDED TAX, CONSUMPTION TYPE

The differential incidence of the retail sales tax and the value-added tax, consumption type, is nil, because both taxes have the same aggregate base.[2] The consumption tax (retail sales tax) is imposed on the amount consumers pay (*ex* other tax, if any) for consumption goods, and the value-added tax, consumption type, is imposed on the amount paid to factors for producing those goods. These remarks of course abstract from friction and like imperfections in the market.

C. CRITERIA

(1) Consensus Criteria

The definitional problem involving producers' consumables and capital goods (Chapter 8, Section B.4.A) is troublesome under the retail sales tax also. To check tax-free diversion to households of goods ostensibly purchased by business firms, retail sales tax administrators prefer to define a sale at retail to include fuel, supplies, office furniture, and other producers' goods, including certain capital goods, that do not appear physically in the product that is sold, and that may be usable by consumers. Some jurisdictions, but not all, exempt certain types of machinery and other capital goods that obviously would be useless for a household. Some extend the exemption to livestock feed, seed for farm purposes, fertilizer, and industrial fuel.

2. See notes 20 and 21 below and Appendix to this chapter.

A few, among the states of the United States, exempt more or less all producers' goods, including consumables and capital goods.[3] Still, in most jurisdictions producers' goods are estimated to account for from 20 to 25 per cent of total retail sales tax revenue.[4] It is not known how much of this represents capital goods.

Small business firms present a more serious administrative problem here than under any other sales tax, owing to the important role they play in retailing. A large part of the tax base will be lost, including value added at earlier stages by large producers and wholesalers,[5] if exemption is granted to the small retailer, or if he succeeds in evading the tax. Withdrawal of taxable goods for consumption by the proprietor and his family will be a larger proportion of the tax base than under the other sales taxes. On the favorable side, no administrative problems arise from vertical integration or from intra-firm transfers.

Counter-cycle changes in the tax rate will induce a smaller amount of perverse anticipatory reaction under a retail sales tax than under any of the other broad-based sales taxes, for reasons given in Chapter 8, page 238 (manufacturers' sales tax). With respect to a discretionary counter-cycle policy, therefore, the retail sales tax is the most efficient member of the sales tax family, provided of course that it is imposed by the central government.

If the retail sales tax is a state, provincial, or local tax, its rate will be changed, if at all, cyclically, not counter-cyclically. Its built-in flexibility is an embarrassment for these government units. Fortunately, from this point of view, the sensitivity is probably less than unity, since consumer purchases will fall less sharply than whatever investment expenditures are exempt, and less sharply, also, than household incomes.

In principle, the consumer retail sales tax creates less excess burden than the turnover tax. It exerts no pressure toward changing methods of production or distribution with respect to vertical integration or early-stage value added, and does not tax capital goods. In practice, however, as we have just seen, departures from this ideal base are widespread, and exert pressure toward inefficient methods of doing business and methods of manufacture.

The taxation of capital goods under what is supposed to be a consumers' retail sales tax is likely to hamper growth (see the discussion of growth under the income tax in Chapter 12, pages 331–32 below). If it is a local tax, or a state tax, it discourages capital-intensive production within the taxing area. Some movement of capital-intensive production out of the city or state will occur until marginal cost to the industry remaining within the city or state has declined enough to allow the producers to offer the same price on their products as do capital-intensive out-of-city producers. Imports from those producers, if taxed at all, are not taxed more heavily than imports from labor-intensive producers. City producers of capital goods, as

---

3. Due, *Sales Taxation*, pp. 298–99, and index, "Producers' goods."

4. *Ibid.*, p. 299. The Swedish tax applies to purchases of buildings and machinery. A complex series of rulings distinguishes producers' consumables (not taxable) from the taxable capital goods. See Martin Norr, Claes Sandels, and Nils G. Hornhammer, *The Corporation Income Tax in Sweden* (3d ed.; Stockholms Enskilda Bank, 1966), pp. 46, 178.

5. See page 250 below.

distinguished from capital-intensive city producers, are not harmed directly by inclusion of capital goods in the tax base if they also have a market outside the city. They can sell for export tax-free and are commonly more or less protected from outside competition by a use tax imposed on the local purchaser. Of course their sales may decline appreciably if the market for their capital goods is largely within the city.

The goods-and-services type of retail sales tax does not, in principle, tax services rendered to business firms. Accordingly, encouragement to retain old machinery and keep it going by intensive servicing and repair is offered by a retail sales tax that strikes sale of new machinery, just as it is by a similar manufacturers' sales tax.

(2) Conflict Criteria

The retail sales tax is probably somewhat progressive by income relative to the turnover tax or the other single-stage taxes, for reasons given in Chapter 8, Section A.4.B. A retail sales tax that exempts food is probably progressive relative to one that does not, especially if the tax is a local one. Producers and processors of food located outside the taxing area and able to sell to many markets will not be benefited much if the taxing locality exempts food, just as they would not be harmed much if a food exemption were repealed.[6]

Households with incomes that are low, but not so low that they pay no income tax, can benefit appreciably from a tax credit given against income tax on account of sales tax presumed shifted to them.[7] But the credit tends to discriminate against large families at a low or modest income level who are exempted from income tax by the allowances for dependents and are therefore unable to use the credit for sales tax. They can be indemnified only by a cash payment. If this is not feasible, exemption of food is the next best way to assure relief to a large family of low income. Exemption of dwelling rental, paid or imputed, is the next best.

For a country that wishes to aid depressed areas within its boundaries by exemptions from a general sales tax, the retail sales tax is an excellent instrument, provided the aim is to help all consumers living in the area, not all factors working in the area. Under a nationwide retail sales tax the goods arrive as yet not taxed, at retail stores throughout the country. A simple exemption of retail sales, limited to the depressed area, assures complete tax exemption in a manner not feasible under a turnover tax. Most of that exemption, if not all, will be reflected in correspondingly lower prices to consumers. Owners of factors employed in the depressed area who themselves live

6. In Norway, food is taxed, under an unusually severe retail sales tax of 11.11 per cent, but it is simultaneously subsidized to an even greater degree. Here, taxation of food is clearly dictated by administrative convenience; it is deemed easier to operate a cross-hauling system of subsidies and taxes than it is to undertake the close examination of the books of general stores that sell foodstuffs and many other commodities that would be required by a foodstuffs exemption alongside taxation of a store's remaining trade. See Due, *Sales Taxation*, pp. 264, 269.

7. Such a credit is given in several United States sales taxing jurisdictions.

outside the area will not reap any benefit from a retail sales tax exemption except as expansion of purchases in the area increases the rewards to factors employed there.

If the retail tax reaches capital goods used within a city, or state, the economic growth of that geographical unit will be checked, in the sense that a smaller capital stock will be located there. But the economic growth of the residents of that area may be scarcely affected, since they can so easily export their capital to the rest of the country at no perceptible decline in return on capital. Given perfect mobility of capital, the economic growth of the country of which the taxing jurisdiction is but a small part will be affected imperceptibly as capital is spread a trifle more deeply over the rest of the country, to earn just a trifle less than it could have earned if the city's tax did not reach capital goods.

A city's balance of trade with the rest of the country tends to improve under a retail sales tax; an incremental flow of money to the city is induced. In this instance, the taxing unit does not control the supply of money, and enough money can flow into its jurisdiction from the rest of the country to support a higher level of prices locally without appreciably affecting the rest of the country. No parallel, of course, can be drawn with devaluation. The terms of trade ex-tax are unchanged, on the assumption of perfect elasticities of export demand and import supply.

Difficult problems of intergovernmental coordination are raised by the retail sales tax. The taxing city may claim the right to count as retail sales all sales to state or national departments or enterprises located in the city, and it may also attempt to tax sales made in the city by state or national retail enterprises. The former issue is in practice the more important (see Chapter 25).

If the city's tax system already includes the income tax, its real yield is reduced by the higher price level in the city that results from the retail sales tax. Even the money yield of a city real estate tax will be affected, but only slowly, by a fall in values if rentals and imputed income of homeowners are included in the retail sales tax base; otherwise, little effect may be expected. Price-indexed social security payments may increase.[8]

An increase in the city real estate tax rate does not directly affect the retail sales tax base. A city income tax is unlikely to raise money factor rewards; therefore it too will have little effect on the retail sales tax base. An increase in an excise tax automatically increases the sales tax yield, if the sales tax base is inclusive of the excise tax.[9]

3. Goods-Only Retail Sales Tax

Retail sales taxes commonly exempt sales of most consumer services, chiefly on administrative grounds. A major part of the total value of such services is supplied by

8. As was expected in Sweden in 1960 (Martin Norr, "The Retail Sales Tax in Sweden," *National Tax Journal* [June, 1961], 14: 174).

9. As in Sweden, for certain excises (*ibid.*, p. 179).

small firms or by professional men. To be sure, services are taxed implicitly insofar as they are rendered to business firms and become embodied in taxable goods sold at retail. The value of legal services rendered to a manufacturer of textiles, for example, and the services of wholesaling and retailing the textiles are all embodied in the taxable retail sales price of the textiles. But the services of a doctor or a barber rendered directly to the consumer are exempt under the goods-only variant of the retail sales tax.

A large proportion of the national income is produced in the service industries in a highly industrialized high-income economy: about one-fifth, excluding government, and nearly two-fifths if wholesale and retail trade are counted as service industries. A much smaller proportion of course is embodied in goods taxable at retail under a goods-only retail sales tax.

Dwelling rental is universally exempted from retail sales taxes. This policy is dictated by the difficulty of collecting a tax on imputed rent of owner-occupied dwellings. Without such a levy, inclusion of rental payments in the retail sales tax base would be grossly discriminatory. Taxation of the sale of building materials is common under "retail" sales taxes, including materials used in construction of dwellings. Some jurisdictions tax construction contracts, a wider application of the same idea. On balance, however, the typical retail sales tax gives preferential treatment to dwelling accommodation.

Services sold direct to the consumer consist of late-stage value added. Exemption of these services, under a goods-only retail sales tax, converts the tax into one that discriminates somewhat against early-stage value added, despite the fact that the tax is not imposed until the final sale to consumer. Consumers will be induced to purchase rather more of the exempt services relative to all other consumer products. The implications of this type of discrimination have been explored above (see Chapter 8, Section A.3). An important difference appears, however, if the tax is a local tax.

Consumer services, although not usually imported by a country, may be imported by a city from the rest of the country. By exempting such services, a city goods-only retail sales tax does not push consumer demand toward the products of domestic city factors quite as much as a national goods-only tax pushes consumer demand toward the output of domestic national factors that are producing these services.

Still, there is some such pressure, some shift in demand toward the products of city factors, if a city substitutes a goods-only retail sales tax for a goods-and-services tax. The proportion of consumer services that is imported, even by a city, is less than the proportion of goods that is imported. The favorable change experienced in the city's balance of trade upon introduction of a retail sales tax is therefore larger under a goods-only tax.

The goods-only tax compares unfavorably with the goods-and-services tax in equity aspects; the exemption of services is justified chiefly on administrative grounds.[10] The excess burden is also heavier, owing to this discrimination. Insofar

---

10. But administration is not simplified if the logic of the tax is carried so far as to try to distinguish the (nontaxable) service element from the (taxable) goods element in, for instance, a restaurant meal, as in Sweden (Norr, *op. cit.*, p. 179).

as an exemption of services benefits consumers it probably makes the tax more regressive with respect to consumer expenditures, hence also with respect to income.

4. Hybrid Single-stage Sales Tax

There has been devised a sales tax that falls on a retail value in some instances and only on the wholesale or manufacturers' value in other instances; it is therefore a hybrid single-stage tax. Retailers with sales volume below a certain small amount per month or per year are denied a tax license, that is, they are kept outside the tax suspension area (see Chapter 8, Section B.1). Sales to them by a wholesaler or manufacturer are therefore taxable, as if they were consumers, but at the wholesale or manufacturers' price. This hybrid tax is useful in a less developed country where small shops, market stalls, and peddlers account for a large part but not the major part of retail trade. As the country develops, a larger proportion of total value added at retail becomes taxable as more business is transacted in stores with a turnover above the exempt minimum. The hybrid tax is thus a transitional tax, providing a gradual entry into a complete retail-tax system.[11]

B. VALUE-ADDED TAX[12]

1. Conceptual Basis

The value-added tax is the latest and probably the final stage in a historical development of general sales taxation at the national level that has eliminated the uneven impact of the turnover tax and the manufacturers' and wholesalers' sales taxes. The

11. For favorable comment on this type of tax in Honduras, see John F. Due, "The Retail Sales Tax in Honduras: A Breakthrough in Taxation for Economic Development," *Inter-American Economic Affairs* (Winter, 1966), 20(3): 55–67.

12. The comprehensive value-added tax was imposed first by Denmark, effective July 3, 1967, then by France and Germany, effective January 1, 1968. The French tax replaced a value-added tax that had been restricted to manufacturers (optional for wholesalers) and a separate tax on services, as well as a local tax on retail sales. The German tax replaced a turnover tax; the Danish tax, a wholesalers' sales tax. The Netherlands will replace its turnover tax with the value-added tax, effective January 1, 1969. The remaining European Economic Community nations (Belgium, Luxembourg, and Italy) are expected to effect a similar replacement by 1970, to comply with the directive of the E. E. C. Commission, which adopted the recommendation of the Community's Fiscal and Financial Committee Report (Neumark Report) (see Chapter 25 below). The Swedish government is presenting a bill to replace the retail sales tax, which includes in its base some producer good by the value-added tax, effective January 1, 1969. All of these value-added taxes are of the consumption type, i.e., they allow full deduction in year of purchase for capital goods. For some perplexing transitional problems, see J. C. L. Huiskamp, "A New TVA Paradox," *Bulletin for International Fiscal Documentation* (January, 1968), 22: 2. In the United States the state of Michigan experimented for some ten years with a very low-rate value-added tax that was comprehensive in principle but restricted by many exemptions and high minimum deductions; the

alternate final stage of development, the retail sales tax, either will be reserved for state, provincial, and local governments, for reasons given in Section A above, or will serve as an adjunct to the value-added tax to permit differences in sales taxation rates among countries without requiring border control.

A. TYPES OF VALUE-ADDED TAX: CLOSED ECONOMY

The value-added tax is imposed on the value that a business firm adds to the goods and services that it purchases from other firms. It adds value by processing or handling these purchased items with its own labor force and its own machinery, buildings, or other capital goods. It then sells the resulting product to consumers or to other firms. The difference between the sales proceeds and the cost of the materials, etc., that it has purchased from other firms is its value added, which is the tax base of the value-added tax.

The items that a firm purchases from other firms consist of raw materials, semi-manufactured goods, supplies used up in the process of manufacture or handling, services (e.g., banking, insurance, advertising), finished goods ready for resale to consumers (in the case of retailers), and finally machinery, equipment, and other capital goods. The treatment accorded to capital goods differs, however, depending on the type of value-added tax employed. Four types can be distinguished.

(1) Gross Product Value-added Tax[13]

Under this type of value-added tax purchases from other firms that are deductible from sales exclude purchases of capital goods, e.g., machinery, buildings, equipment, furniture, vehicles. "Capital goods" includes any asset that will not be used up entirely within the tax year of purchase. Moreover, no depreciation can be deducted in subsequent years. This tax offends so against some of the consensus equity criteria that it is unlikely to be widely used.[14] If an asset with a life of, say, seven months is purchased in the period January–May of a calendar-year tax year it is deductible; if it is purchased after June 1 it is nondeductible. To be fully consistent, no deduction should be allowed for purchases that go to increase year-end inventory over year-beginning inventory, and in a subsequent year no offset against sales should be allowed for a drawing-down of inventory. This tax therefore puts heavy pressure on firms to use methods of production that do not require capital assets

tax was repealed in 1967. A value-added base has been used in Brazil, Greece, and Turkey for a manufacturers' sales tax. The value-added tax was recommended by the Shoup Tax Mission to Japan in 1950 for use by the prefectures but was never put into effect. The standard reference for a history and analysis of the value-added tax is Clara K. Sullivan, *The Tax on Value Added* (New York: Columbia University Press, 1965). The basic rates of the European value-added taxes range from about 10 per cent to 20 per cent on a base excluding the tax itself. See Carl S. Shoup, "Value-Added Tax Experience in Denmark, and Prospects in Sweden," *Finanzarchiv* (1969), 28, No. 2.

13. See Sullivan, *op. cit.*, index, "Gross product type of tax."

14. It was employed by France, 1948–53. See *ibid.*, Ch. 2.

and that do not involve frequent year-to-year fluctuations in physical volume of inventories.

In a closed economy with two factors, if C is consumption, I is gross investment, W is wages, P is net profit after depreciation, and D is depreciation, the aggregate base of the gross-product value-added tax is:

$$\text{Gross National Product} \equiv C + I \equiv W + P + D.$$

(2) Income Type of Value-added Tax

This value-added tax resembles the gross product value-added tax in not permitting deduction of capital goods purchased from other firms, but as a (delayed) offset it allows the value-added tax base to be reduced by the amount of depreciation that occurs during the year, just as does an income tax. Similarly, as does an income tax, it requires that an excess of year-end inventory over year-beginning inventory be included in the tax base and allows an excess of year-beginning inventory over year-end inventory to be deducted. For example, if a firm in Year 1 does nothing but employ its own labor to build up inventory, its sales are zero and its purchases from other firms are zero so that its value added as an excess of sales over purchases from other firms is also zero, but the income type of value-added tax requires that to this zero figure there be added the increment of inventory. If in Year 2 the firm sells off the entire inventory, its value added is tentatively the full amount of the sales (purchases from other firms being zero also in this year), but from this tentative figure there can be subtracted the decrease in inventory.

In a closed economy the aggregate base of the income type of value-added tax is net national income $\equiv C + I - D \equiv W + P$.

(3) Capital-exemption Types of Value-added Tax

There are two types of value-added tax that exempt capital, either by exempting income from it, or by exempting the value added in producing it. These are the wages type of value-added tax and the consumption type of value-added tax, respectively.

(A) WAGES TYPE OF VALUE-ADDED TAX

The base of the wages type of value-added tax is obtained, in a two-factor economy, by modification of the base of the income type of value-added tax. A deduction from that base is allowed, in an amount equal to the net earnings from the firm's capital for that year. Normally, this deduction, or exemption, will be simply P, net profits including interest. In a two-factor world, this procedure leaves in the tax base for any given year an amount corresponding to wages paid, since in this world wages plus profit (including interest) equals net national income. Hence, at the cost of some imprecision because of the presence of income from other factors that may fall outside the categories, wages and profits (including interest),[15] this kind of value-added tax may be termed the wages type. A more precise, if more cumbersome, term is investment-earnings-exclusion type of value-added tax.[16]

In a closed economy the base of this wages type of value-added tax, where Y_f is net national income as reward to factors (or, as the same total, Y_p, as net national product), is $Y - P \equiv C + I - D - P \equiv W$.

(B) CONSUMPTION TYPE OF VALUE-ADDED TAX

The other type of value-added tax that exempts capital does so by allowing deduction, in the year of purchase, of the full value of any capital good purchased from another firm, instead of, as under the income type of value-added tax, delaying such deduction until depreciation occurs year by year. It allows no adjustment for depreciation in other years (if it did so, it would be deducting the price of the capital good twice). In effect, this tax grants 100 per cent accelerated depreciation, which is equivalent to tax exemption.[17]

The base of this tax, in a closed economy, is $W + P + D - I \equiv C$, since $GNP \equiv C + I \equiv W + P + D$. Or, as just noted, net national income as reward to factors, Y_f, is by definition equal to Y_p, net national product, which is the sum of consumption goods and capital goods produced in that year, less an allowance for capital goods used up in the course of this production. Since $Y_f \equiv P + W$ (in a two-factor world in a closed economy), and $Y_p \equiv C + I - D$, it follows that $C \equiv P + W - I + D$. This latter expression is the base of this value-added tax for any one firm and hence for the closed economy as a whole. When a firm subtracts from its sales its purchases only of currently used-up goods and services, what is left is its payments to the factors it hires and that part of the cash flow from its sales that reflects the wearing down of its capital goods and its decrease, if any, in inventory. For example, if a firm does nothing in a certain year but wear down its machinery and pay some labor, to produce goods that it sells at a profit, its value added is tentatively the value of its sales, since its purchases from other firms are zero. This sales volume equals factor payments (here, wages and profits) plus depreciation, i.e., $W + P + D$. If, as is the case under the type of value added-tax now being discussed, a firm is allowed to subtract the full value

---

15. Thus for some purposes it may be useful to exclude from profits (and interest) the rent of land, where land is defined as a capital asset not produced either by labor or the wearing out of other capital. Marshallian quasi-rent in the sense of return on capital goods that were produced before the value-added tax was imposed may need to be excluded in discussing incentive effects of the tax. See Chapter 16 below, pages 386–90.

16. The term "interest-exclusion variant of the consumption-type concept" in Shoup, "Theory and Background of the Value-Added Tax" (*Proceedings, Forty-Eighth National Tax Conference*, 1955; Sacramento, Calif.: National Tax Association, 1956) is too narrow, in a world of risk and imperfect markets, where profit is viewed as something additional to interest (and may be negative). Furthermore, when this "variant" is considered in a two-factor world where labor receives wages and capital receives profit and interest, it deserves definitional status as a "type," along with the consumption type of value-added tax.

17. See the discussion of accelerated depreciation in the chapter on income taxation below, Chapter 12, pages 301–302.

of any capital goods it buys from other firms, its taxable value-added base is $W + P + D - I$, which, as shown above, is by definition equal to C. Hence this type of value-added tax may be termed the consumption type of value-added tax. It has the same aggregate base, for any one year, as a retail sales tax on consumer goods and services, that is, a general consumption tax. That this is so can be seen intuitively by noting that in a closed economy inter-firm purchases and sales cancel each other, leaving only the final retail sales total as the tax base, provided that retail sales is defined to exclude the sale of capital goods.

The amount C is equal to W if, and only if, $I = P + D$. This follows from the definitional equation above for the base of the tax, i.e., $W + P + D - I \equiv C$. If $C = W$, then $P + D - I = 0$, and $I = P + D$. Similarly, under the wages type of value-added tax, the base of that tax, W, equals C if, and only if, $P + D = I$.[18]

The consumption type of value-added tax has the same base as that which John Stuart Mill, Irving Fisher, and some others have proposed for the income tax; they would reach it by techniques that are essentially the same as the techniques just described, but designed for application to a progressive-rate tax collected from households. They would simply exclude from taxable income all returns from capital; or they would allow full deduction of saving, and since definitionally, realized saving equals realized investment, they would therefore allow the equivalent of deduction of expenditures on capital goods (see Chapter 13, Expenditure Tax).

For any one firm in any one year the base of the consumption type of value-added tax may be negative; indeed, a rapidly expanding firm may show a negative value added for many years in a row. The rationale of this type of value-added tax calls for a prompt payment by the government, or reduction of tax otherwise due in the same year, in an amount equal to the tax rate applied to this negative base.[19] A carry-forward to reduce a future year's positive value-added will not suffice, unless it is enlarged by an interest factor, since delay in tax relief is equivalent to reduction in tax relief.

It has been argued with respect to the value-added taxes that their economic effects may differ from those of their definitional equivalents, the income tax and the general consumption tax (retail sales tax).[20] Intuitively, this result seems unlikely if

18. This condition will be satisfied along the optimal growth path for a boundless golden age of natural growth, where the fraction of output accumulated is unchanged over all time, as shown by Edmund Phelps ("The Golden Rule of Accumulation: A Fable for Growthmen," *American Economic Review* [September, 1961], 51: 638–43).

19. For practice under the French value-added tax as it stood prior to the recent reform, see the description of the "buffer rule," the transfer of excess credit from a commonly owned subsidiary to the parent corporations, and the treatment of exports, in Martin Norr and Pierre Kerlan (correspondent), *Taxation in France*, World Tax Series, Law School of Harvard University (Chicago: Commerce Clearing House, 1966), pp. 1013–15.

20. See William H. Oakland, "The Theory of the Value-Added Tax: I—A Comparison of Tax Bases," *National Tax Journal* (June, 1967), 20: 131–33, with respect to the consumption type of value-added tax as compared with the consumption tax (retail sales tax), and Ezio Lancellotti, "Effetti Differenziali di Imposte ad Identica Base Complessiva," *Rivista di Diritto Finanziario e Scienza delle Finanze* (March, 1968), 27: 24–54. For the reasons why Oakland's conclusion appears unwarranted on the basis of his analysis, see Carl S. Shoup, "Consumption Tax, Wages Tax, and Value-Added Tax, Consumption Type," *National Tax Journal* (June, 1968) 21: 153–61.

not impossible.[21] The definitions given above, however, are in terms of national income accounting identities for a given year. These identities, not being behavioral relations, say nothing directly about incentives, and it is incentives that must be considered (along with the income effects, which are given by the national income relations) if the several types of tax are to be compared for their economic effects. It can be shown that definitions in terms of incentives, rather than in terms of national income accounting identities for a given year, are consistent with the conclusions that the economic effects of the value-added tax, consumption type, and of the general consumption tax (retail sales tax) are the same. Moreover, these two taxes are seen to be equivalent, in this incentive sense, to a wages tax. Regardless of what the national income accounts for the aggregate economy show for a given year, the three types of tax are equivalent in their incentive effects: the two capital-exemption types of value-added tax, and the consumption tax (retail sales tax).[22]

B. Types of Value-added Tax: Open Economy

In an open economy, the analysis above must be supplemented, particularly for the consumption type of value-added tax (the gross-product type of value-added tax will not be covered here, in view of its relative unimportance practically).

In a two-country world, if both countries wish to impose the consumption type of value-added tax, that is, if they wish to exempt value added in producing capital goods or in accumulating inventory, in the year of investment (and tax it as it is consumed in later years), the formula, sales less all purchases from other firms, remains valid. If, for example, all that happens is that Country 1 manufactures, with its labor alone, a machine that it sells to Country 2 for $100, the government of Country 1 collects tax on sales by the Country 1 firm, Firm A, including sales for export, minus purchases from other firms, that is, on $100 − 0 = $100, while the government of Country 2 gives to its Firm B a tax credit on Firm B's negative value added of $100 (sales by Firm B, zero, minus purchases from other firms, including imports, $100). Total tax collected by the countries together is zero. National income in Country 1 is $100, saving $100, and investment (claim against Country 2), $100. Income in Country 2 is zero, investment zero (+ $100, spent on machine; − $100, claim against Country 2).

The formula given above is that for an origin-principle value-added tax, coupled with a tax rebate for negative value added. The destination principle would exempt Firm A's export sale and would impose a tax on Firm B's import purchase; Country 1 would receive no tax revenue; and in fact neither would Country 2, since the import tax would be offset by the tax rebate for negative value added. If the value-added tax rates were the same in the two countries, the world tax would be the same under either of the two principles, namely, zero. Under the origin principle Country 1 would collect tax on $100 and Country 2 would give tax rebate on $100. Under

21. See Musgrave, *The Theory of Public Finance*, pp. 350–51.
22. See Appendix A to this chapter.

the destination principle neither country would collect or rebate any tax—a much simpler outcome for both tax administrator and taxpayer.

If the tax rates in the two countries differ, the world tax is still zero under the destination principle, but not under the origin principle; under this latter principle the world tax will be positive if the exporting country's tax rate is greater than that of the importing country, negative in the reverse instance. Evidently, if the world aim is not to tax value added in the form of net investment in the year of net investment, but only later as consumption occurs, the destination principle is better suited for this goal in a world of differing tax rates than is the origin principle.

If Firm B in Country 2 pays interest on its debt to Firm A in Country 1 in succeeding years, the world-wide concept of the consumption type of value-added tax is maintained either by (a) not allowing Firm B to deduct the interest payment (as a "purchase" from Firm A) and not requiring Firm A to include it in "sales," or (b) counting it as a purchase by B and a sale by A. Financial flows therefore need not invalidate the formula for the consumption type of tax, if these flows are treated consistently in the paying and receiving countries.

The identity between retail sales and total value added (consumption type) does not obtain in any one open economy except by chance, but it does still obtain for the world as a whole. In the example just given, retail sales in Country 1 are zero, although value added is $100, and retail sales in Country 2 are also zero, although value added there is minus $100. If, instead, Country 1 produces consumer goods that are exported to and consumed in Country 2, no capital goods being involved, value added is $100 in Country 1 and zero in Country 2, while retail sales are just the reverse. In terms of national income components, in an open economy, where X is exports, M imports, and I capital goods purchased or created for own use,

$$C + I \equiv W + P + D - X + M,$$

that is,

$$W + P + D - I \equiv C + X - M.$$

But the destination principle excludes X from and includes M in the tax base; that base, distinguished from the $W + P + D - I$ definition of value added, does equal retail sales, C.

Under a wages type of value-added tax it is the destination principle that is the less suitable. It would require that each import be broken down into its wages element and profit element; the import duty should, for consistency, be applied only to the wages element. Import-competing goods will have paid tax at prior stages only on the wages spent in producing them. Similarly, each export will need to be broken down into these two elements, so that a tax rebate can be given for the value-added tax paid domestically at earlier stages on the wages element.

The origin principle entails no such complications for the wages type of value-added tax. But the tax base in any one country will be the wages paid in that country, whichever principle is adopted. Moreover, no tax refunds on account of the exemption of profits will be required; in this respect the wages type of value-added tax is simpler, in a world-wide sense, than is the consumption type of value-added tax under the origin principle.

An income type of value-added tax is equally simple to administer under either the destination or the origin principle. Exports and imports are either wholly exempt and wholly taxable, respectively (destination principle) or wholly taxable and wholly exempt.

c. Rentals and Interest

Rentals and interest pose the problem, not of whether they shall be included in the tax base, but to whom they shall be attributed: the payor (tenant or debtor) or the payee (landlord or creditor).

An individual who leases a parcel of land to a business firm may himself be viewed as a firm, engaged in the business of leasing. Under this approach, the value added represented by the rent paid is attributed to him, as a business firm, not to the business that uses the land. This view seems appropriate, since the only alternate view is somewhat forced: the landowner is considered to be within the using firm, the rental payment is an intra-firm transfer, and the value added is attributed to the using firm, the lessee.

Interest payments raise the same question. Is the interest that is paid to an individual portfolio investor by the debtor business firm to be counted as value added by that firm? Or shall the investor be viewed as himself a firm that creates value by lending money? Now it is this latter interpretation that seems forced, so passive is this type of investor. Interest payments are commonly considered to reflect value added within the debtor firm. But there will be occasions when a creditor is much more active in helping make decisions how the money shall be used than is the landowner with respect to managing or otherwise influencing the use made of the land. Whatever the decision, the total value added will be the same, for a closed economy. It will the same for an open economy, when the creditor or landlord resides in a different country, only if the geographical rules of attribution determine that the activity occurs within the country, whoever is held to be the active agent, and if the source rule is then applied (see page 292).

A rented building or piece of equipment will yield a value added that is less than the rental paid, since rent of such properties includes an allowance for depreciation. Depreciation does not add value, it merely transfers value from the thing that is wearing out to the product that it helps produce. Accordingly, a deduction is allowed either for depreciation (income type of value-added tax) or for the full cost of the capital good in year of purchase or of construction by the user (consumption type of value-added tax), or for the full amount of the rental payment (wages type of value-added tax).

2. The Three Methods of Computation of Tax

a. In General

Since value added is produced only by factor activity, it can be computed, for any one firm, by adding the factor payments made by that firm, including profits. This is the "addition method" of computing value added. It is appropriate, however, only for the income type of value-added tax, which includes in its base the rewards to all factors, including interest and profit. Profit is net after depreciation, as under the income tax. Inventory accounting is the same as under the income tax. If the firm constructs its own capital good rather than purchasing it, this addition method captures the value thus added by the firm.[23]

But for the consumption type of value-added tax, the "subtraction method" is the appropriate one. From its sales the firm deducts its purchases from other firms, including purchases of capital goods. The difference is the value that it adds by its own activity, except that the firm's net return on its capital goods is effectively exempted by the deduction allowed in full in the year of purchase of the good (see the discussion on pages 253–55). Under this subtraction method for the consumption type of value-added tax, no account needs to be taken of capital goods produced within the firm and no inventory accounting is required. It would be awkward to use the addition method to compute the base of the consumption type of value-added tax, since to the net profit figure there would have to be added depreciation and the excess of opening inventory over closing inventory (deducted, as a part of cost of goods sold, in computing net profit), with subtraction of capital goods purchased or produced within the firm, and subtraction of an excess of closing inventory over opening inventory.[24]

A third technique, the tax-credit method, is a variant of the subtraction method, and is gaining wide acceptance. To the firm's total sales, without any deduction whatever, there is applied the value-added tax rate. From the tentative tax thus obtained there is subtracted the similar tentative taxes shown on the invoices of firms that have sold materials, etc. to the firm in question. In place of subtracting purchases from sales and applying the tax rate to the difference, tax on purchases is subtracted from tax on sales. Commonly, the matching is on a monthly basis; from the tax on a given month's sales there is subtracted the sum of the taxes on purchases made by the firm in that month.[25]

---

23. If a capital asset is resold after some use, the tax base for the year of resale should, for consistency, include the excess of the sales price over depreciated basis (or allow deduction of a shortfall), and for this the addition method is the simpler also, since profit is, or can readily be, computed to include this item.

24. If a capital asset is resold after some use, the subtraction technique is the simpler, under the consumption type of value-added tax; sales are defined to include sales of used capital goods, and deduction is allowed for purchase of used capital goods. The French manufacturers' value-added tax contained a curious provision whereby, if a depreciable asset was resold within five years of purchase, the deduction that had been allowed on purchase was retroactively cancelled, and was reallowed only for a pro rata part indicated by the number of years the original purchaser had held the asset. See Norr and Kerlan, *op. cit.*, p. 1019. This provision amounted to imposing a turnover tax on the first sale of a used capital good at a rate declining with the age of the good.

25. The French value-added tax on manufacturers required a lag of one month. The tentative tax on sales for June, for example, was reduced by the taxes shown on invoices paid in May (Norr and Kerlan, *op. cit.*, pp. 1013 and 1041). This peculiar feature reflects an attempt to gain a month's revenue when the production tax was changed from a single-stage tax to a value-added type of manufacturers' sales tax. (The past tense is used in the footnotes in this chapter when reference is to the French value-added tax as it stood prior to its reform in 1967).

The tax credit method can be especially useful if it is desired to reduce the rate of the value-added tax at some stage in the productive and distributive process, say the raw materials or farm products stage, for administrative reasons, without reducing the total tax paid on total value added. The reduced tax at the earlier stage simply gives rise to an equally increased tax at a later stage. The determinative tax rate on the entire value of any commodity will be the tax rate applicable at the last stage, typically the retail stage. This result cannot be achieved under the addition or subtraction method, as the following comparison demonstrates, where Stage 3 is the retail stage. The rate on total value added is 170/3,500 under the subtraction or addition method, i.e., 4.857 . . . per cent; it is 5 per cent under the tax credit method.

Stage	Purchases from other firms	Value added[26]	Tax rate applicable	Tax paid	Cumulated tax
1	0	1,000	5%	50	50
2	1,050	500	4%	20	70
3	1,570	2,000	5%	100	170

Under the tax-credit method, the cumulated tax paid depends solely on the rate applied at Stage 3:

Stage	Tax paid	
1	50	[5 per cent on 1,000 sales = 50, less zero tax credit]
2	10	[4 per cent on 1,500 sales[27] = 60, less 50 tax credit]
3	115	[5 per cent on 3,500 sales[27] = 175, less tax credit of 60, that is, less 4 per cent on 1,500 sales]

The cumulated tax is 175, i.e., 5 per cent of $3,500, as against 170 under the addition or subtraction method, because the 1 percentage point of tax relief given at Stage 2 by the 4 per cent rate has been negated, under the tax-credit method, since the rate at the last stage is 5 per cent. The tax credit method retroactively enforces a uniform tax rate, this rate being the statutory rate applied at the latest stage.

If, however, one or more of the earlier stages of value added are completely exempt, the tax-credit method fails to record the correct amount of cumulated tax paid unless either (*a*) the stage so exempted is the very first stage, typically the raw materials stage, or (*b*) either (1) at the exempt stage there is a refund of prior tax paid or (2) a shadow tentative tax is computed that can be shown on the invoice issued by the exempt seller and claimed as a credit by the one who purchases from him. If, no tax at all being due at the stage in question, no tax credit is taken by the exempt seller, all record of earlier tax paid is lost, and no account can be taken of it at later stages where taxation resumes. This difficulty can be illustrated by revising the numerical example given above as follows. Let the tax to be paid on value added at each stage be as indicated, under an addition or subtraction method:

26. The value added, if computed by subtraction, is net of value-added tax. Thus, in Stage 2, purchases inclusive of tax are 1,050 and sales inclusive of tax are 1,570, a difference of 520, but taxable value added is only 500.

27. Sales are computed net of tax. See preceding footnote.

Stage	Purchases from other firms	Value added[28]	Tax rate applicable	Tax paid[28]	Cumulated tax
1	0	1,000	5%	50	50
2	1,050	500	exempt	0	50
3	1,550	2,000	5%	100	150

Under the tax-credit method, tax paid would be:

Stage 1: 50 (5 per cent on 1,000 sales = 50, less zero tax credit)
Stage 2: 0 (zero per cent on 1,500 sales, hence no use of tax credit of 50)
Stage 3: 177.50 (5 per cent on 3,550 sales = 177.50, less credit for tax paid at Stage 2, i.e. zero = 177.50)
Cumulated Tax   227.50

If the zero rate is applied only at the first stage, the tax-credit method works satisfactorily; there is no over taxation.

The exemption, at one of the stages, may be granted only to small firms in that stage, as a means of reducing administrative costs relative to revenue. Then, if the stage in question is an intermediate one, the tax-credit method concentrates its overtaxation on commodities handled or processed by those small firms; large firms gain a competitive advantage. If the stage in question is that of manufacturing, for example, a wholesaler buying from a small exempt manufacturer suffers the full weight of the tentative tax upon resale, since his vendor had no tentative tax to record on the invoice.[29] The small manufacturer might be allowed to enter on his invoice to the wholesaler the taxes recorded on invoices for goods he had purchased. But then the tax administrator would have to check on the small manufacturer periodically to make certain that he had not been falsifying, and it is to avoid just such checking of books and records that the exemption is granted.

If the small exempt firm is a retailer the tax-credit method does not destroy previous tax credits, but it does lose a modest amount of revenue, equal to the tax rate times the value added by the retailer.

Under the subtraction or addition method, exemption of the small firm at an intermediate stage does not give rise to over-taxation. On the other hand, revenue is always lost by the exemption; there is no catching up at a later stage, as there is under the tax credit for an earlier-stage exemption. On balance, this failure to regain the revenue, equal to the tax rate times the value added by the exempt firm, seems less serious than the injustices that can occur under the tax-credit system.

The size of the firm to be exempt could be stated in terms of value added but, as an indicator of the facility with which tax administration and taxpayer can enforce and comply with the law, gross receipts seems a better base for the exemption. Of two firms with the same small amount of value added, one may be a bulk handler of

28. See footnotes 26 and 27.

29. The same disadvantage existed under French law when the small vendor was not exempt from the value-added tax but was allowed to "pay the value-added tax on an estimate of presumed sales (*forfait*) . . . rather than on actual turnover." (See Chapter 8, Section A.4.A, for use of the *forfait* under the French turnover tax.) The *forfait*-estimated tax was not allowed to appear on invoices, and, as vendees could credit only tax that appeared on invoices rendered to them, the tax-credit chain was broken (Norr and Kerlan, *op. cit.*, p. 1012).

goods somewhere in the wholesale stage that buys and sells fairly large quantities and hence keeps adequate records and is commercially sophisticated, while the other may be a small shop the sales of which consist almost entirely of value added by the labor of a few employees, perhaps all members of the family.

B. DIFFERENTIAL TAXATION
OF CERTAIN CONSUMER GOODS

If certain consumer goods are to be taxed lightly and others heavily, some being necessaries and some, luxuries, the value-added tax is not as convenient in this respect as is a retail sales tax, but it is better than the other general sales taxes. The turnover tax is a hopelessly inadequate instrument for this purpose, save in the few cases where the finished good contains physically, or economically, chiefly materials not used also in producing other types of final product: milk and jewelry, for example. Cheap clothing and luxury clothing illustrate the impossible cases, where exemption can hardly be granted to early-stage sales of raw materials or cloth, because of uncertainty in which category these intermediate products will appear at retail. The manufacturers' and wholesalers' sales taxes are somewhat better in this respect, but worse in another, for they cannot distinguish between luxury and non-luxury retailing of physically similar goods. It is often the degree of service lavished on the customer at retail that constitutes the largest element of luxury. A modest amount of retail services often characterizes the items called necessaries.

The value-added tax discriminates readily and completely if the tax-credit method is employed, provided always that no gap in the credit chain exists, as explained above. The virtue of the tax-credit method for this purpose is its power to make the overall rate depend on the rate imposed at the last stage of production or distribution, whatever may be the higher or lower rates at various earlier stages.

If the rate at retail on a particular commodity is very low, or zero, the retailer must be allowed a carry-over of excess tax credit, or a tax refund, if the rest of his sales, taxable at the standard or luxury rates, do not generate enough tentative tax to absorb prior tax on all his purchases.[30]

Exemption of the final product may be intended not as a complete exemption but only as an exemption of value added to that particular product at that final stage. The tax credit can be restricted accordingly. Such a product may be termed quasi-exempt. A final-stage vendor selling both taxable and quasi-exempt goods will have a tentative tax of zero on the quasi-exempt goods, but in turn will be denied tax credit for value-added tax shown on invoices to him covering (1) the quasi-exempt goods, or (2) materials that he physically incorporates into such goods, or will be denied the credit for tax on a pro rata share of the cost of capital goods that are used in producing both quasi-exempt and taxable goods.[31]

30. Excess tax credit may also arise because a vendor sells for a price less than he paid, or because his vendee defaults, or because the goods are stolen or destroyed (*ibid.*, pp. 1014–15.)

31. As was done in France, with respect to exports. The complexity encountered in implementing the pro rata rule is described in *ibid.*, pp. 1015–20. The effect of the non-

The subtraction and addition methods are not well suited for discrimination among types of consumer goods. The tax collected at the last stage, on the retailer's value added, cannot so readily be adjusted for early-stage taxation that is now seen to have been inadequate for luxuries or excessive for necessaries.

c. INTERNATIONAL TRADE

(1) Destination Principle

If the value-added tax is truly comprehensive and is levied at a single rate, the destination principle can be implemented easily and precisely both for rebate of cumulated tax on exports and for the compensating tax on imports.

The export rebate, under the subtraction or addition methods of computing value added, is simply the product of the tax rate times the amount paid by the exporter for the goods he is to export. Under the tax credit method the export rebate equals the tentative tax shown on the invoice given to the exporter-purchaser.

The import tax is even simpler to compute; any inaccuracy in statement of import value and consequent over- or underpayment of import compensating tax will be precisely offset on the first domestic sale by the importer. He will have a larger value added to pay tax on, under the subtraction or addition method, if he has understated value upon importation, or a smaller tax credit to apply against the tentative tax under the tax-credit method. Indeed, in principle no tax at all need be collected upon importation other than by the ultimate user. In practice, however, the value-added tax will not apply a uniform rate to all stages of value added of all goods and services, as already noted. Under these circumstances, neither the subtraction nor the addition method supplies the information needed to compute precisely the export rebate or the import compensating tax. Unless some information items are included on each invoice, a differential-rate value-added tax will prove almost as difficult to implement for exports and imports as is the turnover tax.

The tax-credit method, on the other hand, does provide the precise information, on cumulated tax paid, provided that the credit chain is not broken.

Export exemption can sometimes be pushed back one stage by allowing a firm that manufactures for export to make its purchases from other domestic firms free of tax on those firms.[32] In principle, the vendor firms then should be allowed a refund for value-added tax accumulated at earlier stages; otherwise no such vendor firm can afford to sell to the manufacturer-exporter at a price reduced by the full amount of the tentative tax.

Vertical differentiation of tax rates likewise creates difficulties with respect to taxation of imports. If, for example, the importing country applies a low rate to agricultural value added within its borders and desires that the cumulative tax on goods containing agricultural value added be correspondingly reduced, the value of

creditability was softened by allowing the non-creditable value-added tax to be subtracted in computing net profit for the income tax (*ibid.*, p. 1021).

32. As was done in France, within certain limits (*ibid.*, pp. 1033, 1035).

an imported good must be decomposed into its agricultural and nonagricultural elements of value added if the import tax is to be computed so that it will be truly compensating and not in part a protective duty for agriculture.

The tax-credit method here, as for exports, destroys the differential aspect of the regime by recouping at a later fully taxed stage all the tax relief granted to import-competing goods through a lower tax rate at an earlier stage. Both imports and import-competing goods are subjected to a cumulative tax at the full rate.

If one of the earlier, pre-import domestic stages (other than the first stage) is exempt, this tax-credit method fails to give credit for tax paid prior to that exempt stage, because the tax-credit chain is broken. Imports meanwhile do not lose any tax credits and pay a smaller cumulative tax, under the tax-credit method, than import-competing goods. The result is an inadvertent subsidy to imports.

(2) Origin Principle

As with the turnover tax, so also with the value-added tax, a change from the destination principle to the origin principle is of less significance to the government treasury and to the economy at large than under the single-stage taxes. Wholesale and retail value added are normally taxed by the country of consumption under either principle. But the revenue aspects are more important under the value-added tax than under the turnover tax. The origin-principle value-added tax does not allow the importing country to tax the value added in the exporting country. In terms of the numerical illustration on page 210 (note 6), when value added is 50 in A and 50 in B (destination country), a value-added tax rate of 22 per cent is required to yield 22 in tax, and under the origin principle the tax on A's producers for export would rise from 0 to 11 instead of from 0 to 6; B's tax would decline from 22 to 11 instead of only to 16.

The three methods—subtraction, addition, and tax credit—are all equally well adapted to use of a single-rate origin-principle value-added tax with respect to exports.

Imports, in contrast, are bound to present a difficult problem for the origin principle if the tax-credit method is used. A hypothetical import tax must be computed at the tax rate of the importing country, and this hypothetical tax must be allowable as a credit against the actual tentative tax on the first domestic sale of the imported goods.

If the importing country instead simply allows credit for the tax paid in the exporting country, the origin principle is converted into the destination principle in the sense that the rate of tax of country of importation determines the combined tax of both countries (the country of export of course keeps the tax revenue it has collected). If the tax paid abroad exceeds the first tentative domestic tax, the theory of the tax credit calls for a refund of the excess. If there is no such excess the importing country's tax rate is automatically applied to the total value.

The subtraction and addition methods need no adjustment to operate correctly under the origin principle for imports.

The tax credit method encounters still more difficulties under an origin-principle value-added tax that imposes different rates at different stages simply for administrative reasons. In export, over- or undertaxation may occur. For example, farmers might be taxed at a low rate, in the expectation that the revenue shortfall would be made up automatically at a later stage. But if the farmer exports, this reduced tax will never be made up.

On imports, the existence of vertically differentiated rates implies that the hypothetical tax that must be computed for use as a credit, under the origin principle, must be computed at the rate applicable to the last stage, the retail stage. Suppose, for example, that domestic farmers are taxed at a low rate, manufacturers and retailers at the standard rate. Farm products are imported to be processed. The aim of the origin principle is to tax only the value added in the importing country, at the standard rate. If credit is given only at the low tax rate paid by farmers, the imported product pays more than the standard rate of tax on value added in the importing country.

The subtraction and addition methods need no adjustment to reach the goal of taxing only domestic value that is added to the foreign imports at rates of tax identical to those applying to similar values added to goods that have been produced domestically.

Evidently, the origin principle and the tax-credit method are somewhat incompatible, though perhaps not so much so that a country moving to the origin principle need give up use of the tax-credit method.

3. Allowance for Other Taxes

If the value-added tax is not allowed as a deduction in computing the base for an income tax paid by the same firm, the income tax base includes an amount that is not available to the firm as profit. Since value-added tax rates commonly range from 10 to 20 per cent and corporation income tax rates from 40 to 50 per cent, this question is an important one.[33]

The depreciation base of a capital asset for income tax purposes must be so computed as to take account of the treatment allowed under the value-added tax. If full deduction of the capital asset cost is allowed in the year of purchase (consumption type of value-added tax) the depreciation base for income tax must be the cost of the capital good, which will include the value-added tax paid by the vendor, less an amount equal to the value-added tax rebate or allowance, if depreciation is to be restricted to the amount of capital investment made by the business firm.

4. Incidence in an Open Economy

The analysis in Chapter 8 of the open-economy incidence of a turnover tax is applicable to any of the value-added taxes, making allowance for the fact that they

33. France, with rates at or near these levels, allowed deduction of value-added tax in computing profit for income tax. See Norr and Kerlan, *op. cit.*, pp. 310–11, 396–97.

do not discriminate against non-integrated industries or early-stage value added. Since the value-added tax can easily be applied to exports, while exempting imported value added, a subordinate jurisdiction that enjoys a fairly inelastic demand for its chief export may be able thereby to export some of the tax. And insofar as the demand is not inelastic, there remains the possibility of exporting some of the tax to nonresident factor owners.[34]

5. Differential Incidence

Since the value-added tax, consumption type, is used in this work as the reference tax for ascertaining differential incidence with other broad-based taxes, the relevant analysis will be found in the chapters on those taxes. Incidence of the value-added tax itself, without reference to some other tax, is a meaningless concept, for reasons given in Chapter 1, Section B, and Chapter 8, Section A.2.

The differential incidence of the wages type of value-added tax is perhaps slightly progressive, partly because its base includes, in fact, something more than wages (i.e., non-wage forms of economic rent and quasi-rent in a transition period) and because the deferring of tax relief on capital to the year of income receipt can reflect a real burden on capital in an economy where money markets are imperfect or at least constrained.

The differential incidence of the income type of value-added tax is presumably somewhat progressive, since the tax includes in its base the net return from investment, which the consumption type does not do. This conclusion is strengthened by the fact that, in order to raise the same amount of revenue in any given year in an economy where net capital formation is positive, the value-added tax, consumption type, must carry a higher tax rate. The supply of capital is probably no more elastic than the supply of labor, unless the taxing jurisdiction is very small.

6. Criteria

The consumption type of value-added tax satisfies the consensus criteria better than any other general sales tax except possibly that on retail sales of consumer goods and services, which has the same base in a closed economy. In an open economy, however, the value-added tax, even of the consumption type, requires an allocation of cash flow from the firm's capital goods between taxing jurisdictions, which implies an allocation of the outlay for these capital goods between those jurisdictions. This kind of problem can be especially troublesome for a large firm that operates in several taxing jurisdictions, but the problem is more one of technical details than concepts.

34. On both these grounds the automobile industry in Michigan may have exported a substantial part of the value-added tax that it paid.

With respect to counter-cycle full employment policy, the value-added tax will probably show greater perverse anticipatory reactions to discretionary rate changes than the retail sales tax. Competitive relations will not be changed in principle, but in practice it may prove more difficult for a series of vertically non-integrated firms to change their price lists by just the amount of the tax change than it will be for a vertically integrated firm; each point of sale from one firm to another is a point of potential friction or resistance when a price change is made.

Most of the conflict-of-interests criteria can be satisfied fairly well by the consumption type of value-added tax. Differential tax rates for various commodities, designed to make the tax progressive, and lighter on large families, are more difficult than under the retail sales tax, unless the tax-credit method is employed. The same remark applies to geographical discrimination aimed at benefiting consumers in depressed areas. For benefiting factors in such areas, the value-added tax is more adaptable than the retail sales tax or perhaps any of the other sales taxes (see the remarks above on a small open economy, a state or city for example). And the requirements of economic growth can be readily met by exemption of capital goods to a degree not feasible, because of evasion through diversion of such goods to household use, with the sales taxes not based on value added. As to the remaining criteria, the value-added tax is much like the other general sales taxes.

The income type of value-added tax, because it requires depreciation accounting and inventory accounting, is more likely to violate the equal-treatment criterion in one or another of its six aspects. The need for such computations tends to make the problem of allocating profit among taxing jurisdictions more difficult, if not more important. The wages type of value-added tax may be easier to handle, for allocation, since it is the only one of the value-added taxes that exempts the entire cash flow from a capital asset.

With respect to the conflict-of-interests criteria, the income type and the wages type probably do not differ much from the consumption type, except as the income type may tend to discourage investment and hence growth.

APPENDIX TO CHAPTER NINE

This appendix compares the value-added tax, consumption type, the value-added tax, wages type, and the consumption tax (retail sales tax), not in terms of national income identities for the entire economy for a given year, but in terms of the behavioral relations describing the action of entrepreneurs. For this purpose it is necessary to deal with a particular venture that stretches over a period of years, not with a single year's summation of: the beginning-year results for some ventures, an intermediate-year result for earlier ventures, and an end-year result for still other ventures—the kind of summation that the national income identities require.

In a riskless, perfectly competitive system any given investment must, in terms of its cost in the year of investment, equal the present value of the future cash flow from that investment, i.e., it must equal the stream of profits net of depreciation, plus the stream of depreciation, all discounted to a present value, at the market rate of interest. If the cost of the investment were less than that present value, competing entrepreneurs would enter and drive the future profits down, and perhaps the cost of the present investment up. If it exceeded that value, the entrepreneur would not make the investment. Let the stream of future net profits, discounted to a present value, be designated by $P_{f,\,d}$ and the stream of that part of the cash flow that represents depreciation be designated by $D_{f,\,d}$. Then the cost of the investment in the year of investment, $I_p = P_{f,\,d} + D_{f,\,d}$.

A series of investments undertaken in successive years give rise to streams of P's and D's that overlap in any one year (except the first). For any given year, the national income definitions, as already noted, supply no reason to expect that the aggregate amount in that year of I and P and D will be such that $I = P + D$. For any given year the summation of the P's and the D's represents a mixing of the components of various ventures started at various points in time and of varying lengths of life. There is no discounting involved. This procedure is essential for describing the events of that particular year, which is what national income accounting does, but it throws no light on the incentives needed to induce investment. These incentives must be stated in terms of the I for a single investment or venture, and the future-years' P's and D's that it gives rise to, discounted to a present value for the year in which the investment I is made. For example, if the national income accounts for Year 100 are being made up, there may be summed the P for that year from Venture 1, which was started in Year 1, the P for that same year from Venture 2, which was started in Year 2, and so on. In this summation each dollar of the first P of course accounts for as much as each dollar of the second P. But for an understanding of behavior, the P dollars in Year 100 deriving from Venture 1 count for less than the P dollars in Year 100 deriving from Venture 2, since an explanation of why Venture 1 was undertaken must discount the P dollars of Year 100 received from that venture back 100 years, while to explain the undertaking of Venture 2 we need discount the P dollars of Year 100 from that venture back only 99 years. The behavioral relation asserts, not that $I = P + D$, but that $I_p = P_{f,\,d} + D_{f,\,d}$.

In present-value terms, if a concern employs only labor in the present year to create some consumer goods that will be consumed in the present year and in addition employs only labor to create a capital good, its wage payments, under competition, will be such that $W_p = C_p + I_p = C_p + P_{f,\,d} + D_{f,\,d}$ where W_p is wages paid this year, and C_p is consumer goods consumed this year produced by the labor that received part of the W_p.

As this firm considers what its CVAT[1] base will be, in present-value terms, it sees that the base can be expressed as follows: $W_p - I_p + P_{f,\,d} + D_{f,\,d}$. This expression equals W_p, that is, the CVAT base in present-value terms for a given firm equals its wage payments of this year (the base of a wages tax), where the cost of the investment is wages, if and only if $I_p = P_{f,\,d} + D_{f,\,d}$. But it is just this behavioral relation that must hold, to induce the investment. Accordingly, in such an economy, for

---

1. CVAT stands for consumption type of value-added tax; CT, for consumption tax (pure retail sales tax).

any given firm the base of a wages tax is the same as the present value of the base of a CVAT.

Concerns do not of course use only labor. But insofar as a concern uses up a capital good in a given year to produce consumer goods or other capital goods that it sells in the same year, the CVAT liability that it incurs thereby was presumably foreseen in the earlier year when the decision was made to create that capital good (moreover, its CVAT liability from sale of the capital goods is offset indirectly by the tax credit granted to the purchasing firm). The only current decision that is affected by CVAT liabilities is the decision with respect to the employment of labor, at least in the absence of errors and surprises. The CVAT may therefore be regarded, from a behavioral point of view, as a tax on labor, and the simplifying assumption made above, that the firm employs only labor, is in these circumstances a useful abstraction for analysis.

What, now, of a consumption tax, in similar terms? The base of a consumption tax, for consumption now and consumption in future years, made possible by employment of labor this year, is, in present value terms, $C_p + P_{f,\ d} + D_{f,\ d}$, provided that P and D represent consumption in the year in which they occur. Let us assume that they do; we shall return to this point in the next paragraph. This expression for the base of the consumption tax, in present value terms, equals the base of the CVAT, which is $W_p - I_p + P_{f,\ d} + D_{f,\ d}$, if and only if $I_p = P_{f,\ d} + D_{f,\ d}$, for if this latter relation holds, setting the two bases equal to each other yields $W_p = C_p + I_p$, which is true here by definition. The base of the consumption tax equals the base of the CVAT and both equal the base of a wages tax, in present-value terms for a given firm or venture, in a two-factor economy.

The assumption that $P_{f,\ d}$ and $D_{f,\ d}$ represent discounted consumption streams rests on the fact that no business firm is going to purchase a capital good unless it believes that the product from the use of this capital good will be either consumed, or used to produce another capital good the product of which will be consumed, or . . . will be consumed. The purpose of any capital good is to produce, at one or more removes, consumer goods. The outlay on a capital good this year equals the present value of the stream, irregular or not, of consumer goods made possible by that capital good (less allowance, of course, for future complementary labor), however remote in time is the emergence of the consumer goods, and however many transformations the capital good has to undergo meanwhile. For simplicity, it has been assumed that the capital good is made this year wholly by labor. But if it is made partly by the wearing out of capital goods produced earlier, this same reasoning applies.

We have seen that for any one year, for all firms together, wages paid may well not equal consumption of that year. But in present value terms, a firm deciding whether to use its labor to produce a consumer good for consumption this year or to use it to produce a capital good must, if it is to maximize its profit, be receiving what is in effect a market signal, transmitted to it perhaps through several other firms, that ultimately the consumer goods attributable to this capital good will be worth just enough in those future years so that their value, discounted to the present year, will equal the value of the alternative product that could be made this year with the given amount of labor, namely, consumer goods for consumption this year. This is so, even in an economy that is accumulating capital.

From the viewpoint, then, not of macro identities for any given year, but of the choices that the firm faces between using labor to make a consumer good or a capital good, in a two-factor closed economy, the CVAT, the wages tax (or wages type of value-added tax) and the CT all inflict exactly the same tax penalty, in present value terms.

CHAPTER TEN

Excise Taxes; Monopoly Revenue

A. EXCISE TAXES

1. Conceptual Basis

A SYSTEM OF EXCISES is a series of taxes imposed on specified commodities, usually at differing rates. But much the same result may be achieved by varying the rate of a general sales tax with respect to a few commodities.[1] Thus a value-added tax at 10 per cent that taxes certain luxuries at 15 per cent and foodstuffs at, say, 6 per cent may be viewed as a uniform-rate value-added tax of 10 per cent supplemented by an excise tax of 5 per cent on the named luxuries and a subsidy of 4 per cent on food-stuffs.

Toward the other extreme, a series of excises may approach the status of a general sales tax if the taxable goods are numerous, and are grouped into a few, not very different, rate categories.[2] In any event, the characteristic excise (or subsidy) feature is that the commodities or services affected are named, not defined in general terms, e.g., goods sold in the course of business.

Certain excise taxes exert strong substitution effects, and therefore alter consumers' budget patterns substantially. Others have only modest substitution effects; these are the excises on "addictives," the consumer goods that are habit forming. The household's budget pattern is altered chiefly through the income effect of these taxes, the most notable of which are taxes on tobacco, liquor, and gambling. Except for certain grades of spirits, they are not luxuries, that is, (a) the demand for them is not highly income-elastic, and (b) they appear in low-income budgets.

1. The value-added tax of 20 per cent of the price including tax (25 per cent of price excluding tax) in France was reduced to (a) 10 per cent for producers' consumables (e.g., coal, fertilizers, sulphur), and, among others, "many widely consumed prepared food products," household soap, and books, and (b) 6 per cent for some widely used commodities, including foods (e.g., wheat, flour, sugar), and was raised to 25 per cent for many luxury products (except that rates of 23 or 20 per cent applied to producers who had undertaken to increase exports). In 1963 the 20 per cent rate supplied 84 per cent of the value-added tax revenue (Norr and Kerlan, *Taxation in France*, pp. 1022–27).

2. The United Kingdom's purchase tax is an example.

They are not productive consumption goods; indeed, they lower the consumer's productivity.

The income effect of an excise becomes overwhelming and the substitution effect virtually nil when the tax is imposed on some physiological necessity within a price range where demand for it is perfectly inelastic: table salt in a high-income economy, for example. This kind of a salt tax resembles the uniform-rate general sales tax in its influence on the pattern of consumption, since both taxes exert that influence through an income effect, not through a substitution effect. Historically, to be sure, the rate of the salt tax was at times so high that the demand for table salt was probably pushed back into a price-elastic segment of the demand curve.

As with subsidies, excise taxes may be directed at either consumers or factors of production (see Chapter 6). In fact, however, only a few excises are designed to reduce factor rewards; export taxes (see Chapter 16) are the chief example. The desire to burden only consumers of the taxed article can never be fully implemented, however, save in the rare instances where demand is perfectly inelastic or the less rare instances (see pages 274–76), where supply is perfectly elastic. Accordingly, as with subsidies, the effect is usually divided between consumers and factors.

The purchasers of the taxed product are in some instances business firms, particularly with respect to expense-account distilled spirits. That part of the excise not absorbed by factors in the taxed industry then becomes widely diffused among consumers and factors in all sectors. The same is true of a large part of the tax on motor fuel and of the entire tax on business vehicles, including trucks.[3]

Being aimed at households as consumers (rather than as factor suppliers), either directly or through business firms in general as in the examples just given, excises are always on the destination basis (see Chapter 8).[4] An origin-basis excise would rest largely on domestic factors with respect to that part of the output exported, unless the vendee countries imposed a similar tax. Even then, the tax would not perform its function, since it would be Country A's and Country B's aim each to burden its own consumers, not each other's consumers. But the origin principle may be useful in a common market that desires to eliminate border control (fiscal frontiers), if the commodity is consumed chiefly within the country of production.

For any excise tax there are two tax rates that give the same yield, one on the low side of that rate that produces the maximum yield, the other on the high side of that rate. Sumptuary considerations, that is, reduction of negative externalities,[5] dictate

3. If the revenue is used for highways, there may be no net burden on the firm.
4. But subordinate jurisdictions, cities for instance, may face legal or practical problems in taxing imports.
5. Including in negative externalities certain social opportunity costs. For example: tobacco-growing land might yield foodstuffs instead. "It is the policy of the Japanese government to restrict tobacco production severely in any case, in order to have more land available for producing food" (Carl S. Shoup, Director, and Howard R. Bowen, Jerome B. Cohen, Rolland F. Hatfield, Stanley S. Surrey, William Vickrey, and William C. Warren, *Report on Japanese Taxation* [Tokyo: General Headquarters, Supreme Commander for the Allied Powers, September, 1949], vol. 2, p. 156).

use of the high rate, but in fact all sumptuary tax rates are on the low side, when indeed they are not aimed at the maximum yield. To be sure, rates of evasion and of compliance costs are more unequal from taxpayer to taxpayer, under the higher rate, but that disadvantage would not be decisive if the sumptuary aim were taken seriously.

2. Incidence

The incidence of any one excise tax can usually be expressed in partial-equilibrium terms, for reasons given above.[6] The degree of forward shifting, if the tax is levied on the seller, can be measured by the change in price of the taxed commodity, and the degree of backward shifting by the decline in marginal cost ex-tax. If the tax is levied on the buyer, "price," for this purpose, is what he pays to the seller plus the tax he pays to the government. It is immaterial whether the tax is imposed on the buyer or the seller, apart from institutional rigidities or other frictions.

Since the incidence of an excise tax in a closed economy has been explored rigorously by a long line of economists, starting with Cournot is 1838 and including, for major contributions, Due in 1942, the standard conclusions will be only briefly stated here,[7] and attention will be focused on certain neglected aspects of some importance, particularly (1) the four extreme cases created by perfectly elastic and perfectly inelastic demand or supply functions under competition; (2) the restricted number of generalizations valid for monopoly or monopsony taxation; (3) the effects of introducing into the analysis the cost and demand functions of untaxed substitutes or complements; (4) the effects of introducing transportation costs, including a tax on such costs.[8] No attempt will be made to trace the incidence of particular excises, for example, those on liquor, tobacco, or gambling,[9] or those on luxuries.

Under competition, the tax is divided between a rise in price of product and a fall in the marginal cost of production (ex-tax), or, more loosely speaking, the tax is divided between consumer and producer, in the ratio of the slope of the demand curve to the slope of the supply curve, if the slopes are taken with respect to the quantity axis ("quantity slopes"), so that the slope measures the decrement in price per unit increase in quantity. If, as is the usual practice, the slopes are taken with respect to the price axis ("price slopes") the theorem reads: the tax is divided

6. See Chapter 1, Section B, and the exception there noted for extremely heavy excises.

7. For the short-run adjustment of the atomistically competitive firm to a unit or ad valorem tax through the two separate stages when (1) price has not yet risen at all, (2) price has risen, but no firms have yet left the industry, see the step-by-step analysis by John F. Due, *The Theory of Incidence of Sales Taxation* (New York: King's Crown Press, 1942), pp. 17–21. A highly condensed summary of the two stages together is given in Musgrave, *Theory of Public Finance*, p. 288, note 2. See also Chapter 6 above, p. 154.

8. For incidence under large-group monopolistic competition, see Due, *The Theory of Incidence of Sales Taxation*, ch. IV, "Monopolistic Competition and the Incidence of Special Sales Taxes," reproduced in Musgrave and Shoup (Eds.), *A. E. A. Readings in the Economics of Taxation.*

9. But see Chapter 16.

between buyers and sellers in the ratio of the slope of the supply curve to the slope of the demand curve,[10] i.e.,

$$\frac{dq_s}{dp} \bigg/ \frac{dq_d}{dp}.$$

To express this theorem in elasticity terms, the numerator and denominator are multiplied by the ratio of price to quantity, i.e.,

$$\frac{dq_s}{dp} \cdot \frac{p}{q} \bigg/ \frac{dq_d}{dp} \cdot \frac{p}{q}.$$

The tax is thus seen to be divided between buyer and seller in the ratio of the elasticity of supply to the elasticity of demand.[11] These conclusions hold for small changes, or for large changes if the demand and supply functions are linear.

It follows that if supply is perfectly elastic, a tax on the seller causes price to rise by the full amount of the tax, whatever the elasticity of demand.[12] The incidence of the tax is entirely on the buyer. The more elastic the demand, the greater is the reduction in quantity purchased. Similarly, if demand is perfectly elastic, a tax on the seller does not change the price at all, whatever the elasticity of supply. Incidence is entirely on the seller. The more elastic the supply, the greater is the reduction in quantity purchased.

A perfectly inelastic supply curve forces the seller to bear the entire tax. The degree of elasticity of the demand curve affects neither (a) the price, which remains unchanged if the tax is on the seller, or falls by the full amount of the tax if the tax is collected from the buyer, nor (b) the amount purchased.

Finally, a perfectly inelastic demand similarly forces the buyer to bear the whole tax, and the degree of elasticity of supply affects neither price nor quantity purchased. Price rises by the full amount of a tax on the seller.

Studies that distribute the burden of an excise tax by income groups have assumed that the tax is fully shifted to the consumer. The implied assumption seems to be, not that demand is perfectly inelastic, but that supply is perfectly elastic. How reasonable is this assumption?

A perfectly elastic supply indicates that the factors can be moved to another

---

10. For a statement of the theorem in terms of quantity slopes, see Musgrave, *Theory of Public Finance*, p. 295; for a statement in terms of price slopes, see Leif Johansen, *Public Economics*, pp. 276–77.

11. Since the tax, t, is divided into the rise in price, dp, and the remainder of the tax $t - dp$, we have, by the theorem noted above, that dp (the part of the tax that rests on buyers) is to $t - dp$ (the part of the tax that rests on sellers) as the elasticity of supply is to the elasticity of demand:

$dp/(t - dp) = E_s/E_d$, where E_s is the elasticity of supply, and E_d, the elasticity of demand, whence

$$dp/t = E_s/(E_s + E_d),$$

which is the "well-known Dalton formula," as Bent Hansen terms it (*The Economic Theory of Fiscal Policy*, p. 90); see Hugh Dalton, *Principles of Public Finance* (4th ed., London: Routledge & Kegan Paul, 1954), p. 51.

12. Short of perfect elasticity, and similarly abstracting from indeterminate or non-equilibrium instances in the three cases following.

untaxed industry or industries at no reduction in rate of pay, or, in an open economy, that an alternate untaxed market is available. The studies in question usually deal with a closed economy. Some factors can indeed move without reduction in reward, notably when they are engaged in producing or handling a number of commodities in the course of a day, one or a few of which are singled out for taxation. Thus if a retail shop is in this position, the store owner will decline to deal in the taxed article unless he can obtain the customary rate of return; he can easily reassign his factors (store clerks and the building itself) to the untaxed lines solely. Thus no part of a tax on cigarettes, for example, will usually be absorbed by a grocery store, not even over a short period.

Somewhere in a preceding stage, however, specialization will be encountered: at the cigarette factory, if not before. There, the level of factor use in the taxed trade will be reduced slowly. The capital equipment is specialized and will be used as long as it yields a normal return on the value in its next best use (often scrap). The supply of labor will be slightly inelastic, because of the less than perfect mobility consequent upon specialization. If the taxed industry is growing, complete forward shifting requires merely a reduction in the rate of flow of capital and labor into the industry. But if it is shrinking, a generation or more of backward shifting to labor and capital in the manufacturing sector may occur. This fact is one reason why legislators are commonly unwilling to impose an excise tax on a declining industry, no matter how well the product itself may fit the specifications for an excise.

Finally, the land from which the raw materials come is usually specialized to some degree. Even in a growing economy the landlord absorbs some of the tax; the specialized land is not used as intensively as it would have been. Marginal cost of the raw material is less than it would have been. The price of the finished good at retail at any given moment in the future is in principle higher than it would have been, by something less than the tax. But since the raw-materials element is normally but a small proportion of retail value, the backward shifting will be slight. On the whole, the common assumption of complete forward shifting of an excise tax is in most cases close enough to reality to be a useful approximation, if the tax rate is moderate,[13] and the industry is growing.

Under a heavy excise tax the proportion of raw materials cost to retail value is even smaller than indicated immediately above. In these circumstances the supply conditions for the raw material can be virtually ignored in estimating the incidence of a still further increase in the tax rate. Indeed, even the supply conditions of all the factors in the industry are then of little significance. The commodity is already in perfectly elastic supply with respect to a large part of its retail price, the part reflecting the existing excise; the government will not allow any of the commodity to be sold if it does not get its tax. Price wars are correspondingly limited, in percentage terms, by existence of a heavy excise tax.[14]

13. The heavy United Kingdom tobacco tax, on the other hand, may conceivably be borne in some degree by the foreign producers of particular types of tobacco.

14. In Britain, a price war in cigarettes reduced the retail price from 76 cents per pack of 20 cigarettes to 71 cents for expensive brands, and from 49 cents to 45 cents for cheaper brands. Of the 76 cents (or 71 cents) 58 cents goes to the government in excise. The tax is based on the amount of tobacco, by weight; some filter cigarettes, containing less tobacco, are taxed

If the excise is levied on a very narrowly defined commodity, both supply and demand are likely to be extremely, though perhaps not perfectly, price-elastic for some distance from the pre-tax equilibrium point. Consumption falls greatly under the tax, until a small core of specialized producers and taste-hardened consumers share between them a modest total tax bill.

Supply of the narrowly defined commodity will in a few instances be fairly inelastic, while demand remains very elastic. Factors can become specialized in a narrow field, producing a commodity for which consumers have ready substitutes. The reverse is not so likely to occur. A narrowly based excise may therefore be shifted almost entirely backward to factors.

The remarks up to this point are appropriate for a perfectly competitive industry, but not for a monopoly, which never encounters the four extremes of elasticity-inelasticity. A perfectly elastic demand exists only for an undifferentiated, hence not monopolized, commodity. No monopolist will operate at a level of output where the demand for his product is of unit elasticity or less, for he then could always increase his profit by raising his price. Perfectly elastic and perfectly inelastic supply do not exist for a monopolist, since he has no supply function, only a cost function.

In turn, however, the monopolist presents two extreme cases of his own: (1) Under constant costs, there occurs the apparent paradox that, although no factor rewards are reduced, the buyer does not pay the full tax; price rises by less than the tax. The balance of the tax comes out of the monopolist's pre-tax profit, which is not a factor reward.[15] (2) When supply is physically limited short of the output the monopolist would otherwise produce under an excise tax, the full burden of the tax rests on the monopolist.

The number of possible outcomes under a tax on a monopoly is greater than under a tax on a competitive industry: for example, under a unit tax the price may rise by more than the tax, when marginal cost is increasing,[16] an outcome not possible under competition, except for related commodities (see page 278 below). The few generalizations that can be made with respect to a unit excise tax on a monopolist are therefore worth noting:[17]

    1. Under a unit tax, large or small, the price of the taxed product will always be

less and cost less (*New York Times*, January 14, 1967, p. 10). If factor supply were perfectly inelastic, price could fall by no more than 24 per cent from the 76-cent level.

    15. See James M. Buchanan, *The Public Finances*, rev. ed. (Homewood, Ill.: Irwin, 1965), pp. 452–53. Buchanan's diagram illustrates the linear demand case, but the statement also holds for any negatively sloped demand curve that is concave to the origin or that is no more than moderately convex. See Joan Robinson, *Economics of Imperfect Competition*, pp. 79–80: "the effect of the tax [on price] will be greater the more concave is the demand curve, and less the more convex is the demand curve." In her terminology, a curve is concave when it is convex to the origin, and convex when it is concave to the origin (*ibid.*, p. 23). See also Carl S. Shoup, *Shifting and Incidence Theory: Taxes on Monopoly* (privately distributed, Columbia University, revised, September, 1950), pp. 15–16.

    16. See F. Y. Edgeworth, "The Pure Theory of Taxation," reprinted in Musgrave and Shoup, *Readings in the Economics of Taxation*, p. 284. Edgeworth remarks that the rise in price is more likely to be less than the tax, rather than greater, for reasons he gives in his footnote 108, *idem*. If the price were to rise by more than the tax, under increasing costs, the demand curve would have to be very convex to the origin (see note immediately preceding).

    17. Taken from Shoup, *op. cit.*, pp. 10–21.

increased and therefore the amount purchased will decrease.[18] This conclusion applies also to an ad valorem tax.

2. For small changes in tax, the following conclusions hold, regardless of the particular cost or demand conditions at the initial equilibrium (elasticity, curvature, and sign of marginal cost):[19]

(*a*) The ratio of the rise in price to the rate of tax per unit will be: the ratio of (1) the marginal demand, defined as the change in absolute number of units sold, per unit change in price (the slope of the demand curve with respect to the price axis), to (2) the rate at which the monopolist's *marginal* pre-tax net revenue (marginal pre-tax profit) is tending to change per unit increase in price (not per unit decrease in output). Marginal net revenue is rate of change in total net revenue per unit increase in price.

(*b*) The increase in price will be very much larger than the tax if the marginal net revenue is tending to change very little per unit increase in price.[20] If the tax is imposed on someone who is buying from the monopolist, a consumer or retailer, for example, the tax will of course induce the monopolist to raise his price, when, if the tax had been levied on the monopolist, he would have raised his price by more than the tax.

(*c*) The greater the rate at which marginal cost (increase in total cost per unit increase in *output*) is increasing, per unit increase in output, the smaller will be the rise in the monopolist's price under a unit tax.[21]

(*d*) The more the marginal demand is tending to increase in absolute terms, per unit increase in *price*, the smaller is the rise in price caused by the tax.[22]

3. If both the demand function and the total cost function are linear, price will rise by just half the tax, whether the tax is large or small.[23]

4. The effect of a change in the slope of the demand curve is not a meaningful question in the monopoly case, since such a change alters the initial, non-tax equilibrium point, and thus makes comparison impossible.[24]

If the supply and demand functions of the taxed commodity depend upon the prices of one or more other commodities, the standard results no longer obtain necessarily, either for competition or for monopoly.[25] If two commodities are rival in

18. *Ibid.*, p. 10.   19. *Ibid.*, pp. 11–16.

20. Or, as Marshall put it, if total net revenue is tending to change slowly (*Principles*, 8th ed., pp. 483–84, footnote).

21. Shoup, *op. cit.*, pp. 14–15.

22. *Ibid.*, pp. 15–16. See also note 16 above.

23. "This theorem was discovered independently by Knut Wicksell, *Lectures on Political Economy*, 1901, Vol. I, p. 93; Joan Robinson, *The Economics of Imperfect Competition*, 1933, p. 77; and Raymond Garver, 'The Effect of Taxation on a Monopolist,' *Am. Eco. Rev.* September, 1932, p. 464. Neither Cournot nor Edgeworth states it" (Shoup, *op. cit.*, p. 17, note). Conclusions depending on curvature and direction throughout the demand and marginal cost curves are given in Shoup, *op. cit.*, pp. 17–18 and 64–67, where George N. Raney extends certain theorems developed by Joan Robinson.

24. See Due, *op. cit.*, p. 39, and Shoup, *op. cit.*, pp. 19–20. The slope of the marginal cost curve or the curvature of the demand curve can be changed without disturbing the initial equilibrium point; see Shoup, *op. cit.*, pp. 15–16 and 59, and above, items (*c*) and (*d*).

25. Edgeworth demonstrated this fact for the monopoly case in his article, "The Pure Theory of Taxation," and for the competitive case in a bracketed addition to the article when

production and consumption,[26] a tax on one of them may cause the price of both to fall; a tax on the other may raise its price by more than the tax, even under competition. The fall in the price of the taxed commodity does not, however, imply that more of that commodity is purchased under the new low cum-tax price.[27]

If a cluster of competitive firms is located at one point in space, and another cluster of firms in the same industry at another point, and if transport costs are positive, a marketing boundary will develop somewhere between the two points. If transport costs are proportional to distance and are the same for both clusters of producers, and if both industry clusters operate under identical costs, the boundary will bisect vertically a straight line joining the two clusters of firms. If a transportation tax is imposed on one of the clusters of producers, such that their transport costs per mile are larger by a constant amount than the transport costs of the other cluster,[28] the boundary line becomes a circle surrounding (but not centered on) the point at which that cluster of producers is located. The center of the circle will be on the far side of this point, that is, on the side away from the initial vertical boundary line, but will draw nearer to it if the tax is increased, and the circle consequently contracts. The untaxed cluster of firms can therefore capture customers located on the far side of the taxed cluster, if those customers are far enough away to make the difference in transport costs outweigh the fact that the untaxed shipper is more distant from the customer than is the taxed shipper. A tax on the commodity at the factory, on the other hand, allows the taxed cluster of firms to hold customers on the far side, that is, away from the untaxed cluster. The straight-line boundary,

the latter was published in his *Papers Relating to Political Economy*, vol. 2, p. 124 (reprinted in Musgrave and Shoup [Eds.], *Readings in the Economics of Taxation*, p. 295). Harold Hotelling independently extended the analysis to the competitive case in his article, "Edgeworth's Taxation Paradox and the Nature of Supply and Demand Functions," *Journal of Political Economy* (October, 1932), 40: 577–616. See also R. G. D. Allen, *Mathematical Analysis for Economists*, Examples 41 and 42 to Chapter 2, p. 60; Martin J. Bailey, "Edgeworth's Taxation Paradox, and the Nature of Demand Functions," *Econometrica* (January, 1954), 22: 72–76; and William Vickrey, "Can Excises Lower Prices?" in R. W. Pfouts (Ed.), *Essays in Economics and Econometrics* (Chapel Hill: University of North Carolina Press, n.d.).

26. Specifically, if, under competition, the demand for the taxed commodity A varies directly, and the supply inversely, with the price of commodity B, while the demand and supply functions of B vary similarly with the price of A.

27. In the example given in Allen, before a tax is imposed,

$$\text{demand for wheat,} \quad x_1 = 4 - 10p_1 + 7p_2$$
$$\text{demand for rye,} \quad x_2 = 3 + 7p_1 - 5p_2$$
$$\text{supply of wheat,} \quad x_1 = 7 + p_1 - p_2$$
$$\text{supply of rye,} \quad x_2 = -27 - p_1 + 2p_2$$

where p_1 is the price per bushel of wheat and p_2 the price per bushel of rye. A tax t_1 per bushel is imposed on wheat producers and one of t_2 per bushel on rye producers. Substituting $p_1 - t_1$ for p_1 and $p_2 - t_2$ for p_2 in the supply relations above, and letting $p_2 = 0$, we find that the price of wheat falls from $219/13$ to $(219 - t_1)/13$, while the price of rye falls from $306/13$ to $(306 - 3t_1)/13$. The quantity of wheat purchased, under the tax on wheat, is $4 - 10[(219 - t_1)/13] + 7[(306 - 3t_1)/13]$. When no tax was in force this quantity was $4 - 10(219/13) + 7(306/13)$. The quantity of wheat purchased thus decreases by $11t_1/13$, although the market price of wheat, including tax, has fallen by $t_1/13$. But the quantity of rye taken increases by $8t_1/13$. A tax on rye will raise both prices, the rye price by more than the tax.

28. A motor fuel tax is an approximate example (abstracting from use made of the revenue).

instead of being changed to a circle, is bent back into a hyperbola.[29] Intuition suggests therefore that a transportation tax will do more damage to the producing firms than will an equal-yield tax on the product at the factory.

If the two clusters of competitive firms are replaced by two single firms, each firm will be a monopolist within its own marketing territory, and one of a two-firm oligopoly at the boundary. The applicability of the cost and pricing assumptions above is correspondingly weakened if not invalidated; the conclusions just stated require that each firm charge each customer a price equal to a certain price quoted for delivery at the factory plus the cost of transport, so that the price to each customer rises by just the amount of the increase in the transport tax, or the commodity tax at the factory.[30]

In an open economy that imports an excise-taxed commodity that is marketed by firms that handle many other items simultaneously, virtually the entire incidence of the tax will be on the consumer. The supply of the commodity from the outside world can be taken as perfectly price-elastic in the usual case, and the supply of domestic marketing service is perfectly elastic for the reasons discussed on page 275. This conclusion holds even if the taxed good is also manufactured domestically, provided that the decline in amount taken by consumers is not so large as to eliminate imports (see Chapter 8, Section A.2).

The consuming country may conceivably be so large a customer that the import supply to it is not perfectly price-elastic; in that event its consumers will force the foreign supplier to bear part of the incidence and the price to the consumer will rise by less than the tax.[31]

3. Criteria

Given the aims of the excise taxes, most of them satisfy some aspects of the consensus equity criterion, equal treatment of those equally circumstanced. Irrelevant circumstances, defined as in Chapter 2, Section A.1.A, do not usually intrude. Impersonality is commonly preserved; there are few one-taxpayer clauses in excise tax laws.

Certainty, however, may be impaired for many business firms because of the difficulty of defining precisely the commodity that is to be taxed. This difficulty is often overcome at the cost of injecting qualitative or quantitative discontinuities. How much fur must a coat have on it (and on the inside or the outside?) before it becomes a "fur coat"? Any definition that is precise enough to remove uncertainty

29. With a directrix parallel to the initial marketing boundary, on the far side of it (away from the untaxed cluster).

30. These remarks on transport costs and taxes are derived from the analysis in R. G. D. Allen, *op. cit.*, pp. 80–82, and Examples III–36, III–37. Allen's analysis, based on the work of Erich Schneider, is in terms of two firms, but does not explore the implications of monopoly raised here. It must be noted, too, that in practice transport costs are not linear.

31. The United Kingdom tobacco tax and petroleum taxes may be illustrations; all tobacco and petroleum consumed there are imported.

is apt to offend common sense by its boundary lines. At what price per pair do shoes enter a "luxury" category? How are household soap and luxury soap to be distinguished from still other soaps?[32]

The discontinuities under the taxes on addictives are chiefly quantitative, for two reasons. First, these commodities have no close substitutes, by definition of an addictive. Secondly, if there is a luxury grade of the addictive, or if a grade is more than usually dangerous socially owing to concentration of the drug element, or owing to certain psychological elements, as in some forms of gambling, that grade can be defined in quantitative terms: percentage of alcohol content by volume, for example (compare the task of defining luxury soap). Alternatively, or in addition, the dividing line can be drawn in terms of price per unit, again an easier task for these commodities than for luxuries.

The degree of evasion is equal for all, under an excise tax, only when evasion is virtually zero. This goal can be achieved when a few large firms account for all the trade and when the tax administrators cannot be corrupted.[33] The higher the excise, the easier it may be to achieve zero evasion, since a high tax rate imposes so great a working capital problem on a new firm that entry may be very difficult; the few established firms remain in complete control even in a rapidly growing economy. But when evasion does exist, it is always very uneven, especially under taxes on distilled spirits and gambling.

Compliance costs are more likely to be roughly equal than evasion rates, under a given excise. As a percentage of total cost they are large under the spirits tax, because the tax law commonly requires that the distillery be constructed and operated in specified ways to minimize the possibility of evasion; but if the costs do not differ much from one firm to another, they cannot be condemned on equity grounds.

The built-in flexibility of the yield of luxury excises is high, by definition of luxury, but the efficiency of that flexibility[34] is probably low; the reduction in the consumer's tax bill, as his income falls, compared with what that bill would be under a poll tax of equal yield initially, seems more likely to be saved than spent, at least in the short run. The addictives contrast on both counts with the luxuries. The demands for addictives are not income-elastic, but the small decline in yield of these excises that does occur is probably efficient, since most of the revenue comes from low-income and moderate-income households, insofar as it has not come out of specialized factor rewards.

Reduction in excise tax rates, especially rates on alcohol and tobacco, is less appropriate to promote full employment than is reduction of a broad-based sales

32. Compare "soap," "household soap," and "soap de luxe," taxed, respectively, at 20 per cent, 10 per cent, and 25 per cent under the French value-added tax as it stood prior to 1968. The range of rates and the scope of exemptions were so wide that "a French business advisor asserts that a basic question in business planning in France is to determine exactly how the contemplated activities will be treated under the value-added tax" (Norr and Kerlan, *Taxation in France*, p. 1023, note 137). "A taxpayer's guide uses 13 closely printed pages to set forth the products that are subject to the luxury rate of 25% and the related or similar products that are not" (*ibid.*, p. 1026, note 151).

33. The United Kingdom excises on alcohol, tobacco, and petroleum are examples.

34. See Chapter 22, Section D.4.

tax rate. Excise tax rates are commonly higher than sales tax rates; counter-cycle rate changes would probably be a larger percentage of ex-tax price. The perverse anticipatory reactions of consumers or business firms would be correspondingly stronger. So too would be the beneficial income effects (see Chapter 22, Section B.1), but among low-income families those effects might well be to alter rates of expenditure on food, clothing, and medicine more than on the taxed commodities. On balance the score seems unfavorable to the excises. Moreover, it appears odd, distributively, to require the smokers and drinkers to be responsible for, or allow them alone to obtain the benefits of, countering cyclical tendencies.

Excises probably impose only a small excess burden on consumers of luxuries and a moderate excess burden on consumers of addictives.

The demand for a luxury good is fairly sensitive to a change in income, by definition of a luxury. Only a small proportion of a consumer's income is ordinarily devoted to any one luxury good. Also, the demand for a luxury is probably not very sensitive to a change in price, unless the luxury is so narrowly described as to have close substitutes. The net result of these three facts is a rather low elasticity of substitution and a consequently small loss of consumer surplus and small excess burden on consumers, since that excess burden depends on the elasticity of substitution (rather than on price elasticity as ordinarily defined).[35]

The demand for an addictive, in contrast to that for a luxury good, is not very sensitive to a change in income (as with luxuries, the income elasticity is positive; addictives are not inferior goods). Addictives resemble luxuries in that only a small proportion of a consumer's income is spent on any one addictive, extreme cases aside, and price elasticity is usually low. The net result is an elasticity of substitution that is probably somewhat larger than for most luxuries, producing a correspondingly somewhat greater excess burden on the consumer, although one that is still moderate compared with the excess burden created by taxes on standard varieties of food, shelter, and clothing.

In other words, the loss of consumer surplus under compensated demand curves, i.e., ordinary demand curves reformulated to eliminate the income effect of changes in the price of the commodity, is probably small under taxes on luxuries and small to moderate under taxes on addictives.

On the producer side of the market the distinctions between luxuries, addictives, and other goods are of course meaningless, and no a priori conjectures about relative loss of producer surplus under the three types of excise appear warranted.

Since the consumption of most addictives commonly imposes discomfort on others, a tax that induces a reduction in consumption of these consumer goods reduces negative externalities. In effect, we start, under no tax, from a second-best situation. The moderate excess burden that taxes on addictives create for the consumer is therefore offset, more or less, by their reduction of excess burden through reduction of negative externalities. But the gain on this latter account will not be great, as consumption will not in fact decrease greatly under the tax.

The more that consumption decreases under a given tax rate, the greater is the gain on externality account and, probably—certainly, if the income effect is kept

35. See Appendix to this chapter.

constant—the greater the loss on elasticity-of-substitution account. For a given revenue yield, except the maximum, we have seen that every excise offers two alternative rates of tax. At the higher rate the gain on externality account will be the greater, but so too will be the loss on substitution account. It cannot be said a priori whether the net gain on these two accounts will be the larger (or the net loss smaller) at the higher rate than at the lower rate of tax.

Excises commonly induce or even require more expensive methods of doing business; taxes on distilled spirits are a good example. In effect, the cost curve is shifted upward, in addition to the upward shift representing the tax rate itself (or the downward shift in the demand curve if the tax is collected from consumers). There is a corresponding loss of consumer and producer surplus without any off-setting tax revenue.

Excise taxes may exert import effects on quality of product, and on selling effort. Both of these effects imply excess burden.[36]

We turn now to the conflict criteria, for the excises.

An excise tax that is only partly shifted to consumers distributes the rest of its burden erratically as to income or wealth class, since the owners of the particular factors that have to absorb part of the tax may be at any income level.

This erratic element is small when the supply is almost perfectly price-elastic. Luxury excises in a highly open-economy, less developed country are therefore distributed progressively by income class, except as evasion is easier for the rich and as accurate definition of luxuries is difficult. But one of the most important of all luxuries in less developed countries is not imported, except as some of its physical constituents are imported, for example, luxury housing. A heavy tax on such housing throws some specialized domestic factors out of work and forces the domestic factors remaining in the building trades to accept lower rates of reward; a part of the luxury tax is then probably distributed regressively. The services of household servants, similarly, are not imported and are not perfectly elastic in supply.

The taxes on addictives make no pretense of progressivity by income or wealth. That part of the tax on an addictive that is borne by the consumer is either regressive or erratic in distribution by income. Alcohol, to be sure, can be packaged in luxury form, chiefly by allowing the consumer to absorb more alcohol with less water (spirits as against beer) and by affording him the social status that goes with paying a high price for slight improvements in taste and appearance (17-year-old Scotch). Tobacco and gambling, in contrast, are much less amenable to stratification of the product between luxury and non-luxury levels and so lose even the modest ability of the liquor tax to be something less than sharply regressive.

The tax on motor fuel, considered apart from the use made of the revenue, is in part a tax on the factors producing motor fuel, except in small countries that import their petroleum. In part it is a tax on private-car owners and, to the extent that motor fuel is consumed in business use, in part a tax diffused among consumers who buy motor-fuel-intensive products, or among factors that work with motor fuel.

36. See the intensive treatment of these two effects, *inter alia*, in Ned Shilling's forth-coming *Economic Effects of Excise Taxes* (New York: Columbia University Press, 1969), especially Parts II and IV.

Excise taxes take no account of horizontal-equity standards; indeed, the taxes on addictives flout them. In some countries the great disparity in tax burden among families of the same composition and income is welcomed on the grounds that the sinful should contribute more to the public purse. Allied to this is the argument that any family that finds the burden too heavy can escape by giving up the addictives; the tax is a voluntary contribution. The element of hypocrisy here lies in the belief, held at the same time, that these are good taxes because consumption does not decrease.

Some excise taxes favor depressed regions within the taxing country insofar as (1) depressed regions are largely subsistence economies outside the money circuit and (2) the tax is shifted forward. These regions will purchase little of the commodity taxed, just because household money incomes are so low. Moreover, households in these regions may be able to produce the taxed good, or a close substitute, for home use, liquor particularly. If the depressed areas are producers of raw materials for the taxed goods, they may suffer severely from that part of the tax that is shifted backward. But since ownership of the raw materials is commonly in persons who live outside the depressed area, it is somewhat ambiguous to say that the area suffers. Excise taxes are never shifted to foreign consumers, since exports are invariably exempted (see Chapter 24), but part of the tax may be exported by backward shifting.

The excises possess the advantage of being virtually unusable for discrimination by color, race, or social status. Occasionally an excise can be narrowly based on a product used chiefly by consumers of a given race or color, but these instances are rare.

Economic growth can be promoted by excises, just because they are so selective. Even a broad system of excises can avoid taxing producers' goods, except a few goods that are so easily turned to consumer use and so difficult to police after purchase that they must be taxed even when sold to producers.[37] Gainful consumption and even all productive consumption can be exempted by limiting the excises to luxuries. The portion of luxury taxes that is shifted forward will however come in some degree out of saving. The taxes on addictives are another matter. The resulting reduction of real disposable income in many low-income households will almost surely induce a decline in productive-consumption purchases. The household's income elasticity for milk and medicine may well prove greater than that for liquor and tobacco.

An excise tax on commodities that are complementary to the enjoyment of leisure will on the one hand reduce the price of leisure, since the rewards from work are taxed (the taxed item is purchased in part from wages), and will on the other hand increase the price of leisure by taxing goods that are consumed in the process of consuming leisure. The latter effect reduces the amount by which work would otherwise be lessened by the excise. But the complementarity between any given good and leisure is usually rather weak, if not for any one person then surely for the economy as a whole. Moreover, it would be difficult to collect taxes at rates high

---

37. Examples under the United Kingdom purchase tax are "commercial motor vehicles, office requisites, and various supplies" (Due, *Sales Taxation*, p. 207). See Chapter 8, Section B.4.A.

enough to exert an important effect. Since the negative effect, of the one tax, on work is also weak, however, the net result may well be almost zero, with respect to effect on the supply of labor.

In a world of certainty, an excise tax induces some movement of factors out of the taxed industry, the extent of the movement, we have seen, depending on the elasticities of demand and supply. In a world in which every venture, within and outside of the taxed industry, is equally risky before the excise is imposed, the conclusions reached for a world of certainty need to be modified or at least qualified. The immediate effect of the excise tax, before any movement of factors has occurred, is to lower the amount of profit on all prospective profitable outcomes of a venture in this field, and to increase the loss on all prospective loss outcomes of such a venture. Thus the mean return of every venture in the taxed field is reduced. But it is possible that the variance of the outcomes of any venture in the taxed field may be lowered by the tax, either lowered absolutely or even relative to the mean return. Thus the outmigration of resources may be less than the fall in the mean return alone would suggest, for it appears plausible that under a given mean return more investment will be made in an industry the smaller the variance of the after-tax outcomes; the investment world is probably dominated by risk-averters rather than by risk-seekers or risk-neutralists. On the other hand, variance may increase under the tax, either absolutely or at least relatively to the mean, as the mean return falls.

Accordingly, the movement of resources out of the taxed industry may be greater or less than in a world of certainty. Nothing more can be said pending further analysis of the probable patterns of change in variance relative to change in mean return, first, immediately after the tax is imposed, and secondly, after migration of factors has produced a new equilibrium within the taxed industry.

Total social risk-taking in the economy may be increased, if the effect of the excise is to widen the variance of outcomes of ventures in the taxed industry absolutely, and perhaps even if the widening is only relative to the mean return. Risk averters may be willing to undertake ventures outside the taxed field more risky than had been undertaken before, in view of the increase in risk (if that occurs) in the taxed industry.

An incremental surplus on balance of payments can be achieved in less developed countries by an excise tax system, since so large a proportion of luxuries are imported. Taxes on addictives serve the same end in an industrialized economy, if the raw materials for the taxed addictive are imported.[38]

None of the excises are suitable for diverting consumer expenditure to public-purpose outlays except for the rather weak substitution effect they exert by not taxing such outlays. The effect is weak because there are so many other uses of income that also are not subject to the excise taxes.

The problems of intergovernmental and intragovernmental coordination discussed under the turnover tax (Chapter 8, Section A.4.B) do not arise here, since excises are normally not imposed on the kind of goods and services purchased by governments.

38. As in the United Kingdom, with the tobacco tax. See Carl S. Shoup, "Tax Tension in the British Fiscal System," *National Tax Journal* (March, 1961), 14: 1–40, esp. p. 22.

4. Intra-system Reactions on Yields

Backward shifting of an excise tax, by reducing the money amount of factor rewards, reduces the money yield of an income tax. Forward shifting does not decrease the income tax yield, since the consumer is usually not allowed to deduct the excise tax element in the cost of his consumer's good, in computing taxable income. The yield of a general sales tax will automatically increase with an excise tax if the sales tax is imposed on total selling price including excises, and if the excise tax is in fact shifted forward at least in part. The excise tax itself is not sensitive to changes in the rates of other taxes.

B. MONOPOLY REVENUE

To obtain revenue in lieu of taxation, governments in some private enterprise economies operate monopolies in the production or distribution of liquor or tobacco products, or, less frequently, salt or playing cards.[39] Certain forms of gambling are monopolized for the same purpose, notably the lottery. In one country the monopolies return only a modest profit as such, but serve as evasion-proof tax collectors.[40] Other government monopolies, notably the post office, railroads, telephone, telegraph, and radio and television are more commonly drains on the government fisc than contributors to it.

1. Choice of Commodities or Services to Be Monopolized

A community will commonly tolerate, and a government is commonly disposed to exercise, a certain ruthlessness in suppressing illegal competition that may not be acceptable in enforcing a tax law. And there may be something inherently easier in suppressing competition than in collecting taxes. Accordingly, it is usually easier to enforce a government monopoly than a tax. This point is valid only when the industry would not be a monopoly or oligopoly if in private hands, for in these instances tax collection should be relatively easy, unless the private firms themselves control the government.

Moreover, the public may rebel against a burden that is explicit in a tax rate

39. Notably France, Germany and Italy, but not the United Kingdom or the United States federal government. See the World Tax Series volumes on these countries.

40. The Swedish wholesale and retail liquor and tobacco manufacture monopolies yield revenue primarily in the form of taxes at stipulated rates levied on sales by the monopoly enterprise. See Martin Norr, Frank J. Duffy, and Harry Sterner, *Taxation in Sweden*, World Tax Series, Law School of Harvard University (Boston: Little, Brown, 1959), pp. 143–44, 146–47.

which it will accept if it is buried in a price. The "tax" imposed by the government monopoly is fixed in its "rate" by the administrative decree that sets the price of the product. These implicit tax rates are commonly high, relative to excise tax rates.

Even if enforcement of the excise tax is perfect, more revenue can be obtained from a government monopoly than from the excise tax if the industry is monopolized when in private hands. A tax on output will always induce a private monopolist to reduce his output. At this lower level of operation the monopolist's profit before tax will be smaller than at the initial level of operation. At any given level of operation the yield of a tax on output cannot exceed what the monopoly profit would be at that level under no tax. Hence a tax on output, because it drives the private monopolist to operate at a less-than-maximum pre-tax profit, must yield less than the government could get by taking all the profit from operation at the higher level.

If the tax applies to the profit, not the output, of a private monopoly, the government can of course get as much revenue by taxing at a 100 per cent rate as by operating the monopoly itself, unless it can discriminate more than the private monopolist in prices charged to customers or paid to factors. Moreover, a private monopolist may hold price and therefore profit somewhat below, and maintain output somewhat above, the level that would maximize profit, owing to fear of potential competitors, a fear that the government need not experience.[41]

The likelihood of a government monopoly rather than an excise tax is increased if the commodity or service can be produced or marketed profitably without co-products or sidelines. The government can then avoid involvement in articles or services that it has no desire to deal in. Another condition favorable for a government monopoly is that the chief raw material for the commodity in question be not used to produce any other commodity. The government can then monopolize not the production of the finished good but the distribution of the raw material. It will control directly the total amount of the raw material produced within the country and imported, and allocate quotas to particular domestic producers, thereby reducing the amount of the raw material that is diverted to illegal private processing. Tobacco is an example.

Profitable coordination of many small or medium-sized plants is commonly so difficult that it can be accomplished only by the most skillful and profit-motivated effort. The problem is somewhat like that of efficiency in farming. Distilling of whiskeys in some countries illustrates this point and helps explain why whiskey is taxed rather than monopolized.

A subordinate political unit, a province, state, or city, which cannot prohibit imports from other parts of the nation, will not monopolize the production of tobacco products or liquor within its borders, but will take over, instead, the wholesaling or retailing of these commodities, since a substantial part of these services can be imported only with difficulty if at all.[42]

41. If the industry is a perfectly competitive one when in private hands, the problem of comparing maximum revenue under taxation and under government monopoly cannot be analyzed in the straightforward manner above; that case is not covered here.

42. These considerations help explain why many states of the United States operate retail liquor monopolies, but none of them, production monopolies.

Finally, if the product is marketed through a large number of retail outlets, a government monopoly does, while an excise tax of course does not, afford an opportunity to pay off political debts by allocating the outlets to particular individuals.

Outside of the scope of the remarks up to this point fall those monopolies that are inherently governmental—coinage, for example—and that therefore pose no problem of choice between monopoly profits and taxation.

2. Incidence

If the government monopoly is simply an alternative to a private monopoly, the incidence of the government's monopoly profit rests entirely on those who would obtain the monopoly profit under private operation and no tax. This conclusion of course assumes that the government monopoly does not come about through the government's purchasing the business from an already existing private monopoly at a price that capitalizes the monopoly's profit.

If the government monopoly is an alternative to a perfectly competitive industry employing specialized factors, the partial equilibrium incidence of the government's monopoly profit is much the same as would be that of a per-unit tax levied on the competitive industry at a rate equal to the spread between the monopolist's price and marginal cost at his monopoly equilibrium point.[43] In general, the conclusion reached in Section A.2 on the partial equilibrium incidence of a per-unit excise tax applies, and the incidence of the government's monopoly profit is divided between consumers and factors in proportions determined by the elasticities.

3. Criteria

A government monopoly can raise revenue while observing more closely than do taxes on the industry the consensus equity criterion. The price mechanism of the market is the means employed, which produces impersonality, certainty, and continuity in the (implicit) tax function, Evasion may be troublesome, as clandestine producers and conniving consumers seek to bypass the government monopoly, but equality of rates of evasion has little meaning here. Costs of compliance are virtually nil. The amount of resources the government would have to spend to prevent evasion might be greater or less than under a tax; this relationship must vary widely from one industry to another.

43. For precision it must be assumed that the monopolist discriminates in payments to the factors, extracting their rent (or owns the factors). Then "the marginal-cost curve to the monopolist would also be an industry marginal-cost curve for the competitive case," and "The effect of shifting from competition to a [private] monopoly . . . is very much as though a tax [equal to the difference between price and marginal cost] had been levied on the output of the industry and turned over to the producers or monopolists [that is, in the present case, to the government monopoly]" (Vickrey, *Microstatics*, p. 287).

If a business recession develops, a private monopolist would in principle reduce his rate of output, since the demand curve for his product will be shifting downward. He might either raise or lower his price, depending on the form of the new curve. If the government monopoly thus reduces its output, in an endeavour always to maximize its profit, it will increase unemployment. But maximizing net revenue from a government revenue monopoly in a recession is just as inappropriate to a counter-cycle public finance policy as would be maximizing revenue from an excise tax at that time. The monopoly would seek smaller profits, or even a loss. And in a boom period it might set its prices above the maximum-profit level.

The conflict-of-interests criteria are not easily applied to government monopoly revenue in general. It depends on whether salt or diamonds are being monopolized, or ships or lottery tickets. But if, as here, the issue is narrowed in each case to the question whether there shall be government monopoly, or taxation, monopoly is preferable insofar as discriminatory pricing can be employed more accurately to achieve a particular distributive aim than can a series of different tax rates, and exemptions, under a tax on the same commodity. In principle, it should be easier to discriminate directly than through the intermediary links of taxation and the private business firm. Consumers at different income levels, belonging to families of differing size and composition and located in one or another part of the country, could be more readily given differing treatment than under a sales tax. In practice, however, there has been little departure from uniform pricing, at least by revenue-raising monopolies, as distinguished from monopolies run at a loss or with only a normal profit.

Economic growth, external equilibrium, and maintenance of the labor supply seem unlikely to be fostered by a revenue-oriented monopoly as compared with what they would be under a tax on the industry in question. The kinds of goods monopolized are usually not purchased by subordinate or higher levels of government. Some intra-fiscal-system reactions may occur, just as under a tax; an increase in the government monopoly's prices will decrease its own income tax revenue and that of its subordinate governments, if the monopolized commodity is a deductible expense.

On the whole, government revenue-raising monopolies compare favorably with excise taxes on the same industries, under these criteria, but the criteria do not cover certain special issues posed by government ownership as against private ownership. There is, for example, the potential abuse of the concentration of economic power in governmental bodies, power that could otherwise be spread thinly throughout a competitive industry or, if concentrated in a private monopoly, might be viewed by government officials as something to be checked rather than strengthened. Further issues are: Is government operation more efficient, technically, than private, and in particular does it respond quickly to technical change? Is it more responsive to consumer preferences? Is it able to limit wasteful or extravagant promotion expenditures?

APPENDIX TO CHAPTER TEN

Let it be assumed, as in the text above, that the demand for a luxury good is usually not very sensitive to a change in price, but is sensitive to a change in income, and that only a small proportion of one's income is normally devoted to any one luxury item.

Let E_p be the price elasticity (it is normally negative)

E_i be the income elasticity (it is positive, for luxuries)

E_s be the elasticity of substitution (it is negative)

a be the proportion of income spent on the article.

$$E_p = -aE_i + (1-a)E_s^1$$

If, then, E_p is a numerically small negative number, the two negative terms, $-aE_i$ and $(1-a)E_s$ must both be small numerically. For a luxury, the first of these terms, $-aE_i$, is small under the assumption that the coefficient a is a small fraction, applied to a fairly large income elasticity, E_i. But if the coefficient a is a small fraction, the coefficient $(1-a)$ is a correspondingly large fraction, and, since it is large, E_s must be small numerically in order that $(1-a)E_s$ may be small numerically. The fact that E_s is small numerically means that the excess burden of a tax on the luxury must be light.

Demand for an addictive is assumed to be not very sensitive to a change in income, but otherwise to resemble the demand for a luxury. Since both E_i and the coefficient a are numerically small, the term $-aE_i$ is numerically very small. Hence the elasticity of substitution, E_s, may be appreciable (though indeed not large), even if E_p is small. There is therefore probably somewhat more danger of excess burden under taxes on addictives than under taxes on luxuries.

In terms of compensated demand curves, the excess burden on consumers is zero if such a demand curve is vertical, i.e. compensated demand is perfectly inelastic.[2] Price rises by the full amount of the tax, and the tax revenue equals the reduction in consumer surplus. Producers do not suffer.

The excess burden on consumers is also zero if the compensated demand curve is horizontal, i.e. compensated demand is perfectly elastic. Consumers have no consumer surplus to lose. Price does not rise at all under a tax.

Consequently, as the compensated demand curve, under alternative assumptions as to its position, pivots on its initial equilibrium point from a vertical position to a horizontal position, excess burden on consumers first rises, then declines. At some position in between the extremes just described this quantity reaches a maximum.

If the compensated supply curve is perfectly elastic, the maximum excess loss of

---

1. See, e.g. Alfred W. Stonier and Douglas C. Hague, *A Textbook of Economic Theory* (3d ed.; London: Longmans, 1964), pp. 74–76, and Milton Friedman, *Price Theory* (Chicago: Aldine Publishing Company, 1962), p. 55 (using the Slutsky substitution concept).

2. An ordinary demand curve, i.e. uncompensated, that is perfectly inelastic will nevertheless reflect some elasticity of substitution if the income elasticity of demand for the commodity is negative (the commodity is an inferior good); the two elasticities exactly offset one another. See Musgrave, *op. cit.*, pp. 146–47 (but use "substitution effect" in place of "price effect").

consumer surplus will appear when the demand curve is so sloped that it cuts the price axis exactly at the point where the new horizontal supply curve (the old curve, raised by the tax) also cuts that axis. Sales of the taxed commodity are zero, and the familiar triangle for excess loss of consumer surplus is at a maximum. One side of this triangle, represented by the rate of tax, remains unchanged as the demand curve pivots downward from a vertical position to the position just described, while the other side of the triangle, represented by a segment of the supply curve ex-tax, steadily increases. If the demand curve pivots still further so that it cuts the price axis below the intercept of the supply-curve-with-tax with that axis, the first of these two sides of the excess-burden triangle now decreases, while the second side (which is now the horizontal distance from the price axis to the initial point of equilibrium) remains unchanged. Excess burden decreases. Outwardly, nothing alters as the demand curve thus pivots further, since the market for the good has already been killed; we are dealing with a corner solution. But excess burden becomes smaller, as the slope of the compensated demand curve approaches the horizontal. If it is horizontal, excess burden is zero.[3]

3. See John G. Head and Carl S. Shoup, "Excess Burden—the Corner Case", *American Economic Review* (forthcoming).

CHAPTER ELEVEN

Income Taxes: I

A. CONCEPTUAL BASIS AND SCOPE

INCOME TAXES ARE either universal or partial. The partial income taxes are uniform, quasi-schedular, or schedular. The universal income tax places the personal exemption so low that virtually every household pays income tax or, if the number of dependents is large, at least must file a return. This is the mass income tax, initiated during World War II.[1] The universal income taxes happen also to be uniform, in the sense that they each employ a single (progressive) rate schedule.

The partial income tax allows personal exemptions so high relative to the median household income that only a minority of households pay tax. Almost all wage payments and most salary payments are thereby exempted. The tax is virtually one on property income, including income from human capital, particularly training for the professions, and on economic rent from superior inborn ability. If a single progressive rate scale is used by this tax, it is a uniform partial income tax.[2] If differing rate schedules apply to different types of income, it is a schedular partial income tax.

Schedular rates are commonly supplemented by a progressive rate scale applicable to the taxpayer's total income from all sources. If the progressive rate scale is heavy and if the schedular rates are low and proportional, and not far from uniform, the tax is only a quasi-schedular income tax. In contrast, if there is no progressive rate scale applicable to total income, or only an unimportant one, and if the schedular

1. Notably in Australia, the United Kingdom, and the United States. If the French employers' payroll tax (not a tax for social security) is considered a part of the French income tax system, France is another universal income-tax country (see Chapter 16 below).

2. The German income tax exemplified the uniform partial income tax after the German tax reduction of 1958: "It is estimated that . . . less than one-half of all persons who are gainfully employed are obliged to pay income tax and that the great majority of these pay tax at the minimum rate of 20 per cent" (Gumpel and Boettcher, *Taxation in Germany*, p. 138). In 1959, 60.8 per cent of Germany's national income (net product at factor cost) was "gross income of employees" (*ibid.*, p. 36), that is, DM 116.9 billion, since the national income that year was DM 192.2 billion (*ibid.*, p. 32). Tax withheld on wages and salaries under the income tax in 1960 was DM 8.1 billion (*ibid.*, p. 122). But as per capita income increased in the succeeding years, the German tax apparently became, by 1968, a mass income tax.

rates are notably progressive and differ materially from one another, the tax is a true schedular income tax. Few countries impose a true schedular income tax; many impose the quasi-schedular tax.[3]

Another classification distinguishes countries that tax only income originating in the country ("source principle") from those that tax all income paid to residents of the country ("residence principle"), including income earned abroad.

A small and declining number of countries[4] comprise the first group, exempting their residents from taxation on all income earned abroad, from either investment or labor. The residence-principle countries in fact also tax, if only at flat rates, domestic-source income flowing to nonresidents. Some of them even tax foreign-source income flowing to nonresidents, if the recipients are citizens of the taxing country.[5] Consequently, "world-wide principle" is a more appropriate term than residence principle to distinguish that income tax from the source-principle tax. The distinction is further blurred by the credit that many of the "world-wide" income tax laws allow the taxpayer for income taxes paid to foreign countries on income arising there, or, less generously, deductibility of such taxes in computing taxable income. Thus the circle almost closes; what seems at first to be the opposite of a source-principle tax ends by resembling it.

With these reservations in mind, and for simplicity in exposition, the term "residence principle" will be used here to designate those income taxes that do not formally enunciate a strict source principle.

The income tax has not evolved as steadily and rapidly as has the sales tax from an economically uncoordinated version (the turnover tax and, correspondingly, the extreme type of schedular income tax) to an economically sophisticated type (the value-added or retail sales tax and, correspondingly, the universal income tax). The earliest income tax of modern times was a uniform partial income tax.[6] To be sure, changes in partial income taxes in recent years have all been in one direction, away from the schedular and toward the uniform income tax. On the other hand, there is little indication that the universal income tax will supplant the partial income tax. The advantage of historical perspective gained in Chapters 8 and 9 (Sales Taxes) at the cost of analytical repetition is therefore not obtainable here. The analysis to follow will consequently start with the most general type of income tax system, the

---

3. The true schedular tax is found in some of the former colonies of France. In Cambodia three different progressive-rate schedules apply to: unincorporated-business profits (top rate, 62 per cent), income from real estate (top rate, 80 per cent), and salaries and wages (top rate, 40 per cent). Tax at flat withholding rates is collected at the source on income from securities. The *impôt général sur le revenu* (top rate, 50 per cent) does not apply to income subject to the profits tax or the wages and salaries tax and supplies a negligible part of the income tax revenue. Corporations (*personnes morales*) are taxed at 25 per cent (40 per cent on real estate corporations) (Japan Tax Association, *Asian Taxation, 1965* [Tokyo: Japan Tax Association, 1966], pp. 1–10). A universal tax could be a schedular tax, but in practice it is not, aside from the schedular element in the British tax, that is, the favored treatment accorded earned income.

4. Chiefly some of the Latin American countries and, until recently, France.

5. The United States is an example.

6. The United Kingdom income tax of 1799–1802 and 1803–1816. See Shoup, *Ricardo on Taxation*, pp. 219–24. Although income was classified by schedules, the tax was not a schedular tax in the sense defined here.

universal income tax. This tax is usually imposed on a residence basis or a world-wide basis. The schedular types of partial income tax are commonly on a source basis.

B. UNIVERSAL INCOME TAX

1. Aggregate Tax Base Relative to That of a Value-Added Tax

The differential incidence of the income tax will be analyzed in terms of a value-added tax, for reasons given in Chapter 1 above. Consequently, it will be useful to compare the two taxes with respect to size of tax base. It will be seen that, abstracting from the personal exemptions and whatever non-business deductions the income tax allows, the base of the income tax is considerably the larger. This is so, even when the value-added tax is of the income type and therefore reflects deduction only of depreciation and obsolescence, not the cost of capital goods when purchased.

In this comparison, the concept formulated by Haig is taken to be the basic one: income is "the increase or accretion in one's power to satisfy his wants in a given period in so far as that power consists of (*a*) money itself, or, (*b*) anything susceptible of valuation in terms of money," or, "more simply stated," "Income is the *money value of the net accretion to one's economic power between two points of time.*"[7] Economic power, in this sense, of course includes consumption occurring during the period.

There are several reasons why the income tax base, so defined, is the larger. First, the income tax does, and the value-added tax does not, apply to factor payments made by national, state, or local governments, and by churches, charitable organizations, and similar non-profit-seeking bodies, all of which are customarily exempt from the value-added tax. A large proportion of total wages and salaries paid therefore falls outside the value-added tax base but within the income tax base.

Second, capital gains and losses, defined as gains or losses on assets not held for sale in the ordinary course of business, are ignored in computing even the income type of value added, except possibly as they reflect realized changes in value of assets used by business firms. Consequently, an income tax that included all capital gains and

7. Robert Murray Haig, "The Concept of Income—Economic and Legal Aspects," in R. M. Haig (Ed.), *The Federal Income Tax* (New York; Columbia University Press, 1921), p. 7, reprinted in Musgrave and Shoup (Eds.), *Readings in the Economics of Taxation*, p. 59. Others who employed a similarly broad concept in defining income for tax purposes include Georg Schanz, "Der Einkommensbegriff und die Einkommensteuergesetze," *Finanz-Archiv* (1896), 13: 1–87, and Henry C. Simons, *Personal Income Taxation* (Chicago: University of Chicago Press, 1938), pp. 59–102. See also Richard Goode, *The Individual Income Tax* (Washington, D.C.: Brookings Institution, 1964), pp. 13–17; Roswell Magill, *Taxable Income* (New York: Ronald Press, 1936, revised 1945); Fritz Neumark, *Theorie und Praxis der modernen Einkommensbesteuerung* (Bern; Francke, 1947), pp. 34–50; Stanley S. Surrey, "The Federal Income Tax Base for Individuals," *Columbia Law Review* (June, 1958) 58: 815–30; Paul H. Wueller, "Concepts of Taxable Income," *Political Science Quarterly* (March and December, 1938, and December, 1939). Professor Seligman's history and appraisal of income taxation in several countries reveals many aspects of the problem encountered in the earlier days of income taxation: E. R. A. Seligman, *The Income Tax* (New York: Columbia University Press, 1911). For references to the (usually) narrower definition of income, which would define it as consumption expenditure, see the references give in in Chapter 13 below.

allowed deduction of all capital losses would certainly distribute the aggregate tax base differently among the factor owners, compared with the income type of value-added tax. But would the two aggregates differ in size? Do capital gains exceed capital losses?

In a world without risk, there would be no return on assets less than the return expected initially, hence no decrease in the value of any asset, and hence no capital loss. A return on human economic rent could be embodied in an asset, say, a patent or a copyright, that would then yield a more than normal return. The asset could show a gain over its cost, including all the costs of training or education. Otherwise, the only increase in value of an asset apart from adding to its cost would come from accrual of normal interest not separated from the asset: for example, retained corporate earnings that would enhance the value of the corporate shares that meanwhile would have received dividends smaller than the normal rate of return, and discount bonds, paying no interest. Under these no-risk conditions, the aggregate base of an income tax that included capital gains would exceed the aggregate base of a value-added tax (income-type),[8] but the excess would amount only to the accrued normal return that had somehow escaped the value-added tax, plus the capitalized value of the patent, copyright, or other evidence of human economic rent, a quantity that would quite escape the value-added tax as it is currently conceived.

In the real world of risk, or its non-probabilistic companion, uncertainty, capital gains may be presumed to exceed capital losses, over a long run of decades, by (1) the premium demanded for risk-taking by investors who, as assumed here, are on the whole risk-averters rather than risk-seekers, and (2) those gains, just noted, that would arise even in a riskless world. Hence the base of the income tax that takes fully into account capital gains and losses will exceed that of the income type of value-added tax by at least the amount of the risk premium. In practice the disparity of the aggregate bases is widened by the common refusal of income tax laws to allow full deduction of capital losses. As to whether taxation of this risk premium inhibits risk-taking or indeed encourages it is another matter, to be discussed below. At this point we are interested only in defining and comparing tax bases.

A capital gain, in the view expressed here, is not a windfall in the sense of being an outcome that was not among the list of possible outcomes considered by the investor when he purchased the asset. Yet the gain is not the same as income arising from labor, or other non-capitalized incomes, or incomes from flows that are capitalized only for brief periods, into inventory values, for example. The difference

---

8. And *a fortiori* the aggregate base of a consumption type of value-added tax. This statement with respect to that type of value-added tax will be left implicit in succeeding paragraphs. Since the consumption type of value-added tax exempts all returns on capital assets, its base excludes gains from the sale of such assets. The seller includes receipts from the sale, but the buyer obtains a deduction of the same amount (unless he is a household, not a firm, and in that event the asset is not one not held for sale in the ordinary course of business). It seems therefore inappropriate to speak of the "failure" of the consumption type of value-added tax to make allowance for capital gains and losses (cf. Francisco Forte, "On the Feasibility of a Truly General Value Added Tax: Some Reflections on the French Experience," *National Tax Journal* [December, 1966], 19: 349). No inventory accounting is required, hence no question arises of choice between last-in first-out and first-in first-out methods (cf. *ibid.*, pp. 350–51). One of the administrative virtues of the consumption type of value-added tax is that it does not require any accounting at all for capital gains or losses as such (cf. *ibid.*, p. 352).

is that the capital gain reflects but one of a number of outcomes that were possible for the given venture, and materializes only when that particular outcome is seen to be fairly certain. The policy decision, whether to tax or exempt capital gains, therefore cannot be based simply on a decision whether windfalls are to be taxed, or on the treatment to be given to wages, salaries, or other non-capitalized incomes.[9]

The foregoing discussion does not apply to assets held for sale in the ordinary course of business. Such assets do not usually stay in one owner's hands long enough to change appreciably in value, other than by the cost he devotes to processing or otherwise improving them. An important exception is the minimum inventory of raw materials, semi-finished products and finished products that a firm must maintain to support a given volume of sales. This part of the inventory, even if changing continually as to the particular units that comprise it, is a "durable" producers' good that may rise or fall in value over the years as supply and demand fluctuate. The accrued capital gain or loss will never be realized for tax purposes if goods sold are charged with the cost of those particular raw materials and other components most recently purchased (last-in, first-out, or LIFO, inventory accounting), at least not unless sales exceed purchases by so much that the firm has to dip into these base stocks of inventory. The value-added tax will likewise fail to record those gains and losses, under LIFO accounting.

Third, the base of an income tax that strikes both profits and dividends will exceed that of the value-added tax by the amount of the dividends.

Fourth, the income tax, in contrast with the value-added tax, taxes the value added domestically that is embodied in exports, and does not reach the value embodied in imports.[10] This is so whether the income tax is on a source basis or a residence basis.[11] Accordingly, in a capital-exporting country that is in external equilibrium on balance of payments, hence in surplus on balance of trade, the universal income tax base will include an amount that is lacking in the base of the destination-principle value-added tax.[12] This amount, still abstracting from personal exemptions and non-business deductions, is the excess of exports over imports.

Fifth, if the domestic income tax is imposed on a residence basis, or even more widely on a citizenship basis, it will include income of a type not included in any domestic value-added tax,[13] namely, interest and dividends on foreign investment, and labor income earned abroad. It will exclude corresponding income arising domestically but flowing abroad; all such income will be subject to a domestic value-added tax (income type). On balance, the net effect will be a larger value added than income tax base in some countries, the reverse in others.

9. For a somewhat different point of view, see the searching analysis by Lawrence H. Seltzer, *The Nature and Tax Treatment of Capital Gains and Losses* (New York: National Bureau of Economic Research, 1951), Chapter 3, especially p. 82, where the question is put in terms of "the notion of attempting to separate windfall gains from ordinary income. . . ."

10. For proposals to exempt export income, if not to tax import income, see Chapter 24.

11. Aside from the presumably small part of imported value that represents foreign-source income taxed by the importing country under a residence tax.

12. See Chapter 8, Section A.1 and Chapter 9, Section B.1.b.

13. Aside from the presumably small portion of foreign investment income that is embodied in imports.

Important amounts of imputed income are excluded from the bases of both taxes, notably imputed labor income of housewives in the home, which does not even get into national income, imputed net rent of owner-occupied dwellings, and imputed interest.[14]

In summary, abstracting from personal exemptions and whatever non-business deductions are allowed, the base of a universal residence-principle income tax system that takes account of capital gains and losses and that taxes both corporate profits and dividends is in principle appreciably larger than that of a destination-principle value-added tax, even of the income type, and more so if it is of the consumption type, unless the country is so heavy an importer of capital that its unfavorable trade balance funnels large amounts to the fisc through the value-added compensating tax on imports. Accordingly, the income tax will carry a somewhat lower average rate, defined as tax revenue divided by aggregate tax base, than an equal-yield value-added tax. To be sure, the concept of an average rate for the income tax has much less economic significance than for a value-added tax, owing to the progressive rate scale and the lack of integration between corporate and personal income taxes.

In practice, the excess of the income tax base is not quite as large as these differences in principle suggest, owing to the omission from that base, but not usually from the value-added tax base, of certain income not currently attributable to any specific person (for example, interest earned on a certain part of life insurance company reserves) or, if attributable, not immediately available to the quasi-recipient (for example, employers' contributions to employees' pension funds). But these exceptions seem not likely to be large enough to alter appreciably the ratio of the base of a universal income tax to that of a value-added tax.

When personal exemptions are taken into account, and also non-business deductions, the base of the universal income tax may easily be but little larger, perhaps indeed smaller, than that of the value-added tax. The significant point is that, even when these exemptions and deductions are allowed for, they may be outweighed by the fact that types of income reached by the income tax but not by the value-added tax are numerous and important.

2. Incidence

A. OPEN ECONOMY

We consider first an income tax levied on the source principle; foreign-source income is not subject to the domestic income tax. In a two-factor country of capital

---

14. Inclusion of unpaid domestic work might raise the national income total by some 20 per cent. Shoup, *Principles of National Income Analysis*, p. 85. Inclusion of imputed interest would have added $11.1 billion to the adjusted gross income of $349.0 billion in the United States in 1960, and inclusion of imputed net rent of owner-occupied dwellings, $6.8 billion. Goode, *The Individual Income Tax*, p. 322. For the treatment of imputed rent in Sweden, see Chapter 15, Section A.1, footnote 2.

and labor, capital will escape any burden from a newly imposed proportional-rate income tax levied on the source principle if it enjoys a perfectly elastic foreign demand. Such a demand implies that the outflow necessary to keep the after-tax rate of return to the investor unchanged at home will not depress the rate of return abroad, because it is so small relative to the stock of capital in the countries to which it can migrate. This condition is approximately fulfilled in any small country, or in any large labor-intensive (less developed) country, although complete shifting is likely to be hindered by barriers to mobility, notably ignorance, and government control of capital movements.

If a progressive income tax is introduced in this country, Country A, and if the demand for capital in Countries B, C, . . . is perfectly elastic, and if Countries B, C, . . . tax domestic-source investment income flowing to Country A (or any other foreign country) at flat rates, the Country A owners of capital will move different proportions of their capitals abroad, in a manner such that the capital remaining at home, in A, is all subject to a single marginal rate of tax under the progressive scale, so that the after-tax domestic return in A equals the after-tax return obtained abroad, which is the same rate that was obtainable at home before the tax was introduced. Before the tax was imposed in A, the marginal return to investment by A's residents in A equaled the return they could get in B, C, . . . net of the flat-rate tax in those countries (for simplicity, we assume the same flat rate of tax in B, C, . . . on income flowing abroad). After the tax is introduced in A, capital flows will be such that at the new equilibrium the after-tax marginal return to A's investors from investment in A will equal the after-tax return they can get in B, C, ... The domestic before-tax return will have risen by just enough to compensate for the particular marginal rate of tax that becomes the only such rate, in practice, in A. Neither the high-income capitalist nor the low-income capitalist is injured by the progressive tax levied on the source principle. Indeed, a small capitalist may gain from the tax, temporarily. To simplify, let there be two capitalists in A: L (large) and S (small). A progressive income tax is imposed in A. L moves a part of his capital abroad, and before he has moved enough to be subject at home to the same marginal rate of tax as is S if S moves no capital at all abroad, the before-tax rate of return at home rises to a level that, after a marginal rate of tax on L that is still higher than that on S, leaves L with a return equal to that obtainable abroad. S is now receiving more, after deduction of tax, than he did before the tax was introduced. The tax does not harm the large capitalist, and for the time being it benefits the small capitalist. But capitalists abroad are attracted by the new high return in A; large foreign capitalists are additionally attracted if the progressive feature does not apply to income accruing to non-residents. The before-tax return in A is driven down; more of L's capital goes abroad; the before-tax return tends to rise again. Equilibrium is reached when enough foreign capital has flowed in, and enough of L's capital has gone abroad, to result in a uniform marginal rate of tax at home. The net result of the apparently progressive tax in A is a tax that in practice is proportional at the margin of investment.

If all countries impose à progressive tax on residents, but tax only domestic source income, and impose a flat rate tax on such income accruing to nonresidents, high-income residents in any country will have an incentive to invest abroad and low-income residents to invest at home.

In summary, if foreign demand for domestic capital is perfectly elastic, domestic consumers and domestic factors other than capital will bear the entire burden of a source-basis income tax. These other factors suffer a decline in marginal productivity as they are used in larger proportions with the factor, capital, since there will have been a net export of capital. To the degree that foreign demand is less than perfectly elastic, as is no doubt the case for large countries that export a considerable proportion of their saving, this income tax rests partly on domestic capital, whether it is employed at home or abroad.

Suppliers of labor cannot shift the source-tax in the same manner as can suppliers of capital, that is, by exporting the factor while the factor owner remains at home. Aside from some special cases of commuting between countries, the worker must export himself if he is to escape an income tax that is restricted to domestic-source income. Some such migration is to be expected, but it will usually be so small relative to the total domestic labor force that no appreciable rise in wages can be anticipated at home. This conclusion probably holds even for high-salaried professionals and executives. Those who leave the country escape the tax; those who stay bear it.

If a pure residence-basis income tax is introduced, the capitalist can escape it by migrating himself, while leaving his capital behind. The elasticity of demand for capital abroad is no longer significant. But if the migrating capitalist finds himself in another residence-basis country, he will be subject to the full progressive rates of that country's tax, not simply to the flat withholding tax he would commonly pay if he stayed at home and sent his capital abroad. He may gain little, or may even lose, by migration. At the other extreme, if the country to which he migrates imposes a pure source-basis tax, he escapes income tax entirely by going there and leaving his capital behind in the residence-basis country. In view, however, of the flat-rate withholding tax imposed even by the so-called residence-basis countries, he is in fact not likely to escape completely; but migration may still pay, for the high-income capitalist, if not for the capitalist in the lower brackets.

As countries change their income tax laws, the migrating capitalist may be forced to move frequently. In practice, it appears unlikely that substantial migration of capitalists, as distinguished from migration of capital, is being induced by income taxes.

B. DIFFERENTIAL INCIDENCE:
SUBSTITUTION OF INCOME TAX FOR VALUE-ADDED TAX

Some conjectures will now be offered, through differential-incidence analysis, on the change in distribution of disposable family income, by size of family after-tax income, that follows substitution of a progressive-rate universal income tax for a value-added tax of the income type, that is, a value-added tax that allows deduction of depreciation, not deduction of the full cost of the capital good in the year of purchase as under the consumption type of value-added tax. The difference made if the value-added tax is of the consumption type will then be suggested. This differential-incidence analysis, implying a general equilibrium approach, in contrast to the partial-equilibrium analysis of the immediately preceding section, must be used when the economy is a closed one so that there is no tax-free area to which capital or labor can move.

Accordingly, in the present section no distinction can be drawn between source-basis and residence-basis taxation.

Repeal of the value-added tax puts pressure on a business firm to increase immediately the factor prices it pays, if not in absolute terms, at least relative to product prices. Either factor prices rise in money terms or product prices fall, or some of both occurs. On the other hand, the impact of the new income tax is to decrease disposable-income factor rewards, probably in money terms, and certainly relative to prices of products. It follows that, depending on the monetary policy adopted, either (1) product prices fall by the amount of the value-added tax removed, while disposable money incomes fall by the amount of the new income tax; or (2) product prices in money, and money disposable incomes remain unchanged, an outcome that implies a rise in pre-tax factor money incomes; or (3) product money prices fall by less than the repealed value-added tax, while factor disposable money incomes fall by less than the new income tax. In any event the relation between product money prices and disposable money incomes is unchanged in the aggregate. And the change in distribution of the tax burden is the same under all three outcomes, for the following reasons.

The relative marginal productivities of the several types of factor will continue to set the pattern for relative factor rates of pay. The increase in factor rates of pay relative to product prices that must occur when the value-added tax is repealed will be accomplished in a pattern that is not directly influenced by the size of the factor owner's family or the amount of his total income from all sources, since these circumstances do not directly affect the marginal productivity of the factor. But these circumstances do directly determine the pattern in which factor disposable incomes fall relative to product prices as the income tax is introduced. The pattern of increase in factor real rates of pay upon repeal of the value-added tax, which is in fact a proportional income tax without personal exemptions, will differ from the pattern of decrease of factor real disposable incomes consequent upon introduction of the progressive-rate income tax. The net result is a decrease in the real disposable incomes of factor owners whose total incomes are large and whose families are small.

It seems evident that, whether product prices rise or do not rise, in money terms, substitution of a progressive income tax for a proportional value-added tax of the income type (and the more so, for one of the consumption type, which leaves the return to capital untaxed) will benefit low-income large-family households and will disadvantage high-income small-family households. Some in-between households will be about where they were before. High-income salary earners or entrepreneurs may escape part of the income tax by reducing their supply of effort; the result then depends on how the government bridges the revenue gap, if the equal-yield objective is sought.

c. DIFFERENTIAL INCIDENCE: SUBSTITUTION OF CORPORATION INCOME TAX FOR VALUE-ADDED TAX

Let a corporation income tax be substituted for a value-added tax (income type) of the same yield. Income from unincorporated enterprises, taxed under the value-added tax, is now free from taxation. In an industrialized economy the value-added tax rate will probably be about one-eighth that of the corporate tax rate that supersedes it.[15] The immediate impact of substitution of the corporate profits tax for the value-added tax is therefore to decrease corporate profits after tax, at least relative to product prices, and to increase profits in the unincorporated sector, and all other factor payments. Capital will flow into fields predominately non-corporate, notably housing, agriculture, repair services, the professions, and some part of wholesale and retail trade, from corporate-dominated fields, notably manufacturing, extraction of raw materials, and transportation.

This flow will continue until marginal rates of return after tax are equal, or differ because of degrees of mobility, or until marginal rates of expected return differ in a certain pattern because of risk (the differences will not take the form of a simple risk premium).[16] In any event the new equilibrium will see fewer manufactured products produced and more housing, farm products, and possibly trade and professional services. Labor and land specialized to manufacturing and raw materials extraction will lose as their marginal productivities fall, owing to the fact that they are now working with a smaller amount of capital. Labor and land specialized elsewhere will gain.[17]

15. This is an approximation, based on data in Norr and Kerlan, *Taxation in France*, pp. 70, 94, and Gumpel and Boettcher, *Taxation in the Federal Republic of Germany*, pp. 122, 123, 143, and assuming that the newly enacted value-added taxes in those countries (for the rates of these taxes, see Chapter 9, Section B) will yield about the same as the old value-added or turnover taxes, in relation to the corporation income tax.

16. See Aiko N. Shibata, *Effects of Taxation on Risk-Taking in a General Equilibrium Analysis*, ch. 3, "The Effects of the Corporation Income Tax on Risk-Taking" (unpublished dissertation, Columbia University, 1968).

17. See the analysis by Arnold C. Harberger of the effects of introducing a corporate income tax, assuming that "the way the government would spend the tax proceeds, if the initial prices continued to prevail, would just counterbalance the reductions in private expenditures on the two goods [i.e., the corporate-sector product and the non-corporate-sector product]" ("The Incidence of the Corporation Income Tax," *Journal of Political Economy* [June, 1962], 70: 224). For comment on the difference between this problem and that of differential incidence, see Chapter 1 above, Section B. A precise answer for the differential incidence case requires the use of general equilibrium analysis, as in Harberger's article, which is not attempted here. For examples of general equilibrium analysis of differential incidence without risk see Peter Michael Mieszkowski, *General Equilibrium Models of Tax Incidence* (unpublished Ph.D. dissertation, Johns Hopkins University, 1963), chs. 5 and 6, and William H. Oakland, "The Theory of the Value-Added Tax: II—Incidence Effects," *National Tax Journal* (September, 1967). Oakland's article investigates the change in the distribution of real income that results from substituting a value-added tax for a corporate profits tax, which, however, for generality, is assumed to include in its base all profits.

What all this will amount to in terms of income classes is difficult to discern. If the total return on capital is decreased by a change from a value-added tax to a corporate income tax, the differential incidence probably tends to be progressive, since capital is supplied chiefly by the middle- and upper-bracket incomes. Much depends, however, on whether the lower-income consumers spend more on products from the unincorporated sector or on those from the incorporated sector. Probably they buy more from the unincorporated sector.[18] If they do, the differential incidence is still more likely to be progressive.

If the repealed value-added tax had been of the consumption type, it will have exempted investment income, whether corporate or non-corporate. But this fact does not alter the amount or pattern of capital flow out of the corporate sector, when the value-added tax is replaced by the corporate income tax.[19]

The capital flows can be accomplished in a short period, say a few years, in a rapidly growing economy; investment of saving, along with reinvestment of depreciation allowances, if largely diverted from one sector to the other, can reestablish the dynamic equilibrium fairly promptly.

If the total supply of capital is not perfectly price-inelastic, this tax substitution will reduce the amount of capital in the economy and hence lower the marginal productivity of labor, therefore also the wage rate. The differential incidence is then partly on labor. In a rapidly growing economy, or in an economy open to capital flows, this effect may be felt fairly quickly. At the same time, products of capital-intensive industries will rise somewhat in price relative to prices of other products. Thus another part of the differential incidence will be on consumers of capital-intensive products. And in the short run, the differential incidence may be in large part directly on consumers of corporate products, if the tax stimulates use of hitherto unexploited oligopoly or other imperfect-competition power.

Allowance must be made for the fact that the real corporate tax rate is in most countries substantially less than the nominal rate, owing to accelerated depreciation, depletion greater than cost depletion, investment credits, cash subsidies to investment expenditure, and the like. Accelerated depreciation is equivalent to a decrease in the tax rate. As depreciation is accelerated more and more, the implicit tax rate on profits computed under ordinary depreciation approaches zero. It reaches zero when depreciation is completely accelerated, so that the cost of the asset can be written off entirely in the year of acquisition, provided that the law allows carry-back of losses or otherwise guarantees full tax benefit immediately from the complete write-off of the cost of the capital good. Completely accelerated depreciation

18. This also is the view of Mieszkowski, *op. cit.*, p. 105. He adds that "models which allow for different spending behavior for the two groups [of factors] under study are a failure qualitatively. . . . To obtain clear-cut results one is forced to place precise restrictions on production characteristics, such as the elasticities of substitution in the two industries, and the relative sizes of labor and capital employed in the two industries. If this exact production information is required it is clear that a qualitative approach to tax incidence is quite sterile" (*ibid.*, pp. 108–109).

19. Tax rates on income from capital were initially, say, 4 per cent in the corporate sector and the non-corporate sector, or zero per cent in both, depending on the type of value-added tax. Now they are zero in the non-corporate sector and, say, 40 per cent in the corporate sector. In either case a zero differential is replaced by a 40-point differential.

is thus equivalent to tax exemption, and transforms the corporate income tax into a value-added tax, consumption type, so far as corporate income is concerned. In effect, the government supplies part of the capital of the firm and in return takes a proportionate share in future cash flow, i.e., profits before subtracting depreciation. Accelerated depreciation, compared with ordinary depreciation, is equivalent to a no-recourse interest-free loan. It is a no-recourse loan because if the venture fails the government does not attempt to recover from the owners the value of the tax rebate given through 100 per cent accelerated depreciation. On the other hand, it is not truly an equity share, compared with what the government would have under ordinary depreciation, because even under ordinary depreciation the government shares in any unusual profit.

Thus, if a corporation is contemplating construction of a plant costing $1,000,000 it need supply only $600,000, if the tax rate is 40 per cent. The remaining $400,000 will come from its savings of tax on profits from the remainder of its business. By deducting $1,000,000 instead of nothing, in the year of construction, it saves $400,000 in tax for that year. The cash flow from the $1,000,000 plant in future years will be taxed at 40 per cent, since no further depreciation will be allowed. The corporation retains 60 per cent of this cash flow. It contributed only 60 per cent of the capital that made the cash flow possible. The corporation therefore obtains the same percentage rate of return on what it put in, of its own money, as if (1) there had been no income tax and (2) it had financed the entire $1,000,000 itself and had kept all the cash flow.[20]

3. Consensus Criteria[21]

A. EQUITY CRITERIA

The income tax, in practice, falls short of observing the consensus criterion, equal treatment of those equally circumstanced, and its corollary, almost equal treatment of those almost equally circumstanced.

The income tax opens large gaps between taxpayers who would probably be

20. The fact that completely accelerated depreciation, when coupled with complete loss offset, is equivalent to exemption of net return from the asset, under an income tax, was discovered by E. Cary Brown (see his "Business-Income Taxation and Investment Incentives," in *Income, Employment, and Public Policy: Essays in Honor of Alvin H. Hansen* [New York: Norton, 1948], pp. 309–10), reprinted in Musgrave and Shoup, *Readings in the Economics of Taxation*. See also Musgrave, *Theory of Public Finance*, pp. 343–44.

21. Of the great number of technical issues that characterize income taxation, only those deemed most important will be broached either here or under the conflict criteria, and then only in a summary fashion, to demonstrate the distinctiveness of the problems that income taxation gives rise to. For an original and intensive analysis of the more complex economic and equity issues raised by income taxation there is still nothing that quite compares with William Vickrey's *Agenda for Progressive Taxation* (New York: Ronald Press, 1947). Of more recent date are the appraisals and solutions of many of these issues to be found in the comprehensive volumes by Richard Goode, *The Corporation Income Tax* (New York: John Wiley, 1951) and *The Individual Income Tax* (Washington, D.C.: Brookings Institution, 1964) and Joseph A. Pechman, *Federal Tax Policy* (Washington, D.C.: Brookings Institution, 1966).

considered by the community, upon due deliberation, to be equally, or almost equally, situated with respect to relevant circumstances. An example is the difference in taxability of homeowners and renters. The income tax contains many one-tax-payer provisions disguised in ostensibly impersonal language and many other provisions applicable only to small groups. At the same time, despite a high level of specificity, it leaves much uncertain, so that even low-income households resort to low-paid tax consultants, and high-income taxpayers find it worth while to engage experts whose skills would be valuable at the highest levels in the treasury or finance ministry. Qualitative and quantitative discontinuities are even more frequent than in the sales taxes. Rates of evasion are markedly unequal, and the inequalities cut across income and wealth categories more than do those of the sales tax. Costs of compliance are similarly uneven and are positively associated with rates of evasion.

A conceptually pure income tax would be marked by none of these failings. But it is important, first, to realize that in practice no conceptually pure income tax exists and, second, to attempt to understand why it does not. The analysis to follow will therefore be of the real-world income tax, not the hypothetically, evidently unachieveable, logically impeccable type of income tax.

We consider first the relevant-circumstance concept. If the sales tax is given a higher score than the income tax on this aspect of the equal-treatment consensus criterion, it is largely because the relevant circumstances for equal treatment must be defined, for any tax, in terms of initial impact. If they are instead defined in terms of where the tax may rest after shifting, there may be no consensus on the facts. And the shifting analysis may have to be in terms of differential incidence, which involves one tax base that is different from the legal base on which the tax is levied, whereas it is the non-relevant differences in the legal base of some one tax that are the test for inequity of a kind that all will agree is indeed inequity.

The differential incidence of sales tax and income tax with respect to income classes, or wealth classes, or size of household is to be evaluated under the conflict criteria (specifically, distribution of disposable income). The consensus criterion of equity, less significant perhaps socially than the conflict criterion, is here restricted to obvious inequalities in the initial impact of the tax. Only so is it possible to distinguish those changes on which all would agree from those on which disagreement will persist. Such a separation is necessary if tax reform is not to be impeded by misunderstanding.

A sales tax, then, need be equal only in its initial impact on business firms, in the sense that competitive inequality is avoided. This is a goal much easier to achieve than equality of impact on the complex pattern of households under the income tax, for there the equality criterion must include many more relevant circumstances than exist under the sales tax. Moreover, the income tax may share the failing of some sales taxes in being competitively unequal: under the income tax the rates applicable to the profits of unincorporated concerns usually differ from those applicable to corporate profits.

If the income tax were not so strongly supported under the conflict criteria, relative to the sales tax, it might well be considered inferior to the sales tax. But since more importance is usually attached to the conflict criteria than to the consensus criteria, no such community verdict of inferiority emerges, at least in most of the industrialized nations.

We now search for the reasons why communities tolerate failure of the income tax to treat equally certain taxpayers who are similarly situated with respect to relevant criteria. One reason is that for certain types of non-recorded income, the practical result would be an increase in inequality of evasion. Inaccuracies in tax payment would vary greatly from one taxpayer to another; equals would not in fact be treated more nearly equally, on the whole, than when the non-recorded income was exempted.

Non-recorded income is either imputed income or offset income. Imputed income is defined here as income that arises without a market transaction. It accrues to the individual by his use of assets that he owns, or from his own labor, for the direct benefit of himself or his family.[22]

If imputed net rent were included in taxable income, the difficulty of estimating imputed gross rental and depreciation would give rise to much evasion, of varying degree, and doubtless also to some overtaxation. Quite conceivably the increase in inequality in mispayment of tax would be greater than the reduction of the in-equality between renters and homeowners that now exists through legally sanctioned irrelevant standards, that is, renting versus homeowning.[23] Doubtless part of the explanation is that homeowners are often better organized for political pressure than are tenants, and that some communities believe there are certain values inherent in homeowning that are worth subsidizing.[24]

Exemption of home-grown food may be similarly justified. And the largest imputed item of all, the value of work done in the home, chiefly by housewives, but increasingly by the man of the house as carpenter, electrician, and the like, is so difficult to value that even national-income compilers exclude it.

Offset income is a claim that a taxpayer obtains from a market transaction, but that is offset, in whole or in large part, by a simultaneous debt he incurs, or free service that he is given. The taxpayer is operating on both sides of the market at once.

One example of offset income is the apparently free service that a depositor in a commercial bank obtains in the form of checkbooks, the clearing of his checks, and the like, when the bank makes no charge for these services but on the other hand

22. In most of the literature of public finance, the term imputed income is used more broadly, to include also what is here defined as offset income.

23. The United Kingdom's decision to abandon taxation of imputed income from home ownership seems to have been motivated largely by these considerations. The relative amounts of inequality are assumed here to be measurable by the Johnson-Mayer-White techniques (see Chapter 2, Section A.1.B). In the United States, "The exclusion of presumptive [i.e., imputed] income [from home ownership] is not expressed in any code provision but is based solely on custom and usage" (Marvin A. Chirelstein, Langdon Day, and Elisabeth Owens, *Taxation in the United States*, World Tax Series, Law School of Harvard University [Chicago: Commerce Clearing House, 1963], p. 371). This fact argues for the importance of administrative considerations.

24. To the degree that exemption of imputed net rental reflects a conscious desire to subsidize homeowners at the expense of renters because of assumed social benefits (externalities) from homeowning relative to renting, the fact of homeowning is no longer an irrelevant circumstance; it is not truly equals who are being treated unequally.

pays him no interest on his deposit. The bank meanwhile is earning money income for itself by investing the deposit. The depositor foregoes this interest in return for the free banking services. If he is a consumer, not a business firm, individuals' aggregate incomes are accordingly understated. No income tax law requires the depositor to include this offset income, perhaps because the community is unfamiliar with the concept. Even after due deliberation, however, the possibility of unequal treatment among depositors, owing to difficulty of evaluation or enforcement, might weight the balance against inclusion.

Another example of offset income is supplied by any of the cooperative organizations. The essence of the cooperative is that the member is operating on both sides of the market simultaneously.[25] If the consumer has an ownership interest in an organization from which he buys, as in a consumers' cooperative, he may receive income in the form of a price for his purchases that is lower than he would be charged if he instead insisted on receiving a full money return on his capital in ordinary cash dividends or interest. In effect, the investment income earned by the cooperative on its capital is offset against what would otherwise be the price of the consumer goods.[26] This investment income is not here termed imputed income; it arises from the use of assets that the consumer owns only indirectly, and involves a market transaction with a legal entity, the cooperative. Exemption of this kind of income is generally agreed to be based on an irrelevant circumstance, the offset nature of the income, unless the cooperative is being deliberately subsidized through the tax system. In some income tax laws, even explicit "patronage dividends" are exempted.

A similar case is that of the small shopkeeper who sells to himself at a zero price by diverting part of his stock to his family's use. An income tax law that will disregard imputed income and even cooperatives' offset income will commonly not ignore this particular kind of offset income.[27]

Another type of offset income, this one commonly tax-exempt, consists of attractive working conditions or perquisites that induce workers and executives to accept lower money compensation than otherwise.[28] It is as if the employee received

25. The "primary characteristic of mutual organizations is that each member is usually a residual claimant against the organization and is also a supplier to the organization or a customer of the organization, or perhaps all three simultaneously" (*Report of the Royal Commission on Taxation* [Canada], 1966 [Ottawa: Queen's Printer, 1966], 4: 99).

26. The Canadian Royal Commission on Taxation, 1966, though concerned over the tax advantage gained by consumers who "invest in a mutual organization and secure a return on their investment by way of below-market prices for the consumer goods or services they consume or through a rebate on their consumption expenditure by means of a patronage dividend or similar distribution" concluded that it would be "hopelessly difficult" to "revalue all transactions . . . and assess tax on the basis of what the gains would have been at fair market value," and suggested, without recommending it outright, that all mutual organizations be required "to bring into their income *at least* an imputed return on all their assets" (*ibid.*, 4: 103, 105).

27. In the United States, "the cost of products consumed [directly by the taxpayer-merchant and his household] must either be subtracted from the cost of goods sold or added to income" (Chirelstein, Day, and Owens, *op. cit., Taxation in the United States*, p. 371, citing a case "involving food and beverages consumed by restaurant owner").

28. See Hugh Holleman Macaulay, Jr., *Fringe Benefits and Their Federal Tax Treatment* (New York: Columbia University Press, 1959).

a tax-free money supplement to his wage or salary and spent the supplement on purchasing the improved working conditions or other fringe benefits. But he may of course value the benefits at less than cost; then only this smaller amount is offset income to him.

The offset income may be negative. If working conditions are unpleasant, the cost that the firm saves by not eliminating the unpleasantness is reflected in the higher money wages it must pay to attract the worker. The increment in money wage (over what it would be if working conditions were not unpleasant) may however fall short of the cost saved by the firm by not improving the conditions.

The net result of this treatment of positive and negative offset income in the form of working conditions is that the income tax puts pressure on workers to insist on, and on firms to grant, improved conditions of work in lieu of increased money wages, even though the money cost to the firm may be greater than would be an increase in money wages equally satisfactory to the employees. The firm deducts either outlay in computing taxable profit, while the employee pays tax only on the cash receipt.

Taxation of income that, although recorded, is unattributable to any particular person in the year in which it arises, may involve heavy costs of administration and compliance. For the time being it cannot be said whose income it will eventually be. By the time it becomes attributable, the task of reopening a large number of old returns will have become expensive and troublesome, and in some instances, through loss of records, impossible.

Interest that is being earned on reserves of a mutual life insurance company with respect to whole-life insurance policies, in excess of that credited to reserves and made available in cash surrender values or other forms, is unattributable income. The degree to which any particular policyholder will benefit from this part of the company's investment income will not be fixed until his death, or surrender of his policy.[29] If the investment income exceeds the amount impliedly promised in the policy contract, the company may pass the benefit on at once to existing policyholders by a "dividend," that is, a reduction in the contracted premium. But it may instead retain the extra earnings, in order to increase dividends in some later year, or to offer more attractive contracts to the next generation of policyholders. An employer's contribution to a pension fund or a stock purchase plan for the account of an employee whose rights to a share of the fund have not yet vested is another example of temporarily unattributed income. Still another is the income of an accumulating trust, the beneficiaries of which are for the time being not identified.

A flat-rate income tax can be imposed on the trustee or other legal recipient of the unattributed income as a crude type of tentative tax, and this practice is common. Later, when the income becomes attributable to a particular person, his past years' tax returns can be reopened and income tax recomputed, with interest on the tax;

29. The taxation of life insurance companies, stock and mutual, and of policyholders, under an income tax involves many more complexities than that of temporarily unattributable income. For a thorough analysis and suggestions for alternative modes of taxation under the income tax, see Vickrey, *Agenda for Progressive Taxation*, pp. 64–75, and appendix 2.

but in practice this step is rarely taken, owing in part to the cost in time and effort to taxpayer and tax administrator under existing systems of income tax. This cost might well be slight if the income tax employed a cumulative system of averaging income over a number of years.

A quite different problem is that of recorded income that is attributable but temporarily unavailable. An example is an employer contribution to a pension fund in which the employee's rights have vested. The employee is assured that this contribution will one day be paid to him or his estate, either as part of his retirement pension or in a lump sum if he leaves the company or dies. Meanwhile, however, it is not available to him. To tax him currently as if it were available would be to disregard the relevant circumstance of unavailability. Yet to tax him not at all currently would be to disregard another relevant circumstance: undisputed ownership of the income. A solution can be found in partial taxation of the income currently, the balance to be taxed when made available. The usual practice, however, is to defer all taxation of such income to the year of availability. The taxpayer accordingly gains interest on the entire tax. He may also pay at a lower rate in the later year because his total income is then lower.

Another set of problems under the relevant-circumstances test concerns the differing treatment of profits, according as they are earned in a corporation or in a partnership. The difference in amount of income tax payable is commonly so great and varies so erratically between the two forms that it can scarcely be supported on grounds of differences in relevant circumstances.

A related problem is the difference in treatment of corporate ownership capital and corporate creditor capital. These differences, also, are too substantial and erratic to be justified by the test of relevancy. Both problems are discussed in Section 2 below as aspects of excess burden.

Having discussed the relevant-circumstances aspect of equal treatment under the income tax, we turn now to the impersonality aspect. Here this tax reveals perhaps its greatest weakness. Most income tax laws contain provisions that apply in practice to but one or a few taxpayers. The rule of impersonality described in Chapter 2, Section A.1.A.is therefore not observed. Here the only explanation is that the tax, by its personal nature, lends itself to this abuse. Under the pressure of high and progressive rates influential individuals and corporations seek the rich rewards that come from moving income into a year when the taxpayer's other income is lower (see pages 323–28) or from the granting of special deductions.[30] The attempts at

---

30. A striking example of a special provision originally designed for one particular person is that in the United States federal income tax law that waives the limit on deduction for contributions to charitable, religious, scientific, and similar organizations (this limit is 20 per cent or 30 per cent of adjusted gross income, according to circumstances) for a taxpayer who gives so much that he has nothing left with which to pay taxes. This provision was inserted in the law a good many years ago to cover the case of a nun who gave all her income to the church. Wealthy benefactors now make use of this provision by giving, not money, but securities, real estate, works of art, and the like that have appreciated in value. The deduction is computed by using the current value of the property, not its cost to the donor, and the capital gain thus "realized" is not taxed to the donor. Contributions plus federal income tax must exceed 90 per cent of taxable income in the tax year and in eight of the preceding ten tax years.

covert personalization of the income tax law would be fewer if the law had not already been made highly detailed in an effort to reach another goal, certainty, which is the third aspect of the equal-treatment criterion. The wealth of detail existing makes one more slight detail seem innocuous.

But indeed certainty itself is commonly not achieved, at least for the majority of taxpayers. Too much detail produces a law that becomes truly known only to a very few: the drafters and a corps of specialized tax practitioners. This is so, because most of the details are logically interconnected, and a proposed change in one aspect of, say, conducting business abroad may require months of expensive study of the tax law before most of the tax consequences are known, and even the expert will then admit that he may not have found them all. This kind of detail is quite different from the details sometimes encountered in sales tax laws, which are usually tedious and perhaps ambiguous but not interconnected.

Discontinuities in the tax function, the fourth departure from the equal-treatment criterion, are common in income taxes. They arise chiefly from attempts to distinguish capital expenditures and capital receipts from other expenditures and receipts, and capital gains and losses from other gains and losses, and from the need to fix the year in which an expenditure is incurred or a receipt is obtained. The discussion of this last problem, the timing problem, is deferred to Section 2 below.

A receipt that represents a return of capital, or a replacement of it, is excluded from gross taxable income. The reward can be high, therefore, for proving that a receipt is a capital receipt, even when the result is simply to defer an unchanged amount of taxation to a later year, as when a given annuity payment is divided into interest that was earned while the annuity fund was being accumulated, and return of capital contributed to the fund.[31] A damage award has been held includable in income if it represents payment for loss of earnings and profits but not if it is payment for destruction of business property.[32] A distribution to a shareholder may be either income or return of capital, depending chiefly on whether the corporation has any accumulated earnings and profits from which the distribution can be deemed to come. These examples give but a hint of the complexities that arise. The answer is determined by definitions that are sure to treat some almost equally circumstanced persons quite differently in many cases.

When capital gains and losses are ignored or are taken into account only in part, or at special low rates, strange discontinuities develop sooner or later in the income tax function, largely for three reasons:

First, wherever the line may be drawn between a capital gain and ordinary gain, or a capital loss and ordinary loss, the taxpayer commonly discovers courses of action with differing tax consequences that are otherwise close substitutes. A concern may be undecided whether to retain an old machine tool or similar asset, or to sell it and purchase a replacement. If the sale price will be at a loss that is only partially deductible if at all, because it is termed a capital loss, the taxpayer may decide

---

31. The present value of a tax dollar can be cut in half by deferring it twelve years if the deferred tax can earn interest compounded annually, net, after tax, at 6 per cent.

32. Chirelstein, Day, and Owens, *op. cit.*, p. 372.

to get full deduction for the remaining book value by retaining the machine and deducting depreciation.[33] If a grower of timber is to be taxed at full rates on the proceeds of timber he cuts, he may decide to sell the tract just before cutting and so create a capital gain.[34]

Second, as in depressions, wars, or other eras of hardship, the lawmaker is induced to soften the tax burden on business by expanding the definition of capital gain and contracting that of capital loss. The particular stopping points in this process of expansion and contraction are likely to enhance discontinuities, if the previous line had been drawn to minimize them.[35]

Third, because of alleged difficulties in keeping books, or other compliance problems, or because of the possibility that certain outlays can never be recovered by ordinary depreciation, the taxpayer is allowed to write off in full in the year they are incurred expenses that create an asset, even though that asset, when finally sold, is deemed a capital asset, the proceeds to be taxed at capital gains rates. Illustrations are livestock held for draft, breeding, or dairy purposes, but later sold,[36] and oil or gas wells drilled and developed.[37]

Unequal rates of evasion, or more generally, of mispayment of tax, constitute probably the most critical shortcoming of the income tax in most countries. This particular breach of the equal-treatment criterion explains in large part why that tax has developed into a mass, comprehensive levy in only a few countries. It may also explain why, in those countries, there is little integration of the corporation tax and personal income tax. The wage-earner and the moderate-income salaried earner, knowing that they must pay their taxes in full through withholding, and hearing rumors, or more, of evasion of income tax by professional men, farmers, small commercial and industrial firms, and with respect to interest and dividends received by anyone, are not interested in plans to eliminate double taxation of corporate profit, much of which flows to these same groups.[38] A grave danger for the

33. It was the existence of this option that led the United States Congress in 1938 to declare all such losses on sale, ordinary losses (*ibid.*, p. 663).

34. This possibility was one of the reasons why the Congress allowed the gain from timber cutting to be treated as a capital gain. For details on the treatment, see *ibid.*, pp. 881–82.

35. In 1942, Congress granted capital gain treatment to sale, exchange, or involuntary conversions of real or depreciable business property, because "it was thought that ordinary treatment of such gains would impede [these wartime] transfers of properties into the hands of those persons who could use them most effectively" (*ibid.*, p. 693). This provision, combined with that noted in footnote 33, above, gives the taxpayer the best of both worlds.

36. To obtain this benefit under the United States income tax, the taxpayer must be on the cash basis, for if he is on the accrual basis, that is, if he must use inventory accounting, the cost of feed, etc., is not deductible as incurred, being in effect a purchase of inventory. But farmers are not required to adopt inventory accounting, even when inventories are a material income producing factor, on the grounds that small farmers cannot keep inventory records easily and large farmers cannot easily find the requisite bookkeeping personnel (*ibid.*, pp. 884–87).

37. A dry hole, since it yields no revenue, affords, by itself, no opportunity for depreciating the drilling and development expenses in later years. The United States income tax law allows full deduction of drilling and development expenses in any event, in the year of outlay, whether they result in a dry hole or a producing well (*ibid.*, pp. 877–81).

38. To be sure, complete and non-optional integration would be disadvantageous to certain wealthy investors, but the general public is not aware of this.

entire income tax system arises when those who cannot evade demand, as an offset, higher and higher tax rates on the kinds of income marked by evasion. The higher rates breed more evasion, and the spiral may continue until administration of all but the withheld income tax virtually collapses.[39]

The variation in compliance costs from one taxpayer to another is apparently not as serious as that of the variation in mispayment. Absolute compliance costs usually grow with size of income, since a larger income is typically a more complex income. Also, within any one income class, a higher compliance cost is commonly but a sort of fee for obtaining favorable tax treatment.[40]

B. Economic Efficiency Criteria

With respect to discretionary counter-cycle rate changes the income tax offers more choices for distributing the burdens and benefits among income classes than any other tax, so much so that dispute over the alternatives may prevent prompt action. The most important single issue is whether the very low income households, under a universal income tax, should be excluded from participating in counter-cycle measures. In any event, taxpayers' anticipatory reactions make the personal income tax more suitable for infrequent, large changes in tax rate than for small changes spaced only a few months apart. These issues are elaborated in Chapter 22 below.

The yield of a universal progressive-rate income tax may decline more slowly in a recession than does national income. All depends on how the decline in national income is distributed and by how much the successive bracket rates differ. To increase the progressivity[41] of a tax may in fact be to decrease its built-in flexibility, for the increase in progressivity might occur over a range of income levels within which incomes fall very little, perhaps because they are composed chiefly of interest and dividends.[42]

The efficiency of a given degree of built-in flexibility, that is, its effect on employment, is much less for the corporate income tax than for the personal income tax. The decline in corporation income tax yield as profits fall results chiefly in a reduction in bank loans and increases in holdings of cash or the equivalent. A decline in that part of the personal income tax that impinges on profits of partnerships and sole proprietorships has similar consequences.

A more powerful instrument is a tax on investment spending, or alternatively a deduction, or credit against tax, for such spending. Counter-cycle suspension and reintroduction of such a tax, or deduction or credit, will affect investment spending

39. Something not far from such collapse appears to have occurred during certain periods in France and Italy.

40. In the United States the individual who can minimize his tax by itemizing his non-business deductions foregoes the convenience of using the standard deduction.

41. For alternative definitions of an increase in progressivity, see page 327.

42. See William Vickrey, "Some Limits to the Income Elasticity of Income Tax Yields," *Review of Economics and Statistics* (May, 1949), 31: 140–44.

appreciably.[43] But the lag may be substantial, or at least unpredictable, and there are troublesome questions of whether to base the cut-off and resumption dates on expenditure planned, committed to, started, or completed.

In a capital-importing country the efficiency of the corporate income tax's built-in flexibility for that country may be even less, with respect to giant international corporations that find use in other countries for tax saved in a country where business is in a recession.

An individual paying income tax could be made better off without making anyone else worse off if he were allowed to pay a lump-sum tax equal in amount to what he does pay under the income tax. He could then choose between his existing situation and one in which he worked more, that is, took less leisure, yet paid no more tax. That choice is not open to him under the income tax. The amount of excess burden that he experiences because he is denied this choice depends on his elasticity of substitution of leisure for disposable money income. If that elasticity is great, the lack of choice means correspondingly more to him, and the excess burden is correspondingly great. The elasticity of substitution is defined as the percentage change in the ratio of leisure to disposable money income per unit percentage change in the rate at which the worker is willing to substitute disposable money income for leisure, along a given indifference curve for money income and leisure. If the indifference curve is fairly flat, the elasticity of substitution is high in absolute terms, that is, it is a large negative number, and the excess burden is large.

Since the elasticity of substitution is not directly observable, an approximation is taken by estimates of the price elasticity of the supply of labor. General observation of labor force activity in countries with high income tax rates suggests that thus far, at least, there has not been a great deal of excess burden imposed by the income tax.[44] This conclusion must be qualified by the effect of the income tax on the distribution of labor among different occupations. The premium wage paid to attract labor to industries or locations where working conditions are less favorable (see page 306 above) is not exempted from the personal income tax. Compared with, say, a poll tax or a corporation income tax of the same yield, a personal income tax creates a difference between the rate of transformation and the rate of substitution in consumption. Wage gross of tax, and hence price of product, in the less attractive industry, must exceed wage gross of tax in a more attractive industry by more than the differential that the worker demands in take-home pay. Less of the product of the former

43. But see the divergent views of econometricians with respect to the United States experience of 1966–67, in a forthcoming publication by the Brookings Institution.

44. Harberger's estimates based on United States data lead him to conclude that the excess burden from the personal income tax arising from the labor-leisure choice may be of the order of $1 billion a year. The tax yielded about $42 billion in 1961. (The percentage, 2.4, is not much above that of administrative costs of many taxes in some countries, though indeed considerably more than that for administering the income tax in the United States.) Harberger points out that the excess burden could be considerably reduced by a broadening of the income tax base that would allow the same revenue to be raised from a generally lower schedule of marginal rates. His computations indicate that, compared with a tax that would not distort choice between labor and leisure at the margin, top-income bracket taxpayers would work about 11 or 12 per cent more, and lowest-income bracket taxpayers, from 2 to 3 per cent more (Arnold C. Harberger, "Taxation, Resource Allocation, and Welfare," in *The Role of Direct and Indirect Taxes in the Federal Revenue System*, pp. 42–52).

industry is produced, and there is a corresponding presumption of excess burden.

By taxing income from an investment and at the same time giving no relief to saved income as against consumed income, the income tax opens a gap between the following rates of substitution: (1) the rate at which future goods can be produced, per unit of present goods foregone, and (2) the rate at which the consumer can make the same substitution. The first rate, the transformation rate, must be greater than the consumer's rate, to make room for payment of the income tax. Under a poll tax, or no tax, these two rates would be the same.

This divergence of rates gives rise to a presumption of excess burden, by the reasoning applied in the immediately preceding section.

The methods of production and distribution that are changed because of the income tax are chiefly financial methods. Physical changes of the type commonly induced by the turnover tax are rare. But, relative to our base for comparison, i.e., the value-added tax (even of the income type), the income tax induces corporations to become partnerships, and vice versa, depending on circumstances; generally, though not always, promotes debt financing in place of ownership ("equity") financing, and always discourages financing by non-convertible preferred stock, since dividends paid are commonly non-deductible; promotes centralization and decentralization of legal structure; induces earlier or later realization of capital gains or losses; and drives some would-be tenants into home ownership—to name some of the most pervasive cases.

If the income tax law does not tax capital gains or allow capital losses, a successful corporation's earnings are taxed once at the corporate level and, in the absence of some credit or similar device, again by the personal income tax, to the extent that they are distributed as dividends to individuals. A partnership's profits are commonly taxed only once, that is, to the owners, but the tax applies whether or not the owners draw the profits out of the business for personal use or reinvestment elsewhere. The applicable tax rate, moreover, depends on the proprietor's or partner's income from all sources; it may well be higher than the corporate tax rate. High-income investors can buy the shares of expanding corporations that retain most or all of their earnings and, if the shares have an active market, can draw down what income they need periodically, free of all tax except the corporate tax already paid, by selling a few of their shares, which presumably are increasing in value fairly steadily. But a low-income investor owning shares in a corporation that declares most of its earnings in cash dividends pays a combined individual and corporate tax at a rate well above the rate that applies to his wages or his profits from unincorporated enterprises.

These discrepancies are not removed if the corporate tax has the same incidence as the value-added tax, in the sense that the corporation's pre-tax profits would be the same under either tax. In that event, the wealthy investor bears no more burden than he would under the value-added tax, while the low-income investor clearly does so.

If the corporation incurs deficits, the shareholder cannot reduce tax on his other income by taking his share of the deficits into account, but a partner or proprietor with other income can offset his share of his firm's loss against such income.

The differences in tax under the two forms of ownership organization vary so widely from one investor to another that they cannot be eliminated through a discounting of the tax differentials in market prices of shares relative to sales prices of partnership or proprietorship interests. A change to a system that would treat all shareholders, partners, and proprietors alike would advantage some corporate investors, relative to owners of unincorporated interests, and disadvantage others.

If the law taxes realized capital gains and allows deduction of realized capital losses, the discrepancies may be reduced somewhat. But sale of a partnership interest or of a sole proprietorship can give rise to taxable capital gains or deductible capital losses. And if accrued gains and losses on property transferred by gift or at death are not taken into account, and the donee or heir is given a new basis, amounting to the value of the property at time of such transfer, for computing gain or loss on later sale, those accrued gains and losses are forever exempt from tax or are denied deductibility, respectively.[45]

In the overlapping ranges of small corporations and large partnerships and proprietorships the usual income tax system, whether or not it takes account of capital gains and losses, exerts erratic pressures to convert from one form of ownership organization to another. The stable business firm whose modest-income owners need to draw down all its profits for personal consumption or for other forms of saving will welcome the unincorporated form that averts the taxing of distributed profits more than once. A growing firm, owned by high-income individuals who wish to reinvest all its profits, will welcome the corporate form that shelters them from the highest-bracket individual rates (commonly higher than the highest corporate rate) and promises an eventual opportunity to convert the reinvested earnings into personal income by sale of their stock that will yield a capital gain taxable not at all or at a low rate. If the seller receives, not cash, but shares in an acquiring corporation, the law may not "recognize" the gain, even though the shares are readily salable.[46] If, in addition, there is no tax on gains accrued upon gift or at death, fortunes can be built up free of personal income tax.

Some income tax laws allow a firm and its owners to be treated for income tax purposes as if the firm had the legal form that in fact it does not possess. Thus a small corporation may be exempted from tax if the shareholders declare in their returns their portions of the year's earnings; or partners and proprietors may exclude their parts of their concerns' earnings if the firms themselves pay the corporation income tax.

Of the many methods that have been employed in various countries to reduce the discrepancies in treatment of profits from corporations and unincorporated concerns, none seems particularly effective, at least with respect to corporations that retain indefinitely a large proportion of each year's profits. To tax their shareholders consistently with other equity owners requires full taxation and full deduction of capital gains and losses, under a system of cumulative averaging, buttressed perhaps by frequent, periodical accounting of accrued gains and losses. For corporations that

45. The "stepped-up" basis for accrued gains and "stepped-down" basis for accrued losses is the rule in the United States; in the United Kingdom the accrued gain is taxed on gift or transfer at death.

46. This is so in the United States.

distribute currently all or most of their profits, full deduction of dividends paid in computing taxable corporate profit is an approximately correct procedure. Alternatively, a credit to the shareholder for corporate tax paid on a "grossed-up" dividend[47] can be granted. Transition to either of these systems from any of the present systems would give rise to substantial windfall gains and possibly some losses, through changes in the prices of corporate shares.

Creditor capital, in contrast to ownership capital, is treated fairly uniformly by most income tax laws, whether the money has been loaned to corporations or to unincorporated enterprises. The interest earned by the business and paid to the creditor is taxed but once, in the hands of the creditor. If the debtor defaults, the creditor can usually deduct from his other income the loss on the bad debt, even if the debt is evidenced by a negotiable security and the tax law ignores capital losses in general.

But creditor capital is treated quite differently from equity capital, in a corporation. Interest is taxed only once, when it reaches the creditor, while we have seen that corporate profits may be taxed either more than once or only once and at a rate lower than a wealthy individual would pay on interest income. A corporation acting to maximize the welfare of its owners is faced with a tax-weighted problem of the optimum mix of creditor and ownership capital. In many instances this mix will differ from what it would be under no income tax, or, in macro-economic terms, from what it would be under a value-added tax of either the consumption or the income type. The difference normally takes the form of more creditor capital under the income tax, at least for growing firms, which finance a larger proportion of their expansion by borrowing than they would otherwise do. Static firms might be expected under pressure of high income tax rates to buy in much of their common stock with obligations issued for this purpose, but such a reaction seems to have been rare. To be sure, the government would have to increase the income tax rate, to make up for the loss in revenue, but no one corporation acting by itself could cause the rate to increase perceptibly. The explanation probably is that tax pressures have little effect in the face of traditional practices dictated by financial prudence that has its roots in the Great Depression or even earlier crises.[48]

If interest were disallowed as a deduction to corporations, many small firms would disincorporate. Many large firms would sell their plants to insurance companies or other financial firms, pay off their debt with the proceeds, and lease back the plants. If, to counter this, the income tax law disallowed rental payments as a deduction, symmetry would require that only the interest element in the rental payment be disallowed; this element might be difficult to measure.

47. See Appendix to this chapter.

48. If the capital markets were nearly enough perfect to allow the Modigliani-Miller theorem to operate (total market value of firm is independent of its debt-equity structure, apart from taxation), the income tax discrimination against equity relative to debt would influence the relative amounts issued more than it does in the existing imperfect markets. See F. Modigliani and M. H. Miller, "The Cost of Capital, Corporation Finance and the Theory of Investment," *American Economic Review* (June, 1958), 48: 261–97, and "Comment" by D. E. Brewer and J. B. Michaelson, and "Reply" by Modigliani and Miller, *ibid.* (June, 1965), 55: 516–27. See also Ronald F. Wippern, "Financial Structure and the Value of the Firm," *Journal of Finance* (December, 1966), 21: 615–33.

An income tax that strikes intercorporate dividends, even if only at a reduced rate, promotes mergers and consolidations that would not be consummated in absence of the income tax. In the other direction, graduation of the rate scale of the corporate profits tax rewards the large corporation that can break itself up into a number of small corporations, as when a company owning many retail outlets incorporates each store separately. Taxation of capital gains upon realization of the gains, but not upon accrual, will impede mergers unless the definition of realization is watered down to exclude swaps of stock and similar transfers common to mergers or reorganizations. On balance, a given income tax system may therefore hinder or promote corporate legal decentralization. Even if the effects cancel out approximately in the aggregate, a substantial excess burden would exist from use of the less efficient forms in each case.

APPENDIX TO CHAPTER ELEVEN[1]

The goal of integration of the corporate and personal income taxes is here taken to be the elimination of extra taxation of that part of corporate profits declared in dividends or realized in the form of fully taxable capital gains to the shareholder, without allowing undistributed corporate profits, or profits realized to the shareholder in capital gains not fully taxed, to be undertaxed. Extra taxation or undertaxation is measured in comparison with the amount of personal income tax that is imposed on a like amount of salary income or income from an unincorporated enterprise.

First to be considered is the extreme case where corporate profits after tax are fully declared in dividends.

If no credit or other relief is given, the rate of extra taxation is found by the following formula: if c is the corporation income tax rate, and m the individual's marginal rate, the rate of extra taxation is $c(1 - m)$ (see note at the end of this appendix for derivation of this and the following formulae). The lower the individual's marginal rate, the larger will be the expression $(1 - m)$, and the larger the rate of extra taxation. In the numerical examples below the corporate tax rate is assumed to be 52 per cent, low-income taxpayer A's marginal tax rate 20 per cent, and high-

1. Much of this appendix is based on, or taken directly from, Carl S. Shoup, "The Dividend Exclusion and Credit in the Revenue Code of 1954," *National Tax Journal* (March, 1955) 8: 136–47. Among the many treatments of the integration problem, aside from those in the books on income taxation already cited, the following may be noted: Cesare Cosciani, *The Effects of Differential Tax Treatment of Corporate and Non-Corporate Enterprises* (Paris: European Productivity Agency, Organization for European Economic Co-operation, 1959); Daniel M. Holland, *Dividends under the Income Tax* (Princeton, N.J.: Princeton University Press, 1962) and *The Income-Tax Burden on Stockholders* (Princeton, N.J.: Princeton University Press, 1958); National Tax Association, Committee on Federal Taxation of Corporations (Robert M. Haig, chairman): Final Report, *Proceedings of the 32nd Annual Conference on Taxation* (Columbia, S.C.: National Tax Association, 1940); and Stanley S. Surrey, "Income Tax Problems of Corporations and Shareholders," *Tax Law Review* (November, 1958), 14: 1–53.

income taxpayer B's marginal tax rate 40 per cent. The corporation distributes in dividends all its profit after corporate tax, i.e., 48 per cent of pre-tax profit.

Since the lowest-income stockholder pays the highest rate of extra taxation, a tax credit to a shareholder equal to some fraction of the corporate tax on his share of the profit reduces the tax of the low-income stockholder by a greater percentage than it reduces the tax of the high-income stockholder. But the reduction is less than proportional to the degree of previous discrimination against the low-income stockholder.

Let a tax credit of, say, 4 per cent of the dividend be granted to each shareholder. The rate of extra taxation declines by 1.92 percentage points for everyone (48 per cent of 4 per cent). Hence the reduction is a smaller proportion of the higher original rates of extra taxation, which attached to the low-income shareholders. The disparity between the low-income and high-income shareholders is widened by the credit provision, in the sense that the rate of extra taxation on the low-income stockholder is a greater multiple than ever of that on the high-income stockholder. Low-income taxpayer A's rate of extra taxation is reduced from 41.6 per cent to 39.7 per cent, a reduction of 4.6 per cent; that of high-income B's is reduced from 31.2 per cent to 29.3 per cent, a reduction of 6.2 per cent. The ratio of the rate reduction to the original rate of extra taxation is given by the formula:

$$(k - ck)/(c - cm),$$

where k is the dividend credit.[2]

Indeed, for taxpayers in the very highest income brackets, where the rate of extra taxation is very low to begin with, this fixed amount of extra-rate reduction by the dividend credit brings such taxpayers close to the point of zero extra taxation. Consider, for example, an individual in a marginal rate bracket of 80 per cent. Under no credit, his rate of extra taxation is only 10.4 per cent of the original corporate profits before all tax. Under a 4 per cent credit, the rate of extra taxation is 8.48 per cent. If the taxpayer is in a 91 per cent bracket, his original rate of extra taxation, 4.68 per cent, is reduced to 2.76 per cent.

These low rates of extra taxation in the high brackets, and the large proportionate reduction in them by the credit, reflect of course the very heights of the individual rates themselves; if the rate approaches 100 per cent, there is slight room for extra taxation.

There is, moreover, a point at which the fixed reduction given by the credit goes beyond the initial extra taxation and thus transforms extra taxation into deficient taxation. This break-even point, where the reduction in the rate of extra taxation, resulting from the dividend credit, just equals the initial rate of extra taxation, is reached when the marginal rate applicable to the individual equals this expression: 100 per cent, plus the dividend credit rate, minus the ratio of the credit rate to the corporate tax rate. When the individual marginal rate exceeds this expression, the credit produces deficient taxation of corporate distributed income.

Under a 52 per cent rate for the corporate tax and a 4 per cent credit, the break-even point occurs when the individual marginal rate is 96.3 per cent. If the corporate

2. See notes to this appendix, note 2.

rate is instead, say, 47 per cent, while the rest of the income tax system remains unchanged, deficient taxation appears at the personal marginal rate of 95.5 per cent (these computations abstract from the problem of undistributed profits). And if the credit is made higher, say 15 per cent, the break-even individual bracket rate goes down further. Under a 52 per cent corporate tax it becomes 86.2 per cent and under a 47 per cent corporate tax, 83.1 per cent.[3]

If all the corporate profits are retained in the corporation, no dividends at all being paid, the shareholder subject to a marginal rate of personal income tax that is lower than the corporate tax rate is still overtaxed, and all shareholders whose marginal rate of tax is higher are undertaxed, at least until the resulting increment in share value is taxed as a capital gain (if ever), and perhaps even then. Even if the capital gain is ultimately taxed, the high-bracket shareholder is favored relative to the low-bracket shareholder, if only because of the interest lost by the latter on the tax differential of the year the profit was taxed.

If the corporation retains only part of its disposable profit, results intermediate to those described above follow. Accordingly, under a tax credit to the shareholder as described above, no generalization applies to taxpayers at all income levels. Those who had been heavily extra taxed are granted a slight percentage reduction; those who had been paying less on their share of corporate income than on salary income are now allowed to pay still less.

For taxpayers with a total income so small that none of their share of corporate post-tax profits, considered as marginal income, would bring their income above the exemption level, under the personal income tax, the credit device alone can never reduce the extra taxation, which in this case is the rate of the corporate tax. For those taxpayers only part of whose dividends fall in the taxable area, the credit device can lessen, but not eliminate, the extra taxation. For taxpayers all of whose dividend income is taxable at, say, a 20 per cent rate, the extra taxation could be eliminated only if the dividend credit were set at $86\frac{2}{3}$ per cent instead of the 4 per cent assumed above, given a corporation income tax rate of 52 per cent. But if such a huge credit were applied to everyone, deficient taxation would appear, of course, as soon as the individual bracket rate exceeded 20 per cent.

Holders of outstanding preferred stock would find the market value of their stock enhanced by the credit. For example, an investor in a 40 per cent marginal bracket who is just willing to pay $100 for a $6 preferred stock is getting a return of 3.6 per cent after tax. Under a 4 per cent credit, he pays 24 cents less tax, and thus retains $3.84 of the dividend. This is an increase of $6\frac{2}{3}$ per cent in his after-tax income, and he is then willing to pay $106\frac{2}{3}$ for the share. What will happen in the market depends, however, on the pattern in which marginal buying of such shares is distributed among purchasers of varying income tax status. A large part of the market for preferred stocks is made up of others than individuals. Nevertheless, a large credit, say 25 per cent of dividends received, is scarcely acceptable unless it is denied to holders of preferred stock that was outstanding before the credit was announced. Preferred stock issued after the credit was announced might be granted the credit on the ground that, in their negotiations for issuing such stock, the common stock-

3. See notes to this appendix, note 3.

holders, as represented by the board of directors, can obtain a higher price for the preferred stock than they could in the absence of the credit, and can thus recoup indirectly the extra tax on that part of the net income allocated to service preferred stock.

Does the problem just posed exist also for common stocks? Have present owners of common stock, by and large, purchased their holdings, whether from former holders or from issuing corporations, with no expectation whatsoever of diminution in extra taxation? If they have done so, the case for reducing extra taxation on outstanding issues of common stock is correspondingly weak. Those whom the extra taxation has truly harmed, the former holders of the common stock and those who were deterred from buying new issues, can no longer be identified and recompensed for the tax injustice. The existing holders reap windfall gains under the tax credit. This point does not of course weigh against reducing the extra taxation with respect to new stock issues if there are any practicable ways of making a distinction between outstanding stock and stock issued after the announcement date. In any event the problem would be mitigated if approximately full taxation of capital gains could be achieved before a truly substantial credit was put into effect (see page 323).

But substantial tax relief on distributed profits will probably not be acceptable to the community at large, as long as undistributed profits provide the sanctuary they do to investors of very high incomes. There will be objection to any plan under which the high-income investors are relieved of extra taxation on distributed profits, while being granted continued occupancy of a tax haven represented by the combination of a corporate tax rate below the individual's marginal rate and exemption of capital gains if the security is held until death or is passed down the generations through *inter-vivos* gifts. Even a taxable capital gain may not redress the balance if it is given a highly preferential rate and if realization is postponed many years beyond the date of accrual.

Another, and more nearly complete, technique for integrating the corporate tax and the individual income tax is a credit to the shareholder at the full corporate tax rate, the dividend being, however, "grossed up" as follows. If the corporate tax rate is, for example, 50 per cent, $100 of dividends actually received would be entered on the taxpayer's income tax return as $200 of dividends constructively received. A tentative tax on the individual's entire income would then be computed in the usual way, and a credit of 50 per cent of $200, or $100, would be granted against that tax. If the credit exceeded the tentative tax, a refund would be given by the treasury.

With regard to distributed income alone, this method eliminates deficient taxation at high-income levels, and extra taxation, but does not solve the problem of windfall gains. It does nothing with respect to undistributed profits. Moreover, unless the corporate tax rate were close to the lower-bracket individual rates, the number and size of refunds might prove awkward. And to explain the rationale of the grossing up to the public would take time and skill.

It is this failure to solve the problem of undistributed profits, even with grossing up, that is the most serious defect of the credit-to-shareholder method. That method is equivalent to a flat-rate tax on corporate profits with a deduction given to the corporation for dividends declared,[4] that is, a tax on undistributed profits— provided that the corporation is allowed something like an indefinite carryback of dividends paid in excess of current year's profits. But no tax on undistributed profits levied on the corporation can do more than the roughest kind of justice, unless it is a true forcing-out tax, to be described below. Undistributed profits give rise to tax benefits to high-income shareholders without eliminating tax penalties on low-income shareholders. An undistributed profits tax collected from the corporation, whether at a flat rate or at progressive rates, strikes all these shareholders proportionately.

Much of the extra taxation, especially at the lower income levels, could be removed by lowering the corporation tax rate. But this, like the credit, is open to the windfall objection (capitalized tax), and it makes more urgent than ever the need to reach undistributed profits accruing to high-income shareholders.

For those who believe that a reduction in the corporation income tax coupled with, say, an increase in individual income tax rates, would put pressure on corporate management to lower product prices, and would favor this result, lowering the corporate rate carries an advantage over the credit method, which puts only indirect pressure on management to lower prices, if indeed any pressure at all.

It seems probable that the undistributed profits problem can best be solved with full taxation of capital gains and full allowance of capital losses, as they accrue. To see this, we consider first two alternatives to complete accounting for capital gains and losses in this context, namely, the partnership method, and a forcing-out type of undistributed profits tax. Under the partnership method each shareholder includes in his taxable income his share, distributed or not, in the corporation's earnings for the year. Cash dividends, or indeed any form of dividend, are not taxable. To avoid double taxation through tax on capital gains, the amount of undistributed profit so taxed is added to the basis of his stock for computing capital gain or loss. An excess of dividends received over taxable share in any one year would correspondingly reduce the basis of the stock.

This method is unacceptable in the case of companies where the accumulated claims of creditors and preferred stockholders are so great that large current earnings per share of common stock really mean little or nothing to common stockholders, since these earnings must go to whittle down prior claims that, even so, remain as a seemingly perpetual barrier to resumption of dividends (corporations can get into this kind of a position and stay there much longer than partnerships and proprietorships). In general, the problem of placing a precise, fair market value on

4. A low corporate tax rate on that part of profits distributed in dividends, as under the present German income tax, approximates the credit-to-shareholder method with a credit less than the corporate tax rate. A detailed comparison of the credit-to-shareholder method and its equivalent, the deduction-of-dividends-paid method, is to be found in Carl S. Shoup, Director of Commission, John F. Due, Lyle C. Fitch, Sir Donald MacDougall, Oliver S. Oldman, and Stanley S. Surrey, *The Fiscal System of Venezuela: A Report* (Baltimore, Md.: Johns Hopkins Press, 1959), pp. 117–25. This part of the report was written by Surrey, with the assistance of Oldman.

current undistributed earnings is in many cases quite serious, although commonly no more so than estimating accrued capital gains and losses. On balance the partnership method is almost as satisfactory as accruing capital gains and losses.

An undistributed profits tax heavy enough to force out cash or other assets to the full extent of current earnings probably runs too contrary to firmly established ideas of rights of management; and it may create very difficult working capital problems, as with inventory profits. A tax designed to force out, instead, taxable tickets rather than assets (taxable stock dividends) is no improvement over the partnership method for companies whose shares have no market.

Undistributed profits tend to increase the market value of the shares. The correspondence is not necessarily, indeed not usually, 1 to 1. But if capital gains could be brought fully to account, the accretion to economic power presented by the retention of profits would be fully taxed, even though the precise role played by such retention in creating the capital gain was never determined. All the forces making for the capital gain or the capital loss, including retention of earnings, would be taken account of in one lump.[5]

It appears impossible to solve the problem of "double taxation" (extra taxation) of corporate profits without solving at the same time the problems of undistributed profits and of capital gains and losses.[6]

Notes to Appendix

1. *Rate of extra taxation.* Let the corporate tax, as a percentage of corporate income before all income tax, be c. If all income is distributed, the individual tax applies only to the remainder of the corporate income, that is, to $1 - c$ of such income. If, for simplicity, all such dividend income received by the shareholder in question is assumed to fall within the marginal bracket in which he finds himself, he pays tax at the rate of $m(1 - c)$ on that corporate income, where m is his marginal rate of personal tax. The combined tax rate on that corporate income is thus $c + m(1 - c)$, or $m + c - cm$. The tax rate on salary income of the same amount (viewing it as an alternative to corporate-derived income) is simply m. The difference between the two is thus $c - cm$, or $c(1 - m)$; this is the extra taxation, as a percentage of the income before any tax.

2. *Reduction in rate of extra taxation.* The cumulated tax rate of $m + c - cm$ (see note 1 above) is reduced, through the operation of the credit k, applied to that part

5. The alternative techniques for taking capital gains and losses into account are discussed in the text of Chapter 12, Section 4.A.

6. Cf. the remarks on this point in the *Report on Japanese Taxation by the Shoup Mission* (Tokyo: General Headquarters, Supreme Commander for the Allied Powers, 1949), pp. 105-13. See also William Vickrey, *Agenda for Progressive Taxation*, Chapter 6, including his proposal for a cumulative low-rate annual tax on undistributed profits, pp. 156 ff.

of the corporate income that is paid in dividends after payment of the corporate tax at the rate c. That part is $1 - c$, and the rate of relief is therefore $k(1 - c)$.

3. *Precise elimination of extra taxation by credit.* The "salary tax" rate is simply m. The rate of the dividend tax is: $c + m(1 - c) - k(1 - c)$. When these two are equal, that is, when extra taxation has been precisely eliminated, $m = c + m(1 - c) - k(1 - c)$, and,

solving for c, we obtain $c = \dfrac{k}{1 + k - m}$

solving for k, we obtain $k = \dfrac{c(1 - m)}{1 - c}$

solving for m, we obtain $m = 1 + k - \dfrac{k}{c}$

CHAPTER TWELVE

Income Taxes: II

4. Conflict Criteria

A. EQUITY CRITERIA

DISTRIBUTION OF the income tax by income class or wealth class is almost surely progressive relative to that of the value-added tax, income type (see Chapter 11, section B.2.B). One possible exception is that a large family with a somewhat higher income that a small family may pay relatively less tax than under a value-added tax because of the large number of personal exemptions. Another possibility is that incomes before tax are more unequally distributed under a highly progressive income tax than under a value-added tax, if the supply of high-income talent is quite price-elastic.

The degree of progression of the income tax depends in part on date of payment of tax, as distinguished from date of accrual of income, and the unit of time for which the progressive rate is defined.

A capital gain, for example, that is taxable only upon realization, by sale of the asset, may therefore give rise to no tax liability until some years after it has accrued. Wage income that is set aside in a pension fund and is not taxed until the pension is distributed is another example. The delay in tax payment is equivalent to a reduction in tax rate. Large incomes probably contain proportionately more income on which tax payment is commonly deferred than do small incomes. The progressive rate scale is therefore less progressive than it appears on its face. Deferral of payment could be reduced to a low level by requiring "payments on account," say every two or three years, on accrued capital gains. For symmetry, "allowances on account" would be permitted for accrued capital losses. In the absence of a general system of averaging, an optional system of prorating the accrued gain or loss could be provided, to soften the impact of occasional wide swings in market or book value: for example, the gain accrued over the two- or three-year period would be divided by, say, five (as if it had accrued evenly over a five-year period), the tax on a gain or the tax relief from a loss would be computed on that one-fifth, and the result would be multiplied by five to find the tax or tax relief due on the gain or loss.

For this purpose alone, namely, reduction of tax deferral to an acceptable level, the valuation of the asset every two or three years to determine the approximate accrued gain or loss would not need to be precise. The error in valuation would be automatically offset later when the asset was sold or, if transferred by gift or at death, carefully valued at that time. Valuation for estimating accrued gains or losses is thus a much less demanding task than valuation of property under a real estate tax or a net wealth tax, where an error in valuation, once made, is never corrected by subsequent reappraisal.[1] Some inequality of treatment would remain, of course, since the taxpayer will commonly be paying income tax at different rates in different years because his annual income changes, or the tax law is changed. Even if he is not, interest lost on early tax overpaid or interest gained on early tax underpaid is never offset. But these errors would probably be small in most instances compared with the existing error of allowing deferral of tax on gain or compelling deferral of tax relief on loss for decades, so that the present value of tax due or tax relief claimed is commonly reduced by one-half, two-thirds, or more. The magnitude of this interest-on-tax error seems not to be appreciated in most discussions of this issue.

Accrual accounting for gains and losses would allow elimination of extensive and complex provisions common in existing income tax laws for deferring recognition of gain or loss upon exchange of securities in the course of a merger or other corporate reorganization.[2] Accrual accounting would also almost eliminate the pressure exerted by the realized-gain technique to hold appreciated assets beyond the point they would be held in the absence of the tax.[3]

The unit of time for which the progressive rate scale of an income tax is defined determines the degree of averaging of income over time that is permitted automatically. All income tax laws average income over time; the only question is, what should the automatic averaging period be and should it be supplemented by inter-period averaging? The automatic period generally adopted is of course one year, either a calendar year or a fiscal year (i.e., a period of twelve months starting other than on January 1). An individual whose income arises irregularly throughout the year is taxed the same amount as one with the same income for the year that accrues regularly, month by month, or day by day. If the progressive rate schedule were applied to, say, monthly income the individual with an income irregularly distri-

---

1. But see, for example, Goode, *The Individual Income Tax*, pp. 29, 32–33, where taxation of accrued gains is impliedly put on the same administrative footing as taxation of personal wealth, and Vickrey, *Agenda for Progressive Taxation*, pp. 137–38. Seltzer (*The Nature and Tax Treatment of Capital Gains and Losses*, pp. 289–95) recognizes the tentative nature of the valuations but considers changes in tax rates and in the taxpayer's other income from year to year too important. "These difficulties would be reduced, however, [by] . . . averaging income for several years . . . or . . . a generous carryback or carryforward of net capital losses against ordinary income" (*ibid.*, p. 294).

2. Probably from one-half to two-thirds of the number of pages of the United States federal income tax law and regulations could be dispensed with if accrual accounting for capital gains and losses were adopted, judging from the unpublished findings of research in a joint law-economics seminar at Columbia University in which I participated, a few years ago. In terms of man-hours spent in planning and in litigation the saving might be of a greater proportion than one-half to two-thirds.

3. For an analysis of this "lock-in" problem, see Goode, *op. cit.*, pp. 207–218.

buted over the twelve months would complain of discrimination arising from irrelevant circumstances and would be under tax pressure to enter occupations paying a regular income. Seasonal fluctuations are so pervasive and often so pronounced that no one favors a monthly basis for progression. A two-year period, in contrast, does not yield a result much different from a one-year period unless the taxpayer experiences a pronounced change in annual income. But a lifetime averaging period for application of the progressive rate scale would yield a quite different pattern of tax distribution from the one-year averaging period.[4]

A lifetime cumulative averaging provision would make it a matter of indifference to the taxpayer as to which parts of his life his income is deemed to arise in, so far as the progressive-rate income tax itself is concerned. This is so, even if the taxpayer has an intrinsic time preference.[5] As between two individuals receiving the same lifetime income, distributed differently over their lifetimes, cumulative averaging would cause the same amount of income tax to be due at the same time, say at the end of the averaging period, or alternatively the tax payments required from time to time throughout life would have the same total discounted value. The question of principle, with respect to cumulative averaging over a lifetime, is whether the difference in lifetime pattern of income receipt is a relevant circumstance for determining the discounted value of lifetime tax payable. Proponents of long periods for averaging believe that it is not relevant. Opponents argue that the individual in, say, his seventh decade of life is not the same person that he was in, say, his fourth decade, and that a lifetime averaging system is therefore not the proper basis for progression. But men in their thirties do deliberately defer taxable income to their sixties or seventies, partly to make that income taxable in a lower range of the progressive rate scale. If they will not be the same men then that they are now, they at least act as if they would be, and the impression given to those who lack this opportunity to restructure their lifetime incomes is one of tax avoidance.

A lifetime averaging system, provided it credits the taxpayer with interest on taxes paid, and charges him interest on taxes deferred, would make such restructuring unnecessary and ineffective. Anything that eliminates efforts to reallocate income among the years is the greatest single simplifying device in prospect for the income tax law of any country. Cumulative lifetime averaging would therefore simplify more than accrual accounting with rudimentary averaging.

Accordingly, if lifetime averaging were adjudged somewhat undesirable on equity grounds, there would remain a strong case for it on grounds of simplification

4. A workable lifetime, or very long period, averaging system has been devised by William Vickrey. See his "Averaging of Income for Income-Tax Purposes," *Journal of Political Economy* (June, 1939), 47: 379–97, reprinted in Musgrave and Shoup (Eds.), *Readings in the Economics of Taxation*; and Vickrey, *Agenda for Progressive Taxation*, Chapter 6. Cf. Louis Shere, "Federal Corporate Income Tax—Revenue and Reform," *National Tax Journal* (June, 1949), 2: 117.

5. Intrinsic time preference with respect to consumption does not depend on ability to save and earn investment income. Such ability is not relevant to the argument here, under the restriction assumed that total lifetime incomes of the two taxpayers are the same. Similarly, the existence of a positive rate of interest does not necessarily imply an intrinsic time preference with respect to consumption. See William S. Vickrey, *Metastatics and Macroeconomics* (New York: Harcourt, Brace and World, 1964), p. 15.

of the tax law and consequent savings in administrative and compliance expense. The only proviso is that a country adopting this system must be firm enough in its understanding of it to be sure that, once adopted, the system will be continued unchanged for decades if not forever. An on-and-off "lifetime" cumulative averaging system would be quite unsatisfactory. A short-period averaging system, say one that averages for successive five-year periods, puts the taxpayer whose income exhibits drastic short-term irregularities on much the same footing as the taxpayer with stable income, but it does little for an individual whose lifetime income is concentrated in a decade or two of high earning power. And it scarcely reduces the pressure to restructure part of an income into the retirement period.

A moving-average system is unsuitable. If it averages back over periods both of increasing income and decreasing income it may require the taxpayer to find more cash for tax payment in a year when he is embarrassed financially, in a trough of his income, than if there were no averaging provision. This the cumulative system of averaging will never do. If the moving average operates only for periods of increasing income,[6] it discriminates against one whose income, hitherto stable and high, now falls off: a common enough instance is supplied by the retirement years.

Legislators have shown no interest in lifetime cumulative averaging, in part because most of them are unfamiliar with the possibilities. Moreover, those few policy officials who grasp its implications thoroughly are less attracted by its elimination of anomalies than they are repelled by the fear of the unknown aroused by the thought of committing the country to a plan that, to be effective, must be left unchanged over decades. Also, certain technical problems have not as yet been solved to the satisfaction of everyone, notably those arising upon divorce and remarriage, and change of residence to or from abroad.[7]

The result of these conflicting views has been gradual introduction of a number of ad hoc provisions,[8] designed chiefly or secondarily for averaging; an example of the latter is deferral of certain non-available income to years of retirement (see page 307 above). An ad hoc averaging device may be so crude that as the years pass the provision comes to be supported largely on other grounds.[9]

6. As does the United States averaging system adopted in 1964, which replaced a number of ad hoc provisions. It is available only to those whose incomes have been rising by more than a specified percentage. For an unusual type of moving average, which distinguishes between "fluctuating income" and "extraordinary [i.e. lump-sum] income," see Taizo Hayashi, *Guide to Japanese Taxes* (Tokyo: Zaikei Shōhō Sha, 1966), p. 85.

7. See Vickrey, *Agenda for Progressive Taxation*, Chapter 6.

8. For a list of such provisions in the Canadian income tax law, information on averaging systems in other countries, and a proposal that does not accept the principle of lifetime averaging see, in the six-volume *Report of the Royal Commission on Taxation [Canada]* (chairman, Kenneth LeM. Carter; director of research, Douglas G. Hartle), vol. 3, Taxation of Income, Part A (Taxation of Individuals and Families), Chapter 13, pp. 241–81 (Ottawa: Queen's Printer, 1966). Provisions that are not commonly regarded as averaging devices but that have much the same effect are exemplified by "the allocation of income to earlier years in cases where payment is received for services performed over an extended period of time . . . and through the use of special methods of accounting . . . and inventory valuation. . . . In addition, where events span two or more annual accounting periods, a unitary or 'transactional' approach is sometimes authorized" (Chirelstein, Day, and Owens, *Taxation in the United States*, p. 389).

9. The United States income tax includes in taxable income one-half of long-term capital

Sometimes averaging is restricted to setting off the negative income of one year against the positive income of another, as with the carryover of business operating losses, or to carrying over an unused part, or the whole, of a deduction, say a medical-expense deduction, to another year. The single most powerful ad hoc averaging provision not yet adopted by any country is the carryover of unused personal exemptions. These ad hoc carryovers usually need to be carry-backs, not carry-forwards to years of future income, if they are to benefit the taxpayer in the very year he takes the carryover, which is likely to be a year in which his finances are strained, for a carry-back is more likely to result in a check from the treasury. The carry-forward simply reduces, in a later year, the tax that would otherwise be due at that time.

The demand for averaging grows with rate of progression, defined here as the rate of change in the rate of change of the total tax bill of the taxpayer in dollars per dollar increase in taxable income (the second derivative of the total-tax function) or, more loosely, the rate of change in marginal tax rate per percentage increase in taxable income. The alternative measure of degree of progression, namely, rate of change in effective rate,[10] has three shortcomings if degree of progression is being studied for its incentive effects, as it is in speaking of the demand for an averaging device. First, if, as is customary, the rate scale applies each rate only to the slice of income within the designated bracket, an increase in taxable income small enough to keep the taxpayer well within the same bracket will not change the rate that influences small increments of action at the margin, although the effective rate increases. Second, when the law supplements the bracket schedule with a ceiling on the effective rate, the marginal rate declines abruptly to the effective rate when that ceiling is reached, while the effective rate simply stops rising at that point. Third, if a minimum, lump-sum tax is imposed on income below a certain level, the effective rate falls as income rises to that level, but the marginal rate is zero.

But if degree of progression is used to compare amounts of tax due at various income levels in a study of relative tax burdens, rate of change in effective rate is the more informative measure of degree of progression.[11]

gains or losses, defined as gains or losses on capital assets held for more than six months. A ceiling rate of 25 per cent applies to the full gain, and capital losses may be deducted only from capital gains (with carry-forward, plus $1,000 a year from ordinary income). These provisions date, for the most part, from 1942, when they were enacted largely as a simplifying substitute for the averaging device that had been in force during most of the 1930's, by which the percentage of gain or loss taken into account varied with the number of years the asset had been held. The six-months dividing line was a concession to those who argued that capital gains are not properly income at all, except to "speculators". But by now even the one-half exclusion is supported on these grounds by many who are not aware of its origin as an averaging device.

10. Effective rate is taxable income divided into tax liability. Average rate would be a better term, but "effective rate" has become embedded in public finance literature.

11. See Michael E. Levy, *Income Tax Exemptions: An Analysis of the Effects of Personal Exemptions on the Income Tax Structure* (Amsterdam: North-Holland Publishing, 1960), especially pp. 9–20, 32, and 37–39. Alternative formulae for progression are not discussed in the present work; see Levy, *op. cit.*, *passim*, and sources cited there, especially Pierre Folliet, *Les Tarifs d'impots: essai de mathématiques fiscales* (Lausanne: Payot, 1947), and William Vickrey, *Agenda for Progressive Taxation*, Chapter 13 and Appendix VII. See also Shun-hsin Chou, *The Capital Levy* (New York: King's Crown Press, 1945), Chapters III and IV.

In summary, degree of progression is to be defined by rate of change in marginal rate for inquiries dealing with the substitution effect of the income tax, and by rate of change in effective rate if the income effect is being studied.

The conflict of interests evoked by progression is heightened under a universal (mass) income tax, which by its breadth of coverage offers a wide range of alternatives for progression and a correspondingly wide arena for dispute. Only societies with stable social structures can employ successfully a highly progressive mass income tax. Other socieities resort to heavier sales taxation or to inflation. The social pressures are not mainly conflicts between the poor and the rich, for the rich do not possess enough in the aggregate to help the poor a great deal; if the poor are to gain appreciably through the public finance system it must be at the expense, largely, of the middle-income and lower-middle income classes. Intense conflicts are generated in the course of deciding on the size of the personal exemption,[12] the first bracket rate, and the degree of progression through the range where the bulk of the taxable income is found.

Those countries where the income tax strikes only a small proportion of residents get most of the tax from foreign corporations. Here there is little internal conflict; the tax can produce appreciable sums without disruptive social tensions. The corporations themselves often object only mildly, in view of the credit against tax at home that is commonly allowed for income tax paid to the foreign country. In effect, the poor state uses the income tax to tax the rich state, and that state is usually so rich that it scarcely notices the burden.

Families with the same incomes, but differing in certain other respects, are commonly treated differently under the income tax.[13] We consider here differences in type of income, family size and composition, and uses made of income. The conflict of interests is now between persons differently circumstanced in attributes other than income or wealth. These conflicts are less intense with respect to family composition and uses of income because any one individual is more likely to find himself in the future, or to have been in the past, in the opposite camp. Most single persons get married, or have been married; many families move through the stages of no children, one child, and so on; many healthy persons become ill and most sick persons get well. It is chiefly the type-of-income differences, as foreseen by any one household, that appear likely to be permanent.

Under the universal income tax and also under the uniform partial income tax, labor income is in some countries taxed at a lower rate than investment income. If the difference in treatment is small it probably reflects only lip service to the idea advanced by Mill that labor income needs to be given relief if its recipient is ever to accumulate to the point where he too may receive a considerable investment income. If the difference is appreciable, but is confined to the lower income brackets, it may reflect a desire by legislators to increase the supply of paid female labor in factories,

12. Perhaps the refusal of Congress to change the $600 exemption in the United States over the post-war period (since 1948), even in the face of a rising price level, is testimony to the degree of conflict that is latent in this issue. See Pechman, *Federal Tax Policy*, pp. 65–72.

13. See Harold M. Groves, *Federal Tax Treatment for the Family* (Washington, D.C.: Brookings, 1963).

shops, and homes.[14] If this appreciable difference in tax treatment for labor income extends into high-income levels,[15] it also reflects a fear that the best brains of the country may emigrate; mobility of this type of labor causes as much concern as mobility of capital. Other grounds advanced for a preferential rate on earned income are absence of provisions for deducting depreciation of human capital that has been created by nondeductible outlays; indirect allowance for sacrifice of imputed income from leisure, since that imputed income is never taxed; and compensation for a relatively small rate of evasion or avoidance.

Families of differing size and composition but with the same family income are under most income tax laws treated differently, in an attempt to adjust progression to a per-person basis. In part the differential treatment reflects a desire to avert behavior of a type deemed socially undesirable (secret divorces,[16] secret marriages). Attempts by the government to encourage or discourage population growth explain some of the differences.

If there were no such differentiation at all, the members of a household would be required to lump all their incomes, one exemption would be given, and one progressive rate scale applied to the aggregated income. No country goes quite that far. The first step toward differentiation is to allow an exemption, or tax credit, for every member of the household, though not necessarily the same amount for each. The next is to allow the filing of a separate return by each member of the household who has income of his own. The last step is to allow or require a splitting of the aggregated incomes between husband and wife, and possibly also children; in effect, an artificially more or even less even allocation among separate returns. But since no system requires inclusion of an estimated imputed income from the housewife's work, equal per capita exemptions for every family member together with income splitting[17] weights the scales heavily against the single person. Over a lifetime the discrimination is less than it might seem, for the reason already noted: most single persons become, or have been, married.

The use that the family makes of its income influences the amount of income tax due. The various provisions differ markedly in their rationale. Deduction of con-

---

14. In the United Kingdom, as of 1960, "Wives in the lower income classes are encouraged by the income tax provisions to seek paid work outside the home; wives in the upper income classes are discouraged from doing so" (Shoup, "Tax Tension and the British Fiscal System," *National Tax Journal* (March, 1961), 14: 26).

15. It was so extended in the United Kingdom in 1961.

16. In the United Kingdom, "If the wife has income of her own from property, or earnings, it pays the high-income couple handsomely to dissolve the marriage [and thus avoid a compulsory joint return]. . . . [They] continue to live together as before, and only the Inland Revenue (and the counsel and the court) know that they have in fact been divorced" (*ibid.*, p. 26, March, 1961).

17. For example, the United States income tax. For a thoroughgoing application of the principle that the family is the appropriate taxing unit, see *Report of the Royal Commission on Taxation* [Canada], vol. 3, Part A, Chapter 10 ("The Tax Unit"), which for this purpose defines the family to include generally the children 21 years of age or less. When a child ceases to be a member of the unit, "unrealized gains on property withdrawn by the child from the original family unit should be taxed as income to the original family unit . . ." (p. 137). See also the formula, devised for the transfer taxes, of the concept of the family unit, which has implications also for income taxation, in Harold M. Groves and Wallace I. Edwards, "A New Model for an Integrated Transfer Tax," *National Tax Journal* (December, 1953), 6: 353–60.

tributions to religious, charitable, and similar organizations are equivalent to government subsidization of those organizations. It is a type of subsidy that is designed to bypass the budgetary process, for reasons given in Chapter 2 above.

Deduction of interest on personal indebtedness incurred for any purpose whatever is logically a necessary corollary of taxing investment income. If deduction were not allowed and investment income continued to be taxed, households would be put under tax-induced pressure always to meet an excess of expenditure over income by selling assets outright, never borrowing against them.

Deduction of taxes paid to subordinate jurisdictions is chiefly a form of vertical fiscal coordination, discussed in Chapter 25 below. It may also reflect a desire to subsidize homeowning without using the budgetary process.

Deduction is commonly given for outlays that cannot be anticipated and that may put severe financial pressure on the household, and that may vary greatly in amount, even over a lifetime, among households with the same average income over that long period .The chief illustrations are major medical expenditures and loss or damage from fire, storm, or other casualty, to the degree uninsured.[18] The medical expense deduction will become less important as free medical service by the government is extended.

A single standard deduction to be taken in lieu of these itemized deductions and expressed as a percentage of income before deductions amounts to disallowing all such deductions except as in the aggregate they exceed the standard percentage; allowance is given only to the excess. This kind of limitation accords well with the reasons for granting the deductions described in the immediately preceding paragraph, but it weakens the budgetary bypass stimulation and fiscal coordination, and contradicts the rationale of the deduction for interest paid.

If the residents of a depressed region are granted lower income tax rates, or higher exemptions, the effect may not be substantial, since many families in a depressed region will have incomes too small to have been taxed before. Those who have enough work at high enough wages to benefit from the tax relief accorded this region may have to meet competition from an inflow of workers from regions where the income tax is still in full force.

Part of the second-round benefits from tax relief will accrue to residents of prosperous regions, since residents of the depressed region who are well enough off to

18. The German individual income tax provides a blanket allowance for extraordinary financial burdens reflected in expenditures of a type that are not specifically deductible. The reasoning is that "A Taxpayer who necessarily incurs expenditures higher than the great majority of other individuals with similar income, net worth, and family responsibilities, is entitled to a reduction of his income tax. An expense is necessarily incurred if the taxpayer cannot avoid it for legal, moral, or factual reasons, and if the expenditure serves the needs of the individual situation and is reasonable in amount. . . . The typical example of an unavoidable extraordinary expenditure . . . is that which results from an accident or a prolonged illness of the taxpayer or a member of his immediate family." The individual's taxable income is reduced "by the amount by which the total amount of the extraordinary expenditure exceeds the portion thereof which the taxpayer can reasonably be expected to bear himself. This portion varies between zero and 7% of the taxpayer's net income . . ." (Gumpel and Boettcher, *Taxation in Germany*, pp. 614–15). Specific allowance is made for extraordinary financial burdens arising from care for dependents other than dependent children, expense of domestic help, and expenditures on account of physical disability (*ibid.*, pp. 615–16).

have been paying tax will spend part of their income tax relief on imports from the rest of the country, if not from abroad. A reduction in rates of tax on business profits, insofar as it benefits the owners, will thereby benefit in part the flourishing regions where many of the owners of firms in the depressed regions will be living.

Capital will flow into the depressed region only if it can be persuaded that the low rates or exemptions are there to stay for some time. If it is so persuaded, enough may flow in to raise appreciably the wages of workers in that area. The competitive position of firms already there, with respect to markets outside the region, is not enhanced very much by reduction of a tax on profits, the quantity sought to be maximized.

Internationally, a country cannot export its income tax in the way it can export part of a sales tax. If foreign capital or foreign labor is to be reached under the income tax, it must be working in the taxing country, hence making at least some use of that government's free services. The sales tax, in contrast, may under certain conditions burden foreign firms or consumers who make no direct use of the country's free services. A partial reply is that they either consume the products of the country or send products to it, and in either case benefit indirectly from the existence of a government there.

In a biased community that employs a universal income tax, the mechanics of the tax open the way, in a manner that the sales tax does not, for discrimination on the basis of race, color, or creed. The same discrimination, only less widespread, is feasible under a partial income tax.

Those who dislike fiscal illusion and do not wish to conceal the burden of a tax find the income tax to their liking, with one exception. The universal type of income tax can be enforced only by withholding the tax from wages and salaries, and a withholding system can be devised so accurately that most workers never need to fill out an income tax return.[19] Even if they are notified of the amount withheld they may focus so upon the take-home wage that they are scarcely conscious of the income tax. If withholding is of a less refined, and less expensive, variety,[20] there is much more tax consciousness. The universal income tax is thus a fairly adaptable instrument on this score, with respect to the great majority of taxpayers.

B. Reallocation Criteria

Economic growth is affected by the income tax, relative to the value-added tax, consumption type, because it drives a wedge, as the latter tax does not, between the rate of return earned by capital and the rate of return realized by the owner of the capital. The consequences in an extreme case in an open economy have been suggested above. Here, the analysis is confined to a closed economy and is in terms of differential effects.

19. As in the United Kingdom. See Alan P. Murray, "A Proposal for Cumulative Withholding," *National Tax Journal* (June, 1962), 15: 184–93.

20. As in the United States.

The initial effect of substituting an income tax for a value-added tax, consumption type, is to reduce the rate of return paid to the capitalist. For the moment, considerations of risk are disregarded. The negative income effect of the reduction in the rate of return to the capitalist resembles that of a reduction in an interest rate,[21] but it is here offset in the aggregate by the positive income effect from repeal of the value-added tax. Since capitalists, even small ones, are likely to have larger incomes than most non-capitalists, the net effect of the tax change, on income account, is probably an increase in current consumption, that is, a decline in current saving and investment. The substitution effect of the income tax relative to that of the value-added tax, consumption type, is entirely in the direction of increasing present consumption. On both income and substitution account, therefore, this tax change is almost certain to check economic growth.

The effect of an income tax on risk-taking must ultimately be analyzed in a general equilibrium setting, one that assumes that some other source of revenue is reduced, or some government expenditure increased. It will be convenient to start with the latter assumption, under the quite artificial restriction that the government spends the money in the same manner that the taxpayers would have done, and abstracting from the income effects of the free services dispensed as a result of the government's purchase of goods and services with the income tax moneys. The results are not those of an income tax alone,[22] but they prepare the way for consideration of a realistic problem, i.e., the effects of substituting an income tax for, say, a value-added tax, consumption type, And under this somewhat artificial type of general equilibrium approach it is easy to utilize some significant conclusions that have been reached under a partial-equilibrium approach that studies an individual investor's portfolio reactions to a tax change.

The change in pattern of private investment among ventures of varying degrees of risk, upon introduction of this public finance measure, depends on what aspects of the probability distribution of a venture's possible outcomes the investor is sensitive to. A common and plausible assumption is that he is sensitive to the mean and the variance of these outcomes. Under these conditions it can be shown that introduction of a proportionate rate income tax with full loss offset induces the investor to increase his portfolio's pre-tax mean income and variance; he increases the degree of risk taken by himself and the government together.[23]

Some details of actual income tax laws as they affect risk-taking are now considered.

Loss offsets are commonly extensive, but far from complete. A loss on a venture can normally be deducted (except under some schedular or quasi-schedular income taxes) from operating income earned on other ventures by the same individual or

---

21. A change in an interest rate has both a substitution effect and an income effect. Even if an individual has no "intrinsic time preference", i.e., "a given rate of expenditure produces just as much satisfaction if it occurs later as it does if it occurs immediately," the income effect of a reduction in the rate of interest may outweigh the substitution effect, and he may save more than under the higher rate of interest (William S. Vickrey, *Metastatics and Macroeconomics*, p. 15).

22. As already noted in Chapter 1, Section B.

23. See Appendix to this chapter.

corporation, at least in the same year, and even in earlier or later years if, as is now the case in many laws, some carry-back or carry-forward is allowed. With respect to a portfolio investor, if his capital gains are taxed, his capital losses are usually deductible against the capital gains of the same or even other years, and under some laws an unabsorbed capital loss can be deducted, to a limited degree, from ordinary income.

A business firm's operating loss may even be deducted from the profits earned in an earlier year by another firm, if the income tax law permits a carry-back after a merger of a loss-heavy firm with a profitable firm.

In view of the restrictions on loss offset, the individual income tax almost surely decreases partners' and sole proprietors' demand for ventures that carry a high degree of risk as computed before tax.

A proportionate corporate income tax is another matter. Large corporations commonly engage in a great number of ventures simultaneously, and so possess a substantial guarantee of loss offset for any one venture, save in exceptionally bad years. Thus a high proportionate-rate corporate income tax may induce corporate boards of directors to undertake ventures more risky (before tax) than they would consider under no tax. Much depends on what kind of a utility function those policy makers operate by. It might well be a linear function (constant marginal utility of income) rather than quadratic (diminishing marginal utility of income). Something depends on the degree to which that utility function incorporates shareholders' preferences and takes account of their liability under the individual income tax. A director of a large, widely held corporation, whose own personal wealth is for the most part in forms other than shares in this company, probably does not consider the individual income tax that may become payable by the shareholders when he votes on an investment project that the company's engineers have put before the board; he asks what the rate of return on the venture may be after corporate tax only. On the other hand, a director of a corporation, large or small, in which a family or other concentrated group has a large interest probably does consider the eventual individual income tax, or asks whether it may not be entirely avoided through the declaration of dividends in the form of shares of stock (nontaxable) and through the shareholder's passing on the stock at death or by inter-vivos gift with a stepped-up or transferred basis.

Complaints by investors about the limitations of loss offset have commonly been met by assuring the risk-taker that if the venture turns out well he will be taxed on a favorable basis. If the venture is in the natural-resource field, the investor may be allowed to deduct depletion far in excess of cost. In effect, the dispersion of possible outcomes is for this investor reduced very little by the presence of the income tax, nor is the expected return much reduced.

But most of these ventures that are extremely risky when undertaken singly can be undertaken in bundles by large business firms; through pooling, the degree of dispersion for the large corporations is greatly reduced, even when there is no income tax. Yet the extra allowance for depletion and the like is commonly available to all investors in the industry, large and small, individual and corporate. The result is a flow of capital and labor into these extractive industries, from other industries, a flow that increases output and lowers prices of their products relative to those of other products, and increases economic rents for the owners of resources that are specialized in these industries. It should be possible, technically, to limit the extra depletion tax relief to those taxpayers that do in fact undergo exceptional risk, that is, unusual degree of dispersion, but no such refinement appears to have been adopted, even in countries with high income tax rates.

With respect to differential effect on risk-taking, income tax vis-à-vis value-added tax, consumption type, the significant fact is that the value-added tax exempts the return from capital goods, or, rather, does the same thing insofar as investment incentives are concerned by allowing deduction of the cost of the capital good in the year of purchase. To be sure, not all capital is given this equivalent of exemption of return from it; capital tied up in financial assets, e.g., accounts receivable, is never deducted in computing taxable value added. But the return on real capital, including inventory accumulation, is effectively exempted.[24] In effect, of the total expenditure on the capital good the government supplies the funds for a part (a part equal to the tax rate) and the private investor receives a return on the remainder, which is all that he in fact finances himself, a return that neither is taxed, nor affords a tax rebate if it is negative. Under the income tax, in contrast, there is either a tax on the return to the capital the investor has put up, if the venture yields a profit, or a tax rebate or offset if the venture yields a loss.

Evidently, the value-added tax of the consumption type does not reduce the mean return and the variance from a venture, as does an income tax, at least when those quantities are expressed as percentages of the capital the investor puts up himself (as distinguished from the part the government puts up, by allowing tax relief on purchase of a capital good). If the investor's utility for income is quadratic (decreasing marginal utility), substitution of a complete-loss-offset income tax for a value-added tax, consumption type, should, by an extension of the partial equilibrium analysis above and in the Appendix to this chapter, increase the amount of social risk taken, if the income tax is imposed at a flat rate.

Compared with a value-added tax, income type, the income tax should exert no differential effect on risk-taking, aside from the progressive rate scale and other special features, since the two taxes are conceptually alike in their treatment of favorable and unfavorable outcomes. A loss is allowed to reduce other taxable value-added, e.g. from the firm's wage bill. In contrast, the turnover tax, as has been noted in Chapter 8, Section A.4.B, or any other sales tax that strikes producers goods, takes no account at all of losses. Whether the outcome of the investment is favorable or not, the tax included in the cost of the capital good is the same. Variance of outcomes from the real investment may thus be increased by the turnover tax, and because of this possibility that tax presumably causes more capital to settle in the less risky industries than under either the income tax or the value-added tax, consumption type. All this, to be sure, is but sketchy conjecture, in a field that is yet to be explored in depth.

24. See the corresponding analysis of completely accelerated depreciation, in Chapter 11, Section B.2.C.

An income tax affects the balance of payments through both the balance of trade and the international movement of capital. Since the effects of the several types of income tax differ less than the effects of the various type of sales tax, discussion of this point is deferred, in contrast to the treatment in Chapter 8, to Chapter 24 (see also Chapter 25, p. 647).

The effect of the income tax on the supply of labor has been discussed in Chapter 11, Section B.3.B in terms of excess burden, on the assumption that the wage before tax remained unchanged. The effect of the tax on the wage rate, and through that on the supply of labor, must be discussed in differential terms.[25] If high-wage labor (of executives, professional men, and the like) responds more to the substitution effect that does low-wage labor, and not very strongly to the heavier income effect that the income tax imposes on it relative to that under an equal-yield value-added tax (even of the income type), replacement of the value-added tax by a progressive personal income tax will reduce the amount of high-wage labor and increase that of low-wage labor. This may be a likely outcome, at least in some of the highly industrialized economies.[26]

Under the usual assumption of diminishing marginal utilities of income and leisure, a proportional rate income tax can always be found, for a given taxpayer with fixed tastes and opportunities to trade leisure for income, that will induce him to supply more labor than he will under any progressive-rate income tax schedule that takes the same amount of tax revenue from him. That same amount of revenue (if it is not the maximum revenue that can be extracted from him) can however be obtained by more than one proportional rate of tax; for a low tax rate on an income representing a certain amount of work there can be substituted a higher tax rate on a certain smaller income representing a smaller amount of work. Then there may in general be one or more progressive rate schedules of equal yield to these proportional-rate taxes that will induce this taxpayer to work more than he will under the second of these proportional rates. But there will be no progressive-rate schedule that will induce him to work more than he will under the most work-inducing proportional rate.

In the more important case of a group of individuals, with varying tastes and opportunities to trade leisure for income, no such general conclusions hold; it is impossible to say a fortiori whether the most work-inducing proportional tax rate schedule will induce more or less work than the most work-inducing progressive rate schedule of the same yield.[27]

More than any other tax, the income tax affords opportunities to stimulate households and firms to make outlays that serve a public purpose, that is, give rise to socially positive externalities (see Chapter 2, Section B(2) (f)). The stimulus to giving is increased by the progressive rate scale, as income increases. Is such an

25. For a note on how the individual price-taking firm might be expected to react to a tax on payrolls in the short run, see Chapter 16, page 410.

26. See footnote 44, page 311, Chapter 11, on Harberger's findings.

27. See Robin Barlow and G. R. Sparks, "A Note on Progression and Leisure," *American Economic Review* (June, 1964), 54: 372–77, and J. Head, "A Note on Progression and Leisure: Comment," *American Economic Review* (March, 1966), 56: 172–79, and "Reply" by Barlow and Sparks, *ibid.*, 180.

increase in inducement to giving consistent with the policy that underlies deductibility of these contributions?

In practice, gifts to religious organizations aggregate to a larger sum than do other types of donation in the lower income groups.[28] It is in these groups that the tax stimulus to giving is the least. This is as it should be, in the view of those who believe that expenditure for religious purposes is not an appropriate expenditure for government, whether made directly through the budget or indirectly through income tax deductions. Another view is that government should support religious institutions, but only indirectly, through tax relief to donors and tax exemption for the institutions, in order to avoid social tensions that might develop in the course of the budgetary process: in deciding, for example, how much of the budget for religious support should be allocated to each organization.

Direct appropriation by government may be more efficient, per dollar of government expenditure, or revenue loss, than is stimulation by tax concessions. The private giving stimulated by the deductibility of the donation may easily be less than the tax revenue thus foregone.

To maximize private giving for a specified revenue loss, the government should probably share more heavily in the contributions made by low-income households than in those made by high-income households, that is, reverse its current procedure under a progressive tax rate system. Much of this tax concession to the rich is probably wasted in the sense that they would give a large part of what they now give, even if the government's share were only 10 or 20 per cent instead of 60 or 70 per cent; they would do so because they are rich. The low-income groups are here assumed to respond more to the tax concession, that is, the elasticity of demand for charitable giving (demand by the donor) is, by this argument, greater for the low-income household than for the high-income household.[29] The goal of maximizing private giving for a given revenue loss is itself a value-judgment assumption, however; for social purposes it may be worth sacrificing efficiency for obtaining what is deemed a better distribution of private giving by income class.

Intragovernmental coordination involves chiefly these questions: Shall the government tax the salaries and wages that it pays? Shall it tax the debt interest it pays? The almost universal answer in practice is Yes to the first question and No to the second. This response may seem odd, in view of the facts that impairment of progressivity is more serious when interest on debt is exempt, since each wage salary, but not interest on each bond, can in principle be adjusted to offset the degree of progressive tax escaped by the particular individual, and since much of the bond interest is received by individuals in the very high bracket rates. Also, the option to borrow or not to borrow is much greater than the option to vary the amount of labor engaged. Perhaps the explanation, in the face of these considerations, is a belief that, given the proposition that it would be too obvious a breach of progres-

28. For data on the United States, see C. Harry Kahn, *Personal Deductions in the Federal Income Tax* (Princeton, N.J.: Princeton University Press, 1960), p. 82. For a comparison of the United States provisions with those of other countries under income tax, death tax, and gift tax laws, see Jeffrey Schaefer, "Tax Incentives to Promote Charitable Giving, for Selected Countries," *Bulletin for International Fiscal Documentation* (October, 1966), 20: 413–16.

29. See Shoup, *Federal Estate and Gift Taxes*, pp. 64–65.

sivity to exempt government employees without reducing salaries and wages from those in the private sector by different proportions at different income levels, such a readjustment of compensation would be too delicate a process. The selling of debt, on the other hand, this argument would run, is an impersonal process; it can be accomplished in large blocks through middlemen. The resulting breach of progressivity, though more serious, is less obvious, and hence is more acceptable to the public. Also, a certain readjustment downward of the interest rate is accomplished by the market. It is of course an incomplete adjustment, since it is the same for all purchasers of the obligations, regardless of the rate of income tax escaped. Finally, total debt service is a figure publicized more than the total government wage bill; and a low coupon rate on an issue of debt expresses apparent economy in a way not open to the government as an employer. These somewhat spurious arguments seem to be all that can be cited to explain the difference in treatment actually accorded in most countries to government interest payments as against government salaries and wages.

The income tax is almost never deducted in computing the base of any other tax imposed by the same government; in this it is virtually unique.

In a number of jurisdictions the income tax paid the previous year is deducted from the income of the current year to arrive at the current year's taxable income. Under this provision a higher nominal rate is required to obtain a given yield over a long period of years. Over a short period, the tax rate would have to be changed every year if each year's yield were to be the same as it would be under a stable tax rate but without allowing deduction of the previous year's tax. If deduction is allowed of the previous year's tax, an unchanged proportional rate will amount to a fluctuating rate on income before subtracting income tax. This equivalent fluctuating rate will swing, in alternate years, above and below the long-term rate that it will eventually reach, through a dampening of these fluctuations.[30] Another undesirable consequence of allowing the income tax of the previous year to be deducted is that it discriminates against irregular income even more than the usual income tax, if rates are progressive.

5. Intra-System Reactions on Yields

An increase in income tax rates does not usually change, through reactions of the market in the private sector, the base of another tax, except possibly that of the property tax. By reducing the after-tax return that is capitalized to arrive at the value for a property tax, an increase in an income tax may reduce the base and hence the yield of a property tax. But this effect is apt to be only partial, and delayed, because of lag between changes in income and changes in assessed values. The yield of the income tax, on the other hand, is sensitive to changes in rates of other taxes, insofar as they are allowed as deductions in computing net taxable income.

30. See Shoup, *The Tax System of Brazil* (Rio de Janeiro: Fundação Getúlio Vargas, 1965), pp. 50, 85.

If the price level rises, under inflationary finance, the yield of the progressive-rate income tax will increase in real terms as long as the price rise is moderate. If prices rise by 50 to 100 per cent a year or more, the real meaning of the exemptions and brackets becomes so different from what was envisaged that both taxpayer compliance and administrative effort fall off, and the yield may no more than maintain itself in real terms, if that. Under a rapid and long-continued inflation the exemption and rate brackets will either be changed frequently or will be stated in some real unit, such as the money amount of a minimum annual wage that itself is changed to keep up with inflation.[31] In either case the income tax loses its power to increase its yield in real terms and thus automatically loses its power to reduce the share of the task of resource diversion that is allotted to inflation.

The equity of the tax also suffers along with the real yield where only a part of the tax is paid with a significant lag, as when taxes on salaries are withheld but taxes on profits are paid in a following year. And a tax on capital gains is likely to become so erratic in its impact as to lead to abandonment of this part of the tax altogether.

C. PARTIAL INCOME TAXES

1. Aggregate Base Relative to that of Value-Added Tax

Under a partial income tax the personal exemptions are so high that they outweigh the broader conceptual scope of the income tax base relative to that of the value-added tax. A considerably higher average tax rate is therefore required to obtain an equal yield.

2. Incidence

A. OPEN ECONOMY

Under a schedular tax system capital outflow can never equate marginal tax rates among the various domestic capitalists. Mortgage interest, for example, will remain taxed at, say, 8 per cent and proprietorship profit at 10 per cent. But in a small, capital-mobile economy, the pre-tax rates of return will rise by differing amounts, through flow of capital abroad, to compensate for the differences in domestic tax rates. Thus the schedular rate differences do not, under these circumstances, impose differential burdens; they merely change the proportions in which various types of capital are used at home. The schedular tax on investment in general is in such an economy shifted to consumers and labor. This conclusion must of course be modified to the extent that certain types of capital are not mobile and so cannot take advantage of rates of return prevailing abroad.

31. As in Brazil, 1963–64 (see Shoup, *The Tax System of Brazil*, pp. 28–34).

If the foreign demand for domestic capital is less than perfectly elastic, some of the tax burden rests on the capitalists, but there is still no differential burden as among the types of capitalist, despite the differences in schedular rates. In general, then, the ostensible aim of the differences in the schedular rates is defeated by mobility of capital in an open economy, even if home capital must accept a somewhat lower rate of return abroad, because of the pressure it puts on the market there, than it was earning at home before the tax was imposed.

The residence basis is not used for schedular taxes that impose varying rates on varying types of capital income. It would often be difficult for the domestic tax administrator to disprove a taxpayer's contention that his foreign-source income was from that type of capital that is accorded the lowest tax rate.

B. DIFFERENTIAL INCIDENCE

Since a partial income tax strikes almost all income from capital but only a small part of labor income, such a tax would make disposable incomes less unequal than under a universal income tax, but more so than under a corporation income tax.

3. Consensus Criteria

The partial income tax may score a little better than the universal income tax under the equal treatment criterion, because it is less extensive and is thereby exposed to somewhat fewer occasions for discrepancies. Still, the more serious defects of the universal income tax remain important under the partial tax, since that tax will in practice reach many if not most homeowners, beneficiaries of trust funds, and shareholders and partners and sole proprietors. On the other hand, it will avoid, by its high personal exemptions, a large part of the problems posed by imputed labor income, income from cooperatives and insurance companies, non-money wages, contributions to pension funds, and the like; and the degree of dispersion of rates of evasion will perhaps be less than under the universal tax. Dispersion in costs of compliance will certainly be less under the schedular form of the partial tax, for that form relies heavily on collection at source. But the schedular form provokes new difficulties, as each item of income must be assigned to its proper schedule. Qualitative discontinuities and an increase in uncertainty are common results of a schedular tax.

The partial income tax is probably more sensitive to cyclical fluctuations than the universal income tax because the personal exemption is so high, but if it is very high the personal incomes remaining taxable may consist largely of fairly stable investment income. In any event the effect on employment of whatever built-in flexibility there is must be rather low; on balance, the partial income tax is likely to be a poorer stabilizer than the universal income tax.

The partial income tax creates the same kinds of excess burden through divergence in rates of substitution as does the universal income tax except that wage labor is commonly not involved, owing to the high personal exemptions. Ownership organization and methods of financing are apt to be less affected under those schedular systems that apply the same rate scale, often a graduated one, to business earnings of all description, whether corporate or non-corporate, and regardless of the size of the owners' other types of income. Dividends are not taxed under these systems. Some schedular systems apply to corporate incomes a graduated rate scale that is also applied to individuals' income (excluding dividends); the tax differential between corporate and non-corporate enterprise is usually still not as great as under the non-schedular systems. But the resultant degree of progression of the corporate tax rate scale gives even more inducement to split an enterprise into a number of corporations, each with an income small enough to enter only the lowest income bracket. Since these income tax systems commonly do not take account of gains or losses on corporate securities, they encourage a formal sort of corporate legal decentralization.[32]

4. Conflict Criteria

A schedular tax that allowed averaging of each type of income separately, over the years, could be much less progressive than the rate structure would suggest, if the various types of income fluctuated out of phase. In an extreme case, let a taxpayer receive one type of income that fluctuates from zero in Year 1 to 100 in Year 2, back to zero in Year 3, and so on, while he receives another type of income that fluctuates from 100 in Year 1 to zero in Year 2, to 100 in Year 3, and so on. If each schedular income could be averaged separately over the years, this individual would pay, each year, two taxes on 50 of income. Under a non-schedular tax he would pay one tax on 100 each year. In practice, it appears that such averaging has not been permitted under the schedular taxes. A policy that segregates even one year's income into several compartments is not likely to be sympathetic to the combining of several years' incomes.

Size and composition of the family influence the amount of tax paid under the uniform partial income tax, but the schedular tax, at least in its extreme form, gives no allowance for dependents, although it does not necessarily require all the family's income under any one schedule to be lumped.[33]

Deductions for outlays not made in order to obtain income do not fit readily into a schedular system; there is no one type of income more than another from which heavy medical expenses or contributions to charitable organization, for example, should be deducted. Commonly, such deductions are not allowed.

A partial income tax can differentiate geographically in favor of low-income regions even less effectively than the universal tax, the personal exemptions being so

32. See Chapter 11, Section B.3.B.

33. In Venezuela, for example, the tax is computed separately for earnings of husband and wife, although such earnings are community income (Shoup and others, *The Fiscal System of Venezuela*, p. 95).

high that few persons will have been paying income tax in the depressed region before geographical differentiation is introduced.

The effects on allocation of resources under the universal income tax will obtain also under the partial income tax, schedular or non-schedular, with due allowance for differences in rate scales, offset provisions, and the like.

APPENDIX TO CHAPTER TWELVE

The assumption that the investor is sensitive only to mean return and variance[1] implies (aside from restrictions on the nature of the distribution) a quadratic utility function for sure-thing income, the function being limited to values where marginal utility is positive. Such a function implies that the indifference map describing the investor's sensitivity to the mean return and the variance has the following characteristics, provided (1) the investor maximizes expected utility and (2) he is a risk-averter, not a risk neutralist or a risk-lover, that is, for him the marginal utility of sure income decreases as income increases. With mean return measured on the vertical y-axis and risk defined as standard deviation measured on the horizontal x-axis, the indifference curves slope up to the north-east, convex to the origin. Thus the slope of any one curve increases as the standard deviation and mean increase. For any given standard deviation (any given point on the x-axis) the slopes of the indifference curves become steeper as the mean return increases; the lower indifference curves are flatter than the higher ones, for a given degree of risk.[2] This

---

1. For a discussion of the usefulness of considering higher moments, see Marcel K. Richter, "Cardinal Utility, Portfolio Selection and Taxation," *Review of Economic Studies* (June, 1960), 27: 152–66, especially pp. 154 and 155; and J. Tobin, "Liquidity Preference as Behavior Towards Risk," *Review of Economic Studies* (February, 1958), 25: 65–86. The pioneering analysis of Evsey D. Domar and Richard A. Musgrave, "Proportional Income Taxation and Risk-Taking," *Quarterly Journal of Economics* (May, 1944), 58: 387–422, reproduced in summary form in Musgrave, *The Theory of Public Finance*, pp. 312–22, implied, by its definitions of what the investor is sensitive to [(1) risk defined as the mean value of the probability-weighted loss outcomes of a venture rather than as the standard deviation of all the probability-weighted outcomes, (2) gain defined as the mean value of the probability-weighted gain outcomes, and (3) the mean value of all probability-weighted outcomes ("yield")], that, if he is an expected-utility maximizer, he has a linear utility function for money income, with a kink in the line at zero yield. Such a utility function cannot give rise to the type of indifference curves (the same type as those assumed in the text above) used by Domar and Musgrave. See Marcel K. Richter, *loc. cit.*, pp. 155–57. Still, as Richter notes, the Domar-Musgrave conclusion that a proportional income tax with complete loss offset will induce a risk-averting investor to prefer a venture with a social risk greater than that of the one he would have chosen in the absence of such a tax, is not necessarily invalid under the assumptions appropriate to that type of indifference curve between mean return and risk defined as standard deviation.

2. Derived from Richter, *loc. cit.*, p. 154. Richter shows that $\sigma^2_y = (\alpha/\beta)\,\bar{y} - \bar{y}^2 + \text{constant}$, where α and β are the coefficients in the quadratic utility function and $\bar{y}$ is the mean return, and that therefore "the indifference curves will all have identical slopes at the same $\bar{y}$." This quadratic relation can also be used to show that at the same σ (as well as at the same σ^2) the slopes increase as $\bar{y}$ increases, where σ (or σ^2) is on the x-axis and $\bar{y}$, on the y-axis.

fact amounts to saying that as this kind of investor's mean return is reduced he becomes more willing to assume risk in the following sense. At a low mean return he is indifferent between a slight increase in mean return and a considerable decrease in risk (the indifference curve slopes upward only gently); at a high mean return, and the same risk, he is indifferent between a considerable increase in mean return and a slight decrease in risk (the indifference curve slopes steeply upward). Thus, when he is moved down to a lower mean return, this investor with a quadratic utility function for sure-thing income will be ready to increase his private risk-taking considerably if he can obtain a small increment in mean return.

Given this type of indifference map for mean return and risk, a public finance measure that reduces the mean and the risk of a venture by the same proportion places that venture on a lower indifference curve but at a flatter segment. It can be shown that under these circumstances an increase in the rate of a proportional income tax with full loss offset leads to a shift in investment pattern such that the investor's portfolio pre-tax mean income and variance rise.[3]

If the government can treat the investor even more generously, by reducing the standard deviation while leaving the mean return unchanged, it may be able to attract investors to more risky ventures even if the slopes of the indifference curves do not follow the pattern described above, depending on how the investor's indifference curves change slope as risk changes for a given mean return.

The way in which the government might reduce risk for the investor while leaving his mean return unchanged may be illustrated as follows. Let a certain venture, under no taxation and no subsidy, offer the prospect of returning a total of either 150 or 90 from an investment of 100, the two outcomes being equally likely. The mean gross return is 120, the mean net return (i.e. after recouping the amount invested) is 20 and for both the gross return and the net return the standard deviation is 30. Now let the government announce that a subsidy of 10 will be paid if the gross outcome turns out to be 90 (a net loss, before subsidy, of 10) and that a tax of 10 will be imposed in the event of a net return of 50; this amounts to a 100 per cent subsidy in the event of loss and a 20 per cent tax in the event of gain. The gross-return outcomes are now 100 and 140. The mean gross return remains at 120 and the mean net return at 20, while the standard deviation, for both gross return and net return, falls from 30 to 20.

If, on the other hand, the loss offset is given only at the same rate as the positive tax, the mean gross return and net return will both be reduced. The mean gross return will be reduced by a proportion smaller than the tax rate, the mean net return by a proportion equal to the tax rate. The standard deviation of both gross return and net return will be reduced by a proportion equal to the tax rate. In terms of the example above, if the tax rate is 20 per cent, the gross return under this tax, with complete loss offset, will be either 150 minus 10 tax, that is, 140, or 90 plus 2 tax rebate, that is, 92. The standard deviation of the gross returns or the net returns is reduced (from the no-tax situation) from 30 to 24, i.e., by the tax rate, 20 per cent.

3. Richter, loc. cit., p. 161. For a general equilibrium analysis of this point, under a corporation income tax, see Aiko Shibata, op. cit., Chapter 3.

The mean gross return is reduced only from 120 to 116, a reduction of but $3\frac{1}{3}$ per cent. The mean net return, i.e., after depreciation, is reduced by a proportion equal to the tax rate, that is, from 20 to 16.[4]

4. For analysis of effects of taxation on risk taking, see also Harry M. Markowitz, "Portfolio Selection," *The Journal of Finance* (March, 1952), 7: 77–91; Rudolph G. Penner, "A Note on Portfolio Selection and Taxation," *Review of Economic Studies* (January, 1964), 31: 83–86, and "Uncertainty and the Short-Run Shifting of the Corporation Tax," *Oxford Economic Papers* (March, 1967), 19: 99–110; William F. Sharpe, "Capital Asset Prices: A Theory of Market Equilibrium under Conditions of Risk," *The Journal of Finance* (September, 1964), 19: 425–42; and Jan Mossin, "Taxation and Risk-Taking: An Expected Utility Approach," *Economica* (February, 1968), 35: 74–82. Mossin's analysis requires no assumption about the investor's utility function, aside from risk aversion, or about the distribution of outcomes, but does require that the yield on one of the assets be known with certainty.

CHAPTER THIRTEEN

Expenditure Tax

A. CONCEPTUAL BASIS

A PROGRESSIVE-RATE TAX on a household's total consumption expenditure is either a supplement to the income tax or a substitute for it. As a supplement, it is imposed on only a wealthy few, chiefly to check or to penalize consumption deemed extravagant or ostentatious, or to reach indirectly, when the money is spent, income obtained in forms that escape the income tax, notably capital gains. In this form the expenditure tax yields a negligible amount of revenue. Experience with it has been limited to two countries, for about a decade.[1]

As a substitute for the income tax, including the corporation income tax,[2] the expenditure tax becomes either a mass expenditure tax, corresponding to the universal income tax, or a uniform but partial, that is selective, expenditure tax. No

1. This is the type of expenditure tax enacted in India in 1957 and Ceylon in 1959. See Walter W. Brudno, Charles K. Cobb, Jr., and Nani A. Palkhivala, *Taxation in India*, World Tax Series, Law School of Harvard University (Boston: Little, Brown, 1960), p. 422; K. C. Khanna, "An Expenditure Tax in India," *Bulletin for International Fiscal Documentation* (September, 1964), 18(9): 353–63; and "World Tax Review," *Bulletin for International Fiscal Documentation* (May, 1966), 20(5): 201–202. The initial Indian tax applied to that part of the annual expenditure of an individual or a Hindu undivided family in excess of Rs. 30,000 (1 rupee was worth approximately 21 cents in 1960), but taxpayers with incomes, after income tax, of not over Rs. 36,000 were exempt (*Taxation in India*, p. 425). "The imposition of the expenditure tax was the subject of considerable public controversy and aroused strong opposition. The Select Committee had to provide numerous exemptions and allowances . . ." (Khanna, *loc. cit.*, p. 360). The tax supplied one-tenth of one per cent of the national tax revenue in each of the four financial years ending in 1959–62. It was repealed in 1962 at the request of a new finance minister. When the finance minister who had introduced the expenditure tax was reappointed (1964), he reintroduced the tax (*ibid.*, p. 361). It was again repealed, in 1966, because of administrative difficulties and the fact that the yield was only about Rs. 60 lakhs (Rs. 1 lakh = Rs. 100,000), much the same as the yield of the earlier tax (*Bulletin for International Fiscal Documentation* [May, 1966], 20[5]: 201–202).

2. An alternative program would retain the corporation income tax. But this system is internally inconsistent unless the corporation income tax is viewed as one to be shifted forward to the consumer (Cf. Nicholas Kaldor, *An Expenditure Tax* [London: Allen and Unwin, 1955], Chapter 5, "Company Taxation"). "If the system of personal income taxation were replaced by a personal expenditure tax, the logical counterpart in the field of business taxation would be to abolish all taxes on undistributed profits and to turn the present [British] investment allowance (at any rate, initially) into an investment tax" (*ibid.*, p. 177).

experience is available with either of these types of expenditure tax. With one exception (Kaldor)[3] the most vigorous proponents of the expenditure tax as a substitute for the income tax (J. S. Mill and Irving Fisher, among others) wrote before the era of mass income taxation and before corporation income tax rates on the order of 50 per cent; the implied rate schedule of the expenditure tax they had in mind and the number of households it would cover are those of a modest, though not extremely mild, tax restricted to middle- and upper-income classes.

Mill and Fisher emphasized a concept of income that is equated with consumption. To tax that part of income saved and also, in later years, the interest earned on the saving is in this view to tax the same thing twice, since the present value of the saving is but the discounted reflection of the stream of future interest.[4] An undercurrent of apprehension that capital formation would thereupon be less, at least within the taxing country, than under an expenditure tax may be sensed, but Mill and Fisher would have been bound to adhere to an expenditure tax even if it would have decreased saving, relative to an income tax.[5] Substitution of an equal-rate expenditure tax for an income tax amounts to an increase in the rate of interest received by the saver (except in the unlikely event that the market rate of interest falls pari passu), without the income effect that accompanies such an increase, at least as to taxpayers in the aggregate, since the total amount taken in tax is stipulated to remain unchanged. In the aggregate, then, the change in tax policy represents an inducement to saving, on substitution account. The taxable base of the expenditure tax will be the smaller, hence a higher tax rate will be required to yield the same revenue.[6] But since this higher rate applies of course to both present consumption

3. Kaldor proposed "a restricted initial application of the principle . . . in the replacement of the present surtax [in the United Kingdom] by a tax on expenditure" [op. cit., p. 15). He concluded that "because of its administrative complexities it would never be a suitable tax for 15 million taxpayers" (ibid., p. 224), but there is a clear implication that it would be a suitable replacement for a partial income tax.

4. To tax both is therefore "to disturb, by artificial interference, the natural competition between the motives for saving and those for spending" (J. S. Mill, Principles of Political Economy, Ashley ed. [London: Longmans, Green, 1926], p. 814).

5. So too, it appears, would Marshall, although he favored taxing property "on inheritance and in some other ways . . ." (A. C. Pigou [Ed.], Memorials of Alfred Marshall [London: Macmillan, 1925], "The Equitable Distribution of Taxation" [written by Marshall in 1917], p. 350).

6. See A. R. Prest, "The Expenditure Tax and Saving," Economic Journal (September, 1959), 69: 483–89, and his Public Finance in Theory and Practice, 3d ed. (London: Weidenfeld and Nicolson, 1967), pp. 48, 81–86. If the tax rates are proportional, and if x is the income tax rate, e the expenditure tax rate, and c the fraction of income after tax (either income tax or expenditure tax) that is spent on consumption goods (ex the expenditure tax if any), then for equal yield,

$$e = \frac{x}{c\,(1 - x)}$$

This formula is a compound of (1) the formula for translating a tax rate on a base that includes the tax itself (the income tax rate is usually stated in this manner) to a tax rate on the same base but excluding the tax itself (the way an expenditure tax rate would presumably be stated), and (2) the formula for allowing for the fact that the expenditure tax base will be smaller still by reason of saving. The formula for part (1) is derived as follows. Let T be the tax revenue, B the tax base including the tax, t_x the tax rate on the base excluding tax, and t_i the tax rate on the base including tax. For equality of yield, $T = t_x\,(B - T) = t_i B$, and, substituting $t_i B$ for T,

and future consumption, it does not imply any weakening of the substitution effect of replacing an income tax by an expenditure tax. The aggregate income effect will be distributed differently among different income classes, and probably in a manner that will lead to still more of an increase in saving (on income account) to add to the stimulus given on substitution account. The difference on income account may not be great, however, since neither the income tax nor the expenditure tax is assumed here to reach down into the low-income groups. But it seems clear that on balance this particular tax substitution must lead to an increase in saving.

Under a progressive-rate expenditure tax, some households can save tax by post-poning part of their spending to a later year when their total spending will be lower, but others can save tax by moving spending up to an earlier year. It may pay a young couple to dissave heavily, chiefly through borrowing, to increase their current low rate of consumption. Over their lifetimes, this action may level off their humped curve of consumption spending by spreading parts of the hump over the two ends. The interest factor on the earlier paid tax of course mitigates against a completely uniform spreading.

The expenditure tax is to the income tax as the consumption type of value-added tax is to the income type of that tax. The consumption type of value-added tax is likely to be the preferred form, as that tax spreads.[7] It might be inferred that the reasoning that supports the consumption type of value-added tax would induce replacement of the income tax by the expenditure tax. But no such trend is apparent. The explanation may be that in the community's judgment a tax that is designed to vary with family status and level of well-being must be based on ability to consume rather than on actual consumption. This ability cannot be reached, on a family-by-family basis, under any kind of value-added tax.

An income tax that allows deduction of saved income is equivalent to an expenditure tax only if it also requires that the deduction be algebraic, so that a negative saving is added to taxable income.[8] While many income taxes allow limited deduction of certain non-consumption uses of income, payment of life insurance premiums (up to some limit) for example, they usually do so regardless of whether the taxpayer saves or dissaves in the aggregate. Accordingly, none of the income tax proposals or laws approach closely an expenditure tax.

An expenditure tax may grant a dual personal exemption, one in terms of expenditure, and a higher one in terms of income. Then the expenditure tax is at one point a step function of income. For example, let the first $30,000 of expenditure be exempt, and let no one be taxable unless his income exceeds $36,000.[9] Then a taxpayer with $36,000 income whose expenditure is well above $30,000 incurs a heavy expenditure tax by increasing his income by one dollar.[10] This case would, to be sure,

we have $t_x = t_i/(1 - t_i)$. Thus a tax rate of $\frac{1}{10}$, for example, on a base including tax is equivalent to a tax rate of $\frac{1}{9}$ on a base excluding tax.

7. See Chapter 9, Section B.1.

8. As Irving Fisher's proposal did; his was a true expenditure tax. See Irving Fisher and Herbert W. Fisher, *Constructive Income Taxation* (New York: Harper, 1942), p. 8.

9. See the provision in the Indian law, note 1 above, page 345.

10. The increment in income may increase only the expenditure-tax bill, for it may be of a type exempt from the income tax (Brudno, Cobb, and Palkhivala, *op. cit.*, p. 425).

imply dissaving if the income tax itself was nearly $6,000 or more. Still, this notch feature violates the criterion of nearly equal treatment of taxpayers almost equally circumstanced. It imposes a rate of more than 100 per cent, or several thousand per cent, on the first dollar (or first cent!) of income above the exemption level.

If the income exemption were lower than the expenditure exemption, the number of taxpayers encountering this notch problem would be fewer. Those whose incomes were just at the exemption level could even be dissaving somewhat, without facing an expenditure tax bill upon receipt of one dollar more of income. Under the reverse relationship of the exemptions, unless the income tax itself fills the gap between the two exemptions, a taxpayer who is saving some of his income may nevertheless have to pay a heavy expenditure tax if he gets one dollar more of income. The number of these cases could of course be reduced by defining the income exemption in terms of disposable income, i.e., income after income tax.

Household expenditure can in principle be computed simply by subtracting from income the household's increase in net worth,[11] provided only that the definitions of expenditure and income are symmetrical. For example, if a gift made by the taxpayer is not deductible in computing his taxable income, computation of taxable expenditure by subtraction from income of the increase in net worth will automatically include the gift in taxable expenditure.[12] Again, if the household's real estate tax is deductible in computing income, it is automatically excluded from taxable expenditure, by the income and net worth method. That method will therefore yield the desired total of taxable expenditure only when any outgo that is not deductible in computing taxable income is also intended to be included in taxable expenditure. However attractive aesthetically such symmetry may be, few countries are likely to observe it. Gifts *inter vivos* and transfers at death, although universally not deductible in computing taxable income, are not likely to be called taxable expenditure as long as those transfers are taxed separately under gift and death taxes.[13] Losses by theft, or by fire or other casualty, although deductible in some countries in computing taxable income, are not likely to be regarded as undoing the expenditure made on the items initially, for purposes of the expenditure tax.[14] For certain other income-tax deductions, symmetry will no doubt prevail. Other taxes, the real estate tax for example, that are deductible for computing taxable income, would probably not be regarded as taxable expenditure.

11. There are several ways in which the constituent items necessary to reach the increment in net worth and the item representing income could be ordered in the process of computation (Kaldor, *An Expenditure Tax*, pp. 192–93, 215, and Fisher and Fisher, *op. cit.*, p. 8).

12. Let n_1 be the net worth at the start of the period and n_2 the net worth at the end of the period: Δn the increase in net worth, and y, the income. If g is the gift, and e the other expenditures.

$$n_1 + y - g - e = n_2, \text{ so that}$$
$$y - (n_2 - n_1) = g + e$$
$$y - \Delta n = g + e$$

13. The Indian tax exempted gifts and, evidently, transfers at death (Brudno, Cobb, and Palkhivala, *op. cit.*, p. 423). Kaldor urged taxation of gifts as expenditure, with some exceptions, as a safeguard against evasion (*An Expenditure Tax*, pp. 201–205).

14. Kaldor (*op. cit.*, pp. 210–11) would require that insurance have been taken out, if any expenditure tax relief were to be granted.

The expenditure tax itself would presumably not be deductible in computing taxable income. If it were, there would be a substantial reduction in the degree of progressivity added to the tax system by introduction of the expenditure tax. Nondeductibility, however, implies that the expenditure tax itself is a form of expenditure, if expenditure is defined as taxable income minus the taxpayer's increase in net worth.

An expenditure tax of a very restricted sort, designed merely to replace part of the high rates of a progressive income tax, would change somewhat the distribution of taxation among high-income households and might effect a change in the economy's aggregate saving, amount of risk-taking, and work. But the change would be small. This group of taxpayers supply a modest part of total saving, and their work habits would not be altered much by the changes in their real disposable incomes. These remarks assume that the corporate income tax would continue, and that capital gains and losses are taken into account in the income tax.

Accordingly, the analysis below disregards this very restricted type of expenditure tax and is directed to one that replaces entirely a partial uniform income tax, including the corporation income tax. Nothing is said about an expenditure tax that would replace a universal (mass) income tax; the formidable administrative problems facing a mass expenditure tax make detailed discussion of it unfruitful at this time.

The expenditure tax is assumed to be progressive, imposed on expenditure ex the expenditure tax; marginal tax rates may therefore rise above 100 per cent. It is of course not applicable to corporations or other business entities. The comparison for differential analysis, where needed, will be as usual with a value-added tax, consumption type. This comparison is of special interest here, since the expenditure tax is in principle imposed on the same aggregate base as that of the value-added tax, in a closed economy, except for the personal exemption and allowances for dependents.

B. INCIDENCE

1. Open Economy

The expenditure tax is a destination-principle tax; the product of a country is not taxed in the hands of consumers if it is exported, while imports are taxed when consumed. No compensating import tax is needed; in effect, the consumer pays a use tax (see Chapter 9, Section A.2.A) on everything he buys. The tax can even be made to cover embodied imports, that is, services that the individual consumes while abroad.[15]

15. The Indian expenditure tax applied to expenditure incurred outside India by citizens ordinarily resident in India. The tax was given an income-tax flavor by being imposed on expenditure abroad made from income or capital accrued or realized in India by nonresident citizens (and citizens "resident but not ordinarily resident") and by resident aliens (Brudno, Cobb, and Palkhivala, *op. cit.*, pp. 430–31).

In contrast to the value-added tax, the rate of tax on any particular import depends on the personal circumstances of the consumer, notably the total of his consumption from all sources. A foreign producer of luxuries must assume that his goods will bear a heavier average tax that do necessaries. He sees the problem, if he thinks of it at all, as one of reduced consumer demand. But if the foreign producer's supply to the taxing country is perfectly price-elastic, the consumer will be unable to shift any of the tax, back to the foreign producer, whatever the rate may be. Producers of import-competing goods will therefore escape any of the burden of the expenditure tax just as they do the burden of the turnover tax, or value-added tax (see Chapter 8), as long as demand does not fall so far as to eliminate imports. Producers for export bear none of the tax.

The households of a country that absorbs so large a part of the output of another country that the supply to it is not perfectly elastic will shift part of the tax to the producers of that country. In general, and speaking rather loosely, a large country will shift part of its expenditure tax to producers in small countries, especially producers of specialized luxuries, and a small country will shift little or none of its expenditure tax to producers in large countries.

2. Differential Incidence: Expenditure Tax and Value-Added Tax

Substitution of an expenditure tax for a value-added tax (consumption type) would in part advantage factors specialized in the production of necessaries relative to those specialized in the luxury trades. By income classes, these factors may be supposed to be distributed randomly. To this extent, the differential incidence by income classes would be nil. But the substitution would also favor low-expenditure consumers against high-expenditure consumers; on balance, the substitution would doubtless be progressive by income class.

Substitution of an expenditure tax for a personal income tax would enhance the disposable incomes of those who save and decrease that of those who dissave. For those parts of these taxes that affect households as consumers rather than as producers, and if income classes are measured by income for a given year rather than by income over a period of years, the differential incidence would be regressive, provided that identical progressive rate schedules were employed. In practice, the rate schedule of the expenditure tax might well be more progressive, if only because the rates can exceed 100 per cent (on the base computed ex-tax) and would have to be more severe in an average sense, to yield the same discounted value of revenue.

Many of the low-income households that would be taxed more heavily under the expenditure tax than under an income tax or even a value-added tax would be those living off retirement pensions and other forms of savings. For these persons the expenditure tax is a crude lifetime averaging device. But it operates quite differently from cumulative lifetime averaging under an income tax, which never requires more tax, in any given year, under any fixed rate schedule, than would be payable without the averaging device. The expenditure tax does require more tax, from retired dissavers, then would an income tax with an equal yield over the life span.

If income classes are defined in terms of lifetime incomes, substitution of an expenditure tax for a personal income tax is somewhat less regressive by income than just indicated, but still regressive, at least for an identical rate schedule.

The more inelastic the supply of saving, the larger is the proportion of the tax relief to saving that is captured by savers rather than by consumers of things made by capital-intensive processes, and the more regressive is the substitution of expenditure taxation for personal income taxation.

C. CRITERIA

1. Consensus Criteria

The expenditure tax has some advantage over the income tax with respect to the aim of treating equally circumstanced persons equally, and almost equally circumstanced persons almost alike, if only because the complex field of corporate profits and corporate distributions is bypassed, as are also capital gains and losses —unless expenditure is computed by subtracting the net-worth increment from income.

Certain non-recorded expenditure, imputed or offset, may not be reached by the expenditure tax law, imputed net rent being again an important item.[16] But non-attributed expenditure is far less frequent, if it exists at all, than non-attributed income, and there is no expenditure analogous to non-available income.[17] For much the same reasons, the expenditure tax will observe the rule of impersonality less well than a value-added tax, but better than an income tax. The optimum level of certainty may be as low as, or even lower than it would be under a personal income tax. There is the same problem of distinguishing between personal and business expenditures, including business entertainment expenditures, and there are a few new ones: distinguishing between expenditure and reciprocal gifts; between consumption expenditures and investment (but non-business) expenditures; between expenditures that do and those that do not have to be averaged,[18] or that give rise to

16. Apparently, such income was not taxed under the Indian expenditure tax, and the purchase of a dwelling for one's own use was apparently not taxed (Brudno, Cobb, and Palkhivala, *op. cit.*, especially p. 428, Chapter 15).

17. See Chapter 11, Section B.3.A.

18. "Prior to the [Indian] Finance Act of 1959, expenditures 'by way of investment' in bullion, precious stones, and jewelry were exempt." By that act, taxable expenditure included "Expenditure 'by way of capital expenditure' on the purchase of bullion, precious stones, jewelry, furniture and other household goods, automobiles and other conveyances, or any other articles 'for the personal use' of the taxpayer or any of his dependents," and all such expenditure had to be spread over a five-year period pro rata (Brudno, Cobb, and Palkhivala, *op. cit.*, pp. 426–27).

an option to average. Discontinuities are not great except as definitional problems create abrupt qualitative boundary lines. Rates of evasion must be very unequal, and cost of compliance no doubt varies widely. The average level of evasion (see Chapter 2, Section A.1.A) would be of significance, and the effort required to keep evasion down to a given level would be somewhat greater than under a personal income tax, since the information required, in addition to the taxpayer's income, would include that needed for a tax on net worth, with certain adjustments.[19]

The expenditure tax probably falls between the income tax and the value-added tax with respect to built-in flexibility. The efficiency of the built-in flexibility may be greater than for either tax. The taxpayer with room to maneuver may come to discount temporary income tax increases and decreases, continuing his expenditure over the entire cycle much as he would if the income tax rates were not changed, while an expenditure tax, or expenditure tax remission, known to be temporary will, because it is temporary, repress or stimulate expenditure.[20] Against this is to be set the perverse effect engendered by expectations that the expenditure tax will be reduced or increased.[21]

The expenditure tax does not change the ratio of possible consumption later to consumption now except as the level of spending varies, so that expenditure is subject to different marginal rates in the earlier and later years (unless averaging is used). If this variation in annual expenditure can be closely estimated and is fairly well assured, it may induce a good deal of shifting of consumption from now to later, or from later to now. By thus altering the rate at which consumption now can exchange against consumption later, the progressive-rate expenditure tax moves the household away from a Pareto optimum (with reservations, in a world of second-best), and creates excess burden. Insofar as saving offers imputed income in the form of , and a like amount of imputed expenditure on, prestige, power, and security, the expenditure tax discriminates in favor of this form of expenditure, against money expenditure, and so creates another type of excess burden. It may thus induce a wealthy person to hold his land idle if he can obtain prestige or some other psychic benefit that would be reduced if he put the land to work.

2. Conflict Criteria

Although the progressive-rate expenditure tax is progressive vis-à-vis the value-added tax, with respect to long-period income, it can be highly regressive among certain groups, if measured against the income of any one year. The community would need to have a fairly sophisticated concept of progressivity not to be impressed

19. For a somewhat more hopeful appraisal of the administration of an expenditure tax, see Kaldor, *An Expenditure Tax*, pp. 213–23. For the transition problem, especially the anticipatory hoarding of cash and double taxation of those living off capital that had been accumulated from taxed income, see *ibid.*, pp. 220–22.

20. On these points, see Kaldor, *op. cit.*, pp. 177–78.

21. See Chapter 22, Section B.1.

by the complaints of elderly persons living on annuities that they were being taxed more heavily than other households that enjoyed larger incomes.

The tax must take into account the composition and size of the family, if only by implication. If the law is silent on this score, and implies that each person is to be taxed separately on his own expenditure, a way is opened for husband or wife to incur expenditure on behalf of the spouse, financed by inter-spousal gifts, that will be artificial, yet difficult to term evasion rather than avoidance.[22] Expenditure on behalf of a dependent child will have to be attributed to one spouse or the other. The alternative of a compulsory joint return seems even less defensible than under the income tax, where the large incomes contain saving that may well benefit chiefly one member of the family. The benefit of family expenditure is more evenly divided among the members. Expenditure splitting would come closest to conforming to the rationale of the expenditure tax, and the revenue loss would be less than from splitting under the income tax, since under separate returns expenditure would be more nearly equally divided among, or on behalf of, the several members of the family than is income.

Some income taxes take into account both composition of income, especially the schedular taxes, and composition of expenditure, as in allowing deduction of medical expenses and other non-business outlays. An expenditure tax can take account only of the latter.

Geographical distribution of the tax will generally favor large countries at the expense of small countries (see page 350 above), but even the large country will be able to export only a small proportion of its expenditure tax.

The expenditure tax is unpromising as an instrument of differential taxation to aid depressed areas within the taxing country. Exemption of depressed areas from the tax would have to be on a residence basis. The direct benefit to most households living in the area would be small, since their expenditure levels would be so low as to exempt them anyway or to tax them at low rates. Some wealthy persons might take up residence in the depressed area, but most of their purchases might well continue to be made from firms located elsewhere, even from firms in other countries, all these purchases now being exempt.

Since it is collected directly from households, the expenditure tax is more vulnerable to manipulation for discrimination against ethnic, color, or status groups than are taxes collected from business concerns.

Saving, we have seen (Section A above) will be promoted by an expenditure tax, relative to an income tax. And if an expenditure tax were announced as temporary, say for five years, and if the announcement were believed, the tax might well cause massive saving, not fully matched in later years by dissaving.

With respect to risk-taking, the expenditure tax exerts no differential effect vis-à-vis the reference tax, i.e., the tax on value-added, consumption type. As does that tax, the expenditure tax in effect exempts the return from capital goods by taxing

22. This was the route taken by the Indian tax for all except undivided Hindu families: "Each spouse is taxed separately on expenditure incurred by him for his own benefit and out of his separate funds. . . . A spouse is . . . subject to tax on expenditure made on his behalf . . . by the other spouse" (Brudno, Cobb, and Palkhivala, *op. cit.*, p. 424).

only consumer goods. The progressive rate of the expenditure tax may make some difference, but it is not obvious, from the viewpoint of those who produce the goods to sell to the taxed consumer, what that difference might be.[23]

The country's balance of trade would experience an incremental surplus under an expenditure tax, since it is a destination-principle tax, and, as the tax would have no effect on financial flows, the balance of payments would improve.

The substitution effect with respect to work versus leisure would be small because the tax would not extend to the bulk of wage- and salary-earners. Among the rest, those who work chiefly to save and not spend later would not find the price of leisure much lowered. And if spendthrifts are not very sensitive to the price of leisure, they too would not work much less. On the whole, there would probably be a somewhat larger supply of labor under the expenditure tax than under an income tax of equal yield.[24]

As a stimulant to public-purpose outlays, donations to charitable organizations for example,[25] the expenditure tax may be either more or less effective than the income tax. It tends to be more effective because, for equal yield, the rates will be higher, hence the amount of tax saved by giving to a charity rather than by spending on oneself is greater. But it tends to be less effective in that it offers a third possibility, postponement of spending on oneself, at a better price than does the income tax, and a fourth alternative, indefinite accumulation of wealth through reinvestment of income, quite free of tax.

The manner in which the expenditure tax meets most of these criteria, consensus or conflict, depends on the treatment accorded expenditure on owner-occupied housing and, in an advanced economy, on automobiles and other expensive consumer durables. If the expenditure is taxed in full in the year made, and if the rates are steeply progressive and not averaged, many wealthy consumers may decide to rent rather than purchase, with consequent effects on distribution of the tax by income classes, on risk-taking, and even on location of business. These repercussions can be only partly avoided by a rule that spreads the expenditure over a few years. The logical procedure is to impute an expenditure equal to the interest foregone plus the depreciation and obsolescence suffered each year.[26]

---

23. The conclusions reached in Kaldor, *op. cit.*, pp. 118–20, are not accepted here, since the numerical example on p. 120 seems to imply that the consumer attaches no value to the option to consume the last £1,000 a year tax free, under no tax, compared with no such option under the expenditure tax. Moreover, the analysis assumes that an income tax induces the investor to take less, instead of more, risk.

24. Cf. Kaldor, *op. cit.*, Chapter 4, "Taxation and the Incentive to Work."

25. "Expenditure incurred within India for a public purpose of a religious or charitable nature is exempt" (Brudno, Cobb, and Palkhivala, *op. cit.*, p. 428).

26. The alternatives of taxing imputed expenditure and spreading the initial expenditure are discussed in Kaldor, *op. cit.*, pp. 196 ff. Kaldor seems to attach little or no importance to interest earned by deferring tax (*ibid.*, p. 197).

D. INTRA-SYSTEM REACTIONS ON YIELDS

Typically, the income tax will not be deemed a taxable expenditure, but the expenditure tax will not be deductible in computing taxable income.[27] An increase in income tax rates will therefore not affect the expenditure tax yield directly, but it will do so indirectly, by reducing, though of course by a smaller amount, expenditure on goods and services. An increase in rates of the expenditure tax will have no effect on the income tax revenue, except very indirectly as it induces the taxpayer to earn more, or less, income. Very likely the expenditure tax will include in its base excises and sales taxes on the things purchased.[28] Then an increase in an excise or sales tax rate will automatically increase somewhat the yield of the expenditure tax as long as demand for the product is of less than unit elasticity. But an increase in the expenditure tax rate will have no direct, special effect on the yield of the excises or sales taxes. Their yield may fall, of course, as households buy fewer units of everything when the expenditure tax is increased.

27. This was the procedure in India (Brudno, Cobb, and Palkhivala, *op. cit.*, pp. 192–93, 429).

28. Again, this was the procedure followed in India (*idem.*).

CHAPTER FOURTEEN

Property Taxation: Net-Worth
Tax, Capital Levy, Death and Gift Taxes

A. VARIETIES OF TAXES ON PROPERTY

"Property taxes" includes taxes on stock and transfer of, and flow from, property: taxes based on the value, area, soil classification and the like as of a given date; taxes that take a proportion of money income or crop yield in a year; and taxes on sale, lease, gift, bequest, or other transfer of rights to property. Property taxes are therefore the counterpart of payroll taxes but take forms that the latter cannot, since future labor is not usually capitalized. Together, the taxes cover all factor activity: taxes on capital and taxes on labor.

The economic and social consequences of any one of these property taxes depend chiefly on whether the tax

(1) applies to all property in general (G) or is restricted to one or a few types of specified property (g),

(2) is a personal tax in the legal sense, so that the tax official must ascertain the owner of the property in order to levy and collect the tax (P) or is an impersonal tax that can be levied and collected without regard to ownership (p),

(3) is levied on a net base after subtraction of liabilities (N) or on a base gross of liabilities (n),

(4) is imposed at a flat rate (F) or not (f),

(5) is deductible in computing the base of an income tax payable by the owner of the property (D) or is not deductible (d), and

(6) is imposed upon transfer of the property (T) or on stock or flow (t).

Only 5 of the 64 possible combinations from this list of six characteristics have been employed extensively. Another five or so may be included by listing all the varieties from country to country. The net-worth tax, for example, is usually levied at progressive rates, but there is at least one exception.[1] And exemptions from the tax are in some countries so extensive as to restrict it to a few types of property.

1. Germany.

357

The five widely used combinations are:

GPNfDt   net-worth tax
„   dt   capital levy
„   dT   death and gift taxes
gpnFDt   real estate and business property taxes
„   DT   taxes on transfers for a consideration

Most of the fifty-odd combinations that have not been used at all are unacceptable or at least unattractive for various reasons. A general tax on all forms of property (G), for example, must be levied on a base net of liabilities (N) if it is not to bankrupt low-income households that are heavily in debt. And once liabilities are taken into account, the tax in this G form cannot be levied and collected without ascertaining who owns the property, since the liabilities must be matched against the aggregate of property values in any one case; the tax cannot be impersonal (p). Being a personal tax (P), the general property tax (G) invites use of a progressive rate (f).

B. NET-WORTH TAX[2]

1. Conceptual Basis; Importance

The net-worth tax, or net-wealth tax, is regarded, in the few countries that use it, as a supplement to the income tax, helpful for three reasons. First, since it does not strike human capital, it serves somewhat the same purpose as does an earned income allowance in countries that do not levy a net-worth tax.[3]

Second, it indirectly strikes at imputed property income that escapes the income tax, notably the net imputed rental of owner-occupied dwellings, the imputed liquidity income derived from holding cash and low-yielding securities, and, where these objects are not specifically excluded from the tax base, the imputed income from viewing, and having others view, jewelry, art objects, and the like.[4]

Third, if the income tax does not reach capital gains, or does so only after a long period of accrual, the annual tax on net worth affords the only means of tapping those increments promptly.

2. The net-worth tax, or net-wealth tax, is found in Ceylon, Colombia, Denmark, Finland, Germany, India, Luxembourg, Netherlands, Norway, and Sweden. It is not imposed in France, Italy, the United Kingdom, or the United States. It is levied usually on the basis of residence, not location of property, and usually does not apply to corporations. The rates either range from about 0.1 per cent to 1.5 per cent on a progressive scale, or are flat at 1/2 of 1 per cent or (Germany) 1 per cent. See World Tax Series volumes and references in footnotes therein. For an analysis of economic effects of net worth taxes, see Alan A. Tait, *The Taxation of Personal Wealth* (Urbana, Ill.: University of Illinois Press, 1967), *passim*.

3. Notably the United Kingdom. Generally, the countries that use the net-worth tax do not give an earned income allowance under the income tax: for example, Germany and the Netherlands.

4. But in Sweden, down to a reduction of no more than 50 per cent of its original amount axable net wealth cannot be more than thirty times the taxpayer's combined net income before tax) from all sources (Norr, Duffy, and Sterner, *Taxation in Sweden*, p. 642).

Countries that impose heavy real estate taxes do not levy a net-worth tax.[5]

In contrast to the income tax, the net-worth tax commonly avoids extra taxation by exempting corporations.[6] Yet this exemption does not allow undistributed profits to go free of tax, since retention of profits tends to increase the value of the corporate shares, and this value is subject to the personal net-worth tax.

The personal exemption is usually not high enough to restrict the tax to extremely wealthy individuals, but the number of taxpayers is nevertheless far below the number of income tax payers. At rates that apparently average about $\frac{1}{2}$ of 1 per cent to 1 per cent, the tax commonly accounts for no more than 1 or 2 per cent of a country's tax revenue, if that.

The rate of the net-worth tax is in all countries set at a level that will allow the tax to be paid out of the income from the taxed asset, for all but very low yielding assets.[7]

If the net-worth tax were a universal, impersonal (*in rem*) tax at a uniform rate, the tax bill could never equal or exceed the income from the property, no matter how high the rate of tax. If it did so, the property, yielding no income after tax, would possess no value, and the tax itself would be zero.[8] But if, as is the case in practice, the tax is not applied to all property holders at a uniform rate, it can exceed the income from a certain property held by a certain individual, and still not reduce the market value of that property to zero. The property will have a positive value for (1) those who are exempt from the tax, either because their net worth is so small, or because they live abroad and can remove the property from the jurisdiction of the taxing country, and (2) those who are taxable, but at a low rate.

A lifetime cycle of saving and then dissaving, starting from zero capital and returning virtually to zero, is common to many households. The usual exemption of so much per person under the net-worth tax therefore makes it predominantly a tax that becomes effective in one's middle age, for those groups that accumulate but do not inherit or bequeath a substantial amount of property.

2. Incidence in an Open Economy

Partial equilibrium analysis for an open economy[9] suggests that if a small capital-importing country imposes a net-worth tax on a source basis[10] domestic capital that is internationally mobile will migrate and foreign capital will cease to flow in, until

5. Germany is an exception.

6. Germany, Luxembourg, and Norway are exceptions.

7. See, for instance, Gumpel and Boettcher, *Taxation in Germany*, p. 153.

8. See Appendix below, p. 380.

9. See Chapter 2, Section B.

10. George Jackson Eder, John C. Chommie, and Hector Julio Becerra (*Taxation in Colombia*, World Tax Series, Law School of Harvard University [Chicago: Commerce Clearing House, 1964], pp. 440–43), indicate that Colombia's net-worth tax is on a source basis; see especially the rules for determining where shares of stock are held (*ibid.*, p. 443). Moreover, deduction is allowed for all indebtedness of the taxpayer, including even debts owed to creditors outside Colombia (*ibid.*, pp. 452–53).

the rate of return in the taxing country has risen by enough to cover the tax. No new investment will be made in the country, whether to replace depreciated assets or to expand, until the tax has thus been fully shifted, in part forward to consumers, in part laterally to co-factors. In the extreme case, the tax will be fully shifted even if domestic capital is not perfectly mobile. This occurs when the supply of foreign capital is perfectly elastic and is so important a part of the total supply that the rate of return rises by the full amount of the tax before the inflow of foreign capital falls to zero.[11]

Under a residence tax, however, foreign capital employed in the country is exempt, and the domestic capitalist must emigrate with his capital to escape the tax. Few will care to do so. Most of those to whom the tax will apply will be infra-marginal residents; varying degrees of fiscal pressure are required to overcome "the natural reluctance which every man feels to quit the place of his birth, and the scene of his early associations."[12] The limited number of low-tax jurisdictions that supply suitable refuge suggests that even a fairly high rate of net-worth tax will not induce substantial emigration. Much depends, of course, on what the revenue is used for. Thus the capital-importing country's resident capitalists will be unable to shift the tax, since foreign capital employed in the country will be exempt from it. But this statement may hold in full only for non-risk capital.

If, as appears likely, the amount of saving available for investment of a kind that carries little or no risk is in almost perfectly inelastic supply, the rate of return on such investment will decline by the full amount of the tax, in this economy. Potential saving available for risky ventures, on the other hand, may well be sensitive to the reduction in the expected (mean) return relative to the dispersion of possible out-comes that is a feature of the net-worth tax because, in contrast to the income tax, it does not, in one sense, grant full loss offset in the event of an unfavorable outcome (see page 366 below). Such potential saving may then turn into consumption, or into safety-seeking capital, driving the pre-tax rate of return on such capital below what it was before the tax was introduced. In either case the before-tax mean rate of return on risk capital is forced up by the tax. A part of a purely residence-basis tax thus fragments into burdens on consumers buying and co-factors producing products made in risky businesses, and on owners of safety-seeking capital. Co-factors in and consumers of safe industries are benefited by the tax.

Commonly, in fact, both source and residence principles apply, source for capital supplied by foreign residents, residence for capital owned by residents. Then in a capital-importing country that is small, if equilibrium is reestablished while capital imports are still positive, the after-tax rate of return on safe capital and the after-tax mean-variance pattern on risk capital must be the same as under no tax, else the flow of foreign capital, the supply of which is presumed to be perfectly elastic, will not continue.

11. The reasoning is analogous to that employed for a turnover tax, in Chapter 8, Section A.2, where the supply of imports is assumed to be perfectly elastic, while the supply of import-competing goods is not.

12. David Ricardo, *Principles of Political Economy and Taxation*, Sraffa (ed.) (Cambridge: Cambridge University Press, 1952), pp. 247–48.

If the inflow of capital to the taxing country is so large relative to the world supply that it is not perfectly elastic in supply to that country, the pre-tax reward to capital in the taxing country declines as that inflow decreases; part of the tax is exported to the remaining foreign capitalists.

In a capital-exporting economy a pure source tax will not be borne by domestic capitalists as long as they can divert enough more of their capital to a perfectly elastic demand abroad, to raise the before-tax rate of return by the full amount of the tax. This result is likely only if the country is small. If the residence basis is used, the domestic capitalist cannot thus escape the burden of the tax, unless he migrates.

A residence-basis tax sometimes allows credit for foreign net-worth tax paid on the resident's property located abroad, up to a rate equal to the resident country's tax rate.[13] To this extent the residence-basis tax becomes a source-basis tax. If country A is initially not imposing a net worth tax, while Countries B, C, . . . do so, on a source-basis or source-and-residence basis, introduction of a residence-basis tax in A, with credit for foreign tax, does not increase the tax on its residents' capital that is invested in B, C, . . . unless A's tax rate exceeds one or more of the rates in the other countries. But it does increase the tax (from zero) on A's residents' investments in A. The initial equilibrium in distribution of A's residents' capital between A and B, C, . . . is thus disturbed; an incentive is given investors in A to move capital to B, C, . . . until the pre-tax rate of return in A rises by enough to restore the earlier relationship between post-tax rates of return on investment by A's residents in A and in B, C. . . . The applicable analysis with respect to incidence is that of a source tax, not a tax based solely on residence or on residence and source.

3. Differential Incidence: Net Worth Tax and Value-Added Tax

Substitution of a net worth tax for a value-added tax, consumption type, poses unfamiliar quantitative problems. The rate of the annual net worth tax, in place of being, say, 1 per cent, would have to reach 10, 15, or 20 per cent.[14] Even the maximum-revenue rate might not produce as much revenue as the usual value-added tax of 10 to 15 per cent. These percentage rates of net worth tax at the high levels represent, we recall, far larger percentages of income taken by the tax.

Business firms, having been paying under the consumption type of value-added tax no tax on income created by capital, and a substantial tax on labor income and other non-capital factors, would now pay no tax on value added by labor and other non-capital factors and a very heavy tax on value added by capital. In an economy of two factors, a tax on wages would have been replaced by a tax on capital, in behavioral terms.[15] In the short run, when all factors are in rather inelastic supply,

13. For example, Germany (Gumpel and Boettcher, *Taxation in Germany*, p. 163).

14. In Germany, in 1960, the 1 per cent net worth tax yielded DM 1.1 billion, against DM 16.1 billion from the turnover tax.

15. See the distinction between national-income definitions of value-added and behavioral definitions, in Appendix to Chapter 9, page 267.

relative product prices would not change much. Product prices would not change relative to factor prices. Instead, the disposable income of capitalists would decline severely relative to other disposable income.

Over the longer run, in a closed economy, the amount of capital offered for safe ventures might be only a little lower than otherwise. Capital for risky ventures would decline in volume until its mean yield had increased somewhat, though not by the full amount of the tax differential (see page 366 below). Some capital would move to safe ventures, pushing down the rate of return there. On balance, labor and other factors would gain, probably even those working with risk capital.

If the net worth tax is substituted for the progressive part of the personal income tax, above the levels where property income becomes important,[16] much of the open-economy analysis above is applicable, where the move is from a zero tax on capital to a heavy tax. The differential-incidence approach adds the fact that simultaneously a tax on other factor incomes is repealed. Although the other factors are far less mobile internationally than is capital, there are many skilled and internationally mobile executives and professional men among those whose real disposable income would be increased by the tax change. Fewer of them would emigrate, and more would enter the country. As a result, the marginal productivity of capital should rise, thus reducing the decline in disposable income of capitalists.

4. Criteria

A. CONSENSUS CRITERIA

The equity criterion of equal treatment is not closely observed under the net worth taxes, even at the prevailing low rates. Admittedly irrelevant circumstances are allowed to influence the amount of tax, chiefly in the valuation process, where crude methods, or values fixed long ago, are accepted partly because otherwise the degree of evasion would vary too widely.[17]

16. Such a comparison, together with consideration of effects on saving, risk-taking, and work, is given in A. T. Peacock, "Economics of a Net Wealth Tax for Britain," and R. C. Tress, "A Wealth Tax Is a Wealth Tax," *British Tax Review* (November-December, 1963), pp. 388–409.

17. Under the German net-worth tax the value of real property is that determined by the most recent principal assessment, which, as late as 1963, was that of January 1, 1935. However: the physical characteristics and the condition of the property are considered as they exist on the date for which the redetermination is made. . . . The difficulties of computing the value of the property for a date more than a quarter century past are obvious, especially where a rental value must be determined for property that was not rented or not even in existence in 1935 (Gumpel and Boettcher, *op. cit.*, pp. 722–23).
As to securities:
In default of sales, the fair market value of an investment is estimated. In order to safeguard the equal application of the law [equal, it appears, only within each subgroup], the government has developed special formulae which are applied in the valuation of unlisted investments, especially membership rights in limited liability companies and in closely held corporations. According to the method formerly applied, . . . the fair market value of a company was computed as the mean between its net worth (based primarily on the assessed value of the company's property) and earning capacity (based on the average profits of the

The laws are reasonably impersonal and achieve a fair degree of certainty, but at the cost of many discontinuities. Some of them are qualitative; exemption is commonly granted to certain personal and household effects but not others, or at least only up to a certain figure.[18] Definitions must be given for "resident," for varieties of family status (spouses "permanently separated"; "child"), for a foreign tax that is substantially similar to the domestic net-worth tax (so that it may be credited against the domestic tax), and for the practice of a profession as distinguished from purely scientific or artistic activities.[19]

Some of the discontinuities are quantitative: exemptions may disappear suddenly rather than dwindle;[20] standard procedures must sometimes be supplemented.[21] Degrees of evasion vary substantially among taxpayers, except where arbitrary but readily enforceable rules of valuation are employed. The compliance cost may not be appreciable except for business firms.[22]

Since the decline in income from an asset in a business recession is usually not permanent, the capital value of the asset might be expected to fall by less than the recession dip in income. But conjecture about future income may range very widely in periods of speculation and depression. If net-wealth tax values were frequently and truly assessed the tax might easily show a greater cyclical sensitivity than an income tax. Changes in interest rates, however, would tend to maintain values in recessions and limit their increase in booms. Probably the built-in flexibility of a proportional net-worth tax is greater than that of a graduated income tax that is based largely on wage and salary income, but smaller than that of an income tax limited to investment income, including corporate and non-corporate profits. The effectiveness of the built-in flexibility must be rather low, since the tax is normally small relative to the resources of the wealthy upon whom it is imposed. Some

company for the preceding three years). In recent years this method has been abandoned in favor of another, . . . which puts greater emphasis on net worth and gives less weight to earning capacity (*ibid.*, p. 708).

18. The German net-worth tax exempts "the furnishings and equipment of the taxpayer's home, such as furniture and carpets, and objects for the personal use of the taxpayer and his family, such as clothing, linen, and books . . ." (*ibid.*, p. 735). But jewelry and similar items are taxable if their total value exceeds DM 10,000, and art objects are included if their total value exceeds DM 20,000 (except objects created by a German artist who is living or died within the past fifteen years) (*ibid.*, p. 734). But all precious metals or stones, and pearls not converted into jewelry, are taxable (*idem.*).

19. *Ibid.*, p. 725.

20. "A taxpayer who is over 60 years of age [the exemption vanishes suddenly at sixty years] or who can reasonably be expected to be incapable of self-support for at least three years [another sharp dividing line] can claim an additional tax-free amount of DM 5,000 if his total property . . . before exemption is not more than DM 100,000 [still another sharp boundary line]" (*ibid.*, p. 157).

21. In Germany, "a new assessment of net worth tax . . . must be made [in between the regular valuation dates, which may be several years apart] if the value of the taxpayer's total property" is more than DM 100,000 different from its value as of the last preceding assessment, "or more than one-fifth of the last assessed value. In the latter case, the change in value must further amount to more than DM 50,000 if the present value is higher, or more than DM 5,000 if it is lower" (*ibid.*, p. 161).

22. For an analysis of administrative problems of a hypothetical net-worth tax in the United Kingdom as a substitute for surtax, see G. S. A. Wheatcroft, "The Administrative Problems of a Wealth Tax," *British Tax Review* (November-December, 1963), pp. 410-22.

perverse changes in yield may occur. Securities values often fall before a depression takes hold, indeed while boom-time inflationary pressures still seem intense. And asset values may rise fairly sharply at the first signs of recovery from a depression; the net-worth tax might tend more than any other tax to slow up recovery through its automatic response.

Excess burden is created by the net-worth tax because, as does the income tax, it reduces the ratio at which future consumption can be substituted for present consumption. Saving will almost surely decrease if the net-worth tax is substituted for a value-added tax, consumption type, or even income type (see Chapter 12, Section 4.B, page 332). There is an important exception to this statement. In so far as the asset yields an imputed consumption of liquidity or status display, for example, the net-worth tax does not disturb the ratio of present consumption to future consumption; it taxes both, equally. But it penalizes these forms of imputed consumption compared with ordinary consumption, and so creates another kind of excess burden. An individual possessing $100,000 in cash can spend it all on luxuries this year or he can hold it in non-appreciating, no-yield assets and, with interest at 5 per cent, derive an imputed consumption of $5,000 a year in status display, etc. Under no tax, the present value of the stream of future imputed consumption is $100,000. Under an income tax it is still $100,000. But under a net-worth tax it is less than $100,000, because yearly imputed consumption cannot be as much as $5,000 while maintaining the capital intact and paying the annual net worth tax.

By disturbing the ratio of future ordinary consumption to present ordinary consumption the tax also disturbs the ratio at which most workers are willing to sacrifice leisure for income, since one of the options concerning use of income has been altered. The disturbance of this ratio is not an extra excess burden to be added to the one just noted; rather, it reflects that excess burden. But the reflection takes observable form in a reduction or increase in the amount of labor supplied under the net worth tax, compared with no tax.

B. CONFLICT CRITERIA

Even a flat-rate net-worth tax meets well the conflict criterion of progressive incidence by income, relative to the value-added tax. The damage the net-worth tax does to incomes of co-factors and to consumers of products employing capital-intensive processes is probably small, and distributed randomly by income class. But in small countries importing capital or, under a source-basis tax, exporting capital, the net-worth tax may be shifted to a degree such that its true differential incidence is regressive.

The net-worth tax can be adjusted to differences in family size and composition as readily as the income tax. If separate returns are required by husband and wife, a progressive-rate net-worth tax will induce intra-family transfers of property to minimize tax. Aggregation of family wealth and splitting, as under the income tax in some jurisdictions, seems indicated. The problem of interests in trusts, however, is virtually insoluble.[23]

23. See Wheatcroft, *op. cit.*, pp. 415–16.

Stimulus for charitable and other contributions, and relief for medical expenses, could be fully implemented under a net-worth tax only by allowing the current year's outlay for such purposes to be deducted constructively in computing net worth of the current year and all succeeding years. The current year's outlay would have reduced net worth, for the current year and all succeeding years, but by no more than any other outlay, including outlays for ordinary living expenses. For the extra stimulus, the fictional ("constructive") second deduction would have to be allowed.

Exemption of capital located in a depressed area within a country will tend to raise wage rates and employment there over a period of years. Since the tax does not reach labor income, the exemption will not directly induce an in-migration of labor that might check that rise. But the effect is apt to be modest, and slow. Not much of the net worth tax is likely to be exported to other countries.

The net-worth tax can be misused to discriminate by color, race, or status, since it is a personal tax, but the discrimination can be directed only against those who have risen enough, economically, to have accumulated capital.

Among the reallocation criteria, those of promotion of growth and of increase in amount of social risk taken are the most significant for the net-worth tax. The net-worth tax stimulates the use of property to yield money income rather than imputed income, for the tax is the same in either event (in contrast to the income tax), and only money income will help pay the tax. Land otherwise held idle will tend to be devoted to producing money income. In this sense the net-worth tax promotes economic growth. But if the land, or cash, or jewelry held "idle" yields an imputed income to the owner, income that he "consumes" as he receives it, any diminution in that kind of income that must occur when he puts his capital to work is an offset against the money income now earned, in computing the net increase in aggregate income.

It might be thought that even with respect to money income that is to be saved, the net-worth tax offers less deterrent to effort and saving than an income tax, because an increment to income is taxed at a substantial rate under the income tax but only at a low rate under the net-worth tax. And the income tax is repeated on a smaller scale each year by being imposed on the net return from that saving. The net-worth tax, however, is repeated every year also, and its discounted present value must be the same as that of this year's income tax and the present value of the string of smaller income tax payments, if the same present value of tax revenue is to be taken from the taxpayer. On the other hand, the option of consuming the capital, even if it is not exercised, may provide more incentive under the more deferred tax (the net-worth tax). Something depends, also, on how "equivalent present value" taxes are defined here, which includes the problem of whether a social or at least a governmental rate of discount of future tax payments shall be used that differs from the taxpayer's own rate of discount.

With respect to risk taking, the major issue is whether the net-worth tax reduces the loss in the event of an unfavorable outcome, by allowing a loss offset as the income tax does, or at least may do, or whether it increases the loss under such an outcome as does an ordinary excise tax. In the former case the dispersion of possible outcomes of a given venture is always reduced by the tax, a fact that tends to encourage risk taking by risk averters.

The answer is rather complex, for it depends on what two alternatives are being compared. If the net-worth tax is in force, and if the taxpayer is debating whether to undertake a certain venture rather than hold his funds idle, he will see that if he accepts the venture and then suffers a loss, the net-worth tax reduces that loss in the sense that if he did not undertake the venture his idle funds would still be taxed. To be sure, the tax takes a part of his diminished net worth if he undertakes the venture and incurs a loss, but it will take the same proportion of his idle funds if he does not undertake the venture. By thus taking the same proportion of either amount (the undiminished idle funds or the depleted investment value) the tax narrows the absolute difference between these two from what it would be under no tax. In this manner the net-worth tax provides a loss offset, one which never requires direct payment from the treasury.

But if we start with the assumption that in any event the taxpayer does undertake the venture, and compare his situation in the event of a loss under the net-worth tax with that under no tax, we see that his loss is larger under the net-worth tax than under no tax. The income tax, in contrast, reduces his loss in this kind of comparison, as it does also in the first comparison above, where the outcome under holding funds idle is compared with the outcome under the losing venture, and the difference is then compared with the similar difference under no tax. The latter is the more significant comparison for policy purposes, and so the net-worth tax can be said to resemble the income tax in allowing a loss offset, but it does so only because it pushes the holder of funds to employ them rather than hold them idle, either in a world of risk or in a riskless world. This pressure, in a world of risk, makes the loss outcome less serious to the entrepreneur; had he not undertaken the venture he would have "lost" part of his funds anyway, since the net-worth tax would have taken a part of them.

If the net worth tax extends to private corporations but not to government-owned enterprises, the latter can attract capital on better terms than competing private enterprises. The competitive advantage may also appear in other ways.[24]

The net-worth tax is far less of a burden than its nominal rate would indicate where, as is common, it is deductible in computing income subject to the income tax.[25] Deductibility, however, requires a higher marginal rate on either the net-worth tax or the income tax, to obtain the same revenue, and this increases the net disincentive exerted by the two taxes together to work, accept risk, and the like. By its nature, the base of the net-worth tax is reduced by payment of other taxes.

24. For the German experience, see Gumpel and Boettcher, *op. cit.*, pp. 155–56.

25. Such deduction is allowed in Germany for individuals but not for corporations (*ibid.*, p. 355). Deduction is not allowed in Sweden (Norr, Duffy, and Sterner, *Taxation in Sweden*, p. 262), but is allowed in Colombia (Eder, Chommie, and Becerra, *op. cit.*, p. 246).

C. CAPITAL LEVY

1. Conceptual Basis

A capital levy establishes a heavy tax liability according to property ownership as of one date. Tax payment is normally spread out over a decade or two. Any particular property owner's total liability will usually be so large that he could not possibly meet it even by restricting his purchases of real resources for the year to zero. To pay in full in the year of liability he would have to transfer real estate and securities to the government or, by selling or borrowing, induce others in the private sector to supply the money to pay the tax. This they might do by restricting their own use of real resources, but in part they would probably activate idle balances or persuade the banking system to create money. Usually a government that wants money stocks activated or increased will accomplish these ends by selling its own obligations to the holders of money pools or to the banking system, thus avoiding the social and administrative strains inherent in levying a tax so heavy and demanding payment so quickly that the taxpayers must sell or borrow.

The emphasis placed on circumstances as of a particular date, to fix the tax liability, usually reflects a recent catastrophe, normally a war. Some persons will have lost much property, others will have emerged relatively free of loss, owing largely to chance. The members of the latter group can be identified only if some date not too far distant from the date of the catastrophe is chosen. They are asked to share retroactively the burden of the disaster. What they pay is handed over to the other group; or alternatively the other group is taxed less, for ordinary budget purposes, than otherwise. Or the contrast may be between all who own property and all the rest of the community, including those who never owned any appreciable amount. Those without property may now be living on so low a level, owing to the results of the catastrophe, that they are deemed to have a moral claim to much of the current resources over the years ahead that the property owners will otherwise command for themselves, by the gradual transformation of their machines, buildings, and the like into salable products. The capital levy does not prevent this process of transformation; it merely deflects part of the product to the group that came out of the catastrophe without property.

A peculiar question of sharing the burden arises when a large stock of money has been created during the war or other disaster but has not been allowed to drive prices up, thanks to rationing or other direct controls, which are not expected, however, to continue indefinitely. If much of this money is now destroyed by a radical scaling down of money in a currency reform in order to keep prices at their existing level, and if a capital levy on real estate and other tangible property is then proposed, can one of the grounds for such a levy be that the owners of tangible property should in part recompense the owners of money, who have seen, say, nine-tenths of their money stock taken from them? The answer is no; the owners of money have not suffered by the currency reform and hence need no recompense. A crude quantity theory of money can be invoked here, since the money destroyed is many times, say ten times, greater than the amount needed to support the existing price level at full employment and at an interest rate about as low as it can be driven. If nine-tenths of their money has not been taken away, the holders of money would have had to deal with a price level roughly ten times as high and would have been no better off.

Holders of money claims, bonds and insurance policies for example, are in a different position from holders of money. The real value of their claims will depend not only on whether their claims are cut down but also on what is done to the stock of money. We consider three possible combinations.

First, enough of the money stock is destroyed to keep the real value of those claims unchanged; the claims themselves are not reduced. They are then as logical a target for the capital levy as is real estate.

Second, the money stock is not reduced, controls are ended, and prices rise greatly. The holders of bonds, insurance policies, and the like are thereby subjected to a special and very heavy capital levy, one that the owners of real estate and other tangible property escape. There are now no grounds for including the bonds, etc., in the base of the regular capital levy.

Third, the money stock is reduced, and the face value of the bonds and other fixed money claims are reduced in the same proportion. The holders of these claims suffer a loss in real terms, relative to their situation in the first case above, and similar to the loss they incur in the second situation. Again, there are no grounds for including the bonds and other claims in the base of the regular capital levy.

At the same time, the second and third situations do not justify payment of any recompense to the holders of bonds, etc., for the real loss they have suffered, except perhaps to the degree that their loss is greater than that inflicted by the regular capital levy on the owners of tangible goods. In no case are there grounds for paying any part of the regular capital levy proceeds to holders of amputated cash balances.[26]

The earlier discussions of a capital levy, up to World War II, viewed it as a means of reducing a large domestic government debt incurred during wartime. A certain symmetry is introduced by such a measure; a government bondholder always capitalizes the expected stream of receipts (interest and amortization), but no taxpayer ever capitalizes the equivalent stream of subtractions from his income that will cover these payments.[27]

26. The point is emphasized because there seems to have been some confusion of thought on this issue in post-World-War-II Germany, where the capital levy (Equalization of Burdens Law) was justified by its proponents partly on the grounds that "the Currency Reform of 1948 had effected a radical scaling down of cash holdings, bank balances, and monetary claims, without corresponding losses in the value of land and such real estate and business property as had been preserved, so that some compensation for lost savings, investments, and insurance claims had to be devised" (Gumpel and Boettcher, *op. cit.*, p. 174).

27. Ricardo valued this symmetry. See Shoup, Ricardo on Taxation, Chapter 11, and sources there cited. See also A. C. Pigou, *A Study in Public Finance* (2d ed., 1929), Part 3, Chapter 6, and his *The Political Economy of War*; and J. Hicks, U. K. Hicks, and L. Rostas, *The Taxation of War Wealth* (Oxford: Clarendon Press, 1941, 1942).

2. Incidence

A capital levy is a legal obligation resting on particular pieces of capital equipment or particular business firms or particular individuals which or who were in existence at a certain point in time. The equipment or the ownership interest in the business firm must decline in value relative to equipment produced later or to ownership interests in new firms.[28] If such a tax has been quite unanticipated and is considered certain not to recur, it exerts no substitution effect, only an income effect, as does a poll tax.

The incidence of that tax in an open economy, in partial equilibrium terms, is on the owner of the property as of the date the tax is announced, even though the assessment date in the law is later. The implications for foreign trade or movement of capital are nil. There will be no opportunity for the incidence to be affected by the elasticities of demand or supply at home or abroad. If the capital levy is anticipated, the incidence is on the owner as of the date of anticipation, which in practice means varying dates for varying degrees of anticipation by different persons. If this prospective tax can be avoided by exporting capital, that is, by transferring ownership to a nonresident, and if the country is large, the foreign buyers will gain and domestic sellers will lose, as either the currency falls in value under the impact of capital flight, or the ownership interests fall in terms of domestic money. But this is an effect of the tax other than its incidence, since no tax is paid on such property. In practice, however, the capital levy is likely to include all capital with a situs in the taxing country regardless of residence of the owner.[29] If the capital levy is thought likely to recur, the events that make up the incidence of the annual net-worth tax will be the effects of the capital levy.

The incidence of an unanticipated capital levy as a substitute for a value-added tax, over the period of time when the capital levy is being collected, is one that benefits factor owners and consumers in general, as the value-added tax is repealed, and burdens a certain cohort of property owners. For any one person, the pattern of this differential incidence will change over the years, as his economic fortunes rise and fall, only because the burden of the value-added tax on him would have changed correspondingly. The burden of the capital levy on him changes not at all as his fortunes change. The capital levy can have no "dynamic incidence," as the value-added tax can have;[30] more precisely, the dynamic incidence possibilities in the

28. In Germany, "The capital levy [50 per cent of the net worth of individuals and entities computed as of June 21, 1948] is payable with interest from 1949 to 1979. The obligation for its payment continues to exist even if the net-worth on which it is computed has disappeared or lost its value; however, administrative relief is available. . . . As a burden which is imposed on the person of the debtor, liability for the capital levy passes to the purchaser of a business only if there is an agreement to this effect. . . . The release, however, of the transferor requires the consent of the finance office, which is rarely granted. . . . Corporations, limited liability companies, and other entities of the commercial law . . . must show the present value of the capital levy . . . in an annotation to their balance sheet" (Gumpel and Boettcher, *op. cit.*, pp. 175–76).

29. In general, this was true of the German capital levy (*idem.*).

30. See Douglas Dosser, "Tax Incidence and Growth," *Economic Journal* (September,

differential incidence depend solely on the value-added tax, not at all on the capital levy.

The differential incidence is progressive in the sense that most of those who bear the capital levy were, before the levy was announced, in the upper-income ranges.

3. Criteria

The circumstances which, a capital levy implies, are relevant for equal treatment of equals include one that is unique in the tax system: the fact of ownership of property at a date fixed in the law, and not, impliedly, at any other date for decades to come. This provision adds to the usual qualitative and quantitative discontinuities that mark a general tax on property (see page 363 above) a severe time discontinuity. Under the pressure of high rates on this narrow (temporal) base, the law and regulations become extremely detailed in an effort to remove uncertainties and to refine the concept of equally circumstanced among this time-specified group of tax-payers.[31] A decided loss of impersonality must be one result. And even the degrees of evasion and of compliance costs must be very unequal. Administrative problems of valuation require use of circumstances, in defining equals, that are by common consent not relevant: for example, use of assessed values for certain properties, but not others, as of a decade or so earlier, at a lower price level.[32]

The administrative problem of the capital levy will be much smaller if a well-administered net-worth tax and death-gift tax have been in effect for some time. While the capital levy scores poorly under the consensus equity criterion, it shares a high ranking with the poll tax on absence of excess burden, aside from anticipatory effects.

Since the incidence of an unexpected capital levy is clearly on owners of the factor, capital, the tax is progressive by income, relative to the value-added tax, even if the rate is proportional. The progressivity is partial, since many individuals with high incomes from human capital will own little property subject to the tax. Family composition has usually been taken into account, by personal exemptions. The tax rate has sometimes varied with composition of wealth, and with location of tax-payer or property within the country.[33] Economic growth is hindered only by the

1961), 71: 572–91, and for further discussion of this concept, A. P. Bain, "Tax Incidence and Growth: A Comment"; A. R. Prest, "Observations on Dynamic Incidence"; and Douglas Dosser, "Incidence and Growth Further Considered," *Economic Journal* (September, 1963), 73: 533–53. See also Chapter 23 below, Section B.

31. "The [German, 1948] Equalization of Burdens Law, together with its numerous amendments and supplementary laws, implementing ordinances, and regulatory decrees, is one of the most extensive and complex pieces of fiscal legislation . . ." (Gumpel and Boettcher, *op. cit.*, p. 175).

32. In Germany, real property under the 1948 capital levy was valued as of January 1, 1935 (*ibid.*, pp. 713, 722).

33. Accompanying the German Equalization of Burdens Law (1948) there were (1) a 100 per cent tax on profits from the redemption of mortgage loans "to capture the fortuitous gain of a mortgagor whose obligation under the mortgage was reduced to one-tenth of its face value

income effect of the tax and by anticipations it may give rise to. Apart from such anticipations the capital levy can have no effect on amount of social risk taken. An incremental deficit on balance of payments would arise if taxpayers, under pressure to pay large sums at once instead of by the more usual installment plan, tried to borrow abroad; an incremental surplus is achieved by including under the capital levy property owned by foreigners. No effect on the supply of labor is to be expected, again save as anticipations lead to emigration.[34]

If the amount paid as capital levy is deductible in computing taxable income for the income tax,[35] the true rate of the capital levy is for most taxpayers much less than the nominal one, since those with enough property to be subject to the capital levy are in most instances paying a fairly high income tax marginal rate. Estimates of the net yield of a capital levy must therefore allow for the accompanying decrease in income tax revenue.

D. DEATH AND GIFT TAXES

1. Conceptual Basis

No income tax, it appears, has ever included gifts and inheritances in taxable income.[36] Estate and inheritance taxes preceded the income tax in most countries. The government's supervision of transfers at death, to safeguard heirs and enforce social aims regarding distribution of such property, encouraged development of an

by the Currency Reform," and (2) a 100 per cent tax on "book profits arising from the conversion of the balance sheets of commercial and industrial enterprises from the pre-1948 currency . . . to the new currency . . ." (*ibid.*, p. 175). As to the equitableness of such taxes, see discussion in Section 1. Under the German levy, "special rules apply to taxpayers domiciled in West Berlin" (*ibid.*, pp. 175–76).

34. For analysis of economic effects of a capital levy, see Shun-hsin Chou, *The Capital Levy*.

35. The Germany capital levy following World War II is not deductible, excepting its interest element (*ibid.*, p. 355).

36. Such inclusion was recommended by the Royal Commission on Taxation [Canada] (Ottawa: Queen's Printer, 1966), vol. 3, Chapter 17. In the United States, the Income Tax Bill of 1894 included inheritances in income (the tax rate was only a flat 2 per cent), but the entire income tax was declared unconstitutional (William J. Shultz, *The Taxation of Inheritance* [Boston: Houghton Mifflin, 1926], p. 153). Henry Simons urged that "all inheritances, bequests, and (large) gifts *inter vivos*" be included in taxable income of the recipient, "as the only practicable method . . . for successfully avoiding evasion through distribution of property prior to death," but he added that "a case could be made for retention of moderate estate taxes" (*Economic Policy for a Free Society* [Chicago: University of Chicago Press, 1948], p. 67). Simons had presented his case in detail in his earlier work, *Personal Income Taxation* (Chicago: University of Chicago Press, 1938), Chapter 6. His proposal retained some of the features of the transfer taxes, e.g., special exemptions for widows and other dependents incapable of self-support, and it called for retention of the transfer taxes as supplementary levies, preferably as "a cumulative personal tax on beneficiaries with respect to gifts, inheritances, and bequests . . ." because this is a kind of accumulation that can be taxed "with least adverse effect upon the morale of an enterprise economy; and opinion generally supports especially heavy taxation of 'income' in this form" (*ibid.*, p. 144).

administrative cadre who became experts in a certain type of complexity. Income tax laws without powerful averaging devices were ill equipped to handle bulges in taxable income caused by some gifts and inheritances. And the amount of tax that should be paid on such transfers has in most communities been considered to vary with factors or aims that the income tax cannot readily take into account: (1) the degree to which the transfer is a true windfall, (2) the degree to which the transfer represents, or causes, a socially unacceptable concentration of wealth in the hands of one person or family, and (3) the desire to use the transfer tax as a rough substitute for an annual net-worth tax.

The weights given to these aims largely determine the choice between an inheritance tax and an estate tax,[37] and the decision whether to impose a tax on lifetime gifts and, if so, at what rates relative to those of the death tax.

The inheritance tax emphasizes taxation of windfalls. The greater the degree of legitimate expectation, as shown by the relationship of the heir to the decedent, the lower is the scale of rates usually applied. But the windfall criterion is not used exclusively or consistently; if it were, it would call for a low rate of tax on a transfer to a distant relative or even to one not related, if there were no close relatives living to defeat a lively expectation. Windfall taxation implies little need for a gift tax, since most gifts are to near relatives or to charitable or religious organizations.

The estate tax, in contrast, can take no account of the windfall element, at least in the purest form of estate tax, which simply imposes a single progressive rate schedule on the decedent's entire estate. But the estate tax does strike heavily at a large aggregate of wealth, measured by what the decedent himself controlled. The concentration of wealth may have existed for some decades, but the tax law serves notice that the price to be paid for accumulation will be high unless the accumulator disposes of most of his property by lifetime gifts or, in some countries, leaves it to charity or the church. A cumulated gift tax-death tax, that is, a unified transfer tax, would be a still more effective weapon against accumulation, but such a tax is rarely found.[38] Under this levy, the tax rates on any one donor are progressive according to the aggregate of his lifetime transfers and his transfers at death; the transfer tax is a unified donor tax.

To avert concentration of wealth in a second generation of persons, more than a unified donor tax is needed. Any one heir may receive gifts and bequests from several donors and decedents. A unified tax on the donee, that is, an accessions tax, is required. Its rate schedule would be progressive according to the total value of bequests and gifts received by any one donee-heir in his lifetime, regardless of the

37. The inheritance tax, levied on each heir, usually at rates varying with size of inheritance and relationship to decedent, is imposed by more countries than is the estate tax, which is imposed on the estate at rates varying with size of estate and sometimes with the pattern of bequests from the estate. France and Germany, for example, impose an inheritance tax. The United States federal government and the United Kingdom impose an estate tax. Practice varies widely among the states of the United States. Italy imposes both types of tax, and at times in the past France and the United Kingdom have imposed both. See the various volumes of the *World Tax Series* for the respective countries.

38. For the unified transfer tax on the donor in Italy and Colombia, see Carl S. Shoup, *Federal Estate and Gift Taxes* (Washington: Brookings Institution, 1966), pp. 12–13, note 2, and sources there cited.

number or type of donors or decedents. With one exception,[39] no country, it appears, has ever imposed a complete accessions tax.

To truly break up concentration of wealth caused by gifts and bequests requires still heavier tax rates, aimed solely at property that can be identified as having been transmitted through several generations. After a certain number of generations, perhaps indeed after only one or two, the tax rate on such property might reach 100 per cent, as proposed by Rignano. The blow could be softened by allowing a life annuity or term annuity yielding the same income, for the generation following the imposition of the 100 per cent rate.[40]

The third aim is to consider property as a relevant circumstance in determining who are equally circumstanced for purposes of taxation. In the present context this aim calls for a transfer tax structure that will reach property rather regularly, say once a generation, and so serve as a substitute for a wealth tax collected once a year. A gift tax now becomes even more important than under the anti-concentration aim, to reach gifts to a younger generation. But exemption must be granted to transfers during life or at death to members of the same generation. This aim also requires that inter-spousal gifts or bequests be exempt, at least up to the amount in which they will normally be given.[41] An estate tax can be equipped with the appropriate exemptions, but an inheritance tax is a still more flexible instrument for this purpose. Both taxes are vulnerable to trusts that tie up property so that title to it is not transferred as often as once a generation. The only comprehensive formula for a transfer tax the present value of which will be independent of the number or ages of persons through whom the property is routed is that of the Vickrey bequeathing-power tax.[42]

Property accumulated early in life and then destroyed by consumption or business losses can of course be reached only by an annual net-worth tax, or indirectly by the progressive rates of an accessions tax, if the progression is based on the net worth of the donee.

The three aims of death and gift taxation often conflict. Transfer to a spouse should be exempted if the tax is aimed at windfalls or is a substitute for a net-wealth tax but should in some instances, where both spouses are wealthy, be taxed if the aim is to prevent or penalize concentration of wealth. Transfers to sons and

39. An accessions tax was in force in Japan from 1949 to 1952. The case for an accessions tax in Japan was given in *Report on Japanese Taxation by the Shoup Mission*, vol. 2, Chapter 8. An incomplete accessions tax is on the statute book in Colombia and Italy. See Shoup, *Federal Estate and Gift Taxes*, p. 13, note 3.

40. As suggested by Hugh Dalton, in his *Principles of Public Finance* (London: Routledge and Kegan Paul, 1954), p. 83, for application to a part of every estate in excess of a minimum value.

41. This amount will commonly be one-half the estate, if the estate is large and if there are children destined to receive, sooner or later, the entire estate. Under these circumstances, to leave the widow the entire estate would cost more, under a progressive rate schedule, than to leave half to her and half to the children, even if all the estate could be passed to her free of tax, unless she survived for so long a period that the value of the tax on her estate, when discounted back to the date of death of the first decedent, was greatly reduced.

42. William Vickrey, *Agenda for Progressive Taxation*, Chapter 7 and Appendix 4. For comment on Vickrey's proposal, see Alan A. Tait, *The Taxation of Personal Wealth*, Chapter 11.

daughters should be exempt under windfall taxation but taxed under the once-a-generation test. That test calls for taxing doubly a transfer to a grandchild, which however should be exempt under a windfall tax and taxed lightly, in the usual instance, if the aim is to discourage concentration of wealth.

A weighted mixture of the three aims will produce a type of transfer tax that will appear erratic and inconsistent to one who is not aware of the compromise made to accommodate conflicting ends. Transfers made by or to those in the lower ranges of wealth would be taxed almost entirely on the windfall principle. The usual net-worth tax would exempt these families. Higher up the wealth scale, the transfer tax would attempt to tax all property once a generation, as a substitute for a net-worth tax. The windfall element would still be taken into account but would no longer be the sole occasion for the tax. At the highest wealth levels the tax would be shaped primarily to reflect the community's concern over the social dangers of great accumulations of individual wealth.[43] These considerations indicate that a carefully designed system of death and gift taxes need not present a superficial uniformity of structure.

The need to be clear about the aims of death and gift taxation is nowhere more evident that in the formulation of a regime for trusts. Transfer of property into a trust is commonly taxable, whether the trust is set up by a lifetime gift or by a bequest. What happens thereafter varies remarkably from country to country, and within any one country it depends upon the form of the trust or, in those countries the laws of which do not recognize a trust, upon the form of the substitute disposition of the property. In the simplest case, income from the property that has been placed in trust is paid regularly by the trustee (the legal owner of the property in the trust) to the beneficiary or beneficiaries. The commonest form of this simplest case is a trust with income to the surviving spouse for her lifetime; at her death the trust is dissolved and the property passes outright to the remainderman or remaindermen, usually the children of the couple, who have been named as such in the trust instrument. Another common form of trust pays income to the surviving spouse, then, after her death, to the children; upon the death of the last child, or, pro-rata, upon the death of any of the children, the property passes out of the trust into the hands of the grandchildren. This maturing of the remaindermen's interests is in some countries not considered a taxable transfer; in others, it is. On the one hand, the transfer from original donor to remaindermen was legally consummated at the time the trust instrument was set up; on the other hand, the remaindermen do come into possession of something over which they have had only potential power of complete ownership. If a taxable transfer is deemed not to occur when the remaindermen's interests mature, the road is open to skip, not just one generation of death or gift taxation, as in this instance, but two or more; the trust instrument may specify that upon death of the children the property shall stay in the trust, the income now being paid to the grandchildren, and not until they have died shall the property move out of the trust. This procedure cannot be extended indefinitely; in most jurisdictions that permit the trust, interests designated in the trust instrument

43. For details, and a suggested implementation of this set of weights, see Shoup, *Federal Estate and Gift Taxes*, pp. 107–11.

must vest within a period not exceeding the length of lives in being when the instrument becomes effective plus 21 years, or (the precise rule varies from jurisdiction to jurisdiction) some period approximating this.[44] Still, generation-skipping presents a serious threat to the efficacy of the death and gift tax system. Even if only every other generation avoids the transfer tax, half the base of the tax is lost.

Those jurisdictions that attempt to tax the property at the time the remainder-men's interests mature, or, more generally, whenever a life interest expires, whether or not it is succeeded by another life interest,[45] have encountered attempts to outwit the law, attempts that have been on the whole fairly successful. One device is the discretionary trust; the trustee is given power to distribute the income, annually, among any one or more of a number of named beneficiaries. Evidently, until all but two of these beneficiaries have died, the death of any one beneficiary creates no interest of value for the other beneficiaries that they did not already possess; each one is still at the mercy of the trustee and may receive nothing at all from the trust. It has been held[46] that under these circumstances there is no tenable legal basis at all for taxing the property upon the death of one of the (potential) beneficiaries, since no new legal interest will thereby have been created.

The appropriate treatment of trusts depends on the relative weights given to the several aims of transfer taxation. Suppose, for example, that the widow is the life tenant, and the children are the remaindermen. If the aim is to tax property once a generation, or to tax windfalls, there need be no tax upon expiry of the widow's life interest, but if great concentration of wealth is to be prevented, such a tax is called for, if the amounts involved are large. If it is the great-grandchildren who are the remaindermen, the children and grandchildren being the life tenants, the aim of taxing property once a generation requires taxation upon the expiry of each life estate (on a pro-rata share of the property); windfall taxation, in contrast, calls either for no tax, or at the most, for one, when the grandchildren's life interests expire.

2. Incidence

In an open economy the taxing country can shift a part of its death and gift taxes to another country by including in the tax base property located in the taxing country but owned by nonresidents. "Located in" means, for practical purposes, seizable by the taxing country to satisfy the tax if the owner does not pay. This limits the taxable foreign-owned property to real estate and possibly shares in or debts owed by domestic corporations, since those corporations can be prevented from sending

44. See Shoup, *op. cit.*, p. 34 and, in Appendix B thereto, Robert Anthoine, "Testamentary Trusts," p. 153; and Gerald R. Jantscher, *Trusts and Estate Taxation* (Washington, D.C.: Brookings Institution, 1967), pp. 24–29, 35–36, 55. Jantscher's volume is an authoritative statement and analysis, primarily from the economist's point of view, of the complex problem of trusts under the estate tax.

45. The United Kingdom is the most notable example.

46. In the United Kingdom.

dividend or interest payments to the tax-delinquent owners or creditors. If the tax burden is to be truly exported, however, the property must have been foreign-owned at the time the death or gift tax was introduced, or increased, or anticipated to be introduced or increased, since subsequent foreign purchasers would have discounted the prospective series of taxes in the price paid. The discounting can of course be only approximate, in view of the uncertainty both of amounts and of timing of the future taxes.

By the same reasoning, residents of the country may be bearing some part of death or gift taxes levied by other countries.

Even in a closed economy partial equilibrium analysis is useful in ascertaining the incidence of the tax, since the revenue is usually so small relative to total tax revenue or national income, and since the tax impinges not on all property but only on certain property at certain occasions. But incidence cannot, as it can with excises, be described in terms of a rise in price compared with the tax rate. Only the change in distribution of wealth and income can conceptually be quantified.

The tax reaches only a small portion of the total capital stock of a country. In a rapidly growing economy that is accumulating capital swiftly there is at any one point of time a relatively large proportion of the capital stock that has been accumulated recently enough so that it has not been subject to a death or gift tax and is not likely to become so subject for another decade or two or even more. Indeed, a part of this portion will never pay transfer tax because it will be consumed. On the remainder of this portion the present value of the prospective transfer taxes is too small to exert an appreciable influence on either the prospective donor's actions at this time or on those of the prospective donees or heirs.

The incidence of the tax is largely on the heirs and donees, in the sense that if it were repealed they, and not the prospective decedent or donor, are the ones whose net worth or level of consumption, or both, would increase. This conclusion implies that the prospective testator or donor does not reduce his own consumption or increase his own supply of work appreciably in order to make up to his heirs and donees a part of the prospective decrease in their gifts and inheritances arising from the tax. Although little direct information is available on this point, general observation suggests that the basic exemptions are usually so high and the starting rates so low that the prospective testator-donor's concern over the resulting impairment of his heirs' or donees' standards of living is too mild to induce him to sacrifice any of his own consumption or leisure. The income effect of the tax on him is therefore to reduce his saving.

Since the prospective tax can be reduced by increasing consumption or reducing work, the substitution effect on the donor-testator also tends to lower the amount that the heirs or donees will receive. If this effect were great, the stock of capital would be reduced by more than the amount of the tax. Any reduction in the stock of capital will increase its marginal productivity and reduce that of labor, and in this sense the death and gift taxes indirectly burden labor incomes and increase the incomes from those blocks of capital that do not, for reasons given above, pass through these taxes. So far as the substitution effect is concerned, however, these changes in productivity are not likely to be appreciable. The amount of capital taxed is, we have seen, relatively small; moreover, the consumption habits of those wealthy enough to be threatened with a transfer tax are fixed to a degree such that little increase will be induced by the prospect of saving future death or gift taxes. The income effect, however, may be appreciable in its effect on productivities, unless the amount of capital caught in the tax is a very small proportion of the total.

3. Criteria

A. CONSENSUS CRITERIA

The death and gift taxes score poorly on the consensus criteria, except that of economic efficiency. Equals are frequently treated unequally, and those almost equal are often treated quite differently.

Circumstances that all would agree are irrelevant are allowed to influence the amount of tax paid. An illustration is the discretionary trust described above, at least when, as is common, the trustee, perhaps a bank or trust company, simply carries out a plan of distribution formulated by the settlor, known to all the beneficiaries, and relied on by them, much as if it had been spelled out in the trust instrument. The discretion then exists only legally, not de facto. The one-taxpayer clauses in estate and gift tax laws rival those in the income tax, in covert favoritism if not in numbers. Even a high degree of detail in the tax law has not prevented great uncertainty over the amount of tax that will be attracted, or repelled, by any given course of action. A small quantitative change, say in the proportion that a reversionary interest bears to the whole interest, can cause a large change in tax, and so too can small qualitative differences that are difficult to define: for example, distribution from the corpus of a trust of more than enough to preserve the standard of living of the beneficiary.

The degree of evasion perhaps varies no more than under the sales tax or income tax, but probably no less. And the differences in cost of compliance are great. The general level of evasion is meaningful, too, in the sense that the tax rates would probably not be decreased if evasion were reduced. In some countries evasion is so great and widespread as to be a common scandal.

In general, then, the death and gift taxes start with a heavy handicap in their failure to conform to the equal-treatment-of-equals principle in the consensus aspects of that principle.

In the efficiency sector, they are of little assistance to counter-cycle policy. The sensitivity of the yield is low, and the efficiency of that sensitivity also is low. The impact of changes in rates of tax, on private-sector use of resources, would occur with large leads and lags. But on Pareto-optimum grounds these taxes do well, with one important exception. The only rate of substitution they disturb is that between present goods and future goods, and they disturb that so little that the amount of excess burden created must be small. The exception refers to the change these taxes induce in methods, timing, and allocation, in the transfer of property, through more extensive and intensive use of trusts, and of novel forms of trust, in more gifts *inter vivos*, in the passage of more, or possibly even less, property to the types of heirs or donees that enjoy low rates under an inheritance tax. The aggregate of such change for the economy as a whole is, however, easily overstated. By far the greater number of decedents, donors, and donees, representing probably by far the major part of wealth transferred, proceed no doubt much as they would in the absence of death and gift taxes, because they are not sophisticated enough to seek the kind of legal advice that will reduce their prospective taxes of an uncertain date, or to accept this advice when sought.

B. CONFLICT CRITERIA

The criterion of progressivity by income or wealth can be met by the death-gift taxes only indirectly and erratically. It is important however only with respect to the third aim of such taxes, that of approximating a low-rate annual tax on wealth. Windfall taxation and anti-concentration taxation have nothing directly to do with this criterion of progressivity.

Family composition can be taken into account, but more easily by an inheritance tax than an estate tax. The estate tax puts more pressure on the family to rearrange its ownership pattern. To see this, consider the following cases.

(1) All the family's property is in the husband's name, and he dies first. The high progressive rates apply, because the aggregate of the property is so large. If he leaves it all to his widow, and if she then passes it (less the tax paid on the first transfer) on to the children at her death, tax rates almost as high apply again, usually in a short time, although in some tax laws the second impact is mitigated by provisions that lighten the tax on property previously taxed within a given period.

(2) All the property is in the husband's name, but the wife dies first. There is now only one tax, at high rates, before the property reaches the children (assuming no transfers *inter vivos*).

(3) The property is evenly divided between husband and wife, and the surviving spouse is the sole heir. There is one tax on one-half the estate followed by a tax on the entire estate (less the tax paid on the first transfer). The resulting tax has a present value, as of the first decedent's death, in between those of the tax in the other two cases, whichever spouse dies first.

For risk-averters, the estate tax therefore exerts pressure on the family to distribute property evenly between the spouses, save in those few cases where it is fairly certain that the spouse that owns no, or less, property will be the first to die. This pressure can be reduced by allowing either spouse to pass tax-free to the surviving spouse an amount equal to one-half the decedent spouse's estate (the "marital deduction"). Now the tax will be the same as in (3) above, if the property is all in one spouse's name, provided that the property-owning spouse dies first. And if the non-property–owning spouse dies first, the total tax is as in (2) above, that is, the lightest of the three cases. The marital deduction will, however, still leave some inducement to divide property evenly before death, including the case where, if the property were not evenly divided, the spouse owning all or a major part would probably be the one to die first, in the following circumstances.

(4) The property is divided equally between the spouses; the first spouse to die, say the husband, leaves all his property to the children, thus foregoing the advantages of the marital deduction. The surviving spouse lives off the income from the one-half of the property that she already possessed, and on her death passes this property on to the children. The present value of the two taxes, at date of death of the first decedent, will normally be smaller than that of the taxes that obtain in case (1) above under the marital deduction, that is, when the spouse owning all the property leaves it all to the surviving spouse, paying tax only on half of it, because of the marital deduction, and the surviving spouse passes the property (less the first tax) on to the children.[47] To be sure, the second spouse has more income, and the children have less, in case (1) than in case (4).

Various provisions have been considered that would eliminate entirely, or almost so, this pressure on risk-averters for equal division of the family property before death, but they all encounter formidable difficulties.[48] The inheritance and accessions taxes, on the contrary, do not vary with interspousal distribution of property.

A depressed area within the taxing country can raise the market value of its real estate by securing exemption of it from death and gift taxes, but the gain, which is once for all, may well accrue entirely to a nonresident of the area. And the exemption is not likely to induce construction of factories or development of mines within the area. The depressed area may be able to attract a few elderly persons of wealth if it is empowered to grant exemption to residents with respect to all of their property wherever located. Being intensely personal, these taxes can be exploited to discriminate, in practice if not in law, against racial, ethnic, or other groups, provided the discriminees are wealthy enough.

For the allocation criteria the death and gift taxes are not very significant except with respect to economic growth, to which they are adverse, and stimulation of public-purpose outlays by the private sector, which they can encourage.

The conclusion reached above, that neither the decedent-to-be nor the prospective heirs are likely to consume much less or to work much more because of the tax implies that it comes chiefly out of saving. Under some conditions, to be sure, the prospective heirs may live more cautiously and, after receiving the tax-reduced inheritance, will consume somewhat less, than if there were no transfer tax. In fact this decrease in consumption seems unlikely to represent a large proportion of the tax. But the possibilities, if not the probabilities, are larger than with most taxes, since two sets of households are involved. Both the decedent-to-be and the prospective heirs might react strongly, each cutting down their levels of consumption to

47. For numerical illustrations of this and the preceding cases, see Shoup, *op. cit.*, pp. 51–52.

48. See G. S. A. Wheatcroft, *Estate and Gift Taxation, A Comparative Study* (London: Sweet and Maxwell, 1965), pp. 137–43. The most promising possibility may be to give the surviving spouse an option to declare a constructive distribution of ownership of the property between the spouses as of the first death, for tax purposes. Thus, cases (1) and (3) could be transformed into case (2). A complete interspousal exemption would equalize the tax for cases (1), (2), and (3), but case (4) would then still usually yield a smaller tax. For further analysis of this point, see a forthcoming article by Harold M. Groves in *National Tax Journal*.

meet the tax. Thus a death tax of say $100,000 might reduce the accumulated and discounted value of consumption as of the date of tax payment by as much as, say, $200,000. Saving would be greater than in the absence of the tax.

The effect of the death and gift taxes on investment spending seems minor and chiefly indirect. The likelihood that the individual will have to pay such a tax some-time in the future may increase his preference for liquidity, thus putting an upward pressure on the interest rate. In particular, closely held firms may slow or stop their expansions as their owners reach an age when death taxes should be prepared for; often, however, expansion continues after a merger into a larger company, since the former owners of the small concern are now in possession of a readily marketable security. Property tied up in trusts may be more risk-averting than it would have been. But, since the tax is never levied directly on a business firm or an investor as such, it has no direct effect on risk-taking.

A favorable increment in the balance of payments may be obtained by exempting foreign-owned bank deposits and such other short-term investments as the taxing country might be able to reach if it chose to do so, except that when tax rates are increased, foreign-owned real estate may be put on the market and the proceeds of sale repatriated.

By exempting gifts or bequests to religious, charitable, and educational institu-tions the death and gift taxes can stimulate transfers to them.[49] These exemptions, or deductions, may allow a wealthy family to maintain control over the wealth even after it has ostensibly been given away. Moreover, by granting a larger subsidy to taxpayers with larger estates, the government is probably losing more revenue than it needs to, to induce a certain volume of such transfers.[50]

4. Intra-System Effects on Yields

Usually the death and gift taxes are not deductible in computing the base of any other tax. No other tax is deductible in computing the base of these taxes, with the possible exception of income tax paid on income earned by the estate after the decedent's death and before the assets are distributed.

APPENDIX TO CHAPTER FOURTEEN

Let r be the market rate of interest, assumed unchanged by the tax, y the annual flow of a perpetuity, t the rate of annual tax on the capital value of the perpetuity, and v_t the present value of the perpetuity under the tax. The tax bill, $T = tv_t$.

The annual flow to be capitalized under the tax is $y - tv_t$; hence the present value

49. Accordingly, many countries grant such an exemption, in whole or in part. See Jeffrey Schaefer, "Tax Incentives to Promote Charitable Giving, for Selected Countries," in *Bulletin for International Fiscal Documentation* (October, 1966), 20(10): 413–16.

50. See page 336 above, and Shoup, *op. cit.*, p. 64.

of the perpetuity under the tax is $(y - tv_t)/r$. Thus $v_t = (y - tv_t)/r = y/(r + t)$. Hence v_t approaches zero as t becomes indefinitely large. For example, if the tax rate were 80 per cent of the capital value, per year, a perpetuity of $100 a year at 10 per cent market rate of interest would be worth $111.11. If the tax rate were 200 per cent per year of the market value, that market value (of a perpetuity of $100 a year) would be $47.62.

If the market rate of interest changes because of the tax, to become xr in place of r, the market value of the disposable perpetuity under the tax will be

$$v_t = (y - tv_t)/rx = y/(rx + t).$$

Since the market value when no tax is imposed is $v = y/r$, the tax does not change the market value of the perpetuity when $y/(rx + t) = y/r)$, that is, when $x = 1 - t/r$, provided that r is greater than t, since x is limited to positive values.

In the particular case where the tax causes the interest rate to fall in proportion to the tax rate, so that the interest rate under the tax, $rx = r(1 - t)$, we have an unchanged value for the perpetuity when $1 - t = 1 - t/r$, that is, when $r = 1$, i.e., when the initial market rate of interest is 100 per cent.

The value of the perpetuity under the tax, v_t, will exceed the value of the perpetuity under no tax, v, when $y/(rx + t) > y/r$, that is, when $rx + t < r$, or $x < 1 - t/r$. Thus, if the market rate of interest drops only slightly because of the tax, from r to $0.9r$ (here, $x = 0.9$), we have, if the value of the perpetuity is to rise under the tax, $t/r < 0.1$, that is, the tax rate must be less than one-tenth the initial market rate of interest. For example, if $r = 0.04$, $x = 0.9$, and $t = 0.003$, $v = \$2,500$ and $v_t = \$2,564$.

CHAPTER FIFTEEN

Property Taxation:
Real Estate Tax, Taxes on
Transfers for a Consideration

A. REAL ESTATE TAX

1. Conceptual Basis

IN ITS MOST GENERAL FORM, the real estate tax is imposed on all immovable property: land, buildings, and those fixtures and machinery that are more or less permanently attached. The tax is separable, for economic analysis, into (1) an ad valorem excise on a consumer good, housing, whether rented or owner-occupied, and (2) an ad valorem tax on a factor, business real estate, which is used in the production and distribution of almost all consumer goods and services and capital goods. Business real estate consists of factories, farms, warehouses, retail shops, transportation and power infrastructure and equipment, and the like.

In an industrially advanced economy, aggregate real estate value will be divided about equally between housing, including the value of land on which the dwellings stand, and business real estate. But the two taxes differ markedly in open-economy incidence, in differential incidence, and in the degrees to which they meet the consensus and the conflict criteria.

Associated with the real estate tax in some jurisdictions[1] is a tax on certain personal, that is, movable, tangible property, notably business inventories, and a tax on some types of securities, claims, and the like ("intangibles"). These taxes are noted incidentally in the present section.

Farm real estate is here considered a factor of production, since the housing element is usually minor.

The factor, real estate, is itself produced in part from other forms of capital, and from labor. In part it is supplied by nature in an amount that can be increased only with great difficulty: land chiefly in its aspect of supplying space at a given location.

1. Especially in certain states in the United States.

The real estate tax is in no country an important national tax, perhaps because nothing at the national level justifies special taxation of this particular producers good, and because dwelling accommodation is a poor object for excise taxation, being neither a luxury nor an addictive.

As a provincial, state, or local tax the real estate tax is important only where those subordinate units have power to vary the level of the types of service that affect the value of real estate: police protection, fire protection, education, and refuse removal, for example. And if those units possess other taxing powers of significance, the real estate tax plays a smaller role or none at all.[2]

In less developed countries local government units are usually given little responsibility. They collect little or nothing in real estate tax. Perhaps both phenomena reflect per capita incomes too low to permit the luxury of local government services as the industrially advanced countries know them. Moreover, in warm-climate countries buildings are less substantial. An equal cubic-foot real estate tax will amount to a much larger percentage of cost of construction in the warmer climate. And except where the terrain compresses large cities, as in a narrow valley, there may be little intensive application of buildings to land, with corresponding increases in land values. But these considerations do not explain the absence of heavy urban real estate taxation in many countires.[3]

Heavy taxation of idle land, designed to induce owners to put it to productive use, has so far not been markedly successful. Land taxation to recoup the unearned increment and to stimulate improvements has also made little progress. A land tax graduated by size of holding, to break up huge individual holdings, has been used in a few countries.[4]

2. Thus the real estate tax is important, meaning here equal to more than 2 per cent of the national income, only in Australia (2.0), Canada (5.2), Denmark (2.3), Ireland (3.8), New Zealand (2.3), the United Kingdom (4.2) and the United States (4.3). The percentages are for recent years, from Dick Netzer, *Economics of the Property Tax* (Washington, D.C.: Brookings Institution, 1966), Table 1–3, "Property Taxes in Selected Countries in Recent Years"; no data are given for Spain or Switzerland. The tax supplies 100 per cent of local-government tax revenue in Australia, Ireland, and the United Kingdom. In at least two other countries where local governments are strong, the real estate tax is weak. In Germany, in 1964, it produced only 16 per cent of local tax revenues (79 per cent came from the local trade tax [*Gewerbesteuer*]); this share has been steadily declining at least since 1955, when it was 25 per cent (Commission for Fiscal Reform, *Gutachten uber die Finanzreform in der Bundesrepublik Deutschland* [Kohlhammer, Stuttgart, 1966], p. 215). The assessed values are still those of 1935. For an appraisal of the *Grundsteuer* see *ibid.*, pp. 104–106. In Sweden, the separate local real property tax was abolished in 1955; instead, an income is imputed to real estate (2.5 per cent of the assessed capital value) and is included, as a minimum, in the base of the income subject to the local income tax (rates, 13 to 15 per cent). Norr, Duffy, and Sterner, *Taxation in Sweden*, p. 105. In Japan, local governments rely heavily on income taxation, individual and corporate. The real estate tax rate is nominally 1.4 per cent in most municipalities; it may not exceed 2.1 per cent (Taizo Hayashi, *Guide to Japanese Taxes, 1967–68* [Tokyo: Zaikei Shōtō Sha, 1967], pp. 13–27). The real estate tax amounts to 1.2 per cent of the national income (Netzer, *loc. cit.*).

3. Caracas, in Venezuela, and Rio de Janeiro, in Brazil, illustrate intensive application of capital to land. Such areas have a rich land and buildings base on which a substantial real estate tax could be, but is not, imposed.

4. Notably in Australia and New Zealand. For a general survey and critique, see George E. Lent, *The Taxation of Unimproved Land Value* (Washington, D.C.: International Monetary Fund, 1966).

In some countries the real estate tax is a percentage of capital value of the property; in others, a percentage of current rental received from, or attributable to, the property. If taxable rental value were in fact net rental after depreciation and current maintenance, the difference between the rental value base and the capital-value base would not be great, since market value reflects anticipated net rentals, which usually turn out to be, in the aggregate, not far from net rentals. Those countries that tax on a rental basis commonly use, however, a gross rental figure, i.e., before deducting depreciation and expenses,[5] and those that profess to use net rental tie the allowable deductions so rigidly to the amount of gross rental[6] that the tax varies from property to property more directly with gross than with true net rental.

The following analysis will draw conclusions first for the capital-value tax, and then note how they need to be modified for a gross-rental tax. Still a third version views the real estate tax chiefly as a payment for fire protection, street maintenance, and other government outlays that, as they rise, enhance the value of the property. Cost-benefit analysis suggests that a real estate tax resembling a specific (i.e., per-unit) excise tax would correspond more closely to the cost caused to the government by any particular property than does a capital-value or gross-rental real estate tax. This kind of tax, imposed at so much per square foot of land or floor space, or cubic feet of structure, will be examined briefly toward the end of this section. As with any tax based primarily on cost-benefit analysis, its importance is the more limited, the less willing one is to set criteria for a tax on the assumption that the existing distribution of income and wealth is satisfactory.

The effects of a tax restricted to land value are given in the analysis below of a tax on both land and improvements.

2. The Tax on Housing

The incidence of a tax on housing may be explored with partial equilibrium analysis for any one local unit. A city, town, county, or even province or state is an open economy engaged in "foreign" trade within a common market. It is normally so small, relative to the rest of this market, that even a high mobility of capital and labor between it and the rest of this market would not affect prices or factor rewards in the rest of the market. Similarly, resort to this external market by consumers in the taxing city would not push prices up in that market.

The city's expenditures financed by the tax are indeed largely devoted to hiring or buying factors, chiefly labor, residing in the very same dwellings that are taxed, and the free services dispensed by the city government go almost entirely to city residents and city business firms. Accordingly, only differential incidence (or "budget incidence" in Musgrave's terminology) is significant in the last analysis. But as a first step, partial equilibrium analysis can be employed, because of the large tax-free area, that is, the rest of the country to which the factors can move and

5. As in many countries in Latin America.
6. As in the United Kingdom.

from which consumers in the city can buy goods and services. That area is tax-free of course, only in the sense that the particular increase in the housing tax, or the introduction of it, that is under study is assumed not to be occurring in the rest of the country.

The tax, or tax increase, that is imposed on housing is assumed to apply also to business real estate in the same city, since in practice this is what occurs. Factors engaged in on-site residential construction cannot therefore move into a tax-free construction sector within the taxing city. But the incidence of the tax on business property, or rather on the factor real estate, is analyzed separately in Section A.3.A below.

A quite different analytical problem is posed by a study of the effects of more or less simultaneous, independent increases in the housing tax by virtually all local units within the country. Now a partial equilibrium approach is not useful at all; no factor has a tax-free area to move to, no consumer a tax-free area to buy from. Differential (or budget) incidence is the only valid concept. The incidence analysis below concentrates initially on the actions of a single decision-making unit, a single city, county, or the like. A brief conjecture on the broader incidence is then offered.

The housing tax is an excise tax that is imposed on the destination principle. To be sure, construction materials enter the city without paying tax at the border, but, when they are complemented by labor at, and fixed on, the site within the city they become subject, as part of the dwelling, to an annual tax, whatever their origin may have been. For a certain substantial part of the value of the dwelling this origin-destination distinction never arises, namely, that part represented by labor at the site. This segment of total value is never imported. Only in mobile homes is labor at the site a small, or negligible, percentage of total value. Exports of housing are exempt, or rather exports of materials later to be embodied in housing elsewhere are exempt.

Thus a small, entirely open geographical unit is able to impose a heavy tax on the destination basis without border control. It can do so only because the tax applies to a large-item consumer good that cannot escape the eye of the tax collector; in this respect the real estate tax on housing is a "use tax" (to be distinguished from a "user tax"), similar to that on automobiles under a retail sales tax.

The discussion turns now to the partial equilibrium incidence of the dwellings-tax part of the real estate tax.

A. INCIDENCE

The dwellings-tax part of the real estate tax in a given city is imposed on a product, dwelling accommodation, that can be supplied only at increasing cost. To put more and more cubic feet of dwelling accommodation on a given parcel of land, as by pushing an apartment house higher and higher, is to encounter increasing costs because of technical factors, for example, increased diameter of pipe needed throughout the building, disproportionate absorption of otherwise usable space by elevator shafts, and the like, not to mention the added expense of hauling materials to higher floors in the course of construction.

At some height the cost of constructing another usable unit of dwelling space, say an apartment of some standard size and quality, is so great that it equals the amount that dwellers are willing to pay for a usable unit at that location. The apartment house is pushed that high and no higher.

Let us suppose for simplicity that the height of the apartment above the ground does not influence the demand for it. Then the same dwelling rental is paid for each apartment in the building, although the cost of constructing each apartment differs from the cost of each of the others. The closer it is to the ground, the less does each apartment cost to construct. Since the rental just covers the cost of the highest-up apartment, it more than covers the cost of the others, by varying amounts, and these varying surpluses, aggregated, make up the site rent. The landowner cannot charge more, or the builder will take his capital elsewhere. He need not charge less site rent, since competition among builders, who ask only the normal return on their capital, will force the land rent up to that figure.

Let a real estate tax now be announced, while a large number of competing apartment houses that are perfect substitutes for one another are still in the planning stage. Let the tax be levied as a percentage of the rent. Such a tax strikes of course the rent paid for the marginal dwelling units (as well as all the other units); these units are on the top floor of each building, where rental is just enough to cover the cost of construction. Before the tax was announced each apartment house was planned to rise, say, 20 stories high. But now the 20th story cannot pay for itself; the rental will not cover both construction cost and tax (no land rent at all is being paid from the dwelling units on the top story), unless demand for dwelling units in all these buildings is perfectly inelastic in the relevant price range. Otherwise, the height of each building must be reduced until cost of construction of the marginal dwelling unit is so reduced that, together with the tax, it is covered by the rental offered when that smaller number of dwelling units is put on the market. Rental per dwelling unit rises somewhat, as households bid for a smaller number of units; cost ex-tax declines. Part of the tax rests on tenants, and part on the owners of the sites, since aggregate land rent will decrease for each site. The builder bears none of the tax, since his capital and effort are in perfectly elastic supply to these ventures; he and his construction workers can go elsewhere.

If the demand for the dwelling units at these sites is perfectly elastic in the relevant price range, construction must be reduced on each apartment house until the construction cost of a dwelling unit on the top floor of each structure is lower than that of the initially planned marginal unit by the full amount of the tax. None of the tax rests on the tenants; all of it rests on the owners of these sites.

As with other excise taxes, the excise tax on dwelling accommodation is divided between the two sides of the competitive market in a ratio that depends on the relative elasticities of demand and supply, the elasticity of supply being given by the increasing-cost schedule of "growing" more dwelling units on a given site. The specialized factor that accounts for this increasing cost is here the site.

If there is no tax, and each building is built to 20 stories in height, aggregate tenants' rental for any one building is divided in a certain proportion between the building capitalist, to cover a normal return on the investment in the building, and the owner of the site. Under perfect competition, and no tax, the elasticity of demand for apartments in these substitutable apartment houses can vary without changing the point of equilibrium, provided that the new demand curve intersects the unchanged cost curve at that initial point, which is represented by the 20th story. Evidently, then, this proportion does not determine the ratio in which a real estate tax will be divided between the tenants and the site owner, for that ratio, we have seen, varies with the elasticity of demand (given the elasticity of supply). The tax on rentals is therefore not to be divided into a tax on building rent (that part of the rent that goes to recompense the capitalist builder) and a tax on site rent in the same proportion that the building rent bears to the site rent.[7]

Let the tax be a percentage, not of aggregate tenants' rental, but of the capital value of each parcel of land plus its building. The tax will still strike the top story of each planned building, the marginal dwelling units of each site, and so will force construction to halt at a lower story, unless demand is perfectly inelastic in the vicinity of the margin. In the absence of a tax, and with construction up to the 20th story, the value of the land, determined by capitalizing the site rental, will bear a certain proportion to the cost of the building. But this ratio is no more informative about how a tax will be divided between tenants and site owner than is the ratio of site rental to building rental. The division of the tax will depend in part on the elasticity of demand. If demand is perfectly elastic, none of the tax will be borne by the tenants.

If a tax is imposed only on the site rentals, or on the capital values of the sites as determined by capitalization of the site rentals, it does not increase the cost of supplying the twentieth story, because this last story yields no surplus on any of the buildings, to pay land rent. Hence the tax does not alter the height of the buildings in the planning stage, and does not affect the rental the tenants pay. All of the tax rests on the site owner.

If the tax is levied only on the cost of constructing each building, construction will stop somewhere below the twentieth floor (unless demand is perfectly inelastic). Prices of all dwelling units on all floors will rise by the same amount, by something less than the tax (unless demand is perfectly elastic). But the tax bill will be smaller, per dwelling unit, the lower the floor, i.e., the lower the cost of construction. The difference between the rise in price and rise in tax on these inframarginal (lower-floor) dwelling units will go to the land owners in land rent.

Up to this point the tax has been assumed to rest only on a group of competing apartment buildings that are perfect substitutes, an assumption made for ease of exposition of the principles underlying shifting. But now let the tax be extended to all dwelling units in the city.

Various groups of dwelling units compete with one another, to varying degrees,

7. See Edgeworth's objection to statements to this effect by McCulloch, J. S. Mill, and Sidgwick. "The Pure Theory of Taxation," from F. Y. Edgeworth, *Papers Relating to Political Economy*, Vol. II, reprinted in Musgrave and Shoup, *Readings in the Economics of Taxation*, pp. 278–79.

from close competition (close substitutes) to negligible competition, for a host of reasons, including differences in time or other cost of transportation to place of work, distance to markets or schools, neighborhood environment, and so on. No a priori statement can be made as to how much of a real estate tax (other than a tax restricted to site rent) will be paid by tenants, how much by landlords, for any given apartment house, by considering the elasticities for that building alone. We face a complex problem in the taxation of rival products, one that has scarcely been formulated, let alone researched, in the literature of public finance. A few generalizations can be made if some highly unreal simplifying assumptions are accepted concerning the reasons for differences in demand for dwelling units at the various locations throughout the city: for example, the Pierson assumption that the difference between prices paid for housing at different sites reflects some cost, say transportation, that would itself be unaffected by a real estate tax, or the Edgeworth assumption that the difference reflects a difference in the "quantity" of housing that can be obtained from a given input, a difference that can be affected, in absolute amount, by a tax on housing. These ramifications will not be pursued here.[8]

Single family houses can be discussed in much the same terms of increasing marginal cost of dwelling accommodation on any given site. The last $1,000 (say) spent in making a dwelling more attractive (more rooms, better construction, etc.) is just covered by the capitalized value of the increment in rental, or for a homeowner, increment in satisfaction, that this $1,000 outlay achieves. The preceding inputs on the house will more than have paid for themselves; they leave a surplus that goes to site rent. The last $1,000 leaves no such surplus. A tax on value of house, or value of house and land, or on rental value of house, or of house and land, reduces the amount of money spent in constructing the house at that site, unless demand is perfectly inelastic.

Once the structures have been fixed on the land, an increase of a tax on the structure resembles an increase of the land tax, since the supply of that particular structure is now not affected by the tax, unless the tax is so heavy that the owner of the structure loses less by paying demolition costs to avoid the structure tax, or, by reducing maintenance outlays, accepting lower rentals and (in principle) obtaining a lower tax assessment.[9]

Considering now all local, state, and similar units in a country, and assuming that they simultaneously impose or increase the tax on housing, we ask, in closed-economy terms, what the differential incidence of the housing tax is, using the value-added tax (consumption type) as the base for comparison.

Much depends on the period of time assumed. The housing tax is a tax on a stock; the value-added tax is one on a flow. The pattern of factor flows among industries, and of consumer purchasing flows among products can be changed quickly compared with the pattern and total of stock of a certain durable good. In the

8. For an analysis of these two assumptions, and a general statement of the incidence of the tax, see Herbert A. Simon, "The Incidence of a Tax on Urban Real Property," *Quarterly Journal of Economics* (May, 1943), 57: 398–420, reprinted in Musgrave and Shoup (Eds.), *op. cit.*, pp. 416–35.

9. See James Heilbrun, *Real Estate Taxes and Urban Housing* (New York: Columbia University Press, 1966).

very long run, when even the stock will have reached its new equilibrium of pattern and amount, replacing a value-added tax by a housing tax would create a net adverse pressure on certain land and on labor and capital equipment specialized in the production of housing, and on households spending more than the average proportion of the family budget on housing. This latter group are probably for the most part low-income households; the disadvantaged labor factors might be anywhere in the income spectrum: the disadvantaged owners of dwelling land and of specialized capital equipment for constructing housing are probably in the upper income groups. In the absence of studies using general equilibrium models we may perhaps conjecture that the differential incidence of the housing tax is somewhat regressive with income, but very irregularly so.

Finally, the simultaneous increase in the housing tax all over the country may be regarded in the international setting, reverting thus to an open-economy analysis. The analysis given above can be repeated, but under an assumption that the mobility of factors to an untaxed area is almost nil for labor and fairly low for most capital.

B. CRITERIA

Under the equal treatment of equals test the housing tax scores much better than the widespread criticism of real estate taxation might suggest. The number and importance of irrelevant circumstances that affect the amount of tax due are not great, compared with, say, the income tax. A tax that purports to tax all housing, except that specifically exempted, does so to a closer approximation than a tax that purports to tax income does with respect to all income. There is no gap in the housing tax comparable with that found in the income tax for imputed income.

Housing tax laws avoid personalization without any loss in certainty and contain few quantitative discontinuities. Qualitative discontinuities are fewer here than in the tax on business real estate (see Section A.3.B below). Cost of compliance is equal for all, being virtually zero. Only in degree of dispersion of rates of mispayment, both within the group of dwelling owners or renters and between them and the business-real-estate taxpayers does the housing tax fail to observe the equal-treatment criterion closely. The average degree of underassessment of the real estate tax as a whole, though large, probably does not in most countries create much injustice for other taxpaying groups in the community. If the underassessment were rectified, real estate tax rates would probably be lowered promptly and almost proportionately (see Chapter 2, Section A.1.A). Indeed, a part of the disparity between valuation of dwellings and of all other property is in many jurisdictions a reflection of community consensus that the excise tax on housing should be imposed at a lower rate than the general business tax on real estate as a factor of production.

Data revealing a wide range of assessed to true value show that the criterion of equal mispayment is far from being observed,[10] but if only a few cases are at the extremes, the degree of inequity may not be great after all.

10. See the summary of *Census of Governments* information on ratios of assessed values to sales price for real estate (not merely housing) taxed in the United States, in James A. Maxwell,

On the Pareto-optimum test the housing tax scores very poorly, at least if no account is taken of the use made of the revenue (see Chapter 21 below). The demand for dwelling accommodation is perhaps fairly price-elastic in the middle and upper ranges of income; such families can purchase many good substitutes for increments of dwelling, considering the amount of dwelling they consume. They can easily move to longer cars and shorter houses, richer food and somewhat closer quarters, finer clothing and less substantial building materials. For a low-income family, already cramped in housing accommodation, demand may be less elastic, and the excess burden may not be so substantial, since its income elasticity of demand for housing may be rather high, and a large proportion of household income is spent for housing, at least in the absence of rent control. But if the excess burden is moderate, the non-excess part of the burden is heavy by usual standards. No other tax strikes so severely, relative to other expenditures, an outlay that is so large a proportion of the total family budget of a low-income household. A capital value-tax of 2 per cent is equivalent to a tax of 20 per cent on gross rental, if rental is 10 per cent of capital value (say, 5 per cent for depreciation and maintenance and 5 per cent for net return). There is a good case for imposing the housing part of the real estate tax at a much lower rate than the business-property part, since the latter does not concentrate its pressure so heavily on one aspect of the consumer budget, an aspect that is relatively more important in the low-income budget—again aside from rent control.

The insensitivity of the housing tax to a decrease in national income is another reason why it is more suitable for local than for national finance. Indeed, what built-in flexibility there is may merely cause the tax revenue to rise less rapidly, since the tax is based on a stock of durables that is continually increasing, even in periods of recession, in most countries. It will be quite unusual for a year's depreciation and obsolescence of the housing stock to exceed the value of new housing constructed.

The housing tax does moderately well under the conflict criteria of the distributive type and could be much better adapted to them than it usually is.

At a uniform tax rate, that part of the tax that rests on landowners is progressive with income, in an irregular way, since ownership of wealth does not appear until a very low income level has been passed, and it thereafter increases more than in proportion to income. But this progressivity may be no more than formal. A large part of the tax that rests on land, in the heavily taxing jurisdictions, has long since been discounted in the purchase price of the land, so that what appears to be a somewhat progressive tax is no burden at all to the present owners. To be sure, if the tax were repealed or lowered, the benefit would be distributed progressively.[11]

How regressively distributed the buildings part of the housing tax may be depends on consumer habits that vary somewhat from country to country. But those

Financing State and Local Governments (Washington, D.C.: Brookings Institution, 1965), pp. 137–46.

11. The absence of a heavy real estate tax in many Latin American countries explains in large part why the land values in the residential areas of cities in those countries are strikingly higher than land values in similar sections of cities in the United States.

countries in which lavish expenditure on housing is the greatest symbol of affluence happen to be those in which the real estate tax is light; under pressure of a world-wide uniform housing tax, differences in consumer tastes might turn out to be less than they now appear. If this is so, the housing tax is least regressive in those countries where the rate of the tax is low.

The income concept to be employed in defining progressivity or regressivity for this tax is long-period income rather than current income. A temporary decline in income will not normally force the household to move to a lower-priced dwelling.

The burden of the housing tax on the low-income family is substantial in those countries where the rate is, say, 2 per cent or more. If, to continue the illustration above, the low-income household spends 30 per cent of its income on dwelling rental, actual or imputed, the tax amounts to 6 per cent of income; and if, say, two-thirds of the tax rests on the dweller rather than on the landowner and the factors engaged in building dwellings, the burden is 4 per cent of income. This is a heavy flat rate tax for a low-income family; only in countries with a per capita income that is high and not extremely unevenly distributed can the lowest income classes be called on to pay this much tax for dwelling accommodation. Only such countries can afford the luxury of responsible local governments that finance themselves in large part by a dwellings tax. An undeveloped country is unlikely to make heavy use of a dwellings tax until its per capita income has risen considerably, that is, until it becomes partly developed.

Even the wealthy countries mitigate the burden of the dwellings tax on the very poor, and sometimes on the not-so-poor, by exempting the first, say, $5,000 of the value of an owner-occupied property, by providing public housing erected under tax-exemption or tax-reduction provisions, and the like. Exemption in this manner of a minimum capital amount for houses and, indirectly, of a minimum rental for apartments reduces regressivity. On the other hand, deductibility of the tax in computing the base of the income tax for a homeowner under progressive income tax rates increases regressivity.

Discrimination among homeowners, but not among tenants, according to their age, or status as veterans of wars, has proved feasible; discrimination according to number of children in the household has apparently not been tried but should be administratively practicable. All such provisions could be extended to tenants by reducing the tax bill of the owner of the house or apartment in some proportion to the age pattern or family size of his tenants' households. Competition among land-lords would pass most of these tax benefits on to the tenants. The lack of imaginative programs in these directions has perhaps been due to the habit of lumping the housing tax with the business property tax and so considering it somehow to be impersonal, not to be varied with the circumstances of the owner or tenant. The low level of administrative effort commonly allowed for enforcement of the dwellings tax has discouraged even these simple departures from a nominal uniformity. Meanwhile, if no special provisions of this kind are made, the housing tax probably rests more heavily on the families with more children, since they presumably spend a larger proportion of a given income on dwelling space.

Geographical discrimination through the housing tax in favor of depressed areas is feasible in large cities, in provinces and states, and perhaps also in smaller cities. But the depression to be mitigated is that of consumers of housing, not that of owners as such, and, unless the discrimination increases the physical supply of housing, the consumer tenant will gain nothing. The homeowner will of course benefit even if the supply of housing does not increase, because of his dual status as owner and consumer. Exemption or a low tax rate on new single-family housing in a depressed area may achieve little if there are few moderate-income or high-income families in that area who can buy the new dwellings and, placing their old ones on the market, depress prices there. Building new single-family housing that the very poor can buy even with a moderate subsidy is usually not feasible. Tax exemption or a low tax rate granted to dwellings that are for rent, in contrast, may well increase the supply of new housing for the poor (see Chapter 7, pages 186–90).

The housing tax lends itself all too easily to discrimination by color, ethnic, or status group when the dwellings are single-family houses or when an entire area is homogeneous in these respects.

The dwelling tax is on the whole conducive to economic growth. Much of the burden falls on households that have no choice but to reduce consumption to meet the tax. At extremely low income levels, to be sure, some of this consumption foregone would be gainful (see Chapter 23, pages 592–93), and growth would therefore be hampered; this is another reason for conjecturing that in a very low-income country a high-rate real estate tax on modest dwellings is not appropriate.

As to inducement to invest, the dwellings tax impairs incentives only with respect to this one type of investment, which, though as genuine as any other in providing for future wants by use of current resources, is in its luxury forms viewed with disfavor by advocates of economic growth, at least for less developed countries. This judgment implies dislike of the current distribution of income from which saving is made and emphasizes the fact that the growth criterion in any form is a conflict-of-interests criterion.

The effect of the housing tax on risk-taking is discussed in Section 3.B below, together with the effect of the rest of the real estate tax. The balance of payments of the taxing city with the rest of the country will be put incrementally in surplus by the income effect of the tax, to the degree that the incidence of the tax rests on persons residing in the city rather than on nonresident landlords. The substitution effect, deflecting demand from materials and supplies for housing, may worsen the city's balance of payments, if those materials and supplies are produced within the city and the rival commodities, outside the city. Otherwise, the effect will be favorable, since a part of the on-site labor no longer needed may go into the city's export trades.

That part of the dwellings tax that is not absorbed in land rent probably induces more work by dwellers of almost all income classes except the highest than does an equal-yield income tax or sales tax. The increase in work is probably greatest in the low-income groups, in view of the relatively heavy pressure of the tax at those levels. These remarks assume that the marginal effects of the tax are not perceived as clearly as, and do not exert the continuing day-by-day pressure of, those of a sales tax or income tax. One who considers working longer hours and, with part of his extra earnings, housing his family a little better, is no doubt discouraged from doing so by dwelling rentals or home-purchase costs higher than would obtain under no dwellings tax; the substitution effect is not quite zero. But since this kind of a decision, that is, to change dwelling accommodation, is not taken frequently, there may elapse a long period when a rising rate of dwelling tax exerts no appreciable aggregate substitution effect on decisions within the community with respect to accepting overtime work, moonlighting, refraining from absenteeism, and similar actions.

Intragovernmental aspects and intra-system relations are important only in those few local units that impose an income tax. If deduction of the same unit's real estate tax is allowed to homeowners in computing taxable income, an increase in the dwellings tax will decrease the yield of the income tax. Landlords will deduct the dwellings tax as an expense, and, to the degree that they do not recoup the tax in increased rents, the yield of the income tax falls. An increase in the city's income tax rates may cause property values to decline and so also the yield of the property tax.

3. The Tax on Business Real Estate

The factor tax on business real estate, in so far as it is shifted forward, is a production tax (on a particular factor) on the origin principle and not at all, in contrast to the excise tax on housing, on the destination principle. To be sure, if a parcel of business real estate is moved into the taxing area, a mobile warehouse for example, it becomes taxable, and real estate produced in the taxing area but sent elsewhere for use, a pre-fabricated factory, for example, pays no property tax in this first area. The distinction between the origin and destination principles, however, does not involve factor location or factor geographic flow, but only the product of the factors. Clothing, for example, will not be given relief for whatever part of the real estate tax is embodied in its price when it is exported. It is being taxed, indirectly, through a tax on one of the factors (real estate) that produces it.

The rest of the factor tax, the part not shifted forward, is an (origin-principle) income tax levied on a source basis, not on a residence basis.

A real estate tax on factories, shops, and the like could conceivably be levied on the destination principle. A producer for export would be relieved of the real estate tax on the land and building he used and would be given a rebate of real estate taxes presumed paid at previous stages of production of the good. He would be over-compensated, to be sure, since some part of the tax, as just noted, would have been absorbed by domestic owners of real estate and so would not have constituted a competitive threat for him in his external markets. But such overcompensation is a feature of all destination-basis tax systems; the export rebates assume, in principle, that the entire tax is embodied in the price of the product. On the import side, producers for the domestic market would be protected from goods made elsewhere by a compensating import tax, which again would include overprotection, since some of the domestic real estate tax would not go into the price of domestically produced goods.

This picture of a destination-principle tax on business real estate is quite unreal, however, at least for a local government unit. Without the power to exercise fiscal control at its borders, the taxing city cannot implement the destination principle, at least not for imports. In any event the task of estimating the amount of real estate tax embodied in the price of an export, or escaped on an import, would be a perplexing one, entirely apart from attempting to distinguish the part shifted from the part absorbed by factors.

The business real estate tax, then, resembles the excise tax on housing in being capable of operation without border control, but for quite a different reason: the origin basis inherently requires no border control.

A. INCIDENCE

A single, small local political unit that attempted to increase substantially its real estate tax on business property while other geographical entities were not raising theirs would render its producers unable to compete with firms in the other areas at the old prices, until they cut back output by reducing the intensity with which they utilized land until costs at the new margin were low enough, and a higher point on the demand schedules for their products was reached, to allow the tax to be fully absorbed at this new margin. There is no exchange rate that can substitute for this process, by depreciating. Specialized and immobile factors, particularly real estate itself, would thus have to absorb the tax and would fall accordingly in value. In this analysis, the intensive and extensive margins of building described above for dwellings exist for factories and commercial structures, but now the "crop" is a producers' good, not a consumers' good. Office buildings, retail stores, wholesale warehouses, and factory buildings utilize land more or less intensively and extensively. The convenient concept of a floor or story is not so easily used, aside from office buildings. But there is always an intensive margin of building on a given plot of land, even for a one-story supermarket, in terms of incremental durability, appearance, and interior fixed equipment. And there is an extensive margin of land use, linked with costs of transportation.

The occupying firm's demand for building space, in contrast to the household's demand for dwelling space, is a derived demand, dependent on the demand for the firm's own products and on the supply of other factors that the firm may use more intensively as a partial substitute for building space.

Insofar as the firm's customers, in or out of the city, can easily turn to other firms in other cities, that firm's demand for building space is far more elastic than the household's demand for dwelling space. Although any given household can contemplate moving to another city, its mobility is less than the mobility of much of the demand of customers of the business firms. To be sure, some of these firms render services chiefly to inhabitants of the same city, who cannot readily switch their demand to firms in other cities. And even when the firms sell their products outside the city, a particular city may offer economies of scale to a certain branch of activity; the "front office" activity in New York City, for example, is so substantial that demand for space by certain business groupings is fairly inelastic. The expenses of the central office of a nation-wide or international concern, located in a metropolitan area, are but a small fraction of the total sales of the company, and that part of the real estate tax borne by this tenant is a small part of those expenses. If, as is usual, there is no good substitute for the metropolitan area as a home for the central office, the company's demand for rental space will be very inelastic. The city government collects what for it are large sums by indirectly raising by a negligible percentage the price of the thousands of items the firm sells. For other types of business, for example, certain types of manufacturing by smaller enterprises, there are close substitutes for location in such a city, and the city's tax is a larger percentage of the sales revenue of this firm. The aggregate demand by such firms for space in the city may thus be fairly price-elastic. The real estate tax reduces the number of such firms or their size (abstracting from the services rendered by the city, financed by this revenue), and a large part of the general-business tax segment of the real estate tax comes out of landowners.

In addition, the firm can use other factors as substitutes for some of the taxed factor. If customers are to be impressed, more expensive furniture may offset a decrease in size of office. Similar considerations, we have seen, influence a household's demand for dwelling space. But it is not clear whether these substitution possibilities are stronger for the business firm than for the household as a consumer of dwellings.

In general: the business real estate tax of a single local area, assuming no other areas to be imposing such a tax (or a tax increase confined to this area) will be passed forward little if at all to consumers in other areas, and will not burden consumers in the taxed area appreciably, since imports enter tax-free, except as transport costs or the sheer inability to transport (e.g., certain retail services) provide a measure of protection.

In a city that is static or declining for reasons unconnected with the real estate tax, that tax can rise very high without affecting the volume of business done in the city. The tax on buildings is then one on quasi-rent. Building rentals, and land rentals with them, will fall pari passu with the increase in tax rate. But in practice it is difficult to ascertain why a city is stagnant or declining; the continued prospect of high real estate taxes can easily stifle a potential economic renaissance. In principle, however, an increase in the tax rate discourages location only in a growing city, or in one that is replacing or renovating its buildings.

If the business real estate tax is being imposed, or increased, all over the country by roughly the same amount, its differential incidence is almost random with respect to income class (the consumption type of value-added tax is the base for comparison). General observation does not suggest in what income strata there fall those households that buy proportionately more of goods or services in the production of which real estate is a significant factor. Land owners suffer somewhat. The marginal productivity of capital will fall as part of it is pressed out of one sector (real estate) into others.

In an international open-economy setting, under partial-equilibrium analysis, the business real estate tax, being on the origin principle, exerts pressure toward devaluation of the currency. If elasticities are perfect, domestic exporters cannot shift any of the tax to export purchasers, and producers of import-competing goods cannot shift any of the tax to domestic consumers. These remarks abstract from the concomitant services to business firms by the government. In those countries that impose the tax on business real estate at a substantial rate, it is the only heavy tax that, while increasing the marginal cost of producing almost all commodities and services, is nevertheless imposed on the origin basis. If each of these countries accounts for a substantial amount of total foreign trade,[12] the demand for their exports is not perfectly elastic, and they can shift part of the tax to foreign buyers. At the same time, foreign supply to these countries is not perfectly elastic; import-competing producers can shift some of the tax to domestic consumers.

B. CRITERIA

The business real estate tax will be appraised here only as it differs appreciably from the housing excise tax. This factor tax scores poorly on qualitative discontinuities; the borderline between immovable property (real estate) and movable property (tangible personal property) itself shifts continually with technological developments. At what point, for example, does a wall become a partition? If the line is drawn to exempt all machinery that is not permanently attached to the building, a premium is placed on using less efficient, lighter machinery, and on arrangements that make the degree of attachment seem not permanent.

If the tax includes certain movables, notably inventories, another discontinuity becomes important, now in the time dimension. The day of the year on which the inventory is held must be specified, or, if artificial fluctuations in inventory are to be avoided, an average value must be computed for a number of days. If the tax includes even certain intangibles, bank deposits, for example, a large number of days' values must be averaged if these movables are not to be shifted in and out of taxing jurisdictions in great amounts around the tax date.

The tax diffuses its pressure over many consumer goods, but induces consumers to buy more of products made with little use of real estate, and it promotes inefficiency in production of any one commodity by inducing some substitution of non-realty means of production.

On balance, the business real estate tax is probably somewhat progressive by income, relative to a housing tax that does not exempt low-cost housing and perhaps even relative to a value-added tax. It cannot discriminate purposefully among households of different patterns of consumption, size, and the like. A lower tax rate in a depressed area will benefit owners of real estate there, resident or non-resident, and will increase the area's employment, but only over the long run, and then only if the taxpayers are persuaded that the tax relief will last for many years.

Not much of the business real estate tax will be exported (see under "Incidence" above), unless "exporting" includes capitalization of the tax on land owned by a non-resident.

12. As do, notably, the United Kingdom and the United States.

Those who attempt to discriminate by race, color, or status, either against owners of business real estate or against consumers of products made with the help of taxed real estate, find this tax not useful to them, except in areas where it is known that the owners and the consumers are all of one group.

The tax probably comes more out of saving than does the housing tax, in view of its differential incidence; in this respect it hinders economic growth. Whether its substitution effect encourages current consumption is not at all clear. If all consumer goods were made by capital-intensive methods and all capital goods were made by labor-intensive methods, the chief effect of the tax might be to induce less efficient methods of producing consumer goods. In any event the tax presumably deters a certain amount of investment unless the supply of capital is perfectly price-inelastic.

As to risk, the business real estate tax differs from the income tax, for the tax bill is not zero or negative when the firm's profit is zero or negative. If a firm borrows to purchase a taxable capital good, it must pay the real estate tax whatever may happen to its equity capital. Every one of the possible outcomes of a venture is thereby made somewhat worse, as under the net worth tax, save in the rare case where the tax may be completely shifted. Accordingly, relative to the value-added tax, consumption type, the real estate tax may reduce risk-taking, for the reasons advanced in the discussion of the net worth tax, in pages 365–66 above.

For any one city, the general-business part of the real estate tax, being an origin-principle tax, affects external equilibrium in just the reverse direction from that of the housing tax. In the common case where elasticities of demand and supply are perfect for the city's exports and imports, an increase in this part of the real estate tax does not change the terms of trade, but throws the city's balance of trade into incremental deficit.[13] If all local units increase the real estate tax rate over a period of years,[14] the balance of trade of the entire nation is worsened. Again, this statement abstracts from the services rendered free to business firms, financed by this tax. And it applies only to that part of the tax that is not absorbed in land rent or other factor rewards.

A marginal pressure against work is probably exerted by the business real estate tax more strongly than by the dwellings tax; the effects are presumably much like those of the turnover tax.

Exempting real estate held by charitable, religious, educational and similar organizations creates a differential between what a household can get for its money spent on itself and what it can get indirectly by giving money to such an organization to acquire real estate. But the inducement to the donor is weaker than the inducement offered by the income tax, where the donor's own tax can be directly and immediately reduced, through deduction of the contribution.

If, as is to be expected, the real estate tax drives down the price of land, these tax-exempt organizations benefit from the tax in so far as they wish to buy land. Those that wish to sell some of their land are of course disadvantaged.

13. See the reasoning for an origin-principle turnover tax, in Chapter 8.
14. As in the United States, 1950–67.

No international double taxation occurs under the real estate tax, for it is a long-established practice in every country to disregard the residence of the owner; the location of the property fixes its taxability.

If the state or local property tax paid by a household is deductible in computing that household's taxable income under a national income tax, an increase in the property tax rate falls partly on the taxpayer and partly on the national government, which must then raise its income tax rate to maintain the yield. In effect, the local unit exports part of the real estate tax to the rest of the nation. But if all local units increase their real estate taxes more or less together, as is commonly the case, the property owners of any one local unit may lose by the deductibility provision.

If the national government increases its income tax rates, local real estate tax revenues may fall, as real estate's disposable income declines, and hence its taxable value.

An increase in the real estate tax rate by a governmental unit that also levies an income tax will bring in less net revenue than the product of tax rate and tax base, since income tax revenue will fall because the real estate tax is deductible, at least by business concerns, in computing taxable income. The yield of a sales tax, on the other hand, will not be directly affected by an increase in the real estate tax rate.

4. Gross Rentals Real Estate Tax[15]

The gross-rentals real estate tax will be analyzed here only as it differs from the capital-value tax in its incidence or with respect to the several criteria.

"Gross rental" for real estate must be carefully defined if equals are to be treated equally. The definition employed here excludes that part of gross rental, if any, that is paid because the landlord agrees to supply furniture, furnishings, equipment other than fixed assets, electricity, gas, water, or super-standard maintenance, or because the tenant is granted an option to renew. It includes the real estate tax itself if the tenant is responsible for payment of the tax.

Owner-occupied real estate is assumed to be taxed on an imputed gross rental, and vacant structures and unimproved land on an imputed best-use gross rental, as are also structures or land not being put to their best current use in terms of gross rental obtainable. Many gross rental taxes in fact do not reach these imputed or potential amounts, and consequently do not, as does the capital-value tax, stimulate a present-value-maximizing use of land and of already existing structures.

The ratio of gross rental to capital value varies, since some buildings are less solidly or less luxuriously constructed than others that rent for the same amount. Their rentals go more to cover maintenance and depreciation, and less to net return on capital. A gross rentals tax will therefore encourage the building of long-lived,

15. See the analysis by C. Lowell Harriss, in Shoup, Harriss and Vickrey, *The Fiscal System of the Federal District of ·Venezuela* (privately printed, New York City, 1960), Chapter IV, "Real Estate Tax"; James Heilbrun, *Real Estate Taxes and Urban Housing* (New York: Columbia University Press, 1966), Chapter 10; and Dick Netzer, *Economics of the Property Tax*, pp. 192–97.

luxurious, maintenance-free structures, while the capital-value tax will encourage the type of structure that has a short life unless heavily maintained by painting, repairs, and the like. Correspondingly, the differential incidence of the gross rentals tax will vary from that of a capital-value tax, but in just what pattern, it is not clear. Land may or may not bear more of the gross rentals tax than of the capital-value tax, over the long run. In the short run, given the existing stock of buildings, the base of the gross rentals tax will be larger than that of a net rentals tax (the equivalent of a capital-value tax), and the tax rate lower. If the tax were assessed in two parts, one tax bill being sent to the landowner and the other, based on gross rent less land rent, to the building owner, the landowner's tax would be smaller than under a similar two-billing assumption for a net rentals tax.[16]

The gross rentals tax will be somewhat less satisfactory than the capital-value tax with respect to consensus equity, because a few additional discontinuities will usually appear, owing to the difficulty of defining taxable gross rental precisely. Most of the definitional difficulties, however, will be simply the counterparts of those found in defining real estate under the capital-value tax.

If tenancy rather than ownership is the prevailing pattern, administrative injustices will be less under a rentals tax than under a capital-value tax, since appeal can be made to the numerous rental contracts of similar properties. In the urban areas of less developed countries, residential property is more commonly rented than owner-occupied, and so too in the largest core cities, as distinguished from the suburbs, in industrialized countries.

In a business recession short-term rentals should in principle fluctuate more than capital values, which reflect in large part an average anticipated rental over a period of years. The rentals real estate tax is thus more sensitive than the capital-value tax.

Excess burden in the form of tax-induced changes in methods of doing business will be created by a gross rentals tax because the tax will lead the contracting parties to place as much as possible of the expenses of maintenance and similar outlays on the tenant, at least as much as can be done without arousing the tax official to go back of the contract and set a standard rental value on the real estate.

As noted above, for a given quality and quantity of accommodation supplied, a building can either be constructed solidly and expensively, to last for a long time and to require little maintenance, or be constructed cheaply, to require frequent reconstruction and large maintenance outlays. The gross rentals tax, being of the same amount in either case, does not affect the decision which method of construction to use. But the capital-value tax exerts pressure to build cheaply and spend much on maintenance. As extreme cases, let us suppose one building that never wears out and requires no maintenance and another building that must be so heavily maintained as to be in effect rebuilt every day. The first building has a high capital value, the second building virtually none. Without any tax, let them be equally attractive to tenants and equally costly to provide: the annual interest on the one equals the annual maintenance expenditure on the other. A tax on gross rentals will leave them still equally costly to supply. A tax on capital value will render the durable type of building the more costly to supply. In this sense the gross rentals real

16. See Heilbrun, *Real Estate Taxes and Urban Housing*, p. 128.

estate tax creates no excess burden, while the capital-value tax does. The contrast is simply another illustration of the familiar theorem that a tax on consumption spending does not, while a tax on income or capital value does, alter the rate at which future consumption can be substituted for present consumption. For the same reason, maintenance of a kind that increases the value of a building beyond enabling the owner to charge more rental only for the period of maintenance expenditure is discouraged by the capital-value tax.

If the use made of the tax revenues is considered, from a cost-benefit point of view, the tax rate should be lower, the more solid the structure. A flimsy building that requires much maintenance is more of a fire hazard and puts a greater burden on the refuse removal department. This link with expenditure may counterbalance the excess burden of the capital-value tax noted above.

As to distribution of the tax burden by income or wealth class, the gross rentals tax is probably more regressive, since the well-to-do tend to inhabit dwellings that are more solidly built, hence attract a larger share of the tax, if the tax is based on capital value.

5. Length, Area, or Volume Tax

A real estate tax may be based, not on money values at all, but on physical quantities. This variant differs from the gross rentals variant much as the specific excise differs from the ad valorem excise. But the rationale is quite different; it is that the real estate tax is in part simply a price for services rendered and should vary with the cost of the services. The cost of a certain government service may vary more directly with the number of front feet of the lot, or the area of the lot, the area covered by the structure, the square feet of floor space or the cubic-foot content of the building than with gross rental or capital value.

A tax on front footage, a length tax, varying from one part of a city to another, and a tax on area of the land would rest entirely on the landowner. The tax might drive out of urban "cultivation" land on the extensive margin, which could escape the tax by reverting to agriculture. In that event the pressure of unchanged demand for building space would raise the intensive margins of building generally throughout the city, causing higher marginal costs. But these higher costs to building occupiers would not reflect, in the usual terminology, a shifting of the footage or area tax. And the tax would exert no direct effect on the margins of building, hence no direct effect on the cost of goods and services, including dwelling service, produced in the city. Land values would fall (abstracting from the fire protection and other services rendered in exchange for the tax).

A tax on floor area or cubic volume would in contrast strike directly at the margin of building. If only usable area or volume were included in the tax base, thus excluding stair landings or elevator shafts, for example, the effect might be like that of a tax on gross rentals, if gross rentals were the same per square foot or cubic foot throughout the building.

Under the consensus equity criteria these physical-unit taxes might rank higher than the more sophisticated, hence more difficult, money-base taxes. But severe discontinuities would exist, at least in definitions of floor area or of volume of a building. None of these physical-base taxes would be sensitive to a change in national income. The land taxes would create no excess burden, but the floor area and volume taxes would alter substantially the design of buildings, depending on how the tax base was defined.

As to the conflict criteria, the length-area-volume taxes on buildings would be regressive relative to the money-base taxes, since they would take no account of the quality factor that is so important in satisfying the demand of the well-to-do, whether as dwellers or shoppers. Imposed on land, these taxes might be progressive relative to the money-base taxes, depending on how land ownership is distributed by income class. For factories, the building taxes would put a premium on crowding as much movable property into as little real property as possible. Large families, willing to trade off quality for more space, would pay more under the other taxes.

For the reallocation type of conflict criteria, no general statements for comparison with the money-base taxes can be made. No doubt the effects on growth, risk-taking, and the other goals would differ, but precisely how, or even just in which direction, must be studied in detail case by case.

B. TAXES ON TRANSFERS FOR A CONSIDERATION

1. Conceptual Basis and Scope

Taxes on transfers for a consideration differ from sales taxes in being imposed chiefly on transfers of ownership to portions of a more or less fixed stock, notably real estate and securities.[17] Occasionally these transfer taxes are linked with production, as when a newly constructed building is taxed upon sale to its first user or where the

17. The most widely used are the taxes on transfer of shares, bonds, and other securities, under rates that vary from about ¼ of 1 per cent (United States, federal government, on shares, and France and Germany) to 2 per cent (United Kingdom), and taxes on real property transfers, often at higher rates but with many exemptions: e.g., United Kingdom (2 per cent, but reduced rates under £5,000), German (federal, 2 or 3 per cent, and states, up to 4 per cent, but the base is "assessed value," which is still the 1935 value [Gumpel and Boettcher, *Taxation in Germany*, pp. 208, 713], and exemption is granted to transfers of one-family houses and cooperatives and to transfers between ancestors and lineal descendents); France (16 per cent, but housing and certain acquisitions for modernizing, etc., are taxed at 4.2 per cent [newly constructed housing is taxed under the value-added tax] and the 16 per cent tax on the transfer for a consideration of a business enterprise or of its clientele is reduced to 4.2 per cent on inventory, and on acquisition of real property "with a view toward the creation of a new industry in an area with high and chronic unemployment" [Norr and Kerlan, *Taxation in France*, pp. 174–75; quotation, p. 163]).

Most of these systems make heavy or exclusive use of stamps affixed to the pertinent document, to collect the tax, and if, in the United Kingdom, for example, "a transaction . . . is not consummated by means of utterance of a written instrument [it] is not subject to [stamp] tax . . ." (Walter W. Brudno and Frank Bower, *Taxation in the United Kingdom*, World Tax Series, Law School of Harvard University [Boston: Little, Brown, 1957], p. 96).

tax applies to the issuance of securities that a newly formed corporation is selling to obtain the proceeds needed to initiate production. Receipts and bills of exchange, defined sometimes to include bank checks, are in some countries[18] subject to stamp tax, which is to this extent a sort of crude sales tax of the turnover type.

To focus ideas on the main attribute of these heterogeneous taxes, the following analysis will assume that the stock of things that is subject to tax upon transfer is fixed in total. A sale then simply redistributes ownership of part of the stock.

Transfer taxes of this kind are taxes on changes of opinion with respect to desirability of holding the asset, chiefly a change of opinion regarding future prices. At an initial equilibrium the units of the stock are distributed among various persons in a manner such that no one wishes to trade at the prevailing bid and ask prices. The market has been cleared, and no sales will take place until at least one person alters his propensity to hold. When he does, he will raise the bid price, or lower the asking price, and can then trade with someone whose propensity to hold has remained unchanged. "Holders" as here defined includes those who hold zero units or negative units, that is, are short of the commodity.

If all holders' propensities change in the same direction and by the same amounts, no trades will occur, but the bid-asked prices will fall or rise. If a large number of the holders alter their opinions on future prices in one direction and another equally large number change theirs simultaneously in the opposite direction, a heavy volume of trading will occur, but, in the extreme case, the bid and ask prices will be the same as before.

These observations apply chiefly to well-organized markets in securities and commodities (wheat, sugar, and the like). Real estate markets are so fragmented that each potential transfer constitutes a market by itself. A sale occurs if the actual holder and a potential holder of this property find that the former's selling range, say $10,000 and up, overlaps the other's buying range, say $12,000 or less. By negotiation they arrive at a price somewhere in this range. But the limits of the ranges are determined partly by what the seller thinks he could get from others and by the price at which the buyer believes he could persuade others to sell comparable properties.

In the usual case, a transfer tax prevents a sale when the change in opinion does not pass a minimum; the size of the minimum depends on the rate of the tax and the shapes of the demand functions. Once the change in opinion passes this minimum, a per-unit tax has no influence on the course of action. But since in the normal course opinions of many holders are changing frequently and by varying amounts, the aggregate effect of the tax is to reduce the volume of transactions in any given time period. The percentage by which it reduces transactions is greatest in times when opinions are fairly stable, or where they all change almost uniformly. Volume of trading is low, even under no tax. The transfers that do occur reflect only a narrow overlap between buyer's range and seller's range, and so will be repressed by even a light tax. But in periods of convulsion, when a massive change of opinion occurs in a large segment of the market but in the rest of the market not at all, or not to the

18. For example, the United Kingdom (2d. per instrument, and higher on some of those not payable on demand); Germany (DM 0.15 for each DM 100 or fraction, checks excluded).

same degree, or perhaps even in the opposite direction, the overlaps are wide and even a heavy tax will not reduce by very much, in percentage terms, the physical volume of transactions.

The tax affects the allocation of the stock, if it is imposed before the market is cleared. Suppose that initially the stock is all in the hands of one subgroup, "S" (for "sellers"), who come to the market where the other subgroup "B" (buyers) are waiting to purchase some of the stock of this good if the price is right. The price that clears the market, in the absence of a tax, is, we assume, one that leaves some of the stock in the hands of the S group. If a per-unit tax is in force, the market will be cleared at a price lower to the sellers and higher to the buyers (the tax fills the gap) than the price that obtains in absence of the tax; and the number of units transferred from S to B will be smaller.

If the initial equilibrium has been reached in the absence of a tax, and the tax is then introduced, it will not, by itself, induce further trading. No seller can get as high a net price as he could just before the tax was introduced, yet no seller was willing to sell at that price at that moment. No buyer can buy at a lower price than before. The importance of the tax, then, lies in the influence it exerts when disequilibrium occurs.

2. Incidence

The incidence of the tax can be analyzed in partial equilibrium terms and measured by the proportions of the tax borne by the buyers and sellers. These proportions will depend upon the relative elasticities of demand. "Supply" is not a necessary concept in the case of a fixed stock, since those who are about to sell some of it can be described in terms of their demand for the commodity.[19]

The incidence is not related to the amount of profit or loss that the seller is realizing on the sale, except as that amount influences his elasticity of demand. The transfer tax is therefore not even a rough substitute for the taxation of capital gains[20] and the allowance of capital losses under the income tax.

Successive purchasers of a parcel of real estate or a share of stock may be buying free of part of the transfer tax, since the prospect of such taxes may have been discounted, in part at least, in the price of the real estate or security when the tax was introduced or raised. There is little tax-free area for capital to resort to, but, when a large difference in transfer-tax rates among various types of property exists, some part of that difference may be expected to be discounted.

19. See, for example, Alfred W. Stonier and Douglas C. Hague, *A Textbook of Economic Theory*, 3d ed. (London: Longmans, Green, 1964), pp. 26–29.

20. See Charles Kennedy, "Stamp Duties as a Capital Gains Tax, *Review of Economic Studies* (1956) 23(3): 241–44; Carl S. Shoup, "Comment," *ibid.* (October, 1957), 25: 53–57; Kennedy, *ibid.*, "A Reply" (October, 1957), 25: 58.

3. Criteria

These transfer taxes, generally known as stamp or registration taxes, fall short of several of the criteria of consensus equity by a wider margin than any other tax. Relevant circumstances are difficult to isolate; certainty exists only for the taxpayer who possesses skilled help in analyzing hundreds of descriptions in the law and regulations;[21] small qualitative differences, usually in legal status, often make the difference between taxability and exemption; the cost of compliance must be grossly unequal. In some countries outright evasion is perhaps not very high because the penalties are so severe relative to the size of the tax. One of these penalties is unenforceability of the contract. There do not appear to be many instances of extreme personalization.

The transfer taxes are fairly sensitive to changes in business activity, especially in the real estate and financial investment sectors, but the efficiency of the built-in flexibility must be rather low. With their multitude of rates these taxes are not promising candidates for counter-cyclical action.

They create excess burden by hindering reallocation of a fixed stock when opinions on best use have altered in a divergent manner.[22] And if these tax rates are high, as are some of those on the transfer of real estate, they induce uneconomical tax-dodging methods of effectively, if not legally, transferring control over the property.[23]

The transfer taxes no doubt fall more heavily on the well-to-do and the rich than on the poor, except for what indirect effect they exert, perhaps not appreciable, on

21. "The [United Kingdom] law of stamp tax is extremely complicated due to the multiplicity of transactions to which it applies and the variety of rules applicable to the different documents which are subject to the tax" (Brudno and Bower, *Taxation in the United Kingdom*, p. 94). "We are still encumbered by a list of stamp duties that fills over eleven pages of the Annual Report of the Commissioners of Inland Revenue but produces little more than one per cent of the total tax revenue" ("The Nuisance of Stamp Duties," *Midland Bank Review* [London] [May, 1959], p. 3). See the mass of detail in what is still but a summary of the French registration taxes (Norr and Kerlan, *Taxation in France*, pp. 156–200) and stamp taxes (*ibid.*, pp. 248–55). In Germany, "The yield of the capital transfer taxes is low in comparison with the cost of collection, and their abolition is strongly recommended" (Gumpel and Boettcher, *Taxation in Germany*, p. 196).

22. The interference of the transfer taxes with efficient allocation of property has been a familiar theme in English-speaking countries ever since Ricardo wrote in 1817 that taxes on the transfer of property "prevent the national capital from being distributed in the way most beneficial to the community." Ricardo quoted Say to the same effect. See Shoup, *Ricardo on Taxation*, p. 57.

23. Under the French tax on transfer of real estate, "In the past, an option to buy real property . . . was generally not required to be registered, and registration tax was not due unless and until the property was formally transferred. As a result of traffic in these options, the tax administration found that, in effect, property was being transferred at secret prices in arrangements that permitted evasion of tax. The Finance Act of 1964 therefore provided that all such options, and transfers thereof, relating to real property, interests therein, leases, or business enterprises, must be registered, under penalty of nullity, within 10 days of their acquisition. Only a specific tax of 10 F is due on such registration . . ., but it is presumed that the requirement of registration will prevent evasion of tax in later transactions [but how?]" (Norr and Kerlan, *Taxation in France*, p. 161).

the accumulation of capital. A tax on stock transfers, for all its erratic distribution among the upper income groups, scores better on this point than a tax on tobacco. The transfer taxes of course are quite incapable of being tailored to varying family patterns, with the possible exception of taxes on real estate transfers. Transfer taxes can be exported to a considerable degree, especially the securities transfer taxes levied by a city, state, or a national government on an exchange located in a nation-wide financial center.[24] The real estate market in a depressed area can be enlivened a bit by exempting properties located there from heavy transfer taxes.[25]

The rates of tax, except occasionally on transfer of newly constructed buildings, are commonly so low that they represent little threat to accumulation of capital. A large part of the stock transfer tax revenue is generated by transactions of a kind. that do little to aid either capital accumulation or proper allocation of capital. Reallocation of land use that might increase productivity appreciably can be checked by taxes in the 10 to 20 per cent range.[26] Risk-taking may be discouraged by the prospect that it will cost transfer-tax money to get out of a venture, whether it is a successful one or not. The expected (mean) return is lowered, at least for those types of venture that the initiator commonly sells to an investor if it proves successful or sells for salvage value otherwise; and the variance is probably not decreased. External equilibrium is not directly affected except in the few great financial centers, where a heavy tax on security transfers might induce financial capital to seek other markets. Public-purpose outlays can be given some stimulation by exemption from a substantial real estate transfer tax.[27]

A transfer tax is reduced to half its nominal weight if it is deductible in computing a corporation's taxable profit that is subject to a 50 per cent income tax. Deduction, for both corporate and individual income tax, is in fact usual, if the transfer has a business purpose.[28]

An estimate of the yield to be expected from an increase in the rate of a transfer tax must usually therefore allow for the adverse effect on income tax yield. No taxes are deductible in determining the base of the transfer tax itself.

24. New York State certainly, and the United States and the United Kingdom probably, export a large part of the securities transfer taxes they impose.

25. See note 17 above.

26. As in France.

27. As in Germany (Gumpel and Boettcher, *op. cit.*, p. 207).

28. Thus the 16 per cent tax on purchase of a business in France is deductible by the purchaser in computing his taxable income (Norr and Kerlan, *op. cit.*, pp. 178, 396).

CHAPTER SIXTEEN

Taxes on Labor Income;
Export and Import Taxes;
Other Taxes and Para-Taxes

A. TAXES ON LABOR INCOME

1. Concept and Scope

IN A TWO-FACTOR WORLD of capital and labor, a tax on labor is the same in incentive terms as a value-added tax, consumption type (pages 266–69). That tax allows complete deduction of the cost of capital goods in the year of purchase. It thereby achieves the same incentive effects as it would if it disallowed that deduction but exempted the annual earnings on the investment while allowing deduction of depreciation. The same point has been made in the chapter on income taxation (Chapter 11, pages 301–302) in demonstrating that fully accelerated depreciation is equivalent to normal depreciation with a zero tax rate on net income from the investment. A tax that was levied on all value added except the annual earnings of capital would of course be the same as a tax limited to labor income, in the two-factor world. Therefore the equivalent of such a value-added tax, namely, the consumption type of value-added tax, is equivalent to a tax on labor income, in terms of economic incentives. And the two are equal for any given year if gross investment equals profit plus depreciation.

The presence of a third factor, "land," complicates the comparison of the value-added tax, consumption type, with the labor income tax. The word "land" is used throughout this chapter to mean a durable producers' good not made by labor or by use of a capital good. At the margin of land use, to be sure, intensive or extensive, and whether agricultural or urban or factory land, the only claimants to the product are capital and labor, and the two-factor analysis applies. But the infra-marginal product yields a surplus in the form of land rent, which does appear in the base of the value-added tax, even the consumption type. Unlike the net return on machinery or buildings, the rent of land cannot be exempted indirectly by exempting the value that is added in the course of creating it, since by definition land is not created.

But since a tax on labor income and a tax on value-added, consumption type, are identical with respect to incentive effects at the margin of land use, and since the aggregate amount of land rent is apparently small relative to the aggregate return on manmade capital instruments, to say nothing of the total wages-salary-fee bill, it will be instructive to start by assuming that a tax on labor income is, in terms of incentives, nothing but a tax on value added, consumption type, in disguise, and then to note the differences between the two arising not only from the presence of land but also from certain institutional differences.

The most notable of these differences is the fact that the tax on labor is universally on the origin basis, whereas the value-added tax, consumption type, is as yet on the destination basis. The tax on labor income is almost universally linked with a system of social security benefits.[1] The labor-income tax often exempts, or in practice fails to reach, much or all of the labor income of the self-employed: the farmer, shopkeeper, artisan, active partner or proprietor of larger businesses, and professional men. In social security systems the tax often applies only to that part of one's labor income below a specified ceiling.

The distinction between return on man-made capital goods and rent of land, that is, return on a producers' durable good not made by man, has lost much of its usefulness as analysis has concentrated on the short run and on quasi-rents, and on the existence of economic rents in labor incomes, and has emphasized that land has had to be "produced" by being discovered and organized or, in agriculture, preserved. But in public finance the distinction has continued to prove useful in explaining reactions to increases in the real estate tax in a growing economy, in conjecturing about the effects of tax increases limited to land values, and in like matters. The view taken here is that the distinction is also helpful in understanding the comparative effects of a tax on labor income and a value-added tax, consumption type.

Even if the aggregate base of a tax on all labor income could be computed indirectly by finding the aggregate of value added, consumption type, the preferred method, of course, would be direct summation of all wage and salary payments made by a firm, or received by an employee, including payment for labor devoted to constructing producers' goods, plus some estimate of the labor element in the income of the self-employed. This direct method is better understood by the public, and in a social security system it emphasizes labor income, upon which benefits are based in part. And if the tax is to be collected from the worker rather than the employer, the indirect method of computation would be far too awkward. Even if a tax on labor income is to be collected from the employer, the indirect method of computing the base of that tax involves one step that might be troublesome, that is,

1. It is debatable whether the employers' payroll tax in France is a part of the French income tax system or a separate tax on labor income (it is not linked to social security). The French wage- or salary-earner, after computing his income tax on total income including labor income, is allowed 5 per cent of his labor income as a credit against the tax. The payroll tax is 5 per cent except for two upper-bracket rates of 10 per cent and 15 per cent. In effect, the French employers' payroll tax may be regarded as a crude form of withholding tax. Nevertheless, experience with the French employers' payroll tax will be cited in subsequent footnotes, since many of the technical problems are the same as under a payroll tax proper, or a general tax on labor income. See Norr and Kerlan, *Taxation in France*, pp. 204–219, 445–63. For the United Kingdom's selective employment tax, see footnote 5, Chapter 24.

isolating the land-rent element in any total rental payment. The remainder of the rental payment, representing interest and depreciation on the structure or equipment, should not be deducted from value-added (consumption type). The full cost of constructing the structure or equipment, including the labor cost, will already have been deducted, in the year of construction. To deduct the cost of construction once more, in the form of the depreciation and interest elements in a rental payment, would therefore be to subsidize capital goods.

The presence of a value-added tax, consumption type, in the tax system therefore does not in practice reduce the administrative task of computing the base for a tax on labor income. If the value-added tax is of the income type, however, and if its base is computed by the addition method, that is, by summing labor payments, and other payments to factors, the presence of this tax does facilitate administration of a separate tax on labor income, since the amount so computed for the value-added tax can be employed also for the labor-income tax.

2. Incidence

In its long-run incentive aspects, we have seen that a labor income tax resembles a value-added tax, consumption type. Its long-run differential incidence can therefore in a very general sense be taken as that of the value-added tax, and is to be found in the other chapters on taxation, by substituting "labor-income tax" for "value-added tax, consumption type." In particular, the long-run effects on relative prices of products and of factors to be expected from substituting a labor-income tax for a general income tax should be about the same as those to be expected from substituting a value-added tax, consumption type, for a general income tax, since over the long run the land-rent element does not, and the other types of income do, appear as costs at the margins where prices are determined. Even the economic rent in labor income appears at the margin, as the posesssor of it weighs the rewards of another hour of artistic or other endeavor against the sacrifice of leisure. Thus the long-run differential incidence of a turnover tax against a labor-income tax can be expressed by the same general remarks as those in Chapter 8, Section A.3.

Accordingly, although the particular pattern of differential incidence may not be clear in any one instance, a tax on labor income cannot be said to burden only labor income. This conclusion holds whether the tax is collected from the employer or the employee. The general theorem that it makes no difference, as to incidence, which side of the market the tax is collected from is as valid here as elsewhere, though the element of friction may be given more weight than in the case of, say, an excise tax.

Since for any one year labor income will in practice differ from consumption, these long-run conclusions based on incentive equivalence must be modified by use of a short-run general equilibrium approach, a task not attempted here.

The literature on the incidence of payroll taxation is a partial equilibrium analysis that proceeds under an assumption that the wage inclusive of tax is the same as the wage when there is no tax. It is thus a study of the worker's reactions under a wage tax that is assumed to rest entirely on him. The standard conclusion reached is that in the normal instance where the marginal utility of income declines as income increases and the marginal utility of leisure declines as leisure increases, the worker's reaction to the income and substitution effects of a proportional-rate tax on his labor income may be either an increase in hours of work offered at the unchanged before-tax wage, though not to the point where he would be earning as much disposable income as before the tax, or no change, or a decrease.[2]

Even in a partial equilibrium setting, however, it is not to be supposed that the wage rate inclusive of tax will remain unchanged. The individual firm in competition must take the net wage that the worker receives as given, not immediately alterable by it alone; the supply of labor appears to the firm as being perfectly elastic. If the new tax is collected from the firm it cannot decrease the wage and expect to retain any of its workers. If the tax is collected from the worker, the firm must expect to increase the wage it pays. The firm's only immediate recourse is to reduce output to the point where it is losing the least under the new high wage cost and unchanged product price, just as it does under an excise tax on its output. As all firms act similarly, the supply curve for labor as a whole takes effect, and so does the demand curve for the industry's output. Each firm finds it loses less, now, by retracing its steps partway with respect to output. Losses are still being incurred; some firms leave the industry; but now the general equilibrium character of the problem becomes evident, for "the industry" is the entire economy, and further use of partial equilibrium analysis is probably not fruitful.

In an open economy the fact that the tax on labor income is imposed on the origin principle, that is, no rebate or exemption is given on exports and no compensating tax is levied on imports, will make no difference over the long run if exchange rates are flexible and if there are no capital or investment flows,[3] but since these conditions are seldom satisfied this distinction between the labor-income tax and the value-added tax, consumption type, is of considerable practical importance. The origin basis has been used with payroll taxes for several reasons. First, they are commonly linked, though loosely, with benefit payments. Second, there is a widespread intuitive belief that the monetary authorities will not permit a rise in prices from a tax that is imposed directly on a factor input but will do so if the tax is on output. Third, an analogy is drawn with the income tax, which has been supposed not to enter marginal costs. Although a graduated income tax with personal exemptions and non-business deductions can indeed not enter marginal costs in a uniform manner, a flat-rate no-exemption payroll tax does enter marginal costs, obviously, in a uniform manner (it will be recalled that it should make no difference which side of the factor market the income tax or the payroll tax is collected from). Fourth, there is no convenient way to ascertain how much payroll tax has been paid in the course of producing a good for export, or what the proper rate of a compensating import tax should be, although the problem is to be sure no more difficult here than under the cumulative turnover tax.

A country that changes from a payroll tax to a value-added tax, consumption

2. For a thorough analysis see Musgrave, *The Theory of Public Finance*, pp. 232–40.
3. See Chapter 8, Section A.1.

type, will in practice thereby be moving from the origin principle to the destination principle and thus covertly devaluing its currency for trade purposes.

In the short run, then, before the ultimate adjustment of the exchange rate, the differential incidence of the labor-income tax tends to rest partly on foreign consumers, if demand for exports is not perfectly elastic, and may benefit foreign factors if the supply of imports is not perfectly elastic, since imports are now tax-free while the labor engaged in the import-competing industries is now taxed.

A special case arises when the jurisdiction levying the tax on labor income is so small that a part of the labor force can easily move, or commute, to work in a tax-free area, as when only one of several cities in a metropolitan area imposes a payroll tax. Production within the taxing city must decline until marginal cost has decreased by the amount of the tax. The adjustment under the origin tax must in this instance take place through migration of labor and capital to other cities, since devaluation of the currency is not possible.

3. Criteria

As to the consensus criteria, the tax on labor income probably scores about the same as its close relative, the value-added tax, consumption type, except as more or less difficulty is encountered with institutional differences, for example, ceilings on taxable wages, formulae for distinguishing earned income from investment income, and exemption of firms based on number of employees rather than on amount of sales. As is the value-added tax, the tax on labor is difficult to collect from small business firms and from households.[4] Discontinuities develop from the difficulty of distinguishing taxable wages or salary from (*a*) pensions that are not being paid in consideration of work in earlier years, (*b*) earnings by salesmen and others obtained other that under an employer-employee relationship, (*c*) tips, (*d*) expense allowances, (*e*) payments under profit-sharing contracts. Policy issues arise in deciding whether taxable payroll should include amounts paid by the employer to pension and similar funds, vacation pay, unemployment compensation, pensions paid for work done in earlier years, benefits in kind (it is difficult to value them), and alimony paid by the firm at order of a court.[5]

These problems are not really escaped under the value-added tax, but they tend to become obscured by concentration on sales, and on purchases from other firms, under the subtraction method or the tax-credit method.

Discretionary rate changes for counter-cycle purposes encounter distributive objections. If the amount of old-age benefits payable depends at all on the recipient's payroll-tax history, counter-cycle variations in the tax rate will disturb the pattern of payments among individuals in a manner not consonant with the principle of linkage of benefits with tax payments. Similar considerations weigh against varia-

4. In France, "As a practical matter, any person with only one domestic servant, whatever his age or family status [which determine legal exemption], enjoys a *de facto* exemption from the employer's payroll tax" (Norr and Kerlan, *Taxation in France*, p. 209).

5. *Ibid.*, pp. 210–14.

tions in the rate of a payroll tax when the amount of unemployment compensation a worker can receive depends in part on how much payroll tax has been paid on his wage.

If low-income families are to be insulated from counter-cycle changes in tax payable, as is suggested in Chapter 22, the payroll tax is unsuitable, since it usually carries no exempt minimum and often has a ceiling on the taxable wage.

Elimination of land rent from the tax base reduces built-in flexibility, though it enhances the average efficiency of the flexibility that remains.[6] Elimination of land rent also increases the excess burden per dollar of tax revenue, since a tax on land rent is one of the few that do not disturb rates of substitution. If coverage by the labor-income tax is incomplete, as when the self-employed are not taxed, or when the tax does not apply to a worker's earnings beyond a certain level, rates of substitution of one type of labor for another are thereby disturbed.

The differences under the conflict criteria between the labor-income tax and the tax on value added, consumption type, are likewise minor, although the fact that the tax does not apply to land rent makes it doubtless less progressive by income than is the value-added tax. Distribution of the tax burden geographically as between the taxing country and other countries is affected in the short run by use of the origin principle, as already noted. With respect to depressed areas within the taxing country, exemptions under the labor-income tax should provide more leverage than under a tax that includes land rent, since land rent reflects a geographically immobile factor, and its owners are often located in other areas.

Economic growth might be somewhat greater under the labor-income tax since the tax relief granted to land rent would probably go largely into saving, except perhaps in some undeveloped countries. But the labor-income tax cannot, as is so often mistakenly assumed, drive producers to more capital-intensive methods or induce them, generally, to modernize their methods of production, any more than can its virtual twin, the value-added tax, consumption type. Neither tax can make machinery cheap relative to labor, since labor makes machinery (machinery does not make labor), and an increase in labor costs forces an equal percentage increase in cost of machinery, as long as the rate of interest as reward for sacrificing liquidity and for waiting and the rate of profit as a reward for risk-taking remain unaltered. Only if the tax that increases labor money costs also reduces the rate of interest or the rate of profit will capital-intensive methods of producing be favored relative to labor-intensive methods. These rates will probably be changed by the general equilibrium consequences of the substitution of the labor-income tax for some other tax, but there seems no reason to expect that they are more likely to fall than to rise.[7]

6. If the payroll tax has a ceiling on the taxable wage, its yield would not decline at all in a recession if the entire decrease in labor income was concentrated above that ceiling, by a decline in overtime and by transfer of workers to lower-paid jobs. While this extreme outcome is virtually impossible, the decline in taxable income can easily be of a much smaller percentage than the fall in the total wage bill.

7. See E. J. Mishan, "The Emperor's New Clothes: The Payroll Tax Stripped Bare," *Bankers' Magazine* (July, 1961), pp. 17–22. For a general analysis of the effect of an increase in money wage rates on techniques of production and the real wage of labor, and for references to earlier discussions on this point, see Paul A. Samuelson, "A New Theorem on Nonsubstitution," in his *The Collected Scientific Papers of Paul A. Samuelson* (Cambridge, Mass.: The

In an open economy, however, some substitution of capital for labor may occur under a payroll tax, since the domestic payroll tax will not raise the cost of producing capital equipment abroad, and such equipment can be imported. Eventually, even this possibility of substitution may be reduced, if not eliminated, if the increase in imports leads to a devaluation of the currency.

As to risk-taking, since the payroll tax from the incentive point of view is the same as a value-added tax, consumption type, in a two-factor economy [see Chapter 9, Section B.1.A.(3).(B)], it may be said to have zero differential effect on risk-taking, relative to that tax. In the real world where all factors cannot be neatly reduced to two, this relation of the two taxes is only approximate. An intragovernmental coordination problem is posed by the question whether the taxing government shall extend the payroll tax to cover its own employees and those of its enterprises. If it does not do so, and does not reduce the wages it pays, and if private-sector disposable wage rates decrease as a result of the tax, the government will have to ration its jobs by non-wage methods, as workers seek to move from the private sector into government employment. The need for rationing would be avoided by reducing government wages pari passu with the reduction in disposable wages in the private sector, but this adjustment would be difficult to make accurately. It would be made automatically by the market if the government subjected its own employees to the payroll tax.

Intergovernmental complications would be more substantial, more difficult to resolve. They would be vertical-relation problems, chiefly, since horizontally related governmental units normally have few persons working within each other's jurisdictions. A local unit can export part of the burden of its payroll tax by taxing state or provincial and national government personnel working within its boundaries, if wage rates inclusive of tax exceed the old wage rates. Taxpayers in other horizontally related jurisdictions will be called on to make up most of the added cost thus imposed on those governments. In effect, the local unit obtains a disguised grant in aid.

If, on the other hand, a local unit exempts the personnel of other governments, it lowers somewhat the wage rates they have to pay in this locality, and so indirectly transfers money to them. The payroll tax on the private sector must be at a higher rate to yield equal revenue.

If a national government's payroll tax applies to all personnel of all subordinate governments, some kind of not easily discernible redistribution of income among these areas must be the result. If the tax exempts all subordinate-unit personnel, it

M.I.T. Press, 1965), vol. 1, pp. 520–35. The conclusion reached by Samuelson, "Should it happen that subsequent accumulation or adjustments of composition of capital goods were to lead back to the previous interest rate, then there could indeed be no lasting substitution of 'capital' for labor and no change in real wages not attributable to technological change" (p. 533), is the same as that reached by Mishan. The contrary view, nevertheless, is widely held. Thus the French employers' payroll tax is said to serve, in principle, as "an incentive to modernization, re-equipment, mechanization, automation, and a more efficient use of labor resources" (Norr and Kerlan, *Taxation in France*, pp. 206–7, and sources there cited, including a United Nations document). The question of course is not whether labor can be made absolutely more expensive by the tax (presumably it cannot in real terms), but whether it is made more expensive relative to capital.

thereby supplies a grant in aid to all these units, to the degree that they can pay a lower rate of wage than the private sector.

4. Intra-System Reactions on Yields

Even when the payroll tax is not deductible in computing taxable income, it will automatically reduce the yield of a personal income tax, save in the unlikely event that the total wage bill is not reduced. That part of the income tax imposed on profits will also decline, again unless total profits after payroll tax, which is here assumed deductible, are not reduced. These partial equilibrium observations are of course of limited value is dealing with this kind of tax. In an open economy, a substantial emigration of employees would so reduce property values as to decrease appreciably the yield of a real estate tax.

B. EXPORT AND IMPORT TAXES

The present section deals with taxes that are not imposed on domestic production domestically consumed. It therefore excludes the export and import taxes levied as part of a general sales tax system or an excise system. The taxes in question are selective; a general tax on all exports but not on home consumption of the exported articles is rare, or nonexistent, and so too is a general tax at a uniform rate on all imports.[8]

1. Export Taxes

A. CONCEPTUAL BASIS AND VARIETIES OF TAX

A pure export tax is imposed only on the domestic factor activity that is embodied in exports. It therefore allows deduction of import content. If that content is small, the export law will commonly not trouble to allow for it. And if a small part of the

8. In recent years a uniform-rate tax on all imports has been enacted or contemplated in a few countries as a temporary measure to retain external equilibrium pending a decision whether devaluation may be necessary. A permanent type of tax on all imports is found occasionally under the name of consular fees, when these are heavy enough to exceed by far the administrative costs of the consular offices incurred in checking on valuations on invoices and the like. In general, however, practice offers only restricted opportunity to make use of the theorem that a uniform-rate tax on all exports comes to the same thing as a uniform-rate tax on all imports (A. P. Lerner, "The Symmetry between Import and Export Taxes," *Economica* [August, 1936], 3: 306–313). But there is occasion to make use of Ronald I. McKinnon's "Intermediate Products and Differential Tariffs: A Generalization of Lerner's Symmetry Theorem" (*Quarterly Journal of Economics* [November, 1966], 80: 584–615).

domestic output is sold on the domestic market, the tax may be collected at point of production with no exemption for domestic consumption.

A transit tax is levied upon export value after subtraction of domestic value added, if any. It is to be distinguished from a transportation tax, which implies taxation of domestic value that is added by domestic transportation. The transit tax goes far back in history, but is rare today.

Included here are taxes that are not formally export taxes, being levied on production, profits, or as royalties, but that apply to products the domestic consumption of which either is allowed for in computing the tax or is very small.[9] Included also, in principle, are those multiple exchange-rate systems that amount to taxation of one or another type of export; but these systems are so different from ordinary taxation that discussion of them is deferred to page 424, on para-taxes.

Marketing boards impose what are in effect export taxes when they monopsonize the domestic output of a product and then sell virtually all of it on the world market. To the extent, apparently rare thus far, that they experience years of deficit as well as years of surplus, they combine implicit taxation in some years with implicit subsidization in other years. To draw an analogy from income taxation, they impose a 100 per cent tax on excess price, against which tax there is set off a carryover of deficiency of price from other years.

Export taxes are confined almost entirely to countries that export chiefly raw products. The tax is per unit or a percentage of gross receipts for agricultural products; but for the extractive industries, which are often dominated by one or a few large firms, a special tax on profits is a common adjunct. The rate of the per-unit tax or of the percentage-of-gross tax in some instances rises as the price of the exported commodity rises.[10]

9. Imposts on petroleum companies in undeveloped countries are the chief examples of export taxes not formally so designated. These include exploration taxes on concessions, royalties as a percentage of gross revenue, and "make-up" profits taxes, for example, a provision that all taxes together shall not amount to less than 50 per cent of the operating profit before any taxes. See, as an illustration of this make-up tax and other implicit export taxes, Shoup and others, *The Fiscal System of Venezuela; A Report* (Baltimore: Johns Hopkins Press, 1959), pp. 97–101.

10. "Almost all the major tropical agricultural products are now subject to export duties. In Asia, export duties are imposed chiefly on rubber, jute and jute products, coconut products, rice, tea, coffee, cocoa, spices, vegetable oils, wool, cotton, and some textile products. In Latin America, there are export taxes on sugar and sugar products, coffee, cocoa, bananas, cotton, wool, hides, meats, and other products. In Africa, export taxes (including marketing boards' surpluses) apply to cocoa, coffee, cotton, coconut products, palm oil, sisal, tobacco, spices, and groundnuts. In various countries, duties are also levied on exports of tin, copper, iron ore, bauxite, diamonds, and a few other minerals" (Richard Goode, George E. Lent, and P. D. Ojha, "Role of Export Taxes in Developing Countries," *International Monetary Fund Staff Papers* [November, 1966], p. 458). In any particular country, the presence or absence of an export duty can be appraised only after consideration of existing measures of direct control, ownership, and size of producing units, share if any in protected foreign markets, and similar background factors. For an illustration of the wide variety of backgrounds that can exist for a given crop in a certain geographical area, see Louis Shere, *Sugar Taxation in the Caribbean and Central American Countries* (Washington, D.C.: Pan American Union, 1952). Malaya supplies an example of simultaneous use of a graduated export tax and a special profits tax (on tin); see Clive Edwards, *Public Finances in West Malaysia and Singapore* (Canberra: Australian National University Press, forthcoming), pp. 198–99 (mimeograph).

B. INCIDENCE

The limiting case of no shifting at all of the export tax to foreign purchasers is probably approached very closely when one country, supplying only a small part of the world market, imposes such a tax. The demand for that country's output is perfectly elastic, or nearly so. If, however, all the producing countries, acting independently but under the common pressure of need for revenue in financing development programs, raises their export tax rates on a particular product more or less simultaneously, the demand will be considerably less than perfectly elastic. An appreciable amount of the tax may then be paid by foreign purchasers.

A large part of the tax may become shifted to foreign purchasers if the world supply is diminished owing to weather conditions, crop disease, or lagged responses to earlier price declines, as with tree crops. The world-market demand curve may well be steeper where the new supply curve intersects it, relative to the steepness of the supply curve, because less essential uses of the commodity will have been given up.

A sudden upward shift in the world-market demand for a commodity seems likely to be accompanied by a change in elasticity at the point of equilibrium. These shifts of demand are commonly associated with war or fear of war, which create considerable inelasticity in demand for a range of quantity centered on the initial quantity. If all the exporting countries increase their export tax rates as the price increases, they can get a considerably larger proportion of the tax revenue from the foreign purchaser than they could before the demand curve shifted, assuming that the supply is not perfectly inelastic. This conclusion does not necessarily hold for an upward shift in demand that results simply from boom conditions in the consuming countries; the elasticity of demand for a given quantity may not then alter greatly in the relevant range.

Whether the exporting countries will in fact act together when the world price rises dramatically depends in part on the type of export tax they impose. If they employ export taxes with rates graduated according to price, all prevailing tax rates will automatically be higher, more or less simultaneously. Extra revenue will be obtained in part at the expense of the foreign purchaser—always assuming some degree of elasticity in the supply.

Some part of the export tax will be shifted back to factors, in any event. We have seen that almost all of it will be shifted backward when the country supplies a small part of the world market. Most of this backward shifting is divided between the owners of specialized land, owners of trees, and the like, and laborers who are fairly immobile. Wholesalers and other traders may also be specialized enough to be vulnerable.[11] A burden that is not counted in the concept of shifting is the loss of income to those less specialized factors that leave the industry when output is reduced by the tax, and the loss of consumers' surplus on those units no longer purchased. Over the long run output will be reduced more and more, since elasticities both of supply and of demand will presumably increase as adjustment is made to the disturbances of demand or supply functions. Tax revenue declines as these elasticities grow, and

11. See Goode, Lent, and Ojha, *op. cit.*, pp. 465–66.

if the tax rates are repeatedly raised in an attempt to maintain revenue, a series of successive short-run inelastic responses will be superimposed on the long-run responses.

A special case is presented when production responds to price changes with a long lag, for example, from eight to thirteen years for plantings of cocoa trees to harvesting.[12] This year's tax increase is then shifted, first, entirely to current factor owners, except as harvesting is less thorough and gathering from wild trees is on a smaller scale. Many years later, when the reduction in plantings will have affected output, the tax becomes shifted entirely to the then consumers (except as harvesting and gathering are more thorough). But if by that time the tax increase is no longer in force, plantings will increase, and a cobweb-type cycle of price and quantity swings will have been set in motion. A tax rate that is steady over decades, at least in ad valorem terms, may be necessary if the waste of resources consequent upon repeatedly disappointed expectations is to be avoided.

An export tax on profits will be shifted entirely to factors, not at all to foreign purchasers, at least if profit is narrowly defined as the excess over what the capital in question can earn elsewhere. If the capital is foreign capital, backward shifting means exporting the tax. Taxes on profits of petroleum companies in less developed countries are of this type, except as the companies have unutilized opportunities in other countries. Again, simultaneous action by all the natural-resource countries will shift abroad a tax that otherwise will tend to disappear as foreign capital moves elsewhere.

c. CRITERIA

Export taxes, except those imposed on profits, belong to the excise tax family, but the goods they strike are almost all intermediate goods, sold by business firms to other business firms. Because they are more easily defined, they suffer less from uncertainties and discontinuities than do many excises, while resembling excises in the lack of irrelevant circumstances and in their impersonality. Abstracting from corruption of tax officials, evasion probably is more nearly equal for all and closer to zero than it is under most excises, since the taxed objects are subject to control at the border. Cost of compliance, too, is more nearly equal.

Insofar as an export tax is shifted backward to domestic factors, its sensitivity to changes in the national income of the exporting country tends to stabilize prices and employment, if the national income changes originate in the export sector. But to the extent, probably modest, that the incidence of the tax is upon foreign purchasers, the sensitivity of the tax exerts no direct effect on the national income of the exporting country. Accordingly, a graduated tax imposed by all the exporting countries is likely to be less stabilizing, for any one country, than would be an additional flat-rate tax imposed by that country alone.

The efficiency of the export taxes' built-in flexibility depends on its incidence. For the part of the tax that is borne by domestic factors it also depends on the spend-

12. *Ibid.*, p. 469.

ing habits of those factors, but no a priori statement on this point seems valid. Similarly, the usefulness of an export tax rate reduction will depend on the incidence of the tax. If a rate reduction causes no change in the export price, the increased disposable income will stimulate domestic employment. Otherwise, some or all of the rate reduction merely stimulates spending by households or firms in other countries, and the question then becomes whether the foreign reprecussions will be significant for the taxing country (see Chapter 24 below).

In contrast to what occurs under other taxes on sales or transfers, no perverse anticipatory reactions by consumers will be generated by a counter-cycle policy, since the consumers will not be affected by it (under the no forward-shifting assumption). These reactions will be confined to domestic firms but may be quite strong; an exporter sensing that a reduction in tax rate is about to be made will defer exporting. This action may not, however, have much effect on domestic factor activity; the deferral may merely add to inventories.

The export taxes create considerable excess burden in production; to the degree that they are shifted backward they tend to divert domestic factors from employment in the taxed industry and to the degree they are shifted forward they tend to induce inefficient combinations of inputs abroad.

The distribution of the export tax burden by income or wealth class seems quite untraceable with respect to that part of the tax that is shifted to foreign purchasers. The backward-shifted part may be either roughly progressive or roughly regressive depending on whether capital or labor bears most of that part. The portion that rests on land rent will tend to be discounted in a lower selling price for the land; those who buy the land after the tax has been introduced will not then be really burdened by the tax, although superficially they will appear so.

If a depressed region is allowed to export its produce tax-free, virtually the entire benefit of the tax remission will accrue to owners of land in that region, who may however be living elsewhere, and to laborers residing there. Production in that region will be increased until marginal cost equals what in other regions is marginal cost plus tax. In principle, then, exemption from an export tax should prove a notable stimulus to a depressed region. This conclusion holds even if most of the tax is shifted to foreign purchasers.

An appreciable part of the tax probably comes out of domestic saving, or domestic gainful consumption, and to this extent the tax checks economic growth. It no doubt holds investment in the taxed industries below what it would otherwise be, but in some countries this investment may be merely deflected, with less efficiency to be sure, to other domestic industries.

That part of an export tax that rests on domestic factors will produce an incremental surplus in the balance of payments as imports decrease owing to the reduction in domestic disposable income, under partial equilibrium analysis.[13] If the demand for exports is perfectly elastic, all of the tax rests on domestic factors. But unless the supply of exports is perfectly inelastic, factors will move out of the export trade, export physical volume will decrease, at unchanged prices, and the balance of

13. For an analysis that takes account of simultaneous reduction of other taxes, see Chapter 24 below.

payments will to this extent worsen. This latter reaction is apt to be larger than the decrease in imports unless the supply of exports is not far from perfectly inelastic. Evidently, a small country heavily engaged in a world market may well incur an incremental external deficit if it imposes an export tax.

If the demand for exports is not perfectly elastic, the volume of exports will not be reduced so far, and a somewhat better price will be obtained on the exports that continue, so that the incremental deficit externally caused by the tax will be less. If the foreign demand is of less than unit elasticity, the incremental result may be a surplus, depending on how elastic is the domestic supply of exports (the less elastic it is, the less inelastic need the demand be, to create an incremental surplus).

That part of a backward shifted export tax that rests on labor appears to the laborer in the form of a lower wage for working in the export industry. Those laborers who leave this industry for other jobs or for leisure, and who therefore do not technically speaking bear any of the incidence, will get lower pay than they used to get in the export industry, and those who remain there will get lower pay there. Depending on the relative strengths of the income and substitution effects, more or less labor in the economy as a whole may be offered.

Allowance must be made for a decrease in income tax yield and eventually in the yield of property taxes when an export tax is imposed, save in the unlikely case where it is all shifted forward to foreign purchasers.

2. Import Taxes

"Import taxes" here includes only those taxes that are imposed if the commodity is imported but that are not imposed if it is produced domestically. If the commodity cannot be produced domestically, it is still pertinent to ask whether it would be taxed if it could be produced domestically. If it would, the import tax is simply another destination-principle excise; the analysis in Chapter 10 can be extended to cover it, and no more need be said here.

This branch of taxation has been the subject of much analysis, particularly with respect to its incidence, in international trade theory, which does not need to be repeated here. The purpose of the tax is either, or both, to draw money for the domestic treasury from the foreign supplier and to subsidize, through higher prices to consumers, domestic production of the commodity. On the consensus criteria the import taxes make a somewhat poorer showing than do the export taxes, chiefly because they deal with more complex products. The sensitivity of their yield can be considerable, since the taxed imports are often largely luxuries, subject to ad valorem rates. They create great excess burden, especially in promoting inefficient domestic production.

No general statement can be made concerning their distribution features, except that a depressed area may be capable of stimulation by exemption of import duties on producers' goods or consumers' goods going to that region. The effect of the import taxes on total investment in the country may well be positive, but economic growth, in the sense of accumulating capital equipment, may not lead to a higher standard of living, because of the inefficiencies in production fostered by these taxes. They always produce an incremental external surplus. The effect on volume of work seems indeterminate. The yield of a general sales tax may increase, if the base of that tax includes, as it commonly does, import duties.

C. OTHER TAXES, AND PARA-TAXES

1. Other Taxes

A. EXCESS PROFITS TAX

An excess profits tax is a tax on profits created by barriers to entry into an industry or to expansion of firms already in the industry. Two cases may be distinguished: short-lived excess profits and long-lived excess profits. Short-lived excess profits are caused by sudden and massive but somewhat temporary shifts in demand or supply, as in wartime, or owing to weather conditions. The barriers to entry or expansion, though they would eventually give way, are sufficient for a while to insure excess profits. Long-lived excess profits rest on barriers that are much stronger, much more durable, and which can be erected to insure excess profits even in the absence of shifts in demand or supply. Short-lived excess profits are computed by comparing current profits of a firm with profits of the same firm in a not distant past period, before the shift in demand or supply occurred. Long-lived excess profits are computed as the excess of the actual percentage return on capital over some normal return.

This second concept of excess is especially difficult to formulate in law and in practice. Certain types of restriction of entry are supported by the government to provide rewards for extraordinary effort and skill, as through patent protection. To tax profits that are above the normal rate of return would in these instances defeat social policy. Secondly, if "normal" is taken to mean "average actual," a profit rate for a firm or industry much higher than the average may merely reflect a high degree of risk in the industry; the favorable outcomes are counted, as they occur, but the unfavorable ones never appear in the records.

A hitherto depressed industry that has been losing capital and labor steadily over a long period may be deemed eligible to earn short-lived excess profits, on grounds of compassion, or to allow accumulation of working capital and funds for capital equipment. The two methods of computing excess profits just noted may for this reason be offered to business firms as alternatives to be selected by the firm, so that the method used will in each case be the one most favourable for the firm in question.[14]

Because of these and other problems, a substitute for excess profits taxation has

14. This has in fact been the usual procedure in excess profits taxes in wartime.

been sought in control of the massive shifts in demand and in direct attack on socially undesired restriction of entry or expansion. The greatest shift in demand in wartime is from private-sector demand to government demand. Sophisticated procurement practices can restrain the government's demand to just the levels needed to induce the required shifts in resources. Renegotiation of contracts after performance to eliminate profits deemed in retrospect excessive is a supplementary tool, a type of excess profits tax or para-tax. Nationalization of heavy industries that are typically beneficiaries of war-induced shifts in demand replaces excess profits revenue by government enterprise profits or eliminates the profits by price reductions.

These substitutes have worked satisfactorily enough in advanced industrial countries to induce them to dispense with the excess profits tax in periods of limited war,[15] and, since periods of unlimited war are assumed to afford no occasion for excess profits, it seems likely that excess profits taxation is a closed chapter in industrialized economies, with two possible exceptions. If recurrent inflationary pressures are met by wage and price controls, these controls may become formalized into counter-cycle excess wage and excess profits taxes. If a limited war leads to stringent wage controls, the demand by labor for some kind of excess profits tax will be very strong.

Economies that are less industrialized, less competitive, and more marked by class conflicts may in some instances retain on the statute book the excess profits taxes that are now there, and a few other countries may join them. The low yields of that tax in those countries, however, indicate either that the occasion for the tax is not pressing or that administration and compliance are lax.

B. TAXES ON BETTING

Revenue from taxes on betting is defined here to include excess profits of a government lottery.

"Betting" covers three types of chance-taking: zero-information betting, as in the purchase of a lottery ticket; information betting, as in placing a wager on someone else's horse; and skill betting, as in betting on one's own horse. The effects of a tax differ among these types of betting because they differ in the degree to which the bettor believes that he can increase his chance of winning by expending money or thought or other effort. In zero-information betting the bettor believes that no expenditure of money or effort on his part will obtain him information that will improve his chance of winning. A tax on such betting is not a tax on effort. In information betting the bettor, while realizing that nothing he can do will influence the outcome, believes that his chance of winning can be improved by reflection or study, or by the purchase of opinions or facts. In skill betting the bettor believes he can influence the outcome by application of his own skill, as in training his own

---

15. The United States–Vietnam war is an illustration. The United States employed an excess profits tax in the Korean War.

horses, or selecting a jockey, or, in a game of cards, by his own skill directly applied. A tax on information betting or skill betting is a tax on effort.

These distinctions are based on what the bettor believes. He may be mistaken in his belief, but his beliefs guide his action, and if a tax is to change his course of action it will do so in accordance with his belief as to which of the three categories of chance-taking he is engaged in. For a few bettors a lottery may represent information betting as they consult astrologists for favorable dates. But it appears that the vast majority of those who buy lottery tickets do not exert themselves to win.

Horse and dog racing, football contests, and the like attract both types of betting, most of it information betting. Most of the information betting is based on an erroneous appraisal of the value of the information, but there is commonly a small group of professionals who make a modest living out of betting.

The horseman who bets on his own horse and the card player who bets on himself are far closer to the investor in business in their motivations and reactions than they are to the zero-information bettor or the information bettor. The chief difference remaining, with respect to motivation, is that in a business venture there are usually an infinite number of possible outcomes, or at least a very large number of possible outcomes, for any given venture, while a bettor commonly faces a finite and sometimes rather small number of outcomes.

In zero-information betting, a lottery for example, the operator sells an expected (mean) return, coupled with a certain variance (dispersion of possible outcomes around this mean), which may be translated into the coefficient of variation (square root of the variance, that is, the standard deviation, divided by the mean). The demand for lottery tickets is of course sensitive to the mean return offered, for any given size of ticket, and to the dispersion. If the lottery operator desires to maximize his profits, which he will presumably do if he is a private firm, he will seek that combination of expected return and dispersion that will give him the largest profit at the point where his marginal revenue equals his marginal cost. A purchaser of a lottery ticket, if he thinks about this point at all, will conclude that his mean return and variance are the same as those of all his fellow bettors.

The information bettor, in contrast, believes that his mean return is higher than that of the majority of his fellow bettors. The aggregate demand of all such bettors is therefore probably higher, for any given expected return for the group as a whole, than under a lottery. From this point of view, there is more tax money to be taken from this group than under a lottery, or more operator profits, for an operation involving a given mean return for the group as a whole (the mean return is of course a cost to the operator). But these information bettors may be just as sensitive as the lottery patrons to a given reduction in the mean return. The hard core of professionals who make a modest living off betting at the races will be even more sensitive. Also, the resource-absorbing expenditures will be a larger part of the total receipts, since it is more expensive to stage a race than to draw tickets from a fishbowl. This cost disadvantage will be overcome if the demand for admission to the race track by non-betting spectators is sufficiently strong.

Illegal competition from enterprises that evade taxation or encroach on the government monopoly will be greater than under a lottery, since the bettor believes, rightly or not, that lottery drawings are more easily fixed or faked by unscrupulous private enterprise operators than even races and the like. If the lottery attempts to overcome this suspicion by using numbers generated by some activity that is quite independent, e.g., the last three digits of the volume of sales on an exchange, some bettors will come to believe that they have the power to predict such numbers, and so become information bettors.

On balance, information betting seems likely to yield a larger maximum revenue or monopoly profit than zero-information betting, for a given outlay (cost).

Skill betting is not a lucrative object of taxation, or government monopoly, because relatively few persons are in a position to engage in it on a scale that makes a tax administratively feasible. A tax on gambling at cards is an illustration. Moreover, these chance-takers will be more sensitive than the other two types to changes in the share returned to them in the aggregate and may be unwilling to pay as much for an objective aggregate mean return as the other two groups; they are more sophisticated, more aware of their own limitations.

The incidence of a tax on betting is divided chiefly between the bettors and the owners of the firm that supply the service; the other factors of production account for but a small part of the total proceeds and are probably not highly specialized to this field. If, as is usual, the private firm supplying this service is a monopolist or imperfect competitor, so that he faces a sloping demand curve, a per-unit or ad valorem tax will come in part out of his profits even if he operates under constant costs (see Chapter 10, page 276). An atomistically competitive betting industry, if it can exist at all, will pay back in prizes a correspondingly large share of the gross revenue under the pressure of competition, and virtually all of the tax will rest on those who bet.

The betting taxes score fairly well on equal treatment of equals. They obviously impose an excess burden in the Paretian sense if externalities are not taken into account, but, since the negative externalities here are so great (for example, grocery stores protest when dog racing is legalized in the neighbourhood), the betting taxes may easily, on balance, improve a second-best world. In fact, however a betting tax may indirectly increase the amount of betting, as it supplies government with a motive to legalize what has hitherto been underground, and to stimulate a taste for betting.

Gambling taxes probably take a larger proportion of the income of the poor than of the rich, though the difference in proportions may be far greater by some other classification, notably, the propensity to bet, which varies widely within any one income group. The betting tax is inimical to economic growth in a low-income country, insofar as households spend more on betting, tax included, than when betting is untaxed. Households for whom betting is an addictive (see Chapter 10, Section A) will reduce productive consumption when a betting tax is imposed, reducing the national income.[16]

16. For details of one of the most extensive systems of taxes on betting, that of the United Kingdom, see G. B. Graham, "Taxes on Betting and Gaming," *British Tax Review* (September–October, 1966), pp. 309–20.

2. Para-Taxes

Para-taxes are financial measures taken by a government that contain a tax element, that is, a compulsory contribution to the government. The three chief examples are multiple exchange rates, forced loans, and renegotiation of contracts. Renegotiation will not be discussed here.

A. MULTIPLE EXCHANGE RATES

Multiple exchange rates are of two chief types. One type simply sets one rate at which the government will sell foreign exchange to anyone and another, lower, rate at which it will buy foreign exchange from anyone. Under the second type the government sells foreign exchange to some persons or firms or for some types of import at a higher rate than it sells exchange to other persons or firms or for other imports; or it buys at different rates. Rarely, some one group of persons or firm will have the same rate quoted to it for both sales and purchases.

The tax element in these devices can be isolated, conceptually, by comparing what happens under the multiple exchange rate system with what would happen under a single-rate system, or at least what would happen in the absence of the particular kind of discrimination under study. For any specific situation the analysis at once becomes far too complex an exercise in the theory of international trade to be pursued here. The following remarks state the chief issues, from the point of view of para-taxation, and offer a few examples.

Suppose that the first type of differential-exchange-rate system noted above is repealed, being replaced by a uniform exchange rate compatible with external equilibrium. This rate may turn out to be in between the two differential rates, but this outcome is not inevitable. The equilibrium rate might be above the higher of the two differential rates, or below the lower.[17] If it would be above the higher of the two differential rates, the profit the government is making on the differential rates, comes entirely out of the pockets of the exporters. And in addition importers are better off than under a single equilibrium rate. Part of the tax on exporters goes to the government; part bypasses the treasury and goes to importers through the low prices at which they can obtain foreign exchange. If this result is to obtain, demand for foreign exchange must be very price-elastic and supply of foreign exchange, very price-inelastic. The total tax element in the differential rate system may be measured in principle by what the limit is to the willingness of the suppliers of foreign exchange to pay openly as tax, in domestic currency, rather than having to live under the multiple-rate system.

A similar analysis would apply if the equilibrium rate were beneath the lower of

17. See Shoup and others, *The Fiscal System of Venezuela*, Appendix A, "The Differential Rate in Venezuela."

the two differential rates. If it fell in between, both suppliers and demanders of foreign exchange would pay an implicit tax.

If foreign exchange is sold to one person or group at one price and to another at another price, depending on what they want to import,[18] the result is much the same as if a free market in exchange at a uniform rate for all were coupled with a series of import taxes on the several commodities. If the various classes of foreign exchange, for example, Class IV for importation of automobiles, are auctioned off every so often, to clear the market by the price mechanism, the tax analogue would be a family of frequently changing import tax rates.

If a sales rate is set so low that it does not establish equilibrium for that particular class of foreign exchange, which then has to be rationed through exchange control, the analogous public finance measure is an import subsidy.

Under a system of differential rates to types of exporter, those exporters who are being paid less than they could obtain under an equilibrium single exchange rate are being taxed, and those who are being paid more are being subsidized.

B. FORCED LOAN

We consider first the kind of forced loan ("compulsory loan," "refundable tax") that gives the lender a non-negotiable debt certificate that is not redeemable at his pleasure but only on a stipulated, or alternatively at an as yet unannounced, date. This type of forced loan contains a tax element for some of the lenders but not for others. Whether the lender is an implicit taxpayer depends on the relation of his rate of substitution of future money for present money to the rate of interest paid on the loan.

To isolate the tax element, let us abstract from differences in interest rates, and also from profit rates, and consider an economy with but a single rate of interest. In general, the forced lender will be indifferent between (1) the forced loan and (2) a tax, smaller than the forced loan, of an amount such that, were this tax imposed on him, he would then freely subscribe to the redemption amount of the loan with the balance of the money that the government wants from him. Consider for example a non-negotiable bond paying no interest, redeemable in ten years (but not before) at $100, and issued at $75. The implied rate of interest is 2.9 per cent. A certain individual, whose borrowing power and net worth are both zero, would buy such a bond freely only if it were offered to him at $20 instead of $75. And if the government were imposing on him a tax of $60, let us assume that he would buy the bond freely only at $15 or less. To obtain $75 from him by a mixture of taxation and voluntary bond purchase the government must, therefore, levy on him a tax of $60

18. For a statement of the tax equivalents of exchange rates differentiated by commodity, see Meade, *The Balance of Payments* (London: Oxford University Press, 1951), pp. 268–72. For an analysis of the auction system in Brazil, where the import rates were not five, one for each category, but as many as there were auctions in some twenty of the principal cities ("Rates vary . . . even from one day to the other in the same city as well as between one city and another") see E. Gudin, "Multiple Exchange Rates: the Brazilian Experience," *Economia Internazionale* (August, 1956), 9(3): 8.

and offer him, for $15, a bond to be redeemed in ten years at $100. A forced loan of $75 from him is the same from his viewpoint as a tax of $60 and a voluntary subscription of $15 for the $100 ten-year bond. The implicit tax element in the forced loan of $75 is $60 (not, note, $55, that is, $75 minus $20). The implicit interest paid him is also $60.

Unfortunately, in real life, the information supplied in this illustration cannot be obtained. The government consequently operates in the dark with a taxing instrument that is regressive with income and wealth. On the lowest income groups the implicit tax element may be far larger than any that would be politically acceptable as an explicit tax.

For this compulsory lender, government borrowing in place of taxing does not entirely postpone the fixing of the pattern in which the sacrifice, represented by the government's use of real resources, is to be distributed, as does a voluntary loan (see Chapter 18). Instead, the forced loan fixes much of the sacrifice irrevocably. The $100 that he will receive upon repayment of the loan does not alter this conclusion, for this $100 is to him merely the $15 of an earlier point in time.

The figures used in this numerical example may appear extreme to those who possess financial reserves. But they probably approximate the state of mind of low-income families, especially those already in debt.[19]

If the government bond issued for the forced loan is negotiable, the tax element is easily measured by the excess of the price the lender must pay for the bond over the price it will command in the market. This statement of course holds, no matter what may be the lender's rate of substitution of present for future dollars.

Compulsory lending is sometimes misnamed compulsory saving. The amount of additional saving induced by the forced loan, that is, the incremental reduction in consumption spending, will normally be less than the amount loaned, since some of the loan will be subscribed with funds raised from the sale of assets.[20]

19. Proposals for a forced loan that would take substantial sums from low-income families have been followed by riots in more than one country in recent years, as in Chile, where the government planned to set aside in bonds one quarter of an expected 20 per cent wage increase as an "enforced savings" measure, with an equal mandatory contribution from employers (*New York Times*, November 24, 1967). The Chilean government abandoned the plan (*ibid.*, January 31, 1968).

20. For further aspects of the forced loan in a war and postwar setting, see Carl Shoup, "Forced Loans," in Tax Institute, *Curbing Inflation through Taxation* (New York: Tax Institute, 1944), pp. 126–36.

CHAPTER SEVENTEEN

Tax Administration

A. GOALS OF TAX ADMINISTRATION

The goals of tax administration differ widely from country to country. At one extreme the goal is simple: maximize tax revenue with the given administrative resources. No attempt is made to achieve any of the six aspects of the consensus criterion of equity, for example, equality in degree of tax error among taxpayers, equality of cost of compliance, and an optimum balance between certainty and impersonalization (see Chapter 2).

This extreme attitude is found in many low-income countries as well as in some wealthy ones, where tax administrators act as if the government cannot afford to strive for any goals that will cost revenue. Other countries, in contrast, pay at least some attention to the six aspects of equity.[1]

B. CONCEPTS[2]

Erroneous tax payments are either underpayments or overpayments. Underpayments may arise from evasion, overpayments from extortion, and either may result from non-observance or administrative ineptness.

Evasion is either (a) understatement by the taxpayer or his agent of the tax due or simply of the quantity or value of the taxable object or (b) failure to pay a tax on time, unless these actions or failures result only from ignorance. Evasion may occur with the connivance or assistance of a government official; it is then bilateral evasion.

---

1. On these issues, see Roy Blough, *The Federal Taxing Process* (New York: Prentice-Hall, 1952), *passim*, especially Chapters 7 and 8.

2. Seligman's classical formulation of shifting and incidence and allied concepts includes alternative means of "escape" through "evasion," which in his terminology embraces both legitimate and illegitimate activity, with further subdivisions. See E. R. A. Seligman, "Introduction to The Shifting and Incidence of Taxation," from *The Shifting and Incidence of Taxation*, 5th ed., reprinted in Musgrave and Shoup (Eds.), *Readings in the Economics of Taxation*, pp. 202–13.

The conniving or assisting party may be the tax assessor, or the tax auditor, that is, an official who determines the amount of the tax base or the amount of the tax from an examination of the taxpayer's records, or it may be the tax collector. In many countries the functions of assessment and collection are sharply divorced, being performed by two quite distinct governmental agencies, apparently on the theory that a taxpayer will find it more difficult to corrupt two men than one. But experience indicates that corruption of either is often sufficient.

Non-observance is understatement or overstatement of tax liability or failure to pay tax or to apply for a refund, solely because of ignorance of the law or regulations.

Administrative ineptness here implies failure by the tax assessor to state correctly the value of the tax base or the amount of tax, owing to ignorance or carelessness. Extortion, the administrative counterpart of evasion, implies deliberate overassessment or overcollection of the tax. The taxpayer pays more than he should, legally, under threat of being assessed a still larger amount. All of the money thus paid may go to the government, or alternatively the tax official may keep all or part of it for himself. Extortion is to be distinguished from bilateral evasion by the fact that under bilateral evasion the taxpayer pays a smaller total sum than he should legally, part of this payment going to the tax official as a bribe. If in any of these instances of extortion or bilateral evasion the government receives less than is legally due it, the government official is an embezzler. Embezzlement may thus exist either with extortion or bilateral evasion.

Avoidance of tax is a legal reduction in the amount of tax that would otherwise have been due, by a change in the taxpayer's behavior that is motivated almost entirely by the prospective tax saving.

The term "protesting" is introduced here to denote a concept not hitherto formalized in public finance literature. It refers to attempts made by the taxpayer to achieve acceptance by the government of an interpretation of the tax law that will reduce his tax bill from what it would have been under the interpretation that was accepted before his protest. Protesting implies of course a zone of uncertainty with respect to the amount of tax due, within which the taxpayer and administrator reach a compromise, or which is eliminated by a judicial decision.

Cost of compliance is cost, other than the tax itself, undergone by the taxpayer or his agent (say an employer who withholds tax from wages) in the course of observance and protesting. It does not include loss of net income arising from avoidance, or the cost of evading.

C. TYPES OF TAX ADMINISTRATION

Six types of tax administration may be distinguished, according to the degree of participation they require of the taxpayer or his agent, and the kind of response they elicit from the taxpayer. Each type of administration is usually associated with particular taxes.

1. At one extreme the taxpayer is wholly passive. If he cannot even appeal the

assessment, his only action is to pay the tax bill that is presented to him. Few of today's taxes answer to this description: a poll tax is one.[3] The tax on windows must have been of this type. The hearth tax, on the other hand, required cooperation from the taxpayer at least to the point of opening the door.[4] Government monopoly profit, regarded as a tax, falls in this group.

Under this type of tax, evasion must be bilateral, through corruption of a tax official. There can be no protesting, and there is no cost of compliance. Carelessness or ignorance on the part of the tax assessor or collector can do more damage than under any other tax. But extortion is difficult, since the tax base is so obvious.

2. In the next group the taxpayer has a right of appeal, though he is still wholly passive at the initial assessment. The modern real estate tax is of this type in many countries.[5] Protesting is therefore possible, but not unilateral evasion. Opportunity for extortion is now appreciable.

3. In the third group of taxes certain information must be supplied by a third party—never by the taxpayer himself—to the tax officials, as an aid to them in assessing the tax. An example is the reporting of dividends or interest paid, under an income tax. For evasion the taxpayer now has the choice of attempting to corrupt either the agent or the tax official. Another, indirect, example is the invoice that the vendor under a value-added tax gives to his vendee, which the latter must show to substantiate his claim for deduction from his sales, incomputing his own value added. Here, it is to the interest of the third party to act in a manner that incidentally will increase the tax liability of the taxpayer in question. An understated invoice means less tax on the vendor, more tax on the vendee. And the vendee would of course like to see the vendor overstate the invoice. This clash of interests is of little importance to the government with respect to total revenue obtained, since the tax gained from one taxpayer is lost to the other, if both pay tax at the same rate. But these conflicts of interest may increase inequality of rate of evasion.

4. In the fourth group of taxes the taxpayer's participation increases notably; he must file a return that gives the tax office information for computing tax due. Most income tax systems are of this type, with respect to all save those for which the precise tax on total income or schedular income is withheld at source. Sometimes the taxpayer need simply submit certain specified pieces of information; sometimes he must fit the pieces together and compute his taxable income. The tax official then calculates the tax due and bills the taxpayer. Unilateral evasion is now possible, and protesting assumes importance as the taxpayer debates whether a certain inflow should be omitted from his statement on the supposition that a court would hold it nontaxable, or an outflow claimed as a deduction. Non-observance by the taxpayer is also possible, and he undergoes a cost of compliance. Opportunity for extortion is greater than under any other group.

3. Some, but not all, varieties of the *forfait* system of assessing sales or income taxes make the taxpayer virtually passive; see Chapter 8, page 219.

4. In Great Britain, the 1696 tax of "two shillings on each house, with higher amounts on houses having more than a stated number of windows . . . was preferred to the hearth tax [repealed in 1688] because it was assessable with less invasion of the privacy of the householder" (Shoup, *Ricardo on Taxation*, p. 213).

5. Including the United States.

5. In the fifth group of taxes computation of tax liability together with payment upon filing the return is performed by the taxpayer's agent. The chief example of the fifth group is collection at source of the income tax. In an extreme form of collection at source, the tax is for all practical purposes levied on the payor; thus, if he pays interest, he is not allowed to deduct that interest in computing his own taxable income or profits, but in return he is given the legal right to reduce his contractual payment to the payee by the amount of the tax.[6] Under these circumstances the identity of the payee is of no concern to the tax official. Precision in withholding is attained under this system only if a single flat rate applies to both payor and payee, and if the incomes of both are above the personal-exemption level, if any. Otherwise there must be some provision for the payee to make himself known and claim refund of tax if he is nontaxable because his total income falls below the personal exemption or other deductible amounts; such provision is usually made in the systems of withholding income tax from wages and salaries.

Under the pure withholding system, evasion is limited to the agent. But the agent is subject to great temptation, for the stakes are large. They are the sum of the taxes on many taxpayers, if he is an employer withholding tax from many employees or a debtor withholding from many creditors. The temptation may be somewhat easier to resist in that he must picture himself even more clearly as a thief than if he evaded tax on himself; here, he steals either from the government or, if the employee or debtor is ultimately held liable, from him. And this mechanism does not lend itself to extortion.

Unless the taxpayer can file to claim a refund, observance and cost of compliance are relevant for the withholding agent alone. Protesting is possible only after the tax has been paid.

6. The sixth group consists of the self-assessed taxes. Here the taxpayer is put under the greatest pressure, for he must supply all relevant information, compute the tax base, calculate the tax, and pay the tax, or some installment of it, when he files his return. Now he has ample opportunity to evade unilaterally by supplying false information or delaying payment, and opportunities, too, for bilateral evasion by corrupting assessors, auditors, or collectors. Protesting occurs from the moment he starts to make out his return and is inevitable when he responds to requests from the tax administration to explain or defend items on that return. He must pay strict attention to oncoming dates for filing and payment and, if he is not to be guilty of non-observance, study complex instructions. If he engages tax consultants, cost of compliance may be an appreciable percentage of the tax; if he values his own time, it is sure to be. Extortion is more feasible than when third parties supply the information and pay the tax.

Taxes on business firms are commonly of this sixth type, but few taxes on households, except the personal income tax in one country,[7] the death and gift taxes in most countries, payroll taxes on account of domestic servants, minor license fees, and the like.

6. This is the traditional British system of withholding, other than on wages and salaries.
7. The United States, both for the federal tax and for most of the states that impose income taxes.

In countries where administrative difficulties are so great that choice of taxes must be based on ease of administration, the system will obtain most of its revenue from taxes in the low-numbered groups above, where the taxpayer must practice corruption if he is to evade, where observance is simple or not needed, and where there is little scope for protesting. These taxes usually cost more to administer, per dollar of revenue, than those in groups 4, 5, and 6, but they bring in substantial amounts under conditions that would prevent the high-numbered taxes from operating at all, or only with grossly unequal rates of evasion. The issue is not always one of business taxes as against taxes collected from households. The difference between an external-indicia or crude *forfait* business tax and one based on true figures of sales or profits is about as great administratively as is that between a poll tax and a self-assessed personal income tax.

Even under the most favorable circumstances, two vexing problems remain: What is the optimum of tax protesting to cultivate, or allow, and what is the optimum trade-off between certainty and impersonalization?

An optimum amount of taxpayer protesting is that amount which reduces the deviation of tax paid from true amount of tax due to the point where any further reduction in the difference is not considered worth the incremental cost in real resources that it requires. What this point is, is a matter of opinion that will vary among observers, and no consensus on it can be hoped for. At least it will be useful to realize that, although protesting does serve a social purpose, it costs something and so cannot, presumably, be carried to the point where the deviation of tax paid from true tax due is zero. Indeed, the true tax due can never be known exactly, for it is that amount that would be due if all possible points of dispute were adjudicated. Protesting that falls far short of the optimum will induce tax assessors, auditors, and collectors to become arbitrary or indifferent; excess tax will be paid. Protesting that goes far beyond the optimum, especially protesting by large business firms and wealthy individuals who dispose of highly trained legal and accounting talent (much of it trained in prior government service), will be a waste of the economy's resources.

The trade-off between certainty and impersonality is effectuated largely through (a) regulations and rulings made public by the tax officials as their interpretation of the law and (b) appeal to higher administrative levels or to the courts.

As published regulations and rulings become more detailed, taxpayers become more certain of the tax consequences of a given course of action. The extreme is reached in "advance rulings," where the taxpayer asks, and is told, what the tax consequences will be of a particular course of action that he is contemplating. He describes this course of action in some detail, and the tax officials are bound to stand by their conclusion even if further reflection convinces them that they conceded too much.[8] The greater the number of these individual rulings, the more personalized

8. Many of the problems of operating a modern tax system in a complex industrial economy can be understood by studying this problem of advance rulings. See International Fiscal Association, *Studies on International Fiscal Law*, Vol. 50b, Reports for the 19th International Congress on Financial and Fiscal Law (London, 1965), Second Subject, Advance Rulings by the Tax Authorities at the Request of a Taxpayer (London: British Branch of International

the law becomes in administration. Two taxpayers almost similarly circumstanced will be treated quite differently, since a line must be drawn somewhere. If, to avoid this, large numbers of taxpayers are lumped together in vaguely defined categories a sharp sense of discrimination is averted, at the cost of much additional uncertainty.

D. ALLOCATION
OF ADMINISTRATIVE EXPENDITURES;
DETERMINATION OF AGGREGATE EXPENDITURES

If a fixed amount is available for administering a given tax system it can be allocated to maximize revenue, to maximize accuracy of payment (that is, to minimize the difference between total tax paid and total true tax due), or to equalize the degree of accuracy among taxpayers (roughly speaking, to equalize rates of evasion and non-observance), or some weighted approach toward all of these goals may be taken.

To maximize tax revenue the administration must so distribute the fixed amount of resources in enforcing the several taxes and, for each tax, must so allocate resources among techniques of administration that the return on the marginal dollar of administrative expense is everywhere the same. When this pattern has been achieved, no revenue is to be gained or lost by transferring a small amount of administrative resources from enforcing one tax to enforcing another, or by engaging more auditors and discharging some collectors, or by distributing more tax instruction booklets and litigating fewer cases. Average-cost data are useless for this purpose; they merely stimulate unprofitable controversy about allocation of overhead costs. Marginal costs point the way to revenue maximization, and they require no information on overhead costs.

A harsh definition of revenue maximizing would imply that the tax officials purposefully assess and collect more tax than they know is due, by taking advantage of the taxpayer's ignorance or unwillingness to protest. Even a milder definition implies that the tax office will spend little time and money training its officials to avoid overassessment that results from their own ignorance, or to keep the taxpayer fully informed of his rights.

To maximize accuracy rather than revenue involves, therefore, calling the taxpayer's attention to errors he is committing against himself and returning to him tax that he has overpaid either because of his own mistakes or because of initial errors by the tax official. Now the fixed administrative resources must be so distributed that a small shifting of resources at the margins will cause about as much inaccuracy to arise, for or against the taxpayer, in one place as the inaccuracy it eliminates in another.[9] A time element is now injected, since promptness in making the tax refund increases the present value of the degree of accuracy obtained.

Fiscal Association, 1965); includes national reports from fourteen countries. For a discussion of the function of regulations and rulings under the United States federal income tax law, see Roy Blough, *The Federal Taxing Process* (New York: Prentice-Hall, 1952), pp. 152–62.

9. For a description of this standard and an application of it, see Ronald B. Welch, "Measuring the Optimum Size of a Field Audit Staff," *National Tax Journal* (September, 1954), 7: 210–21.

Under the standard of maximizing accuracy, the government must decide to litigate a tax case even when it is probable that the taxpayer will win, if a court decision one way or the other will so reduce uncertainty that erroneous payments in the future will be reduced.

The third goal is to equalize the degree of accuracy of tax payment among taxpayers in place of minimizing the aggregate amount of inaccuracy, given a fixed total of administrative resources to employ. In practice, this means chiefly equalizing rates of evasion, although non-observance, administrative ineptness, and extortion must also be considered, just as they must be in aiming at minimizing total inaccuracy.

This goal calls for assigning a large proportion of the fixed resources to check on taxpayers in areas or in groups where tendencies to evasion are strong, whatever may be the marginal cost of obtaining revenue there. Under the income tax, small business firms in some, perhaps most, countries evade a larger percentage of their tax than do wage-earners whose tax is collected largely by withholding. A massive transfer of administrative resources from supervising withholding to enforcing the tax on small business firms could conceivably so increase the rate of evasion under withholding and so reduce it for small business firms that the two rates would become equal, but total income tax revenue collected would almost surely decline. The significance and the feasibility of equating rates of evasion depend a good deal on how the groups are defined. Ideally, the goal is to equalize the rate of evasion for every household (and every firm), but this version of the equalization aim is too impracticable to be considered seriously.

If the amount of resources available for administering a tax system is not fixed, and if revenue maximizing or accuracy maximizing is the aim, it might at first appear that money should be appropriated for tax administration until the incremental dollar of cost yielded just one dollar's increase in revenue, or in accuracy. But this would be to overlook the fact that in tax administration real resources are being used up to implement a system of transfer payments, that is, taxes, not to produce output. That implementation is itself a valuable commodity, but its value is not necessarily to be reckoned in terms of the dollars taken in. An additional $100 of manpower and material used up in order to transfer say $300 from taxpayers to the government may or may not be worth while; there is nothing in the excess of $300 over $100 that proves it, as there is, presumptively, when by spending $100 more the government can create a service, say police protection, for which the taxpayers would pay $300 if they had to. The difference in the two figures of $300 in this example is a major qualitative difference. What the community must ask itself is, how much it would pay, if it had to, to get that extra $300 in tax revenue, and the answer depends on how much the community values what the $300 will be spent for. If an additional $250 worth of manpower and materials has to be used up to render an increment in police service that the community values at $300, and if in addition it costs $100 to collect the tax revenue that is required (here, $250), the process viewed as a whole (transferring the money by taxation and using men and materials to create the additional police service) is not worth while. There is also a psychic cost to be counted in the degree of harshness toward, or closeness of supervision of, taxpayers.

In fact, governments commonly stop far short of the point where marginal cost of collecting tax revenue equals marginal tax revenue, or marginal tax accuracy.

Since they do stop short of that point, rates of accuracy among taxpayers can be equalized at any given level of revenue collection or level of aggregate accuracy, these levels being expressed relative to 100 per cent revenue collection or accuracy. But it remains true that, once rates of accuracy are equalized, the total of resources engaged, whatever that total may be, could be reallocated to obtain more revenue at the expense of incurring inequality in rates of accuracy or to obtain more total accuracy. The necessity of choice among these goals remains, even when resources available are unlimited, unless they are so vast that each of the goals can be achieved completely (with the qualifications expressed above concerning a goal of 100 per cent revenue collection).

E. SELF-ENFORCING TAX SYSTEMS

Assessors, auditors, and tax collectors being expensive, fallible and sometimes corruptible, a search continues for a tax system that is self-enforcing, one that reduces the role of the tax official to that of storing records and receiving freely tendered tax payments. New hopes are stirred by new devices. But in the end they all come down to reliance either on a desire for pecuniary gain by someone other than the taxpayer or on fear by the taxpayer or his agent that he will lose either money or freedom. Neither stimulus amounts to much without some degree of active administration; realistically, the goal cannot be a completely self-enforcing system staffed by completely passive administrators. But some of the devices depend heavily on rewards and punishments coupled with a substantial decrease in direct control of the taxpayer.

The desire for pecuniary gain is played upon by arranging matters so that a non-taxpayer can benefit if the taxpayer fails in attempted evasion. Three devices of this type are at hand.

The first is of little consequence in terms of total revenue. The beneficiary is himself a taxpayer, whose tax liability decreases as the other's tax increases. If, as noted on page 429, the value-added tax rate that the beneficiary pays is the same as that applicable to the would-be evader, his corrective influence brings the government no net revenue, but there may well be a gain in total accuracy. If his tax rate is lower, he can be tempted to connive, on a promise to split the illegal gain. If it is higher, he is the one who is tempted to evade.

The second class of devices enlists the interest of consumers in seeing that business firms observe the tax law, notably retailers under a retail sales tax. Retailers are required to prepay the tax by purchasing coupons, tickets, or stamps. These pieces of paper must then be handed to or divided with the consumer, or with any other purchaser who is not subject to the tax. The coupons handed over must carry a face amount corresponding to the tax payable by the retailer upon the sale. The government then gives a value to the coupons in the hands of the consumer by redeeming them for some fraction of their face value if they are put to a certain use, say given to a charitable organization, or by offering the consumer a chance to get them redeemed at full face value, or even much more, in a lottery drawing where the numbers drawn are those printed on the coupons. The value, actual or expected, of the coupon to the consumer must of course be less than the tax on the retailer, else the government's net revenue would be zero or negative. The consumer is therefore tempted to connive with the retailer by splitting the evaded tax with him on better terms than the government offers. But when any one retailer must deal with dozens or hundreds of persons a day for small amounts, as must the ordinary retail merchant, he finds connivance impracticable. A moderate use of the coupon system, coupled with somewhat less money spent on assessors, auditors, and tax collectors, perhaps decreases evasion by retailers who deal in small items, foods for example, with many customers. But it probably induces connivance with retailers who deal in large items, refrigerators for example, where connivance is practicable.[10]

This device, which relies on transfer payments rather than resource-absorbing expenditures, as when more tax officials are employed, probably reduces total evasion somewhat for a given amount of resource use devoted to tax administration, but it almost certainly increases inequality of evasion and in this respect is an unsatisfactory substitute for an increment of assessing, auditing, and collecting.

A difficult sub-optimization problem is that of setting the optimal expected value on the coupons, in the lottery case. In practice, the systems that give the non-taxpayer buyers or sellers a pecuniary motive to prevent evasion are used chiefly in countries or local areas that are industrially underdeveloped, with low incomes.

The third device that plays on the desire for pecuniary gain is the reward to tax informers. The government offers to pay for information on tax evasion. Probably all governments use this device to some extent, including those that pride themselves on the degree of taxpayer compliance. The informer's interest lies in seeing that evasion is practiced, but uncovered. Connivance is replaced by blackmail. An informer system must be used in moderation if a society is not to generate intolerable animosities among its members.

Fear of loss of money or freedom operates in either of two forms. First, if the taxpayer reduces his liability under one tax, he automatically increases it under another. Second, if he evades or fails to observe the tax law he runs a risk of incurring penalties.

An example of the first is a tax on excess inventories, to accompany a sales tax.[11] The retailer whose reported sales fall short of his purchases plus mark-up by more than a normal amount is deemed to be accumulating excessive inventories, whether they exist in fact or not, and is taxed on the accumulation. Of course, the tax might

10. In the United States, the state of Ohio used a coupon plan until recently, for its retail sales tax; the consumer's half of the coupon had a certain value for donation to charitable and similar organizations. For a detailed analysis of and proposal for an integrated plan of administration that would employ the lottery feature, see Albert Gailord Hart, *An Integrated System of Tax Information: A Model, and a Sketch of Possibilities under Latin American Conditions* (New York: School of International Affairs, Columbia University, 1967).

11. No such tax appears to exist, but it was proposed by Benjamin Higgins, in his *Economic Development* (New York: Norton, 1959), Chapter 23.

as well be assessed on presumed sales; in either case the tax assessor or auditor must have a record of the purchases made by the taxpayer.

A "self-checking" system of taxes[12] is one wherein one or more taxes, levied for reasons quite apart from their administrative compatibility, increase as the taxpayer understates his liability to still another tax. A taxpayer may be subject to a tax on his income, his expenditure, and his net worth. Understatement of expenditure leads to a corresponding increase in net worth, if net worth is computed as last year's net worth plus the excess of this year's income over this year's expenditure. But understatement of income will reduce the sum of the three taxes. If, instead, expenditure is computed as this year's income minus the increase in net worth, an understatement of this year's net worth will increase equally the expenditure figure. But again, understatement of income will be profitable. And if income is defined as the sum of expenditure plus the increase in net worth, the taxpayer gains by understating either this year's expenditure or net worth. The self-checking feature in this system is therefore of limited scope.

This last example also illustrates a somewhat different point: if the taxpayer's understatement of expenditure or net worth is later discovered he must also pay additional income tax.[13] This is a self-reinforcing penalty system of taxes rather than a self-checking system, because the derived tax base (here, income) increases with the other two bases instead of decreasing with one of them, as under a self-checking system.

Self-checking means chiefly that the incremental administrative effort required by adding one of these taxes, say a tax on net worth, to an existing system that includes the other two (income tax and expenditure tax) may be made less than that required to administer a net-worth tax without those taxes. But still less effort might be required to obtain a given amount of revenue, if the rates of the income tax and expenditure tax were raised in lieu of introducing a net-worth tax.

The second form in which fear is utilized is the traditional and universal one of a threat: the taxpayer or his agent are on notice that if they evade, and if they are discovered, they will be forced to pay fines, interest on the tax, or extra tax, or will be jailed, or denied the right to leave the country, assume public office, obtain patents and trademarks or business licenses or construction permits.[14] A rather different type of threat is that he may be forced to sell his property at less than his reservation price.

These threats are meaningful only as the taxpayer knows that informers, or assessors, auditors, and collectors are active and may discover his malfeasance. The more impressed he is by this array of detectors, the smaller need be the penalty to hold the body of taxpayers down to any given level of evasion and to any given dispersion of evasion rates. The larger the penalties, the smaller need be this array,

12. See Nicholas Kaldor, *Indian Tax Reform: Report of a Survey* (New Delhi: Department of Economic Affairs, Ministry of Finance, Government of India, 1956), pp. 2, 13–14.

13. For an example involving a net-worth tax, an accessions tax, and an income tax, see Shoup and others, *Report on Japanese Taxation* (Tokyo: General Headquarters, Supreme Commander for the Allied Powers, September, 1949), vol. 1, pp. 86–87.

14. See the description of the "solvencia" system, in Shoup and others, *The Fiscal System of Venezuela*, index, Solvency Certificates.

or at least the smaller need be the impression it gives. Since an increase in the array of informers and officials absorbs productive resources, while an increase in the level of penalties does not, it might appear that a socially optimum enforcement system could be attained by dismantling almost all the enforcement apparatus and setting the penalties at heights far above those that customarily obtain. But the rate of substitution increases so rapidly that society would find itself imposing penalties that, in the event, it would not be willing to enforce, for reasons that, although obscurely formulated, are nevertheless deeply felt; the penalty would be deemed grossly excessive for the crime, even though the proponents of such a system could reply that, in view of the small chance of being found out, the penalty multiplied by its probability would be only a modest one. The resulting increase in degree of dispersion of evasion because of differing attitudes toward risk among evaders or potential evaders would also cause uneasiness.

There is therefore in any society some socially optimum combination of intensity of enforcement effort and intensity of penalties. No society is likely to depend wholly on enforcement (penalties zero) or wholly on penalties (enforcement zero, infractions discovered by chance). But since this issue has rarely been debated explicitly, it must be a coincidence if existing combinations of enforcement and penalty are at this social optimum. Some explicit study of the problem will probably induce a change from present practice, in one direction or the other.

Penalties can be compared in money terms, whether they are set in those terms explicitly or not, by ascertaining how much the taxpayer would be willing to pay to have the penalty lifted. Penalties then fall into two groups: those the money value of which is set by the government and those the money value of which is set by the taxpayer himself.

The first group consists of the usual fines, interest charges, percentage increases in tax, and similar explicit statements in law or regulations. The second group divides into two parts.

The first part consists of those provisions that allow the taxpayer to set his own explicit money penalty, the chief example being the stipulation that the taxpayer, while being permitted to set any value he wishes on his taxable property, must be ready to sell the property at that same value, or at some specified percentage of it, say 120 per cent, to the government, or, in some versions, to any private person.[15]

15. In France, "To combat the use of false statements of consideration in documents transferring property subject to registration tax, the government may exercise a right of pre-emption. . . . This right permits the administration, in certain circumstances, to acquire the property transferred at the value stated by the parties plus 10%. . . . The decision to exercise the right of pre-emption is solely within the discretion of the tax administration. . . . The fact that the buyer may have disposed of the property to a third person between the date of his acquisition and the date that the right of pre-emption is exercised does not bind the administration [but the right must be exercised within three months of registration of the documents for sale]. The administration may evict the third person. . . . The right of pre-emption is not often exercised; it was used only 62 times between 1942 and 1951, for example, out of 190,000 transfers. . . . The right has, however, given rise to a good deal of litigation. Its existence remains a constant threat to tax evasion" (Norr and Kerlan, *Taxation in France*, pp. 198–200). For a proposal to establish a somewhat similar system to induce accurate self-assessment under a real estate tax, see John Strasma, "Market-Enforced Self-Assessment for Real Estate Taxes [primarily in Latin America]," *International Bulletin for Fiscal Documenta-*

In the latter case, the informer system is being used, the entire penalty going to the informer. Then the usual possibilities of blackmail exist.

The striking feature of this device is that the taxpayer himself sets the level of the penalty he will have to pay if he is discovered. The penalty is the difference between (1) his true reservation price for the property, which of course is higher than its market value, else he would be selling it, and (2) the value at which the property can be taken from him, a value that he sets when he declares the value of his property for tax purposes. He would not, if the market value were clearly established, set a taxable value so low that the price at which he would have to sell if requested would be at or below that market price. Instead, he would set a tax price that, although perhaps itself below the market price, would put the forced-sale price above the market price. But he would be vulnerable to blackmail if his reservation price exceeded the forced-sale price. The higher the reservation above the forced-sale price, and the greater the probability that others will know what his reservation price is, the greater is the expected value of the penalty he faces in the form of blackmail for not setting the taxable price, not just at the market price, but high enough, perhaps well above the market price, to make the forced-sale price not less than his reservation price. Such a penalty will probably appear too capricious to be acceptable in most societies.

But in fact the device is suggested chiefly for environments in which no one is sure what the taxed property would bring if it were put on the market. In these circumstances the taxpayer might take the chance of setting the tax value at a level that puts the forced-sale value somewhat below what he conjectures the property would fetch on the market, or rather, at about the level that he thinks others think will prove to be the market value.

Under these conditions, the taxpayer may vary both the degree of attempted evasion and the potential penalty for that degree of evasion, with the restraint that these two are positively linked, usually by a linear function. For example, if the property tax rate is 2 per cent of the self-assessed value, a decrease of $100 in that value saves $2 a year forever. At 10 per cent discount, the present value of tax saved is $20. The cost is an increment of $100 in the potential penalty, in the simplest case, where the forced-sale value equals the self-assessed value. If the chance of being found out is 1 in 5 and if the taxpayer is neither a risk averter nor a risk-seeker, he will be indifferent to decreasing or not decreasing his taxable value by $100. Again, the society in which he lives may not allow the penalty to be enforced, especially if the informer-buyer is from outside.

The second part of the second group of penalties are those that, while stipulated by the government, carry no explicit money figure; the taxpayer compares them, weighted by the probability that he will have to undergo them, with what he gains from evasion. In this sense, he is allowed to set the money value of the penalty.

tion (September and October, 1965), 19(9): 353–64; 19(10): 397–414. Under this plan, "any person or company could make a bid for self-assessed property at 10% or more than the market value declared. If the owners declined to sell, the tax value would be raised to the amount rejected and a fine would be levied, to be shared with the frustrated bidder" (ibid., p. 413). This last provision makes the plan an informer system.

The chief examples are prison sentences and the denial of certain permits, referred to above.[16]

16. Penalties, as with other aspects of enforcement of a tax law, must be suited to the social and political environment. See, for example, the recommendations by Stanley S. Surrey and Oliver Oldman, in their "Report of a Preliminary Survey of the Tax System of Argentina," *Public Finance* (1961, Nos. 2 and 3/4), 16: 155–82, 313–42, and Stanley S. Surrey, "Tax Administration in Underdeveloped Countries," in Institute International de Finances Publiques, *Finances Publiques, Stabilité Financière Intérieure et Balance de Paiements* (Paris: Editions de l'Epargne, 1955). For an analysis that introduces "costs of apprehension and conviction [and makes] . . . the probability of apprehension and conviction an important decision variable" by, *inter alia*, converting non-monetary punishments into their monetary equivalent or worth, see Gary S. Becker, "Crime and Punishment: An Economic Approach," *Journal of Political Economy* (March/April, 1968), 76: 169–217 (quotation from p. 201).

CHAPTER EIGHTEEN

Government
Borrowing; Inflationary Finance

A. GOVERNMENT BORROWING

1. Concept and Scope

THE FIRST SECTION of this chapter is concerned with receipts from the sale of financial instruments by the government: (1) to individuals or firms in the private sector (including commercial banks) (2) to induce the private sector to release manpower and other real resources and (3) to finance the purchase of those resources or to make welfare payments or subsidies.[1] The discussion assumes full employment and a stable price level.

Sale by a government of its obligations to its own sinking fund, or to its own agencies, a social security fund for example, is not borrowing, as that term is understood here. Sale to some other government's sinking fund or agency in order to raise money for expenditures is borrowing. The other government is not a part of the decision-making group that constitutes the government in question. From the borrowing government's point of view the lending government lies in the private non-bank sector.

The kind of government borrowing covered in the present chapter usually implies future taxation to service the debt. It is therefore a device to substitute future

1. The distinction implied here between borrowing and inflationary finance is essentially that employed by R. J. Ball in *Inflation and the Theory of Money* (Chicago: Aldine Publishing Company, 1964, p. 275): "The Government can finance expenditure in excess of receipts by the creation of money, so adding to the cash base of the commercial banks, or by borrowing, where borrowing here implies obtaining funds either from the public or the financial system without adding to the cash base of the banks." But in the relatively few instances where the commercial banking system's loans to the government in no way displace credit for the private sector, the government may best be viewed, for purposes of the present discussion, as financing by the new-money (inflationary) method rather than by borrowing. Even then, of course, the sale of the government obligations to the banks is not in itself stimulating; it is the subsequent expenditure of the money that is inflationary. Cf. Earl R. Rolph and George F. Break, *Public Finance* (New York: Ronald Press, 1961), pp. 527–29.

taxation for current taxation. The criteria of Chapter 2 will be applied in order to discover the conditions under which such substitution is deemed feasible and acceptable, and to compare the various techniques of borrowing.

The transfer of resources to government use requires that the private sector reduce its spending on investment goods or consumption goods. We consider first the extent to which consumption spending may be reduced.

Those individuals who hold assets and whose net worth is reduced by the fall in market value of outstanding securities consequent upon the issue of government securities may reduce their current consumption slightly because of this (negative) income effect. Their net saving for the year will already have been reduced, on an accrued basis, by the fall in security prices, so that a reduction in consumption will not necessarily imply an increase in saving, as seen from the individual's point of view.

The increase in income from the increase in interest rate tends to increase consumption of present goods as well as of future goods. If the income effect outweighs the substitution effect, the lender will actually increase his current consumption somewhat from what it would be under a lower interest rate. In any event the decrease in consumption, if any, is likely to be slight.

The prospect of more taxation in the years ahead, to service the new debt issue, may conceivably induce a restriction in current consumption. If the stream of future additional taxes is fully discounted, the bond issue will cause the private sector to consider itself, on balance, poorer by an amount equal to the bond issue— unless the bonds are issued to allow reduction in existing taxes or unless the private sector views as a discounted asset the future service, say education, to be made available by the bond issue. The bond issue by itself, that is, the exchange of cash for bonds, makes no one feel richer or poorer. The discounted tax stream to service the debt, by itself, is felt as nothing but a burden.

But discounting future taxes to this degree can scarcely occur, since no one can be sure on whom the taxes will fall. A consistent probability reckoning by all households would in principle lead to discounted tax streams multiplied by probability fractions that would sum, for all households, to the amount of the bond issue, but there is no reason to expect such consistency; each household, insofar as it considers the matter at all, is making its own computations independently. In a community of fearful, pessimistic households the probability-weighted discounted streams might even sum to an aggregate greater than the bond issue. Indeed, a government that wanted its bond issue to induce a reduction in current consumption would do well to remind its constituents repeatedly of the new tax burdens awaiting them. The more usual reaction, for both households and government, is to pay little attention to future taxes. Only as taxes are levied to cover interest on the new issue will some reduction of consumption be sure to occur, and then only to an amount equal to some fraction of the current tax payment alone.

One unusual case of instant discounting of a large part of future taxes to service a debt issue occurs when a local government that relies, and is expected in all future years to rely, solely on a property tax, raises the rate of that tax to service a new bond issue. The value of land, and to a lesser degree that of buildings, should in principle fall by the discounted value of the future stream of taxes. It is difficult however to observe this in any precise degree. And whatever reduction in consumption occurs is certainly much smaller than this fall in value.

From the conclusions above regarding consumption it follows that the resources transferred to government by a bond issue will be chiefly those that would have been used to increase the private-sector stock of capital equipment. In a macro comparison with an increase of taxes in place of a bond issue, the bond issue is seen usually to siphon resources more from private capital formation and less from consumption than would taxation, although there are some forms of taxation, notably the death and gift taxes, that closely resemble borrowing in this respect.

2. Incidence

"Incidence" implies a burden, which comes to rest on someone. The sense in which a public debt can be a burden must therefore be determined, if "incidence" of a government debt is to have any meaning.

In a partial-equilibrium sense, government borrowing by itself, abstracting from the taxes that will be later employed to service the debt, and abstracting too from the use made of the bond-sale proceeds, imposes no burden on anyone except those whose assets suffer a decline in market value owing to the accompanying rise in the rate of interest. If these declines in value are regarded only as collateral effects, there is no incidence of the government debt. The purchasers of the securities move to a preferred position by exchanging their cash for the securities.

If the taxes imposed to service the debt are taken into account, there is a burden, and an incidence, but it is that of these taxes, not of the debt. It can be explored by means of the differential analyses of Chapters 8 to 16, by injecting a time element into the comparison of the two taxes: one heavy tax now, against a number of smaller annual taxes payable in later years.

The resources used up by the government as it spends the proceeds of the bond issue are of course current, not future resources. Accordingly, if the subscribers reduce their investment spending by more than taxpayers would have reduced theirs if the tax-financing method had been used, a future generation finds that it has less capital equipment to work with than if taxation had been employed in place of borrowing. In this sense, a burden has been placed on future generations by the decision of the earlier generation to finance by debt rather than by taxation: the future generations are worse off than they would have been had taxation been employed.[2]

2. It seems to be a widely held view that debt finance, relative to tax finance, can burden a future generation in some way other than by causing the future generation to inherit a smaller amount of capital stock than it would have inherited if tax finance had been employed. (See W. G. Bowen, R. G. Davis, and D. H. Kopf, "The Public Debt," *American Economic Review* [September, 1960], 50: 701-6, reprinted in James M. Ferguson, *Public Debt and Future Generations* [Chapel Hill: University of North Carolina Press, 1964], and the review of the Ferguson volume by Richard A. Musgrave, *American Economic Review* [December, 1965],

To say that in these circumstances the burden has been "shifted to" the future generation is, however, to imply that if the earlier generation had chosen taxation it would have burdened itself. But such a choice, freely made under no compulsion from anyone, can hardly be a burden, any more than a donation freely made is a burden to the donor. And it is freely made; at least it is not made under any compulsion from future generations, which are not yet in existence. In this sense, that is, with respect to comparative burdens of different generations, taxation and the consequent reduction in consumption is no more a burden to the earlier generation than a gift by a philanthropist is a burden to him.

Finally, in the year when the debt is redeemed no burden is created thereby; no real resources are absorbed. This fact does not prevent each taxpayer of that date from believing that he bears a burden. But this feeling is a collective illusion, arising from neglect of the fact that by redeeming the bonds the taxpayers are freed from a stream of future taxes equal in present value to the taxes being paid to redeem. This illusion of burden at the time of debt redemption is the counterpart of the illusion of no tax burden when the debt is issued.

In one sense, however, the feeling of burden is no illusion. When the bonds are redeemed by taxes the uncertainty that existed for each potential taxpayer is removed; some who, if they did look ahead, feared they would have to pay to service the debt are now relieved of that apprehension, since they happen not to be called upon to pay the debt-redemption taxes; others, who had been looking ahead in an optimistic mood, are shocked to find that they are being taxed, for redemption, more than the discounted value of what they had been expecting to have to pay. What the taxing for debt service (interest and redemption) does is to fix, irrevocably, the allocation of the burden, if burden is defined as a decrease in a household's conventionally computed[3] net worth (not just decrease in consumption). Such

55: 1227–1228), and Otto Eckstein, *Public Finance* (Englewood Cliffs, N.J.: Prentice-Hall, 1964), pp. 110–11. But if the distinction between possessing a certain stock of capital goods and inheriting them is kept in mind, it will be seen that only through the "Ricardo–Pigou effect," that is, only through a reduction in the size of the capital stock inherited, can debt finance burden a future generation. (See Carl S. Shoup, "Debt Financing and Future Generations," *Economic Journal* [December, 1962], 72: 887–98, reprinted in Ferguson, *op. cit.*). If a first generation sells its earlier-purchased government bonds to an overlapping second generation, which reduces its consumption in order to buy the bonds, the second generation's reduction in consumption is voluntary and hence is no burden on it. If the first generation spends the proceeds on consumption, it must later bequeath a smaller real capital stock than would be the case if it had not so sold its bonds and spent the proceeds, and this reduction in real bequest is a burden on the second generation. If the two "generations" are not linked at all by inheritance, they are not distinct generations, i.e., distinct groups with successive life spans in the same political community, in a sense meaningful for policy decisions by that community. On the local level, to the degree that tomorrow's residents of a given city will have no inheritance links with today's residents, as families flow into and out of the city, the issue involves successive residency spans, not successive life spans. The "proposition that loan finance postpones the final settlement of an expenditure burden, simply because it postpones the final reduction in net worth which is implicit in taxation" (Musgrave, *loc. cit.*) is a proposition regarding distribution of burden among members of a given generation, not as between generations, since taxation for debt redemption creates no burden for the generation of redemption in the aggregate; this taxation is accompanied by elimination of an equal present-value amount of future taxation (see text above).

3. That is, not computed on the probability basis noted on page 442.

taxation fixes the burden bit by bit as interest is paid and fixes the remainder of the burden when the debt is redeemed.

The view taken here is that it seems unfruitful to conceptualize and allocate an "incidence of debt," as distinguished from the incidence of the taxes levied to service the debt, even though the resources used up are those of the date the debt was issued. The using up of the resources is certainly not a burden, if the society chooses freely to employ them in this manner, through government, rather than let the private sector use them. A differential incidence concept, on the other hand, is quite useful, e.g., the effect on distribution of disposable real incomes of substituting borrowing, together with the future taxes to service the debt, for current taxation; this might be termed the differential tax-debt incidence.[4]

The issuance of public debt makes it possible for an individual to do something he could otherwise never do: leave a negative true estate, as defined below, without leaving debts of his own.[5] If the government finances a certain expenditure by borrowing from this individual rather by taxing him, it takes money from him, in either case, and leaves him with a debt certificate rather than a tax receipt. If he wishes to consume more, during his lifetime, than his lifetime disposable income would be under the tax financing, he cannot, of course, do so if tax financing is in fact used, but he can do so if debt financing is used. He can sell the debt certificate (but of course not the tax certificate) to someone else. The purchaser may be either of the current generation or, if the generations overlap, of the younger generation. If the purchaser is of the current generation, and reduces his lifetime consumption by the amount of the purchase, from what it would have been if the taxing method had been used to obtain money from the other person, the younger generation inherits as large a stock of capital goods as it would have done if the taxing method had been used and it also, presumably, inherits the bond. If the purchaser is of the younger generation, the younger generation inherits correspondingly less capital equipment than if taxation had been used. In this latter case, the individual who bought the government bond initially may be said to have left a negative true estate, in the sense that his lifetime consumption has exceeded his lifetime income less the resources the government used up. The negativeness of his estate lies in the facts that (1) he "bequeaths" to the younger generation a tax liability to service the debt, a liability that would not exist if the taxing method had been used, but (2) does not bequeath the bond that entitles the younger generation to receive the interest and repayment of the principle. They have to work to get it, i.e., they sacrifice consumption or saving to buy the bond. The presence of just one such person in the community makes the younger generation poorer than they would be if the taxation method had been used.

This case is an extreme instance of the individual who decides to consume more in his lifetime if he is sold a government bond than if he must pay tax. In this sense his

4. Or, more simply, "differential debt incidence." See John G. Head, "The Theory of Debt Incidence," *Rivista di Diritto Finanziario e Scienza delle Finanze* (June, 1967), 26: 179.

5. The concept of a negative estate was developed by William Vickrey, in "The Burden of a Public Debt: Comment," *American Economic Review* (March, 1961) 51: 132–37, reprinted in Ferguson, *op. cit.* See also the analysis of this concept in John G. Head, *op. cit.*, pp. 190–91.

true estate is smaller than his financial estate. In any event, including the case of the negative-estate individual, the real burden on the future generation lies in the fact that they inherit a smaller capital stock (owing to the larger consumption on the part of the first generation) than they would have, had the first-generation individual been forced or induced to forego that larger consumption, by being given a tax receipt in place of a debt certificate.

3. Criteria

The choice between issuing an increment of public debt and raising current taxes is in practice made on the grounds of the criteria listed in Chapter 2, although the relative weights given to the several criteria will differ, largely because of differing relevance, from those used in choosing one tax rather than another tax. To sharpen the comparison, the discussion here will usually abstract from the future taxes that the issuance of debt implies, but on occasion these taxes must be taken into account for a meaningful statement. When they are, this will be noted explicitly.

Further, the choice among types of debt instrument is guided by the same criteria, with a still different set of weights. The single criterion sometimes implied in the literature on government debt, namely, minimization of the total interest bill, has rarely been accepted, even by hard-pressed governments. This criterion treats the security purchasers as if they were foreigners, relative to the taxpayers who are to service the debt. The implications of this point of view for debt marketing techniques are explored in Section 4 below.

Debt issuance can almost always be conducted in a manner that treats equally circumstanced persons equally, chiefly because it is free of the elements of compulsion or of gift that characterize taxation on the one hand or unrequited transfer payments and free government services on the other. The exceptions occur when a particular issue is restricted to a certain class of buyers. The definition of that class is likely to create discontinuities that seem unjust, as when a security carrying an interest rate above the market rate is offered to certain financial intermediaries to help them meet contractual obligations that had been incurred when interest rates were much higher,[6] or is offered to small savers in the form of bonds that are non-negotiable but constantly presentable at any time for redemption.[7] Those who fall just outside the privileged category because they do not quite fit a description or are just over some quantitative line are likely to feel aggrieved.

6. This was done by the federal government of the United States shortly after World War II to assist life insurance companies to meet their obligations under contracts that had been entered into when the market rate of interest was very much higher. Mutual savings banks were also allowed to purchase these "Investment Series" 2.5 per cent 18-year bonds. See Carl S. Shoup, "Les restrictions à la négotiabilité de la dette fédérale aux Etats Unis," *Revue de Science et de Législation financières* (July–September, 1949), 41: 245–46.

7. The United Kingdom and United States savings bonds are illustrations. The prices at which the government stands ready to buy back the bond varies in a way that gives the holder a larger interest yield the longer he holds the bond.

Excess burden is created by the issuance of debt insofar as debt illusion exists. Each potential taxpayer destined to help, possibly, to service the debt believes himself richer than he really is, and so tends to spend more or work less than he would if he were aware of his probability-weighted liability to service a part of the debt. In this sense, of doing something he would not do if he were fully aware of the circumstances, he may be said to carry excess burden. It needs to be emphasized that it is not the holder of the debt, as such, who is deceived. He is quite correct in believing that if he lost his debt certificate he would lose something of value. The excess burden arising from debt issue cannot be defined without reference to future taxes. This burden is therefore not a feature of the debt issue itself.

Sometimes the securities carry features designed to move the holder closer to an optimum position than certain gross imperfections of a second-best world otherwise allow. The United States savings bonds for small savers were designed primarily to obviate a recurrence of the post-World War I liquidation of government bonds on a large scale by small owners who had been persuaded to "borrow and buy." When interest rates rose after the war, some of the banks that had loaned these small "investors" most of the money for purchase of the bonds sold some of them out as the market value of the bonds sank to unanticipated depths.[8]

Issuance of marketable debt, by itself, influences distribution of income only indirectly, by its tendency to raise interest rates and to depress the value of outstanding marketable securities, governmental or private. The latter result is roughly progressive with wealth, but it is once-for-all, in the year of issue, and is cancelled as the securities approach maturity. As they do, the increase in the interest rate that occurred in the year of issue becomes correspondingly more significant in increasing the share of total income going to the well-to-do. A complete statement must assume what taxes are being imposed that would not be there if the debt had not been issued. At the time the debt is issued, say in wartime, taxes may already be so heavy on the well-to-do that another increment of tax finance will come out of the poor. In those circumstances, debt finance is a means of sparing the poor, provided that in the later years taxes on the rich will be so light, with the reduction in military outlays, that they can be taxed in those years to service and retire the debt.[9]

The family status of the security purchaser has apparently never been taken into account in fixing the rate of interest or terms of redemption, but such a differentiation is not impossible, if the security is made nonmarketable. A higher rate of interest might be needed to induce a large family of low income to reduce its per capita consumption by purchasing a bond than a smaller family of the same income. On this score, current taxation is much easier adapted to differences in family composition,

8. For a history and analysis of the savings bond in the United States shortly before, during, and shortly after World War II, see Henry C. Murphy, *The National Debt in War and Transition* (New York: McGraw-Hill, 1950), pp. 35–43, Chapter 15, and pp. 225–26.

9. "The crucial question is whether, if we had financed the War [World War I], let us say, two-thirds out of taxes instead of one-third, the *additional* burdens would have fallen more heavily on the rich than the subsequent peace-time taxes which the borrowing has made necessary. As to this, the answer is absolutely certain. A heavy increase in war taxes could not have fallen on the very rich, for the simple reason that our system had already gone as far as possible in this direction . . ." (John Maurice Clark, *The Costs of the World War to the American People* [New Haven, Conn: Yale University Press, 1931], p. 76).

and for a large family a smaller (not a larger) amount of taxation is needed than for a small family, to induce a certain uniform per capita restriction of consumption.

Geographical discrimination within the issuing country seems also not to have been practiced in terms of debt issue. But geographical discrimination in borrowing abroad is commonplace. The several foreign markets, except for securities actively traded in, tend to be more or less compartmented. Minimization of the total interest bill now is an obvious goal of the borrower. The result of these two facts is a tendency to fit the borrowing terms to the particular markets.

Economic growth is inhibited by debt finance in place of tax finance, unless the adverse incentive effects on investment exercised by the once-for-all heavy tax are a good deal greater than those exercised by the taxes necessary to service the debt and by the increase in interest rates caused by the debt issue. The debt illusion, or no-tax illusion, we have seen, tends to let consumption spending proceed unchecked.

Among types of debt instrument, those with a distant maturity are probably more likely to be purchased by rich households and correspondingly more likely not to reduce consumption spending. Perpetuities, by which the government does not obligate itself to redeem the debt, but retains the right to do so, were especially suitable for the wealthy families of Britain and France in the economically stable world of the late nineteenth century. The fact that they fluctuate in market value by the same percentage as does the long-term interest rate makes them unsuitable investments for families of little wealth who may have to sell them in emergencies.[10] Debt of twenty, to thirty or forty years to maturity, on the other hand, may be quite attractive to institutions that mobilize the savings of low-income families, and the availability of such debt may reduce consumption by facilitating the pooling of those savings.

A distant maturity date makes the security akin to a perpetuity initially. A debt that does not mature until fifty years later is not very different in the eyes of the purchaser from a perpetuity. For example, the present value of a dollar fifty years hence, at an interest rate of 5 per cent compounded annually, is only $8\frac{7}{10}$ cents. The basic difference from the perpetuity is that once the terminable security is issued it

10. The instabilities of interest rates and price levels of the twentieth century have finally eliminated the perpetuity altogether. This form of debt was employed in the United Kingdom as early as the mid-eighteenth century, if not earlier, and reached its greatest acceptance more than a hundred years later under the name of Consols ("consolidated annuities," a term originally applied to the 3 per cent Consols of 1751, which were converted in 1888 into stock bearing interest at $2\frac{3}{4}$ per cent to 1903, and $2\frac{1}{2}$ per cent to 1923, but which were in fact redeemed in 1889 (Henry Higgs [Ed.], *Palgrave's Dictionary of Political Economy* [London: Macmillan, 1926], vol. 1, p. 390). In France, annuities were issued under the name of *rentes*. The last issue of perpetuities in either country was the ill-fated Dalton $2\frac{1}{2}$ per cents of 1947, issued immediately after World War II at nearly 100; in 1968 they sold as low as 33. In France no perpetuities have been issued since 1949 (François Bloch-Lainé and Pierre de Vogüé, *Le trésor public et le mouvement général des fonds* [Paris, Presses Universitaires de France, 1960], p. 97). The perpetuity is also useful to guardians or trustees in a society in which settlement of property for several generations ahead is accepted as a correct social and economic procedure, for example in the entail of estates and in various long-period forms of land tenure. This attitude goes especially well with an accumulation that is large relative to the present and foreseeable needs of the family in question, so that a steady income of, say, 3 per cent provides more than ample means.

changes its aspect steadily as the years progress and ultimately becomes a very short-term security, akin to money.

For direct appeal to the small saver, that is, to the household most likely to reduce consumption somewhat to meet an incremental purchase of securities, a maturity of not more than ten years or so is probably the most attractive. Protection against fall in market value is an even more important feature for this class of investor. The danger of a wholesale cashing-in of such bonds in the event of an inflation is apparently slight, to judge by the experience of the United Kingdom and the United States since 1940; and if interest rates rise, the rates on these bonds, including those outstanding, can be increased by enough to induce retention.

The relative rates of growth of different industries can be influenced by the government's decision on the type of debt to issue. If the government persistently employs short-dated debt, the consequently reduced supply of long-term debt will lower the long-term interest rate somewhat, relative to short, compared with what the pattern would be if the government issued only long-term debt and kept refunding it constantly to keep it long. Investment will be stimulated in industries the capital of which takes the form of long-lived equipment and buildings, which can be financed more easily by long-term debt than by repeated short-term borrowings, and will be checked in industries that carry large inventories, especially seasonally fluctuating inventories, which are typically financed by short-term borrowing.

Risk-taking is either increased or decreased depending in part on how the once-for-all current tax compares in this respect with the future taxes to service the debt. The type of debt issued makes some difference. A lottery bond, for example, tends both to reduce risk taking, by drawing money from risk-seekers, and to increase risk-taking by its example. But the effect in this instance is probably small, especially if the lottery bond is of the conservative type used in recent years, whereby all the interest that the entire issue would normally pay is placed in a pool from which the prizes are distributed.[11] The response to these issues has not been notable.

Borrowing domestically may create an incremental surplus on balance of payments relative to taxation for two reasons, at least in a less developed country. The balance of trade will improve if investment goods are largely imported, and most consumers' goods are produced within the country. This conclusion assumes that borrowing comes more out of investment spending than does taxation. Secondly, net capital inflow will be increased as interest rates rise. In a high-income industrialized country, on the other hand, imports may be chiefly of raw materials or consumer goods. Borrowing may then produce an incremental deficit on balance of trade, relative to current taxation. When the debt is redeemed by taxation, and consumption spending is thereupon checked appreciably while investment spending is increased, the reverse conclusions apply: the less developed country experiences an incremental deficit in its balance of payments in the year of taxation and redemption, compared with what the balance of payments would have been if redemption had been postponed. Borrowing abroad of course produces an incremental surplus in the year of debt issue and a decrement in years of interest payment and redemption.

The supply of labor is almost surely reduced in the initial year by the issuance of

11. As in Berlin and the United Kingdom after World War II.

debt in place of the once-for-all lump of taxation, owing to the debt illusion. In the year of redemption, the supply of labor is almost surely increased, as some households feel poorer and none (mistakenly) feels richer. A heavy annual interest bill also must reduce the volume of labor, since the net income effect is zero, and the substitution effect of the taxes imposed to finance the interest is positive. On balance, over the whole life of the debt, the value of the change in the supply of labor, discounted to or accumulated to some one date, is almost certainly negative. But the size of this decrement depends greatly on the type of debt issued and the relative types of tax under a debt policy and no-debt policy. If the debt is sold to the upper-income groups, the income effect of the debt illusion probably changes the supply of labor from those groups by an insignificant amount. Perpetuity financing thus probably reduces the supply of labor less than savings bond financing, assuming tax patterns unchanged.

The chief problem of intragovernmental coordination is whether the issuing government shall tax the interest income from its own bonds. Under a progressive income tax, a large tax-exempt bond issue must carry a coupon large enough to attract purchasers who are taxed at less than the highest tax rate. This tax-exempt coupon gives the subscribers who are in higher tax brackets a greater inducement than they need, with respect to at least a part of what they subscribe. The government pays out more money in interest than it saves in income tax and at the same time reduces the real rate of progression of the income tax. Nevertheless, it appears that, with one outstanding exception,[12] governments with progressive income taxes exempt the interest on their own bonds.

Estate and gift tax laws, on the contrary, rarely if ever exempt the issuing government's own bonds. But the privilege of tendering such bonds at par value in payment of those taxes may on occasion be a valuable privilege, which probably costs the government more than it obtains in a lower coupon rate.

4. Minimizing Interest Bill

In the unrealistic case of a government that desires to minimize the interest bill on its debt to the non-bank sector, it will attempt to break up that sector into non-trading groups, selling its securities on different terms to each group.

The general rule for minimization is monopsonistic purchasing at differential prices (here, at differential interest rates). Non-negotiable securities are sold competitively within each market in amounts and on terms such that the marginal proceeds to be obtained from further lending by increasing the interest rate by a given small increment is the same, per dollar of incremental interest paid out, in all the markets. For example, let the rates of interest be 4 per cent in competitive market A, 6 per cent in competitive market B, and 7 per cent in competitive market C. Markets A, B, and C are isolated from each other; lenders in C cannot resell their holdings of government debt to persons in A or B. If an increase in interest paid on

12. The United States.

all securities in all three markets of, say, 0.01 percentage point would yield in all three markets the same ratio of (1) incremental proceeds from sale of bonds to (2) the increment of aggregate interest charge (including of course the additional interest to be paid on bonds already sold), then the aggregate interest bill is at a minimum. If this ratio is not the same in all three markets, the interest bill can be reduced by selling more debt in the market where the ratio is the highest and with the proceeds redeeming a like amount of debt in markets where the ratio is lower.

Although the investing public has access to many fairly good substitutes for a government bond, the substitution is not so close as to preclude application of monopsonistic principles in the purchase of funds by the government, especially in times of war or other crisis when the private capital market is severely restricted. But an intensive application of these monopsonistic principles, particularly in normal times, would give rise to serious social and political tension, with charges of favoritism and discrimination.[13]

In a single market the interest bill can be minimized over the short term by refunding constantly into whatever maturity date happens to be the cheapest; but this is to lose all control over liquidity. Moreover, since changes in interest rates cannot be foreseen, there is no guarantee that this technique would make the aggregate interest charge over, say, a decade or more any lower than a random policy of refunding. Thus, for example, the long-term rate may be the lowest in the year when refunding must be accomplished, but the next year it may be enough lower to have made it worth while to sell one-year securities the preceding year, had this been foreseen. A call date will give the government an opportunity to take advantage of changes in the interest rate structure; on or after the call date the holder must surrender the security for repayment at par, at the request of the government. But, because of the increased uncertainty he must bear, the investor will demand at least a slight increase in rate of interest if he is to be subject to a call date, and the further in advance of the maturity date the call date is, the greater the premium.[14]

To raise a given increment of money in a single competitive market at the lowest possible cost, the government must issue a variety of securities and follow the marginal rule described above for the separated markets. Each type of security is offered to the point where the ratio, incremental proceeds per dollar increase in annual debt charge, is the same for each type of security. The different types of security should not, of course, be issued in package form, unless marketing difficulties make the package approach unavoidable.[15]

13. In 1948 the United States had outstanding in the hands of the public five different types of non-negotiable securities, but for none of them could the restriction on marketability be explained chiefly by a desire to minimize the total interest charge, and for two of them this goal was obviously not in mind (Shoup, *loc. cit.*, pp. 242–49, 252–54).

14. At the extreme, the call date would be the day following the date of issue; the security's holder's uncertainty as to the date he would be required to turn in the security would be at a maximum. The reverse procedure is exemplified by the savings bond where the holder is given a series of "puts." (See page 446.)

15. As perhaps they did in the England of the Napoleonic war and postwar periods. The British debt offerings of those days included "the Omnium," which for one offering consisted of the following package: "the main unit, £100 in 3 per cent stock [perpetuities] [and] . . . the following 'douceurs' (sweeteners): an annuity of 13s. for 77 years, £25 in 4 per cent stock, and

If the interest paid by the government is taxed by it, the marginal rule should be cast in terms of the net interest burden on the government. Under a progressive income tax the net interest burden is equalized at the margins of borrowing only by selling so many securities to higher-income lenders that gross interest rates to them are pushed to levels higher than that which obtains for the low-income lender.

State and local governments, in contrast to national governments, weight heavily the goal of a minimum interest bill, since so much of their borrowing is "abroad." But the possibilities of breaking up the market are correspondingly less, since for any one state or local government security the investor has available so many close substitutes that monopsonistic purchase of funds by any one state or municipality is difficult if not impossible.

5. Minimizing Danger of Treasury Embarrassment

Governments that are not completely stable financially and that do not possess large political and economic reserve powers of taxation to tide them over emergencies must consider how to avert possible embarrassment of the treasury, in their choice of debt maturities. If all or most of the debt is very short term, or if the security holders have been given "puts," the government may someday find itself in acute financial embarrassment that leads to unplanned money creation. A short-term debt allows investors' uneasiness, fear, or panic to feed upon itself. A somewhat similar danger is that holders of the short-term debt may attempt to convert large amounts into foreign currencies in times when balance of payments problems threaten the stability of the home currency relative to foreign currencies.

B. INFLATIONARY FINANCE

1. Concept and Scope

This chapter deals with only one type of inflation: that arising from the issue of new money by the government,[16] or at its order, to obtain some of the real resources that it desires by bidding them away from the private sector through a rise in prices that continues over a period of years. Emphasis is on appraisal of new-money creation as an instrument deliberately employed, along with a certain amount of taxation, to transfer resources from the private sector to the public.

Excluded from analysis here, therefore, are the types of inflation, whether

four tickets in a lottery for an extra £10 per £1,000 subscribed" (Shoup, *Ricardo on Taxation*, p. 144, and sources there cited).

16. The new money discussed here is therefore usually money created within the government sector (see note 1 above).

evidenced by a rise in prices or repressed by direct controls, that occur when the government and its agencies are not themselves financing an appreciable part of their outlays by creation of money. These excluded types are (*a*) inflation arising from an increase in private-sector demand for domestically produced capital goods, or inventories, fueled by credit created for the private sector; (*b*) inflation resulting from monetary wage increases in excess of productivity increases; (*c*) inflation induced by an increase in foreign demand for domestic products.[17] Action by the government to slow or to stop these types of inflation by the use of public finance instruments is discussed in Chapter 24 below.[18]

Also excluded from the present chapter is the hypothetical type of inflation, the rate of which is announced in advance, which is assumed by everyone to be certain to occur and which does occur. This kind of new-money finance, which is but part of a broader fiscal-monetary stabilization-redistribution framework, lacks the characteristic that is essential to the inflations that are the subject of study here: uncertainty as to speed and duration of the rise in prices. The uncertainty is chiefly in the minds of the public, but even the decision-makers cannot control closely the inflation they deliberately invoke.

New money is emphasized, rather than an increase in the velocity of an existing money stock, because the increment of real resources that the government can draw away from the private sector by increasing velocity is relatively limited. It is accomplished by giving incentives to government bond dealers and their co-workers to seek out even the smallest pools of idle money throughout the economy, to absorb new issues of government securities.[19]

Inflation that is an effective tool to force the private sector to relax its hold on resources cannot of course be repressed inflation; the rise in prices is an essential part of the process. The inflation is a purposeful action directed to the same end as taxation and borrowing. The government is not to be viewed as somehow struggling under a catastrophe that it did its best to avoid. Governments that inflate sometimes like to give that impression, but they will in fact have chosen consciously not to impose additional taxation, or not to enforce fully the taxes already levied, or not to borrow, or not to forego certain expenditures. Evidently, new money finance that induces a rise in prices must possess in the policy-makers' minds some advantages over these alternative courses of action. The task facing the public finance student is to ascertain what those advantages are and to compare them with the drawbacks.

17. The rise in prices assumed in this chapter includes the rise that is traceable to a more or less constant, positive, coefficient of expectations (ratio of difference between expected and actual price levels to the actual change in price level). But the analysis abstracts from possible instability of the price level in the sense of hyper-inflation. For a summary of these concepts, see R. J. Ball, *Inflation and the Theory of Money*, pp. 39–45.

18. The analysis in the present chapter, as distinguished from that in Chapter 24, is therefore concerned more with the kind of inflation that has characterized, particularly, certain Latin-American countries in the postwar period, than with the problems to which Ball's treatise is addressed, the "problems of inflation in the context of developed economies which are relatively industrialized, with developed financial institutions and in which organized labour plays a significant role" (*ibid.*, pp. 24–25).

19. This action appears to have been taken, to a significant degree, in the United States in the 1950's and 1960's.

The framework of appraisal used in Chapters 8–16 above will prove equally useful here: first, to explore the incidence of inflation; second, to set it against the consensus and conflict criteria by which communities commonly appraise their other public finance instruments. Alternative methods of creating new money will not be discussed here; the choice among them does not much affect the answers to the questions posed below, of incidence and criteria.

The countries that have used inflationary finance to divert resources to government have commonly maintained their exchange rates, whether multiple or single, at fixed levels for months or even years while the internal price level was rising. Devaluation of the currency by a considerable percentage is then followed by another period of nominal exchange-rate stability and continually rising prices. Use of this combined procedure will be assumed in most of the analysis to follow. The consequences of inflationary finance would be appreciably different under a freely fluctuating exchange rate; what those differences would be can for the most part be deduced from the explanation of what happens under irregularly spaced devaluations.

As with a general sales tax, quantitative estimates of the effect of inflationary finance can be given only in a general equilibrium setting where at least one other part of the environment must change when inflationary finance is introduced; the "consequences" mentioned in the preceding paragraph, when quantitatively assessed, are always those of introducing inflationary finance and changing something else. Only differential incidence is meaningful, except with respect to foreign as against domestic consumers and factors, where, as with the major taxes, a brief excursion into partial-equilibrium analysis will be fruitful.

If the analysis to follow seems sometimes to imply nothing but a crude quantity theory of money and the price level, it is only for brevity of exposition in a setting where the new-money issue is large and the interest-rate markets are disorganized.

2. Incidence

A. OPEN ECONOMY

In an open economy, inflationary finance is the equivalent of an origin-principle tax.[20]

If the demand for exports is perfectly elastic, the exportables manufacturing industry must reduce its output as costs in domestic currency rise, until marginal costs in domestic currency are back to where they were initially. Domestic consumers of these exportables (including the government itself) escape the pressure of inflation, except as it raises the costs of domestically marketing these goods.

If, in the process of reducing output and lowering marginal costs, so much

20. This fact has been noted by Professor Marion Hamilton Gillim, in "Some Fiscal Aspects of the Latin-American Free Trade Association," in Shoup (Ed.), *Fiscal Harmonization in Common Markets* (New York: Columbia University Press, 1967), vol. 2, pp. 527–29.

domestic demand for the exportables is attracted that equilibrium can be reached with exports zero, the burden of the inflationary finance with respect to production of these goods does not rest wholly on factors in the export industry; part of it is borne by domestic purchasers, including the government.

While some domestic demand will certainly be diverted to exportables, as costs in that sector are reduced relative to costs of non-traded goods, it seems straining even this partial equilibrium analysis too far to assume that an equilibrium will be reached with exports zero. Accordingly, as with the origin-principle sales tax (Chapter 8, Section A.1), factor rewards, at the margin, in the export industry, may be assumed in the usual case to be reduced by the full amount of the inflation-induced rise in prices, as long as the exchange rate is not altered.

Domestic prices of all domestically produced goods rise under the initial impact of the inflationary financing, but the prices of imports do not rise, as long as the supply of imports is perfectly elastic in foreign currency prices and the exchange rate remains unaltered. The production of import-competing goods will have to be reduced until, even under the inflationary pressure, marginal costs in domestic currency are kept where they were initially, in view of the fact that import prices will not have risen, given the fixed exchange rate and no import quotas. This pressure on import-competing producers can become very severe if the exchange rate, at least for imports, is kept unchanged for a considerable period of time while domestic costs are rising under the new-money financing. Consumers, including the government, meanwhile remain exempt from the inflation tax with respect to their consumption of imports, and import-competing goods, until devaluation or import restrictions are decreed.

If the foreign trade elasticities are less than perfect, the incidence of inflation is spread more widely within the domestic economy. Part of it, too, will rest on foreign purchasers. Less of the burden will fall on domestic factors producing (1) exportables or (2) import-competing goods. Imports remain "tax-free" only in the sense that the costs of producing the pre-inflation quantities are not increased. The demand diverted to them under this origin-principle "tax" will induce an increase of imports, now at a rising foreign-factor cost, hence at a rising domestic price of imports. Since inflation's pressure on the import-competing factors will be reduced, domestic consumers both of imports and of import-competing goods will now have to yield real resources to the government under the inflation.

When the rise in domestic prices has created so great a deficit on balance of payments that devaluation is decreed, the devaluation is unlikely to be enough to restore everyone approximately to his pre-inflation relative economic status, after allowance for the increased use of real resources by the government. An over-devaluation will for a time place exporters and import-competing industries in an even better position than before inflation began, and domestic consumers of exportables, imports, and import-competing goods in a worse position than they were initially. But these facts are attributable only secondarily to inflation.

B. DIFFERENTIAL INCIDENCE:
INFLATION AND VALUE-ADDED TAX

If inflationary finance is substituted for a value-added tax (consumption type) in a closed-economy general equilibrium setting, the differential incidence will be largely on the holders of claims fixed in money value in proportion to the size of those claims.

If the rate of inflation were steady and perfectly forseen by everyone, and if all contracts (e.g., loan contracts) were therefore instantly revised to take account of the inflation, i.e., were "indexed," the incidence of inflation would be that of a tax on cash balances.[21] Cash balances would initially be reduced in real terms because the cost of holding a cash balance would have risen to be the sum of interest foregone plus the depreciation in real value of the cash balance owing to the rise in prices. Thus the immediate reaction to the announcement of the inflation would be a decrease in cash balances, but in each year thereafter cash would be added to these balances in an amount necessary to keep them at their new (low) level in real terms. This repeated withdrawal of cash from the market for goods and services would make the private sector unable to prevent the government from obtaining real resources by its continual issue of new money to bid up prices.

In fact, of course, real cash balances do not remain unchanged during inflations; when the price level rises at a greater percentage rate than the quantity of money, real cash balances decline. The base of the inflation tax, in real terms, shrinks.[22] The government's call on the resources of the economy is further diminished by participation of other money-creating authorities, typically commercial banks, in the taxing process (though they may in turn inadvertently pass on part of this revenue to their borrowers, by not raising interest rates enough).

Redistribution of real income occurs partly because many old contracts cannot be renegotiated at once and partly also because no one can know what the rate of rise in prices will be. Initially, at least, there is considerable redistribution from long-term creditors to long-term debtors. Other lags in adjustment, perhaps with respect to wages especially, will redistribute income from employees for a time. In most of these instances, what one part of the private sector loses, another part gains. The ability of the government to obtain real resources through inflation still depends on its share of the implicit tax on cash balances.

If these tendencies are to be quantified for incidence analysis, differential incidence must be the concept employed. The results under an inflation must be compared

21. See Milton Friedman, "Discussion of the Inflationary Gap," in his *Essays in Positive Economics* (Chicago: University of Chicago Press, 1953), pp. 254–57, and *Dollars and Deficits* (Englewood Cliffs, N.J.: Prentice-Hall, 1968), Chapter 1, "Inflation: Causes and Consequences;" Martin J. Bailey, "The Welfare Cost of Inflationary Finance," *Journal of Political Economy* (April, 1956), 64: 93–95, 101.

22. See Phillip Cagan, "The Monetary Dynamics of Hyperinflation," in Milton Friedman (Ed.), *Studies in the Quantity Theory of Money* (Chicago: University of Chicago Press, 1956), Section VII, "The Tax on Cash Balances." "The note-issuing authorities 'collect' all the revenue; however, when prices rise in greater proportion than the quantity of money, . . . part of the revenue goes to reduce the real value of the outstanding money supply." *Ibid.*, p. 78.

with those under a reference tax, here, the value-added tax, consumption type. This differential incidence rests in large part on the holders of cash balances, since the value-added tax does not strike cash balances as such. But since incidence in this context includes the entire change in distribution of real disposable income, no general a priori statement seems possible, in view of the uncertain lags in adjustment and mistakes arising from inability to forecast the course of the inflation.

These possibilities of forcing a reduction in private-sector use of resources by driving up the price level with new money may seem so limited as to prompt the question, How can the inflationary technique be considered a major resource-obtaining instrument for government, on a par with a general sales tax? The answer probably is that it cannot and that, if differential incidence is to be computed, a continual rise in prices of, say, 20 or 30 per cent a year should be compared, for equal-resource releasing power, with only 5 percentage points or so on a value-added tax, not 10 or 20 points, and certainly not 20 or 30 points. "Equal-yield" comparisons in money terms mean nothing here. The sales tax revenue at the initial price level is to be compared with: (a) the new-money revenue deflated by the price index, minus (b) the loss in real value of other government revenue, or (b') plus the increase in real value. If, for example, the government's revenues in Year 1 dollars were: value-added tax, 100 and other taxes, 100; if, after substitution of new-money finance for the value-added tax the government obtains from new money 250 and from other taxes 150 in Year 2 dollars; and if the Year 2 price level is double that of Year 1, this government revenue mix, 62 $\frac{1}{2}$ per cent new money and 37 $\frac{1}{2}$ per cent other taxes, obtains only the same amount of real resources that was initially obtained by a mix of 50 per cent from value-added tax and 50 per cent from other taxes. In this second period, new money of two and a half times the amount of the first-period value-added tax revenue is required merely to maintain the government's real revenue. The amount of new money required, when deflated by the price index, is one-fourth greater than the first-period value-added tax revenue, as it needs to be because of the loss of value of other tax revenue. It is therefore easy to exaggerate the role that new-money finance plays in any one year in pulling real resources away from the private sector. The new-money revenue, even when deflated, can be large relative to the tax revenue it replaces, without obtaining additional real resources for the government.

A partial offset is of course the decrease in real value of government expenditures that are fixed in money terms. This decrease might better be viewed as a part of the implicit tax represented by inflation. And once inflation has progressed for some time, so that no new debt can be issued (unless indexed), the real amount of such fixed expenditure becomes small if not zero.

3. Criteria

The new-money technique scores highly on the consensus type of equity criteria. This fact explains in part why inflationary finance is used in countries where the social and political environment is such that beyond a certain level of taxation almost any tax falls far short of satisfying those criteria, chiefly because impersonality in the drafting and administering of tax laws is not highly developed.

The new-money method does not purport to establish any tests of relevance as to membership in taxed groups, all of the members of any one group being treated equally. The new-money method is highly impersonal: there are no one-taxpayer clauses under inflation. There are no substantial discontinuities, qualitative or quantitative. There is no evasion at all in a formal sense, since there is no law to evade and cost of compliance is zero, since there is no law to comply with. But inflationary finance fails to meet the test of certainty; it is the essence of the kind of inflation discussed here that the household or the firm faces great uncertainty regarding the consequences of any particular course of action it undertakes. And evasion occurs in a more fundamental fashion when some persons are able to protect themselves against or even profit from inflation; they release no resources for government use.

Even the uncertainty that characterizes inflationary finance speaks in favor of it to legislators in a country where social and economic conflicts are so great that consensus on how to distribute the burden, beyond a modest level of taxation, is virtually impossible to achieve. In addition, a certain amount of illusion that inflation hurts no one weights the decision toward partial use of the new money technique.

With respect to the Pareto-optimum criterion, inflation creates no formal differences in rates of substitution, but the gross uncertainty it produces is a source of errors by producers and consumers who attempt to clear markets, errors that leave a trail of shortages and gluts. Another inefficiency arises through collapse of certain methods of doing business, especially in finance; long-term mortgages disappear, and apartment houses have to be built entirely with equity money, construction sometimes being delayed until the next floor is sold.

Under some circumstances inflationary finance may be progressive by income class, at least relative to the value-added tax.

An example is a less developed country where a great majority of the workers, small farmers and small shopkeepers or artisans, and all of those in the non-monetized sectors of such an economy, hold little in cash balances and have little or no savings accumulated in fixed-claim form, either directly or through pension funds or insurance policies. Such claims are held chiefly by the upper-income groups and by substantial business firms. In advanced industrial societies, however, fixed income claims are held by all but those in the lowest income groups. This extensive holding of fixed claims helps explain why inflationary finance is so much less politically acceptable in those countries than in the others. In a fairly open economy, much depends on how consumption of imports and of import-competing goods, and of exportables, is distributed by income classes.

As between families of different size and composition but equal income and wealth, inflationary finance may benefit the larger family, since such a family will be saving less, and so will be less exposed to erosion of real value of savings. On the other side is the fact that the large family has little leeway for anticipatory consumer buying.

Geographical distribution of the burden under inflationary finance includes the possibility that the foreign purchaser will bear part of it if the demand for exports is less than perfectly elastic, as noted earlier. In less developed countries many of the largest firms are foreign-owned, and the losses they suffer from having to hold cash balances, accounts receivable, and the like show up clearly in the accounts they render to shareholders when a devaluation of the currency has made their real loss quite visible. Accordingly, much of the burden of inflation in open, less developed economies has probably been exported.

For a depressed region within the inflating country, new-money finance can scarcely be tailored to advantage that region. But if the region is depressed by a heavy load of debt, inflation may benefit it on balance, since neither depressed firms nor depressed households usually possess much in fixed money claims. No discrimination against ethnic, color, or other similar groups is possible.

The overriding distributive feature is the one referred to briefly above, and stated in more detail in Chapter 2, namely, the absence of any need ever to make an explicit decision on how the burden shall be distributed, even initially. It is this freedom from the need to make up one's mind in order to reach an explicit compromise that is so attractive in a turbulent political environment. Inflationary finance is rarely found under dictatorships, for dictators do not have to compromise; they find it easy to decide where the burden shall rest.

The effect of inflationary finance on economic growth is the most important issue under the reallocation criteria. Growth here means not the achievement of full employment, for that is assumed, but an increase in the ratio of investment spending plus gainful consumption spending to non-gainful consumption spending (for definitions, see Chapter 23, pages 592–93). Investment, for this purpose, excludes the hoarding of consumer goods by households or unusual increments of inventory motivated by the fear of a further rise in prices.

Whether this ratio is higher under inflationary finance than under, say, a value-added tax and stable prices seems very uncertain. Consumption now becomes preferable to saving money for consumption later, if the household would be somewhat in favor of saving under a stable price level. But investment spending now becomes preferable to investment spending later, and investment goods can be stockpiled by business firms to a degree impracticable for the household and its consumer goods. The inefficiencies noted above under the Pareto-optimum heading tend to reduce investment. When the exchange rates are fixed while prices rise, imports are stimulated. If imports are more capital goods than consumer goods, investment spending is fostered at the expense of consumption; if imports are simply of producers' consumables, for example, raw materials, the tendency may be either way. Exports are reduced, and more exportables are sold on the domestic market. Again, the effect on growth depends on whether the exportables are capital goods.

Private risk-taking is increased by inflationary finance, but not for a reason that commends this measure to those who favor more risk-taking. Inflationary finance increases the social risk of almost every venture, by the wide range of possibilities it creates for any given supply or demand function. The dispersion of possible outcomes in nominal money terms increases, and probably by more than the expected income, so that the coefficient of variation increases. In contrast to taxation, inflationary finance creates no distinction between social risk and private risk; the investor keeps all he gets and bears the entire loss himself.

An incremental deficit in the balance of trade is created by inflationary finance, as by any other origin-principle tax. Since the inflow of foreign capital is unlikely to be greater under inflation than under taxation, new-money finance will almost surely produce a larger incremental external deficit than would taxation.

The supply of labor is likely to be affected but slightly by inflationary finance. The income effect of such finance is chiefly on those who supply factors other than labor (except possibly in exporting and import-competing industries). The only substitution effect on work against leisure is the narrowing of options as to what the worker can do with his wages, certain types of saving now being unfeasible or inadvisable. If wage lags impose heavy burdens on the worker, the income effect is likely to overcome the substitution effect, since the former is a fact and the latter is a forecast, one very difficult to make.

Since inflation is a tax that cannot be made selective, even the government pays the tax if it holds fixed claims, cash or other, as it commonly does. Government officials may not be as careful as those of private business firms to reduce cash holdings to a minimum and may even fear the public's reaction to this implicit forecast of further inflation.

The intra-system reactions under inflation are among the most important aspects of this method of financing. Since the money yields of the government's taxes rise, a sufficiently progressive tax system sturdily administered and widely accepted would cause the substitution of new-money finance for some part of the tax system to be gradually succeeded by substitution of taxation for inflation. In practice, however, a degree of tax progression that would force inflationary finance to burn itself out, as under a highly progressive income tax, creates in that burning-out process anomalies so marked that evasion grows, enforcement wanes, and the tax itself is either discredited or rescued by restating the progression in units of constant purchasing power.[23] Other, non-progressive taxes, a flat-rate sales tax, for example, are not thus discredited by inflation. Accordingly, a long period of inflationary finance will restructure the tax system. A smaller role will be played by the personal income tax, per-unit excises, specific customs duties, and ad valorem taxes that are based on estimated values rather than on money transactions, the real estate tax being the chief example.

Taxes that allow a gap between date of accrual and date of payment likewise fall into disfavor under inflationary finance. The chief casualties are again the income tax, except as it is withheld at the source or paid on an estimated basis, the real estate tax, and death taxes. The loss of real purchasing power to the government owing to this lapse of time may seriously reduce or even completely offset the potential real revenue from the issue of new money.[24]

The third technique of government financing, borrowing, is virtually destroyed by

23. See Chapter 12, page 338, above for the technique employed in Brazil.

24. See Paul J. Strayer, "The Effect of a Rise in Prices upon the Income Tax," *Bulletin of the National Tax Association* (March, 1939), 24: 165–76, and Jacob Viner, "Taxation and Changes in Price Levels," *Journal of Political Economy* (August, 1923), 31: 494–520.

inflationary finance. The indexed bond is feasible only as a means of instilling confidence at a time when there is as yet only the threat of inflation. Once inflation is well under way, the more the government promises to guard certain groups against it, holders of indexed bonds, for example, the greater is the inflation it implicitly forecasts, since the resources to make good on these promises are recognized by all as not likely to be forthcoming from added taxation.

The effects of each of the three main revenue-raising techniques on the other two are seen not to be symmetrical. Inflationary finance destroys borrowing and on balance weakens taxation. Borrowing reduces tax yields only as it reduces spending of a kind that is taxable and does not make inflationary finance more difficult, though it may make it less appealing or at least less necessary. Taxation reduces the amount subscribed to a given government security issue but does not hinder the adoption of inflationary finance.

BOOK THREE
Macro Public Finance

CHAPTER NINETEEN

Framework of Macro Public Finance

A. PUBLIC FINANCE GOALS

THE PRIMARY PURPOSES of the public finance system are to supply the money for government purchase of goods and factor services, to distribute free of charge to households and firms the government services that are produced through use of these goods and factors, and to finance and distribute transfer payments. In the course of achieving these aims, decisions must be made as to what services shall be rendered, how much of each, and to what households and firms they shall be given. Transfer payments call for similar decisions. And on the financing side, a choice must be made among the countless possible patterns of taxation, or mixtures of taxation, borrowing, and new-money finance.

These choices are made in the light of certain ends that the community sets for itself, either unanimously, when the end is one that everyone approves of (full employment, for example, considered apart from price increases that it may engender), or by some rule for taking decisions[1] when interests conflict, as they do with respect to the distribution of real disposable income.

These ends were labeled "criteria" in Chapters 2–18 above. Each public finance instrument, in a very broad sense of that word, was appraised in turn, in isolation from the other instruments. The degree to which the ends could be achieved had to be stated in comparative terms of more or less, rather than in terms of concrete objectives. It would hardly make sense to ask whether the personal income tax could get the economy on to a growth path of, say, 3 per cent a year. But in Chapters 21–24, where each end is considered by itself, in the light of all the public finance instruments available to help achieve it, an implicit quantifying of the end, an assignment of some sort of value to it, is necessary if the analysis is to be useful. In fact, there will be little or no explicit quantification in this and the following chap-

1. These rules are the subject of a rapidly growing literature. They are not covered in the present work, except for analysis of Wicksell's unanimity rule and a reference to Lindahl's analysis, in Chapter 21. See also page 519, note 12, in Chapter 21, which refers to the work of Downs, Buchanan and Tullock, and Olson. See also Musgrave, *Theory of Public Finance*, chapter 6 ("Budget Determination through Voting"), and the references to Blough and Cosciani in Chapter 2 above, footnote 4.

ters, but implicitly the idea of a specified figure for the end is always in the background. There would be little purpose to scanning all the instruments available, to move toward a certain end, unless the end was ultimately to be specified quantitatively or at least in some form of ranking.

An even stronger impulse toward quantification of ends is the fact that in principle the policy-maker must consider not only all the instruments simultaneously (as do each of Chapters 21–24), and not only all the ends simultaneously (as do each of Chapters 4–16 and Chapter 18), but both at once. In principle, an entire system of means and ends has to be formulated, to be expressed by a series of more or less interdependent relations. Now, some form of quantification is clearly essential, if we are to discover how to achieve all the ends by employing suitable values of all the instruments.

This last-mentioned task, the supreme one of the policy-maker, is not attempted in the present work for any specified system; that is something for a large group bringing diverse skills to bear. And indeed our knowledge of how the economic and social system responds to one or another stimulus or deterrent is as yet so imperfect, and the system-wide approach is still so unfamiliar, that there is little even to report on so far. The present chapter, then, attempts to sketch the principles on which such an approach can be built. In doing so, it follows fairly closely the paths developed by Bent Hansen and Leif Johansen. Its chief purpose is to promote a mode of thinking about public finance problems, a basic approach that may at least help to avoid gross inconsistencies and to remind us always that one cannot afford to become too engrossed with some one end, forgetting that the measures taken to achieve this end will quite likely affect appreciably the degree to which other ends can be achieved.

To emphasize the implicit quantification of the ends and their interdependence, the term "criterion" is now replaced by "goal." There are a few criteria, moreover (as defined in Chapter 2), that are better thought of as attributes that are desirable for all instruments, not quantifiable goals, particularly the aspects of consensus equity (except, possibly, indexing degrees of inequality). Intergovernmental fiscal coordination is another instance; the types of coordination to be employed are those that facilitate achievement of the goals by use of the instruments. Because any particular system of fiscal coordination can be appraised only in the light of the whole system of instruments and goals, discussion of it is deferred to the last chapter, Chapter 25.

Certain other criteria discussed in Chapter 2 and in some of the succeeding chapters are omitted from consideration in the following chapters either because of their relatively minor role or because they appear implicitly in the discussion of other criteria-goals: degree of explicitness, or awareness, of tax burdens, and promotion of public-purpose outlays.

In one instance three of the criteria are merged into one goal: degree of risk-taking, amount of work supplied, and rate of economic growth are discussed together under the goal of a certain rate of economic growth.

Most of the goals covered in Chapters 21–24 can be achieved, or at least approached, by actions taken outside the public finance field. Distribution of income can be affected by wage controls and price controls, and by commandeering goods and services for government use. The foreign exchange rate can be supported by import quotas. A complete discussion of how to achieve the goals considered in these chapters is therefore not to be found in the present work, which does not extend to comparing the efficacy of public finance measures with direct controls or other non-public finance measures. Such an analysis must be developed in a book of much broader scope than this one.

Still, most of the goals discussed in Chapters 21–24 are in practice achieved or approached chiefly by financial measures, many of which are public finance measures. Some of the instruments are those of monetary policy, in the sense that they may best be analyzed by those whose expertise is in the field of money and banking rather than in that of taxation, distribution of government services, and the like. The line of separation between monetary policy and fiscal policy is discussed on page 469 below, where it will be seen that there is no unambiguous demarcation between the two policies that is very useful. Two groups of students, those of public finance and those of monetary economics, will overlap in their research and writings. The point to make here is that public finance instruments do not comprise the total of financial instruments.

Since the present analysis covers only public finance measures it implicitly assumes something about the non-public-finance measures. The effects of the public finance measures will differ, depending on the particular non-public-finance measures that are in effect. The implicit assumptions here about those measures are those applicable to most of the private enterprise economies in peacetime, including absence of price and wage controls and rationing. Monetary policy is assumed to be used to affect the amount of credit available and the terms on which it can be obtained; more detailed assumptions about monetary policy will be supplied as needed.

A precise definition of a distinct instrument is given in Section C.1 below; for the moment, an instrument may be thought of as a certain tax rate, or rate of flow of transfer payments, or rate of issue or redemption of government debt, or of expenditure by government on goods and services, or rate of flow of a certain free government service. The use of any one of these instruments, considered in isolation, changes the government's cash balance. It will be assumed here that this change is in the government's cash balance at the central bank. Such a change, strictly by itself, that is, considered apart from concomitant changes in private-sector balances, has no economic consequences of importance for the present analysis, if indeed any at all, and can be ignored. The simultaneous change, if any, in the private sector's cash balances and the consequent change in the commercial banking system's reserves with the central bank are of course of economic significance. The point to be made here may be seen by supposing that the government increases its cash balance at the central bank by selling the bank newly issued non-interest-bearing obligations. So far, nothing of consequence has occurred. If the government now transfers that balance to its deposit accounts with the commercial banks, the commercial banks gain reserves. Hence the level of government deposits in the commercial banks is an instrument, more conveniently labeled, perhaps, a monetary instrument than a public finance instrument. But the cash balance held by the government in the central bank is viewed here as being, strictly in itself, of no interest to the present analysis.

If a postulated decrease in tax rate, or increase in rate of government expenditure, is so large that the cash balance becomes negative within the time period covered, it will be assumed to be brought up to zero, or any positive amount (the amount does not matter, as just explained) by sales of non-interest-bearing obligations to the central bank—or by the simple printing of money, which is held in the government's cash vaults.

In more general terms, an "instrument" is a variable, the value of which can be set by the policy-maker precisely, with no uncertainty, and regardless of any other action that is being taken by the same policy-maker or any one else. It is an exogenous and autonomous variable: exogenous because its value is not influenced by the values of the dependent variables, for example tax revenue or level of employment, and autonomous because its value is not influenced by the values assumed for the other policy variables (level of government spending or tax rate, for example) or any other exogenous variables.[2]

An instrument is therefore to be distinguished from its own immediate results that are not, however, goals. Let us suppose, for example, that a tax rate is lowered to achieve a reduction in tax revenue and an increase in the stock of money in the private sector, all with the goal of stimulating employment. The tax rate is an instrument. The tax revenue is neither instrument nor goal; it may be termed a medium (or channel, or vehicle). The same is to be said of the stock of money in the private sector. Thus the medium is valued not for its own sake but only as a means of achieving a goal. There are two reasons why the amount of tax revenue or the size of the privately held money stock cannot be regarded as an instrument. First, it depends in part on the values assumed by other mediums in the system, and by other instruments if they are regarded also as dependent variables, hence it is not exogenous. Second, it depends in part on the values taken by exogenous elements in the system, including the values taken by other instruments if they are regarded as exogenous; hence it is not autonomous.

Speaking more loosely, the tax revenue is not an instrument because the government cannot decree with certainty that the revenue shall be a specified amount. This is so, even when a real estate tax rate is arrived at by dividing a desired revenue by the aggregate amount of taxed property. For one thing, tax delinquency must be estimated, and its amount depends on factors not under the control of the policy-makers. The real estate tax rate alone is the instrument.

The amount of government debt held by the private sector may be regarded as an instrument, if the government or its agent the central bank is postulated to be able to fix this amount, through open market operations, regardless of what the private sector tries to do and regardless also of the values the government selects for other policy variables. The ratio of money stock to government debt in the private sector cannot be viewed as an instrument, unless the size of the money stock is both exogenous and autonomous, which, as already indicated it is not, except perhaps

2. See Bent Hansen, *The Economic Theory of Fiscal Policy*, trans. by P. E. Burke (London: Allen & Unwin, 1958), p. 6.

under assumptions too strenuous to be very useful. As examples outside the public finance structure, the market interest rate is only a medium, while the discount rate of the central bank is an instrument.

The distinction often attempted between fiscal policy and monetary policy seems seldom if ever to have been unambiguous and helpful at the same time. Fiscal policy, or public finance policy, might be defined as the setting of values of all instruments that imply payments to and from the government. But this definition includes transactions in the credit market, by the treasury, the central bank, and any other government branches, departments, or bodies. Insofar as such transactions result in a change in the stock of money held by the private sector they are commonly thought of as part of monetary policy. In order to exclude from fiscal policy those transactions with this result it has been suggested that fiscal policy be said to deal with the size, and monetary policy with the composition, of the "net national debt," defined in the following particular way: net national debt is for this purpose "the difference between (gross) national debt (including notes in circulation and money at call) and the public claims (including central bank exchange reserves and claims on the private sector). . . ."[3] An objection to this terminology is that the technical problems posed by government debt, as that term is ordinarily understood, are very different from those involved in issuing or redeeming currency ("non-interest-bearing consols"). The former group of problems has been analyzed extensively in public finance literature. For the public finance student, at least, it is usually more confusing than helpful to include currency in the public debt or, more generally, to define net national debt as in the quotation above.

When government bonds are sold to the private sector in exchange for currency and deposits, several economic issues are thereby posed simultaneously. Some of them are best attacked by the monetary theorist, some by those specializing in public finance, and some by joint effort of the two. It is here that the attempted distinction between fiscal policy and monetary policy causes the most confusion. It is not very useful analytically to base the distinction on whether the treasury or the central bank is buying—or selling—the government obligation.

Some tax instruments resemble monetary instruments more than they do other tax instruments. The chief example is a speed-up of tax payments.[4] In effect, the taxpayer is required to purchase his own tax obligation, which has tentatively accrued but has not yet come due (tentatively, because until the income year is over, the tax based on that year's income is of course not fixed). The government engages in a compulsory alternative to an open-market operation; it requires the private sector to buy, not government obligations but its own obligations held by the government.

Perhaps the most useful approach is to move the argument to a lower level of importance by speaking of fiscal (or public finance) instruments and monetary instruments, rather than of fiscal policy and of monetary policy. In any event,

3. Hansen, *op. cit.*, p. 31.

4. The near crisis in the money market in the United States in the fall of 1966 was precipitated in part by the new provisions of the income tax law placing corporations more nearly on a current-payment basis. The continuance of high interest rates through 1967 was attributed partly to the same instrument.

monetary theorists alone will study bank reserves as their special province, public finance theorists alone will study income tax rate schedules as technical specialists, and both will study government transactions in the credit market.[5]

B. COMPULSORY, DONATIVE, AND VOLUNTARY INSTRUMENTS

From the viewpoint of the household or the firm, public finance instruments are either (1) compulsory, (2) donative, or (3) voluntary. The chief examples, respectively, are (1) tax rates, (2) flow of transfer payments of the unrequited type,[6] and flow of free government services, and (3) level of government purchase of goods and services and stock of government debt or stock of money held in the private sector.

The household or firm, in acquiescing in the government's use of a compulsory instrument, or in welcoming its use of a donative instrument, experiences a compulsory, or donative, change in its disposable income. Its net worth therefore changes correspondingly unless the donative flow must be consumed as it is received, which is usually the case with respect to free government services.

When the government purchases goods and services, the sellers experience a voluntary increase in income and, at least momentarily, in net worth, except as they merely draw down inventories.

When the value of the instrument, amount of government debt held by the private sector, is altered by purchase or sale of its obligations by the government on the free market, the household or firm does not, by its own act alone, experience a change in net worth or in its level of consumption. It merely swaps money for obligations or vice versa. Yet it suffers from a micro illusion; as will be noted in Chapter 22, the change in the level of the money stock or the government debt is of use to the government only when it alters prices of assets. But if it alters these prices it must change the net worth of the private sector as an aggregate. An example is sale by the government of its own debt in order to check inflationary pressures by increasing the rate of interest. The prices of outstanding securities fall. Correspondingly, in a depression, the government may purchase securities from the private sector with newly created money, but unless, in doing so, it raises the prices of securities (lowers the rate of interest), the action will have little or no stimulative effect.[7] Yet to any one

5. For most purposes, Musgrave's definition of "pure fiscal policy," that is, equal changes in expenditures and tax yield, seems inconveniently narrow; his definition is accompanied by definitions of three "mixed" fiscal and liquidity policies, and of three "pure" liquidity policies. Monetary policy and debt policy are involved in both of these groups of three (*The Theory of Public Finance*, pp. 526–28). Compare the implied definitions in *ibid.*, pp. 410 ff. We may agree with Bent Hansen that it is "not absolutely clear how the line between fiscal policy and monetary policy should be drawn nor is it altogether clear whether such a distinction on the whole is useful" (Hansen, *op. cit.*, p. 30).

6. Including the "money rain" postulated in some analyses (see Musgrave, p. 410, note 2, and p. 415, note 1).

7. If income is defined as consumption plus increase in net worth, the income of these security holders is changed by the change in market values. But it will be convenient to speak of the compulsory or donative instruments as affecting "disposable income," while the voluntary instruments are said to affect "net worth" if they change the market prices of assets.

transactor, his sale of government obligations is an exchange that does not affect the value of his remaining holdings or the holdings of others. The term, "voluntary instrument" thus remains appropriate, despite the compulsory or donative element, that is, the decrease or increase in net worth suffered or enjoyed by those already holding securities. These holders are subject to an implicit tax or are given an implicit transfer payment, based on market values of their holdings.

The voluntary aspect of the government's purchase of goods and services and of its security transactions explains much of the relative roles played in public finance policy by changes in tax rates, changes in level of transfer payments and of government purchase of goods and services, and government operations in the securities markets.

The power to employ compulsory instruments is in most countries reluctantly, if at all, surrendered by the legislature to the executive,[8] especially if the power is to be exercised by a board or small group that is partially detached from the elected executive, as is a central bank board of directors in many countries. The power to alter the flow of transfer payments and of purchase of goods and services is not extensively delegated because such a change implies that sooner or later there will be a roughly corresponding change in the compulsory instrument, tax rates. For short periods, however, the executive may be empowered to speed up or slow down the rate at which a given total of expenditure is to be made.

The power to use a voluntary instrument that seems not to imply the use of a compulsory instrument is in contrast commonly delegated extensively, notably the power to buy and sell government securities on the open market.

The board, or other small group, or the single official to whom power to employ the instrument is delegated can normally decide more quickly than the legislature whether to act. Since the particular voluntary instruments that are used can be put into effect immediately once the decision is reached, policy changes with respect to the government bond market will usually be implemented well before changes in tax, transfer, or expenditure policy. And since the more of one that is effective, the less, normally, is the need for the other, a further consequence is that the mixture of voluntary and compulsory-donative policy instruments will on the whole consist more of voluntary, that is, market-transaction, instruments than it needs to on substantive grounds. Changes in open-market policy will therefore commonly precede changes in rate of expenditure on goods and services, which in turn will commonly precede changes in tax rates or the level of transfer payments.

To be sure, tax revenues and transfer payments react quickly to changes in national income, while open-market operations of course possess no built-in flexibility at all, and expenditures on goods and services, very little. These facts tend to make the compulsory and donative instruments rather more important, at least for the goals of full employment and of price stability, than the immediately preceding paragraphs would indicate.

8. The power of the executive to change tax rates or other tax provisions is being steadily enlarged in many countries, but the power is usually given only for short periods of time, and exercise of it must usually be ratified by the legislature within a specified period of time after the executive has acted. See J. van Hoorn, Jr., "Are All Tax Laws Laws?," *European Taxation* (June, 1967), 7(6): 121.

C. INSTRUMENTS IN RELATION TO GOALS

A goal is a value of a variable that the policy-makers would like to see attained: zero unemployment within a certain time or maintenance of price stability for a certain period. A shortfall or an overshooting of the goal is to be measured in similarly quantitative terms. But for some goals a statement of quantity to be achieved, or of amount of overshooting, or shortfall is much more difficult than these two examples would suggest. The goal of a Pareto-optimal allocation of resources is a case in point. But if no quantitative measure, however rough, is given, it is not possible to rank combinations of public finance measures with respect to the degree to which they succeed in approximating the goal. This point will be taken up with respect to each goal in Chapters 21–24. The solutions offered are not very satisfying. In general, public finance is only at the beginning of the formidable task of sorting out means and ends, defining units of measurement for ends, assigning a value to each end, and then selecting the means to achieve or approximate the ends. The chapters in Book Three will have accomplished the task set for them if they travel at least a short way down the road to this overriding goal of consistent use of means in relation to specified ends. In practice, complete attainment of a goal is often seen to be impossible, at least for the goals specified, for reasons now to be given.

1. Number of Instruments, Number of Goals[9]

First, there may be more goals than there are instruments available. To be sure, an excess of number of goals over number of instruments does not always make achievement of all of the goals impossible. It does so when each of the instruments affects progress toward each of the goals (the system is completely interdependent) and the relations are linear and independent. Each instrument is of course independent of every other instrument, as already specified above in the distinction between instruments and other variables.

Thus a completely interdependent system of simultaneous independent linear equations is postulated, one equation for each goal.

The linear relationship is an especially strenuous assumption, but it is useful conceptually for understanding the nature of the problem. Moreover, small changes from given values of nonlinear functions may often be treated linearly. If the relations are not linear, no general statement can be made about the requisite number of instruments, given the number of goals.[10] Each system would have to be examined to ascertain, if possible, how many instrument values would be needed.

9. See Bent Hansen, *The Economic Theory of Fiscal Policy, passim,* but especially Chapter 1, and Leif Johansen, *Public Economics,* Chapter 2, for a rigorous development of the relationships of instruments to goals.

10. See Robert Dorfman, Paul A. Samuelson, and Robert M. Solow, *Linear Programming and Economic Analysis* (New York: McGraw-Hill, 1958), p. 350.

But those fully interdependent systems where the number of unknowns did not equal the number of equations would in general reflect unusual relationships. The equal-numbers approach seems still a useful working rule, subject to its being found invalid in any particular case.

The independence of the relationships that is specified is an algebraic independence. It may happen, by economic coincidence, that the values of the series of instruments that yield the desired value for a certain goal also yield the desired value of another goal, yet the relations may still be independent in the algebraic sense; the system still cannot be solved for the goal values if the number of instruments is less than the number of goals (the system being assumed wholly interdependent).

Thus what is postulated here, for purposes of discussion (unless otherwise specified), is a completely interdependent system of simultaneous independent linear equations, one equation to each goal, in which the number of unknowns (dependent variables, here, the instrument variables) must equal the number of equations if there is to be a unique set of values of those variables that is consistent with the stipulated goal values.

If all the goals but one can be overshot (or undershot) without disadvantage, and if one goal is to maximize or minimize some value, the problem may then be formulated as one in linear programming. The number of instruments can now fall short of the number of goals, yet values of the instruments can be found that will minimize or maximize the value of the "objective function" while meeting or more than meeting the requirements set forth in the inequalities, which are to be regarded as restraints on the minimization or maximization process. In public finance linear programming has been developed thus far only in a very abstract manner, and if it is used by the policy-maker it will probably be employed only in lower levels of sub-optimization. Linear programming does not yet seem to promise much for the generalized approach that is the main subject of the present chapter.[11]

An instrument, we have seen, is an exogenous and autonomous variable. But to be a distinct instrument, the variable must affect the goal values in a distinct manner. It is not enough that the devices differ in legal description. If two such devices, say two taxes that are legally distinct, affect goal values in the same ratio, they are but one instrument for purposes of counting instruments and goals. In a system of two goals and two taxes, for example, let a reduction of one percentage point in the rate of tax A approach one goal by three times as much as does a reduction of one percentage point in the rate of tax B, and let it simultaneously draw the economy away from the other goal by three times as much as does a unit rate increase in tax B. Then no combination of rates of the two taxes will permit achievement of the two distinct goals (two goals are distinct if achievement of one does not imply automatic achievement of the other). The two tax rates are only different scale models of the same instrument. But if a reduction of one percentage point in tax B draws the economy away from the second goal two times as much, or four times as much, as

11. See Carl S. Shoup, "Linear Programming in Public Finance," *Finanzarchiv* (August, 1963), 22: 464–83, and Douglas Dosser, "Notes on Linear Programming and Public Finance," *Finanzarchiv* (January, 1964), 23: 279–87.

does a point reduction in tax A, the two tax rates are distinct instruments. If the values that can be given them are not constrained, they can be set so that both goals are achieved.

A distinct instrument is therefore an exogenous autonomous variable that alters the values of the goals (strictly, alters the values of the progress being made toward or away from the goals) in ratios that differ from those by which some other exogenous autonomous variable alters those goal values.[12] Or, in other words, two legally distinct instruments are economically distinct if they differ in the relative effects on goals in the sense that a unit change in one goal value achieved by changing the value of one of the legally distinct instruments is accompanied by a change in another goal value different from that which occurs under a change in the other instrument that also achieves a unit change in the first goal value.

The way in which a number of instruments equal to the number of goals will allow attainment of the goals, under the assumptions given above, and in the absence of some problems to be discussed below (constraints on the values of the instruments, risk, and dynamic complications) will now be illustrated by the simplest kind of example: two instruments and two goals. Let us consider an individual income tax rate and a corporation income tax rate, to be manipulated in order to achieve zero unemployment and to maintain a certain rate of exchange with zero surplus or deficit in the balance of payments. It is assumed that achievement of either one of these goals does not automatically entail or preclude achievement of the other.

Let us suppose that (1) initially, there exist both unemployment and an external deficit; (2) the external deficit can be reduced by a decrease in imports induced by an increase in the rate of the individual income tax on domestic households[13] (the revenue to be added to the treasury's cash balance at the central bank), although this public finance instrument will simultaneously increase domestic unemployment; (3) domestic unemployment can be reduced, because of favorable incentive effects, by a reduction in the corporate income tax rate, financed by drawing on the treasury's cash balance at the central bank, but at the cost of an increase in imports of capital goods.[14] If these two tax instruments differ in their relative effects on domestic employment and imports, some combination of an increase in one tax and reduction in the other will reduce unemployment and the external deficit to zero. Ordinarily there will be but one combination of individual income tax rate and corporation income tax rate that will do this. Thus, if a one percentage point increment in the personal income tax rate reduces the external deficit greatly but increases domestic unemployment only slightly, while a one percentage point decrement in the corporation income tax rate increases the external deficit but slightly while reducing unemployment greatly, the required combination is some increase in the personal

12. This definition of a distinct instrument is useful only insofar as the assumption of linearity is retained. If the relations are nonlinear, that which in a linear system is a single instrument becomes itself, by this definition, an indefinitely large number of instruments, since at different values of the device an incremental change in the value will alter the values of goals in different ratios.

13. For simplicity, any simultaneous increase in exports is ignored. Foreign repercussions are not taken into account.

14. For simplicity, any decrease in exports is ignored.

income tax rate and some decrease in the corporate rate from the initial levels of these rates.

This illustration indicates why two instruments that are legally distinct may not be economically distinct. If, in this case, it took, say, 4 percentage points on the corporate income tax to reduce the external deficit by the same amount as a one percentage point increase in the personal income tax (consistently with what was assumed above), but if it also took 4 percentage points reduction in the corporate income tax to reduce unemployment as much as did one percentage point reduction in the personal income tax (contrary to the assumption above), any increase in the personal income tax coupled with any decrease in the corporation income tax rate would come to the same as an increase in the personal income rax tate followed at once by a decrease in the personal income tax rate by one-fourth as much as the corporation tax rate would be decreased. In effect, only one distinct instrument is available.[15]

2. Constrained Values of Instruments

Second, even when the number of instruments equals or exceeds the number of goals, some of the instruments may be usable only over limited ranges of values, for several reasons.

As the instrument is used more and more intensively, its effect may depart from the linear relationship postulated for the system, probably becoming weaker, and possibly even reversing its direction. "The tobacco excise alone, to whatever levels it be raised, cannot suffice to solve a problem of a serious balance of payments deficit,"[16]—even, we might add, in a country importing all its tobacco.[17] As the tax rate is increased from a moderate level, it will no doubt decrease the payments deficit, in such a country at least. But if the rate is raised to the point where total expenditure on tobacco, including the tax, decreases, consumer purchasing power, released for other purposes, is spent partly on imports, and at some point imports begin to rise as the tax rate is increased further, instead of continuing to fall.

Certain values of an instrument may be inconsistent with the mechanism of the economic system in question. A tax of more than 100 per cent on corporation profits is an example. This case might be regarded as a special instance of the phenomenon noted in the paragraph immediately preceding.

Certain values of the instrument may be deemed inconsistent with certain aims or goals not expressed in the set of economic goals in the particular interdependent system under examination. Those values of those instruments are therefore deemed inadmissible. In a broader interdependent system those hitherto unspecified goals would be included specifically. The values in question would not then be considered

---

15. See Appendix to this chapter.

16. J. Tinbergen, *Economic Policy: Principles and Design* (Amsterdam: North Holland, 1964), p. 26.

17. See Chapter 10 above, page 284.

inadmissible; of course they might, or might not, occur in the resulting set of instrument values required for reaching all the targets. This broadening of the interdependent system is technically appropriate when the constraints on the instrument variable arise from reactions that are germane to the public finance field. Thus, if, "when income taxes are increased beyond a certain figure, evasion will assume large proportions, leading to much extra cost in the broadest sense,"[18] it is technically appropriate for an analysis of public finance, in place of setting more or less arbitrary constraints on the income tax rates for this reason, to set up equal treatment of equals as a goal and solve for the entire system including this goal. In such a system, one instrument would be government expenditure on tax administration.

A purely formal difficulty arises when certain values of the instrument fall outside the definition of the instrument. A corporation income tax of a rate less than zero would commonly be regarded as a subsidy, not a tax, hence a different instrument. But the definition of a distinct instrument that is used in the present work does not prevent the subsidy and the positive tax from being regarded simply as different values of the same instrument (see also Chapter 6 above, on negative taxes). Administrative questions may still make the negative tax differ qualitatively from the positive tax sufficiently to warrant maintaining the distinction for purposes other than the counting of instruments and goals.

If constraints on the instrument values render one or more goals unattainable, they may be made attainable by employing additional instruments, even if they too are constrained. Number of instruments must now exceed number of goals, to make them all attainable, but in practice this requirement is not necessarily a cause for concern. Many instruments are available; more can be invented.

The point just made can be illustrated most simply by assuming that there is only one goal, and initially only one instrument, which is so constrained that it cannot achieve that goal. One more instrument, even though constrained, may suffice. Let the goal be an external deficit of zero, which can be achieved by an increase of 15 percentage points in the personal income tax rate. The community, however, is assumed not to tolerate an increase of more than 10 percentage points. An increase in the corporate income tax rate is therefore employed as a second instrument. We assume that an increase of 45 points in the corporate tax rate will itself reduce the deficit to zero; but the community will tolerate no more than 30 points of increase. Let the relationship of the two taxes' effects be linear, so that each percentage point on the individual income tax reduces the external deficit by three times as much as does each percentage point on the corporate income tax rate. The goal of zero external deficit can be reached by any one of an infinitely large number of permissible combinations, but not by a corporate income tax increase alone or an individual income tax rate increase alone.

18. Tinbergen, *op. cit.*, p. 25.

3. Dispersion of Possible Outcomes

Third, the use of any instrument involves risk, in the sense that the precise outcome cannot be known in advance, and the policy-maker must contemplate a series of alternative possible outcomes, which yield a certain expected value (mean) and a certain dispersion about that expected value (variance). If the instrument is assigned a value extreme enough to make the expected value reach the goal value, the dispersion of possible outcomes may be unacceptably high. The policy-maker may prefer a less extreme value for the instrument, one that will not yield an expected value equal to the desired goal value but that will promise less risk, that is, less dispersion of possible outcomes.

Dispersion, for this purpose, may be measured by the coefficient of variation (standard deviation divided by the mean). If overshooting the "goal" is deemed beneficial, the mean is to be computed by assigning positive values to the overshoots and negative values to the shortfalls, and the true goal is then to maximize the mean. Usually, however, the goal will be an extreme value that cannot be overshot, say zero unemployment, or zero change in the price level or in the foreign exchange value of the currency, and the only possible outcomes will be either attainment of the goal or some degree of shortfall.

To illustrate this discussion of policy risk in a very elementary manner, let us consider the goal of zero unemployment in an economy where unemployment is currently 4 per cent. Alternative tax reductions to stimulate the economy are being considered. Possible outcomes, with probability weights, are believed to be as given in Table 3. A cautious policy-maker, a risk-averter, may decide that the first tax

Table 3   Expected Value and Variance of Unemployment under Alternative Tax Reductions

Probability	Level of Unemployment over a Specified Period
Tax Reduction No. 1	
0.2	5 per cent
0.8	2 per cent
Expected level of unemployment	2.6 per cent
Variance	1.44 per cent
Standard deviation	1.2 per cent
Coefficient of variation, 1.2/2.6	0.46
Tax Reduction No. 2	
0.3	6 per cent
0.7	1 per cent
Expected level of unemployment	2.5 per cent
Variance	5.25 per cent
Standard deviation	2.29 per cent
Coefficient of variation, 2.29/2.5	0.92

reduction measure in Table 3 is the preferable one, although it carries a lower expected value (higher expected unemployment).

Still other probability distributions may be relevant, for example, a distribution of the possible periods of time that will have to elapse before a given value will be reached. And when it is recalled that the policy-maker will be dealing with an interdependent system, hence with a number of expected values, one for each policy end—stable price level, stable exchange rate, a given rate of growth, and so on—and a corresponding number of dispersions of possible outcomes, it will be seen that he faces a formidable problem in deciding among alternative sets of instruments that differ in the degrees of risk they imply for the corresponding sets of goal values.

4. Dynamic Difficulties

Since the instruments must be used on a system that is dynamic in the sense both that the value of at least one variable depends on the rate of change in the value of at least one other variable over time, and that there are lags in the planning process,[19] the structure of the relations may be so imperfectly understood that there can be little hope of achieving the goal except by coincidence, even if the system were subject to no exogenous influences that give rise to risk as discussed in Section 3 above.

5. Specialized Instruments

Let us suppose that in a wholly interdependent system all the goals are being met, save one. An effort to reach that remaining goal by a change in the value of some one instrument alone cannot succeed, for, if all the other goal values that are obtaining are to be kept unchanged, while at the same time progress is to be made toward the as yet unattained goal, every one of the instruments must be changed in value. This is so, because the change in value of some one instrument alone, in an effort to reach the unattained goal, will cause the system to depart from all the other goal values, which are prevailing and desired. In a wholly interdependent system, it will be recalled, a change in the value of one instrument affects the values obtaining for every one of the goals.

Under these circumstances it is ambiguous to label some one instrument as being especially relevant or important or efficient for the achievement of some one goal; it is of little or no use to consider the size of the partial derivative of the function for the goal, with respect to the instrument in question, the values of all the other instruments being assumed unchanged.

In practice, however, the values of the other instruments may on occasion need to change by only a negligible amount. The partial derivative just referred to then yields a close approximation to the ratio of a small change in goal value achieved to

19. See Chapter 22 below, Section C.

a small change in the value of that instrument that is observed when the entire system has reached a new equilibrium, all the other goal values achieved remaining unchanged, and all the other instrument values having changed slightly, perhaps negligibly. In this case, the instrument in question may be termed a specialized instrument.

If the nature of the goal and the distance to it from the prevailing value are such that the goal can be reached only by altering the actions of most of the firms and households in the economy, it is unlikely that any specialized public finance instrument for that goal can be found. If, in contrast, the desired goal value is so close or refers to so narrow a part of the economy that only a small proportion of firms and households must be induced to change their conduct, and that not to an extreme degree, some one public finance instrument, or group of closely similar instruments, will often prove sufficiently specialized. If, for example, the external account is only slightly in deficit, an increase in the tobacco tax may be able to place the account in balance, without appreciably altering the values of other goals already achieved.

In a more extreme case, the system is not at all wholly interdependent; a change in the value of a certain instrument affects progress only toward one goal, without affecting even in a negligible amount the values achieved for other goals. Such an instrument may be termed a completely specialized one. A hypothetical case of this kind has been suggested by Bent Hansen,[20] in which, of three goals, namely, a certain consumer goods price level, full employment, and a certain balance of trade surplus or deficit at a fixed exchange rate, credit policy (interest rate policy) affects only the balance of trade. This result occurs in an extremely open economy, under certain restrictive but not inappropriate assumptions about the relations of these three goals to the three instruments of exchange rate policy, fiscal policy and wage policy, and credit policy. In practice it seems unlikely that this kind of non-interdependence can exist, though there will be many instances where interdependence is so weak that for practical purposes it can be ignored, as suggested above.

If a tax, used as a specialized instrument, is imposed at a rate so high that it yields no revenue, it is a control device resembling licensing, or rationing, or outright prohibition, not a public finance instrument. The expertise of the public finance student is of little assistance here.

6. Isolated Goals

In the extremely open-economy model just cited from Bent Hansen, the value of one goal, the level of domestic prices of consumer goods, is affected only by exchange rate policy, including in this phrase import and export taxes and subsidies. The domestic price level is thus affected not at all by fiscal policy and wage policy, or by credit policy. (This result follows from the extreme openness of the economy.) It is convenient to attach some label to this kind of goal; "isolated goal" is suggested here, to indicate that the goal is isolated from the influence of any instrument save the one. An approximation to an isolated goal exists when only negligible progress toward it

20. *Op. cit.*, p. 399.

can be achieved by use of any instrument other than the one that does contribute appreciably. In practice, an approximately isolated goal seems to be rare, in contrast to the approximately specialized instrument. This is so, even when a goal, and the relevant instruments, are very broadly defined. In Keynesian theory, the liquidity trap affords an example if the goal is full employment and if there are only two instruments, monetary policy, defined as changes in the composition of claims, and fiscal policy, defined as changes in tax rates or expenditure levels, without change in composition of claims.

If all the goals in a system were isolated, all the instruments would be specialized. There would be no interdependence whatever. Otherwise, it is possible for the system to contain a completely specialized instrument but no isolated goals, or an isolated goal but no specialized instruments.

7. Conflict of Goals

Conflict of goals is a common theme in public finance. Equity is said to conflict with allocative efficiency. Full employment is said to conflict with price stability, and the Phillips curve is offered as evidence. In principle, however, there can be no conflict of goals in a linear system that contains as many unconstrained instruments as it does goals. And if the system is self-adjusting, in the sense that it contains one or more goals that it will reach in any event, the number of unconstrained instruments can be fewer than the number of goals and still there will be no conflict.[21] Only if the goals are defined in an inherently self-contradictory manner such that one goal is the opposite of another goal—one goal being price stability, the other being a rise in prices—can there be inherent conflict.[22] The conflicts usually cited arise not because the goals are inherently incompatible but because the instruments assumed available are too few, or their values too constrained, or their effectiveness zero or negative for certain ranges of their values.

21. See Bent Hansen, *op. cit.*, pp. 9–11.

22. More generally, inherent conflict exists if the goals are in logical conflict with one another, either in any event, as when the three goals are expressed as follows:

$$x_1 + x_2 = k; \; x_1 = x_2/k; \; x_1 = 1/(1-k),$$

where $k \neq 1$, or within the definitional framework of the model, as where the sum of the goals set for investment and consumption differs from the goal set for national income, in a closed economy. These examples are from Bent Hansen, *op. cit.*, pp. 25–26. The "interpretation of the expression 'the conflict of ends' which is most in accordance with the meaning usually attached to it" is said by Hansen to be "that the model and the means which it contains do not allow the ends to be fulfilled." The same truth might be put more forcefully by asserting that the alleged conflicts of goals commonly reveal a refusal to think, even intuitively, in terms of a model, and reflect an attachment to partial equilibrium analysis couched in macro terms. In any event, the present analysis agrees with Hansen's view of what the economist must be held to imply, with respect to the kind of phenomenon revealed by the Phillips curve: "If an economist arrives at the conclusion that the ends of full employment and stable value of money are in conflict with each other, he has done so under definite presumptions about the means intended to be used and always dependent on his current knowledge of the economic universe" (*ibid.*, p. 27).

The alleged conflict between full employment and price stability is a good illustration of this thesis. As unemployment falls below, say, 4 per cent, prices rise, because unit costs increase as less efficient labor, more costly labor per hour (overtime), and less efficient plant and equipment are employed, because oligopolistic pricing is revised to take advantage of the increased demand, and for other reasons that do not need to be specified here. But for these specified price-raising forces there exists or can be invented a public finance instrument that at least for certain ranges of its values will restrict the rise in prices relative to its adverse effect on employment by more than does some other instrument that is already being used to increase employment. That such instruments do exist or can be invented is intuitively evident from the definition of a distinct instrument. For example, a subsidy could be granted for overtime work, financed by a tax on, say, the first 50 per cent of everyone's straight-time wage, in order to avoid adverse incentive effects. An ad valorem tax could be imposed on price increases, the proceeds to go as a subsidy to firms that do not increase prices. Such instruments may be dismissed out of hand, and perhaps correctly so, as violating some fundamental criterion, or as obviously exerting too adverse an influence with respect to other goals to allow a solution within admissible ranges of instrument values. Rejection of a proposed measure on such grounds, instead of producing an attitude of hopelessness grounded on an alleged conflict of goals, could better supply incentive to invention of still other instruments. Rejection, in this view, does not prove some inherent incompatibility between the goals of full employment and price stability. An increased rate of government expenditure on goods and services in a fully employed economy might as well be said to be incompatible with a stable price level; it is not, of course, if it is financed by taxation or borrowing, instead of by creation of new money.

This subject may be approached from its other side. In the sense that conflict or incompatibility are commonly said to exist, almost any goal whatever conflicts with every other goal. Two goals and one instrument usually imply this kind of "conflict" of goals, even if an increase in the value of the instrument moves the economy closer to both goals, provided the two goals are not reached with the same value of the one instrument. If they are, they are really not two distinct goals. In correspondence with the definition of a distinct instrument given on page 473, a distinct goal may be defined as one that is not achieved for a value of an instrument that does achieve another goal.

The task of public finance research is therefore (a) to eliminate or reduce the conflict of goals by inventing new public finance instruments, (b) to compute or conjecture the range of values each of the new instruments would need to take, (c) to ascertain whether any of these ranges of values are unacceptably wide, and (d) if they are, to find out what goals outside the sytem those instrument values are incompatible with, since this is what "unacceptable" means.

8. Measurement of Degree of Shortfall

The degree of shortfall in achievement is to be expressed by the size of the gap between the value reached and the goal value, cumulated over the time during which the gap exists.[23] Thus if the goal is zero unemployment, and a certain public finance measure reduces unemployment from 4 per cent to 3 per cent over eight months, and to 2 per cent over the succeeding four months, the degree of shortfall for the year is 3 percentage points times 8 months, plus 2 percentage points times 4 months, or 32 percentage-point months of unemployment.

In this example, no time discount has been employed. Absence of time discount implies that in a world of certainty the individuals who compose the community have no intrinsic time preference.[24] Under this implication, ex post measurement of shortfall involves no discount of the gap that occurs in any particular time period.[25]

In the real world, a discount for risk is to be made in an ex ante estimation of shortfall. The further off the time period for which planning is done, the greater, usually, will be the dispersion of possible outcomes. Intrinsic time preference may now be assumed, if only because of risk.

Intrinsic time preference will have to be assumed for still another reason, the unwillingness of individuals to care as much for their descendants, at least their remote descendants, as for themselves. No community is likely to consider, even in a hypothetical world of certainty, that heavy unemployment for the next 100 years is a worthwhile trade-off for full employment during the succeeding 200 years. The political process, resulting in compromise over a difference of opinion on this as on other reasons for time preference, will establish an implicit intrinsic time preference by which degrees of shortfall over time, suitably discounted, can be expressed in single figures for comparison.

Care must be taken in adding percentages. In a growing labor force, 3 per cent at a later time of course implies a larger amount of unemployment than 3 per cent now. Moreover, welfare weights may be attached by the community to differing percentages at any given time; unemployment of 4 per cent, for example, may be regarded as more than twice as unfavorable as unemployment of 2 per cent. This weighting can be inserted in the process of assigning quantitative values to approaches to the goals and to the rate of approach to a goal per unit change in an instrument. To do so, however, makes it still less likely that the relations will be approximately linear.

An ex-post reckoning of degree of short-fall is not of much interest when it covers a period so long that most of that period can be given little or no weight in successive

23. If the gap is measured along the y-axis and time along the x-axis, the shortfall in achievement is measured by the area underneath the curve. See Chapter 22 below, Appendix C.

24. The existence of a positive rate of interest in a world of certainty would of course not be inconsistent with absence of intrinsic time preference. See Chapter 21 above, page 521.

25. This is not to say that a zero rate of interest should be assumed in distributing inputs over time. If the rate of interest is positive, a lump of unemployment costs the community less, in potential output lost, if it comes later rather than earlier.

policy formulations, that is, successive ex ante estimates of degree of shortfall. The chief reason for measuring the shortfall after the event is to discover ways of doing better next time. To this end, it is conjectured what would have happened over this past period if tax rates, for example, had been different, or if more flexibility had been built in, and so forth. It is too costly to make these conjectures continuously, and the value of the lesson will be lost if no reckoning is made until a decade or more has passed. Probably the most useful length of time for an ex post measurement of shortfall in achievement, when that measurement is undertaken with an eye to improving performance in the future, is the length of the time span for which ex ante estimation was made when policy was formulated.[26]

9. Deducing Goals and Achievement from Real-World Data

In any given country, for any given period of time, the level and pattern of government expenditures and the financing methods employed will reflect a mixture of goals. In the present state of knowledge it cannot be deduced, from what occurs in the real world, at what levels the several goals have been set, and to what degree they have been approached. It is, for example, difficult if not impossible to estimate accurately what proportion of a country's government expenditure, or which particular expenditures, and which segments of the financing structure are traceable chiefly to an attempt by the legislators, the executive, and other policy-makers to allocate the resources of the country efficiently under the Pareto-optimum test, and what other proportions and segments reflect chiefly a desire to alter the rate of economic growth—to mention only one possible inquiry. (The term "chiefly" reminds us that any particular instrument is likely to affect in some degree the approach toward all the goals.) The following chapters undertake the more modest task of indicating the bounds within which the policy-makers must act if they do in fact pursue the goal of optimum allocation, or the goal of a certain rate of economic growth. With these rules in mind, a real-life public finance system may be observed in order to deduce which goals appear to be considered important and which unimportant. If, for example, a certain country is observed to rely chiefly on a series of heavy excise taxes that exercise strong substitution effects, we may infer that the policy-makers of this country do not attach much weight to Pareto-efficient allocation, which demands an absence of such substitution effects, unless these excises reflect an attempt to match benefits and costs, as may occur under a motor fuel tax.

26. An analogy may be drawn with an automobile driver's safety record. Most of the driver's policy decisions, e.g., whether to pass the car ahead, exert their full effect in a short period of time; the driver's planning period for most of his decisions is very short. Accordingly a shortfall from an accident-free record over even a few minutes is significant for learning how to do better in the future by asking how that shortfall might have been avoided. In addition, there are policy decisions, e.g., whether to attend a driving school, that can be appraised only by examination of the driver's record over a long period of time.

10. Usefulness of Instruments-Goals Approach

In view of the difficulties described in Sections 2 to 9 above, the listing and counting of instruments and goals is useful not so much because the numbers will reveal at once whether the entire policy program is inherently achievable with public finance instruments as because they stimulate the policy-maker to search for instruments each of which affects appreciably the approach to only one goal, induce him to ascertain the range over which a constrained instrument may be allowed to vary, and make clear the need for inventiveness in devising new instruments. The listing-counting exercise may also uncover gross inconsistencies in policy, at least if the instrument values tentatively selected by intuition are run through some sort of model, even if only very crude, of the whole economy. Moreover, such a run-through cannot be made without assumptions about instruments to be used in fields other than public finance. How these assumptions are to be made is a problem in total coordination of policy that is not covered in the present work in any detail, yet no macro public finance measure can be appraised without some background assumptions of this kind.

APPENDIX TO CHAPTER NINETEEN

The case where two legally distinct public finance instruments are not distinct economic instruments is illustrated by the following relations, where one of the equations is only a scale model of the other.

Let a_{11} be the change in unemployment per percentage point increase in the corporate tax rate C,

a_{12} be the change in unemployment per percentage point increase in the personal income tax rate P,

a_{21} be the change in import surplus per percentage point increase in the corporate tax rate C,

a_{22} be the change in import surplus per percentage point increase in the personal income tax rate P,

C be the corporate tax rate, in percentage points, and P the personal income tax rate, in percentage points,

U be units of unemployment,

M be units of import surplus.

The coefficients a_{21} and a_{22} are negative.
Let

$$a_{11}C + a_{12}P + h = U$$
$$a_{21}C + a_{22}P + k = M,$$

so that, if the corporate and personal income tax rates were zero, unemployment would be h, and the import surplus, k.

Let us consider first a numerical example for which this system gives no solution:

$$a_{11}=12; \ a_{12}=60; \ a_{21}=-3; \ a_{22}=-15; \ h=0; \ k=25.$$

Set $U=M=0$.

Since, in this example, $a_{11}/a_{21}=a_{12}/a_{22}$, that is, $a_{11}a_{22}-a_{21}a_{12}=0$, there is no solution except that, if $h=-100$, any values of C and P that set $U=0$ also set $M=0$, and the two goals are not distinct; achievement of one implies achievement of the other.

But if $a_{12}=2$, and the other values remain as above, setting $U=M=0$ yields values for

$$C= -0.287 \text{ percentage points (a corporate subsidy)}$$
$$P= \quad 1.72 \text{ percentage points.}$$

If U had been, say, 15 initially, and M, 10, C would have been 1.121 percentage points initially and P, .776 percentage points. Thus, to move from those initial values of U and M to a value of zero for both, C is reduced and P is increased.

If only the corporate income tax rate alone, or only the individual income tax rate alone, could be changed, the two targets clearly could not be achieved; the number of instruments would be less than the number of goals in a completely interdependent linear system.

An alternative way of setting up the problem is that used by Bent Hansen in his *Economic Theory of Fiscal Policy* (p. 13); using this method for the problem just posed, we have:

x_1 = units of unemployment
x_2 = units of import surplus
a_{14} = rate of personal income tax
a_{24} = rate of corporate income tax
a_{13} and a_{23} are uncontrollable parameters,

and

$$a_{11}x_1 + a_{12}x_2 + a_{13} = a_{14}$$
$$a_{21}x_1 + a_{22}x_2 + a_{23} = a_{24}$$

Now, $da_{14}/dx_1 = a_{11}$, so that a_{11} is the units of change in the personal income tax rate per unit increase in unemployment. Thus a_{11} in the Hansen type of matrix is the same as $1/a_{12}$ in the example above, where it was $1/2$.

Similarly,

Hansen's $a_{12} = 1/a_{22}$ of the example above, $= -1/15$
$\qquad\quad a_{21} = 1/a_{11}$ of the example above, $= 1/12$
$\qquad\quad a_{22} = 1/a_{21}$ of the example above, $= -1/3$

This manner of setting up the equations has the advantage of emphasizing that the value assigned to any one instrument, say a_{14}, affects the degree of approach toward all the targets (here, x_1 and x_2), and it gives immediately the value that must be assigned to the instruments, a_{14} and a_{24}, if the target values, x_1 and x_2, are both zero, for then

$$a_{14} = a_{13}$$

and

$$a_{24} = a_{23}.$$

The other way of stating the problem has the advantage of emphasizing that the value reached for any one target depends on the values given to all the instruments. It also allows for easy use of inequalities in place of equations, where overshooting a target is not objectionable.

CHAPTER TWENTY

Size of the Public Finance Sector

A. PROBLEMS OF
MEASUREMENT: CONTENT, NETTING, TIMING

THE COMPONENT PARTS of the government's outlays and receipts have been studied in Chapters 4–18. Attention is now turned to total outlays and total receipts.

Definitions of these totals and of the difference between them, the surplus or deficit, are needed especially for three basic documents: (1) the budget, which presents the government's plan of action for the period ahead; (2) the set of government accounts, which record the outcome of a past period; and (3) the national income accounts. The national income accounts supply the economy-wide totals of national income and gross national product with which the totals of government outlay or receipt included in those same accounts may be compared.

Totals of government outlay and receipts do not construct themselves in any self-evident way. They cannot be computed until conceptual decisions have been reached on (a) what outlays and what receipts are to be taken into account, (b) to what extent receipts and outlays in any given subsector of government activity are to be netted against each other, thus shrinking the totals, and (c) what rules of timing are to be adopted for entering receipts and outlays. The choices made on this third point sometimes affect the totals for a given fiscal year.

These three issues of content, netting, and timing will now be discussed in the light of the uses to which the concepts of totals for receipts and for outlays, and of the resulting surplus or deficit, are to be put. The answer to any particular query on procedure for content, netting, and timing may differ depending on whether the aim is to measure the public finance sector relative to the economy as a whole, to formulate a policy for full employment, external equilibrium, and price stability, to anticipate the treasury's financing requirements, or to submit a plan of action to a legislative body.

For convenience in reference, the several types of outlay and expenditure as defined in Chapter 3 are recapitulated here on page 489.

B. USES OF TOTALS AND OF
SURPLUS OR DEFICIT FIGURES

1. Ascertaining Product Dispensed by
Government on Non-Market Basis as Proportion of Total Produc

The public finance sector, that is, that part of the government that dispenses goods
on a nonmarket basis (see Chapter 1), can be expressed as a fraction of the total
economy. This ratio can then be compared over time and between governmental
jurisdictions.[1] It may be asked whether there exist upper limits to this ratio, and
lower limits, compatible with the functioning of the market-price sector of the
economy.

A. PRODUCT DISPENSED BY
GOVERNMENT (NUMERATOR OF THE FRACTION)

The goods dispensed by the government on a nonmarket basis, and also the
subsidy element in subsidized marketed goods, must be valued at cost, in the
absence of satisfactory data on value to recipients.

If cost is reckoned on a cash outlay basis, so that the cost of a building, for
example, is included in government expenditures in full in the year of outlay, and
no depreciation is taken in later years, an exaggerated idea of the size of the government as a dispenser of services will be given for the year of construction or purchase.
For later years that size will be understated as the building is gradually worn out or
used up economically if not physically in the course of rendering service. A capital
budget thus presents a chronologically more accurate statement of the flow of
government service. The point at issue is not whether the government service itself
is a capital good to the private sector but, instead, how much input is being used up
in the year under review, in rendering the service. Education, for example, is
doubtless a capital good to the recipient of it; and the government, spending money
on free education, is itself investing in human capital. The question remains, How
much is it so investing in any given year? A schoolteacher's salary for the year is a
good measure of the amount of teacher input devoted to the service of educating
children in that year. The total cost of a new school building is not a good measure
of the amount of building input devoted to the service, education, in that year.

If the cost of the service is computed, not by including the initial outlay for the
schoolhouse or other capital asset, but by including the depreciation and obsolescence
experienced year by year, imputed interest on the depreciated value of the building
or other asset must also be included as an expense, since if the service were dis-
continued the building could be sold and the proceeds invested in interest-bearing

1. The socialist countries, even the Soviet Union and China, may or may not show a
higher value for this ratio than do the private enterprise countries.

securities. The imputed interest is also to be entered as an income item. Taking account of imputed interest therefore does not alter the surplus or deficit. A premium for risk-taking could be entered, on similar grounds, as imputed income and imputed outlay.

Types of Governmental Outlays and Receipts

OUTLAYS
  Explicit outlays
    Transfer payments
      Unrequited payments
        Donative payments
          Welfare payments
          Subsidies
          Aid to domestic governmental units
          Aid to foreign governments
        Compulsory payments
          Reparations
      Property payments
        Real assets
        Financial instruments
    Purchases of goods and services
  Imputed outlays
    Depreciation
    Imputed interest
    Imputed risk premium
    Imputed wages to conscripts and volunteers
    Imputed outlays linked with tax relief
    Imputed interest on compulsory loans
    Imputed outlay for defaults
    Transfer-payment element in loans at low interest rates
    Guarantee reserve attributions

RECEIPTS
  Explicit receipts
    Transfer receipts
      Unrequited receipts
        Compulsory
          Taxes
          Certain fees and fines
        Donative receipts
          Aid from domestic governmental units
          Aid from foreign governments
      Property sale receipts
        Real assets
        Financial instruments
          Sale to non-money-creating part of private sector
          Sale to money-creating part of private sector
      Money created within governmental sector
    Receipts from sale or rental of goods or services
  Imputed receipts (counterparts of imputed outlays above)[a]

a. But as to depreciation, see Chapter 3 above, page 52.

Explicit interest paid by government on its own debt domestically held by the banking system is a cost of the services that the banks render to the government, nominally free of charge. Such interest payments are therefore to be included as an element of cost of the services that the government in turn dispenses free of charge. Interest paid to domestic creditors other than banks is the cost of persuading those creditors to restrict their liquidity.[2] It is not a cost of rendering government services, as are imputed interest and interest paid to banks, and so must be excluded from total outlay for the purpose now under consideration. Interest on debt held abroad is a cost of obtaining whatever is purchased with the proceeds of the loan and is to be included.

The welfare type of transfer payment is to be excluded in measuring government as a nonmarket dispenser of output, since it does not in itself reflect creation or distribution of a product.

Aid to other domestic government units is to be included only as a rough substitute for consolidating the governmental accounts to include those units. The substitute is very imperfect indeed, since the receiving units may use the aid, not to dispense products free of charge, but to make welfare payments themselves. Consolidation of all government accounts within the economy is the preferable technique for the purpose under discussion here.

Aid to foreign governments is to be included, as also are reparations, if it takes the form of payment in kind and so reflects the government as a dispenser of particular goods or services on a nonmarket basis. Aid given as general purchasing power must, on the same grounds, be excluded for present purposes (but see Section 2 below), except as it is regarded as a purchase from the foreign government of good will or military assistance that benefits the citizens of the donor country (see Chapter 7 above).

The cost of old buildings, land, and the like must be included, one way or another, since these assets are used to dispense services free of charge. Depreciation and imputed interest, instead of purchase price, again yield the best measure of annual service rendered.

Subsidies by government reflect a direct allocation of resources to the production of particular commodities, which welfare payments do not reflect. For present purposes, stimulation of consumption of a particular product by all persons is to be distinguished from stimulation of consumption of products in general by particular persons.

By parity of reasoning, the deficit from government-operated enterprises is to be included in outlays, as this deficit represents the dispensing of a part of product free of charge. If the enterprise yields more than a normal profit, that excess profit is a form of taxation, not a product, and should not enter into the total of product dispensed by government.

It may be argued that services that are financed by user taxes, say non-toll highways, are to be excluded, as being, in effect, sold on the market, not dispensed free of charge. But the degree of consumer sovereignty is much smaller than with respect to most marketed goods, including the services of the post office. If consumers were

2. See the discussion by Musgrave, *Theory of Public Finance*, pp. 192–93.

to increase their purchase of postage stamps, and hence their consumption of postal service, sharply, the amount of input into the postal service would increase more or less correspondingly and, short of capacity limits to buildings and the like, promptly. And if the sale of postage stamps continued to increase when capacity limits had been reached, creation of new capacity would be undertaken, not as quickly perhaps as with a private enterprise, but still with less political decision-making involved than if non-toll roads began to become congested. Thus inputs into the user-tax-financed highway system do not increase as rapidly at consumer bidding as do inputs into the postal system. (The toll highway is a special case, since it is relatively rare, and competes with the non-toll highway.)[3]

Loans by the government to the private sector are to be excluded from a government outlay total when that outlay total is designed to measure the role of government as a dispenser of product on a non-price basis. If, however, there is a subsidy element in the loan, that subsidy element must be included in the total, for the reasons just given for subsidies in general.

The subsidy element in a loan is either an interest subsidy or a default subsidy. The interest subsidy is the excess of what the government must pay on its own borrowing from the non-bank private sector over the interest rate it charges on the loan. The series of annual interest subsidies on the loan can be discounted to a present value. This capital value, when subtracted from the amount of the loan, leaves as a balance the "hard loan" element of the total loan. The actual interest paid, plus the excess of the redemption amount over the hard-loan element, represents a normal investment return on the hard-loan element.

A default subsidy, or subsidy on principal account, takes the form of either a write-off in the year the default occurs or an advance allocation to a reserve for bad debts.

A government guarantee of a loan by the private sector is, in principle, to be included in government outlays to an amount equal to the anticipated expense.[4] Only a rough estimate, of course, is feasible.

Government redemption, or open-market purchase, of its own debt is obviously not an outlay for present purposes. Transactions within the government are to be excluded, but wage and salary payments are to be entered gross, before deduction of taxes or of employee contributions to pension funds. Contributions made by the government to these funds as employer are to be included if they are on a regular,

---

3. For the wide range of issues involved in this question of presenting a governmental activity's results on a gross or a net basis, see the Staff Paper, "Netting and Grossing in the Federal Budget," and the Staff Memorandum, "Netting and Grossing," in President's Commission on Budget Concepts, *Staff Papers and Other Materials Reviewed by the President's Commission* (Washington, D.C.: Government Printing Office, 1967), pp. 245–76.

4. See Chapter 6, Section C.1.a.(1).(a). For an analysis of the treatment of loans and guarantees in general, see President's Commission on Budget Concepts, *Report* (Washington, D.C.: Government Printing Office, 1967), Chapter 5, "Federal Credit Programs," and the Staff Papers on "Loans, Participation Certificates, and the Financing of Budget Deficits," and "Feasibility of Explicit Recognition of the Interest Subsidy in Connection with Separate Budgeting of Loans," in President's Commission on Budget Concepts, *Staff Papers and Other Materials Reviewed by the President's Commission*, pp. 279–300 and 335–45.

contractual basis, or if their amount helps determine in an ascertainable manner the amount of pension the employee will receive.

The receipts side of the government's budget or accounts is not relevant to this inquiry on the size of government as a non-market dispenser of product. What is being measured is product of a certain type, namely, product dispensed without use of the price mechanism. For this purpose, product can be measured in terms of its cost. The pattern of receipts does not matter, except in the question to be discussed below, of possible economic limits to government as a dispenser of free product (see Sections d and e below).

Refunds of overpaid tax are here considered to be netted against gross tax revenues, not entered as an item of outlay. The outlay counterparts to imputed receipts are to be included, since they are imputed costs of rendering services.

B. TOTAL ECONOMY-WIDE PRODUCT, COMPATIBLY DEFINED (DENOMINATOR OF THE FRACTION)

Once the total of government product has been computed, the question arises whether it can be expressed as a fraction of some economy-wide total, notably gross national product or net national product. In fact, some adjustments to these totals as they are commonly computed are required or some further adjustments to the figure for total of government services.

Gross national product includes all capital assets at the time of their creation and does not deduct depreciation in subsequent years. Yet it includes the full value of consumer purchases, which cover, among other expenses, depreciation. Thus the value of a building constructed to manufacture food products appears in GNP twice, once when it is constructed, and again as it becomes embodied, economically, bit by bit, in the food products that it helps produce over the years and that consumers purchase, until the building is worn out or obsolete. For a government capital asset, however, this double counting does not occur, because there are no consumer purchases, and GNP does not include an estimated value of the free services rendered by government. Thus a highway enters GNP when it is constructed, but the value of the services it yields to consumers as it is worn out over the years is not included in the consumer goods subtotal in GNP for those years. Accordingly, the role of government as a nonmarket dispenser of products is understated when government outlays are compared to GNP. To make the two figures comparable, the government total would have to double-count also, by computing outlay on a cash basis and including it again as depreciation. The imputed service represented by the using up of the highway would have to be included in the government total for each year, in addition to including the cost of the highway in the year of construction. In fact, the national income accounts make no such adjustment. The fault lies in the use of GNP as a total, not in the government accounts. GNP is in fact a total that cannot be defined meaningfully, in economic terms, since it is a mixture of production and consumption, with inherent double counting.

This difficulty does not arise when comparing government outlay with national net product (national income), which is computed after subtracting depreciation from gross investment, so that only net investment is added to consumer goods produced. For complete comparability the government service should be computed on a capital-budget basis; government services to consumers and business would be estimated, at a cost that included depreciation and obsolescence charges for the year in question. Government outlay on capital assets in any year would be included only net of depreciation on assets purchased in earlier years. This excess of new construction value over depreciation of old construction values, this net investment, is indeed not yet a service, but it may be included in the total on the same rationale on which net private investment is included in the economy-wide total. It is a net provision for future services, the discounted present value of those future services, which, when they come to be rendered, will be entered, and at once counterbalanced by a negative entry, disinvestment. In a shrinking economy net investment would be negative, but that should not prevent the value of service rendered during the year from being computed as suggested.

Imputed interest on the depreciated value of government buildings, inventory, road system, and other assets is in practice not included in either GNP or national income. Inclusion of it in the government total, as suggested above, would therefore require a similar upward adjustment in the economy-wide totals. The same remark applies to any imputed risk premium. The ratio of government product to total product would thereby increase.

Welfare payments and grants to other governments are not included in GNP or in national income, under customary methods of accounting, hence no adjustment is needed here.[5]

Subsidies and deficits of government enterprises lower the prices of the subsidized goods purchased by consumers and the cost of subsidized net investment, relative to other goods. The free-good element represented by these subsidies or deficits is to be included in the government total of services dispensed on a nonmarket basis; hence it must also be included in the GNP or national income total, if the government total is to be expressed as a fraction of the economy total. This inclusion in the GNP or national income total can be accomplished by deflating with a price index. Let us consider, for example, a new subsidy on foodstuffs, financed by an increase in the individual income tax, assuming, for simplicity in analysis, that the prices of foodstuffs fall correspondingly, along with personal disposable incomes (personal incomes before tax do not change). The aggregate money value of all consumer products will fall, because of the decline in the foodstuffs component. But since year-to-year comparisons mean little unless they are given in real terms, through deflation, or reflation, by a price index, a price index will be applied, and the new low level of aggregate value of consumer goods will be adjusted upward accordingly. In the previous year there was no government subsidy and no additional income tax. In the current year there are both subsidy and tax. When the current year's total is

---

5. Welfare payments are of course included in the "national income accounts budget" constructed from national income items and government accounts.

adjusted upward by application of the price index, there is no decline in the total;[6] the subsidy is thereby included.

Even if the subsidy is increased until it covers 99.999 per cent of the cost of the consumer good, the same principle of adjustment by a price index applies.

If, on the other hand, the subsidy is 100 per cent, that is, if the good is not sold at a price, but is instead distributed free of all charge by the government, it will not be included in the computation of a price index, under conventional methods of computation. The price index will show no change; it will merely have discarded the item that fell to a price of zero. Aggregate value of consumer goods will now be smaller than the year before, even when the price index is applied. But the GNP or national income total will not be too small, for they include as a distinct item the cost of free government services, reckoned on the basis of factor cost to the government. They do not include government subsidies as such and do not need to include them, as long as any price, however small, remains, that will retain the good in the price-index computation, so that the total will thereby be adjusted upward.

Government free service that is merely an intermediate product to the private sector, not a consumer good, raises the same problem of how it is to be included in the GNP or net national product total. The answer is the same: it should not be included as such, but should be allowed to appear implicitly, through reflation by a price index. Let us suppose, for example, that the government takes over the wholesale foodstuffs business and supplies retailers their customary wholesale services free of charge, that is, the value added by wholesaling. Prices of foodstuffs at retail will decline, as under an ordinary subsidy. Use of a price index, however, will prevent any decline in recorded aggregate real value of consumer goods.

If national income or GNP includes the cost not only of government services in the form of final products, free parks for example, but also the cost of government services to business firms, and if then a price index is used, the real value of consumer goods will be overstated. In terms of the extreme example just given, if the national income total includes the cost of the government's food wholesaling activities and if the resulting national income total is reflated upward by a price index because food prices to consumers have dropped under the impact of this free wholesale service, the wholesale service is, in effect, included twice, and the retail value of foodstuffs is correspondingly overstated. Unfortunately, all national income accounting systems do include the value (the cost) of intermediate services supplied by governments, and so do exaggerate the GNP, or national income, for comparison with the government sector. The role of government as a non-market dispenser of product is thereby understated. In practice, the understatement is not as extreme as would occur in the hypothetical case just given. Governments do not supply whole strata of intermediate services free to the business world. But much of government activity is a producers' good rather than a consumers' good; it reduces the cost of doing business. What is needed in national income accounting is a splitting of government outlays on services into those that create free consumers'

---

6. To simplify, it is assumed here that there are no changes in relative quantities purchased. In fact, there will be, and familiar index-number problems will arise.

goods and those that create free intermediate goods. Even a rough division would be better than the present practice of operating entirely at one extreme.[7]

National income and GNP do not include loans by the government to the private sector. The subsidy element in these loans will in effect be included through reflation by the price index.

Imputed outlay equal to the imputed income from conscript and volunteer service must be added to GNP or national income. The national income and GNP totals do not include the value of imputed labor income in the home, chiefly that from work by housewives. This omission is so substantial that it biases upward by several percentage points the ratio of government-dispensed nonmarketed services to economy-wide product.

Either GNP or national net product can be computed alternatively at factor prices or at market prices, that is, ex all taxes except direct taxes, chiefly income taxes, or inclusive of all taxes. If the government could in fact purchase goods completely tax-free, national income would need to be computed at factor prices, to obtain a comparable denominator. In practice no government buys goods completely tax-free, in the sense that taxes paid at earlier stages are cancelled when the end product is sold to government. The last sale, the one directly to the government, is, however, often exempted. This combination of taxable and tax-exempt transactions suggests that in principle the denominator should be computed on a base approaching but not quite as large as GNP or national income at market prices.

In summary, with respect to current methods of national income accounting and government accounts, the ratio of the public finance sector to the total economy is in some respects overstated, in others understated, and the degree of error is not the same for GNP as for net national product. It is not evident a priori whether the net result is understatement or overstatement.

The fraction expressing the public finance sector as a proportion of the entire economy will use as its denominator national income or domestic income according to the question asked and the surrounding circumstances; in some instances the denominator may appropriately include non-duplicating parts of the one in addition to all of the other. National income, or national product, refers to the economic activity of the residents of the country, wherever that activity may take place.

---

7. These and related issues have been discussed at length by me in my *Principles of National Income Analysis* (New York: Houghton Mifflin, 1947), Chapter 7, "The Government Sector," especially pp. 254–55, 257–58. A briefer statement that takes much the same point of view is to be found in Musgrave, *The Theory of Public Finance*, Chapter 9, "Budget Items in the Social Accounts," especially pp. 186–88. Musgrave, however, appears too pessimistic in concluding that "there is no simple solution to the problem" of intermediate government services, unless "simple" means "precise." The amount (cost) of a government's services that does lower the costs of business firms is indeed difficult to estimate precisely. The second difficulty Musgrave cites is that "data on factor earnings similarly include earnings of factors engaged in the rendering of intermediate services" (p. 188). But this fact seems not relevant to computation on the product side of the national income accounts. If the service reduces costs to the firm, it does not matter, for computation of the deflated net national product total, whether the result is a fall in the firm's product prices or instead a rise in its factor prices, as Musgrave points out (*ibid.*, p. 187). See also Vickrey, *Metastatics and Macroeconomics*, pp. 151–67.

Domestic income, or domestic product, refers to the economic activity occurring within the boundaries of the country, wherever those to whom this income accrues may reside. A factor-importing and factor-exporting country can in principle tax all the income earned within the country plus all the income earned by its residents abroad, by employing both the source principle and the residence principle (see Chapter 11, Section A). In practice, only a small country can go that far without inviting retaliation in kind. It can therefore appropriately include in the denominator of the fraction showing the ratio of the public finance sector to the entire economy both national income and that part of domestic income that does not appear in national income, i.e., investment income accruing to foreign investors, provided their tax administrators are able to enforce this part of the tax law. The upward economic or social limit to the size of the public finance sector (see Section D below) increases thereby in absolute amount, and may also increase in terms of the ratio, if the non-duplicative part added to the denominator can be taxed at a higher rate than the rest (see also Chapter 25, pages 623–24).

c. Historical Trends

The ratio of product dispensed by government free of charge to the total of the economy's product is higher in richer countries than in poorer, at least in the private enterprise economies. (This statement may hold also for the socialist economies.) In some of the richer countries this fact reflects large military expenditures. The reasons for this rise in the ratio, with a rise in per capita income, are still not well understood. The higher degree of urbanization in most of the high-income countries may be one explanation. The differences among countries are not as great as they appear from comparative data on total government outlay, including transfer payments. Higher levels of tax rates reached during wars, coupled with a social consciousness stimulated by wars, have been offered as a partial explanation, but the conclusion applies to total outlay, including welfare payments.[8] Adolph Wagner's "law," formulated in the latter half of the nineteenth century, asserts that government expenditures in a modern state grow, over time, but whether he meant growth as a percentage of the total economy is not wholly clear, and his supporting data were inadequate.[9] A reasonably satisfactory analysis of historical data and of possible trends is yet to be made, on this subject of government-dispensed free product, excluding welfare payments. That task is not attempted here.

Since technological improvements that increase labor productivity in government seem to lag somewhat behind those in the private sector, while hourly wages paid by government must increase to match those made possible by increased productivity in the private sector, the cost per unit for government output rises relative to the

8. Alan T. Peacock and Jack Wiseman, *The Growth of Public Expenditure in the United Kingdom* (Princeton, N.J.: Princeton University Press, National Bureau of Economic Research, 1961).

9. See Herbert Timm, "Das Gesetz der wachsenden Staatsausgaben," *Finanzarchiv* (September, 1961), 21(2): 201–47.

cost per unit of marketed output. For this reason alone, the proportion of national income taken in taxes may be expected to increase unless the government reduces appreciably its total output in real terms relative to the total of marketed output.

D. UPPER LIMITS TO THE RATIO

As government expands the proportion of the national income that it distributes as free goods, financed by taxes, the question arises whether the economic system itself sets any upper limit to this ratio. The answer depends primarily on the effect exerted on the supply of labor. The effect on the supply of capital can be neglected in a socialist country and is probably second in importance to the supply of labor in a private enterprise economy.

As the ratio increases, the recipient of the free government services needs to obtain fewer goods through the market mechanism, if he is to retain his customary standard of living. If, in view of this fact, he works shorter hours, total product declines, and if everyone reacts in this way, the per capita standard of living cannot in fact be maintained. The mixed economic system of free goods (plus taxation) and purchased goods breaks down. The crucial question is thus whether the supply of labor offered freely in the market (not conscripted) can in fact remain undiminished as the proportion of total product that is distributed free of charge increases. For this analysis we abstract from the policing problem, for example, the problem of how to prevent resale of tangible commodities distributed free by the government.

If the good that is dispensed free of charge is a consumer good, not an intermediate good, it exerts an income effect that tends to decrease the supply of labor. But if it is financed by a poll tax or other type of tax that does not increase as economic activity increases, there is an offsetting income effect, tending to increase the supply of labor. In practice, the tax is almost sure not to be of the poll tax type; it will normally also exert a substitution effect tending to decrease hours of work. To take an extreme case, if all goods and services except food were supplied by the government free of charge and if this distribution were financed by a heavy poll tax the individual could not buy any food at all until he had worked a substantial number of hours, since the poll tax would have first claim on his earnings, and once he had reached the point where he could begin to buy food (having earned enough to pay the poll tax) he would find the incremental ratio between food obtained and leisure sacrificed just as it would be under no tax.

But if there were an attempt to finance the free distribution of non-foods by a proportional income tax (less than 100 per cent rate, of course), the individual would be able to start buying food with his first hour of work. After a certain number of hours of work he would have enough food—though not as much food as he would work to get under the poll tax—and the rate of tax on the next hour's work would appear sufficiently heavy to him that he would cease work much earlier than under the poll tax, and therefore much earlier than before the public finance sector was expanded. The total supply of labor would have decreased; the government could not make good on its promises to distribute all non-foods in the amounts in which they had been consumed when they were purchased on the market; and less food too, would be purchased.

But if the goods distributed by the government are producers' goods, intermediate goods, that is, free goods and services to business firms, not to consumers, the outcome is not the same. Let the new government services to firms be of a kind that enables those firms to forego an equal amount of hitherto purchased services. Competition among firms will then, we have seen, reduce final product prices pari passu with the reduction in households' disposable incomes caused by the increase in taxation, or, if the monetary authorities permit it, final product prices and disposable incomes remain roughly unaltered.

As an extreme case, let us consider a government that does nothing but provide certain free services, even free goods, to business firms, financing this activity by individual income taxation. Consumers are assumed to purchase only from retailers, not from firms at earlier stages. The economic limits to this kind of extension of government nonmarket activity may be very far off; perhaps 90 (or 99) per cent of the net national product could be produced and distributed free by the government, yet consumers as factor owners would be willing to work as much as if that percentage were only, say, 10. To push to an extreme the hypothetical case given earlier above, the government might supply all raw materials, all manufacturing, transportation, and almost all retailing value added free of charge to business firms, but with respect to every final product (consumer good) it would supply none of the last 10 per cent of total value added needed to produce and market the good or service. Let this government outlay be financed by a 90 per cent income tax. Although the worker's disposable income will increase but slowly as he increases his hours of work, because the marginal tax rate takes 90 per cent of each wage increment, he will not be discouraged thereby from working, since final-product prices will be correspondingly low. No final product is completely free, so he must work, to obtain any product at all.

If, in contrast, the government tried to distribute 90 per cent of all final products completely free of charge, financing this program by a 90 per cent income tax, while the remaining one-tenth of final products had to be purchased at full cost price, the individual could get nine-tenths of his maximum possible amount of consumer goods even if he worked not at all (or so he would be told; in the event, of course, nobody would get anything much). To get the remaining 10 per cent, full-cost full-price goods, he would have to work full time: a rather unattractive proposition.

E. LOWER LIMITS TO THE RATIO

The lower economic limit to the ratio of government-dispensed free product to total national product is the ratio below which the private sector, attempting to purchase on the market substitutes for government police protection, fire protection, and the like, to an amount that will make feasible production of other private-sector goods, finds the cost so high (because it is so inefficient to produce the service on a marketable basis) that the resources left are not enough to prevent the economy's output per man from declining steadily, because of malnutrition and disease. This decline would continue until the community was broken up by emigration or death.

In a small rural community this ratio may be close to zero.[10] In a modern metropolis, it is probably—to hazard a guess—well over 5 per cent.

2. Stating Welfare Payments as a Proportion of Total Product

Welfare payments were excluded from the discussion in Section 1 above, not being product. They are so important in so many countries that government as a dispenser on a non-market basis is in much of the world far larger than the dispensing of product alone will imply. The problem is, if welfare payments are included in the numerator of the government-to-total economy ratio, how shall the denominator be defined?

GNP, or better yet, net national product, is still a useful denominator even though neither one includes welfare payments, directly, or indirectly (as they do include subsidies, indirectly) through deflation by price indexes.

Welfare payments turn over to certain households a certain part of the economy's output, at the expense of certain other households. It is a part that is not routed through government, to be dispensed by it in kind, but this fact merely means that the choice of the particular items of product will be exercised directly by the beneficiary households, not by the government. Actual production by the government, as distinct from dispensing by it, is not at issue here; for all that was said in Section 1 above, the entire product dispensed by government might have been produced in private firms and purchased by the government, to be handed on free of charge.

Accordingly, welfare payments may be added in to the numerator, along with services dispensed by the government on a nonmarket basis, to obtain a ratio that describes the proportion of total product that is distributed independently of current productive effort by the recipients, or exercise by them of property rights; for short, we say, distributed without appeal to the market. The transferee himself of course utilizes the market mechanism, but only because the market has been disregarded in enabling him to do so.

The composition of the denominator is to be determined by the rules suggested in Section 1 above; there is nothing in the nature of welfare payments to require further adjustments to the figure for the total of the economy's output.

Welfare payments are of more recent growth than government services. And if welfare payments are placed in the numerator, the resulting ratio to national income or GNP will vary more widely from country to country than will the ratio where the numerator includes only government-dispensed product.

In many low-income countries this ratio of welfare payments to national income

10. On the island of Pitcairn, the 90-odd inhabitants supply a certain amount of labor on the roads; aside from this there is no government activity (*New York Times*, August 15, 1967).

is probably close to zero, in part because they are not properly accounted for, as when relief to the indigent is given in the form of low-paying jobs that make little or no demand on the wage recipient. Railroads or other government enterprises are sometimes operated at huge current losses because unneeded workers would otherwise be unemployed and destitute. In very rich countries the ratio of welfare payments to national income may be only moderately high because the general level of income is so high—provided the variance is not too great. It is probably in the middle class of countries that the ratio is likely to be the highest.

Welfare payments resemble free government services to consumers rather than free government services to business firms, with respect to an upper economic limit to the ratio of government's free dispensing to an economy-wide total of product. If, for example, every individual pays 50 per cent of his income in tax and receives a welfare payment equal to half of what he would be earning if working a normal number of hours, and if this payment is not conditioned on the size of his income, he will receive half of what he did before this measure was in force even if he does no work at all. To obtain the other half he will have to work full time.

The lower limit to the ratio of aggregate welfare payments to national income is probably close to zero and in any case can hardly be defined as closely in economic terms as can the lower limit to the free services-to-national income ratio.

3. Ratio for Impact of
Government Sector on Employment and Prices[11]

A budget or set of accounts drawn up primarily with a view to facilitating policy for full employment and price stabilization ("fiscal policy") will need to be, on balance, more comprehensive on the outlays side than are the suggestions in Section 1 above, and will need to specify the sources of funds. But it will exclude all purely intra-governmental transfers, for example credits from the treasury to the social security fund.

The outlays included for the fiscal policy budget will be on a cash basis; depreciation will be irrelevant and so will imputed interest outlay, imputed risk premiums, and attributions to bad debt reserves.

The capital-budget approach recommended in Section 1 will therefore be dispensed with for fiscal policy computations. Property payments for real assets will also be irrelevant. But property payments for financial instruments must now be included, among them the open market purchases by the central bank, and the redemptions of debt by the treasury, the loans, hard or soft, extended by the government to the private sector, and guarantees made on loans within the private sector. Actual defaults by private debtors on government loans are most usefully treated as reductions in government receipts. The "outlay" corresponding to the imputed income from conscript service needs to be included as a reminder, to interpret the economy-wide total of wages paid.

11. For more details on this issue, see Chapter 3, pages 51–53.

The general rule is that any outlay that has a direct or indirect effect on the level of employment or prices must be included, the error to be on the side of including too much rather than missing some relevant item. This attitude reflects the fact that for fiscal policy purposes the total itself, even when expressed as a ratio to some economy-wide total, is of little use. The constituent items differ so markedly in their effect on employment or prices, per money unit of outlay, that a total is too heterogeneous to be helpful. Inclusion of an item that is seen upon examination to be of no effect is an inconvenient error, but failure to include an item that does have some effect is an irreparable error. Moreover, the fiscal policy planner is interested not so much in the total of any constituent item as in the range over which it can be changed for his purposes. An employee contribution to a pension fund affects employment and prices, but if contractual or actuarial considerations forbid changing it, it is literally of no more interest to the fiscal policy planner than the population, the exchange rate, or any other quantity or ratio that he must, for whatever reason, take as given. On the other hand, the central bank must be included in this fiscal policy budget, as indicated by the remark above concerning open-market operations.

On the receipts side, every explicit receipt listed in the recapitulation on page 489 above is relevant, to the extent that changes can be made, except possibly receipts from sale of real assets other than from commodity stabilization programs. The imputed tax element in military conscription and the gifts in kind from volunteer workers are important only in interpreting the total employment figures.

The receipts side will detail not only the tax, fee, and other income items, but the financing plan, distinguishing between new money to be created by note issue or by central bank purchases of obligations, borrowing from the commercial banks, and borrowing from the non-bank private sector.

As to the degree of netting, it will be more helpful to present the data in gross form, in order to uncover differences in effects on employment and prices. The budget or accounts of the postal service, for example, unless that service is declared out of bounds for fiscal policy, are best examined on a gross basis. If unemployment is especially severe among the urban unskilled, perhaps an expansion of the staff of mail carriers is called for, but by how much cannot be deduced from a net deficit or surplus figure for the service. Loans made by the government on a certain program may have stronger or weaker effects (in the opposite direction of course) than loans repaid under the same program, and a net figure for loans would be correspondingly uninformative for fiscal policy purposes.

The calendar date to be attached to an outlay item must, for fiscal policy analysis, be at least as early as that dictated by accrual accounting, and an even earlier date, say date of contract or of letter of intent, may be more appropriate for this economic analysis, since employment or upward pressure on prices will normally occur in the private sector, on account of the government's expenditure program, well before the government's legal liability to pay has accrued.

On the revenue side, the optimum timing for fiscal policy analysis is not so evident. Some taxpayers react to increased taxation only when they feel the cash drain; others react well in advance. But in general, early-date figures will be the more appropriate.

4. Anticipating the Treasury's Financing Needs

The treasury's financing needs are in a sense not needs at all but instruments of fiscal policy in countries that possess highly developed capital markets and that enjoy many options for attacking unemployment and instability of prices or the exchange rate. But in many other countries one of the chief functions of the budget is to reveal to the government whether its plans are practicable in view of the money-market financing they imply. If they are not practicable, the budget data must indicate how far the programs must be cut back. The measurement of the size of the government's operations must for this purpose be not on an accrual basis or on a commitments basis but on a cash basis. Depreciation accounting is of no assistance here, and imputed expenditures are of course irrelevant. Property payments, on the other hand, are just as important as any other payments. Receipts, too, are to be anticipated on a cash basis.

Netting of outlays against receipts must be avoided, for the purpose of anticipating the treasury's financing task, unless they occur on the same day, and even then it may prove misleading to net one against the other, since they may reach or leave different parts of the government's banking or cash depository system.

5. The Budget: Executive Formulation and Legislative Action

In a budget formulated by the executive and submitted by it for legislative action, the procedures followed with respect to content, netting, and timing will affect (a) public understanding and confidence, (b) the efficiency of the legislative process, and (c) choice of efficient methods of operation. These reactions will be mild in a country where the legislature allows itself little power to amend the government's proposals, and they will be weak in countries dominated by a small ruling group, but they will never be completely absent.

A. PUBLIC UNDERSTANDING AND CONFIDENCE

To the public, especially the press, and through the press the business and professional community and members of the legislature with little expertise in these fields, projected totals of expenditures, receipts, and the resulting surplus or deficit are thought of in much the same manner as is the household budget. The dominant note in this thinking is a balance sheet approach. Outgo consists of expenditures for goods and services and for gifts. Purchase of a house is not an expenditure to the full amount of the purchase price in the year of purchase. Loans to others are not outlays, unless they are "soft" loans. Receipts are all inflows that add to net worth; receipts from borrowing are not included. The resulting deficit, if any, must be covered by borrowing, or by more income (in the government sector, more taxation). Or a surplus is available to increase cash or security balances, or reduce debt, or, in the government sector, to reduce taxation.

Public confidence and understanding will be strengthened by defining budget totals and differences in these familiar terms. The fact that the implications of a surplus or deficit are different, sometimes almost the reverse of what they are for the household stands a better chance of being appreciated by the public if the explanation employs words in a familiar sense. If the definitions are familiar, the novel reasoning is easier to grasp. On these grounds, outlays should not be defined to include financial property payments, except for the subsidy element, which should be made explicit. Property receipts should also be excluded. A capital budget for long-lived government-owned assets, with depreciation accounting and even imputed interest cost would be understood by most homeowners, but on balance it probably does not advance understanding and confidence on the part of the public as a whole.

Imputed income and expenditure on conscript account might be presented as an educational device; the surplus or deficit is not affected. Most important of all for public understanding is a statement of proposed financing of the deficit or of disposition of the surplus, including the expected net results from central bank open-market operations. On this item considerable educational effort would be required, but the alternatives, complete omission or a lump-sum item, tend to baffle the intelligent layman who has understood the budget up to this point.

Purely intragovernmental transactions, including those involving trust funds, are to be omitted, on the grounds given above, unless there is an actuarial principle that is to be adhered to strictly; in that event, an information item on this score will reassure the public or alert it to abuses.

Public confidence decreases if the total outlay and total receipts item, hence the deficit or surplus, are subject to sudden and wide swings from market forces that are not subject to government control, yet appear as if they should be. Such swings can occur in financial asset transactions, as when government loans to private mortgage institutions are repaid at an abnormally high rate relative to new loans; a sudden surplus in the government's budget generated in this fashion, if loans are counted in outlays and repayments as receipts, appears suspect to the public, and a sudden deficit is viewed skeptically. These reactions can be avoided by excluding such financial transactions from the budget.

Budget definitions that allow the executive branch to create large, if temporary, changes in the surplus or deficit by changing only the form or timing of transactions also undermine public confidence and reduce understanding.

One example of this kind of change is provided by inclusion, in receipts, of proceeds from sale of participation certificates. In United States practice, these are certificates that represent a pro rata share in a pool of obligations of private-sector debtors to the federal government, reflecting federal loans for housing, certain loans to business, and the like. Title to these underlying obligations remains with the government, which also guarantees the purchaser of the participation certificates against loss in the event of default by the private-sector debtors. If the government counts as an expenditure its loan to these debtors, and if it counts as a receipt repayments by them, or money realized by sale of the obligations themselves to private-sector investors, it is argued that proceeds from sale of participation certificates should also be counted as a receipt, not as a means of financing a deficit. But the government's guarantee makes these certificates the equivalent of ordinary treasury obligations in the eyes of investors. The government could therefore shift from issuing ordinary obligations to the sale of participation certificates whenever it wanted to show a smaller deficit, though the change would be purely a formal one.

Another example of a change in surplus or deficit that occurs owing merely to a formal change in legal or accounting methods occurs when capital assets of a type that the government has been purchasing outright, say post office buildings, are thenceforth leased from the private sector. The current rate of expenditure on the postal service, as reported, drops substantially, until that period far ahead when the owned buildings have worn out and are replaced by leased buildings. A separate capital account, from which depreciation is carried into the budget, will prevent so purely formal a change from affecting the expenditure total and the surplus or deficit so markedly.

If outlays are entered when checks are issued rather than when invoices are received, the executive can sometimes convert a deficit into a surplus by postponing payments near the end of a fiscal year. The fact that next year's deficit will be so much the greater is often not enough to deter the executive from this practice, a practice that, when at last understood, impairs confidence in the budget estimates and the accounts. Even the invoices-issued basis is subject to manipulation. A somewhat less vulnerable basis is deliveries and, on construction contracts, amount of progress in construction.

If only the net result of a government enterprise is to be included in the budget, the question remains whether the enterprise's deficit shall be entered as a positive expenditure or as a negative receipt. Similarly, if the enterprise is profitable, shall the profit be entered as a positive receipt or as a negative expenditure? The amount of the budget surplus or deficit is not affected by this choice, but the total of outlays and receipts is affected. The problem is especially acute if the enterprise does not use capital budgeting and if its net outlays are high in some years and its net receipts are high in others. A waterway[12] that is many years in the making is an example. If every balance, every year, is always entered as a positive item—positive expenditure or positive receipt as the case may be—the size of the total budget over a decade or two is increased, on the outlay side by the capital costs of the early years, on the receipts side by the excess of tolls over maintenance expenses in the later years. For cash flow analysis (see Section 4 above), this procedure is the correct one, but it may mislead the public, especially when some other enterprise, just as large, say the post office, has a more synchronized schedule of capital outlays as against receipts and so reports only a small deficit each year instead of a large deficit for many years and almost as large surpluses in later years. By treating the excess of outlays over receipts as negative receipts the budget total is kept down in the early years; by, instead, treating the excess of receipts over outlays as a negative expenditure, the budget total is kept down in later years. Capital budget accounting is preferable, for public understanding and trust, with such enterprises. A second-best

12. The St. Lawrence Seaway, for example.

procedure is to count receipts as negative expenditures, if the enterprise is to be operated at a net loss over the entire span of years as a matter of public policy.

B. EFFICIENCY OF BUDGET
FORMULATION AND OF LEGISLATIVE PROCESS

Efficiency of the formulation of the budget and of the legislative process refers in this context to the ability of the executive, in formulating the bugdet, and the legislature, in passing on it, to make comparisons intelligently. The comparisons involved are those between alternative programs, between the levels of a program over two or more years, and between an increment or decrement in program and the corresponding increment or decrement in financing by taxes, borrowing, or inflation.

The ability to make comparisons will depend in large part on the answers given to the questions of content, netting, and timing, for both expenditures and receipts, in the budget document while it is being formulated and when it is being examined by the legislature.

For this purpose, a comprehensive type of budget is helpful. Not even intra-governmental transactions will be excluded, if they involve trust fund or similar programs that will otherwise be concealed (as to netting, see below). With every exclusion from the budget document, the executive's and the legislature's ability to compare is somewhat reduced. On the other hand, both executive and legislature are sensitive to public reactions to the size of the totals, and of the deficit or surplus. The information needed for comparisons can be obtained, without swelling the budget totals to a size that would create misunderstanding in the public mind, by retaining the definitions suggested under Section a above, and providing sufficient detail under "means of financing" or "disposal of surplus." Appendices could include any imputed items and intragovernmental items that are omitted from the totals.

Netting, from this ability-to-compare point of view, is not helpful, but it may be tolerated by an executive or legislature that deems it more efficient to leave the choice of methods of operating a government enterprise entirely to that enterprise. This reasoning does not apply to the netting of tax refunds against tax receipts, or to tax withholding from government employees' wages. It also does not apply to some of the intragovernmental transactions, especially those involving distinct legal or actuarial entities, social security or highway trust funds, for example.

Timing designed to improve efficiency of budget formulation and legislative processes is an even more complex matter than revealed in Sections 1 to 4 above.

In some countries a considerable part of the expenditure presented in the budget for a given fiscal year cannot be refused by the legislature, because of binding decisions made in an earlier year. First, a part of this type of expenditure is to be made under permanent authorizations or appropriations: interest on the public debt is the chief example. Second, a part is to be made out of earlier multi-year authorizations, which will have granted the executive a period of two or more years in which to spend the authorized total. Or the payments will be made under formula-type programs authorized in earlier years, which provide benefits or grants to individuals, firms, or subordinate units of government that meet certain criteria (farm price supports and veterans' payments, for example). Third, another part will consist of payments under contracts that were entered into by the executive in a prior year, under appropriations made in that earlier year, if payment under the contract falls due not in that earlier year but in the current year. Even when the legislature must formally approve the current-year expenditure in some of these cases, its control over the amount spent is scarcely more than nominal. In similar fashion the current-year legislature may take action that will effectively commit future-year legislatures to a certain amount of spending.[13]

In other countries the legislature of a given year primarily grants to the executive the power to spend stipulated amounts during that year, rather than power to obligate the government to spend stipulated amounts in that or a future year.[14] But the difference is in many instances more apparent than real. By allowing public debt to be issued currently, the legislature effectively binds future legislatures to spend money on interest, whether or not a permanent appropriation or authorization is voted.

Under "timing," but in a special sense, may be placed the following problem. A capital budget is sometimes opposed on the grounds that it will distort, for the legislator, choice between an investment in bricks-and-mortar capital and investment in human capital, notably education, because the capital budget will place the outlay for a building, say a courthouse, "below the line," that is, not in the total for the budget for the current year, while the outlay for teachers' salaries will go above the line. This issue has been touched on above,[15] but requires emphasis here. A legislature anxious to keep the total of the current year's expenditures low will be tempted, so runs the argument, to build the courthouse and economize on hiring more teachers, if a capital budget is used. But if "schoolhouse" is substituted for "courthouse," it becomes evident that the issue is not one of biasing the legislator in favor of one function (administration of justice) and against another (education), but of bias in favor of spending more on capital and less on labor as inputs for any function whatever. To be sure, if production of a certain government service—and education may well be an example—is inherently more labor intensive than another, say irrigation or reclamation, the former kind of service will tend to lose support,

13. In the United States, the President's budget for the fiscal year ending June 30, 1969, called for outlays of $201.4 billion (gross of adjustments for interfund and intragovernmental transactions and applicable receipts), of which $58.9 billion was to be available for expenditure by the executive without further action by Congress. The remaining $142.5 billion would require action by Congress, but of this, $52.3 billion was based on authority granted in earlier years and thus was to some degree effectively beyond the power of the current Congress to reduce or deny. Joint Committee on Reduction of Federal Expenditures, Congress of the United States, *Staff Report (No. 2) on The Status of the 1969 Fiscal Year Federal Budget as of June 14, 1969* (Washington, D.C.: Government Printing Office, 1968), p. 2.

14. See "Congress and the Budget" [no author], and Maynard S. Comiez, "Notes on Budget Concepts in Selected Developed Countries," in President's Commission on Budget Concepts, *Staff Papers and Other Materials Reviewed by the President's Commission* (Washington, D.C.: Government Printing Office, 1967), especially pp. 5–6, 122–23, 147.

15. Section B.1.a.

relatively. And the service, say education, that is labor intensive in its production may well be capital intensive in its effects; that is, the recipients of education may get most of the benefits from it in future years.

The total of factor activity utilized (not real resources used up) and paid for during the current year is the same for courthouse or schoolhouse as for school-teachers. A legislator who desires to obtain the political benefits that come from activation of factors, especially those in his own district, yet desires to avoid being charged with increasing the current year's total expenditures, can achieve both ends by voting for construction rather than for salaries, if a capital budget is in use.

c. Choice of Efficient Methods of Operation

Choice of efficient methods of operating the government will be hampered if capital-budget accounting is not employed. In the absence of depreciation accounting an outlay to purchase a capital asset now that would reduce out-of-pocket operating costs in a later year will be given less consideration than the facts warrant. In the later years, maintenance outlay will be skimped, even at the (unrecorded) cost of accelerating actual depreciation by more than the maintenance costs foregone, since this cost is not recorded.

CHAPTER TWENTY-ONE

Optimum Output Pattern

PUBLIC FINANCE measures to achieve a Pareto-optimum pattern of output fall into four groups. First, the government supplies free of charge group-consumption goods,[1] some of which are consumed collectively, some not, and raises the tax revenue or other moneys to finance these services.

Second, when a group-consumption good arises as a jointly produced externality with production or consumption of a marketable good, subsidies or tax devices may perhaps be designed that will increase the private-sector output of those marketable goods and their accompanying group-consumption externalities. These same devices may serve to collect part of the cost of production from those who benefit from the group-consumption goods. The externality may be negative, and Pareto-optimum public finance measures then include taxes designed to reduce private-sector output of the goods that create those undesirable externalities, and perhaps to compensate those who suffer from the negative externalities that remain.

Third, a privately marketable good yielding no externalities may nevertheless be subsidized, or taxed, or be supplied directly by the government, below or above cost, on Pareto-optimum grounds, if the good is one that is consumed collectively. It is difficult, if not impossible, for a competitive market to reach an optimum output when demand curves must be added vertically.

Fourth, subsidies or subsidy-tax devices may be used to induce greater private-sector output of goods produced under imperfect competition or in industries of decreasing cost.

All four of these types will be explored in the present chapter, with emphasis on government-supplied group-consumption goods.

1. For definitions of group-consumption goods, marketable goods, collective consumption, etc., see Chapter 4 above, especially Figure 1 and the accompanying text.

A. GOVERNMENT-SUPPLIED
GROUP-CONSUMPTION GOODS

Within the category of government-supplied group-consumption goods, there may be distinguished, as already noted, those that are consumed collectively and those that are not. Some of the collectively consumed group-consumption goods arise as joint-product externalities with services that, although marketable, are marketed by direct rationing rather than by rationing through the price mechanism. Thus an improved milieu from education is a joint-product externality produced with a marketable good, education, that is itself distributed by direct rationing, not by pricing.

The government may be regarded as the supplier of a group-consumption, collective-consumption good when it makes a welfare payment that induces or renders feasible some action by the recipient that benefits the rest of the community. The benefits are usually in the form of an improved milieu of some sort.

In judging whether demand is strong enough under a Pareto-optimum test, to justify supplying one more unit of a group-consumption good, or a collective-consumption good (or one that is both), the demand curves of the individuals interested in the service must be added vertically, not horizontally. The resulting demand for the increment is then compared with its cost; at an optimum level, the sum of the marginal rates of substitution of the users equals the marginal rate of transformation.[2]

Demand curves as commonly constructed imply uniform pricing over all units of product,[3] if not over all buyers, but in the present case there is no reason to postulate uniform pricing over all the infra-marginal units, and of course not even uniform pricing as among users, either for the marginal unit or any infra-marginal unit. With this proviso, we may speak of vertical addition of demand curves.

This rule of vertical addition applies to two classes of goods: (1) collective consumption goods, whether marketable or non-marketable (i.e. group-consumption) goods, (2) non-collective consumption goods that are not marketable, e.g., fire protection. Whenever demand curves must be added vertically, the rule for not

2. See Howard R. Bowen, *Toward Social Economy* (New York: Rinehart, 1948), pp. 176–79 and Paul A. Samuelson, "The Pure Theory of Public Expenditure," *Review of Economics and Statistics* (November, 1954), 36: 387–89, and "Diagrammatic Exposition of a Theory of Public Expenditure," *Review of Economics and Statistics* (November, 1955), 37: 350–56. For the earlier contribution by Eric Lindahl with respect to vertical addition of demand curves, see the discussions and references given by Musgrave, *Theory of Public Finance*, pp. 75–76, and the definitive summary and analysis of Lindahl's theory in J. G. Head, "Lindahl's Theory of the Budget," *Finanzarchiv* (October, 1964), 421–54. For a comprehensive analysis of the public goods concept, see James M. Buchanan, *The Demand and Supply of Public Goods* (Chicago: Rand McNally, 1968). None of these analyses, however, emphasize as does the present analysis the distinction between group consumption and collective consumption, since they usually do not cover specifically the types of service for which exclusion by price is not efficient, or possible, yet which are not collective-consumption services, i.e., do not exhibit a zero marginal cost per user.

3. See John G. Head, "The Theory of Public Goods," *Rivista di Diritto Finanziario e Scienza delle Finanze* (June, 1968), 27: 218.

extending the service beyond a Pareto-optimum level of intensity or quality or period of time (e.g., length of a play) is the rule of unanimity first formulated by Wicksell to be described in Section 1 below.

Let us emphasize that this rule of unanimity applies to marketable as well as to nonmarketable services, as long as they are consumed collectively. It applies, for example, to privately supplied theatrical performances, within the capacity limits of the theater, as well as to publicly supplied mosquito abatement. The discussion to follow will be in terms of nonmarketable services, both those collectively consumed (mosquito abatement) and those not collectively consumed (fire protection). But the applicability of the Wicksell marginal rule to marketable, collectively consumed services (theater performances) must be kept in mind.

Nonmarketable goods that are consumed collectively will be considered first. It will be convenient to deal initially with services for which no intra-group discrimination is feasible, for example, mosquito abatement, as contrasted with television broadcasting that can black out selected areas. The analysis will be of goods that do not arise as joint-product externalities with marketable goods [for these joint-product goods, see pages 524–26 below]. Much of this discussion will, however, apply to the other categories of goods; where it does not, later sections will make this fact clear.

1. Group-Consumption Goods Consumed Collectively

A. No Intra-group Discrimination Feasible

(1) Not Produced as Joint Product with Marketable Good

Among the group-consumption goods, those (1) that are collectively consumed, (2) for which no intra-group discrimination is feasible,[4] and (3) that do not arise as joint products with marketable goods are the ones that have served as examples for Pareto-optimum discussion in the public finance literature, even though they account for few services: deterrence of foreign foes by the military, public health, exploration of space, and some aspects of contract enforcement.

(a). BASIC PARETO-OPTIMUM PRINCIPLE:
UNANIMITY FOR EACH INCREMENT OF SERVICE

The principle of unanimity says, in effect, that each increment in the level of the service for which the demand curves must be added vertically will be worth while, in the Pareto-optimum sense, only if some pattern of covering the cost of that increment can be found that will make at least one person better off without making any one else worse off. If such a pattern for distributing the incremental cost can be found,

4. For a definition of goods for which no intragroup discrimination is feasible, see Chapter 4, pages 70, 73.

no one will vote against adopting it, if he reveals his true preference (deliberate misstatement of preferance to gain a bargaining advantage, or refusal to state any preference at all, are discussed below). Wicksell's unanimity principle was his way of stating what later came to be the modern welfare economics principle that welfare cannot be unambiguously increased by any action that does not make at least one person better off while making no one else worse off. The only way to insure that no one will be made worse off, when the good must be supplied to a group of persons (vertical addition of demand curves) rather than being purchased by each person on the market, is to allow any one individual in the group to veto the proposed incremental action.

If, for example, a public health campaign against tuberculosis is to be strengthened, and if the proposal specifies the tax measure for sharing this increment of outlay on tuberculosis prevention, then no matter how much all the others will gain from this action, one person who will lose by it must be allowed to block the action, under modern welfare (Wicksell) rules. His veto requires that the financing plan be revised in a manner such that his contribution will be reduced to or below the point where his incremental gain is larger than his incremental cost. Let us suppose that the others, though paying more than under the initial (vetoed) financing plan, will still be better off than if no increment were produced. This hurdle once passed, the addition of still another increment of anti-tuberculosis service can be considered, and so on, up to the level of anti-tuberculosis service where, with respect to the next increment, every financing plan conceivable for that increment does no better than leave everyone indifferent whether they obtain that increment or not.

Unanimity is therefore not a rule to be diluted to some sort of qualified majority rule because it is too strong in principle, as long as the Pareto-optimum concept itself is held not too strong in principle. Complete unanimity is the essential feature for an increment of service and its attendant financing if the policy-makers are seeking an efficient allocation in the Pareto sense. The only reasons for not following the unanimity rule strictly, if the goal is simply optimum allocation, are the following. First, from a non-optimal position it is usually possible to move to a Pareto-optimum either (*a*) in a manner that makes some persons worse off than they were in the non-optimal position, or (*b*) in a manner (and to a different Pareto-optimum position) that does not make anyone worse off, and there is nothing in the nature of the Pareto-optimum position itself that dictates which type of move shall be selected (see Section]i] below). Secondly, if the group is small, the unanimity principle may be abused by those who, although knowing that they will be better off under a certain proposed increment (and its financing method), vote against it as a bargaining-bluffing procedure (see Section [ii] below). Third, if the group is large, it is difficult, perhaps impossible, to formulate an agreement and enforce it. Fourth, the procedure is costly.

[1] *Pareto-Optimum Movement,*
Pareto-Desirable Movement, and Pareto-Optimum Position

The possible ambiguity in the principle of unanimity may be discussed in terms of a distinction between what we here call a Pareto-optimum movement, a Pareto-desirable movement, and a Pareto-optimum position.

A Pareto-optimum position is one in which no one can be made better off without making someone worse off. A Pareto-optimum movement is a move from a non-optimum position to an optimum position. Such a move may, or may not, make some persons worse off than they were at the initial, non-optimum position, but that fact does not convert the point that is reached into a non-optimum point. A Pareto-desirable movement is one that makes some one or more persons better off without making anyone worse off.

Rules for government action designed to achieve an optimum allocation of resources therefore need to specify whether they are merely position rules or also movement rules, and, if the latter, whether only Pareto-desirable moves are allowed. The discussion to follow assumes that only Pareto-desirable moves are allowed.

Let us consider, for example, a two-person economy, initially without government services. Both persons, A and B, are willing to sacrifice some marketed goods in order to receive some government service. Let the initial distribution of marketed services between A and B be given. At one extreme, on the first small movement away from the initial position, the government can require A to give up so large an increment in marketed services that the increment of government service he receives only just compensates him for this decrement in marketed services; he is kept on the same indifference curve between government and marketed services that he was on when the amount of government service was zero.[5] He is no worse off, but neither is he any better off. Let A be continually held on this indifference curve as successive increments of the government service are supplied, at the cost of successive decrements in the marketed goods he receives.

As this process continues, A will of course give up less and less of marketed goods for a further increment of the government service, and B must begin to surrender marketable goods if those further increments of government service are to be produced. Eventually a Pareto-optimum point will be reached at which A will still be no better and no worse off than when no government service was being rendered, while B will of course be much better off. In similar fashion at the other extreme, B could be held down to his initial welfare level, and at the Pareto-optimum (Wicksell) point A would be much better off.

Positions on the utility frontier in between the extremes reached under these two formulations can be attained by moving both A and B to higher indifference curves simultaneously, at one or more stages away from the initial stage of no government service. It is possible to make such moves, within limits, because the decrement of

---

5. The resources so released may be enough not only to supply A, and simultaneously B, with the stated initial increment in government service, but also to supply B with more marketed goods than he had when no government goods were being produced. B pays nothing and, in this event, gains in both goods.

marketed goods for A releases resources that produce an increment of government service that benefits both A and B, and similarly for what B gives up. But the moves must be timed carefully if neither A nor B is to be made worse off at any one step in the progress toward the utility frontier. If B is held down on his initial indifference curve for some distance while successive increments of government service are furnished, A is moved to ever higher indifference curves, and a corresponding part of the utility frontier will then have become unattainable without violating the movement version of the optimum rule, by making A worse off than he was at the immediately preceding stage, when he was not on the utility frontier.

Figure 14 illustrates this point.[6] Initially, when no government service is being rendered, A and B are at z. If B is kept on his initial indifference curve when the first

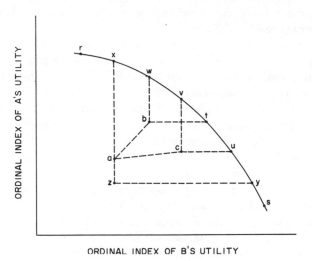

FIGURE 14. Attainable Utility Frontier Positions under Constraints of Given Initial Income Distribution and under Pareto-Desirable Moves

increment of government service is produced (at the cost of fewer marketable goods produced), the parties move up to, say, the point a. If for the next increment of government service the sharing of its cost is such that B gains, but only a little, while A gains a good deal, and they move to point b, it is now impossible to reach a point on the utility frontier southeast of t (from t to y) on the next move or moves, without violating the movement version of the optimum rule by making A worse off than he is at b. But if the sharing of the cost of the second increment had been more favorable to B, so that the parties reached, say, c instead of b, only the range between u and y (instead of from t to y) would be unattainable because of the rule against making A worse off on any move. Similarly, from c no point from v to x is attainable, and from b, no point from w to x, for B would be made worse off (than at c or at b) by a move to points in those ranges.

6. This figure is adapted from Musgrave's figure 4–6, in his *Theory of Public Finance* (see the following footnote).

Positions outside the two extreme points x and y on the utility frontier in Figure 14, say r or s, cannot be reached at all, under the double constraint of (*a*) a given initial distribution of marketed goods when no government service is produced (point z in Figure 14) and (*b*) Pareto-desirable moves. Those positions outside the two extremes could be reached only by at least one move that would make one of the parties worse off than he was just before that move.[7] Yet r and s are Pareto-optimum points.

[2] *Intra-Marginal Deadlock; Cost of Applying Unanimity Rule*

Until the level of the government service has been pushed so high that no financing pattern for another increment can be found that all will agree on, there is a consumer surplus on each increment, in the sense that the sum of the maximum amounts that each user of the service is willing to pay for an increment of it exceeds the cost of supplying the increment. Thus there are an infinite number of ways of sharing the cost of that increment, all of which ways will be better, for all parties, than not having the increment at all. But each of the parties may try to persuade the group to accept a pattern that gives him so large a part of the consumer surplus on the increment being considered that when all these demands are summed, they are seen to exceed that surplus. If no one yields, a deadlock ensues, the increment of service is not supplied, and the level of service actually given remains below any of the levels represented by the utility frontier, the locus of Pareto-optimum points.

If no deadlock occurs, and the parties somehow successfully compromise on the financing pattern of each increment, until the margin is reached, the particular financing patterns they have adopted for the infra-marginal units will influence two things: the level of the service at which the marginal increment is found and the distribution among these individuals of the economy's total real income (goods and services, distributed free and marketed).

That the level of the service will be influenced can be seen by supposing that the financing patterns for the infra-marginal units happen to be, in one case, uniformly unfavorable to those whose tastes for group-consumption goods are above average or, in another case, uniformly unfavorable to those whose tastes for these goods are below average. If those with an inclination for group-consumption goods come out badly in the infra-marginal bargaining, their weakened economic position makes them less able to express their tastes than if they come out well, and fewer of the economy's resources will be devoted to group-consumption goods.

7. Musgrave's "Utility frontier with given income [i.e., initial, marketed-goods-only, income] distribution" in his figure 4–6, p. 83 (similar to Figure 14) is limited to the range x to y by his implicit adoption of the movement version of the optimum rule, since he does not allow either A or B to become worse off than they were in the initial, non-optimum position. Samuelson's more general treatment does not utilize Musgrave's constraint of an initial distribution of marketed-goods income and so can construct an attainable utility frontier that extends beyond Musgrave's x to y range. It also of course includes Musgrave's x to y range. Any point between Musgrave's x and y can be reached by moving A (or B) to a somewhat higher indifference curve than the one he starts with, as increments of the government service are supplied, without moving the other party to a lower one, then holding A (or B) on this new higher curve until a Pareto-optimum point is reached. This is how Samuelson's frontier is reached, except that he allows A (or B) to start on that indifference curve initially.

It remains true, of course, that whatever infra-marginal route is followed to the utility frontier, the end result is achievement of the goal of a Pareto-optimum point, and the efficient-allocation criterion is thus satisfied. But each optimum point will differ from all the others in the distribution of real income that goes with it and in the level of government service that goes with it.[8]

The probability that an infra-marginal deadlock will occur and that the level of service will be below that represented by the utility frontier depends in a somewhat complex manner on the size of the group. The analysis to follow will deal first with small groups of various sizes, a small group being defined as one so small that a threat by one of the members that he will act in a certain way influences the decisions of at least one other member of the group.

The smallest possible group, the two-person group, has been discussed extensively in the public finance literature. It poses essentially the same problems as bilateral monopoly in the field of marketable goods.[9] Correspondingly, no very helpful generalizations have been developed. A deadlock may ensue far short of the utility frontier, if either party refuses to accept a gain achievable from rebargaining in the mistaken hope that the other party can be pressured into accepting a position still less advantageous for him. In any event, if the frontier is reached, no one point on it seems more likely, a priori, than another. The only feature of the two-person group that is encouraging for reaching a Pareto-optimum allocation is that it should be possible for this group of two to scan quickly a large number of alternative financing plans for any one increment of the service and that the number of such plans should be fewer than if the group were larger. These circumstances would facilitate a close approach to the utility frontier, once the group had come so near to it that further progress depended on finding some unusual forms of taxation, tax rates, and so on, that would implement the few sharing patterns that would be acceptable to them.

The typical case in real life is a group that is small, but far from as small as two, with the complication that each member of the group represents a constituency that is itself a large group. Even if there are only two parties, and party discipline under a parliamentary form of government prevails, informal discussions within the parties prior to announcement of the government's bill make the group much larger than a group of two. And even a dictator will find it helpful to gain the assent of others.

As the group becomes larger, the influence on the actions of the group that any one member of it can exert by a threat to withdraw diminishes, finally to zero. The danger of a deadlock short of the utility frontier owing to bluffing and bargaining decreases as the size of the group increases. Simultaneously, however, two other problems arise. First, the cost of scanning alternative patterns of financing in-

---

8. A social welfare function can indeed dictate that just one of the points on the utility frontier shall be *the* optimum, but the view taken here is that no agreement can be reached on a social welfare function and the outcome of conflicts of interest must therefore determine which one of the Pareto-optimum points the society will reach, if it reaches any of them.

9. See John G. Head, "Lindahl's Theory of the Budget," *Finanzarchiv* (October, 1964), 23: 421–54, especially pp. 427, 440–42, 445–47.

creases, both in money outlay and time consumed; the larger the group, the longer it takes for a plan to be understood by all, and the larger is the number of possible alternative patterns of financing. Second, any one member of the group is more inclined to withdraw, or rather not to participate from the beginning, the larger is the group, since he considers that his influence over the outcome becomes smaller. At the extreme, he believes that the outcome will the same whether he participates in the decision making or not. He therefore fails to reveal his preferences, not because he is bargaining or bluffing but because he believes that such preference revelation will neither increase nor decrease the likelihood that he will receive the service under what he considers an acceptable financing plan.[10] If everyone adopts this attitude, nothing is done, even when it is in the interest of all that something be done. For a marketed good, on the other hand, the individual must reveal his preference, by offering the price asked for the good, or be excluded.

Somewhere in between the extremes of a two-person group and a group so large that no one person believes that his preference expression will prove useful to him, there must lie a group of an optimum size in the sense that it maximizes a probability-weighted degree of approach toward a Pareto frontier. But even this statement is too simple. Each alternative pattern of financing is in fact a pattern for distributing the cost not among the group members themselves, but among their constituents, in a representative form of government, or among those who do, and also among those who do not, assist an oligarchy or a dictator to remain in power. A correspondingly gigantic number of alternative financing patterns is available, in principle, for any increment of service; legislator A might agree that his constituents should pay 2 per cent of the cost, yet that 2 per cent could be divided among those constituents in a large number of alternative patterns.

In any event there is no reason to expect real-life groups to be anywhere near this optimum-creating size, since in real life Pareto-optimum efficiency is not the only goal attempted. A conflict of interests over distribution of income, to name but one other influence, might be resolved in a manner that would affect the size of the group, since those whose views had prevailed might conclude that a certain size of group would be helpful in consolidating and maintaining their victory.

Abstracting again from all goals other than optimum allocation, a deadlock far short of the optimum may be made unlikely by certain devices, which, however, reduce almost to zero the probability that the group will ever get as far as the utility frontier. A more or less fixed, accepted system of raising tax revenue is the most notable of such devices. Under this approach it is understood that a proposal to increase the level of a certain service will be accompanied by a limited number of alternative revenue-raising patterns, each of them attainable by marginal adjustments to an existing tax system. Only when some entirely new type of government service is introduced, or a very large increment in an existing service, usually military protection or aggression, are new types of tax considered, and even then the number examined will be small. The scanning patterns may be thus limited for

10. Cf. William J. Baumol, *Welfare Economics and the Theory of the State*, 2d ed. (London: Bell and Sons, 1965), pp. 173–75, and Mancur Olson, Jr., *The Logic of Collective Action* (Cambridge, Mass.: Harvard University Press, 1965) pp. 9–16, 43–52.

reasons having little or nothing to do with the danger of deadlock, but the effect is to narrow the range of proposals that those who bluff can make for placing more of the burden on others, and to reduce the scanning time and effort that are needed even when there is no bluffing.

From this point of view, national tax systems can be divided into two categories. In one, almost all the revenue is obtained from a few taxes, each of which, however, can be varied at many points, for example, income tax rates, exemptions, deductions, concepts of income, relative treatment of corporations, and so on. The other kind of system imposes a large number of small taxes, say a series of revenue taxes on imports and a widespread system of stamp taxes. Either tax system can offer a substantial number of alternative incremental financing plans that are sufficiently different to assist in avoiding infra-marginal deadlock, yet not so many that the group will be tied up indefinitely in arguing over an endless series of competing proposals. Certain jurisdictions, however, must work with a far narrower range of choice, particularly (1) local bodies that may be restricted to a property tax, or a crude form of business tax, and (2) those countries where tax administration and tax compliance are at a level so low that even the national government can operate with only a few types of tax and those few on a very simply defined base. In these circumstances the community as a whole might gain, in the Pareto-optimum sense, if it could administer a more complicated tax system, since such a system would offer more alternatives and so might enable the supply of group-consumption goods to be moved nearer an allocational optimum, provided again that not so many options were available as to so increase the amount of bluffing and to put so heavy a pressure on scanning time and energy that in fact some of the options would never be considered.

If the more complicated tax system is not available, a deadlock far from the optimum frontier can be broken by inflationary finance, for reasons and with results noted in Chapter 18 above. Borrowing is still another way of escaping an intra-marginal deadlock, by postponing the decision as to how the cost shall be shared (see Chapter 18). But often the countries that are most restricted in their choice of taxes are also unable to use inflationary finance steadily because of the resulting external disequilibrium that may be relatively important for them, and cannot borrow much either at home or abroad.

For subordinate units of government, the number of financing patterns available for moving toward a Pareto-optimum can be enlarged by persuading the central government to tax the firms and households in this local area and return the resulting tax proceeds to the local government unit to be spent by it as those firms and households decide, again on the unanimity principle. An income tax may in this way be included in the financing options when otherwise the scanning would be restricted to changes in, say, a real estate tax. The central government, however, is quite unlikely to do this favor for any one local unit alone, perhaps indeed cannot constitutionally do so. All local units must accept this revenue round-trip service, or at least all of a certain type, say all cities of more than a given size. This degree of unanimity will be so difficult to obtain that the technique of the general-purpose grant with revenues returned to area of origin is not likely to be employed simply to help local areas reach their own Pareto-optimum levels of government service.[11]

If, as is common, tax revenues are rising steadily because they are linked with output and per-person output is increasing, and if, as seems likely, the cost of a given level of service per person does not increase with per-person output, an increment in level of government service can be obtained merely by not reducing tax rates as much as otherwise. In principle this fact should not make it any easier to reach a Pareto-optimum level of government service, but in practice it will probably do so. Countries that are growing in per capita income may therefore be expected to come somewhat closer to an optimum level of government service than those that are not.

[3] Level of Service in Excess of Optimum

If the government service is subject to increasing cost per increment in level of service and if large discontinuities exist in the decision process, the group may unwittingly push the level of the service, unanimously, beyond the optimal level. A proposal to increase a large city's police force from, say, 10,000 to 15,000 men may prove unanimously acceptable because the consequent decrease in the crime rate seems to everyone to be worth the cost, even though closer examination would reveal no possibility of unanimous agreement on increasing the police force from 14,000 to 15,000, in view of the relatively small decrease in the crime rate at those levels, where the cost of preventing further crime is much higher (increasing costs) than in the 10,000–14,000 range. When the increase of 5,000 is the unit for considerations, the consumers' surplus on the first 4,000, being greater than the consumers' deficit on the last 1,000, makes unanimous agreement in favor of the 5,000 possible.

This mistake can be avoided by moving gradually toward the optimum, considering only one small increment at a time. As with the scanning of a large number of alternative financing methods, this small-increment decision-making carries its own cost in time and effort. In practice, as government budgets are adjusted from one year to the next, under severe financing restraints, this danger of moving by increments too large is perhaps minimal.

Finally, where several groups overlap, reciprocal agreements to support each other's proposals (log-rolling) may produce agreement on levels of group-consumption service beyond the Pareto optimum, but only, it appears, when the unanimity principle is not strictly observed, some substitute, a majority vote, for instance, being employed.[12]

---

11. In fact there are few if any instances in any country of such a grant. General-purpose grants are usually given on a per capita basis, partly as a means of redistributing disposable income.

12. Buchanan and Tullock tend to fear overexpansion of government service because of extensive log-rolling. Downs, in contrast, believes that the political process, because it is so devoted to maximizing stay in office by maximizing votes for the legislator casting his vote leads to underexpansion of the public sector. See the extended analysis and original insights provided by these authors in James M. Buchanan and Gordon Tullock, *The Calculus of Consent: Logical Foundations of Constitutional Democracy* (Ann Arbor: University of Michigan

(B) PROBLEMS IN ESTIMATING
INCREMENTAL COSTS AND INCREMENTAL BENEFITS

[1] Relinquishing Benefits and Shifting Taxes

For purposes simply of knowing whether a Pareto-optimum level of a given service
has been attained it is not strictly necessary to measure physical units of output (see
Chapter 4, Section B). What is necessary for rational action is that each recipient,
or at least each representative of recipients, be able to estimate the money value of
the increment of service to his constituents and to compare that with the money cost
to them of the tax or other financing programs.

These estimates are more difficult than those that must be made by the purchaser
of marketable goods. A purchaser is now but one of a group. If the unanimous
decision is that the group shall act, the group is usually so large that its action sets
in motion forces in the market sector that may deprive the recipient of part or all of
the benefit he receives initially from the group-consumption good. An example is a
decision to improve a city's school system. A consequent increase in demand for
dwelling accommodation within the city, from families elsewhere who now wish to
move to this city, will force tenants to relinquish part of the benefits of improved
education by payment of higher dwelling rentals, quite apart from the effect of any
tax that is employed to finance the school improvement.

This problem might be dismissed for discussion on an abstract level by assuming
that each member of the group is immediately aware of the degree to which the
benefit will be relinquished. Such an assumption robs the comparison of the government sector with the market sector of its reality, for in fact the task of forecasting
accurately the incidence of benefits of services or burdens of taxes takes time and
effort and is subject to error. In contrast, the single consumer of marketable goods
can be certain that his atomistic purchase will not set in motion forces that will rob
him of the benefits of his purchase, or that will allow him to shift any part of the
cost to others.

[2] Benefits and Costs Spread over Time

If the benefits or the costs, or both, lie partly or wholly in the future, they must be
discounted to the present date or accumulated at compound interest to some single
future date if the totals are to be compared. The question then arises whether everyone in the decision-taking group must use the same interest rate if a Pareto-optimum
level of the service is to emerge from the group decision. The answer is important
for all benefit-cost analysis, including the type being examined in this chapter.

If the world were riskless, if the capital market functioned perfectly, if everyone

Press, 1962), and Anthony Downs, *An Economic Theory of Democracy* (New York: Harper,
1957). For a summary and critique of Downs and of Buchanan and Tullock, see J. G. Head,
"The Welfare Foundations of Public Finance Theory," *Rivista di diritto finanziario e scienza
delle finanze* (January, 1965), 23: 41–50.

could lend or borrow without limit, and if (as in fact is the case) technical productivity patterns existed that yielded a positive rate of interest, each person would adjust his rates of present and future consumption to the single market rate of interest. Everyone's marginal time preference would be the same, while intrinsic rates of time preference could still differ widely from person to person.[13] In this state of affairs no problem arises; future benefits and costs are discounted at the one rate of interest, for comparison of total benefits of an increment of government service with total costs of that increment.

In the real world of risk, imperfect capital markets, and limited borrowing capacity, if not limited lending capacity, no one of the many actual interest rates, all of them reflecting second-best states of affairs, has a clear priority over any of the others. The choice will depend on the weights given to various considerations in the process of sub-optimizing.

One method of computation that must be avoided in any event, if a Pareto-optimum is to be reached, is that of ranking competing projects according to the size of the respective benefit-cost ratios.[14] Under this procedure the benefits and costs of a project for any one year are not netted, to obtain a net benefit or net cost for the year, before discounting[15] to a present value. Instead, the benefit stream is discounted to a present value, the cost stream is discounted separately (though of course at the same rate of interest), and the ratio of the former to the latter is ascertained. This ratio is related to a rate of return on sales. It is not a rate of return on investment. A project with a benefit-cost ratio of present values of, say, $1,000,000 to $800,000, or 1.25, can be upgraded, under this test, by revising it so that equal amounts are lopped off both benefits and costs in some particular future year. Thus if for the twelfth year it is possible to revise the project so that benefits and costs in that year each decline by $400,000, the present value of benefits, if a 6 per cent rate

13. An individual's "intrinsic time preference" is zero if "a given rate of expenditure produces just as much satisfaction if it occurs later as it does if it occurs immediately." William S. Vickrey, *Metastatics and Macro-economics*, p. 15. If the market offers such an individual a zero rate of interest, he will spend equal amounts now and later, since the price of one amount in terms of the other amount is unity, and the satisfactions are the same. But if the market offers him a positive rate of interest, so that he can spend more later than he gives up now, and so receive more satisfaction then than he gives up now, he will save, until he is spending enough more later than he spends now to equate the marginal satisfaction given up now with the marginal satisfaction to be received thereby later. He exhibits a "marginal time preference."

14. As employed, for example, in the United States, commonly to evaluate water-resource projects. Any project with a benefit-cost ratio of unity or more is worth undertaking, in the sense that it will earn a rate of return on investment equal to, or greater than, the discount rate employed in obtaining present values. But a project with a benefit-cost ratio of, say, 1.1 may show a larger rate of return on investment than one showing a benefit-cost ratio of 1.2.

15. For a comprehensive discussion of the "proper" interest rate to employ to discount future benefits and costs in evaluating a government service, see Bernard Sobin, *Shadow Prices for Money in Government Expenditure Policy* (unpublished doctoral dissertation, Columbia University, 1967). See also Joint Economic Committee, Congress of the United States, "The Planning-Programing Budgeting System: Progress and Potentials," Report of the Subcommittee on Economy in Government, December, 1967 (Washington, D.C.: U.S. Government Printing Office, 1967), pp. 5–6. Agreement within the economics profession on the interest rate to use is probably less nearly uniform than might be inferred from the subcommittee's language.

is used, becomes approximately $1,000,000 − $200,000, or $800,000, and the present values of costs, $800,000 − $200,000, or $600,000. The benefit-cost ratio rises from 1.25 to 1.33.[16]

Another ranking to be avoided, generally, is one based on relative amounts of consumer surplus generated by competing projects. If the projects are not mutually exclusive in a physical sense, this criterion is fundamentally misleading, since it diverts attention from a comparison of marginal returns over marginal costs on the competing projects and seems to imply that the size of the project is fixed in advance. Project A, planned on a scale to yield k units of service a year, may show a much smaller consumer surplus than Project B, planned on a scale to yield j units a year (the units are not necessarily the same). Yet if the $k + 1$ unit of Project A will yield a larger ratio of social revenue over social cost than will a $j + 1$ unit of Project B, the scale of Project B should be cut back and that of Project A increased, or, better yet, the scale of both projects increased to the level where marginal social revenue equals marginal social cost. The relative amounts of consumer surplus are irrelevant in determining the scale of Project A and that of Project B.

Even if the projects are mutually exclusive, consumer surplus has no role to play in determining choice of product, if the results of the private market mechanism are appealed to as the criterion, which is the case if the project is one that adds a small increment of product to an already large market (e.g., a dam to add electric power to an already large supply). To take another illustration, if a site can be used for either an apartment house or an office building but not both at once, the project that is chosen should be (for Paretian efficiency) the one that affords the larger producer surplus (economic rent). There is no consumer surplus on this building, if it is only an addition to an already large supply. Producer surplus is the market test because producers of the product do have to pay varying amounts per unit of the product to get the successive units produced (see the discussion in Chapter 15 on increasing costs for dwelling space in a high-rise structure).[17] Consumer surplus is not relevant in these instances. Consumers do not have to pay varying amounts per unit to buy the product.[18]

16. See Roland W. McKean, *Efficiency in Government through Systems Analysis* (New York: John Wiley, 1958), Chapter 7, and comment on McKean by Otto Eckstein, "A Survey of the Theory of Public Expenditures Criteria," in National Bureau of Economic Research, *Public Finances: Needs, Sources, and Utilization* (Princeton, N.J.: Princeton University Press, 1961), pp. 484–86. Eckstein points out practical considerations that may have to be taken into account: "budget money will remain scarce" with respect to future operating costs, "only federal cost" is "the constrained financial resource," and "there is no reinvestment." See also Otto Eckstein, *Water-Resource Development, the Economics of Project Evaluation* (Cambridge, Mass: Harvard University Press, 1958). In the United States, the ratio computed has commonly been that of annualized benefits to annualized costs rather than of present values, but the erroneous ranking that results is the same. For a description and critique see McKean, *op. cit.*, pp. 107 ff.

17. In the market, if the producer surplus is larger for the apartment building than for the office building, the landowner will allow only the apartment building to be constructed on the site, since his land rent is the producer surplus. This conclusion assumes of course that either one of the buildings will be pushed up to a height such that the top floor yields no producer surplus. It also abstracts from economic rents in various elements of the construction industry, which can be disregarded in an example focussed on one building.

18. Much of the benefit-cost, or project valuation, analysis of recent years has been

(C) EFFECT ON OPTIMUM LEVEL OF NUMBERS AND AREA SERVED

[1] Changes in Numbers (Area Constant)

If the number of households and firms in a given area increases through migration or an excess of births over deaths, more resources will tend to be devoted to a group-consumption, collective-consumption good, relative to the amount of resources devoted to a non-collective consumption good, on Pareto-optimum grounds. Per capita cost of a given level of the collective-consumption service necessarily declines exactly in proportion to the increase in numbers served (see Chapter 4). This increase in resources devoted to the collective-consumption good will however be slight if the average income of the new households and firms is very low. And if the increase is one in population due to an excess of births over deaths, the average income of the newcomers is zero, until they grow up to be productive members of the group. When the average income of the newcomers is zero, the per capita cost of the initial level of the service, to those who participate in paying for it, is just what it was initially. The volume of resources devoted to the collective-consumption service will therefore be expected to remain as it was initially, externalities aside, and abstracting from the fact that the advent of the newcomers, especially if they are newborn, will cause the demand for marketable goods to move up. In this latter event, the demand for the group-consumption, collective-consumption good at an unchanged per capita cost may be expected to fall.

If we turn to marketable collective-consumption goods, we observe that capacity limits seem to be reached so quickly, in most instances, that the conclusions stated here are of less interest for those goods than for, say, broadcasting of weather reports and many other group-consumption collective-consumption goods, the level of which can be expanded greatly without encountering capacity limits.

Similarly, the optimum level of the service, for a collective-consumption good, tends to fall with a decline in population. Fewer persons must now divide among them an undiminished total cost. Again, if per capita income rises sufficiently, as it may if the emigrants are of low average income, the optimum level of the collective-consumption good may actually increase.

The expected value of degree of progress toward the Pareto-optimum level of the service will probably increase as the cost per capita of that level decreases; consumer surpluses increase, and each member of the group may devote less effort to enlarging his share of that surplus. This result can therefore occur under immigration, if the service is one of collective consumption. But immigration causes an increase in the number of households and firms who must reach agreement, and

concerned with a variety of special cases, based on particular restraints, which cannot be handled at the general level of the present work. Another part of that analysis suggests methods of placing money values on benefits that are distributed free of charge, a topic that is discussed in Chapters 2, 4, and 5 above. Those projects intended to sell at a price designed to cover cost fall outside the scope of public finance as defined in Chapter 1 above. For a general survey of the literature, see A. R. Prest and R. Turvey, "Cost-Benefit Analysis: A Survey," in American Economic Association and Royal Economic Society, *Survey of Economic Theory*, vol. 3, "Resource Allocation" (New York: St. Martin's, 1966).

such an increase may either increase or decrease the expected degree of progress toward a Pareto-optimum, since on the one hand it reduces the likelihood of deadlock due to bluffing and bargaining but on the other hand increases the scanning problem, as the number of legislators increases.

The decrease in per capita cost of a collective-consumption service that is caused by a household or a firm that moves into the area served is an effect external to this household or firm; it is an externality. So too is the increase in per capita cost that the firm or household causes to those remaining when it moves out of the area served. In deciding whether to move in, or leave, the single household or firm does not take account of the change in per capita cost to those others already in, or remaining in, the area. It will pay those initially in the area to offer prospective immigrants favorable tax treatment, thus compensating them for the favorable externality they cause. Those who threaten to leave may be given similar, favorable treatment to induce them not to create the negative externality. But these possibilities are but another aspect of the bluffing-bargaining process with respect to intra-marginal units of the service. The threatened withdrawal from the group of a particular household or firm takes the form of threatening to leave the area, or threatening not to enter it, thus placing itself beyond the taxing jurisdiction within which the service is rendered.

[2] Change in Area (Numbers Constant)

Up to this point, the geographical area within which the number of recipients increases or decreases has been assumed to remain unchanged. If, instead, the area changes but the number of recipients of the service remains unchanged, the total cost of rendering a given level of the collectively consumed service will normally change. If it increases, the Pareto-optimum level of the service decreases, and vice-versa, since per capita income is now postulated to remain unchanged. As indicated in Chapter 5, total cost probably rises, with area (population and level of service constant), for damage limitation; probably falls with area for deterrence, public health, and externalities from medical care; and is unchanged for the remaining type of collective-consumption group-consumption goods.

(2) Produced as Joint
Products with Marketable Good

The free distribution of education, refuse removal, sewerage, medical care, and cultural and recreational services cannot be justified on Pareto-optimum grounds (however justifiable it may be on other grounds) unless these direct services yield externalities, and in sufficient amount. These direct services, the education itself as distinct from the improved milieu resulting from education, for example, are quite marketable; exclusion of any selected individual or firm is easy, technically speaking. Moreover, these particular services are not collective-consumption goods, aside from certain recreational facilities, and so do not present to the market, as an optimal allocating mechanism, the difficulties that theatres, for example, do, because for theatres individual demand curves must be added vertically within capacity limits.[19] Subsidized goods are of course marketable, by definition of "subsidy."

The Wicksell principle of unanimity applies in determining the optimum level at which any one of these externalities, say the improved milieu from education, is to be supplied. But that principle does not apply in determining the optimum level of the direct service, say education, with which the externality is a joint product. It does not apply to the direct service because the direct service is marketable and is not a collective-consumption good. "Joint product" means here that the proportions in which the direct service and the externality can be produced are not alterable.

The Pareto-optimum level of the output of, say, education, is therefore to be ascertained by adding horizontally, for successive levels of education, the individual demand curves for education as such and adding vertically the individual demand curves for the associated level of the externalities. If the cost of the incremental unit of education and its associated increment of externality is less than the demand price for that incremental unit of education, found in the usual way by horizontal addition, plus the sum of the demand prices for the associated externality found by vertical addition, more of the direct service and its associated externality should be produced, until incremental cost equals incremental price as thus ascertained.

Goals other than a Pareto optimum, for example a certain redistribution of income in kind, will in practice cause the level of education offered to exceed the Pareto-optimum level just described. The conflict of interests arising from this redistribution goal creates a struggle over the proportions in which the cost of education shall be shared, and to this is added the struggle over the sharing of intra-marginal increments of the externality. The two struggles commonly embrace two different-sized groups. Normally, the group of persons benefiting from the improved milieu yielded by education will be a larger group, spread over a wider area, than the group within which the redistribution struggle occurs. Urban areas to which the rural young men and women migrate cannot afford to let rural levels of education be settled by the contest over redistribution of income in kind in those areas, along with whatever the persons there consider to be the value to them of the externalities of education. Accordingly, inhabitants of urban areas have been willing to help finance education in rural areas, usually through taxes paid to a common higher level of government, a state or province, or a central government. But no one urban area has much interest in proceeding alone to help finance education in a particular rural area or even in rural areas in general. Too small a fraction of the externalities created will accrue to the benefit of the residents of that particular urban area. The larger the number of urban areas that can reach agreement to work together, the more will each be willing to contribute toward the purchase of the externalities, up to a number such that the remaining urban areas have little or no chance of benefiting from the externality at all, perhaps because they are so unlikely to receive rural immigrants. Indeed, very few urban centers may show much interest in a country where the rural areas are so poor that the economic power to emigrate is lacking or where migration from rural areas is prohibited by a dictator or oligarchy.

19. See Chapter 4, Section A.2.

Negative externalities for the wealthy arise from education of the poor in those countries where the wealthy feel threatened by the transformation of an illiterate mass into educated individuals. Since the illiterate themselves will gain positive "milieu" externalities, as well as the direct benefit of being educated, two sets of conflicting externalities develop. A Pareto-optimum approach is not very instructive in these circumstances, but insofar as it is applied, it calls for the rich to pay the poor to reject education, down to the level of education so low that it would raise so little fear in the rich that they would not pay enough for a further decrement to match the positive externalities and direct benefits for the poor from that increment—all this, in the context of whatever had been decided under the redistribution aim.

Migrants from districts that have rendered a low level of, say, garbage and refuse removal do not embody the effects of those low levels as much as they do the effects of a low level of education. Moreover, with respect to those who do not migrate, the area that would gain an improved milieu from a higher level of garbage and refuse removal is a much smaller one than it is with respect to education: the neighborhood, perhaps, compared with an entire city or county. Similarly, in countries where the rich fear the influence of education on the poor, they fear much less the influence of an improved level of garbage and refuse removal. For these reasons, grants in aid for garbage and refuse removal are rarer, in any country, if indeed they exist at all, than for education, yet the level of garbage and refuse removal for the poor is perhaps not held down, in the kind of countries just noted, to as low a level as is education for the poor.

Certain marketable goods are offered by the government free, with no compulsion to accept them, in contrast to education and refuse removal. The most important are medical care (to be distinguished from public health) and cultural and recreational facilities. Positive externalities seem to be the only explanation for compelling acceptance of a service. Accordingly, externalities from medical care and recreation must be far weaker than those from education and garbage-refuse removal, except as absence of compulsion is explained by the greater difficulty of policing compulsory use of medical care and recreation.

Since the total cost of providing a certain level of the improved milieu that arises from any of these four services (education, garbage-refuse removal, medical care, culture and recreation), as distinguished from the cost of the services themselves, does not increase as the number of persons enjoying that milieu increases, the remarks in Section (c).[1] above apply to these externalities.

An increase in area alone, that is, dispersion of an unchanged number of households and firms, weakens the influence of the externalities, markedly so for the externalities associated with garbage and refuse removal, medical care, and recreation and culture, less so for those associated with education. A household's uncollected garbage is less offensive or dangerous to another household, the farther removed is the latter. Hence the Pareto-optimum level of the externality, and therefore of the direct service itself, tends to decrease with dispersion. Conversely, as density increases, number remaining unchanged, the Pareto-optimum levels of education and other marketable services that yield externalities increase.

B. INTRA-GROUP DISCRIMINATION FEASIBLE

Among collective-consumption goods that are also group-consumption goods, discrimination among subgroups is feasible only in a few instances. Television broadcasts have already been cited, if certain areas can be blocked out. Another possibility, in this missile age, is military output for damage limitation (see Chapter 5, Section A.1). The chief instances of intra-group discrimination occur with services that are not consumed collectively (for example, police protection), to which we now turn.

2. Group-Consumption Goods Not Consumed Collectively

For group-consumption goods that are not consumed collectively, an increase in the number of consumers of the service requires an increase in total input if the other consumers are not to suffer a decline in level of service. Police and fire protection are typical examples. In terms of Figure 1 in Chapter 4, these goods occupy the area ABJCKD, which, however, contains one empty box, ABJGKD, since there appears to be no instance of a non-collective-consumption group-consumption good that does not permit discrimination among subgroups. Discrimination down to the level of a selected household or firm is of course still not feasible, at least not to the point of providing none of the service at all. No goods in this category appear to be joint products with a marketable good.

The analysis to follow is therefore restricted to the one sub-category of services that are group-consumption goods not collectively consumed, capable of distribution in a discriminatory pattern among subgroups, and not linked as a joint product with a marketable good.

A. APPLICATION OF UNANIMITY PRINCIPLE

(1) Vertically Added Demand and Cost Curves

The total cost of a certain level of a group-consumption good that is not consumed collectively will increase, we have seen (Chapter 4, page 68) as the population in the area that is served increases. In this respect the good contrasts sharply with the collective-consumption case discussed in the immediately preceding Section (1). Now there is a positive marginal cost, not only with respect to the level of the service but also with respect to the number of persons served.

If a household moving into an area where a Wicksell margin has been reached for a certain service has a demand for the existing level of that service so strong that it more than covers the additional cost of supplying this household at that level, the group must reconvene and push the service to a higher level, following the pro-

cedures outlined in Chapter 4. If the new household's demand is so weak that it is
unwilling to cover the incremental cost it causes, the level of the service must be
reduced.

Figure 15, based on Figure 2, Chapter 4, illustrates how the Wicksell level of
service is ascertained by vertical addition of both demand and cost curves, when the

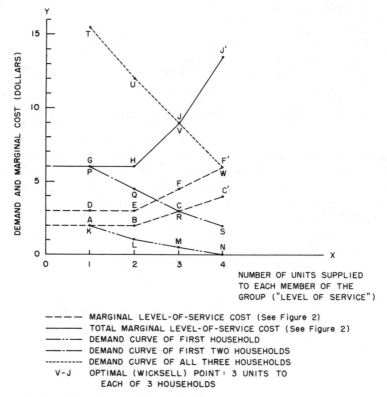

FIGURE 15. Optimal Level of a Group-Consumption Good That Is Not Consumed
Collectively

good is not a collective-consumption good. The three cost curves are reproduced
from Figure 2, and are extended to 4 units. Three demand curves are inserted and
added vertically. The optimal output is 3 units of the service, supplied to each of the
three households. As in Figure 2, the x-axis is distinguished from that of the ordinary
supply-demand diagram by being labeled "Number of units supplied to each
member of the group," instead of simply "Number of units supplied."

The externality created by the entry or departure of the single household or firm,
through its influence on per capita cost, is of the same nature as that discussed for
collective consumption goods in Section (1).(c).[1] above. The effect is weaker. The
per capita cost for the rest of the recipients falls with entry or rises with departure
by something less than that which occurs when average cost varies exactly in pro-

portion to the total number of recipients. And if the per capita cost rises with entry, and falls with departure, the change in that cost is still apt to be less than the reverse kind of change that occurs under collective consumption.

The effect that the incoming household or firm exerts on average per capita cost will in many instances vary with certain market expenditures that it makes. Fire protection provides an illustration. If the incoming household employs fire resistant materials in its dwelling, it reduces the conflagration hazard. It thereby lowers the average per capita cost that the government must finance to reach a certain level of protection from fire. The cost that the household undergoes in spending on fire-resistant materials therefore creates an externality.

To reach a Pareto optimum under these circumstances, this externality must be internalized in some way, perhaps by allowing the tax that is imposed to cover the cost of fire protection to vary inversely with the externality. Thus a real estate tax that finances fire protection might be lower on fire-resistant buildings, lower on properties built close to an existing fire house, lower on dwellings containing no dangerous space heaters, such as the kerosene space heater that is the mobile heating unit of the poor. Glass and steel skyscrapers would pay little or no real estate tax for fire protection. But this pattern of real estate taxation would be difficult to ascertain and to administer impartially. A local business tax would be even less adaptable for this pattern of variation; that tax fails to reach households at all except as they consume the goods produced by the taxed business or supply factors to it.

(2) Intra-group Discrimination

Figure 15 and the figures in Chapter 4 abstract from the possibility that the service can be rendered at different levels to subgroups within the economic or political group, as "group" is defined in Chapter 4. The unanimity principle might appear applicable, not to the group as a whole, but separately to each of the subgroups. Each of the subgroups would then decide on the level of service and the financing pattern to support it, if a Pareto-optimal level of service were the only goal in view. But this argument overlooks externalities created by one subgroup for another, just as a single household or firm creates externalities for the group. A decrease of 10 units in fire protection to sub-area A may pull down the level of protection to sub-area B by, say, 1 unit, if the input to sub-area B is unchanged, because of the increase in the conflagration hazard. For a Pareto optimum, the demand for fire protection to be accorded to a given subgroup must include some element of demand from the other subgroups, and their demands must be supported by a tax mechanism that will allow them to contribute.

At the other extreme, where the externalities are negligible, certain poor districts within a city may be, and in some countries are, entirely exempted from the real estate tax and in turn are provided with no services of certain types, for example street construction, street maintenance, and street lighting. This treatment is feasible because the political subgroup (the poor district) is an "economic group" as that is defined in Chapter 4 above, Section A.2. These points are developed further in the chapter below on intergovernmental fiscal coordination (Chapter 25).

In fact, these requirements for a Pareto optimum have been far from satisfied. This is so, first, because the subgroups are largely income or wealth classes, since the poor tend to live in one area, the rich in another. If each of these subgroups had to determine, itself, the level of fire protection it was willing to pay for, with some aid from other subgroups affected by interdependencies (e.g., conflagration hazard), a poor area would receive a low level of service, probably, while paying a high tax rate on property or income. The level of service would be low because the inhabitants are poor, the tax rates high because a substantial minimum level of service is so important to them. This pattern of service and tax rates would be politically unacceptable, usually. In the second place, the techniques of taxation cannot reach the level of refinement called for by the cost-causing activities of the individual household or firm.

Some group-consumption goods, highways for example,[20] can be offered to some subgroups and entirely denied to others, not according to where the members of these subgroups live or work, but according to what they buy on the market: motor fuel and motor vehicles, in this case. User taxes on motor fuel or motor vehicles are rough instruments designed to allocate resources according to subgroup demands with little or no disturbance to the existing distribution of disposable income. In practice, motor vehicle user taxes fail to match incremental cost caused with increments in tax payable, though not by so wide a margin as the real estate tax with respect to fire and police protection. The motorist or trucker pays the same gasoline tax whether he travels on a rough, narrow, curving road or on a modern highway. Since his mileage per gallon of fuel is less on the former road, he pays more, per mile traveled, on the road that is cheaper per lane-mile to construct, though it may not be cheaper per vehicle mile, given a heavy use of the modern highway.

Taxes that increase with weight of vehicle are useful in approaching the optimum, since the roads that bear greater loads are more costly to construct, if not to maintain.

B. EFFECT ON OPTIMUM LEVEL, AND ON EXPECTED PROGRESS
TOWARD THAT LEVEL, OF CHANGES IN NUMBERS AND AREA SERVED

(1) Change in Numbers (Area Constant)

For a group-consumption good that does not permit collective consumption, protection from crime, for example, we have seen that more persons to serve means an increase in total cost. If total cost increases faster than does population, that is, if cost increases with density, as it may with traffic control for example, the optimum level of the service per person will fall unless per capita income increases sufficiently. Meanwhile the optimum input per person is of course rising, and if input is mistakenly taken for output, the level of service will mistakenly be described as rising

20. Although price exclusion can be applied to some highways, it cannot be applied to the entire highway network, not at least at a tolerable cost (see Chapter 5, Section B.8.A).

with density. By the same reasoning, an outflow of population may increase the optimum level of service per person, if the average cost of supplying a certain level of service per person declines, for an increasing-cost service.

Downward pressure on the Pareto-optimum level of service per person will be greatest if population increases because of an excess of births over deaths. The community's total economic resources are not increased, as they are by immigration of entire families or, still more, of men and women of working age. The increased number of children and old people supply no additional economic resources immediately, while adding to the demands on the unchanged amount of resources. Unless the (non-collective-consumption) group-consumption good is especially designed for those age groups, the Pareto-optimum level per person will almost surely decline as population increases.

The expected degree of progress toward the optimal frontier is probably reduced if, with an increase in population, total cost rises more than in proportion to the increase in community income; there is less consumer surplus to distribute, and so a greater chance that deadlocks will occur through bargaining and bluffing, by the legislators.

(2) Change in Area (Numbers Constant)

As to the five major group-consumption goods not collectively consumed that have been described in Chapter 5, total cost probably rises for three of them when area served increases, while numbers served and level of service remain unchanged: police protection, streets, and flood control and drainage. Since income per capita is unchanged, the optimum level of these services will correspondingly fall as area increases. The opposite result occurs for highways, while fire protection cost for a given level of service first falls, then rises, as area increases (see Chapter 5, Section E).

3. Group-Consumption Externalities from Welfare Payments

Welfare payments can be discussed in Pareto-optimum terms only as they give rise to externalities, but the externalities they create are very general in nature: preservation of the fabric of society, satisfaction of motives of compassion, and so on. Those who are asked to pay, and receive nothing in return but these externalities, probably reach their Wicksell margin far short of the levels that welfare payments have in fact attained; the chief explanations for welfare payments are to be found elsewhere (see Chapter 23).

These externalities are more intensely felt as area decreases (population remaining the same), since exposure to the unrest of others is thereby more immediate. A country largely urbanized is consequently apt to possess a larger welfare-payment system than one chiefly rural, and not just because a rural population may be more self-supporting in periods of depressed business, in old age, or when weak in mind or body.

4. Geographical Grouping by Preference Patterns

If each of a number of groups, as "group" is defined for a group-consumption good, contains a mixture of households with varying preferences for the group-consumption goods in question, everyone can be made better off without making anyone else worse off by migration within the groups so that each group consists of those with similar preferences. At least this is so if all households have about the same income and property. In a heterogeneous group, those whose demand for joint-consumption good g_1 is strong and for g_2 weak will lose much of their consumer surplus on the intra-marginal units of good g_1 as they bargain with the others, whose demand for g_1 is weak (and strong for g_2). The Wicksell margin of g_1 will be reached at a low level of g_1, since even those whose tastes run to g_1 must spend so much to obtain the intra-marginal units. Similarly, those who favor g_2 pay heavily for it and reach a Wicksell margin for g_2 at a low level of g_2. If this state of affairs characterizes two groups, A and B, say two communities, emigration from Group A of those who prefer g_1 and immigration into A of those who prefer g_2 will result in a higher level of production of g_2 in A and a higher level of production of g_1 in B. Both those who prefer g_1 and those who prefer g_2 will be better off than before; if movement between the groups is costless, the two groups will become homogeneous.

If the two groups are merged into one large group, the difficulties encountered in the two smaller heterogeneous groups are duplicated in the single larger group, since it is of the same pattern, if the two small groups were similarly heterogeneous. And the option of migration from one of the groups to the other will have been removed.

This geographical choice available to consumers of government services, first analyzed by Tiebout,[21] reduces the probability of a deadlock short of the Wicksell margin, but of course does not eliminate it. A group of equal-income households with identical preference patterns for, say, public health, and private-sector goods will still face a bargaining-bluffing problem on the intra-marginal units.

If differences in incomes are taken into account, an unstable geographical pattern will result. Poor households will move to rich districts, so that they can get the same government services at lower tax rates than they must pay if they alone constitute a group, whereupon the wealthy, whose taxes now rise as they must help supply services to the poor, move elsewhere.

21. Charles M. Tiebout, "A Pure Theory of Local Expenditures," *Journal of Political Economy* (October, 1956), 64: 416–24, and "An Economic Theory of Fiscal Decentralization," in National Bureau of Economic Research, *Public Finances: Needs, Sources and Utilization* (Princeton, N.J.: Princeton University Press, 1961). For a critical evaluation of local tax autonomy, see Harvey E. Brazer, "Some Fiscal Implications of Metropolitanism," in Guthrie S. Birkhead, ed., *Metropolitan Issues* (Syracuse, N.Y.: Syracuse University, 1962), pp. 71–82.

B. COLLECTIVE-CONSUMPTION
GOODS THAT ARE MARKETABLE

Theatre performances, bridges, occasional toll roads (but not a complete highway network), and the like require, we have seen, vertical addition of demand curves, to ascertain a Pareto-efficient level of the service to be supplied within the capacity limits of the theater, bridge, road, etc.

In the theater, the quality of the performance, insofar as that quality varies directly with the cost, is to be determined by vertical addition, and so too is the quantity dispensed in terms of units of time (how much will the audience pay for, say, a half-hour increment?). For the bridge, the quality of the service may be almost frozen into the structural characteristics of the bridge, and the cost of another time unit of use, for example, keeping the bridge open all night, may be slight, so that in practice there is little vertical addition of demand curves to be done, once the bridge has been constructed and opened. The charge for using the bridge will have been determined in the planning stage, before the capacity and quality were frozen, and at that stage demand curves are in general added horizontally, since, above a certain minimum size dictated by technology, service to another user adds to the total cost; consumption is not collective. So too with the theater building, as distinct from the quality and length of performance within the theater once it is built.

If competition among private enterprises is appreciably imperfect because of the lumpiness of product that is implied by the need to add demand curves vertically, there is an argument, on Pareto-optimum grounds, for the government to supply these collective-consumption but marketable services. In practice, this argument seems to carry little weight. Where governments do operate theaters, they do so, it appears, because of cultural externalities, and when they operate toll bridges and toll highways they do so largely because they connect with free highways supplied by the government.

C. MARKETABLE GOODS YIELDING EXTERNALITIES

1. Positive Externalities

Marketable goods yielding positive externalities are sometimes distributed free of charge by the government, though rarely if ever only because of the externalities. This case has been discussed above, with reference to education, garbage-refuse removal, medical care, and recreational and cultural facilities. When private enterprise markets this or similiar services its output will fall short of a Pareto-optimum unless the government subsidizes the industry.

In principle the unanimity rule should be followed to determine how large, per unit of private-sector output, the subsidy should be. In practice the optimum subsidy is even more difficult to ascertain, because of the greater difficulty that the beneficiaries of the externality face in valuing it, that is, in computing their demand schedules. Most subsidies are supported on the most general of externalities, which are often only contingent: sugar beet subsidies, for example, to prevent disruption of supply in the event of war; merchant marine subsidies designed to facilitate prosecution of some future war; passenger aircraft subsidies to bolster national prestige.

2. Negative Externalities

Negative externalities from privately marketed goods have almost universally been limited, if at all, by direct regulation of amount and technique of production of the good giving rise to the externalities. Pareto-efficient tax-subsidy devices to cope with air pollution and water pollution are currently only in the discussion stage. If the externality is non-separable, that is, if it affects the marginal cost of producing, or the marginal benefit from consuming, another good, instead of being a lump-sum externality (from the viewpoint of the recipient), the principle of efficient allocation requires the following procedure. A tax is to be levied on the marketable output of the private firm or on the consumption of the individual that causes the externality, at a rate such that, at the reduced level of production or consumption under the tax, as determined by the demand and cost functions for the marketable good or the consumed good, the tax on a marginal unit of output or consumption is enough when paid over to the sufferers (themselves either producers or consumers) from the externality, or when spent on repair or abatement to correct or forestall the damage, to compensate them for, or to obviate, the harm associated with the increment of externality.[22]

This last amount measures the damage, at the margin, that the negative externality is causing. Ideally, the tax revenue on the marginal unit produced would be paid to the sufferers; in practice, however, the costs of measuring and evaluating the suffering of individuals or costs of firms affected may preclude such payment even

22. This general statement of principle conceals a number of difficulties in implementing the tax-subsidy approach, including the issue of which party is to be taxed and which subsidized (which one is responsible for the misallocation of resources?), and the problem of how much information will be needed to determine the appropriate rate of tax or subsidy and whether the information can be obtained only with so much inquiry by the government into each firm's cost functions, etc., that the tax subsidy as a market internalizer of externalities turns out to be instead a direct-control mechanism. In any event, as with virtually all of the goals discussed in Chapters 21–24, public finance measures are not the only ones available. Externalities may be handled more or less well, according to one's point of view, by "Bargaining, . . . merger, re-definition of property rights (and sometimes the establishment of property rights), constraints of the zoning type, the establishment of certain 'standards' and . . . centralized directives." Otto A. Davis and Andrew B. Whinston, "On Externalities, Information and the Government-Assisted Invisible Hand," *Economica* (August, 1966), 33: 303–4. For a recent discussion of the issues, see Stanislaw Wellisz, "On External Diseconomies and the Government-Assisted Invisible Hand," *Economica* (November, 1964), 31: 375–62; Davis and Whinston, *loc. cit.*; and the references cited in these two articles.

though good estimates of aggregate diseconomies may cost relatively little to make. On the infra-marginal units of production, the negative externalities would presumably be smaller per unit, and only a portion of the tax on the infra-marginal units would need to be paid to those disadvantaged by the externalities. The remainder of the tax would serve the general purpose of repressing private demand to release resources for government use.

Since these negative externalities are always linked with the production of a particular commodity or service, not with production in general, no broad-scope tax like a general sales tax is useful for this purpose. The tax must be an excise tax or a tax on certain factor mixes, if there are other mixes that permit production with a lower level of the externality.

Although the taxes on addictives reduce the volume of negative externalities somewhat, this achievement, we have seen (Chapter 10, Sections A.1 and A.3), is only a subsidiary goal, as evidenced by the refusal to move tax rates beyond the maximum revenue point. The most likely candidates for excise taxation justified chiefly on grounds of negative externalities are air pollution and traffic congestion.[23] Even in these instances, however, taxation must compete with direct prohibition as a means of regulation, just as, in the opposite instance, a subsidy must compete with free distribution by the government. The case for control rather than taxation depends on whether the government faces financial temptation, if it employs taxation, and whether it can resist temptation. If the socially optimum level of consumption of the commodity is higher than that level of consumption that maximizes revenue from the excise tax, the financial temptation is that of raising the tax rate beyond the socially optimum level, thus reducing consumption too much, a temptation that is relatively easy to resist politically speaking. But if the socially optimum level of consumption is lower than that at which tax revenue is a maximum, the government must raise the tax rate beyond the point of maximum revenue, and the temptation not to press as hard as this is difficult to withstand politically. Gambling, which probably illustrates the second case, may well be encouraged by the government far beyond the level that would be permitted under direct control in which the government had no financial stake.[24]

Even if the regulatory level is on the high-consumption side of the maximum-revenue level of consumption, the results are not likely to be satisfactory, since this regulatory level is itself only a total, which will doubtless mask a degree of regulation that is more than sufficient with respect to the poor, and less than sufficient with respect to the rich. A tax of 20 cents per pack of cigarettes may be enough to force the poor consumer down to a level of consumption that virtually eliminates the danger from lung cancer, but for a middle-income group the rate might have to be

23. For the theorem that an optimal congestion charge (optimal toll) will be just enough to cover the capital cost of the optimal amount of investment in the highway, given constant costs with respect to both capacity and number of trips, see O. H. Brownlee, "Optimal Expenditure for Highways," Institut International de Finances Publiques, *Efficiency in Government Spending* (Saarbrücken: Institut International de Finances Publiques, 1967), pp. 98–104.

24. New York State horses now get only two weeks off each year instead of three or four months as formerly, thanks largely to the appetite of the state's fisc.

$2.00 a pack, while for the wealthy no administrable tax rate would be high enough.

If the industry is privately monopolized, maximum revenue from a unit tax will be less than the revenue from a tax of 100 per cent on the private monopolist's profit. If maximum revenue is sought from a monopoly industry, there is accordingly a strong case for government ownership.[25]

Where the addictive is easily rationed, as by queuing, the government can monopolize and dispense any desired amount at a price that just covers its cost of operation. Gambling at race tracks can thus be rationed by setting the number of races and the number of windows. A government lottery could be run on a cost basis, at whatever level the regulatory criterion might dictate. Government liquor stores, open only at certain hours or on certain days, provide another form of non-price rationing that allows the government to clear the market at a price where demand would exceed supply and so generate monopoly profits in a private enterprise.

D. MARKETABLE GOODS
AND OTHER MARKET IMPERFECTIONS

1. Imperfect Competition

Since production under imperfect competition falls short of the point where the rate of transformation equals the rate of substitution for the consumer, and therefore is not at a Pareto-optimum level, at least for volume (if not for variety), per-unit subsidies to increase output have been suggested. If the imperfect competition is of a kind that gives rise to excess profits, distributive criteria may suggest lump-sum taxes on the subsidized producers. Instead of a subsidy, there might be employed, to stimulate output, a tax the marginal rate of which decreases as output increases.[26] In practice, no such fiscal devices seem ever to have been used. The public would probably misunderstand the aim of the subsidy. The lump-sum tax might need to be readjusted so often that it would exert the very substitution effect it is designed to avert. The degressive tax on output is a newly formulated instrument that seems somewhat more practicable than the subsidy-lump sum tax combination.

In a second-best world, expansion of imperfect competitors' outputs may or may not be capable of making some persons better off without making anyone (except the monopolists themselves) worse off (and they could be compensated), but this uncertainty does not explain the absence of the devices just described.

25. See Chapter 10, Section B, for further discussion of this point.

26. This possibility, suggested by Ned Shilling, is analyzed intensively in his forthcoming book, *Economic Effects of Excise Taxes* (New York: Columbia University Press, 1969).

2. Increasing Returns for an Industry

If an atomistically competitive industry faces decreasing industry-wide costs, which can be obtained only if all firms increase output simultaneously, a subsidy can in principle improve the allocation of resources in the Pareto sense. Perhaps because of the difficulty of identifying such an industry, or the small magnitude of the effect where it exists, no subsidy seems ever to have been paid on these grounds.

CHAPTER TWENTY-TWO

Full Employment and Capacity Utilization

A. THE GOALS

THE GOALS DISCUSSED in this chapter are full employment of labor and full utilization of plant and equipment, as defined in Chapter 2. For brevity, these two goals will be covered by the single phrase, full employment. The fact that they may not always be attained simultaneously will be taken into account in Section E below.

The goal of price stability is discussed separately in Chapter 24, for, in contrast to full employment, it reflects a conflict of interests. But since most of the measures described in the present chapter to stimulate employment can be used, in reverse, to avert a rise in prices, the explicit analysis in Chapter 24 can be correspondingly restricted. The term "counter-cycle policy" and occasional mention of business booms in the present chapter testify to the convenience of discussing in one place the mechanics of achieving full employment and price stability, even though they represent quite different social issues.

Although the term "stabilization" suggests a static economy, the problem in practice is one of assuring employment to a growing labor force and utilization of an increasing stock of capital goods. Comparative statics must therefore be complemented by at least a simple type of dynamic analysis, and degree of failure to achieve the goal must be measured by cumulative unemployment over time.

The goal of full employment must be distinguished from that of economic growth, which differs from full employment, as does price stability, in that it reflects a conflict of interests. Growth policy determines what proportion of the total full employment output shall be devoted to capital formation in the broadest sense; full employment simply implies full utilization of whatever resources are available at the time, regardless of the disposition of the output between capital goods and consumer goods. It will be convenient, for purposes of the present chapter, to assume that the proportion of output devoted to capital goods is such that total income grows at a rate given by population growth and technical progress.

B. PUBLIC FINANCE INSTRUMENTS

1. Changes in Disposable Incomes

Fiscal policy for full employment is implemented either (1) by changing the disposable real incomes of households and firms, or (2) by changing the prices of assets, usually financial assets, that households and firms hold.

Tax rates and formulae for transfer payments are direct instruments for changing disposable incomes, in two senses. A change in the rates or formulae alters disposable incomes immediately. It also alters the endogenous rate of fluctuation of disposable income as national income fluctuates, since tax revenue and volume of transfer payments fluctuate endogenously with the national income. The degree to which they fluctuate depends on the amount of "flexibility" that has been "built into" them by choice of a particular structure of rates, levels of exemptions, and the like. The rate structure, exemption levels, and similar features are thus direct instruments of policy, and the changes in flexibility or sensitivity resulting from a change in these direct instruments may be regarded as changes in mediums, as defined in Chapter 19 above.

Disposable real income includes the free services rendered to households or firms by government. This income goes to those who use the free service or to those whose money incomes increase when the benefit of the service is relinquished to them through the play of market forces (see Chapter 4). If the recipient of the free service is not forced to relinquish the benefit and if he attaches some value to the service, so that he considers that his real disposable income has been increased, he may be expected to save part of this increment in income, according to his marginal propensity to save. But he cannot save part of the free-service income itself; that income must be consumed as it is received. The increment in saving will therefore come out of his unchanged money income, which is to say, his money expenditure on consumption will decline. If his marginal propensity to save is 10 per cent and if a government service costing the government $100 is valued by the recipient at, say, $60, the income effect of this $60 will induce him to cut back his money expenditure by $6. Of course he does not usually trouble to place, consciously, a specific money value on the free service, but he may be expected to act as if he did.

The gap between the $100 cost to the government and the $60 value implicitly placed on the service by the recipient in this illustration reflects an imperfect substitutability of the free service for any of the goods and services the recipient is already purchasing, or, what comes to the same thing, imperfect substitutability for things the recipient would purchase if he were given $100 in cash. If the free government good were, say, free meals costing $100 of a type the recipient is already purchasing for $100, he would decrease his money spending by 10 per cent of $100, not 10 per cent of $60. He could be viewed as reducing his expenditure on meals, tentatively by $100, and using $90 of this $100 to spend on a variety of consumer goods, including even a little on supplements to the government's free meals.[1]

Business firms, also, may be expected to show income effects from the receipt of free government services. The effects tend to be passed on to consumers in lower prices or to factors in higher rewards, so that the results may again be analyzed in terms of an increase in households' real disposable income. But there may be a significant consequence for private investment spending, as when the government supplies certain infrastructure free of charge.

Some basic theorems in fiscal policy must be modified when these income effects of free government services are taken into account. Among them is the balanced budget multiplier theorem. If an increment of government free service, financed wholly by an increment of taxation, is valued by the recipient at its cost to the government, and if the marginal propensity to save is everywhere the same, whether income is entirely in money or partly in money and partly in free government services for consumers, it can be shown that an increment of a government service financed wholly by taxation will result in no change in national income, under the usual assumptions of the balanced-budget theorem, notably the assumption that private investment remains unchanged. Thus if the government increases the tax bill by $100, and spends $100 on goods and services to supply a free service to households, and if the recipient households consider that their real disposable income has been thereby increased by $100, national income will remain unchanged, in place of rising by $100. If the marginal propensity to save is 10 per cent, the recipient households reduce their money spending on consumer goods by $10. The taxpayers reduce their money spending by $90. Total private-sector spending is reduced by the same amount by which government spending is increased. It is as if government were an integral part of the private sector, which had simply changed the pattern of its expenditure. If taxpayers and recipients are the same persons, they in effect spend $100 less on some marketed goods and $100 more on government-supplied services.[2]

Changing the disposable real incomes of the community for counter-cycle purposes raises an important social issue, namely, whether households with relatively low incomes should be required to participate in that policy in periods of boom, and, if not, what this decision implies for periods of recession. Family budget planning at these levels can be seriously disrupted by small percentage changes in disposable income. To be sure, the very tightness of their budgets makes them quite responsive to counter-cycle tax rate changes, since they have little or no slack in the way of non-contractual saving, and few liquid assets. But the corresponding hardship when the tax rate is increased may be considered greater than the benefit conferred by the recession-period decrease in tax rate. On balance, therefore, it may be decided, as a matter of distributive equity, to place the extremely low-income households outside the counter-cycle program. They will then receive no tax reduction in recessions but in return will experience no increased tax as full employment is approached. This is

---

1. See the analysis of indirect rejection of a government service, Chapter 4, Section F and Appendix C, and the references to indirect rejection in the discussion of the various government services in Chapter 5.

2. See Appendix A to this chapter.

the view taken here, but those who differ can readily adjust for that fact in the following appraisals of alternative fiscal instruments for stabilization.

The choice between an increase in government expenditures on free services and a decrease in taxes or an increase in transfer payments, to regain full employment rests on several considerations.

In Chapter 5 we saw that a counter-cycle variation in the level of service will be regarded by the recipients of the service as capricious if not unfair with respect to contract enforcement and other civil rights, fire protection, police protection, street supply, education, and medical care. Contracyclical variation in level of service would be inimical to achievement of the goals set for military outputs, exploration of space, and sewerage and garbage and refuse disposal. Indeed, there will be pressure to vary the level of services cyclically, not contracyclically, with respect to street supply and sewerage. Only in the supply of highways, flood control and drainage, and cultural and recreational facilities can the flow of service be varied appreciably from depression to boom without undue impairment of the program.

On the other hand, we have seen also that the level of input can be varied to some extent without affecting the level of output when the service is rendered with the aid of capital goods or large inventories. Limited changes in the timing of construction projects and changes in stockpiles or other inventories can be made without disturbing appreciably the current level of some military services, supply of highways (but not streets), garbage and refuse disposal, certain cultural and recreational outputs, and possibly, to a minor degree, medical care.

But even when the timing of the capital inputs can be varied without disrupting the normal flow of service, there remains the problem of accurate timing. On large projects there are long lags from decision to bids to contracts to on-site activity, and from the beginning of on-site activity to peaking and ending. Recessions and recoveries cannot yet be forecast far enough ahead to allow these public works or inventory build-ups to be very effective counter-recession instruments.

In summary, government expenditures incurred to supply free services offer little possibility of contracyclical timing accurate enough to avoid interfering seriously with the programs. For prolonged depressions resulting from secular forces, the retiming of expansion of public works programs may prove more suitable.

The present analysis does not cover those government enterprises where output is normally sold at market prices that roughly cover cost (see Chapter 1). Government steel mills, coal mines, chemical works, reclamation projects, and some railway, shipping, and air transport activities presumably afford a possibility of counter-cycle variation of inputs if not of outputs.

The welfare type of transfer payments cannot be varied in a counter-cycle manner, or indeed in any other way, at the discretion of the executive or the legislature without impairing the aims of the programs. A positive built-in flexibility is substantial in some of the programs, notably unemployment insurance (where still more flexibility could be built in to many of the systems), resource-conditioned benefits, and assistance payments, and to a minor degree for old-age benefits.

Subsidies to private enterprises commonly show a perverse built-in flexibility.

Where the subsidy takes the form of an intentional deficit of a government enterprise, notably the post office in many countries, this perverseness can be avoided and indeed the subsidy can be increased by increasing the level of service in a recession.

The discussion of the several taxes in Chapters 8 to 16 has indicated that among them only the income tax and the general sales tax in any of its many forms are suitable and powerful enough for tax rate variation designed to maintain full employment. A third, hypothetical, instrument is a broad-based expenditure tax collected from households.

The income tax, it will be recalled, affords more alternatives in distributing the burdens and benefits of a counter-cycle tax policy, especially in allowing very low income families to remain unaffected by that policy. But this advantage implies dispute and hence delay in formulating and implementing changes. Administratively, too, the change in income tax rates is somewhat more difficult.

These considerations are, however, secondary to the basic question, Under which tax will the policy be most effective? The answer lies in the extent to which the taxpayer anticipates changes in tax rates and the degree to which his anticipations are correct. ·

The following analysis will be in terms of a decrease in tax rates to reduce unemployment, but, with appropriate modifications, the reasoning can of course be applied to tax rate increases designed to maintain price stability. It is implied that the differential incidence of the sales tax as against the income tax is on consumers rather than on factor owners.

If households anticipate correctly the amount and duration of a reduction in the rate of a sales tax, they will revise their time patterns of consumption under the influence of the substitution effect and the income effect of this tax reduction. The substitution effect will induce them to move some of their consumption, in real terms, from the periods before and after the period when the tax reduction is to be in effect, into that period, because the price of consumption then will be lower than before or after.

But the tax reduction also has an income effect; it increases their total consumption, and they will normally move some of that increase of consumption from the tax-reduction period, where it originates, into the periods before and after the tax-reduction period. They lose some aggregate consumption in doing so, since goods cost more in those before- and after-periods, but this fact will not deter them completely. Especially those who have no intrinsic time preference will sacrifice some aggregate consumption over a series of periods in order to achieve a more nearly level flow of consumption. The income effect of the temporary reduction in sales tax rate will therefore be unlike the substitution effect, in that it will tend to increase money spending on consumption in the periods before and after the tax reduction, compared with what that spending would have been if there were no tax reduction but they had the same factor incomes (an inadmissible hypothesis macroeconomically, to be sure). This is not the effect desired by counter-cycle policy; indeed, if the first period lies in part in an inflationary setting, those who desire price stability (Chapter 24) will be vexed by the anticipatory income effect of a correctly foreseen tax reduction designed to check a forthcoming recession. There will of course remain some increase in consumption spending in the tax-reduction period due to the income effect of the tax reduction, an increase, that is, compared with what would obtain if the tax rate were not reduced.

How much spending is diverted from the tax-reduction period by the income effect of that reduction is a subject for conjecture, but no answer to this question is needed in order to compare the sales tax with the income tax in this context. The income tax reduction exerts only an income effect, or almost so. The only substitution effect of that reduction is an increase in the rate of interest obtainable by a creditor from a given rate of debtor interest. Since the increase will be in effect only for a few months or a year or two, it will be of negligible influence. The correctly anticipated income tax reduction will therefore increase money spending more in the periods before and after the tax reduction period than will the correctly anticipated sales tax reduction, which indeed may on balance decrease spending in those periods owing to its substitution effect. The sales tax is the more suitable instrument, in this kind of a world.

Under either type of tax reduction low-income families with few assets and little access to credit will find it difficult to spend their increased disposable real income before it reaches them and may have a time preference so high that the amount of spending they move to the period following that of tax reduction will be small. High-income families may shift only their pattern of saving, more or less automatically. Countries with a low per capita income, especially where income is concentrated in the poor and the very rich, and where installment credit or charge account credit are not available to the poor, will therefore find that the income tax or sales tax rate can be reduced without losing much of the increased consumer spending to an earlier period, where it is not needed (all this, of course, under correct anticipation by households).

The households' anticipation of the substitution effect of the change in sales tax rate may not in practice be as entirely favorable to contracyclical policy as the remarks above suggest. If the authorities delay at all in reducing the tax rate when a recession threatens, the pre-tax-reduction period will include a span of time when no reduction in spending is desired, yet the substitution effect generated by correct anticipation on the part of the households as to what the authorities will in fact do will indeed reduce spending. And such a reduction in this setting will be considered perverse. On this point alone, the sales tax suffers as a counter-cycle instrument compared with the income tax. The perverse anticipation reaction can indeed be dangerous if the authorities repeatedly promise tax reduction but repeatedly refuse to act. It is a nice question whether more damage will be done if the households then correctly anticipate the policy-makers' actions or are instead repeatedly deceived by their promises; probably the latter is the more dangerous.

In fact, of course, no one can anticipate correctly the size or extent of contracyclical tax reductions. At the extreme, where no correct anticipation is possible, that is, where any anticipation is no more than predicting the toss of a single coin, there can be no substitution effect under the sales tax reduction, since the consumer never has an opportunity to choose between high-price and (tax-reduction) low-price periods of consumption. And the income effect of the tax reduction will be concentrated in the period of tax reduction; the consumer will not have had any reason to increase his consumption spending in the earlier period, given the assumption of no correct anticipation being possible, and he will have no motive for postponing part of the use of his potential consumption increment, since he does not know whether the coming period will be one of greater or smaller potential consumption. Now the income tax is at no disadvantage vis-à-vis the sales tax; both exercise only an income effect, one moreover that will be exercised in full, in either case, in the period of tax reduction. And the sales tax cannot give rise to perverse anticipatory reactions.

The real world lies in between these extremes. The ability to anticipate tax rate changes correctly will be the less, the less experienced are the households in contra-cyclical policy, and the longer and less frequent are the periods for which and when the tax rate is reduced. If the income tax is favored on other grounds (e.g., ability to leave poor households undisturbed by the program) it may be thought better suited as an instrument to maintain full employment under conditions that call for infrequent, substantial, long-period changes designed to adapt the community's disposable income to the exigencies of a conventional war, or to a seemingly secular change in the investment spending or consumer spending functions, or to a steadily growing full-employment surplus in the government budget,[3] than it is when the changes must be frequent, minor, and short-lived. And the income tax will fare better in the earlier years or decades of a counter-cycle policy, when households have had little practice in readjusting their consumption time patterns, than in later years. The sales tax, on the other hand, will do better as a counter-cycle instrument, the more familiar households become with this use of it—apart from the possibly perverse anticipatory reaction to the substitution effect. But this reaction is a side effect inherent in the substitution effect and can be minimized only by prompt implementation of policy that is desirable in any event.

2. Changes in Prices of Assets

The second method of implementing a public finance policy for full employment, changing the prices of assets, alters the net worth of those who already hold such assets. By doing so it gives rise to income effects, if income is defined broadly as increase in net worth plus consumption. These income effects might have been included above, under "changes in disposable income." It is useful, however, to distinguish the two income effects by excluding from "change in disposable income" an alteration in net worth brought about by a change in the price of an asset. The

3. A "full-employment surplus" is usually computed, in a year of less than full employment, by comparing the current level of government spending with the amount of revenue that the existing tax structure (existing rates, exemptions, and the like) would yield if the economy were at full employment. The surplus under this reckoning may be larger than any likely excess of investment over private saving, thus (disregarding foreign transactions) indicating an impossibility of reaching full employment under the existing tax structure.

reason for distinguishing them is that in the one case the individual household or firm does, and in the other case does not, regard its own participation in the government's program as something that in itself alters its income or net worth. The response of the household or firm to the government's offer to purchase or sell a security is a voluntary response, and it is the response of a price-taker, not that of a price-maker.

The assets, the prices of which are altered by government intervention in the asset markets, include both financial assets and real assets, for example, farm products and real estate.

Financial assets, for fiscal policy purposes, are principally domestic money, consisting of currency or coin and bank deposits, government obligations, and foreign exchange. They also include on occasion household and business-firm obligations and equity interests: home mortgages, student loans, commercial bills, debentures, bonds, household equity in homes and cars, shares of corporate stock, ownership and creditor interests in financial intermediaries, and so on. A single household that is both a creditor or owner on some accounts and a debtor on other accounts must net out the results for it of changes in prices of financial assets induced by fiscal policy before it can discern whether its net worth has increased or decreased.

Although governments and central banks commonly restrict their dealings in financial assets to domestic money, government obligations or foreign exchange in their efforts to assure full employment, this goal implies, in principle, possible intervention in markets for all types of financial assets, including the stock market.[4]

If all households and firms anticipate correctly the government's offers to purchase financial assets, even if some time well into the future, the prices of those assets will rise at once to the full amount, less time discount, and the income effect is felt at once, well in advance of action by the government. The rate of interest falls at once, and the stimulative action takes effect at once, perhaps indeed considerably earlier than the government desires. This state of affairs contrasts in two ways with that which obtains when everyone anticipates that the government will decrease a sales tax rate, to stimulate employment. First, under the sales tax decrease the reaction cannot be as strong, since for most households and firms current purchasing cannot depart very far from a normal level. Second, a part of the immediate reaction to a prospective sales tax decrease is, we have seen, depressant rather than stimulative. Correct anticipation of the government's financial-assets policy for stimulating the economy therefore does not provoke a perverse reaction temporarily, but it may speed up the desired reaction to an undesired extent. Similar conclusions apply with respect to repressive actions.

4. Earl R. Rolph, in "Debt-Management: Some Theoretical Aspects," *Public Finance* (1961), 16(1): 105–120, emphasizes the role of asset-price changes in fiscal policy, extending the analysis to assets in general; a restrictive policy, whereby a central bank sells title to real assets, is equivalent to a wealth tax (*ibid.*, p. 115). The need for thus broadening the analysis beyond the traditional area of government obligations has been demonstrated by practice. The Japanese government bought heavily in the stock market a few years ago, in an attempt to limit the decline in share prices and promote recovery. The Bank of England routinely purchases and sells commercial bills.

C. SCOPE AND LIMITATIONS OF PUBLIC FINANCE INSTRUMENTS IN A DYNAMIC, OPEN, GROWING ECONOMY

Maintenance of, or prompt return to, full employment must in practice involve the use of many instruments, including some that are not covered in the present work, for example, strictly monetary instruments, exemplified by changes in required member bank reserves, or in the central bank discount rate. Perhaps in principle it could be demonstrated that public finance instruments alone, if they are understood to include governmental purchase and sale of financial assets, could do the job. In practice, constraints on acceptable values of the public finance instruments (see Chapter 19) will induce the policy-maker to utilize non-public finance instruments also. The relative role to be played by public finance instruments can be ascertained only in a comprehensive analysis of business fluctuations, a task of course not attempted here. The remainder of this chapter undertakes the more modest task of suggesting, with elementary illustrations, the directions in which analysis of the effects of public finance instruments may perhaps most fruitfully proceed, now that the static framework of Keynesian analysis has at the very least persuaded most policy-makers[5] not to repeat the mistakes of earlier decades when a business recession was thought to call for an increase in tax rates and a decrease in government expenditures in order to balance the budget.

Keynesian analysis has of course done more than this, by inducing positive action in the other direction, but the amount and timing of such action and the choice between alternative mixes of instruments remain essentially unsolved problems. They remain so chiefly because the static, closed-economy framework of Keynesian analysis needs to be supplemented by analysis—into which public finance instruments can be fitted—of an economy that is dynamic, open, and growing. The analysis needs to be dynamic in the sense that the value of at least one of the variables in the system is related to a rate of change over time in the value of some other variable, and also in the sense that lags are assumed (disequilibrium models).[6] The analysis needs to be in terms of an open economy if it is not to be dangerously misleading to policy-makers in small countries heavily committed to foreign trade and seriously incomplete even for large countries that are rather self-sufficient but are also troubled by a continued deficit on balance of payments account. Finally, unless aggregate income and the full-employment level are taken as growing over

5. As this is written (1968), the older views have not yet lost all their force, as is evidenced by the recovery program undertaken by Germany in 1967, which appears to have been composed in part of pre-Keynesian public finance instruments, in part of Keynesian. In the United States the use of Keynesian public finance policy to promote full employment gained full official acceptance only in the early 1960's; the tax reduction of 1964 was the milestone. With respect to the chief problems involved in implementing a Keynesian public finance policy, some of which now seem quite troublesome in the light of the United States' experience of 1966–67, see Fritz Neumark, "Wo steht die 'fiscal policy' heute?," *Finanzarchiv* (1959), 19(1): 46–71, reprinted in his *Wirtschafts- und Finanzprobleme des Interventionsstaates* (Tubingen: Mohr, 1961), pp. 216–41.

6. See R. G. D. Allen, "A Simple Approach to Macro-economic Dynamics," *Economica* November, 1967), 34: 396.

time, the task of assuring any given degree of approach to full employment and full utilization of capital equipment will be assumed to be much less difficult than it actually is.

The following sections consider each of three major public finance questions commonly posed for a full employment policy, first in a setting of no growth and a closed economy, but allowing in a highly simplified manner for certain lags in private-sector reaction, then in a setting that allows for growth, and finally in one for an open economy. The analysis is intended to be suggestive only, at a level designed to indicate in their simple forms some of the problems yet to be solved in prescribing the use of public finance instruments for a full employment policy.

D. UNCHANGING LEVEL OF FULL EMPLOYMENT

1. Types of Adjustment by Public Finance Instruments

If an economy that is neither growing nor declining in aggregate income is subject to an exogenous shock, say a fall in autonomous investment, the policy questions that are commonly posed for public finance fall into the following three groups.

1. What public finance measures will preserve equilibrium at full employment, or will restore it instantly if unemployment has been allowed to develop?

2. If some unemployment is bound to develop, perhaps because forecasting cannot be wholly accurate, and if instant return to full employment equilibrium is not possible because of lags in response, what public finance measures will maximize the speed of readjustment, and at what danger of failing to achieve other goals, for example price stability?

3. If the government chooses to depend entirely on the built-in flexibility (sensitivity) of the public finance system, how much unemployment will be averted by that flexibility, and in what pattern over time?

The answer to the first of these questions, being an exercise in one-period comparative statics, is of limited value to the policy-maker, who must be concerned with the time lags of real life. Even if forecasting could be accurate, the time pattern of the multiplier effects of the exogenous shock would need to be specified, for comparison with the time pattern in which the effects of a forestalling measure would develop.

2. Forestalling Unemployment or Achieving
Full Employment Instantaneously in a No-Lag Economy

The comparative statics of fiscal policy in a no-lag economy explains how to forestall a departure from full employment in the face of an exogenous shock from the private sector, or how to achieve full employment instantaneously in an economy that has been in equilibrium at less than full employment. The extensive literature in this field[7] will not be summarized here, except to note the types of underemployment equilibrium and the measures that in this kind of a model can move the economy to full employment.

In the classical model,[8] where money wage rates are flexible downward and the interest and saving schedules are assumed to intersect at a feasible rate of interest, fiscal policy for full employment is unnecessary, since no departure from a full-employment equilibrium is possible. In a closed economy of this type the government can only change the rate of growth and the price level.

In the Keynesian no-lag models of a closed economy, the cases of underemployment equilibrium may be distinguished as follows.[9]

(1) The economy is operating with a money wage that is the lowest that workers will accept, but which represents a real wage too high to allow full employment, given the demand for labor and the price level of products. Let the product price level rise, for reasons to be noted presently, and let the minimum money wage that the workers demand remain unchanged. They are now demanding a smaller real wage; their real-wage supply curve shifts to the left (number of workers measured on the y-axis, real wage on the x-axis). Because of the decline in the real wage and the way it has been brought about (see below), more workers are employed. A large enough shift of the real-wage supply curve, through a great enough increase in the product price level, brings employment up to a point where the supply of labor becomes responsive to a change in the money wage at a given level of product prices; employment is then full, by definition of full employment.[10]

---

7. See, e.g., the following expositions. R. G. D. Allen, *Macro-Economic Theory* (London: Macmillan, 1967), Chapters 7 and 8; Richard A. Musgrave, *The Theory of Public Finance* (New York: McGraw-Hill, 1959), Chapters 17 and 18; Paul A. Samuelson, "The Simple Mathematics of Income Determination," in *Income, Employment, and Public Policy* (New York: Norton, 1948); Leif Johansen, *Public Economics* (Chicago: Rand McNally, 1965), pp. 28–50. Allen combines systematic and comprehensive analysis with brevity; Musgrave includes an analysis of the role of fiscal policy in a classical economy and compares policies that change disposable income with those that change only the pattern or amount of financial claims held by the public (including money); Samuelson's analysis includes policy areas outside public finance; Johansen contrasts the multiplier effects of income taxes with those of sales taxes, and extends his analysis to an open economy (but without including foreign repercussions). See also Bernard P. Herber, *Modern Public Finance* (Homewood, Ill.: Irwin, 1967), Chapters 18 and 19, for a mixture of theory and institutional background (United States). For a summary of the successively weaker effects of fiscal stimulus as the Keynesian model is made more complex, see Appendix B below.

8. Musgrave, *Theory of Public Finance*, pp. 407–11, 416–18.

9. There is also a no-solution case. If, as the interest rate is imagined to rise from a level of zero, investment falls so rapidly that it becomes zero even before the interest rate has risen to the minimum level set by the liquidity trap, no solution exists. The interest rate cannot in fact be pushed below the liquidity-trap level, a level that is still too high to allow any investment. The Hicksian IS curve intersects the y-axis, along which the rate of interest, r, is measured (income, Y, is measured along the x-axis), at a point below the intersection of that axis by the LM curve. Under these circumstances an increase in the stock of money does not give a solution for the model and neither does an increase in consumption obtained through tax reduction, as long as investment is zero. A solution can be found only by assuming a suitably large increment of autonomous investment, presumably by the government. See Allen, *op. cit.*, Exercise 7.3, p. 134.

10. See Allen, *op. cit.*, p. 126.

The product price level rises under an increase in demand for products, induced by fiscal policy measures. With the money wage rate of so much per hour remaining constant, while the marginal productivity of labor decreases as output is increased, the price of a product must rise if an increase in output is not to be unprofitable. The increase in demand that supports this increase in product prices may be induced by a lowering of the interest rate, so that investment spending increases, or by an increase in disposable income through tax reduction, to increase consumer spending —provided the obstacles to be described in (2) and (3) below are not encountered. Thus, in the complete Keynesian system, the price level is increased by an increase in the stock of money, and so is real income, and employment, while the interest rate and the real wage are decreased.[11]

(2) Investment, though interest-elastic, is so weak, and the propensity to save is so strong, that investment falls short of full-employment saving at all interest rates, even an interest rate of zero. As a special instance, investment is so interest-inelastic that a reduction in the interest rate even to zero (if that is feasible) not only fails to achieve full employment but scarcely reduces the amount of unemployment. The Hicksian IS curve, which has the interest rate, r, on the y-axis, is placed too far to the left; it intersects the x-axis, which measures income, Y, to the left of full-employment Y. An equilibrium income at less than full employment occurs, at a level of income indicated by the intersection of the IS curve and the LM curve. The issue of new money, no matter how much it moves the LM curve down and to the right, cannot achieve an intersection that represents full-employment income. The IS curve must be shifted to the right, by government expenditure, or by a decrease in taxation that enlarges consumption spending out of a given national income.

(3) Investment is strong enough, and the propensity to save is weak enough, so that at a certain low interest rate full employment income would be attained, but the interest rate is prevented from reaching that low level by the strength of the speculative or precautionary demand for money, relative to the existing stock of money and the price level. The IS and LM curves intersect at a point that represents less than full-employment income. If the LM curve is flat at this point (liquidity trap) an increase in the money stock will not lower the interest rate, and an increase in income can be obtained only by shifting the IS curve, through tax reduction or government spending as explained in (2) above. But if the LM curve is not flat at the point of intersection, an increase in the money stock can lower the rate of interest to the required level, unless it encounters a liquidity trap on the way.

This case (3) resembles case (1). An increase in the money stock might not be needed if the product-price level could be lowered, to release money that would go to lower the rate of interest. But such a lowering may be impossible because the money wage rate is at the minimum that workers will accept. Case (3) differs from case (1) in not taking into account the fall in marginal productivity of labor as employment increases.[12]

11. *Ibid.*, p. 129.

12. For a treatment of case (3) with emphasis on the insufficiency of the money supply, see Musgrave, *op. cit.*, p. 419 (his case "e").

3. Regaining Full-Employment under a Consumption Lag

The second of the two questions posed in Section 1 above assumes that unemployment has arisen because there is some lag in the private sector's planning process and forecasting has proved imperfect. Instantaneous re-establishment of equilibrium is impossible, since a lapse of time must occur, say, between an increase in disposable income and an increase in consumption expenditure. A similar lag may be assumed to prevail between a change in the prices of financial assets and a response of investment spenders.[13]

The degree of stimulation adequate in the instantaneous adjustment models is now inadequate because of the consumption lag. A slightly greater degree of stimulation, excessive in an instantaneous model, would in the lagged model merely hasten the process of recovery. To be sure, a stronger counteraction would be necessary later, to prevent a rise in prices once recovery had been achieved. In principle, however, this requirement seems to impose no barrier to more forceful action as long as unemployment exists. Indeed, at the extreme, the obvious prescription is to reduce taxes and increase transfer payments by so large an amount that full employment is regained as quickly as possible; given the time lag between receipt of income by the consumer and his spending of that income, the goal could not be reached instantly, but it might be attained in a few months (if not in a few weeks) rather than only after a year or so (see Appendix C below).

Alternatively, or concurrently, prices of private-sector financial assets could be pushed up well beyond the level called for in the no-lag model.

A large increase in government expenditures on goods and services, on the other hand, may be physically impossible in a very short period of time without unacceptable waste.

The unwillingness of public officials even to contemplate a massive quick-action tax policy is understandable, in view of their fear that the price level would go out of control. "Out of control" means either that the countermeasures needed once recovery had been completed would be so strong that they would not be politically acceptable, or that because of lagged relationships in the system coupled with a lack of precise knowledge about the lags it would not be possible to prevent recovery from being succeeded by a rise in prices.[14]

13. If there is a time lag "between the moment when the disturbance occurs and the moment when the disturbance affects the end-variables" (Bent Hansen, *The Economic Theory of Fiscal Policy*, p. 436), this "disturbance time lag" gives the policy-maker time to set in motion a program that will forestall, not the "disturbance," but the change in the end-variable. In practice, it seems difficult to discover an example of a time lag involving employment as the end-variable with linkage of disturbance to employment clear enough to allow all lapse from full employment to be forestalled.

14. In fact, of course, the real world is so complex that the economy is more or less "out of control" all the time. Allen, *Macro-Economic Theory*, shows how complex is the task of correcting for a deficiency in demand even when there are no oscillations (before the corrective measure is applied) and when the model involves the multiplier, but not the acceleration principle (investment is autonomous) (see Chapter 18, especially pp. 353–56); and in his preface he remarks: "The models considered here . . . are many stages removed from policy

An especially large increase in the tax rate or decrease in government expenditure would then be needed to halt the price rise. The resulting change in expectations in the private sector might quickly create unemployment. Meanwhile private investment plans would have been disrupted by the rise in prices, leading to inefficient investment spending that would be revealed in underutilized capacity or failure to earn normal profits in the future.

These dangers can be admitted, yet it would be odd if the optimum degree of stimulation in the lag model were no greater than in the instantaneous-adjustment model. Even a recovery policy so strong that it led to oscillations above and below the target level of employment, with consequent bursts of price-level increases, might be considered preferable to a weaker stimulative policy; the reduction of cumulative unemployment over time might be worth the cost. Much depends on the degree of probability attached to the outcome. If, under the quick-action approach, the probability of the system's getting out of control were say 0.2 (the only other outcome being the one desired, probability 0.8), a cautious policy-maker might settle for a slower-acting program where the loss-of-control probability was estimated at, say, 0.05.

4. Built-In Flexibility (Sensitivity)

The third of the three questions posed in Section 1 above asks how much fall in national income will be averted by built-in flexibility.

Built-in flexibility of a flow may be either positive or negative. If it is positive, the flow of money between government and the private sector, whichever way it is running, alters in favor of the private sector when private-sector activity declines, and in favor of the government when private-sector activity increases. Positive built-in flexibility is confined to the usual types of tax and to the negative-tax types of welfare payments and negative-tax subsidies. Negative built-in flexibility is found in few, if any, taxes[15] but is a feature of most subsidies, since the total amount of subsidy paid usually declines as activity in the subsidized business falls off.

Ideally, as long as underemployment exists, the fiscal system should possess positive flexibility whenever employment is falling and negative flexibility whenever it is increasing. In practice, no fiscal instrument is so constructed. The drag exerted by positive flexibility in the recovery phase is the price that must be paid for the reduction in the decrease in national income in a recession. The price is worth

applications" (*ibid.*, p. xii). See also, with respect to various types of lags and their consequences for stabilization policy, A. W. Phillips, "Stabilisation Policy in a Closed Economy," *Economic Journal* (June, 1954), 64: 290–323, and "Stabilisation Policy and the Time-Forms of Lagged Responses," *Economic Journal* (June, 1957), 67: 265–77. For a summary see R. G. D. Allen's "A Simple Approach to Macro-economic Dynamics," *Economica* (November, 1967), 34: 401–5.

15. For example, a tax on idle land (see Chapter 6). The increases that occur in rates of payroll tax to finance unemployment insurance in the United States, in those states that apply merit rating, are examples of formula flexibility (negative) rather than built-in flexibility.

paying, since total cumulated unemployment (man-years of unemployment) over a complete cycle is smaller, despite the drag on recovery, than if the system had no built-in flexibility. In the latter event, the recovery would be at a more rapid rate, but so would the recession, and a deeper trough would be reached.

The revenue decreases due to built-in flexibility must be met by new-money finance, if the maximum stimulative effect is to be obtained, and the revenue increases in periods of inflationary pressure must be impounded, not used to purchase securities.

In a no-lag Keynesian model the amount of decline in national income that is prevented by built-in flexibility is the difference between the new, depression equilibrium income under built-in flexibility and that under no built-in flexibility.[16] But when the time dimension is allowed for, it is the difference between two areas (time measured on the abscissa, income on the ordinate) from peak to peak. If the decline and recovery are each at a steady linear rate, and if the rates are equal, and if troughs are either points or of equal width, the difference in areas of cumulated unemployment is proportional to the difference in depth of trough, and the static formulation of the efficiency of the built-in flexibility is adequate. But if the decline or recovery does not proceed at a uniform rate through time this proportionality does not hold, and the static measure is inadequate. This is the case, even in a simple one-period consumption-lag model (see Appendix D below).

Sensitivity (built-in flexibility) in securities prices refers to the degree of change in market value of a security as interest rates rise or fall independently of government action. Let us say that one security has more positive sensitivity, more built-in flexibility, than another if its market price rises by a greater percentage than the other's in a recession and falls by more in a period of inflationary pressure. A security with a distant maturity date therefore has more built-in flexibility than one that is to mature shortly. For counter-cycle purposes the distant-date security is the more helpful. Because its price falls by more in a boom period, a holder can realize less cash from sale of it than if it were a short-term issue, and the less cash he can realize, the less is his power to add to the inflationary pressure by the purchase of goods and services or real assets. In a recession he experiences a larger increase in his call on cash, and hence on goods and services and real assets, than does the holder of a short-term note.

This point has nothing to do with the so-called locked-in effect, which seems of doubtful efficacy if indeed it exists at all.[17] The issue here is not whether the holder will be deterred from selling his long-term security by the fact that he will thereby realize what is up to this time only a paper loss, but how much he can realize if he chooses to do so.

The final result depends of course on what the purchaser of the security would have done with his money if he had not bought it, at a low price in a boom and at a high price in a depression. But perhaps there may be at least a presumption that he would not have spent it on goods and services.

16. For a thorough analysis of compensatory effectiveness in a no-lag model, see Musgrave, *op. cit.*, pp. 503–12.

17. See Musgrave, *op. cit.*, pp. 604–606.

E. STEADILY INCREASING LEVEL OF FULL EMPLOYMENT

Let us now postulate an economy in which the full employment level of output increases each period, owing to a continual increase in capacity output resulting from net investment in every period.

If the economy tends to fall off from a full-employment, full-utilization equilibrium, owing to some exogenous shock, say a fall in private investment, (a) What does the government have to do to prevent any departure at all from that equilibrium, assuming that it can forecast perfectly, and receives and acts on information instantaneously? (b) What happens if the government takes discretionary action, but not until one period of off-equilibrium income has occurred, while the tax-transfer system has zero sensitivity? (c) What happens if the government makes no discretionary changes, relying instead on the system's built-in flexibility?

1. The No-Lag Model

In the simplest case the percentage rate of increase of output per period is constant over time and the labor force grows by the same percentage. There is no technical progress. Constant returns to scale obtain in a two-factor world of capital and labor. The capital-output ratio is assumed to be rigidly fixed, which is not too unsuitable a postulate for the short period with which the present discussion is concerned. The increase in labor supply arises from immigration or from an internal growth in population, or from an exogenous increase in the hours worked per period per worker. In the first case to be considered there are no lagged variables.

Under these conditions the steadily increasing full employment levels of output and capacity can be attained in any one period if the economy's income, its labor force, and its capital equipment all grow at a rate given by the ratio of the propensity to save to the capital-output ratio, multiplied (in this period-by-period analysis) by one plus that rate of growth (see Appendix E below). In continuous analysis, the equilibrium growth rate is the ratio of the propensity to save to the capital-output ratio.[18] The period analysis, although it involves some unrealistic assumptions about the timing of investment within the period (if that investment is to be available for use throughout that period) is employed here, because it facilitates emphasis of certain timing problems in the use of public finance instruments, discussed in the immediately succeeding paragraphs.

18. See R. G. D. Allen, "A Simple Approach to Macro-economic Dynamics," *Economica* (November, 1967), 34: 399.

A. INSTANTANEOUS CORRECTION BY PUBLIC FINANCE INSTRUMENTS

The only difference between the model described immediately above and the one employed in Section D above, aside from the carry-over of an increased capital stock from one period to the next, is that the labor force there was implicitly assumed to remain unchanged. When this assumption is dropped, an infinite number of patterns of successive full-employment incomes can be postulated in this simple model where there is no linkage from one period to the next except in the total capital stock carried over to a succeeding period. Then, for any one series of such full-employment income levels spread over time, a disturbance can be postulated for the initial period, say a decrease in private investment spending below the level needed to equilibrate total spending with capacity output. The consequent increase in government spending, or tax reduction, that is necessary to offset, instantaneously, this fall in private investment spending can be computed. For most purposes we are still in the comparative statics world, with the important difference that effects on capacity output must be considered. Suppose, for example, that private investment in period n will be a certain amount below the full-capacity full-employment equilibrium value if the government takes no stimulative action. This deficiency in investment we label d. Now, even if the government does take stimulative action, full employment income cannot be attained if that action is simply a tax reduction or an increase in transfer payments that raises consumption spending by an amount equal to d. In this no-lag model, the plant capacity will not be there to make possible full employment output. Since the output of a period depends on the investment made in the same period, and reaches a level dictated by the capital-output ratio, prevention of a decline from full employment output requires that the government induce the necessary amount of private investment, or itself do the investment spending, by borrowing the funds that investors are about to hold idle or are about to abstain from borrowing.

In the next period, $n + 1$, the government will have to continue this policy, or will have to change it, depending on whether the level of private investment promises to remain below that consistent with the full employment, capacity-utilization level. A constantly changing fiscal policy may therefore be called for. This requirement of a constantly changing fiscal policy is implicit in the comparative statics approach, where every period is self-contained. The analysis there could, though it rarely does, string together a succession of self-contained periods and, by postulating continued but erratic changes in private investment, make necessary continued changes in fiscal policy measures.

B. INADEQUATE USE OF PUBLIC FINANCE INSTRUMENTS

Let us suppose that the government fails to take the full, necessary action to maintain investment spending at the level consistent with full employment and full capacity utilization. The government either acts immediately, but only to bolster consumption spending, or delays one period before acting at all.

First, let us suppose that the government, upon learning that private investment in period n will fall, merely reduces taxes on consumers for that period. We abstract from built-in flexibility for the moment. Consumption rises from the low level it would fall to if the government did nothing. But the tax reduction must not exceed that which induces an increase in consumption only to the new period-n capacity output which will not increase as much over that of period $n-1$ as does the labor force. Any stimulation to consumption beyond this amount will merely increase prices. The result must be a certain amount of unemployment, just because the capital stock in period n is now not large enough to accommodate the labor force, which has grown faster. Even if the fall in private investment proves to be only a one-period phenomenon, so that investment resumes its normal level in period $n+1$ (and the government thereupon terminates its fiscal policy action) there is still trouble in period $n+1$ on the employment front. The labor force will not have diminished its rate of growth to match the one-period fall in private investment. That lost period of investment implies a total capital stock that in period $n+1$ and all succeeding periods will be lower than is required for the supply of labor that wants to work with it, until the government makes up the lost amount of investment by reducing consumption spending by this amount in some period and for that period induces an equal increase of investment. Politically, it will not be an appealing program to force even a one-period reduction in consumption on the grounds that this must be done in order to achieve full employment. In the comparative statics analysis of Section D above, in contrast, a return of private investment to the normal level assured full employment while allowing the government to cease its stimulative fiscal policy.

If, on the other hand, the reduced level of private investment continues through periods $n+1$ and following periods, and if the government continues a policy merely of stimulating consumption enough to take off the market the capacity output, that level of output will be increasingly below the level that will absorb the growing labor force, and unemployment will increase each period. The shortfall in degree of approach to the goal of full employment, for any one period, is greater, in absolute amount, each successive period, and the cumulated shortfall over time consequently grows at an increasing rate in terms of units of increment in cumulated loss of employment per unit period.

Meanwhile the shortfall in approach to the other goal, capacity utilization, remains zero, an achievement however that lacks significance in view of the growing level of unemployment.

These conclusions rest, *inter alia*, on the strenuous assumption that the capital-output ratio must remain unchanged; they also abstract from the effect that changes in consumption spending exert on private investment. While these aspects of the analysis are unrealistic, this extreme case calls attention to a type of difficulty in the use of public finance instruments for full employment that is ignored, because it is never encountered, in the static analysis of a zero-growth economy.

If the government reacts by inducing, or itself undertaking, investment spending for privately used plant, equipment, and inventory in an amount equal to that which would have occurred if normal growth had not been interrupted, but does so only after one period of shortfall in investment has elapsed, a lump of unemployment continues thenceforth, just as in the case immediately above, and in addition the income of the period in which investment falls off does not reach even the capacity level.

c. Results of Built-in Flexibility

If, when private investment falls in period n, the government takes no discretionary action but depends wholly on the built-in flexibility of the tax-transfer system, the fall in income in period n is somewhat less than it would be under fixed taxes, and transfers, because consumption spending is somewhat higher than it would be under an inflexible tax-transfer system and no discretionary action. Capacity of course remains inadequate to allow full employment.

2. Capacity-Lag Model

A lag is now inserted in this capacity model, in order to compare the requisite public finance policy with that called for by the earlier lagged model (Section D) that ignored capacity. It will be convenient at first to work with a one-period lag in capacity behind investment (no lag in consumption).

A. One-period Capacity Lag

Investment in one period is assumed to add to the capacity output of the next and all succeeding periods, not to that of the period in which it occurs.

Private investment falls in period n from the level called for by the rate of growth of the labor force. If the government reacts by inducing an increase in consumption spending in period n, it can eliminate unemployment in period n, which, we have seen, it cannot do in the no-lag model [Section E.1.A above]. The decline in investment spending in period n now does not lower the capacity output level of that period. However, there is bound to be unemployment in period $n + 1$, no matter what the government does in $n + 1$, because of lack of capacity. And if capacity is to be expanded to a level that allows full employment in period $n + 2$ (under the assumption of a fixed capital-output ratio), consumption in period $n + 1$ must be reduced, to permit the necessary investment. In contrast to the no-lag model, the government's mistake has now placed it in the very difficult political position of having to restrict consumption below the level it would have reached under no disturbance, with capacity output, in a period when it cannot yet eliminate unemployment.

These answers have assumed no built-in flexibility in the tax system. Such flexibility merely checks the fall in consumption spending. If the government relies entirely on built-in flexibility, the economy's capacity falls further and further below the normal rate called for by the growth of the labor force, as investment spending continues to fall short of that rate. But unemployment may be even greater than that forced by the shortfall in capacity, since aggregate demand will also be lower than normal, as the government continues to rely only on built-in flexibility. By the time exogenous investment spending turns up again, the economy will have foregone more consumption than under discretionary action and will still face a long period of unemployment when demand turns up, owing to a shortage of capacity. Finally, when the government acts, as it will need to sooner or later, it can eliminate unemployment only by a drastic reduction in consumption that releases resources to make good the cumulated shortage in capacity.

B. ONE-PERIOD CAPACITY LAG AND ONE-PERIOD CONSUMPTION LAG

As the next step, let us add the kind of lag used in the comparative statics analysis above (page 551), viz., consumption is a function of the immediately preceding period's income. Matters are now improved in the sense that the government, upon learning at the start of period n that private investment in that period will be below the full-employment level, will have no incentive to fall into the error of stimulating employment in that period by stimulating consumption in that period, for it is too late to stimulate consumption. The fiscal policy for this period must be directed at increasing investment in period n if unemployment in that period is to be reduced. A stimulus that keeps investment at its normal level in period n will avert the inevitable unemployment for period $n + 1$ portrayed in Section a above. Full employment will be assured in period n, and therefore a normal level of consumption spending will occur in period $n + 1$; in each period the government need merely do the only thing it can do to provide full employment currently, that is, stimulate investment spending.

The analysis above, for the capacity-lag model, errs on the pessimistic side, insofar as investment is not exogenous but is a function of consumption spending. It also ignores the possibility of adjustments through changes in the propensity to save and the capital-output ratio. In any event the period-to-period relationships will not be as neat as portrayed here, and actual policy will have to take into account many more factors. But this simplified analysis perhaps indicates some of the cumulative dangers that the economy encounters by failing to take the proper kind of action promptly, a danger that static analysis scarcely hints at and that tends to be obscured in the more sophisticated lag models.

3. Coping with Initial Long-Run Disequilibrium

In the analysis up to this point, an economy was assumed to be initially in equilibrium, then disturbed by a short-term change in some exogenous factor, say a temporary fall in investment. Alternatively, the full employment problem (and the conflict-of-interests issue of price-level stability as well) may be viewed as one of putting into equilibrium an economy that initially is disequilibrated because of a continued difference between planned saving and the amount of investment at a full employment level or some other maladjustment. This problem can arise in the Harrod-Domar type of economy, but not in the neo-classical growth models, where an adjustment of v, the capital-output ratio, assures equilibrium and determines the growth rate. In the Harrod-Domar case the public finance system can in principle be so shaped as to reach the value of s, the community's saving that is necessary, given the capital-output ratio, to assure an equality of the warranted rate of growth with the expenditure rate of growth. The major possibilities have been explored intensively elsewhere,[19] and do not need to be repeated here, especially since they employ much the same type of analysis that has been given in Sections 1 and 2 above.

A neo-classical growth model, with its variable capital-output ratio, may be pushed by some disturbance off of its equilibrium rate of growth, which is determined by the rate of growth of the population. An adjustment process then automatically begins, operating through a change in the capital-output ratio, and the economy eventually returns to its natural rate of growth. The transition period may be regarded as something not to be desired, and from this point of view it deserves at least passing mention in the present chapter, even though no unemployment is involved; or it may be a purposely induced transition, designed to change the rate of growth of the economy through a certain period of time, as a second-best aim in a system where the equilibrium rate of growth is independent of the rate of capital accumulation and so cannot be altered by, say, taxes that change the economy's propensity to consume. The latter point of view is the one taken here, hence further discussion of this case is deferred to Chapter 23.

F. EFFECTS OF OPENNESS OF ECONOMY ON PUBLIC FINANCE POLICY FOR FULL EMPLOYMENT

In an open economy, public finance policy measures exert part of their effects abroad, and the reactions abroad to these effects (foreign repercussions) in turn affect the initially acting country's progress toward the goals of full employment, capacity output, and (see Chapter 24) price stability.

The possible results are numerous; the analysis quickly becomes complex. A comprehensive theory of fiscal policy in an open economy has not yet been developed. It is not attempted in the present analysis, which is limited to emphasizing the differences between results in a closed economy and an open economy by focussing briefly on two extreme cases: completely open economies, and open economies

---

19. Musgrave, *op. cit.*, Chapter 20, Section C, which deals with both the problem of assuring that the actual rate of growth of expenditures will match the required rate of growth, in a Domar model, and the problem "of choosing between various rates of growth" (*ibid.*, p. 483). In this latter connection, see Appendix to Chapter 23.

in which one economy experiences no home leakage.[20] A look at these extreme cases may suggest the type of result to be expected from the real-life, in-between instances.[21] The analysis is restricted to comparative statics.

1. First Extreme Case:
A and B Producing Only for Export to Each Other

Let us consider an admittedly unrealistic two-country world in which Country A exports all its output to Country B and obtains all its consumer and capital goods from Country B, and where B has a similar relationship with A. Let investment spending be fixed in each country. Reduction of the rate of personal income tax in A will increase A's imports of consumer goods by an amount depending on A's marginal propensity to consume out of disposable income. The consequent increase in income in B will in part be saved, in part spent on consumer goods produced in A. It can be shown that in these circumstances Country A, by reducing its income tax, increases the income of Country B by more than it increases its own income, and that this is so, whether the marginal propensity to save is larger or smaller in A than in B.[22]

If the marginal propensity to save is the same in both countries and is the same in A as if A were a closed economy, it may then be shown that the increase in income in A consequent upon the tax reduction in A is less in this open economy than it would be in a closed economy. The amount by which it is less is given by the expression

$$T\left(\frac{1-s}{s(2-s)}\right)$$

where T is the decrease in the tax bill and s is the marginal propensity to save.[23] Thus, if the marginal propensity to save is $1/20$, the increase in income in open economy A from a decrease, T, in the personal income tax bill is less than the increase in income in closed economy A by nearly 10 times the decrease in the tax bill.

The weaker effect, in A, of a discretionary reduction of tax by A, than in a closed economy is the counterpart of the fact that, in the open economy, if A takes no action at all, the consequent loss in income generated will not be all A's. Thus A

20. "Home leakage," in Meade's terminology (*The Balance of Payments*, pp. 54–55), is that proportion of "any given primary increase in national income . . . that . . . does not generate any secondary net increase in demand and so in national income," namely, "that which represents the amount which merely replaces unemployment benefit or which leads only to increased savings or increased tax payments *less* the amount by which the increase in national income induces a further increase in demand for goods for capital development." This definition reduces the dole-tax-saving leakage by the accelerator "negative leakage" that develops from the change in level of income, thus becoming a net leakage concept. But for simplicity in analysis below, the accelerator effect will be abstracted from.

21. Some of the analysis of Chapter 24, Section B (External Equilibrium) is relevant here.

22. See Appendix F to this chapter.

23. See Appendix F to this chapter.

(or B) gains less from its own stimulative measures than it would in a closed economy but has less to lose if it fails to take such steps.

The conclusions reached in the three paragraphs immediately above do not hold, however, if the illustration is made extreme in another respect, that is, if there is no home leakage at all in B. We turn now to this case.

2. Second Extreme Case: No Home Leakage in Other Country

If an increment of income in the other country, B, is re-spent entirely, part of it on domestic output and the rest of it on imports from A, the increase in income in A resulting from a reduction in the personal income tax rate in A is as large as if A were a closed economy. Thus A, by its tax decrease, does as well for itself in the open economy, if B has no home leakage, as it does if it is a closed economy.[24] This is so, whether or not A and B are entirely open, that is, whether or not each country consumes none of its own product.[25] Whatever A spends on B's products must be matched by B's expenditure on A's products, if B's trade is to remain balanced.

For the instantaneous-multiplier case, it makes no difference to A whether B's re-spending is divided between imports and home production in a ratio of 1 to 9, or 9 to 1, or any other ratio. Country A still obtains the full effect of its own stimulative measure. But in a period-by-period analysis this ratio is significant; the larger it is, the more quickly will A achieve any given fraction of the total stimulus. An offset to this consideration, however, is the presumption that in a two-country world initially in equilibrium a high ratio in B implies a correspondingly high ratio in A and a correspondingly high foreign leakage in A. And the policy-maker in A will not welcome this high foreign leakage.

3. Capital Movements

If the country in question is small and capital flows are not controlled, the consequences of fiscal policy measures are difficult to predict and, even if predictable, may be so sudden and so massive that, if favorable, they can lead to gross overshooting of the target and, if unfavorable, may yield a net change in the wrong direction. A decrease in tax rates coupled with creation of new money and consequent low interest rates for the time being can lead to an outflow of capital (abstracting from the effects of change in profitability) that will prevent interest rates from sinking to the desired level, and so may prevent domestic investment from rising to the target level while threatening to exhaust foreign-exchange reserves. Similar difficulties exist for a contractive policy.

In practice, the small countries most likely to be thus inhibited from fiscal policy

24. See Appendix F to this chapter.
25. See J. E. Meade, *op. cit.*, pp. 60 and 131 (note).

are not marked by a high degree of elasticity of capital flows, in or out, in response to changes in interest rates or profit rates. Moreover, capital movements in these countries are likely to be controlled, if more or less imperfectly. In practice, then, each country presents a special case, for determining whether sudden and massive capital flows pose a threat to a fiscal policy program intended to maintain full employment.

4. A Multi-Country World

In the real world, where any one country trades with more than one country (and similarly, for capital flows), the two-country analysis of fiscal policy must be modified by taking into account a number of marginal propensities to import, and similar parameters. The basic results are not altered for the instantaneous-multiplier model. For the more realistic case of period-by-period analysis, the introduction of more than one country into the rest of the world may imply a somewhat longer time for foreign repercussions to exert their full effect, if the need to transfer one currency into another, to clear customs, and to fulfill other tasks set by the existence of national border regulations take appreciable time. On the other hand, it is not evident a priori that a multi-country model implies a greater degree of risk (greater dispersion of possible outcomes about the mean) just because there are a greater number of countries involved.

5. Summary for Open Economies

For an open economy the results of public finance measures intended to retain, or regain, full employment, full use of capacity, and price stability are more difficult to estimate accurately and, aside from the case of sudden and massive capital flows, more slow to take hold than in a closed economy. Moreover, these measures are likely to exert pressure for currency devaluation or revaluation if the fiscal policy is to be continued for a considerable stretch of time. If the country is determined to hold to a fixed exchange rate, its stimulative or restrictive public finance measures may have to be halted before they have attained their goal, presumably because the values that the public finance instruments would have to take are outside the permissible ranges (see Chapter 19, Section C.2). The policy question then centers on the reasons why a country wishes to maintain a certain exchange rate. This issue, exhaustively discussed in the literature of international trade and finance, will not be explored here, but some of the problems that it poses for public finance are noted in Chapter 24.

APPENDIX A TO CHAPTER TWENTY-TWO

The effect on national income multipliers of taking into account the income effect on households who receive free government services has been presented by Martin J. Bailey, *National Income and the Price Level* (New York: McGraw-Hill, 1962), pp. 71–81, in an analysis that covers both tax financing and debt financing. The following paragraphs present some of the implications for a tax-financed increase in government expenditure on goods and services in a more step-by-step, detailed procedure.

An increase in government expenditure on goods and services is assumed to take place in order to produce a government service that is distributed free of charge. This service is considered by the recipients to constitute an increment of income in kind equal in value to its cost to the government. It increases their real disposable incomes by that amount, provided they do not have to relinquish the benefits owing to induced increases in prices of things they buy or decreases in their factor rewards. The government takes, say, $1,000 in tax from each of two individuals, T_1 and T_2, who would otherwise each have spent $800 more on consumption in the next round and saved $200 more. With this $2,000 the government hires unemployed workers, W_1 and W_2, to produce a government service that is supplied free of charge to a recipient, R. Under the assumptions of the balanced-budget multiplier theorem (including the important assumption that investment is not affected), the increase of $2,000 in taxation and in expenditures on goods and services increases national income by $2,000.

But R considers that his total real income is increased by $2,000. All of this particular increment of income of R's is necessarily consumed by him as it is received. If R's marginal propensity to consume out of either total money income or total real income is, say, 0.8, he will save $400 "out of" this income in kind by reducing his money expenditure on consumption by that amount. Thus if his money income is $10,000, of which he normally spends $8,000, he will on this occasion spend only $7,600 in money, which, added to his $2,000 "spending" of the income in kind, gives total real consumption spending of $9,600 out of a total real income of $12,000.

On the next round, if the government's free service is not repeated, R will revert to spending $8,000 out of his $10,000 money (and now, total real) income.

The two workers, W_1 and W_2, spend $800 each out of their $1,000 money incomes.

In place of two similar multiplier chains of money spending resulting from T, an increment of tax bill, and G, an equal increment of government spending on goods and services, where c is the uniform propensity to consume:

$$G: 1 + c + c^2 + c^3 + \ldots,$$

$$T \quad -c - c^2 - c^3 - \ldots,$$

there are two dissimilar multiplier chains of money spending:

$$G: 1 + c - f + c(c - f) + c^2(c - f) + \ldots,$$
$$T \quad -c \quad -c^2 \quad -c^3 \quad -\ldots,$$

where f is the propensity to save, on the part of the recipient of the free service, "out of" the increment of real income (which is also all real consumption) that he obtains from the government, a propensity that he implements by spending less out of his money income ("the" recipient may of course be a group of persons instead of one person). If f is the same as the community's uniform propensity to save out of money income, the balanced-budget multiplier is zero; there is no increment or decrement to national income as a result of the equal increase in taxation and government spending on goods and services. Note that money income as conventionally reckoned on the product side does include the free government service at its cost. The increment of money income is equal to the sum of (1) the value of that service, reckoned at cost, and (2) the aggregate of spending on marketed consumption goods that arises through the multiplier process.

This result of zero change in national income is shown as follows.

In general, when an increment of government expenditure on goods and services is financed completely by tax revenue, and when investment spending remains as it would have been otherwise, the resulting increase in money spending will be zero if the sum of the two multiplier chains above is zero. The first of these chains sums to

$$1 + (c - f)/(1 - c);$$

the second sums to

$$-c/(1 - c).$$

When the sum of these two expressions equals zero, we have

$$1 - c + (c - f) - c = 0$$

or

$$f = 1 - c.$$

Thus, if the two chains together sum to zero, the propensity to save, on the part of the recipient of the free service, out of the real-income real-consumption increment he is given, valued at its cost to the government (a propensity that he implements by saving more out of his money income), is equal to the community's uniform propensity to save out of its money income.

If the sum of the first of the multiplier chains, G, exceeds the negative of the sum of the second, T,

$$1 + \frac{c - f}{1 - c} > \frac{c}{1 - c},$$

then

$$1 - c > f$$

Thus, when the recipient's propensity to save out of his free income in kind is less than the community's propensity to save out of money income, national money income (and national real income) is increased by a balanced-budget increment.

And if his propensity to save out of free income in kind is greater than the community's propensity to save out of money income, national money and real income are reduced.

If the recipient of the free service has to relinquish exactly an amount equal to this income in kind, to others, his money income falls by the amount that it costs the government to give him the service (by definition of "relinquish exactly"). A corresponding increase occurs in the money incomes of others. Their propensity to consume has not been affected. Still, the balanced-budget multiplier will not, because of this relinquishing, resume its value of unity. The recipient of the service will spend a smaller percentage of his now reduced money income than he would have done if his total (unchanged) real income were all of it money income. For example, let the recipient's total income be $1,000 in money, if he does not receive the free service, of which he re-spends $800. If he receives a free service costing $200, let his money income fall by $200 and others' money incomes rise by an aggregate of $200. In this latter case he will probably spend out of his now $800 of money income less than 80 per cent of it, in order that he may be consuming, in total, some 80 per cent of his total real income of $1,000. In that event his re-spending (less than $640) plus the respending by those whose money incomes increased, 0.8($200) = $160, will total less than $800, that is, less than what he would have re-spent in absence of the service.

APPENDIX B TO CHAPTER TWENTY-TWO

The effect on income of an autonomous small increment of either government expenditure on goods and services, ΔG, or taxation (net of transfer payments), ΔT, becomes weaker and weaker as we move from the simple multiplier model to the more complex models of the Keynesian system.[1] In the simple multiplier model, with no taxation, $\Delta Y = (1/s)\Delta G$, approximately, where s is the marginal propensity to save out of income. If the system also contains a lump sum tax, $\Delta Y = -[(1-s)/s]\Delta T$, where ΔT is a small increment of tax. A decrement of tax is absorbed partly by saving, hence gives a weaker result than an increment of expenditure.

When the model is expanded to allow investment to vary with the rate of interest and to take account of the transactions demand for money and of liquidity preference, the expression for the increment in income becomes more complex and the increment itself is smaller. Let $I(r) = S(Y_d) + T - G$ (the Hicksian "IS curve") where I is investment other than exogenous investment, r is the rate of interest, Y_d is disposable income, and $T - G$ is government saving; and let $M = L_1(Y) + L_2(r)$ (the "LM curve"), where M is the stock of money, $L_1(Y)$ is the transactions demand for money and $L_2(r)$ is the speculative or precautionary demand for money, expressing liquidity preference. If a linear model is chosen, and if the rate at which investment is decreasing per unit increase of r is denoted by α, the rate at which the transactions

1. This summary is based chiefly on R. G. D. Allen, *Macro-Economic Theory* (London: Macmillan, 1967), Chapter 8.

demand for money is increasing per unit increase in Y by k, and the rate at which the speculative (precautionary) demand for money is decreasing per unit increase in r by β, it can be shown, by differentiating the two equations above with respect to G, that, in place of $1/s$, we have

$$\frac{1}{s[1 + (k\alpha/s\beta)]},$$

so that, for a small increment of G, with T constant,

$$\Delta Y = \frac{1}{s[1 + (k\alpha/s\beta)]} \Delta G.$$

Similarly, for a small decrement in T, with G constant,

$$\Delta Y = -\frac{1 - s}{s[1 + (k\alpha/s\beta)]} \Delta T.$$

The increase in income is smaller in both these cases if the system contains a tax that increases with income. In the simple multiplier model, the equilibrium condition in the product market is now $Y_d = C(Y_d) + A + (G_0 - T_0) - T(Y)$, where $Y_d = Y - T(Y) - T_0$. Here, A is the autonomous element in the private sector of the system (autonomous consumption plus autonomous investment), and G_0 and T_0 are the fixed expenditure and fixed tax elements in the government sector. By differentiating this equation with respect to G_0, we get

$$\frac{dY}{dG_0} = \frac{1}{s + (1 - s)t},$$

in place of simply $1/s$, so that

$$\Delta Y = \frac{\Delta G_0}{s + (1 - s)t}.$$

Differentiating with respect to T_0, we have

$$\Delta Y = \frac{1 - s}{s + (1 - s)t} (-\Delta T_0).$$

If the variable-tax rate is changed, rather than the lump-sum tax, it can be shown that, if the tax rate, t, is the same at all income levels, a decrease in that rate gives us

$$\Delta Y = \frac{1 - s}{s + (1 - s)t} (-\Delta t) Y.$$

If we include the IR curve and the LM curve in this variable-tax model, we get, for computing the result of an increase in government expenditure, not

$$\frac{1}{s[1 + (k\alpha/s\beta)]},$$

but

$$\frac{1}{s[1 + (k\alpha/s\beta) + (1 - s/s)t]}$$

All of these results ignore the income effect of the increment in free government service that accompanies an increment in G. If this effect is taken into account, the increase in Y resulting from an increment in G becomes still less (see page 541 above).

APPENDIX C TO CHAPTER TWENTY-TWO

Let consumption, C_n, in period n be determined completely by the disposable income of the immediately preceding period, i.e., by $Y_{n-1} - T_{n-1}$. Thus $C_n = \alpha(Y_{n-1} - T_{n-1})$, but all other relationships are instantaneous. For simplicity, tax revenue is assumed zero throughout, and the stimulative measure is taken to be an increase in government expenditures on goods and services, G.

Full-employment investment, I_f, decreases exogenously to a depression level, I_d. The equilibrium level of full employment income, Y_f, is replaced by a depression equilibrium level, Y_d, given by

$$Y_d = (I_d + G)/(1 - \alpha),$$

just as the full-employment equilibrium level is given by

$$Y_f = (I_f + G)/(1 - \alpha).$$

In view of the consumption-spending lag, this new equilibrium level is not reached at once; the economy slides downhill, period after period, unless the government intervenes. Let such intervention, in the form of an increase in government expenditure on goods and services, be financed by new money. It is assumed to begin in the period immediately following the one in which investment declines. To fix ideas, a numerical illustration is presented. Consumption in any one period is 60 per cent of income of the preceding period. At full employment equilibrium in period $n - 1$, national income is 75, consumption 45, investment 20, and government expenditure 10 (see Table 4).

Table 4   Decline in National Income, under Decline in Investment, and No Government Action

Period	C	I	G	Y	ΔY	$Y_f - Y$	$Y_f - Y$ Cumulative
$n - 1$	45	20	10	75		0	
n	45	10	10	65	-10	-10	-10
$n + 1$	39	10	10	59	-6	-16	-26
$n + 2$	35.4	10	10	55.4	-3.6	-19.6	-45.6
$n + 3$	33.2	10	10	53.2	-2.2	-21.8	-67.4
.							
.							
.							
$n + \infty$	30	10	10	50	—	-25	

A fall of 10 in investment occurs in period n. If the government takes no action, and investment continues at its new low level, income will move down period by period toward its new equilibrium level of 50, as indicated in Table 4.

In a no-lag model, an increase of 10 in government spending instantaneously returns the economy to full employment, and keeps it there. In the present consumption-lag model, such an increase halts the decline in income and moves the economy gradually toward full employment (Table 5).

Table 5   Decline and Rise in National Income, under Decline in Investment Followed by an Equal Increase in Government Spending

Period	C	I	G	Y	ΔY	$Y_f - Y$	$Y_f - Y$ Cumulative
$n-1$	45	20	10	75		0	
n	45	10	10	65	-10	-10	-10
$n+1$	39	10	20	69	4	-6	-16
$n+2$	41.4	10	20	71.4	2.4	-3.6	-19.6
$n+3$	42.8	10	20	72.8	1.4	-2.2	-21.8
.							
.							
.							
$n+\infty$	45	10	20	75		0	

By the end of period $n+3$ the cumulative loss in income, owing to the government's delay of but one period in increasing its expenditure to what would be adequate for full employment under an instantaneous multiplier, is nearly one-third the cumulative loss that occurs by then if the government does nothing (-21.8 against -67.4). It is of course an even larger proportion in an earlier period (period n, 100 per cent; period $n+1$, 62 per cent; period $n+2$, 43 per cent). The penalty for delay can be heavy in an economy where consumption is lagged on income. The cumulative shortfall from full employment income over periods $n+1$ to $n+3$ is the lined area ABCDEF in Figure 16. The gain over the same three periods from a do-nothing policy is the stippled area HJKLEDCB.

If the policy-makers were bolder and injected a stimulus greater than that needed to assure full employment in the instantaneous model, the cumulative amount of unemployment would be reduced in this lag model. The new equilibrium level of money national income would be higher, which in this context implies a rise in prices. To avoid that level of equilibrium, the stimulative measure would have to be reduced after a time. In the simplest case, government spending is increased by enough to insure full employment in the period when private spending declines and in the next period is decreased to the permanent level that it would assume also under the no-lag model. In period $n+1$, G in Table 5 becomes 26 instead of 20, resulting in an income of 75 instead of 69; G then drops to 20 in $n+2$ and successive periods, which is sufficient to maintain Y at 75 in $n+1$ and all later periods.

This second policy would be the obvious one to adopt were it not for uncertainty, coupled with the cost of reviewing decisions continuously. If that cost, along with institutional rigidities, makes a fresh decision impossible until several periods have elapsed, a more cautious stimulative policy may seem preferable.

If a fresh decision can be taken at the start of each period, then for any given length of period, the degree of risk is less than if policy can be reviewed only after two—or more—periods have passed. The more remote the point in time at which the effects of the policy decision are being felt, the greater, almost surely, is the dispersion of possible outcomes. If, then, policy can be reviewed at the start of each

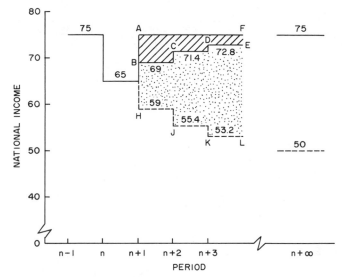

FIGURE 16. Shortfall from Full-Employment Income (from Tables 4 and 5)

period, the shorter the period the better, so far as risk is concerned. But the shorter the period, the greater the cumulative cost over a given time, since the number of reviews will be greater. It is likely that the more frequent reviews will be less costly, per review, though not proportionately so. A period as short as a week carries little risk but high cumulative cost of reviews. A period as long as five years reduces the cumulative cost of reviews but creates great risk.

The length of the period cannot be chosen at will; it is fixed, in the model now under examination, by the assumption that last period's income determines this period's consumption. Consumers may react sluggishly, so that this year's income determines next year's consumption, or they may react quickly, so that this week's income determines next week's consumption. In the former case the policy-maker must deal with a long period, in the second case with a short one.

The ideal type of policy, that is, one having effects only for the decision period, is not available in practice; almost any decision of consequence taken in period $n + 1$ will influence the economy substantially for several periods beyond that.

APPENDIX D TO CHAPTER TWENTY-TWO

Let government expenditures on goods and services, G, remain unchanged, and so too the tax rate, t, of a proportional tax on income yielding a revenue, T. The example presented here is confined to the recession phase: it compares national income, for each period in that phase, under a proportional income tax and under a fixed-revenue tax (Table 6).

Table 6   *Decline in Investment—Effect under Proportional Income Tax Compared with Effect under Fixed Tax*[a]

(1)	(2)	(3)	(4)	(5)	(6)	(7)	(8)
			$T = tY$ ($t = 0.3$) or				*Y under income tax less Y*
Period	C $=0.6(Y-T)_{-1}$	I	$T = 22.5$	G	$Y-T$	Y	*under fixed tax*
$n-1$	31.5	20	22.5	23.5	52.5	75	
n	31.5	10	19.5	23.5	45.5	65	0
	31.5	10	22.5	23.5	42.5	65	
$n+1$	27.3	10	18.2	23.5	42.6	60.8	1.8
	25.5	10	22.5	23.5	36.5	59.0	
$n+2$	25.6	10	17.7	23.5	41.4	59.1	3.7
	21.9	10	22.5	23.5	32.9	55.4	
$n+3$	24.8	10	17.5	23.5	40.8	58.3	5.1
	19.7	10	22.5	23.5	30.7	53.2	
.							
.							
.							
$n+\infty$	24.3	10	17.3	23.5	40.5	57.8	7.8
	16.5	10	22.5	23.5	27.5	50	

[a] Under the fixed tax, equilibrium income is $Y = (I + G - \alpha T)/(1 - \alpha)$.

Under the income tax, when full-employment investment, I_f, falls to a depression level, I_d, national income falls from its full employment level, Y_c, toward a new, depression equilibrium level, Y_d. That level is: $Y_d = (I_d + G)/(1 - \alpha(1 - t))$, just as the full-employment level is: $Y_f = (I_f + G)/(1 - \alpha(1 - t))$.

For the numerical illustration, let $I_f = 20$, $I_d = 10$, and $\alpha = 0.6$, as in Tables 4 and 5 above. Government expenditure on goods and services, G, is here set at 23.50 instead of at 10 as in Table 4, in order that full employment income may be the same as in that table, that is, 75, under an income tax rate of 30 per cent.

As Table 6 shows, by a comparison of the two lines for each period the compensatory effectiveness of the proportional income tax is zero in period n, 11 per cent for period $n+1$ (the 1.8 smaller decrease in income than under the fixed tax, divided by the decline, 75–59, that would have occurred under the fixed tax), 19 per cent for period $n+2$, and 23 per cent for period $n+3$. To the policy-maker these period-by-period figures reveal built-in-flexibility to be even less attractive, relative to discretionary changes in tax rate, than does the usual static compensatory-effectiveness measure. Figure 17 shows the differences graphically. The static compensatory-effectiveness measure overstates the amount of gain to come from built-in flexibility, when the gain is measured as the cumulated amount of unemployment prevented over time.

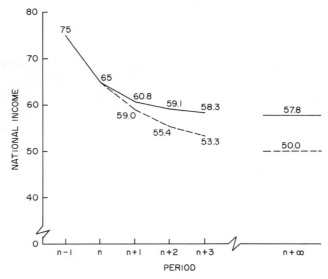

FIGURE 17. Built-In Flexibility of Proportional Income Tax in One-Period Consumption Lag Model

APPENDIX E TO CHAPTER TWENTY-TWO

Let

   s be the marginal propensity to save;

   v be the ratio of investment in any given period to the increase in income in that period over the income of the immediately preceding period;

  Y_t be the capacity output in period t;

  g_c be the rate of growth from one period to the next that makes full use of capacity;

  g_b be the rate of growth from one period to the next that reflects full employment;

   g be the required rate of growth where $g_c = g_b$;

then the relation for steady state growth, g, is

$$Y_{t+1} - Y_t \equiv (sY_{t+1})/v$$

and

$$g \equiv g_b \equiv g_c \equiv \left(\frac{Y_{t+1} - Y_t}{Y_t}\right) \equiv \frac{s}{v} \cdot \frac{Y_{t+1}}{Y_t} \equiv \frac{s}{v}(1+g)$$

Hence

$$g \equiv \frac{s}{v} \Big/ \left(1 - \frac{s}{v} \right)$$

If the time period is made indefinitely short, $Y_{t+1} \approx Y_t$, and $g \approx s/v$.

If, on the other hand, investment takes a period to produce capacity, and v is redefined accordingly,

$$Y_{t+1} - Y_t \equiv \frac{sY_t}{v},$$

$$\text{and } \underset{\sim}{g} \equiv \frac{s}{v}.$$

In an initial period, a given stock of capital and a given labor force produce a certain output. If the next period's investment increases the capital stock by a certain rate, g, the output too must increase at a rate g, if capacity is to be fully utilized, provided of course that the capital-output ratio remains unchanged. But it can remain unchanged, in the face of these assumptions, only if the labor force also increases at a rate g.

Thus the steady-state, full-employment, full-utilization level of income, Y, for any period $n + t$, can be expressed, given the income for period n, as

$$Y_n \left[1 + \left(\frac{s}{v} \left[1 + g \right] \right) \right]^t$$

For example, if Y_n, the income of the initial period, is 100, and if t is 2 (two periods), and if $s = 0.1$ and $v = 2.1$, and if the rate of growth of income is 0.05, then

$$Y_{n+t} = 100 \left[1 + \left(\frac{0.1}{2.1} \left[1 + 0.05 \right] \right) \right]^2 = 110.25.$$

National income per capita, in this model, is neither rising nor falling. The model is therefore commonly referred to as one of steady-state "growth," but it implies no economic growth as that term is defined here (see Chapter 23); it implies only a steadily larger economy.

There is no linkage between periods in this model, except in the amount of capital stock carried over from one period to the next. Accordingly, the assumption of a steady percentage increase in the labor force can be dropped, and full employment and full capacity utilization can be maintained, if only the ratio of saving-investment to national income changes correspondingly. Suppose, for example, that the labor force increases by 50 per cent from period $n + 1$ to period $n + 2$, contrasting with a 5 per cent increase from period n to period $n + 1$ (immigration might be the explanation). Output must increase, from period $n + 1$ to period $n + 2$, by 50 per cent, if the labor force is to be fully employed. In the example above, full employment for period $n + 2$ therefore now implies an output of $105(1.5) = 157.5$, an increase of 52.5 over the output of period $n + 1$, instead of an increase of 5.25. This output is feasible, if investment in period $n + 2$ is likewise ten times greater than assumed earlier, that is, ten times 11.025, or 110.25. The propensity to save must be, therefore, $110.25/157.5$, or 70 per cent, instead of 10 per cent, as earlier.

APPENDIX F TO CHAPTER TWENTY-TWO

The changes in income in A and B, resulting from the tax reduction in A, are shown (for a more generalized case where home consumption of output is allowed for) by the expressions:[1]

$$\Delta Y_a = T\left(\frac{c_a(1-c_b)+m_a m_b}{s_a s_b + m_a s_b + m_b s_a}\right)$$

$$\Delta Y_b = T\left(\frac{m_a}{s_a s_b + m_a s_b + m_b s_a}\right)$$

where

$\Delta Y_{a,\,b}$ is the change in income of A, or B
$c_{a,\,b}$ is the marginal propensity to consume domestic product in A, or B
$m_{a,\,b}$ is the marginal propensity to import in A, or B
$s_{a,\,b}$ is the marginal propensity to save in A, or B
T is the decrease in the tax bill

Hence $s = 1 - c - m$ [in the present extreme case, where $c = 0$, $s = 1 - m$].

In the present case, where $c_a = c_b = 0$, the first expression above reduces to

$$\Delta Y_a = T\frac{m_a m_b}{s_a s_b + m_a s_b + m_b s_a};$$

and since, as above,

$$Y_b = T\frac{m_a}{s_a s_b + m_a s_b + m_b s_a}$$

it follows that, since m_a and m_b are both less than 1, so that $m_a m_b < m_a$,

$$\Delta Y_b > \Delta Y_a$$

That is, Country A, by decreasing its income tax, increases the income of Country B by more than it increases its own income, in this extreme case where neither country consumes any of its own output.

The expressions above can be expressed entirely in terms of T and s in this extreme case, for, as $c_a = c_b = 0$, we have

$$m_a = 1 - s_a$$

$$m_b = 1 - s_b.$$

Hence

$$\Delta Y_a = T\left(\frac{(1-s_a)(1-s_b)}{s_a s_b + (1-s_a)s_b + (1-s_b)s_a}\right) = T\left(\frac{(1-s_a)(1-s_b)}{s_a + s_b - s_a s_b}\right)$$

1. I am indebted to Harry G. Johnson for this formulation of the analysis of this extreme case, and for the derivation of the expressions at the end of this Appendix. For an analysis of the balanced budget multiplier in an open economy, where consumption is also a function of private net financial asset holdings, see Wallace E. Oates, "The Theory of Public Finance in a Federal System," *Canadian Journal of Economics* (February, 1968), 1: 37–44, and sources cited therein.

If we assume that the marginal propensity to save is the same in both countries, the expression becomes

$$\varDelta Y_a = T\left(\frac{(\mathrm{I}-s)^2}{s(2-s)}\right)$$

Under this assumption, the results may be compared with those in a closed economy with the same propensity to save. In such an economy, $\varDelta Y = (\mathrm{I}-s)\varDelta Y + (\mathrm{I}-s)T$

$$\varDelta Y = T\left(\frac{\mathrm{I}-s}{s}\right) = T\left(\frac{(\mathrm{I}-s)^2}{s(\mathrm{I}-s)}\right) > T\left(\frac{(\mathrm{I}-s)^2}{s(2-s)}\right)$$

Thus the increase of income in A is less, in this extreme case of openness, with identical propensities to save, than if the tax reduction occurs in a closed economy with the same propensity to save.

To find the amount by which it is less, we subtract as follows:

$$T\left(\frac{(\mathrm{I}-s)}{s} - \frac{(\mathrm{I}-s)^2}{s(2-s)}\right) = T\left(\frac{\mathrm{I}-s}{s(2-s)}\right)$$

This expression gives the amount by which the increase in income in the closed economy exceeds the increase in income in the open economy, under the conditions stated above. If, for example, s is 0.2, this difference is $(2.22\ldots)T$.

If the illustration is made extreme in another respect, that is, if there is no home leakage at all in B, so that an increment of income in B is re-spent entirely, part of it on domestic output and part of it on imports, $s_b = 0$ in the first two expressions on page 573, and $c_b = \mathrm{I} - m_b$.

Hence

$$\varDelta Y_a = T\left(\frac{c_a(\mathrm{I} - \mathrm{I} + m_b) + m_a m_b}{m_b s_a}\right) = T\left(\frac{c_a + m_a}{s_a}\right)$$

In a closed economy,

$$\varDelta Y = T\left(\frac{c}{s}\right).$$

If $s = s_a$,

$\varDelta Y = \varDelta Y_a$.

Thus A, by its tax decrease, does as well for itself in the open economy, if B has no home leakage, as it does if it is a closed economy.

The derivation of the first two expressions in this note, on page 573, for $\varDelta Y_a$ and $\varDelta Y_b$, is as follows:

Let $c =$ marginal propensity for home consumption of domestic output, and $m =$ marginal propensity to import, so that $s = \mathrm{I} - c - m$, where $s =$ marginal propensity to save. Let $Y =$ change in income, $B =$ trade balance, and C and M autonomous changes in home consumption of domestic goods and in imports respectively.

$$Y_a = c_a Y_a + m_b Y_b + C_a + M_b$$

$$Y_b = m_a Y_a + c_b Y_b + C_b + M_a$$

$$B_a = M_b + m_b Y_b - M_a - m_a Y_a$$

We consider only C_a and M_a, not C_b or M_b.

Let $C_a = c_a T$, and $M_a = m_a T$, where T is the reduction in the tax bill.

$$(1 - c_a) Y_a - m_b Y_b = c_a T$$

$$- m_a Y_a + (1 - c_b) Y_b = m_a T$$

$$Y_a = T \left(\frac{c_a(1 - c_b) + m_a m_b}{s_a s_b + m_a s_b + m_b s_a} \right)$$

$$Y_b = T \left(\frac{m_a}{s_a s_b + m_a s_b + m_b s_a} \right)$$

As to the balance of trade of A:

$$B_a + m_a Y_a - m_b Y_b = - m_a T$$

$$B_a = \left(\frac{- s_b m_a}{s_a s_b + m_a s_b + m_b s_a} \right) T$$

CHAPTER TWENTY-THREE

Distribution of
Disposable Income; Economic Growth

A. DISTRIBUTION OF DISPOSABLE INCOME

1. Change in Distribution

THE EFFECT OF AN entire public finance system on the distribution of disposable income and wealth cannot be known; the question itself is meaningless.[1] The reasons for this conclusion have been given in Chapter 1 above, but it will be useful to repeat them here.

To say, for example, that households with before-tax incomes between $2,000 and $5,000 pay 12 per cent of that income in taxes, directly and indirectly, is to make a statement that is without significance because it is conceptually invalid. It is conceptually invalid because it postulates, for implicit comparison, a state of affairs in which there are no taxes whatever, and no government borrowing or creation of new money, hence impliedly no government services, not even of the minimum type and amount (see Chapter 20 above) necessary to assure existence of the society.

Moreover, the figure, 12 per cent in this example, is a macro economic statement, arrived at by adding the results of a series of partial equilibrium analyses, in which the incidence of each tax is ascertained on the assumption that the rest of the public finance system remains unchanged. Hence, even if an economy completely without government could be imagined, the manner in which the tax-burden figures have been built up would render the findings of doubtful value.

Further, the influence of free government services on rates of wages, interest, and

---

1. This fact is not generally accepted; but see Alan R. Prest, "The Budget and Inter-personal Distribution," in Institut International de Finances Publiques, *Congrès de Prague, The Budget and the Distribution of National Income* (Saarbrücken: Institut International de Finances Publiques, 1968): "We must therefore firmly reject the idea that any such calculations are possible. At the same time, it would be feasible to make calculations about the distributional effects of marginal changes in revenue and expenditure taken together . . .' *Ibid.*, p. 88.

profits, especially through their effect on supply of labor and capital, has been ignored in these computations.

The last two objections are not fatal to the concept of the distribution of burdens and benefits of a public finance system; they can in principle be overcome by the use of general equilibrium analysis that includes the effects of free government services. But the first objection is conclusive; it is the same kind of objection that would apply to the question, Who bears the burden of the wage bill? That question implies comparison with a state of affairs in which no wages are paid but everything else remains unchanged—an obvious impossibility.

That which can be known, in principle, is the change in distribution of disposable real income and wealth that can be achieved by a change in the public finance system or that has been achieved by past changes.

The existing distribution of disposable real income, including free government services in real income, is known; the distribution that would obtain under an alternative public finance system may be estimated or conjectured. The alternative public finance system must not be so rudimentary that the society and its economic structure could no longer exist, but aside from this restraint, the alternative system can be stipulated to consist of a lower level of taxes (in a designated pattern) or borrowing or new-money finance, and a lower level of government services or transfer payments (in a designated pattern). Or, of course, the alternative public finance system may consist of the same level of public finance activity but with a different pattern of taxation, or other financing, or free services or transfer payments, or any combination of these. Finally, the alternative may be postulated as a high level of government services, transfer payments, and financing, up to that uncertain boundary, if any (discussed above in Chapter 20) where the incentive effects of the financing measures and the income effects of the free services and transfer payments so reduce the will to work, take risks, or postpone consumption that again the kind of society and the degree of freedom in the economic structure that are assumed for the analysis could not be expected to exist.

Fortunately, the pressing policy issues with respect to public finance and distribution of disposable income and wealth can be analyzed even under the self-denying ordinance formulated above. If some households in a modern industrialized private enterprise economy have a disposable real income of only from $2,000 to $3,000, while others fall in the $10,000–$12,000 range, and still others show $100,000 or more, the following questions naturally arise:

(1) Since the differences in disposable real incomes (not to mention wealth) are so great, can they be narrowed by some readjustment of the public finance system?

(2) Since large differences can exist, can they be made still larger by readjustments in the public finance system?

The second question is never put quite so bluntly, but it is implicit in any proposal, of which there are many, continually, that reduce taxes on high-income groups.

These questions, limited to the effects of conceivable changes in the fiscal system, rather than attempting to assess the effects of the fiscal system as a whole, can be posed in a historical context or a comparative context: How much, and in what pattern, have disposable real incomes been changed by actual changes in the fiscal system of a country? If Country A adopted Country B's fiscal system, how would Country A's distribution of real disposable income change?

Proposed changes in a fiscal system are commonly supported by appeal to the figures purporting to show the distribution of burden and benefit of the existing entire public finance system. The allegation that, for example, those with incomes of between $2,000 and $5,000 pay 12 per cent of their incomes in taxes while those with incomes of between $5,000 and $8,000 pay only 10 per cent (a hypothetical example, but not too far from what some such studies show) is offered in support of measures that would increase the disposable incomes of the first group relative to those of the second group. The allegation that those with incomes over $100,000 pay, say, 40 per cent of their incomes in tax is offered on behalf of those individuals as a reason for narrowing the gap in the existing total tax burden between them and the lower-income groups. But, in the view taken here, what is really at issue is the degree to which the distribution of disposable real income can be changed—say, made more nearly equal—by changes in the public finance system. This issue is one of conflicts of interest, for which everyone may have his own normative standard, but which is settled by a political and social struggle and compromise. Whatever the standard, it can be neither supported nor opposed by the invalid statement that the existing system in its entirety distributes the tax and government service burden and benefit in a certain pattern. The invalidity of such a statement does not weaken the case of those who propose a change to reduce or increase the degree of inequality of disposable income. All of those who are offended, on general grounds, by the existing degree of inequality desire much the same kinds of public finance change whatever the figures of burden distribution purport to show.

The objections offered here apply only to macro analysis of the entire system. The distribution by income class of the burden of a small excise tax is a valid concept, since a state of affairs may be imagined in which that tax is absent and everything else is almost unchanged, particularly the supply and demand functions relevant to the hitherto taxed industry (see Chapter 1 above). Similarly, the distribution by income class of benefits from, say, free refuse collection is a valid concept. The distribution by income class of a small change in all taxes at once is possible only in the sense that the error inherent in the conceptual invalidity of this idea will be small in relation to the economy's total income; it may be large in relation to the increment in taxation (see the remarks in Chapter 1 on a small change in a broad-based tax).

2. The Mechanics of Comparison

The change in the real disposable income of a household arising from a postulated change in the public finance system may be computed in the following manner. The household in its initial state, as of a specified year, is assigned to a certain disposable money income group according to the money income it receives after deduction of taxes on that income. In the hypothetical state obtaining when the public finance change has worked itself out, the household's after-tax money income will have altered and so will the prices of at least some of the things it buys. It will buy more of some commodities than before, less of others, in the new situation. Its new after-tax money income is then deflated by a cost-of-living index representing the change in its cost of living. This index will differ, depending on whether it is weighted with the initial-period quantities of goods purchased (Laspeyres formula) or with the new, hypothetical-period quantities purchased (Paasche formula), or whether it is an average of those two indexes (Fisher's "ideal" formula). If the change in disposable real income is thought of as measurable cardinally, none of these indexes will do, because a cardinal concept of real income requires more information about the indifference map than is transmitted by any of these indexes. If the change is regarded simply as ordinal (better off, worse off), the index numbers may still give ambiguous answers. Prices and incomes may change in a pattern such that with the new money income the old market basket cannot be purchased at the new prices, while with the old income the new market basket could not have been purchased at the old prices. If E is the index number of money expenditure at the second date or second situation, using the first as a base $(\Sigma p_1 q_1 / \Sigma p_0 q_0)$, if P is the Paasche index, and L, the Laspeyres index, the consumer is certainly better off if E is no less than L and is greater than P, and is certainly worse off if E is no greater than P and is less than L. If E is less than L but greater than P, the answer is ambiguous. If E is greater than L but less than P, "something has gone wrong with the assumptions,"[2] particularly the assumption of unchanged tastes.[3] More generally, a statement that real income has changed by a certain percentage is meaningless unless referred to a specific set of prices.

For most policy purposes, a sufficient approximation will be obtained by using either the Laspeyres or the Paasche index consistently for all households and computing as if cardinal measurement were possible. The new money after-tax incomes, thus deflated for all households, can be compared with the after-tax money incomes in the initial period to ascertain what income groups have benefited from the public finance change and, subject to the reservations just made, by how much. Whether the degree of inequality in distribution of disposable real income has been reduced or increased, and by how much, raises the troublesome question of how to distinguish and rank degrees of inequality. A change in the Gini concentration ratio (the ratio of the area between the Lorenz curve and the 45-degree line to the area below the 45-degree line) does not always give an answer that accords with one's intuitive judgment, which may also insist on considering as a redistribution of income a certain shift in the income structure that leaves the Gini ratio unchanged.[4]

2. J. R. Hicks, "The Valuation of the Social Income," *Economica* (May, 1940), 7: 112.

3. See Carl S. Shoup, *Principles of National Income Analysis* (Boston: Houghton Mifflin, 1947), pp. 222–25.

4. For example, consider the following illustration, constructed by Professor Vickrey: "Suppose, for example, that we are to distribute \$1,100,000 of net income after tax among 100 persons, and that one tax schedule results in 10 after-tax incomes of \$1,100 and 90 of \$12,100 (i.e. the bottom 10% get 1% of income) while another tax schedule results in 1 income of \$110,000 and 99 incomes of \$10,000 (i.e. the top 1% get 10% of the income). Most

Moreover, the 45-degree line in a Lorenz diagram does not measure equal distribution if by that it is meant that every individual has the same amount of income as every other individual of the same age, but a higher income in his mature years than early or late in life.[5]

The coefficient of variation (standard deviation divided by the mean) may be a more useful indicator of whether a certain change in income structure represents what we should like to call a decrease or an increase in inequality (or no change). In any event, these problems are not peculiar to changes in degree of inequality achieved by varying the public finance system.

Changes, if any, in the amount of free services supplied to the household by government must be included if the full effects of the public finance measure on distribution of real income are to be known. These changes will not necessarily be unimportant, for reasons adduced in Section 3.c below.

3. The Possibilities of Change

Most public finance systems can probably be altered in ways that will change appreciably the distribution of real disposable income while not disturbing appreciably the values already reached for other goals. In principle, as explained in Chapter 19, the value of every public finance instrument in use will have to be altered to some extent, on certain assumptions, notably, that the system of instruments and goals is wholly interdependent. In practice, it seems likely that such adjustments need be only minor, though more analysis with general equilibrium models may show this assumption too optimistic. It is an assumption that will be made, however, in the discussion to follow, which in any event is designed merely to open up the subject. Thus it will be assumed that the types of redistributive change catalogued below would not alter appreciably the degree of approach to full employment or to a Pareto optimum and would permit continuance of the rate of growth, the degree of external equilibrium, and internal price stability that would obtain if no such redistributive measure were undertaken. If these assumptions appear at times too strenuous, it may be recalled that to prove them false does not necessarily mean that the redistribution cannot be achieved without disturbing these other goal values; it may mean, rather, that still other public finance instruments than the ones mentioned will have to change their values, in accordance with the framework outlined in Chapter 19.

For economy in exposition it will be assumed in the paragraphs to follow that the goal adopted is that of decreasing the degree of inequality (by some stated amount);

persons would probably express a significant preference for the latter result; indeed in the former case there would be a strong likelihood that some relief, either via public welfare, tax revision, or private charity, would be proposed for the 10 individuals with incomes insufficient to maintain decency and health, whereas the probability of action to redistribute part of the $110,000 income would seem much less likely. Yet the Gini ratio is .18 in both cases." See his "The Problem of Progression," *Univ. of Florida Law Review* (1968), 20: 438–39.

5. See, e.g., W. Allen Wallis and Harry V. Roberts, *Statistics: A New Approach* (Glencoe, Ill.: The Free Press, 1956), p. 258.

the analysis can readily be converted into one appropriate to the opposite goal of increasing inequality.

At certain points, where the assumption of no change occurring in the values of other goals appears too strenuous to be accepted even provisionally, the direction, if not the degree of departure from those goals will be noted. But the task of then indicating what other public finance instruments would need to be varied in value, to maintain these other goal values unaltered while still reaching the degree of change in distribution desired, will not be undertaken. To accomplish that task in even the roughest fashion will require a general equilibrium model of a type not provided by the present work.

A. TAXES

In most of the advanced industrial private enterprise economies the economically feasible tax changes that would most advantage the lowest income groups are, probably, somewhat as follows.

(1) Repeal of Payroll Taxes and Increase in Personal Income Tax Rates

A powerful redistributive measure would be repeal of the employees' and employers' payroll taxes, usually levied to finance social security benefits,[6] the revenue to be replaced by an increase in rates of an income tax, which has personal exemptions (a payroll tax usually does not). The payroll taxes commonly decline, as a percentage of wage before tax, inclusive of employer's contribution, as the wage rises, either because they are fixed amounts per head or because they do not apply above a certain ceiling wage. To maintain the existing relationship between taxation of unincorporated enterprise profits and corporate profits, the corporation income tax would also be increased. The reasons why the differential incidence of this tax measure would be decidely in favor of low-income households and households with large families have been set forth in Chapter 11, Section B.2.b and c and Chapter 16, Section B. The Pareto-like argument that those who receive the social security benefits should pay for them on something not too remote from an actuarial basis has lost much of its force as social security systems have come to cover all but a small percentage of the labor force in many countries, and as the ratio of a cohort's aggregate benefits to the aggregate taxes it paid increases as productivity and the price level increase (see Chapter 7, page 164). But to the extent that the quasi-actuarial argument is accepted, repeal of the payroll taxes would facilitate a full-employment tax policy, since counter-cycle variation in the rates of quasi-actuarial taxes amounts to unequal treatment of equals.

6. But see footnote 1, Chapter 16, as to the employers' payroll tax in France and footnote 5, Chapter 24, as to the United Kingdom's selective employment tax.

(2) Repeal of Part of Payroll Taxes, Increase in Corporation Income Tax

Entire repeal of the payroll taxes could not, in most countries, be compensated for by an increase in corporation income tax rates, because existing after-tax corporate profits are not large enough to supply revenue equal to the payroll taxes even at corporate rates of 80 or 90 per cent as compared with the current rates of around 30 or 40 per cent.[7] But if, say, half the payroll tax were replaced by an increase in corporate income tax rates, it seems likely that at the new equilibrium disposable income would go more to the lower income groups, and less to the upper. This conclusion assumes that capital is fairly inelastic in supply in a closed or not very open economy. It also assumes that movement of capital that could be expected away from the corporate sector into the non-taxed unincorporated sector would not increase capital's share in the national income. And it may need to assume that low-income consumers do not buy more, or at least not much more, from the highly taxed corporate sector (relative to what high-income groups do) than from the unincorporated sector.

(3) Transforming Universal Income Tax into Partial Income Tax

An obvious method available to the few countries that impose a universal income tax ("mass income tax") is to raise the personal exemptions to a level that will exempt most wage-earners and most low to moderate salary earners, replacing the lost revenue by increases in income tax rates above these levels and by an increase in corporate taxation. So much revenue is involved, however, that the rates needed to make up the entire loss would probably not be considered acceptable economically or administratively. This conjecture is supported by the fact that those large industrial countries in which the income tax is not of the universal type make up the revenue by high rates on their general sales taxes, not by extra high rates in either the income tax brackets above the wage line or in the corporation income tax.

(4) Replacing the Housing Tax by a
Value-added Tax or by Increases in Income Tax

In those countries where the real estate tax is heavy, replacement of the housing-tax part of the real estate tax by increases in rates of an income tax, even a universal income tax, would probably redistribute disposable income in favor of low-income groups. This result might be achieved, though to a lesser degree, even if the replacement tax were a proportional-rate value-added tax, consumption type.[8] In contrast to the other tax changes discussed above, however, this change would take some

---

7. The nominal rates are nearer 50 per cent, but accelerated and excess depreciation, investment credits, and investment subsidies reduce the real rate considerably.

8. See Chapter 11, page 253, and Chapter 15, pages 386–90.

time, perhaps indeed decades, to work out its redistribution effects. The stock of housing would climb slowly toward the level it would have reached had the tax never been imposed, and the price of housing at the margin of building would decrease slowly. Part of the benefit would go to owners of land.

While a good deal would be gained in counter-cycle built-in flexibility and discretionary action, something might be lost of the approach to Pareto-optimum levels of government service, since the real estate tax is to a limited degree a suitable benefit tax to pay for fire protection and certain other local government costs that property is partly responsible for. Moreover, a tax on land values alone does not strike at cost margins and so does not influence the pattern of output.

Since the tax to be reduced would be a local or provincial tax and the tax to be increased a national tax, usually, this change in tax pattern would require increased grants-in-aid or similar devices (see Chapter 25 below).

(5) Replacing General Sales Taxes by Increases in Income Tax

Replacing a high-rate general sales tax by an increase in income taxation would require in most countries so massive an increase in income taxation that a partial income tax would be transformed into a universal income tax. If the sales tax had exempted food, as many do, and dwelling rental, as all do (but they usually tax the sale of building materials), the redistributive gain for moderately low income groups might not be appreciable. But the lowest income groups, those below the income tax exemptions, would of course gain considerably.

(6) Replacing Excises or Import Duties by Income Taxation

In a few countries,[9] excise taxes on tobacco and liquor or import duties on some necessities are so high that they impose a considerable burden on low income groups or on certain households in low income groups, relative to what would result from increases in a progressive income tax.

(7) Summary

The income tax, personal or corporate, has been the replacement tax suggested for all these changes, because it alone is powerful enough, except perhaps the as yet untried form of progressive-rate expenditure tax that provides only low personal exemptions. But a combination of other smaller taxes, the tax on transfers *inter vivos* and at death, and the land tax, for example, could achieve a modest amount of redistribution as a replacement for a combination of other small taxes: certain excises and import duties, chiefly.

In the advanced industrial countries, substantial redistribution by tax-system

9. See Chapter 10, Sections A and B.

changes calls for considerable sacrifice by households with incomes in the middle brackets. Those whose incomes reach into the highest brackets taxed at, say, 40 per cent and upward under present laws, do not account for enough total income to allow a material improvement in the disposable income of the poor. The political and social struggle over redistribution is thus to a considerable degree one between households who are in poverty and those who have escaped from it, though not by very much, or whose parents or grandparents can be thus characterized. In some of the thinly populated underdeveloped countries, there may be enough aggregate income among the rich and the well-to-do to lift by an appreciable percentage the extremely low disposable income of the poor, if political and social forces could permit or compel the transfer. It is in just those countries, however, that the income tax is difficult to administer at a level of rates compatible with such a change.

B. TAXES AND UNREQUITED TRANSFER PAYMENTS

In most countries there are found both taxes that burden the lowest income groups[10] and welfare payments or subsidies to aid consumers. There is evidently a cross-hauling from the distributive point of view. This apparent waste of effort may in certain instances be justified, usually by either (1) a desire to redistribute the net advantage within a low-income group, as when aid is given to broken families with dependent children, who buy goods subject to a general sales tax, or (2) the technical difficulty of isolating, so that it alone might be repealed, that part of the tax that burdens the entire low-income group, as when a general sales tax that includes foodstuffs in its base is supplemented by a subsidy on foodstuffs.[11] There remains, no doubt, much cross-hauling of revenue that is difficult or impossible to justify. In sum, it appears likely that an appreciable part of the welfare payments and consumer subsidies merely counter the tax burden on the recipients, yielding no net redistributive effect. The remainder of the welfare payments and consumer subsidies is redistributive.

Further increments of welfare-or-subsidy will benefit the recipient households only if a method of financing can be found that will not in turn decrease their disposable incomes as much as the payments increase them. Massive increments, for example, those proposed under a negative-income-tax or similar devices,[12] can be financed in this way if the payments are restricted to those households below a fairly severe poverty line, for then even a general sales tax will not take away as much from these groups as they get from the income-conditioned welfare payments. The transfer payment obviously opens up possibilities for redistribution of disposable income on a scale unattainable by merely changing the pattern of taxation.

---

10. All phrases such as this are intended only in the tentative differential sense: the tax can be replaced by some other tax such that the disposable income of the low-income group is increased, even after all the other instruments in the system have been readjusted to preserve the other goal values (full employment, price stability, etc.).

11. As in Norway; see Chapter 9, page 247.

12. See Chapter 7.

c. Free Services

Even without increasing the total of group-consumption (nonmarketable) services supplied free by the government, a substantial redistribution of real disposable income could be achieved.

In large urban areas with concentrated slums, it would be technically feasible, though at present politically impracticable, to so repattern free refuse removal that the slum areas would be kept completely clear of rubbish and garbage day and night at the opportunity cost of allowing refuse to pile up uncollected in the more well-to-do areas. The change in real income, whether computed on the basis of what the slum inhabitants would pay if they had to, rather than being thrust back to the former level of service, or what the rich would pay to retain the original pattern of service, or by the cost of the service, would be appreciable, except to the degree that the benefit from the increased service was lost to landowners in higher rents.

A similarly radical redisposition of fire-fighting forces in a large city might reduce the number of deaths from fire in the slum areas while increasing, but probably only moderately, deaths in other areas of the city. Measurement of this benefit to the low-income groups in money terms is difficult but not impossible. Disposable income of the group for the year in question might be deemed to be reduced by the capitalized value of the earning power lost by loss of life, or the loss might be spread over the years to come. But this measure neglects the benefits from fire protection to non-earners, and in any case it neglects some of the values that would motivate this change in pattern of fire protection. At the least, the benefit could be measured in terms of input, that is, cost of supplying the additional fire protection. Similar subtractions would be made for the disadvantaged groups.

Total disposable income might be reduced by this redistribution, since the increment of property loss in the now less well protected wealthy areas could easily exceed the decrement in property loss in the now better protected slum areas. But, as long as the increment of loss did not appreciably affect total output, by denuding business areas of fire protection, the low-income groups would not themselves suffer from this net decline in the community's material assets.

A heavier concentration of police in a slum area might easily so lower the cost of doing business there, not to mention the consequent decrease in theft and destruction of consumer property, that the residents of that area would be considerably better off—at the expense, of course, of those in other areas whose losses would mount as policemen were drained from those districts.

The level of education in low-income areas could be raised, both in terms of input (cost) and in terms of achievement, that is, the level of education absorbed by the children, at the cost of reducing levels in other parts of the city.

Street repair, street lighting, free water supply, sewerage, rodent control (this is linked closely to refuse removal and to housing subsidies), level of free medical and hospital care, all are capable technically of being redistributed radically in many large cities, to the advantage of low-income groups, but of course at substantial disadvantage to the higher-income groups.

When all these possibilities are summed, they amount to redistribution of somewhat the same magnitude as the technically feasible changes in the pattern of taxation, if not in the pattern of tax-cum-transfer payments. This statement applies only to large cities in which there are great disparities in level of service output, if not service input. But such cities, in highly industrialized economies, account for a considerable percentage of the combined population of all those economies.

In smaller cities and towns the levels of service may be less markedly disparate from one part of the city to another, except where ethnic, color, or other class differences have put power in the hands of one group that uses it consciously to discriminate against another.[13] In rural areas the general level of free services is commonly so low over the entire responsible jurisdiction that much less could be accomplished by changing the pattern in which they are distributed within such jurisdiction, though redistribution across jurisdictional boundaries may be more consequential.

A considerable part of the increase in disposable real income to the residents of the low-income areas would be lost by them to those who own the land and buildings in those areas if the service increment attracted households from other parts of the city, or from other cities, to compete, by offering higher rents per square foot, for the as yet unchanged amount of dwelling accommodation in the low-income areas. This possibility is reduced as the area covered by the increase in level of service becomes wider. A large part of the benefits in a demonstration project of better city services limited to a few blocks would soon find its way into the hands of landlords (in the absence of rent control) as households from other poor areas of the city started bidding up the per-square-foot prices, by being willing to live in more crowded conditions in order to get the better city services. At another extreme, a new high level of services applying to all the low-income areas would perhaps— though of this no one can be certain—attract little competition from households in the rest of the city, even though they were being disadvantaged absolutely, not merely relatively, by the postulated decrease in level of service given to them. The greater danger to the newly advantaged poor would probably come from poor families in other cities, or poor migrants who would now swing toward this city in larger numbers. Any massive program of the type described here would very likely need to be accompanied by rent control if its objectives were to be largely attained, or, alternatively, it would need to be accomplished on a nation-wide scale in all cities simultaneously, to avoid loss of benefits in higher rents.

Insofar as the benefits were absorbed in higher rents, rents would tend to decline in areas or cities where the level of service was not increased, or was decreased. The result would be a redistribution of income largely among landlords, rather than from well-to-do to poor.

D. TAXES AND FREE SERVICES

An increase in the level of government group-consumption services, all of it concentrated on low-income areas, and financed entirely by taxation that changes

---

13. Against Negroes in the United States, Indians in certain Latin American countries.

only the disposable real income of upper-income groups is a fourth method of income redistribution. In its technical possibilities it probably ranks above the redistribution of an existing total of services (Section 3 above) and approaches that possible by a combination of higher taxes and larger transfer payments (Section 2 above), provided, again, that the benefits are not siphoned off in higher rents.

E. INTEREST RATES

By purchasing financial assets or by selling fewer securities than it otherwise would, and financing this procedure with newly created money, the government can lower the structure of interest rates, at least for a time. This probably benefits the low-income groups at the expense of the high-income groups. If a rise in commodity prices follows, the distribution of benefits and disadvantages is not clear (see Chapter 18), but on the assumption that the low-income groups are disproportionately in debt, the effects of the price rise complement in this respect the distributive effects of the initial change in interest rates. If prices rise enough to generate expectations of further increases, nominal interest rates will rise, but they may still be declining or remaining steady in real terms. As the rise in prices gains momentum, an estimate of the total redistributive effect becomes very uncertain, except, again, in a society where the poor are chiefly debtors and the wealthy, creditors—and even here there is a countervailing consideration, for the loan market will dry up or loans will become available only at very high real rates if the inflation appears to be getting out of hand.

Redistribution of disposable real income through changes in the interest rate can therefore operate only within modest limits. The issue becomes significant chiefly when the government is choosing among fiscal tools to reduce a moderately excessive aggregate demand, or to stimulate a moderately depressed economy. If the primary aim, aside from full employment with stable prices, is a more nearly equal distribution of income, booms must be checked by higher taxation of the upper-income groups rather than by sale of financial assets, and depressed economies must be stimulated by purchase of financial assets rather than by lower taxes on the upper-income groups. But this policy cycle could scarcely be repeated indefinitely.

A more selective instrument is government lending at a subsidized interest rate to particular types of borrowers: farmers, small business firms generally, homeowners, disaster victims, and so on. The subsidy element is measured by the difference between the rate charged and the rate the borrower would have had to pay in the market. This spread in rates is equivalent to a transfer payment by the government, and can be analyzed under Section 3.B above. If the borrower could have obtained only a smaller loan, or none at all, no matter what interest rate he offered, part or all of the principal amount is itself a transfer payment, equivalent to a reserve for bad debts, and again better analyzed under Section 3.B.

4. Possibilities of Change in Wealth

By inducing a fall in interest rates, the government increases the net worth of creditors and equity owners by the simultaneous rise in the present value of their claims. If the claim matures shortly, the rise in net worth is small, and is more than offset by the decline in investment income obtainable from then on. But if the claim is a perpetuity, the market value the holder now possesses represents, as an alternative to consuming an unchanged amount each year indefinitely, a much larger potential consumption immediately than before the interest rate fell. In this sense of possessing a preferable set of options he is better off than before. Similarly, the real net worth of a household can be decreased by a public finance measure that increases the rate of interest.

Transfers of wealth on a large scale are effected by inflation in a country where debtors are by and large different persons from the creditors. If the debtor owns no property, the redistribution of wealth simply increases his net worth from a negative amount to zero, which is nonetheless a real increase.

In some instances a propertyless class, farm laborers or tenants for example, have been put in a position to purchase land by the issuance of government securities on their behalf that the government requires the initial landowners to accept, and whatever obligation the new owners may face to service this debt has been reduced to a nominal amount by subsequent inflation engineered by the government.[14]

So-called capital levies have in practice turned out to be simply a special form of annual taxation.[15] The proceeds have rarely been used to supply households with substantial amounts of property, save in some cases following natural disasters.

Any increase in a household's wealth can be treated as a combination of increase in income plus a saving of that income, and indeed this is the preferable terminology for rigorous analysis. Everything can be subsumed under change in disposable income. But when the change is large and appears implicitly (shrinkage in real value of debt in an inflation) or is in kind (rebuilding of houses by government after an earthquake), it may usefully be distinguished from a change in income that is not accompanied by a corresponding change in a marketable asset or liability.

A reduction in incomes of one group may in this sense finance an addition of net wealth to another group. An example would be a substantial increase in income tax on incomes above a certain level, to finance the purchase of slum housing by the government, which would then donate these properties to the tenants, or to a low-income group selected on some basis other than current tenancy. The former owners would receive government debt that would be serviced by the increased tax on incomes (there is of course no inflationary finance involved here). Apparently there has been little or no experience with this kind of income-capital redistribution, but something like it may be the only way to improve housing conditions in certain slum areas where the rental technique seems to induce both tenants and landlords to neglect upkeep of the property.

14. The land reform in Japan under the occupation in the late 1940's is an illustration.
15. Chapter 14, page 367.

B. RATE OF ECONOMIC GROWTH

1. Public Finance Measures in Growth Models[16]

The problem discussed here is how to achieve a certain rate of increase in per capita income, over time. The particular rate of increase that is the goal is assumed to have been set by a political or other social decision. Some persons will be worse off and some, better off, under one rate of increase than under another, aside from a "Golden Age" rate of accumulation, which is of no practical importance for the present discussion.[17] Thus the rate that is finally selected as a target will reflect a compromise of conflicting views, or the dominance of one decision-making group.

Chapter 22, on full employment, has utilized part of what is included in models of growth theory. If technological improvement is abstracted from, these models do not require that per capita income be increasing in order to have "growth." Our interest here, in contrast, is confined to measures that generate an increase in per capita income.

The natural rate of growth in the broader sense of growth can be affected by public finance measures that alter the rate of population growth or the rate of technological improvement; an increase in the latter rate will of course increase per capita income. Little is known, however, about the effects on population of family allowances, income tax exemptions or credits for dependents, extra taxation of bachelors, and similar measures that are to be found in certain income tax laws. The rate of technological improvement is probably more amenable to change by public finance measures, but the quantitative relations are highly conjectural. The level of gainful consumption (see p. 592 below), the degree of risk-taking, and a variable amount of labor supplied by a given population of a given age and sex distribution, all of which can be influenced by public finance measures, have been incorporated in few growth models, if any.

Disequilibrium growth models afford a limited opportunity to employ public finance variables. The rate of growth of aggregate income can be moved off its equilibrium path for a time, by public finance measures (see Chapter 22 above): for example, the community's saving may be increased by a new tax, and even though the economy eventually returns to the initial percentage rate of growth, per capita income will then be higher than it otherwise would have been, because of the abnormally high rate of saving that will have characterized the transition period.

16. The most comprehensive and detailed model emphasizing public finance variables is that by Challis A. Hall, Jr., in his *Fiscal Policy for Stable Growth* (New York: Holt, Rinehart and Winston, 1960). See also Musgrave, *The Theory of Public Finance, op. cit.*, Chapter 20 and Chapter 22, Section E; and Warren L. Smith, "Monetary-Fiscal Policy and Economic Growth," *Quarterly Journal of Economics* (February, 1957), 71: 36–55.

17. Given an unchanging investment-income ratio over all time, there will be a unique boundless steady-state rate of growth that maximizes consumption for every generation; it must be such that net investment equals profits. See Edmund Phelps, "The Golden Rule of Accumulation: A Fable for Growthmen," *American Economic Review* (September, 1961), 51: 638–43.

A sacrifice of current per capita consumption will have succeeded in raising future per capita income.[18]

2. Definition of Growth

In their most general sense, measures to promote growth include those that prevent per capita income from declining as rapidly as it otherwise would. If population is outstripping food supply, a reduction in certain types of current consumption may allow greater investment, which will slow down the decline in per capita income.

Aggregate income may be falling but per capita income rising, perhaps owing to emigration of children and elderly persons, or to loss of life through an epidemic or other natural disaster. The increase in per capita income might be greater still, under growth-promoting public finance measures.

In any event, the issue is, whose consumption shall be restricted now, or who shall be induced to work more now, in order that per capita income at some future time may be higher than it otherwise would be—unless some measure can be found that will painlessly increase the rate of technological improvement.

Per capita income is here taken to be that of the inhabitants of a certain geographic area. Income that originates in the area but that flows abroad is therefore not counted in measuring growth. That part of the value of the petroleum, for example, extracted within a country that goes abroad as interest or profits to nonresidents is not included. Income from foreign sources accruing to residents of the country is included. Labor income received by foreign workers temporarily residing in the country is excluded. The definition of aggregate income used in this concept is therefore a residence concept, not a source concept, and the rate of economic growth of a country is measured by the rate of increase in the per-person income of its residents from domestic or foreign sources.

National income, not gross national product, is the aggregate measure, and investment is net investment, not gross. Commonly, gross investment is expressed as a proportion of gross national product; depreciation is subtracted neither from the numerator nor the denominator, and the ratio of gross investment is therefore larger than the ratio of net investment. Some 10 per cent or perhaps even more of gross national product must be gross investment if the economy's capital stock is merely to remain constant, so that net investment is zero.[19] To be sure, measurement of depreciation and obsolescence is highly uncertain. But it seems preferable in this case to employ an inaccurate estimate of a useful concept rather than a fairly accurate estimate of a doubtful concept.

An estimate of income produced in the non-monetized sector must be included in the total; otherwise, public finance measures could promote "growth" simply by inducing movement from non-monetized to monetized sectors. Similarly, imputed

18. See Appendix to this chapter.

19. See T. P. Hill, "Growth and Investment According to International Comparisons," *Economic Journal* (June, 1964), 74: 287–304.

income of housewives and imputed net income from owner-occupied dwellings and other consumer durables are here assumed to be included in national income, although in fact no national income estimates as yet do include imputed income from work in the home.

National income does not include leisure. Indeed, other things equal, the more leisure taken the smaller is the national income. Since leisure is not a free good for most persons, it must be counted as income in the broadest and most generally useful sense of that term. It is, however, not so counted in this chapter, which is restricted to the narrower analysis of growth in rate of output of consumer goods and net investment goods, per person.[20]

3. Public Finance Measures That Increase Rate of Growth[21]

For a given population, and assuming full employment and full utilization, the rate of growth of an economy will increase with each of the following: gainful consumption (including education), investment in the conventional sense, an increase in the intensity and hours of work, technical progress, and, possibly, social risk-taking. The public finance systems that would increase each of these quantities will be sketched in the following paragraphs.

A. GAINFUL CONSUMPTION

Gainful consumption is consumption of a type such that, in the event that it decreases, the output of the economy will decrease, either now or later, by more than the decrement in consumption.

A large part of the consumption of workers with very low incomes in less developed countries is of this type. If these workers are forced to reduce their consumption they are likely to become enfeebled from subsequent illness or malnutrition that reduces their output by more than the reduction in consumption. Per capita income is smaller than it would have been had consumption not been reduced. This statement of course abstracts from the use made of the resources freed by the decrement in consumption. Although the consumption of even the poorest workers includes items, say tobacco, alcohol, or other drugs that do not represent gainful consumption, these items are not likely to be the sole object of retrenchment when the workers are forced to reduce their consumption.

20. Net investment goods are included only because they embody consumer goods to come, either directly or because they produce other producers' goods, etc. If a net investment good is counted in computing the rate of growth, the consumers' goods it gives rise to later must be excluded (by a depreciation deduction) in computing the rate of growth for those later years.

21. Shaping the public finance system of a less developed country to promote economic growth has in recent years become the subject of special monographs; see Ursula K. Hicks, *Development Finance: Planning and Control* (Oxford: Clarendon Press, 1965), and A. R. Prest, *Public Finance in Underdeveloped Countries* (London: Weidenfeld and Nicolson, 1962).

By the same reasoning, most of an increase in consumption by very low-income workers would be, up to a point, gainful consumption.

Consumption by housewives of low-income households is similarly gainful consumption. It is often overlooked because their output is imputed output, not included even in tabulations of national income. Consumption by children in these households is entirely gainful consumption, at least in the first few years of life.[22] After the first few years the child's consumption can vary somewhat, even about a low level, without affecting appreciably his vigor and capacity in his working years.

Growth is achieved by increasing gainful consumption at the expense of productive consumption, where productive consumption is defined as consumption that pays for itself in part or in whole, in increased output, but not more than that.

For comparison with investment of the conventional type, gainful consumption is to be evaluated as a competing use of funds, to ascertain which use will yield a higher return, but after some allowance for the fact that gainful consumption does, and conventional investment does not, provide satisfaction currently (this allowance, however, is not strictly speaking a part of the growth test).

In many industrialized economies, but not in all, even the poorest households receive enough so that there is very little, if any, gainful consumption at the margin in any household. There is correspondingly little or no occasion to alter relative levels of consumption by various households in order to increase the rate of growth, with two possible exceptions. First, perhaps some unproductive consumption can be traded off for productive consumption, or more productive for less productive consumption. Second, special types of gainful consumption may remain to be exploited even in a wealthy economy: education, for example.

With respect to growth-increasing consumption in low-income countries, a policy oriented solely toward growth would reduce all taxes where reduction would increase the disposable real incomes of the very low-income groups, on the assumption that households in this group would spend a very large proportion of the increase on gainful consumption. Such tax reductions would be financed by tax increases on all the higher-income classes. Welfare payments designed to maintain consumption up to the margin where gainful consumption disappears would be introduced.

An increase in disposable real incomes of poor households would probably not induce an increase in births. In fact the number of births might decline. But population might increase, since a reduction in child mortality, especially in the years up to six or so, could be expected from that increase in disposable income. The resources used up in childbearing and child support that under present conditions are largely wasted economically by deaths of infants and very young children (not to mention more important, non-economic considerations) would become to a greater extent investment in future adult workers. The incremental consumption needed to carry the individual through the remainder of his childhood, adult life, and old age might

22. See Carl S. Shoup, "Production from Consumption," *Public Finance* (1965), 20(1–2): 178–202. Many less developed countries would probably attain a higher rate of growth over a span of several decades if they spent more than they do on high-protein foods for their younger children; even at the cost of a lower level of investment in plant, equipment, and public infrastructure.

well be exceeded by his contribution to output in adult life. This result would of course no longer obtain beyond some point of increased pressure of population on resources, unless the workers became highly skilled and had ample capital to work with.[23]

Some increase in the level of certain free services rendered by government, notably public education, would usually represent gainful consumption.

In practice, such a program for low-income countries implies repeal of general sales taxes, and import duties on necessaries. Excise taxes on beer and tobacco would be repealed if a smaller amount of money would be spent on them, under no tax. To finance these tax reductions and the increase in transfer payments, and government services, there would be an increase in income taxes on most salaries and on a substantial part of wages, and on all profits, interest, and land rent, together with increases in luxury excises (including taxes on distilled spirits), property transfer taxes, and the like.

B. CONVENTIONAL INVESTMENT

The volume of private net investment spending will be assumed here to vary directly with the change in income and with the total amount of after-tax profits, corporate or noncorporate, and inversely with the rate of interest, but no specific parameters or relative weights will be suggested.

To increase the rate of growth by inducing an increase in the volume of conventional investment, the public finance system must therefore induce an increase in income—the end becomes a means, must allow post-tax profits to increase, and must lower the rate of interest. The first of these requirements, involving the accelerator, does not by itself permit of an indefinite expansion of the rate of investment, but instead raises the issue of compatibility of a given rate of growth with the assumption of full employment (see Chapter 22).

To increase the amount of after-tax profits, necessarily at the expense chiefly of wages, for any given level of output, the corporation income tax must be reduced and so also that part of the income tax that strikes dividends, and profits of unincorporated business firms, these reductions being financed by an increase in payroll taxes, sales taxes, and the income tax in the lower brackets. The differential incidence of this group of tax changes would almost surely increase the absolute amount of post-tax profits. Some increase in free government services to business firms might also increase profits, although competition might cause most of the benefits to be passed on to consumers (see Chapter 4). In place of reducing tax rates, reduction of the income tax on profits could be accomplished by accelerated depreciation; 100 per cent accelerated depreciation would amount to complete exemption of profits earned on depreciable capital, provided a complete loss-offset were assured (see page 302). Negative taxation of profits could be achieved by investment credits coupled with 100 per cent accelerated depreciation.

23. For a closer consideration of this problem in a public finance context, see Shoup, *op. cit.*

To lower the interest rate the government would need to reduce its volume of debt financing, or, if there were no debt financing, it would need to retire some of its debt. It could also run a surplus in the budget and lend at low, zero, or negative interest rates to private enterprise. Finally, it could follow the familiar pattern of increasing infrastructure and other conventional investment that could then be used by private firms or consumers free of charge.

In an open economy, the low-tax, low-interest rate policy might induce a large inflow of equity capital in search of profits. This inflow would not necessarily lead to growth as that term is used here, since after-tax earnings on that capital would not go to residents. Only as the country's real-wage bill increased as a consequence of the capital inflow would growth occur. A similar remark applies to equity capital repatriated by residents to take advantage of the higher rates now obtaining at home.

c. Incentives to Increase Intensity and Duration of Labor

To strengthen the incentives to increase the intensity and duration of work, the tax system must be recast to make the marginal rate of tax on workers lower relative to the average rate than it has been. The income effect is then increased relative to the substitution effect (see page 335). This might be accomplished to a considerable degree without making the average rate of the taxes on wages and salaries regressive by household income; for example, overtime wages might be taxed at a lower rate than any part of straight-time wages, yet the average rate would remain progressive if overtime was not a large proportion of total time. It would be more difficult, technically, to reduce the rate of tax on piece-work wages above a certain level of intensity of work.

Extremely high tax rates on investment income would put pressure on the recipient to enter the labor force, or to work harder; the high marginal rate here has no distinctive effect on work, except as work is undertaken in order to accumulate capital because of the rate of return that capital offers.

The aim of stimulating the amount of work would also be served by reducing the level of free government services of a type such that, if not rendered by the government, they, or close substitutes for them, would be purchased on the market by the erstwhile recipients of the free service. But services that enhance the ability and the desire to work, medical care for example, would stimulate labor if increased.

The ability to work intensively and for long hours, as distinguished from the economic incentives to do so, has been discussed in Section 1 above, under gainful consumption.

d. Technical Progress

Increased outlays on education will presumably increase technical progress, and there will be some gain from government programs undertaken for other purposes, military and space programs, for example. Free dissemination of technical information by the government will help. Favorable tax treatment for inventors is another possibility. For the most part, however, the public finance system can best encourage technical progress by encouraging investment itself.

E. SOCIAL RISK ASSUMED

Private risk-taking can be encouraged by subsidies to investment or it can be reduced by making more nearly complete a loss offset under an income tax. In either event, the amount of social risk taken may be increased (see Chapter 2, Section B.2.c). Up to a point, this procedure will increase growth, or at least will increase the expected value of growth or reduce the risk associated with any given expected value, owing to the pooling of risks. Beyond this point, the probability of growth increases along with the probability of loss but at a slower rate. A very poor society, facing dissolution if it does not grow, might consider it worth while to encourage this kind of use of resources. For most economies, however, there must be a point beyond which private enterprise must be deterred from taking added risks.

F. SUMMARY

The public finance changes to increase growth that operate through gainful consumption are largely opposite to those that work through increasing conventional investment, and those that work through intensity and duration of work are somewhat of a mixture of the other two. Clearly, no general rule can apply for all countries. Perhaps the less developed countries would grow most rapidly by giving major, but certainly not exclusive, weight to gainful consumption. For already highly developed countries, aside from substantial underdeveloped areas and disadvantaged minority groups, growth is probably maximized by a heavy weighting of the measures that induce and facilitate conventional investment. As to whether the intensity and duration of work can be appreciably affected by changes in the public finance system, little is known, but this factor is probably less important than the other two. The direct effect on technical progress is relatively minor, aside from education, and that on risk-taking is of doubtful value for growth.

4. Implications for Certain Other Goals

If the weighting suggested in the preceding paragraph were used, growth would be increased in underdeveloped countries by a network of public finance measures that on balance might also reduce inequality of distribution of disposable income and wealth. Of course any given reduction in inequality would be reached under such a program only by coincidence, unless the number of instruments were sufficient and sufficiently unconstrained. In the advanced industrial countries the goals of increased growth and of reduced inequality seem, in contrast, to be in conflict, in the sense that within the constraints that normally obtain it would be very difficult both to increase the rate of growth and to decrease the rate of inequality (see Chapter 19, Section C.2).

Full employment is in principle attainable for any rate of growth, but again constraints may make this goal unattainable.

APPENDIX TO CHAPTER TWENTY-THREE

Ryuzo Sato has shown that under certain not extreme assumptions the transition period, i.e., the period during which the system is returning to the equilibrium path of growth, would be 90 per cent complete only after 150 years in an economy with a natural growth rate of 2 per cent, and after 50 years in one where the natural growth rate was 7 per cent.[1] K. Sato has shown that the adjustment period will be reduced if capital goods are less durable, if technical improvements are more embodied, and if the capital elasticity of output is lower;[2] the time may be reduced by as much as three-quarters.[3] Douglas Dosser[4] has demonstrated that the adjustment period can be made still shorter by an active fiscal policy designed for that end, for example, an income tax starting at a rate of 20 per cent and increasing by 1 per cent (i.e., by $\frac{2}{10}$ of a percentage point) each year. Moreover, by introducing a parameter m measuring the effect of taxation on technological advance and the growth of labor effort, Dosser can, for certain values of m, obtain a new equilibrium rate of growth that is different from the original one. In one of his illustrations, an original equilibrium growth rate of 3.5 per cent is replaced, after a 27-year transition period, by an equilibrium growth rate of 3.41 per cent.

1. Ryuzo Sato, "Fiscal Policy in a Neo-Classical Growth Model: An Analysis of Time Required for Equilibrating Adjustment," *Review of Economic Studies* (February, 1963), 30: 16–23.

2. K. Sato, "On the Adjustment Time in Neo-classical Growth Models," *Review of Economic Studies* (July, 1966), 33: 265.

3. *Ibid.*, p. 263. See also his "Taxation and Neo-Classical Growth," *Public Finance* (No. 3, 1967), 22: 346–68.

4. "Adjustment through Fiscal Policy in Neo-Classical Growth Models," unpublished ms., 1968.

CHAPTER TWENTY-FOUR

Price Stability; External Equilibrium

A. PRICE STABILITY

1. Topics, Concepts

AN UPWARD MOVEMENT in the price level other than one provoked by the government to draw resources away from the private sector (Chapter 18) is the type of price rise discussed in the present chapter. The aim usually is to halt or perhaps to limit the rise and seldom if ever to reverse it; in this respect price policy is asymmetrical with employment policy, which attempts to return to a previous level of higher employment. Price policy takes as a base the existing level of prices, whatever the level may have been in the past. No rollback of prices to lower previous levels is usually contemplated; on occasion some modest reflation of prices may be the aim.

Price stability is a conflict-of-interests goal, not a consensus goal as is full employment. Some households and firms will be better off even over the long period if the rise in prices is not checked, than they will be if it is checked, considering the public finance measures that will have to be employed in the latter instance. This may be so even if the total real product of the economy is smaller under inflation.

Public finance measures can slow down or halt a rise in prices either by reducing aggregate demand or by increasing aggregate supply. The latter possibility has been slighted in most analyses.

Forestalling a price increase and halting it are sufficiently different technical tasks to warrant separate treatment. Section 2.A below is concerned chiefly with forestalling cyclical rises in the price level, Section 2.C and Section 2.D, with halting a rise that has been going on for some time.

The absolute and relative efficacy of each public finance instrument in checking inflation will vary considerably, depending on the degree of development of the economy, the importance of the non-monetary sector, and the degree of exposure to international trade and capital movements. Efficacy will also vary with the rate of inflation. The discussion below will consider, in turn, (1) a potential or actual cyclical rise in prices, (2) a slow secular rise due to uneven technical progress or to cost-push forces, (3) a substantial rise of, say, 10 to 30 per cent a year over several years, (4) a rapid rise, more than, say, 30 per cent a year, but short of hyper-inflation, and (5) hyper-inflation.

As in the analysis of Chapter 22 on how to attain full employment, lags must be allowed for; the type of prescription that calls for instantaneous closing of the inflationary gap is of limited value in halting a rise in prices. It may be of more consequence in forestalling a rise. The present chapter offers no specific lagged models, but the tone of the discussion implies period analysis.

2. Checking or Forestalling Price Inflation

A. CYCLICAL RISE IN PRICES

The rise in prices at an annual rate of up to, say, 5 per cent or so that occurs in a high-activity phase of the cycle, or that would occur in the absence of public finance measures specifically designed to forestall it, is here assumed to be due chiefly to increases in real cost that come with overtime pay, use of less efficient workers and less efficient plant and equipment, crowding of existing plant and transportation and storage facilities, higher inventories per unit of sales, and the like. Thus the marginal real costs of production and of transportation, warehousing, retailing, and other aspects of distribution rise. Since factor rates of pay, including profits, do not decrease in money terms, or at least not sufficiently, prices of final products must rise.

(1) Reducing Demand

In the present state of knowledge, including the present stock of public finance instruments (see Chapter 19) a reduction in aggregate demand that is achieved by increasing the usual kinds of broad-based tax will halt a rise in prices, or forestall it, only, it appears, at the cost of a somewhat higher level of unemployment than would otherwise prevail. A rough trade-off is thus required between the rapidity with which price stability is achieved and the level of unemployment that is to be tolerated.

A second major policy issue is whether the direct restriction on private-sector spending should be applied chiefly to consumption spending or to investment spending, or indeed concentrated wholly on the one or the other. To concentrate the restriction entirely on consumption spending, some unfamiliar public finance instruments must be used: either a universal type of expenditure tax (see Chapter 13) or a broad-based sales tax or value-added tax that actually strikes only purchases of consumer goods (see Chapter 9).

An increase in the individual income tax rates will take money from partnerships and proprietorships. Even in an advanced industrialized economy these unincorporated concerns account for a large share, probably more than one-third, of investment spending, notably for housing and agriculture.

Investment spending, in contrast, can be singled out for restraint by familiar public finance measures. An increase in the rate of the corporation income tax will allow perhaps one-third of investment spending to escape, but no consumption spending will be directly taxed. Consumption spending will be checked indirectly to a moderate degree by the effect on dividend payments, which is usually slight in industrialized countries unless the rate increase is severe. Dividend payments may be somewhat more affected in the less industrialized countries where a large part of corporate value-added arises in family corporations whose owners vary their personal spending appreciably with variations in the fortunes of the corporation.

The corporation income tax reduces investment spending both by its income effect and by its substitution effect. The substitution effect will not be strong if the tax increase is thought to be only for a year or two, since much investment spending is made with a view to returns that will flow in over the succeeding five or ten years or more. The increase in tax rate, to be truly powerful in its substitution effect, would have to be thought of as relatively permanent, not as an on-and-off measure designed to cope with cyclical price movements. This is why monetary policy can be so much more effective. A corporation floating a bond issue in a period of cyclically high interest rates knows that it must continue to pay those high rates for a considerable period of time.

The substitution effect can be enhanced by using special taxing instruments that concentrate the restriction even more surely on investment spending. An investment credit (see Chapter 12), for example, may be suspended for a short period, or accelerated depreciation may be temporarily disallowed. These suspensions and temporary disallowances usually carry a high price, however, in anticipatory reactions by taxpayers that increase upward or downward pressures on prices, and in legal disputes over the definition of spending (letter of intent, signing of contract, accrual of liability, payment), especially with respect to capital equipment or structures that take a long time to produce or install. Thus the timing of the impact effects of these measures is uncertain.

The income effect of an increase in the corporation income tax rate will reduce but little the investment spending within the country that is planned by foreign-owned concerns possessing ample financial resources.

An increase in the personal income tax may check consumer spending very little in countries where wage negotiations that are based, ostensibly, on gross pay are in fact influenced by the relation of take-home pay to the cost-of-living index. This possibility is especially significant if wage negotiations can be reopened at any time.[1] An increase in income tax rates then stimulates a demand for an immediate rise in wages, which, if granted, is validated by the monetary authorities. Wages cannot of course increase by precisely the increase in tax for every worker, and even in the aggregate the wage increase may fall short of the increase in personal income tax.

1. The importance of this point depends partly on the proportion of the labor force that is covered by collective wage agreements. "In the United Kingdom. the proportion of earners covered by collective agreements amounts to something like 80 per cent while in the United States only about 35 per cent fall into this category . . . ," and in the United Kingdom agreements there is usually no minimum period before which negotiations cannot be reopened (R. J. Ball, *Inflation and the Theory of Money* [Chicago: Aldine Publishing Company, 1964], pp. 128, 129).

If the corporation income tax rate is high, the income effect of that tax will stiffen the firms' resistance to wage demands stimulated by an increase in the personal income tax, if the firms fear that some part of the wage increase cannot be passed on in higher prices. Thus an increase in the corporation income tax rate, introduced at the same time as the personal income tax is increased, may indirectly hold consumer spending in check. To be sure, it might appear that the substitution effect of a high corporate income tax would weaken the firms' resistance to wage demands, since acceding to those demands will cost less than if the corporate tax rate were lower. But the profit after tax that would be lost if a strike resulted from refusal to grant the wage demands is itself correspondingly less than if the corporate tax rate were low. On balance, an increase in the corporate income tax rate probably increases the firms' resistance to wage demands.

Increases in individual and corporate income tax rates will become less and less effective in checking cyclical price increases as experience teaches consumers and firms how to build up reserves or obtain credit lines in periods of stable prices that will enable them to take in stride the temporary increases in tax rates in periods of boom (see Chapter 22, Section B.1). This precautionary reaction by taxpayers does in itself, however, tend to stabilize prices.

The anticipatory effect of a sales tax rate increase is perverse, but because the consumer has only a limited reserve of purchasing power, he will almost surely react less strongly in anticipation of a rate increase than he will in anticipation of a rate decrease.

Government purchases of goods and services may be reduced in a pattern that bears only on investment spending in either, but not both, of two senses. The government may reduce its rate of acquisition of capital assets or reduce the rate of dispensing those kinds of services that are capital goods to the recipients of them. It is unlikely to be able to do both (and only both) at the same time, because capital-good inputs are used partly to produce current benefits (highway construction for pleasure use) and capital-goods outputs are produced partly by current expenses (teachers' salaries).

A reduction in transfer payments will on the second round reduce only consumer outlays, but manipulation of transfer payments for cyclical purposes encounters strong opposition on contractual and distributive grounds.

Finally, even the sale of financial instruments by the government or its central bank to the private sector reduces both investment and consumer spending by raising interest rates for firms and households, including households that borrow to pay current expenses.

In summary, cyclical price rises can be checked in modern industrialized economies by public finance measures, provided the policy-makers do not insist that only consumption or only investment spending be reduced. There is almost no chance of reducing consumer spending alone, even apart from accelerator effects, given the public finance systems as they are today, and little chance of reducing investment spending alone, even apart from multiplier effects.

(2) Increasing Supply

If the cost to the producer of overtime work can be reduced sufficiently, he can expand output at constant marginal cost by inducing more and more of such work. A subsidy to overtime would have to increase as overtime increased, if unit costs were not to rise, eventually, in view of increasing fatigue of workers and the rising labor-capital ratio. Instead of a subsidy for overtime paid directly to the firm, the worker could be allowed a reduced rate of withholding tax on his overtime earnings, on condition that he pass the reduction along to the producer in a reduced hourly rate for overtime work. That he would consent to do this is so unlikely that the only feasible method appears to be to pay the subsidy directly to the firm. Even this technique, which has never been employed, might encounter formidable technical difficulties. In oligopolistic industries, some understanding on pricing policies would have to be reached with the large firms.

Similar considerations apply to added product that might come from a voluntary speed-up under piece-rate work induced by a subsidy, or tax relief, attaching to the increment in output. This measure would be even more difficult to administer since the output base for computing extra output is less easily established than is the hours base for computing overtime work. But the gain in net output might well be greater. Faster work, to be sure, wears out capital equipment more quickly, but probably not in proportion, and in any event there is less tied up in capital equipment at any moment of time (two concurrently employed machines each with a life of one year tie up more capital than two successively employed machines each with a life of six months).

A logical complement to these measures would be a subsidy to, or tax relief for, employment of those hitherto unemployed because of their relative inefficiency. By the same token, use of inefficient stand-by plant and equipment could be subsidized.

B. Slow Secular Rise in Prices

A slow secular rise in prices due to an uneven rate of technical progress among industries (this is of course not the only force making for such a rise in prices) seems unlikely to be controllable by public finance measures. This kind of rise develops to the extent that, in industries where labor productivity increases steadily, the increase is taken in the form of higher money wages rather than lower product prices. Other industries must then raise money wages to compete for labor and must raise prices if they are to pay the labor. This creeping rise is then validated by monetary instruments, to avert unemployment.

If the slow secular rise in prices is based instead on autonomous increases in money wages resulting from wage bargaining, increases that are supported by monetary instruments, again no public finance instruments seem helpful.

c. Substantial Rise in Prices

No country has experienced a rise in prices of from, say, 10 per cent to 30 per cent a year over several years without a seriously unbalanced government budget. To say that public finance measures shall be employed to check such a price rise is therefore to imply a change in government policy. It might seem that this is an issue already analyzed in Chapter 18. But that chapter only posed the choice between new-money finance and tax finance as it appears before inflation has become a way of life. Stopping a consciously induced inflation is more difficult than refusing to induce one in the first place. The private sector becomes habituated to periodic increases in money wages, a usually overvalued currency that may be undervalued for short periods of time just after a devaluation, absence of a long-term money market, and decision-making procedures for altering product prices frequently. It becomes habituated, too, to a banking system with practices shaped to these ends.

The problem then is, how to manage the transition period to a stable price level, even if the government is completely disposed to do its part by imposing more taxes, reducing expenditures, and taking other deflationary measures. The private-sector inflationary habits must be destroyed, yet without creating so much unemployment over so extended a period that popular pressure forces resumption of inflation.

Virtually no systematic analysis appears to have been devoted to methods of meeting this transition problem through public finance instruments. The following remarks are intended to be merely suggestive.

In the transition period much labor and capital must be redirected, from activities to which they were attracted by inflation, to activities that are penalized by inflation. Salesmen must relearn how to move exportables abroad instead of selling them on a strong domestic market. Import-competing industries must regain the capital and labor that had shifted into the production of non-traded goods and services in order to escape unbearable competition from imports that were in effect subsidized by an overvalued currency. Some of the non-traded goods consist of services rendered by the wholesale and retail trades, and there may need to be a considerable flow of resources from those sectors to those parts of the manufacturing sector that compete severely with imports. Low-income households must realize that savings will now yield them a positive real interest return, so that savings banks and insurance companies may revive. A market for long-term obligations must be reconstructed.

Accordingly, the public finance measures that are employed to check the rise in prices must be of a kind that will encourage these particular transfers of real resources and techniques of financing. Otherwise the transition period may be longer and generate more hardships than the community will tolerate. One rule to follow is that the massive tax increases needed to check aggregate money demand should be imposed at a lower rate on the hitherto disadvantaged sectors, particularly those producing and distributing import-competing goods. After price stability has been in effect for some time, the tax burden can be more evenly distributed among sectors.

On the financial front, taxes should not be increased on fixed-claim intermediaries, notably savings banks and insurance companies, during the transition period and for some time thereafter. Income from bonds and other fixed-income securities should similarly be favored for a while.

Transfer payments, too, will have to be treated generously in the transition period, for they probably cannot be reduced in real terms without considerable distress and social tension. No generalizations with respect to types of government expenditures that can be reduced in such a period seem valid.

Nothing need be said about open-market operations in the period of transition, since the inflation will have destroyed the market for all but the shortest-term securities. But as the economy attains price stability the government might do well to promote sale of its own bonds, granting tax advantages to those who purchase the long-term securities within, say, two or three years.

The rate at which the rise in prices is to be slowed must be consistent with estimates of the speed with which resources can be transferred within the private sector, and the new pattern of financing can be constructed. Thus a rate of inflation of, say, 30 per cent (rise in prices) per year can scarcely be reduced to zero in a few weeks without causing intolerable strain, but a period of a year or two might prove ample.

D. RAPID RISE IN PRICES

If prices have been rising at, say, 50, 75, or 100 per cent a year for a good many years, better results may be obtained, paradoxically, by a shorter period of transition than that allowed when checking a rise of 20 or 30 per cent a year. The pressure of a very rapid rise in prices tends to break down the structure of the economy, to liquefy it. The fortunes of various sectors fluctuate widely, as it becomes more difficult for anyone to foresee the changes in receipts-costs relationships. Resource transfer to the stable-price pattern is easier.

This thesis is supported by experience in checking hyper-inflations. They have been halted sharply; a change from a rate of price increase of 100,000 per cent a year to zero per cent is accomplished almost overnight. The fact that a new currency unit is being introduced does not itself explain how this abrupt change can be accomplished. The explanation may lie in the fact that the economy is so disorganized, so fluid, that it can be forced into the pattern consistent with stable prices quickly. In any event there is no question of slowing down the annual rate of increase from 100,000 per cent to 10,000 per cent, then to 1,000 per cent, and so on, over a period of a year or two or three.

The public finance measures for a transition from very rapid inflation to price stability may accordingly be somewhat less selective, somewhat more uniform and general, than would be appropriate for transition from a substantial but not exceedingly rapid inflation. The fact that larger amounts of tax revenue would be needed to check the faster of the inflations points in the same direction.

3. Checking Price Deflation

In a high-income industrialized economy the likelihood of a falling level of product prices is so remote that no attention need be paid to public finance measures designed to combat either a creeping deflation of prices or substantial, not to mention rapid, deflation. The decrease that occurs in employment during a recession has been discussed in Chapter 22.

But a low-income agricultural and raw materials economy that exports much of its product may have price deflation thrust upon it by changes in supply and demand in the world market for its exports and by flight of capital. Although capital outflow puts a downward pressure on the exchange rate, it also tends to create unemployment at home, and the money wage structure of the kind of country in question may crumble in the face of deflationary pressures. Product prices at home then may fall almost as much as they do in foreign currency.

This decrease in domestic prices induces reallocations of resources and changes in financing techniques that cannot be permanent, since sooner or later the decline must end, with or without government intervention, and the earlier patterns of resource allocation and financing tend to reassert themselves. In this respect deflation differs from inflation.

The simplest way to avert such a decline in the domestic price level is of course devaluation, assuming the relevant elasticities are appropriate. The question remains whether public finance measures can maintain internal price stability or at least slow down the rate of decrease of the internal price level if the currency is not devalued. It seems that this is not possible with any public finance measures that are not themselves covert devaluations: for example, a subsidy on exports and a tax on all imports. The role of public finance in preventing or reducing the rate of decline in the domestic price level of an underdeveloped country therefore appears to be a minor one.

B. EXTERNAL EQUILIBRIUM

1. Definition of the Goal

In principle, external equilibrium can normally be attained without the aid of public finance instruments, and even despite adverse effects of public finance instruments employed for other ends. A devaluation or revaluation of the currency will suffice, barring retaliation, or unusual elasticities for trade or for capital flows. So too will a general reduction or increase in money wages and other money factor prices.

Somewhat the same observation, to be sure, applies to internal equilibrium. If money factor rewards were flexible downward, equilibrium might possibly be attained without government intervention when the real value of the money stock and money claims had increased enough to stimulate a substantial amount of spending. But the use of public finance (and other) instruments for internal equilibrium is considered preferable to a decline in factor prices. Fiscal policy for internal equilibrium accepts floors to factor prices and, in boom periods, economic policy attempts to place ceilings on product prices. The case for a public finance policy that will achieve external equilibrium is similarly attractive and correspondingly limited. It depends upon an assumption that the community has decided, for whatever reasons, that the prevailing rate of exchange shall not be altered by enough to re-establish external equilibrium, at least not for the time being. Foreign-exchange public finance policy is therefore primarily a policy of shaping the public finance system so that a certain exchange rate can be maintained. It is a policy of particular significance to developing countries, since the process of development is likely to put continuing pressure on the exchange rate, both because development implies a greater rate of domestic activity, hence an increase in demand for imports, and because much of the industrial equipment needed for development must be imported.[2] But it is also a policy of special interest even to an industrialized economy, if that economy is suffering both from a deficit on balance of payments (though not necessarily balance of trade) and from domestic unemployment.

2. Types of Public Finance Instrument Suitable

Public finance instruments suitable for maintaining a certain rate of exchange fall into three groups.

The first group of instruments operate through a substitution effect by simulating changes in the exchange rate or changes in money wage rates and other money costs. Second, the government directly changes certain domestic prices by itself operating in the private-sector market. Finally, the government may support the rate of exchange by altering disposable incomes in the private sector, through taxation, subsidies, or free government services.

A. Measures that Simulate Changes in Exchange Rate or Domestic Money Costs

(1) Simulating Changes in Exchange Rate

The public finance instruments that simulate changes in the exchange rate will be analyzed here in terms of a deficit in the balance of payments, but the reasoning can be applied readily to eliminating a surplus.

---

2. Harry G. Johnson, "Fiscal Policy and the Balance of Payments," in Alan T. Peacock and Gerald Hauser (Eds.), *Government Finance and Economic Development*, Organization for Economic Co-operation and Development Conference, Athens, 1963 (Paris: OECD, n.d.), p. 159.

(A) TRADE

To eliminate a deficit on the balance of trade, the most obvious public finance instruments that simulate a change in the exchange rate are a tax on imports coupled with a subsidy on exports or a tax on exports, as the case may be.

A subsidy on exports financed by a tax on imports is essentially a devaluation of the currency for purposes of trade, in goods and services,[3] but not for flows of capital, investment income, remittances, and other non-trade items. In effect, this public finance measure creates an implicit rate of exchange for trade that differs from the explicit rate for financial transactions.

There will be two implicit rates for trade if the rate of import tax differs from that of the export subsidy. If the revenue total differs from the subsidy total, the resultant positive or negative income effects blur the comparison with devaluation.

If the foreign elasticity of demand for exports is less than unity, the subsidy on exports will increase the external deficit. A tax on exports will decrease that deficit. But a fiscal measure composed of a tax on imports and another tax on exports does not simulate a change in the exchange rate, though it still depends on the substitution effect for its efficacy. Care must now be taken in the disposition of the revenue from these two taxes, to avoid an income effect that would worsen the balance of payments. Ideally, the tax revenue should be used to reduce taxes that affect demand for non-traded goods and services[4] and domestic demand for exportables.

If only a tax on imports is imposed, exports being neither subsidized nor taxed, or if only exports are subsidized (or taxed), the fiscal measure is akin to a common type of differential exchange rate system. The tax revenue must be used in the manner just indicated, and the subsidy must be financed by instruments that do not worsen the balance of payments. Thus an export subsidy might be financed by a tax on non-traded goods and services and on exportables consumed at home. A distant approximation to such a measure is supplied by a tax on payrolls of construction and service industries (distribution, insurance, banking, professional, and hotel and restaurant services, for example), the proceeds being devoted to subsidizing payrolls of manufacturing industries, in a country where few services and little on-site construction, but a large proportion of manufactured products, are exported[5] (but

3. In practice, a tax on imports and a subsidy on exports will fail to reach many services.

4. "Non-traded goods and services" is used here to embrace goods and services that are neither imported nor exported, regardless of whether they form only a part or the whole of the finished product. If, as is usual, retail services are produced only at home for home consumption, virtually every final product domestically purchased, at least by households, will contain an element of non-traded services.

5. The United Kingdom's Selective Employment Tax of 1966 seems to have been imposed partly as such an approximation, even though a substantial proportion of the United Kingdom's services are exported. Each establishment (not each firm) was to be classified as either "neutral" (no tax), "premium," or "taxed." See J. P. Hutton and K. Hartley, "The Selective Employment Tax and the Labour Market," *British Journal of Industrial Relations* (November, 1966), no. 34 in Reprint Series: Economics, Institute of Social and Economic Research, University of York and Judith Reid, "The Selective Employment Tax," *British Tax Review* (July–August, 1966), pp. 243–50, and (July–August, 1967), pp. 245–50.

note the reservations with respect to retail and wholesale services in the second paragraph below), and few services are import-competing.

Another type of differential exchange rate system is simulated when a tax is imposed only on those exports the demand for which is inelastic, while a subsidy is given to those exports the demand for which is elastic.[6] Again, the net revenue loss or gain must be met or disposed of in an appropriate manner.

The treatment to be accorded to non-traded goods and services that are complementary in consumption with both imported commodities and home-produced commodities depends on where the complementary relationship is the strongest. Retail services illustrate this point. If imported commodities and exportable commodities are typically sold with more lavish retail service than are non-traded commodities, a tax on value added at retail will improve the balance of trade.

A public finance measure of general scope, with effects similar to those of a uniform-rate import tax and export subsidy, is a change from an origin basis to a destination basis for a general sales tax (see Chapter 8, Section A.1). A milder form of the same measure is retention of the destination principle, but with an increase in the percentage of accumulated sales tax that is rebated upon export, coupled with an increase in the rate of the compensating import tax, under the destination principle. This can be introduced when a country moves from a cascade type of general sales tax under which it has been rebating on the average less than the accumulated tax (and taxing imports inadequately) to a value-added tax of the tax-credit type where the accumulated tax shows up on the invoice and so can easily be deducted in virtually its full amount, and where a completely compensating import tax is less difficult to compute.[7]

Conceivably, this change from origin to destination basis could be limited to imports or limited to exports. While such a measure is unlikely, if only because origin taxation is so rare, the degree of export rebate under a general sales tax of the destination basis has in the past been changed from time to time without simultaneously changing the import compensating tax rate, and vice versa.

The terms of trade will usually alter under these public finance measures; the extent and direction of the change will depend on the elasticities of demand and supply of exports and imports.[8] The analysis on this point is much the same as that for shifting and incidence of excise taxes, given in Chapter 10 above.

The effects of excise taxes on prices and disposable incomes under partial equilibrium analysis in a closed economy differ from the effects that foreign-trade taxes or subsidies exert on balance of payments and terms of trade, for three reasons. First, in the foreign trade case, one side of the market keeps the tax money or has to

6. For a detailed comparison of the effects of devaluation or revaluation with the effects of discriminating export taxes and subsidies, of general import taxes, and of general export taxes or subsidies, see J. E. Meade, *The Balance of Payments* (London: Oxford University Press, 1951), Chapter 23. See also Harry G. Johnson, *International Trade and Economic Growth* (London: Allen & Unwin, 1958), Chapter 7, Section 4, and his "The Balance of Payments," *Pakistan Economic Journal* (June, 1958), 8: 16–28, reprinted in his *Money, Trade, and Economic Growth* (Cambridge, Mass.: Harvard University Press, 1962).

7. As to the destination basis for the income tax, see Chapter 25, pages 647–48.

8. See Meade, *op. cit.*, pp. 309–22.

supply the money for a subsidy. Second, the change in money volume of trade, inclusive of tax or subsidy, is more important in the foreign trade case, which poses a balance of payments problem that is not present in the closed economy. Third, it may be important in the foreign trade case to take account of foreign repercussions, that is, to view the purchaser of exported products (or those somewhere along the line of subsequent purchasers) as sellers to the party (country) levying the tax or granting the subsidy.

(B) FINANCIAL TRANSACTIONS

Devaluation of a country's currency allows the foreigner to invest more in that country, for a given amount of his own currency, but.it also requires that he earn more in that country to obtain a given return in his own currency. Similarly, devaluation makes it more expensive for the domestic investor to invest abroad, but less expensive for him to remit the earnings from that investment. Simulation of a devaluation confined to these financial flows would require a tax on outflow of capital and on outflowing dividends, interest, rentals, and remittances, coupled with a subsidy on import of capital and inflowing dividends, interest, rentals, and remittances. No such complete system of taxation and subsidy for financial transactions seems ever to have existed. Quotas and other direct controls have been preferred to a greater degree even than for trade transactions. But isolated parts of that tax-subsidy system have been employed. Capital outflows have been taxed.[9] Income taxes have commonly included some form of tax, often only at a flat rate, on dividends, interest, rentals, and royalties sent abroad.

A tax on capital outflows makes it more expensive for the domestically based investor to invest abroad, but it does not affect the terms on which he can repatriate earnings from that investment. And of course it does not affect, directly, either inflow of capital or outflow of earnings on that capital. It might therefore be regarded as one-half of a one-sided devaluation of the currency for investment purposes (a "one-quarter devaluation"), except that the increase in the price of foreign exchange to the resident who invests abroad goes all to the domestic government as tax revenue, not to the seller of the foreign currency.

If this tax on capital outflow were coupled with a tax on earnings on capital exported after the capital tax had been put into effect, the deterrent to capital outflow would be still stronger. But investors might not believe that the tax would last, especially since they would realize that the authorities at the later date would be eager to encourage repatriation of such earnings, if the balance of payments was still adverse.

If the country has not hitherto been taxing dividends and other investment earnings that are sent abroad, it can simulate part of a one-sided devaluation by extending its income tax to reach such payments. The foreigner must now earn more, in this country's currency, to obtain a given return in his own currency.

9. Notably by the United States interest equalization tax. See Richard N. Cooper, "The Interest Equalization Tax: An Experiment in the Separation of Capital Markets," *Finanzarchiv* (December, 1965), 24: 447–71.

Again, it is this country's government, not the seller of foreign exchange, that benefits from the rise in price of foreign exchange to this remitter of earnings. Also, in contrast to devaluation, the foreigner cannot invest in this country more cheaply (in terms of his own currency). And of course this taxing measure does not directly affect either outflow of capital or inflow of earnings on that capital. Once more there is something like a one-quarter devaluation for investment purposes.

If the income tax has been levied entirely on the residence basis, foreigners' investment earnings in this country will have been exempt from this country's income tax, whether or not repatriated. If this income tax is now changed completely to a source basis, the simulation of devaluation (for investment purposes) is closer, but still far from equivalent. The income tax is now collected on the foreigner's investment earnings even if he never repatriates them. But if we assume that he will sooner or later repatriate them, the shift from residence to source basis resembles the imposition of a tax on outflow of dividends and other investment income. In addition, it affects the resident who has sent his capital abroad. He now finds it easier to earn a certain amount of disposable home currency on that capital, though he does not have to repatriate the earnings to enjoy the benefit from the shift in principle. Capital flows are not themselves directly affected, and this fact must be emphasized in comparing this income tax change with devaluation. We might say that a change from a residence-basis income tax to a source-basis income tax is tantamount to a one-half devaluation for investment flows (one half of each of two sides of a devaluation), or to a complete devaluation for investment-earnings flows alone. At least this is so if we assume that all earnings are in fact repatriated. The resemblance to a fractional devaluation is the closer, in that the government's revenue gain on foreigners' earnings is offset, more or less, by its loss of revenue on its residents' income earned abroad.

These problems will not be pursued further here, since the aim of the present analysis is only to show the main issues involved in attempting to use the tax or subsidy system as a substitute for a non-public finance measure (devaluation). We note only that the source-residence alternatives are not applicable to the income tax alone. Conceivably, a shift to the residence principle, though difficult administratively, could be made for the real estate tax, which has always been levied on a source basis. Under a residence-of-owner basis, the tax would not apply to real estate held by nonresidents.

This same change of principle could be applied to death and gift taxes, which also have commonly been levied on a source basis, but the aggregate amounts are too small to make much difference. It would be a very selective sort of financial-flows type of implicit devaluation.

Failure to grant credit for taxes paid abroad may amount to a one-sided devaluation of the currency for investment flows (see Chapter 25, Section C.1).

(c) TRADE AND FINANCIAL TRANSACTIONS TOGETHER

A comprehensive system consisting of an import tax, an export subsidy, a tax on financial outflows, and a subsidy on financial inflows would be virtually the same, with respect to balance of payments and terms of trade, as a complete devaluation of the currency. But the operation of this system would require much manpower and other resources that would not be needed at all under a devaluation.

In summary, the tax-and-subsidy measures are useful substitutes for a devaluation that is limited to trade, somewhat less so if limited to financial transactions, and may even be preferred to devaluation on administrative grounds, in view of the difficulties of administering multiple exchange rates. But they are most awkward substitutes for a devaluation that is intended to cover all trade and financial transactions.

(2) Simulating Changes in Domestic Money Factor Rewards

Up to this point only simulation of change in the exchange rate has been considered. Simulation of change in domestic money factor rewards through public finance measures is more difficult. An actual change in such rewards, when they are measured in terms of disposable real income, can of course be engineered by an ordinary deflationary fiscal policy, if there are no floors to factor prices. It is a different matter to simulate such a change, that is, devise a public finance measure that will accomplish for the balance of trade the same result as would an actual reduction of domestic wages and other factor rewards, computed in terms of real disposable income.

A comprehensive uniform proportional subsidy to all producers for all their marginal costs is a hypothetical example. But it would have to be financed by some tax that had no influence on costs, perhaps a poll tax or a tax levied on households only, on the basis of their expenditures or incomes.

Such measures, perhaps because they would be cumbersome, seem not to have been discussed as alternatives to an ordinary deflationary policy.

B. MEASURES THAT CHANGE PRICES
THROUGH GOVERNMENT PURCHASE OR SALE

In between the public finance measures that act on external disequilibrium by price effects, discussed in Section A above, and those that act on it by changing the disposable income of the private sector, to be discussed in C below, are those whereby the government directly changes certain domestic prices by operating in the private-sector market for goods. Thus the government may sell from its stockpiles and build up its cash balance. Domestic prices of grains and metals, for example, are depressed, exports of them are encouraged, and imports are discouraged. If there is an external surplus to be eliminated, the government may create new money to increase its stockpiles.

c. Measures that Operate Through Altering Disposable Incomes in the Private Sector

The balance of trade can almost surely be improved by public finance instruments that decrease the private sector's disposable income. Taxes may be increased and the revenue added to the government's cash balance. To eliminate a trade surplus, taxes may be decreased and the government's cash balance drawn down. Whether these measures will affect the balance of payments in the manner desired is less certain. It may be necessary to exercise directly opposite effects on disposable incomes from capital and those from labor.

(1) Effect on Trade

Under a public finance instrument that decreases the disposable income of residents, imports of consumer goods will decline and so also, for accelerator-based investment, will imports of producers' goods by firms that produce import-competing goods or non-traded goods. Firms producing exportables will minimize the decline in their profits by moving some or all of their hitherto domestic sales to foreign markets. Total imports will decrease in aggregate value save in the exceptional case where they are largely producers' goods of a kind used to produce exportables. Exports will increase in aggregate value save in the unusual case where foreign demand is of less than unit elasticity. These effects would be enhanced if some tax measure could be found that would reduce only disposable incomes of those with a very high marginal propensity to import and to consume exportables. No such single measure of much consequence seems to exist.

(2) Effects on Financial Transactions and Flows

An increase in a tax that is imposed on a source basis will reduce profits of capital employed in the country, except as wages are flexible downward. The resulting reduction in profit rate will cause an incremental capital outflow; foreign capitalists will be deterred from investing in the taxing country, and domestic capitalists will be induced to export capital. This incremental outflow may more than counterbalance the improvement on trade account. The monetary deflation that is implied by holding the tax receipts idle will raise interest rates, attracting creditor capital to the country. At this point the analysis becomes linked with measures needed, if any, to assure full employment.

An income tax, however, is commonly imposed on a residence basis, or at least chiefly so. If an improvement in the payments balance is sought through an increase in some tax, a residence-based income tax rather than a sales tax is the most promising measure, since it will not by itself decrease the after-tax reward to capital employed at home relative to the reward obtainable abroad.

An increase in free government services to business firms operating in the country will exert an income effect that will draw capital into the country and so improve the balance of payments. Freely supplied infrastructure is a notable possibility of special importance in less developed countries where these facilities may be costly to construct and maintain. To be sure, competition may dissipate the benefits to capital, to the advantage of consumers, but some of those consumers will be foreign purchasers of the country's exports.

Borrowing abroad to maintain an exchange rate is usually only a stopgap measure, one that buys a little time. Lending abroad to maintain external stability threatened by a heavy surplus has virtually no limits, especially if it is allowed to become in effect an unrequited transfer payment in the form of a soft loan.

CHAPTER TWENTY-FIVE

Intergovernmental Fiscal Coordination

A. VERTICAL AND HORIZONTAL COORDINATION

FISCAL COORDINATION between governmental units on different levels is commonly termed vertical coordination. Pyramidal coordination might be a better term, to connote the complex network of tax credits, tax sharing, tax aid, and grants in aid that connect the municipalities with their state or province, and the states or provinces with the apex, the national government.

Horizontal coordination connects units at the same level of sovereignty, as with understandings among cities, interstate compacts, and fiscal treaties among nations. Much horizontal coordination is unilateral; many countries grant credit for income tax paid abroad, whether or not the other countries reciprocate. Vertical coordination, in contrast, is always cooperative, in fact if not in form; the different levels of government, usually after strenuous debate, agree on a particular grant-in-aid, tax credit, or other measure.

B. VERTICAL COORDINATION

Vertical coordination is necessary only in a politically decentralized country, that is, one where states or provinces, and municipalities can decide for themselves, within wide limits, how much of certain types of governmental services and transfer payments their residents shall receive and how they shall be financed. Political decentralization is here assumed not to be a goal in itself,[1] but a historical and social phenomenon that happens to exist in some countries and not in others. With respect to those countries where it does exist, alternative methods of providing vertical fiscal coordination are compared, in the following sections, for their efficacy in helping reach the goals that have been analyzed in Chapters 21–24 above. This approach provides a partial explanation of why some forms of coordination pre-

1. This is not to assert that it is not, or should not be, such a goal; the assumption is made merely to limit the scope of the present analysis.

dominate in some countries or states (or provinces), others in others. It will be seen that the tax credit, for example, satisfies those who value (1) local administration of taxes, either because it facilitates equal administrative treatment of equals or because it allows the community to implement its own set of biases or prejudices; (2) a modest degree of fiscal independence, perhaps grounded on an optimum-allocation argument; (3) maintenance of the existing geographical inequalities of income and wealth. The specific-purpose grant-in-aid, on the other hand, draws the support of those whose views on all three of these points are nearly the opposite of those of the tax-credit advocates.

1. Tax Coordination

A. TAX CREDIT

When a superior governmental unit allows a credit against its tax to anyone who pays the same kind of tax to a subordinate unit, it frees the subordinate unit from fear of loss of business or loss of residents to other areas if it imposes or increases the tax. This fear may have been strong enough, in the pre-credit days, to have prevented any subordinate unit from imposing the tax even when all were eager to do so if they could be assured that the others would follow. In this manner the tax credit improves the allocation of resources.

Often the competitive fear will have been mild enough so that the subordinate units will have been levying the tax, but in an uneven pattern from unit to unit and at low rates. Introduction of a credit will then induce the units that have been using only very low rates to increase their rates by enough to absorb the credit. The higher-rate units may tend to retain their initial differentials over the other subordinate units by increasing their rates, even if this means exceeding the credit somewhat. If the credited tax is a new one, however, the subordinate units are likely to start off with rates precisely equal to the creditable amount and to continue this way indefinitely.[2] Or the credit-granting jurisdiction may limit the subordinate unit's rate to the amount of the credit; the tax credit is then scarcely a decentralizing device at all. In general, the tax credit allows the subordinate unit only a moderate degree of fiscal independence, one that is more apparent than real.

The tax credit tends to distort the allocation of resources (in a Paretian sense) by making imposition of the tax by a subordinate unit appear costless to its taxpayers, or at least a bargain. It appears absolutely costless if the subordinate unit is so small that its taxpayers do not believe that the superior unit will raise its own tax rates to make up for the revenue loss that it suffers from their use of the credit. This state of affairs hardly obtains in a federation consisting of only four or five more or less equally sized states or provinces, or fewer. But even here the deterrent effect is mild,

2. As with the payroll taxes to finance unemployment compensation in the United States, apart from the lower rates given under merit-rating plans that favor firms with low unemployment records.

since any one province knows that the loss of revenue it causes to the central government will be made good by a nation-wide increase, of which its own households and firms will pay but a part. Use of the tax credit by any one subordinate unit, viewed apart from the others, therefore creates a negative externality, which presumably moves the entire fiscal system further away from a Pareto-optimal position. But this danger is in practice not a very real one, since, if all the subordinate units make use of the credit, the negative externalities cancel each other. Indeed, if all but a few of the units are using the tax and the credit, the remaining few feel impelled to follow suit if only to make up for what they are indirectly contributing, to the using units.

A full-employment tax policy may be hampered by the tax credit. A central government that desires to lower the rate of this particular tax when unemployment is high will encounter opposition from each subordinate unit, which will fear being exposed to tax competition once the central-government tax rate falls below the creditable rate. Taxes that are in any event unsuitable for counter-cycle variation, the death and gift taxes for example, are on this score alone relatively good taxes for crediting.

The tax revenue that the central government loses through a tax credit is distributed among the subordinate units according to the location of the taxed object, flow, or transaction. The wealthier or busier subordinate units will get more, per capita, from the creditable tax than will the poorer units, compared with an equal revenue loss to the central government distributed by the usual grant-in-aid formulas (see Section 2 below). The tax credit, if applied uniformly, therefore does nothing to reduce geographical inequalities of income and wealth. But if it is confined to inhabitants and business firms in depressed areas of the credit-granting jurisdiction, it can become a fairly powerful geographical equalizing force, as the superior jurisdiction must draw new revenue from all parts of its area to make up for the tax relief it is granting, or the state or local government services it is helping finance in the depressed areas.

B. Tax Deductibility

If it is unwilling to grant a tax credit, the superior jurisdiction may go part way by allowing its taxpayers to subtract the subordinate jurisdiction's tax in computing their taxable incomes. For a given amount of revenue loss to the superior unit this technique may be more effective than the tax credit in reducing tax competition among the subordinate jurisdictions, when the superior unit, say a federal government, employs sharply progressive rates and the subordinate units, say cities, employ only a flat rate or mildly progressive rates. Deductibility of the city tax in computation of the base for the federal tax reduces the net city tax (city tax, less federal tax saved by deductibility) by a greater proportion for the high-income taxpayer than for those with low incomes. And it is the high-income households and corporations that the cities fear most to lose to each other because of local taxation. If the same result were to be reached under a tax credit as under tax deductibility, assuming the same total revenue loss to the federal government in either case, the credit would have to be a larger percentage of the high-income taxpayer's city tax than of the low-income taxpayer's—a formula that might appear too discriminatory to be acceptable, although in fact no more so than deductibility.

In practice, the superior government does not consciously choose between equal-loss credit and deductibility. It usually allows deductibility in full if it allows it at all, and usually limits the credit.[3]

Deductibility exerts far less pressure on subordinate units to adopt the tax in question, perhaps because even a limited tax credit allows a subordinate unit to tax up to a certain level without adding any additional burden, while deductibility never frees any taxpayer completely from the subordinate-unit tax.[4]

The remarks above concerning the tax credit, with respect to distortion of resource allocation and geographical distribution of the revenue foregone by the superior unit of government apply, with less force, to the tax deduction. A full employment policy may be somewhat discouraged; the lower the rate of the superior unit's tax, the more concerned will the taxpayer be about the differences in the subordinate units' tax rates.

c. Tax-Sharing

Under tax-sharing proper, the donor government pays to the donee governments an amount that fluctuates, in total, either with the yield of a certain tax or with the base of a certain tax. It distributes this amount among the donee governments according to the geographical origin of the revenue or of the base. These two modes do not amount to the same thing unless the tax is strictly proportional to the base. Under a progressive income tax, for example, a rich subordinate unit would get a larger share of the total if the distribution were by origin of revenue rather than by origin of base.

If distribution is on some basis other than origin, the device begins to resemble a straight grant-in-aid, except that the amount to be distributed each year is determined, not by an annual appropriation process, but by whatever the yield (or the base) of the tax happens to be. Tax-sharing on a non-origin base is better given a distinct name; let us call it tax aid.

Tax-sharing reduces even the modest discretionary role that the subordinate units play under the tax credit. It takes administration of the tax out of the hands of those units. It guarantees what the credit only strongly encourages, namely, geographical

3. The federal government of the United States limits the credit for state death taxes in just the reverse manner from that of the deductibility technique, allowing a larger percentage of the tax on the smaller taxable estates as a credit; but this is an incidental result of a complex historical development. Tax credits can of course be structured in many different modes. See George F. Break, *Intergovernmental Fiscal Relations in the United States* (Washington, D.C.: Brookings Institution, 1967), pp. 41–45.

4. In the United States, although the federal government allows deductibility of state and local income taxes and does not allow deduction of state retail sales taxes (by consumers), more states impose retail sales taxes than income taxes. The fact that the federal government imposes no general sales tax is of course a partial explanation.

uniformity of tax rate. Tax-sharing does not encourage any one subordinate unit to impose a tax in the expectation that the rest of the country will pay most of it, nor does it allow any unit to opt out of the tax.

A full employment policy through tax-rate changes is inhibited even more than by the credit, unless the sharing is related to the tax base, not the tax revenue: for example, the central government distributes to subordinate units an amount equal to a certain percentage of aggregate taxable income. But quite apart from rate changes, the built-in flexibility of the tax revenue or of the tax base, so desirable for counter-cycle fiscal policy, can create recurring crises and gluts in subordinate-unit budgets. In general, stabilization policy and tax-sharing do not go well together.

Tax aid, which is tax-sharing with distribution on some basis other than origin, opens the way to a reduction of geographical inequalities in disposable income not possible under tax-sharing or the tax credit.

An indirect form of tax sharing occurs when one jurisdiction, say a federal government, exempts from its income tax the interest on obligations of another jurisdiction, say a state or local government. Part of the revenue thus lost goes to the borrowing jurisdiction in the form of lower interest rates for its obligations. Another part goes to high-bracket taxpayers (see Chapter 12, page 337). To induce the borrowing authority to relinquish this advantage, the taxing government may offer an equivalent grant, which would cost it less in revenue because none of the benefit would go to high-income taxpayers.[5]

D. Tax Denial or Tax Restriction

A higher level government will commonly deny to its subordinate jurisdictions the power to levy certain taxes or will place a ceiling on the tax rate they can use, or require that any upward change in tax rate be approved by the legislature at the higher level. These tax denials or tax restrictions usually reflect the desire of the superior jurisdiction not to see a revenue source pre-empted in a scattered geographical pattern that makes that source unavailable for use by that superior jurisdiction, while leaving certain areas not taxed as much as they might be. If in a certain state, for example, some municipalities do, and some do not, wish to impose an income tax of their own, the state cannot allow them complete freedom to do as they wish without producing an uneven geographical profile of income taxation. It is the highest point on this profile that is significant with respect to the state's own income tax policy, unless that point represents a community so small that the combined impact of state and local income taxation there can be disregarded in setting the state's income tax rate. Other areas within the state could stand a higher state income tax, but the opportunity must be foregone unless the state levies its own tax at different rates in different parts of the state—scarcely a politically acceptable procedure, and in most jurisdictions with a written constitution, probably unconstitutional.

5. See Lyle C. Fitch, *Taxing Municipal Bond Income* (Berkeley: University of California Press, 1950), and Richard Goode, *The Individual Income Tax*, pp. 139–45.

These formal restrictions on lower-level tax patterns are not needed by the superior jurisdiction if it has been the first to impose the tax or, at any rate, moves the rates to high levels before the subordinate units make intensive use of the tax. Once it has done so, none of those units dare impose the tax at rates high enough to embarrass the superior jurisdiction.

Sometimes the restrictions reflect the fear of the upper-level government that the common economic base for all taxation will be impaired if the subordinate units are not held in check. This may be one reason why superior jurisdictions sometimes set rate limits even on taxes they have no intention of using themselves.[6]

The restrictions may express a fear that a large number of small units will otherwise impose a tax on a base that is for some households or firms subject to tax by more than one of these units. While this "double taxation" may be justified in some instances, in others it is likely not to be, in the sense that equals are being treated unequally, including unequal compliance costs. An income tax imposed by school districts on a combined residence-source basis, with no credit, is an example.

Local units will be tempted to levy taxes the burden of which can be exported to other local units, at the cost of a reduction in economy-wide income, hence restrictions on local tariffs or differential taxes on exports.

In its extreme form (short of barring any use of the tax), tax restriction permits the subordinate unit to use the tax only by way of a supplemental rate on a base defined by the superior unit. A city or county may be empowered to levy a sales tax in the form of an additional rate on what the state defines as taxable sales. An upper limit, or perhaps a single rate, is always set, and the tax will usually be administered by the superior jurisdiction. Still, the subordinate unit possesses considerably more power and responsibility than it does under a tax credit, tax-sharing, or tax aid.[7]

2. Coordination by Grants-in-Aid

In contrast with the devices just discussed, a grant-in-aid depends not at all on any particular tax imposed by the donor government. Its effects vary, instead, with the degree of decentralization built into it.

At one extreme there is scarcely any decentralization. The donor government so distributes and so conditions the grant that the donee governments are simply its administrative agents. They implement a program that the donor government would otherwise administer directly. For example, let the donor government distribute a grant to any donee government that will spend it on the needy aged in a pattern stipulated precisely by the donor government. No other condition is attached to the grant. The donee government is now under pressure from the aged in its jurisdiction

6. Some of the states of the United States put ceilings on local property tax rates without themselves using that tax.

7. If the subordinate unit administers its own tax (whether as a supplemental rate or otherwise), there is much to be gained from coordination of administration by the higher and lower units, and by agreement on definition of the tax base. For details of development in these fields in the United States, see Break, op. cit., pp. 32–36, 45–50.

to accept the grant, and few are apt to oppose it. The only decentralization is in administration, and this is limited, in view of the conditions set by the donor government. Such a grant is the expenditure-side analogue of a tax credit. With respect to all the public finance goals save one, this kind of grant simply reproduces the conditions of a unitary state, where the donor government would administer the program directly. The exception concerns the equity aspects of administration; something may be gained, or lost, on this score by leaving the day-to-day administration in the hands of subordinate-unit officials.

At the other extreme the donor government attaches no strings whatever to the use of the grant and distributes it by some formula that implicitly or explicitly involves need and capacity, and perhaps effort.[8] This is the general-purpose, or "block" grant.

A. Uniform per Capita Grant for General Purposes

The simplest and most widely used type of general-purpose grant distributes the money on a per capita basis; each donee government receives the same amount per capita. The population of the donee government unit is the implicit index of need for the grant. "Need" in this context means only the size of the job to be done, for example, the number of children to be educated; it does not refer to the amount of local resources available to do the job. By giving every donee government, rich or poor, the same amount per capita the donor government implicitly takes some account of differences in ability, that is, differing levels of local resources per capita: a smaller percentage is added to the rich district's per capita resources than to those of the poor districts. No index of effort on the part of the donee government is involved, either explicitly or implicitly. A rich district may be raising very little money locally to educate its children, but it still receives the per capita grant.

Such a grant implies a high degree of decentralization, unless the rate of the grant is changed from time to time, either to persuade donee governments to follow suggestions or because of temporary fiscal difficulty or affluence of the donor government. Insulation from these influences requires also that the grant be scheduled to increase in money amount per capita, over the years, as national income per capita increases.

The grant expresses non-fiscal values of decentralization in the freedom it gives to donee units to decide how to use the money.

Pareto-optimal distribution of resources between the private sector and public sector is both facilitated and hindered by the per capita block grant. It is hindered by the fact that no one group of persons compares the marginal public dollar spent with the marginal tax dollar raised; there is no opportunity for application of the Wicksell principle. It is facilitated by the fact that the grant lessens the pressure for tax reductions by subordinate units that are competing for business firms and

8. For an analysis of the income and substitution effects of seven such formulas, see Richard A. Musgrave, "Approaches to a Fiscal Theory of Political Federalism," in National Bureau of Economic Research, *Public Finances: Needs, Sources, and Utilization* (Princeton, N.J.: Princeton University Press, 1961), pp. 97–122, and discussion pp. 122–33.

households. As with rate wars under imperfect competition in the private sector, these competitive tax decreases, or failures to increase tax rates, may distort the allocation of resources. The lower the level of governmental unit to which the grant is distributed, the more assurance is there that this inter-unit competition will be lessened. Cities are more fearful of losing a part of their tax base than are states. If the grant is distributed to states they may or may not distribute it among cities in a manner to reduce this type of competition.

If, with the loss of tax base, the cities could reduce the money they have to spend on governmental services by an equal or larger proportion, the competition noted above would not exist, or would be ill-informed if it did. But as Chapter 5 has shown, the total cost of a given level of service per capita does not, for many services, increase in proportion or more than in proportion, to the number of households or firms served. To be sure, if it is the wealthier taxpayers that move, it still pays the rest of the city to compete for them, within limits.

Moreover, no donee government is induced to reallocate its own resources in order to increase its grant revenue; population is beyond its direct control, and there is no other test.

On balance, therefore, it cannot be said a priori whether the general-purpose grant, per capita, improves or worsens the allocation of resources between the public and the private sectors from the technical point of view of Wicksell, Pareto, and modern welfare economics generally.

A general-purpose grant that would vary inversely with some index of economic activity, perhaps the percentage of the labor force employed, would be a stabilizing device especially useful where the subordinate governments' own tax revenues fluctuate markedly with the level of business and they are unable or unwilling to borrow for current expenditures. Such a grant would reduce pressure on these governments to curtail their services at those times.[9]

Distribution of disposable income is made potentially less unequal by the grant itself, for the reasons given in the first paragraph in this section. The net result depends also of course on how the donor government finances the grant, but we are here concerned only with the tendency of the grant itself.

The modifier "potentially," used above, is necessary because the donee government is free to use the grant money in ways that will benefit high-income households disproportionately. A poor state might use the grant money to reduce the top bracket rates in its income tax, or to supply better education to its wealthier districts. The more heterogeneous the donee unit, the greater the possibility of such an outcome. The smaller the donee unit, the less heterogeneous each donee unit will be, in general. A per capita block grant distributed by a federal government directly to cities, villages, and like municipal units rather than to the states that they comprise is less susceptible of being employed disproportionately for the benefit of the well-to-do. Indeed, if the grant could be distributed to the families in each block in each city or village, and to correspondingly small groups in other areas, there would be little chance that any household would benefit more per capita than any other

9. See Paul J. Strayer, "Public Expenditure Policy," *American Economic Review* (March, 1949), 39: 398–99.

household anywhere in the country. But of course the city block is not a government unit. The logical extreme, to assure equal benefit per capita, is distribution by the federal government of a fixed amount of money per person to each household; vertical coordination then vanishes because decentralization has vanished, being replaced by a centrally administered Rhys-Williams social dividend.[10]

The most that can be done to assure equal per capita benefit from a per capita block grant is to distribute it to the lowest-level subordinate unit of government, that is, the smallest unit that is equipped to handle it. The growing proportion of populations everywhere concentrated in large, heterogeneous cities limits the efficacy of such a proposal. Still, a per capita block grant to cities at least gives more assurance of equal benefit than does a similar grant to intermediate levels of government. This assurance is increased in those countries where urban heterogeneity is becoming patterned between core city and suburb, so that a distinct grant can be made to a relatively homogeneous low-income core city. But this remark abstracts from the ability of a core city to export taxation by imposing taxes on business firms located within its boundaries and dealing with the outside world.

B. NON-UNIFORM PER CAPITA GRANT FOR GENERAL PURPOSES

(1) Grants Differentiated According to Relative Resources

More explicit account can be taken of differences in ability to raise revenue by setting the per capita grant at a higher level for poor states or other donee governments than for rich ones. Greater weight is thereby given to distributional factors.

This kind of a grant has been criticized as inefficient economically because it tends to induce resources to flow to regions where marginal productivities are lower. But the definitions of "poor" that are used for allocating such grants do not necessarily imply low marginal productivities. An area is commonly said to be "poor" either on a source basis or on a residence basis. Both computations are per capita; that is, the denominator of the ratio is the number of residents in the area. But the numerator in the one instance is the aggregate income produced in the area, much of which may flow to nonresident capitalists. This ratio shows the source income per (resident) person. In the other instance the aggregate income is that which is received by residents of the area; some of it may come from investments elsewhere. This ratio is residents' income per (resident) person.

An area that is poor under the source-income definition may or may not exhibit a low marginal productivity of labor, or of capital; there is no a priori reason why it should or should not. The area may be poor in the source sense only because its industries are labor intensive, or because they generate little economic rent per worker. Consequently, a grant that favors poor areas defined on a source basis may or may not induce factors to flow where marginal productivities are low.

An area that is poor under the residents' income test is more likely than not to be

10. Except that the Rhys-Williams plan contains a willingness-to-work test. See Chapter 6 above.

one of low marginal productivity of labor, if it can be assumed that low marginal productivity means low wages and that most of the inhabitants of most areas receive chiefly labor income. A grant favoring poor areas defined on a residents' income basis is therefore probably, but not necessarily, favoring areas of low marginal productivity of labor. If the grant-in-aid money is used in a way that increases labor's real disposable income, it is economically inefficient, since it tends to induce labor to flow from areas where its marginal productivity is high to those where it is low (or to discourage the reverse flow).

, At the same time, the marginal productivity of capital may be higher in this area than in others. There is nothing in either the resident's-income figure or the source-income figure to indicate whether the marginal productivity of capital in the area is high or low. If it is high, and if the grant money is spent in a way that increases the return on capital, it promotes economic efficiency, since it speeds up the flow of capital to this area where its marginal productivity is high.

In sum, the source-income figure reveals nothing about marginal productivity, and the residents'-income figure only indicates that the marginal productivity of labor in that area is probably but not at all necessarily low. From this it appears that the only a priori efficiency rule for differential grants is a restricted and negative one, namely, that if the grant money is likely to be spent in a way that benefits residents rather than owners of the capital invested there, it probably, but not surely, should not be given to areas that are poor on the residents'-income test. Labor-force residents should probably, but not surely, be discouraged from locating in such an area.

Even this restricted rule collapses, however, when externalities are taken into account. A child growing up in a family with income that is low because the marginal productivities of its working members are low is likely, just because of that, to possess a low marginal productivity when he or she has matured and joins the labor force or becomes a housewife and mother. Lack of adequate nourishment in childhood and adequate clothing and shelter, cultural stimulus, and the like will reduce the marginal productivity of the adult. That productivity may even become negative, in the sense that the adult consumes more than he produces. This difference is paid by some community, unless the individual is left to starve or die of malnutrition and illness, but there is no assurance that the paying community will be the one in which the adult was reared and where his parents worked. The latter community therefore has only a weak inducement economically to subsidize the parents. A general purpose grant so distributed that this poor community is enabled to and does raise the level of medical care, subsidized food, etc., to such families may increase the economy's total product more, over the decades, than a general purpose grant that is more favorable to areas where labor productivity is higher.

This argument for a grant to areas of low marginal productivity of labor would be undermined if households were perfectly mobile, in the sense that they always located in the areas where their wages plus the free services they obtained, and less the taxes they paid, were not lower than elsewhere, and if wages always equaled marginal product. The latter proposition is disputed, and it is a commonplace that labor is not perfectly mobile, if only because the intangible attractions of the place of residence, together with uncertainties about other potential places of residence make the worker unwilling to move at a slight differential in wages plus free services, less taxes.[11] Under these circumstances a subsidy for moving, financed out of taxes in the rich area, would be economically efficient if set at successively higher and higher levels for the more and more unwilling migrants until the marginal emigrant demanded a subsidy equal to the difference, which will have been steadily shrinking as migration has proceeded, in marginal productivity (capitalized) in the two areas.

No such externalities exist with respect to capital; it has no pre-working life in which it is conditioned. To be sure, the capitalist himself is not to be forgotten, or the entrepreneur.

In general, then, there is no Pareto-optimum efficiency argument against differential grants that give more per capita to poor areas than to rich. At the same time, there is no general argument, on the same grounds, against giving more to the rich areas than to the poor. Each case must be examined to ascertain what the relative marginal productivities are and what externalities need to be taken into account. Neither of these pieces of information can be deduced from data on rich and poor districts, although there may be an initial, if weak, presumption—on efficiency grounds only— against larger per capita grants to areas where residents' incomes per capita are low.

On distributional grounds, a non-uniform per capita grant for general purposes is useful if the aim is to reduce inequality of disposable incomes, defined to include free government services. The "poor" areas must for this purpose be defined as poor in the sense of residents' income per capita, with one qualification. If the donee area is rich in the source sense, the donor government may want to inquire why the residents are not tapping this source of public revenue to a greater degree, since to do so would be to increase disposable incomes plus government services of residents, and perhaps dissipate the need for aid on distributional grounds.

In a federal country of two states, A and B, where the workers all live and work in A, with the capital instruments located there, and where the owners of those instruments all live in B, the residents of A may be able to dispense with vertical coordination arranged through the federal government for distributional purposes by themselves directly taxing the investment income as it flows from A to B, or the capital instruments themselves. But in the real world, State A will be competing with other states, A', A", etc., for capital from B. Over a long period, each of the A states can tax independently of the other A states only to the extent that economic rent is produced by natural resources, or that quasi-rent is produced by non-depreciating manmade resources located within its boundaries. Even this limit cannot be approached in practice, since the wealth of the nonresidents gives them power to influence in many ways the actions of electorate and legislators in the source states.

11. There are of course other aspects of immobility. See Richard M. Bird, for a general discussion of this issue, and the references he gives, in his "Regional Policies in a Common Market," in Carl S. Shoup (Ed.), *Fiscal Harmonization in Common Markets* (New York: Columbia University Press, 1967), vol. 1, pp. 389–94.

(2) Grants Differentiated According to Relative Effort (Sacrifice)

The donor government's grant made on distributional grounds may be conditioned on a showing by the donee government that it is making an adequate effort with its own tax system. If the donee unit is in practice virtually limited to one tax, say a real estate tax, a minimum rate of tax may be stipulated as a condition for aid. This type of stipulation has been attacked as inadequate, a uniform tax rate being said to connote a small effort for a rich community and a great effort for a poor community. But if in both communities the real estate base is in about the same proportion to aggregate local income, the requirement amounts to a minimum percentage of aggregate income being taken by taxation. The more general issue is thus posed: If, of two countries, R and P, both the rich and the poor country take, say, 10 per cent of the national income in taxation, is the poorer country making a greater effort, undergoing more sacrifice, bearing a greater burden than the rich country? The last dollar taken in taxation in the poor country is a greater burden on the taxpayer than is the last dollar taken in taxation in the rich country. But by the same reasoning, the last dollar's worth of free government service rendered in the poor country is a greater benefit to the recipient than is the last dollar's worth of free service received in the rich country. The national income that the poor country consumes in private-sector goods means more, at the margin, to its inhabitants than does that which the rich country consumes; in this sense the poor country may be charged with devoting more effort to obtain private goods than does the rich country.

Accordingly, an equal proportion of national income raised through taxes to supply free services in rich and poor countries does not suggest that the poor country is making a greater effort in the public sector relative to its effort in the private sector. It is worse off than the rich country in both public goods and private goods, because it is a poor country.

Since it is a poor country (or state, or province, or city, etc.) other jurisdictions, particularly a higher-level jurisdiction, may decide to give it assistance through a grant-in-aid. The donor jurisdiction will want to be assured that the donee jurisdiction is making an adequate effort in the public sector relative to its effort in the private sector. An adequate relative effort in this sense need not be a greater relative effort than a rich area is making ("relative" refers to effort in the public sector relative to effort by the same jurisdiction in the private sector). What the donor government wants to be certain of is that the donee government is not holding back, spending relatively little in the public sector because it expects that by doing so it can induce the wealthier jurisdictions to give it grants-in-aid. Once it is satisfied on this score it may then consider the effort that the poor area is making in the public sector, not relative to its effort in the private sector, but relative to the effort that the wealthier jurisdictions are making in their public sectors. It is at this point that comparison is made of relative "sacrifice" among jurisdictions in their public sectors. "Sacrifice," here, is taken to mean the same as "effort."

We return, then, to the question posed earlier, but in this context, which allows us to abstract from the public goods purchased with the taxes raised. If two cities, states, etc., are taking equal proportions of their economies' incomes in taxes, are they making an equal effort in the public sector, undergoing equal sacrifice? To answer this question it will be convenient to start at the level of the individual, moving later to the group.

The ratio of an individual's tax to his income is a valid measure of relative sacrifice among individuals on three conditions. First, the individual's income before tax must be assumed to be unchanged by the tax itself, or if it has been changed, allowance must be made for that fact. If he has shifted the tax in a partial-equilibrium sense, the ratio of tax to income does not measure sacrifice. Second, the test adopted for ranking individuals by amount of sacrifice must (if proportion of tax to income is the test) be equal absolute sacrifice, not equal proportional sacrifice or least aggregate sacrifice.

Third, the individual's utility function must be assumed to be of the type suggested by Bernoulli: above some minimum income necessary for existence, marginal utility of expenditure diminishes in exact proportion to the increase in expenditure. For example, if the subsistence level is $2,000; if A's income and expenditure are $4,000, and B's, $6,000, the marginal utility of a dollar's expenditure to B is one-half the marginal utility of a dollar's expenditure to A. Therefore a $2 tax on B imposes the same absolute amount of sacrifice on him as does a $1 tax on A. This kind of tax distribution is achieved by a proportional tax on that part of A's and B's expenditures (here, also their incomes) that is in excess of a $2,000 exempt minimum. In this instance the tax rate would be $\frac{1}{20}$ of 1 per cent on that part of one's income (expenditure) above $2,000.

If, in contrast, equal proportional sacrifice is the test, a simple comparison of average tax rates does not reveal differences in sacrifice. Under proportional sacrifice, B must sacrifice a larger absolute amount of utility in tax than does A, since the total utility he enjoys is larger than A's. If the Bernoulli law holds, equal proportional sacrifice requires progressive taxation.

Finally, least aggregate sacrifice calls for taking all the tax from the largest incomes, so that no one's income is reduced by taxation until all higher disposable incomes have been brought down to the level of his income.

Anyone whose concept of "equal" sacrifice requires a rate schedule more progressive (or less regressive) than that called for by the equal proportional sacrifice formula, but something short of the least-aggregate-sacrifice formula, must specify some tax rate schedule as a benchmark if he is to rank individuals by the direction in which and the amount by which the sacrifice each one incurs under the existing tax system departs from what in his view is "equality" of sacrifice. This schedule will be progressive unless he believes that the marginal utility of money decreases much less than proportionately with income. Just how much progression he will want in his benchmark tax will depend on his assumptions about the shape of the utility function.

With respect to an individual taxpayer, then, the only definite conclusion is that one may reject the ratio of tax to taxable income after exemption as a test if one rejects either the principle of equal absolute sacrifice or the Bernoulli hypothesis on the shape of the utility function.

In moving to groups, and comparing the sacrifice of one group with that of another, the dispersion of incomes among the groups will be relevant. If the average income in Group A is $4,000 and that in Group B is $6,000, and if some in A have very high incomes and others very low incomes while those in B all have about the same income, the taxpaying ability of Group A is lower, relative to that of Group B, than the averages alone might suggest. This conclusion follows if marginal utility is assumed to decrease as income increases (and, of course, if individuals' utilities can be compared—an assumption that must be made if there is to be any justification for grants-in-aid based on relative sacrifice or effort).

These considerations lead to the practical conclusion that in ranking groups of taxpayers—cities, states, nations, etc.—by amount of tax sacrifice, a hazardous business at best, the most sensible method is to apply to the individual incomes of the community a graduated rate schedule that is assumed to yield the appropriate relative amounts of sacrifice, and compare the resulting tax revenue for the community from this hypothetical schedule with the amount of tax revenue it in fact does raise. To be sure, the question that this exercise tries to answer is fundamentally of dubious validity, at least in any precise sense, for reasons advanced in Chapter 2 above. But if the answer is taken as only a crude approximation it will serve in helping determine how a given total grant is to be allocated among subordinate jurisdictions, when the relative sacrifice already being made by those jurisdictions is to be one of the criteria employed in fixing the relative grants.[12]

As with the individual, so with the group, the degree of effort or sacrifice being made varies inversely with the extent to which it exports the tax burden to other jurisdictions by shifting. An allowance for this might be made by subtracting from tax revenue actually collected a part that is estimated to be shifted elsewhere. Taxes shifted to residents of this area from other areas will presumably be allowed for automatically, as they reduce the factor incomes or raise the prices paid by the residents.

c. Specific-purpose Grants

(1) Non-sharing Grants

The grant-in-aid may be given on the condition that it be spent by the donee government on a specified program. If the donee government is not required to spend on this program, from its own funds, the grant is a non-sharing grant; the donee government is not required to share in the expenses of the program. Such grants are rare; they make the donee government the administrative agent for the donor government's program and invite supervision to so high a degree that the donee government may become, for this program, virtually a branch of the donor government rather than its agent. Since the donee government is free to cut back on its own spending, if any, for this program, this 100 per cent grant is in fact in some degree a general purpose grant-in-aid (compare Chapter 6.C.1.c), on effective-

12. See Appendix to this chapter.

ness of subsidy). Of course even a sharing grant, now to be discussed, may have this effect to some extent.[13]

(2) Sharing Grants

The specific purpose grant may require that the donee government itself spend a stipulated sum on the program. More commonly, it requires that the donee government spend on the program either (1) an amount equivalent to the yield of a specified rate of tax on the donee government's tax base,[14] or (2) a certain matching or partly matching amount, that is, a certain percentage of the total amount spent on the program from both donee and donor sources. This second type will now be analyzed; the conclusions can be applied with little modification to the first type. Although both types are sharing grants, in that the donee unit must share in the total costs of the program, it will be convenient to distinguish between the two types by reserving the term, sharing grant, for the second type, where the donee unit contributes a specified percentage of the total cost. The first type, where the donee unit must impose a minimum tax rate, may be called an effort-conditioned grant.

If the donor's grant is just 50 per cent of the total spent, it is a "matching" grant, although that term is often used to refer to any kind of what is here termed a sharing grant. A 99 per cent sharing grant, where the donor government supplies 99 per cent of the funds spent, will in practice have almost the same effects as a 100 per cent, i.e., non-sharing, grant. In principle, to be sure, there is the same fundamental difference described in Chapter 6 above for subsidies to the private sector. The 100 per cent grant must be either rationed on some basis other than price or given freely up to the point where the donee government is saturated and finds the usefulness of another dollar of grant for the specified purpose to be zero. The saturation amount is likely to be so large, unless the program is very narrowly defined, that rationing is almost always necessary. In contrast, a sharing grant, in principle, is rationed only by price: the donor government stands ready to spend on the particular program as much money as the donee government cares to buy at the reduced price (the price being 1 cent on the dollar when the donor government pays 99 per cent of the program cost). In practice, the donor government usually places an upper bound on the grant, though perhaps a liberal one.

When the donor's share is very large, the rationing is accomplished by donor and donee(s) agreeing on the physical aspects of the program: a certain highway network, for example.[15] But when the donor's percentage is, say, 50 per cent or less, the program is often open-ended. The number of physical units of the program, say the

13. The grant by New York State to New York City for a percentage of the general assistance expenditure (relief payments outside special categories) is probably in large part essentially a general purpose grant; in the absence of this aid the city would still spend a considerable amount on general assistance from its own revenues, more than it does at present.

14. This requirement is common in grants by states in the United States to local units for educational expenditures.

15. As under the United States interstate highway program, where the federal government pays, in general, 90 per cent of the cost.

number of hospital beds, that are purchased by the donee governments then depends on the elasticity of demand by the donee governments for the program's input units and on the elasticity of supply in the private sector that sells those units to the government. The analysis of Chapter 6, Section C.1.c, is now applicable. If supply is perfectly elastic, the donee government's other spending or its revenue policy will be unaltered by the grant only if its elasticity of demand is precisely unity over the range from full price to price less the grant. If that elasticity is less than unity the specific-purpose grant is in effect partly a general purpose grant, since it frees money for other expenditures or for tax reduction or debt repayment. And if it is greater than unity, other services will be reduced or taxes or borrowing increased.

In practice it is likely that the donee government's elasticity of demand for the service units is less than unity, for the following reason. The donor government is presumably supplying the special purpose money because of externalities yielded by the service in question.[16] If there were no externalities a general purpose grant made on distributive grounds would be all that was needed. Before the grant, the donee-to-be will ideally have pushed its own outlay on this service up to the point where the marginal benefit per dollar of expenditure will have been the same for that program as for all others not to be supported by grants. Its elasticity of demand for that program will be high only if that program is a very good substitute for one of the other programs, so that when the price of this particular program declines, the government is willing to cut back sharply on the now more expensive programs for which it is a good substitute. But if the donor government obtains externalities from one of these programs it is likely to obtain them also from the programs for which it is a good substitute. The donor government is therefore likely to include in its sharing grant all or most of these programs. The donee government's demand for the units of these programs considered as one group will then probably be of less than unit elasticity. In practice, then, we might expect a substantial part of any special purpose sharing grant to be, in effect, a general purpose grant.

But if the donor government's grant covers only one of a number of close substitute programs, the donee's demand will be very elastic. The donee government will reduce its spending elsewhere, chiefly in the close substitute grants, to enlarge its own spending on the subsidized program. Since the reduction in spending elsewhere does take place chiefly in the close substitute programs, the grant may in essence play the role of a general purpose grant. Total donee spending, from its own money, on the subsidized program and the close substitutes together may well be less than it would be under no such grant.

To the donor government the marginal utility of the units of the program, arising from the externalities they create, probably decreases as the number of units purchased increases. The donor's share of the cost of the next unit should thereupon decrease, if the donor is to be consistent in paying for what it wants, not making a gift. The grant formula would then contain a large number of bracket rates, that is, marginal rates of grant sharing, decreasing with the number of program units purchased. Alternatively a formula would be constructed for the total grant with a

16. For an analysis of these externalities, see George F. Break, *Intergovernmental Fiscal Relations in the United States* (Washington, D.C.: Brookings Institution, 1967), pp. 63–77.

first derivative with respect to the number of units purchased that would be positive and a second derivative that would be negative. If, as is usually the case, a number of donee governments are involved at once, a differing set of schedules for each would be too complex and open to a (mistaken) charge of unfair discrimination. But one decreasing-rate schedule applied to all might still be better than a single flat-rate sharing schedule.

The specific purpose sharing grant is in intent almost entirely an instrument for approaching a Pareto optimum by taking externalities into account. It has little or nothing to do with full employment, price stability, or external equilibrium. It could be used to promote growth in general by inducing subordinate units to purchase more capital goods, but in fact it is used to promote particular programs rather than growth as such. The redistributive effects of this kind of grant are incidental to its main purpose. They may go either way and for some donees may be important. If the donor's sharing percentage is not large, the high-income donee jurisdictions may draw down much more money from the (open-ended) grant than do the low-income jurisdictions. This fact creates a tendency for disposable incomes to be distributed more unequally, though of course the tendency can be compensated for by a particularly progressive method of financing the grant. If the low-income units do take large amounts, as they may be forced to do in programs that are open-ended also to the users of the service, who may therefore demand and get a large number of units of the service, the low-income jurisdictions can often meet their share only by taxing households of low income or depriving them of other services.[17]

The specific-purpose grant is compatible with a moderate, but not very high, degree of political decentralization, and it is not in itself an expression of decentralization goals that lie outside the public finance area. It is essentially a way for the higher level of government to get done something that it does not itself want to administer but which it is willing to help pay for.

3. Public Finance Goals and Decentralization

The decentralized state equipped with the battery of coordination devices described in Sections 1 and 2 above may now be set alongside the unitary state to inquire how these two types of public finance system, each operating with the best techniques available, compare with respect to the equal treatment of equals criterion and the public finance goals, consensus and conflict. As might be anticipated, the answer is mixed.

The unitary state's public finance system certainly provides more nearly equal treatment to those equally circumstanced, at least on paper. Location is, in principle, not a factor that determines the rate of tax payable. It is said to be not a factor that

17. According to the *New York Times*, September 17, 1967 (Martin Tolchin), the rural woodland counties of New York State are "facing bankruptcy" because of "the vastly increased costs of the Medicaid program," of which they must pay 25 per cent, although they have no voice in setting fees or eligibility standards. The poorest counties have the highest percentage of Medicaid patients.

determines the level of service supplied, but we have seen that even in so relatively homogeneous unitary jurisdictions as cities there is no legal requirement for uniform level of service, and in fact the poor, because of their location, are likely to obtain a lower level of service output if not input, per capita, than the well-to-do (see Chapter 4). And the location of the poor is determined by the fact that they are poor. Still, if the city were divided into independent self-governing boroughs, the variation in level of service would probably be greater yet, unless the richer boroughs made general purpose grants to the poorer boroughs.[18] The level of education in a city and probably over a wider area is somewhat more uniform under a unitary system than under a decentralized system.

The geographical uniformity required by law in the unitary system applies chiefly to taxes and transfer payments, and here practice may easily differ from principle. An income tax may be more laxly administered in one area of a large country than in another,[19] or more harshly enforced.

The decentralized system, if it is without grants-in-aid, provides unequal tax treatment of those who are equal in all relevant respects (except location), chiefly because a decentralized country is decentralized heterogeneously in economic terms. If all families of income below, say, $2,000 lived in one geographical area, say State A, all those with incomes over $2,000 but not over $5,000 in State B, and so on, the existence of state governments would not create unequal treatment of equals in income taxation. Of course, these groups would almost surely not be homogeneous with respect to cigarette consumption; perhaps half in each state would be smokers, and if State A levies a cigarette tax and State B does not, unequal treatment arises.

Meanwhile, those in State A could enjoy only an abysmally low level of free government services from the state unless they were willing to pay much higher taxes than their unequals in State B. Is this unequal treatment of equals? The answer depends on what is regarded as relevant in defining equality of status when free government services are at issue.[20] If the attitude of the market is adopted, those with low incomes are not being treated unequally by being given a low level of free government services; they are getting what they can afford. But if public finance is regarded primarily as a non-price allocating mechanism, the fact that the poor cannot afford to "buy" a high level of services does not disprove the existence of unequal treatment. Recipients of free government services might instead be regarded as are voters: the right to a certain amount of voting power (one man, one vote) is not now linked to the voter's economic status, though it commonly was in earlier times.

And on the revenue side, the economic heterogeneity of the subordinate units guarantees unequal taxation of equals, even if the several units offer the same levels

18. As was done in London, prior to the recent reorganization of the government of that area (Robert M. Haig, Carl S. Shoup, and Lyle C. Fitch, *The Financial Problem of the City of New York* [New York: City of New York, 1952], pp. 62–71).

19. It is common knowledge among tax lawyers in the United States that circuit courts in certain parts of the country are to be preferred, and much ingenuity is expended in attempting to attach a favorable geographical venue to a tax dispute.

20. See J. M. Buchanan, "Federalism and Fiscal Equity," *American Economic Review* (September, 1950), 40: 583–600, reprinted in Musgrave and Shoup (Eds.), *Readings in the Economics of Taxation*, pp. 93–109.

of government services. A poor householder in an enclave of wealthy men fares very well, enjoying a low tax rate even under a flat-rate tax system. A high-income man in a poor state is likely to have to pay high tax rates. These facts set in motion forces that tend to produce a one-sided income homogeneity. Wealthy men go where wealthy men are, not only because of general compatibility, but for tax reasons. Poor men try to go where wealthy men are, and the wealthy try to keep them out, knowing that if they fail they stand to pay higher tax rates if the accustomed level of service is to be continued on a uniform basis for all, save in the unreal case where the marginal cost of serving the in-migrants is so low that it falls even below the small tax-paying ability they bring with them. Boundary lines of local units are drawn by the wealthy, as much as they can influence these matters, to enclose small areas, since the smaller the area the less the opportunity of dilution by entry of the poor. Zoning and other regulations are often designed to discourage immigration of the poor, the ailing, or simply those with large families.

This geographical fragmentation is of course only an expression of the desire of the well-to-do to operate under something as close to a market pricing system as possible: in general, those with incomes above the median rather like the pricing system, while the rest of the populace try to escape from it whenever they can. This tendency to geographical clustering, both voluntary (the well-to-do) and involuntary (the poor) may in a strictly technical sense be described as an approach to a Pareto-optimum use of resources, but like any Pareto optimum, it takes place against a distribution of income that the poor, at least, will try to change. The chief instruments of change are the grants-in-aid, financed by a tax at a uniform rate over all these economically uneven areas.

What the decentralized state or public finance system does is to bring out into the open the struggle between those who want to optimize on the basis of the existing distribution of disposable income, including government free services in that income, and those who want to see that distribution made more nearly equal. This struggle is far less discernible in the unitary state, since the presumption in such a state is that all taxes shall be geographically uniform and all free services shall be at the same level everywhere. This state of affairs does not of course prevent most households in some areas from being poorer than most households in certain other areas. But a unitary fiscal system has no intergovernmental tools with which to improve the lot of the poorer areas—granted that they are better off than they would be under a decentralized system with no grants-in-aid. The bitterness of the impoverished areas in the unitary system may finally erupt into a demand that the system be decentralized centrally, so to speak, with national taxes being levied at lower rates in poorer areas, and with government purchases of goods and services being channeled disproportionately into those areas.[21] Finally a truly decentralized system may emerge, with some governmental units set up in the poor areas to receive grants-in-aid from the central government.

In summary, the decentralized public finance system offers the possibility both of a closer approach to a pricing system and of a closer approach to a system of equal

21. With respect to some of these techniques, see Richard M. Bird, "Regional Policies in a Common Market," in Carl S. Shoup (Ed.), *Fiscal Harmonization in Common Markets*.

real disposable incomes than does the unitary public finance system. Which road the decentralized system takes depends on political and social forces that cannot be analyzed here.

C. HORIZONTAL FISCAL COORDINATION

Horizontal fiscal coordination developed later and more slowly than vertical coordination. Now, with the growth of common markets and free trade areas and the increased flow of international capital, horizontal coordination is increasing in speed and changing in form.[22]

The increase in horizontal coordination has been almost wholly in taxation. Transfer payment coordination is represented chiefly by international aid, discussed in Chapter 7 above. Social security coordination is noted on pages 648-49 below, as are also some of the problems that may arise if government service (government expenditure on goods and services) coordination is attempted.

The chief tools in horizontal tax coordination are the unilateral tax credit or tax deduction, the tax treaty, and tax harmonization.

1. Tax Credit

The tax credit, whereby taxes paid abroad are credited against the domestic tax on the same income, or property, has been granted unilaterally by many of the major capital-exporting nations, chiefly in order to satisfy the criterion of equal treatment of those equally circumstanced. In the absence of the credit, domestic investors investing at home would pay less income tax than domestic investors investing abroad, who would be paying two income taxes. "Equally circumstanced" might be taken instead to mean "similarly located abroad"; an American corporation's wholly owned subsidiary operating in Brazil is in this sense equally circumstanced with a German corporation's wholly owned subsidiary operating in Brazil. Equal treatment if then given only if both the United States and Germany exempt entirely the profits earned in Brazil, leaving Brazil to set the income tax rate, and of course get all the revenue.

A procedure analogous to this is the one followed under sales taxation of the destination principle type (see Chapter 11). That part of the tax base that consists of sales to foreign purchasers who are located abroad is not taxed. The tax base in this instance is sales, not profits. This difference is significant if profit before tax is something that is being maximized, while the total of sales before tax is not something that is being maximized. If before-tax profits are being maximized, the sales

---

22. For the differences in emphasis and goals in discussions of vertical coordination and those of horizontal coordination, see Douglas Dosser, "Economic Analysis of Tax Harmonization," in Shoup (Ed.), *op. cit.*, vol. 1, pp. 19-26.

prices set by the firm and its physical volume of sales will not be affected by the rate of income tax. Differences in the United States and German income tax rates will by this reasoning have no effect on the prices or the physical volumes of sales of the concerns competing in Brazil. Each concern sets prices and output as it would under a Brazilian income tax alone, or under no tax. Equal tax treatment of domestic investors investing at home and those investing abroad can therefore be achieved without distorting competition abroad. Of course, if the Brazilian tax is so high that it exceeds the credit, equal tax treatment is no longer accorded to all types of United States investors (or all types of German investors).

These remarks assume a perfectly inelastic supply of the exported factor, whether capital, technology, or component parts, the pre-tax return from which is to be maximized. In practice, this assumption must be relaxed and some degree of elasticity allowed for. But it may be, even probably is, small, except where the capitalist himself is mobile as to residence.

In a world where capitalists were perfectly mobile, that is, quite willing to change their country of residence just to save tax, the existence of a credit for Brazilian tax would not prevent an exodus of capitalists from the high-rate country, say the United States, to the lower rate country, Germany (it is assumed, unless otherwise noted, that the Brazilian income tax rate is lower than that of either the United States or Germany). At the extreme, all capitalists exporting capital to Brazil would reside in Germany, none in the United States. But of course that does not happen. To be sure, capital itself is mobile, but the United States capitalist who routes his capital to Brazil by way of Germany does not in this way escape the United States tax, which is based on residence of the capitalist.

The real world is closer to the other extreme, where the capitalist is not mobile at all. At that extreme even the absence of a credit for Brazilian tax cannot induce a capitalist to move from the United States to Germany, where a credit is given. What the absence of a tax credit in the United States would do is to induce the United States capitalist to shift his capital from Brazil to the United States, until the pre-tax return had fallen in the United States and risen in Brazil by enough to make up for the absence of the credit. Since the pre-tax rates of return are now unequal because of the tax structure, that structure would be causing an inefficient distribution of capital between the United States and Brazil.

If United States capital invested in Brazil were exempted from the United States tax, or granted a preferential rate, inefficiency would be created in the other direction. United States capital would flow into ventures in Brazil until the pre-tax return in Brazil fell by enough to absorb the rate differential.

The unilateral tax credit given by the capital-exporting countries therefore does better both as to equal treatment of equals and in approaching a Pareto optimum than would exemption, by the capital-exporting country, of profits earned by such capital, leaving the capital-importing country to set the effective tax rate at a uniform level for profits on imported capital from whatever country.

One important qualification must be made to these conclusions. If the United States capital is invested abroad through a foreign corporation that is owned by a United States corporation, as in the examples above, the United States tax is commonly levied, not in the year in which the foreign profits are earned, but in the year in which they are repatriated in the form of dividends, or upon liquidation of the foreign subsidiary. Since delay in tax payment is equivalent to reduction in tax rate (see Chapter 12, Section 4.A), earnings on foreign investment are favored, unless the foreign country's tax rate is as high as that of the United States. To that extent, equal treatment and a Pareto optimum are not attained.

The goal of economic growth has in recent years influenced attitudes toward the tax credit. Capital-importing countries that are underdeveloped are willing to exempt foreign capital from income tax, for a time at least, in order to attract a capital inflow that will accelerate economic growth. They feel impeded, however, by the tax credit. If a capital-importing country reduces its tax rate, the total income tax paid on the income earned by the foreign capital does not decrease. The capitalist's credit against his home tax diminishes pari passu, and there is said to be no more, or less, incentive than before to invest in the underdeveloped country. This conclusion overlooks the fact that the capital-exporting country's tax is commonly not levied until earnings are repatriated. Nevertheless, capital-importing countries feel so strongly on this point that they have requested the capital-exporting countries to grant their capitalists "tax-sparing," that is, to give them credit for the phantom tax, the tax that they would have paid to the underdeveloped country if it had not granted them exemption. Only then, the argument runs, would a tax holiday, say for ten years, mean something to the foreign capitalist.

But tax-sparing would in many cases not add anything to the foreign investor's incentive, and it might even operate to the detriment of the capital-importing country. Let us consider more closely what happens when there is no tax-sparing, but there is a tax holiday in the capital-importing country. The United States income tax law gives credit for tax paid to, say, Brazil, against the United States tax that is imposed on the dividends remitted to the United States parent corporation by its Brazilian-incorporated subsidiary that operates in Brazil. These dividends are presumed by United States Internal Revenue Service regulations to be made out of the profits most recently accumulated by the Brazilian subsidiary. Let a tax holiday be granted as assumed above, and let the Brazilian subsidiary retain all the profits of the first ten years or more, a common policy for new corporations attempting to build up business in a foreign country. When the Brazilian subsidiary does at last declare dividends to its United States parent, those dividends, being considered paid out of the profits of the most recent year, will be treated as dividends from profits that have paid Brazilian tax, and accordingly will be granted a tax credit, even without a tax-sparing provision. Only when the accumulated dividends paid exceed the accumulated earnings from the end of the tax holiday period will there be no credit available. Under these circumstances the tax holiday is effective, not because of a tax-sparing provision, but simply because of the delay in assessing the United States tax on the earnings of the first ten years. This delay will be indefinitely long, if the subsidiary's life is indefinitely long, and provided that the dividends paid to the parent corporation never accumulate to more than the post-holiday accumulated profits. Since a delayed tax is a reduced tax, a United States tax on those first ten years of earnings is a reduced tax, and indeed if the delay lasts for, say, fifty years or more, the present value of the tax is reduced close to zero at usual rates of discount.

What a tax-sparing clause may do is to persuade the parent corporation to call back profits from its subsidiary soon after it is started, in order to get credit for the phantom tax of the first ten years. Repatriation of earnings of the eleventh and following years could be in the same pattern as before, with the same United States tax and credit, or could be less, to make up for the early repatriation of the first ten years' profits. In any event the early repatriation is not to the advantage of the under-developed country and may be to its disadvantage.

The tax credit has no obvious implication for full employment or price stability in the capital-exporting country, except perhaps indirectly through its effect on the balance of payments. By encouraging capital export, relative to no tax credit, the tax credit produces a current incremental deficit in that balance, and may induce a policy of domestic deflation.[23] Future years' balances will be favorably affected as earnings are brought home.

A capital-exporting country that does not allow a credit for foreign taxes paid will commonly as least allow deduction of those taxes in computing net taxable income. The relief from double taxation thus afforded falls far short of the 100 per cent that the tax credit usually guarantees, but the direction of effects of the deduction is the same as that of the credit. The analysis given of the tax credit may therefore be readily adapted to the deduction.

2. Tax Treaty

Bilateral tax treaties, concerned almost entirely with the income tax, have been put into effect among most of the industrialized countries.[24] Few treaties exist between an industrialized country and an undeveloped country, and fewer still between two undeveloped countries.

The treaties have not, as is sometimes alleged, reduced double taxation greatly, if only because there has not been much double taxation to reduce in view of the credit for foreign taxes granted by some of the largest industrial countries[25] and the exemption of foreign-source income granted by some of the others. But these devices have still left pockets of double taxation to be wiped out or reduced,

23. The concept of a tax credit appears simple in principle; in practice, it proves complex. For a comprehensive analysis of the theory and practical problems of the tax credit, see Elisabeth A. Owens, *The Foreign Tax Credit* (Cambridge, Mass: International Program in Taxation, Harvard Law School, 1961). For a critical view of tax-sparing, see Stanley S. Surrey, "The Pakistan Treaty and 'Tax Sparing'," *National Tax Journal* (June, 1958), 11: 156–67.

24. The OECD Council adopted in July, 1963, a Draft Double Taxation Convention on Income and Capital, which might induce revision of the varying bilateral treaties into one or more multilateral treaties.

25. In most of the United States tax treaties, the foreign government, when it did not already do so, has agreed to allow their residents, including United States-owned firms, credit for taxes imposed by the United States on United States source income.

exemplified by taxation of dividends, interest and royalties both by the country of source and the country of residence, even when the latter country grants credit for taxes on profits, as distinct from taxes on distribution of investment income. A roughly equal two-way flow of such receipts between a pair of countries allows elimination of double taxation without either country's being disadvantaged. But if the flow is all one way, there is no such basis for reciprocal action, and this fact helps explain why underdeveloped countries, being typical capital importers, have not entered into tax treaties with the capital-exporting countries.

As to dividends, much depends on the source country's policy with respect to taxation of corporate profits that are distributed to domestic portfolio investors, and of intercorporate dividends paid by subsidiary to parent.

At one extreme, the foreign country may impose on its own corporations and its own residents a completely non-integrated system of income taxation, so that no attempt is made to prevent double taxation of corporate profits and no tax reduction is given to intercorporate dividends. The foreign country may accordingly claim that on dividends flowing abroad it has the right to impose a substantial "withholding" tax, since it will never be able to reach the shareholder directly, as it can when the shareholder is one of its own residents. Only by such a withholding tax, it argues, can it apply roughly equal double taxation on corporate profits earned within its borders irrespective of where the capital came from. The capital-exporting country is presumed to allow a tax credit for the withholding tax, and, if the shares are owned by a parent corporation rather than by a portfolio investor, credit for the corporate tax as well.

At the other extreme, the foreign country may integrate its corporate and individual income taxes to a high degree by exempting intercorporate dividends paid by subsidiary to parent, and by granting a credit or exemption to portfolio-investor shareholders. Now the case for a heavy withholding tax on dividends flowing abroad is weakened, if not destroyed. A tax treaty will stipulate what the withholding rate shall be, and since these treaties are commonly between countries with two-way capital flows, there is a sound basis for bargaining.

Tax treaties are needed to define precisely the rules for application of the tax credit or the territorial principle of taxation. The source rules allocate income, notably profits, among two or more sources (countries). Production, for example, may occur in one country, and the selling activity by the same firm in another country. If two countries differ in their rules of source, double taxation or tax escape may occur, even under a tax credit.[26]

Some tax conventions do not succeed in framing mutually consistent rules of source, or in solving the analogous problem of defining residence, but provide that the two sets of tax officials may reach agreement on apportionment of income.

Differences in definition of income may result in a foreign tax rate higher than the home-country rate, even though the foreign rate is nominally lower. The home country's tax-credit provisions never allow a credit for that part of a foreign tax that exceeds the home country's tax on the foreign-source income. Thus a tax treaty that reduces tax rates on income flowing abroad tends to prevent double

26. Owens, *op. cit.*, pp. 14, 217, 489–95.

taxation arising from differences in definition of taxable income, especially with respect to royalties, which are difficult to allocate, and interest.[27]

Tax treaties commonly make special provision for particular industries the income of which is difficult to allocate. Examples are supplied by the profits of an international transportation company and royalties from exhibiting motion pictures. Often, one country will be given exclusive right to tax the entire profit of a certain type of concern (for example, domestic-flag international carriers).

Transient business and professional men are sometimes exempted by the country of source, in tax treaties, up to a certain amount, or for a certain maximum period of stay. A good deal of nuisance in reporting and getting the tax back by crediting against the home-country tax is thereby avoided.

Resident aliens from a high-income country, like the United States, who are working as executives or other salaried personnel in a low-income country for home-country firms with branches or subsidiaries in the low-income country often find that the personal income tax of the low-income country, being geared to incomes that appear low to one from a high-income country, allows personal exemptions so small and imposes a rate scale so rapidly progressive in terms of the home country's currency that they have little salary left to save in terms of that currency. To reach the savings goals that are typical for their colleagues in the home country, they must be paid salaries that are much higher than those of like personnel in the home country. Tax treaties, it appears, have not been able to solve this perplexing problem.[28] One possibility is that the low-income country could follow the rule already in force in at least one industrialized country (the United Kingdom): tax only the earned income of resident aliens that they "receive in" the country. The employing corporation can arrange to have part of the salary "paid in" the home country, depositing it, for example, in the bank account that the executive keeps there.

Tax treaties are sometimes said to be necessary to allow a high-rate country to get its rates down to the level of a low-rate country from which it wants to import capital and entrepreneurship. The credit device will not achieve that end. But the importance of this issue is perhaps not great, since capital-importing countries are usually low-rate tax countries also, with respect to income taxation.[29]

A vexing problem of allocation occurs when a foreign enterprise, although "engaged in trade or business" in the source country, does not maintain there a "permanent establishment." It may do business there only through a commission agent or it may only purchase goods, not sell them, in that country. Tax treaties may stipulate that the source country will not tax such a concern, in order to avoid harassment out of proportion to the revenue gains. The treaty must then define the term "permanent establishment." If it is narrowly defined, an appreciable amount of

27. See Raphael Sherfy, "Special Problems in Corporate Taxation: Foreign Income," *Tax Revision Compendium* (Compendium of Papers on Broadening the Tax Base) submitted to the Committee on Ways and Means, United States Congress, vol. 3 (Washington, D.C.: Government Printing Office, 1959), p. 2162.

28. Dan Throop Smith, "The Functions of Tax Treaties," in Tax Institute, *Taxation and Operations Abroad* (Princeton, N.J.: Princeton University Press, 1960), p. 290.

29. *Ibid.*, p. 277.

business may be carried on by a nonresident alien or foreign corporation without generating any liability to tax in the host country.[30]

Cooperation in tax administration is a common feature of tax treaties; it is perhaps one of the chief reasons for such treaties.[31] The goals served by the tax treaties, given the existence of tax credits or the territorial principle, between industrialized countries is chiefly that of equal treatment of equals, including the reaching of agreement on definition of equally circumstanced. The treaty provisions have had some effect on income distribution, but it is difficult to generalize on this score. The effect on growth has been minimal or nil, but there has been some slight influence on the balance of payments, chiefly through creating an incremental surplus for capital-exporting countries by somewhat reducing application of the territorial principle.

3. Fiscal Harmonization

A. COMMON MARKETS AND FREE TRADE AREAS

Fiscal harmonization consists of any change in the public finance systems of member countries in a common market or free trade area that is intended to forward the aims of that economic union.[32] Fiscal harmonization is more important for a common market than for a free trade area, for four reasons.

First, in a common market no customs tariffs or export taxes are imposed when goods move from one member country to another, while in a free trade area only goods that originate within that area can cross intra-area borders without paying tariffs; goods that originate outside the free trade area and that enter the area by way of a low-tariff country must pay the difference in tariff when they move on to a high-tariff country within the area. Otherwise, the low-tariff country would become the sole importer for the whole area, and the high tariffs of the other countries would become ineffective.[33] This "anti-trade deflection" provision is not needed in a

---

30. *Ibid.*, p. 282.   31. *Ibid.*, pp. 292–93.

32. A narrower definition but broader in its implications of total harmonization and correspondingly more useful for some purposes is that fiscal harmonization consists of the measures necessary "to establish conditions of taxation and public expenditure similar to those that would exist within a unified economy" ("Report of the Fiscal and Financial Committee [Neumark Report]," *The EEC Reports on Tax Harmonization* [Amsterdam: International Bureau of Fiscal Documentation, 1963], p. 101). To this concept the Neumark Report added "elimination of influences and factors which give rise to distortions of the conditions of competition" (*ibid.*, p. 104). This latter aim is of course not restricted to common markets; it is similar to the goal of Paretian efficiency. But it requires, *inter alia*, precise computation of export rebates and compensating import taxes. For a discussion of the concept of fiscal harmonization, see Douglas Dosser, "Economic Analysis of Tax Harmonization," in Carl S. Shoup (Ed.), *Fiscal Harmonization in Common Markets* (New York: Columbia University Press, 1967), vol. 1, pp. 1–41, and Norbert Andel, "Problems of Government Expenditure Harmonization in a Common Market," *ibid.*, pp. 313–15. See also the definition of a "tax union" in footnote 38 below.

33. See Hirofumi Shibata, "The Theory of Economic Unions," in Shoup (Ed.), *op. cit.*, vol. 1, pp. 172–89, especially the demonstration that the anti-trade-deflection rules give rise to a price differential between physically identical products within a free trade area (*Ibid.*, pp. 177–83).

common market, since the countries of a common market agree at the outset that a uniform system of tariffs shall apply to all imports to the market, whatever the importing country. This greater freedom of internal trade in the common market offers greater rewards to fiscal harmonization; there is more to be lost, in allocative efficiency, by failure to align the public finance systems.

Second, a common market seeks to increase the mobility of labor, capital, and capitalists within the union more than does a free trade area. This enhanced mobility again increases both the rewards to come from harmonization of the internal fiscal systems and the penalties for failure to harmonize.

Third, since border controls in a common market are abolished so far as customs are concerned (they are not, in a free trade area), the way is open for complete elimination of border controls if only the internal tax systems can be revamped so that no rebates of sales taxes are given upon export of goods from one member country to another, and no compensating import tax is levied on imports by one member country from another. The mere psychological gain from complete absence of border control within a common market can scarcely be overrated; it creates a spirit of unity, an expansiveness of outlook, that is a good, if not close, substitute for political unity. In a free trade area border controls on intra-area trade must remain to enforce the anti-trade-deflection rules and to levy purely revenue duties on imports where the importing country produces neither those goods nor close substitutes.[34]

Finally, it seems likely that a free trade area is a holding operation, designed to help its members decide whether they wish to bind themselves more closely in a common market (or join an existing common market). A free trade area is probably either short-lived or ineffective. For all these reasons,[35] the present analysis will concentrate on fiscal harmonization in common markets,[36] with only brief reference to free trade areas.[37]

34. See Hirofumi Shibata, "Tax Harmonization in the European Free Trade Association," in Shoup (Ed.), *op. cit.*, vol. 2, pp. 455–57. If most of the country's international trade moves from and into ports and airports, customs facilities must be maintained there in any case to process imports from non-union countries, and to identify goods coming from union countries and moving into union countries. There is correspondingly less to gain from tax harmonization. It so happens that 95 per cent of trade among the member states of the Latin American Free Trade Association was by sea (in 1961) (Marion H. Gillim, "Some Fiscal Aspects of the Latin American Free Trade Association," in Shoup [Ed.], *op. cit.*, vol. 2, p. 530). This fact does increase the importance of harmonizing taxes on shipping (*ibid.*, p. 531).

35. Another reason in the present-day world arises from the institutional fact that all the European Economic Community countries except France were levying the turnover (cascade) tax, while most of the European Free Trade Association countries were levying single-stage sales taxes (only Austria was using the cascade type of sales tax) at the time these associations were formed. Precise computation of tax to be rebated on export is impossible under the cascade type of sales tax and, in principle, at least, is feasible under single-stage taxes. Replacement of the turnover taxes in the EEC countries by a value-added tax, to assure more nearly correct practice in export rebates and probably also in compensating import taxes, came to be high on the agenda of the EEC countries. See Shibata, "Tax Harmonization in the European Free Trade Association," in Shoup (Ed.), *op. cit.*, vol. 2, pp. 444–46, 460 ff.

36. The European Economic Community, the Central American Common Market (CACM), and the proposed Latin American common market.

37. EFTA and LAFTA. COMECON, the socialist economic union, will not be covered here.

Tax harmonization is one aspect of fiscal harmonization. When tax harmonization is achieved through a binding agreement among member states it may be termed a "tax union."[38]

B. HARMONIZATION IN COMMON MARKETS

In addition to yielding the intangible benefits that come from the feeling of union, a feeling that is enhanced by almost any type of harmonization within a common market, fiscal harmonization proves to be especially significant for equal treatment of equals, allocative efficiency, and economic growth. It is less so for achievement of full employment, indeed may even make that goal more difficult to reach at times, and is of uncertain value with respect to price stability and external equilibrium.[39] Its effects on distribution of disposable income are as yet largely unknown.

Equal treatment of equals in a fiscal system is of no significance if everyone is by definition deemed to be different from everyone else. The larger the number of persons who can be defined as equal in all relevant respects the more powerful is the intuitive appeal of this criterion, and the more important does observance of it become. In a common market, nationality dwindles as a relevant test for "equally circumstanced," and the groups of equals become correspondingly smaller in number and larger in size. The fiscal systems must be revised to take account of this fact. Nationality does not of course disappear completely as a relevant circumstance. Prevailing opinion as to the proper role of the state in economic life will continue to differ from country to country within the union. The conflicts of interest within a country with respect to economic growth, for example, will give rise to different solutions in the different countries. Two common-market families with the same income and family composition, one living in Country A, the other in Country B, may be taxed lightly on their consumption in A and heavily in B, because B desires more rapid economic growth than does A. But this difference in treatment will not necessarily offend the intuitive desire for equal treatment of equals. Still, if the inter-country differences of opinion and policy solutions are quite substantial, the common market will scarcely prove viable. In general, a common market enhances the importance of the criterion of equal treatment of equals.

38. The term "tax union" was introduced by Douglas Dosser, "Economic Analysis of Tax Harmonization," in Shoup (Ed.), *op. cit.*, vol. 1, pp. 10–11, 16–17. A detailed definition is offered by Shibata ("The Theory of Economic Unions," *ibid.*, vol. 1, p. 190): "An international agreement among a group of countries concerning internal taxes, by which the participating countries agree to take (a series of) simultaneous action(s) involving a reorientation of the geographical discrimination prescribed in their internal tax structure. 'Reorientation of geographical discrimination' refers to the modification of taxes imposed on the basis of geographical differences in the location of economic activity, such as country of consumption, country of residence, country of payment, and the like, so that they apply only to group (or non-group) countries." Moreover, "tax union should be differentiated from tax harmonization or tax coordination, for the former involves surrender of a substantial part of individual member sovereignty on tax matters, particularly in the area of tax treatment of non-tax-union members, while the latter generally allows the individual countries to retain substantial autonomy in such matters" (*ibid.*, p. 251).

39. On these points, see G. K. Shaw, "European Economic Integration and Stabilization Policy," in Shoup (Ed.), *op. cit.*, vol. 2, Chapter 11.

Inefficiencies in the allocation of resources among the countries that were prevalent before the common market was formed do not all disappear once the customs network is eliminated. Differences in fiscal systems may still induce inefficient allocations. If exchange rates were free to fluctuate, many if not all of these differences in fiscal systems would become irrelevant, as relative prices among countries were allowed freely to adjust to those differences. But freely fluctuating exchange rates within a common market are somewhat inconsistent with the notion of an economic union. A set of absolutely unvarying rates of exchange among the member countries offers a close substitute for that true mark of complete union, a common currency. Moreover, producers in any one of the member countries would be reluctant to expand output to sell in the now tariff-free area for fear that devaluations could overnight destroy their potential markets, unless accompanied by corresponding inflation in those markets.[40]

Accordingly, it is not to be expected that misallocation of resources arising out of fiscal provisions will be eliminated by allowing exchange rates to alter. The fiscal systems themselves must be changed if the inefficiencies are to be removed. In practice this means that the rates of certain taxes will need to be more or less uniform throughout the common market, notably tax rates on return to capital that is invested by large impersonal economic units, that is, large, widely held corporations. It also implies that if border controls are to be done away with, sales tax rates must be uniform throughout the market, except perhaps with respect to sales taxation at the retail stage. Certain other taxes, particularly those on income from labor, and on real estate, can differ from country to country with less impairment of efficient allocation.

In a common market composed of low-income countries, great structural change to facilitate economic growth will appear more important than adjustment of marginal conditions to enhance allocative efficiency by a Pareto-desirable move making some persons better off without making anyone else worse off. Fiscal harmonization will take a correspondingly different form, one that induces agreement among member countries on fiscal measures to promote technical progress and the creation of human capital. Such an agreement serves to insure on the one hand that growth-promoting measures will be taken, and on the other hand that they will not be pushed beyond what the countries desire by unregulated competition among the countries.

(1) Allocative Efficiency

When a common market is formed, trade within the area is exempted from customs duties and export taxes. Imports are subject to a uniform tariff. If export taxes

40. See the comments on this point in the light of the experience of the LAFTA countries by Marion H. Gillim, in "Some Fiscal Aspects of the Latin American Free Trade Association," Shoup (Ed.), *op. cit.*, vol. 2, pp. 527–30. Professor Gillim notes that inflations and devaluations have so disturbed intra-area trade as to make tax harmonization seem of secondary importance in LAFTA.

exist, they too will almost surely be made uniform, in practice if not by agreement.[41] Also, factor mobility will be enhanced. Under these circumstances, efficiency in allocation of resources within the common market private sector and between the private and government sectors in the member countries can be increased by certain changes in the fiscal systems of those countries. Whether allocative efficiency between the common market and the outside world can also be increased seems less certain; it may be decreased. It will be convenient to consider first sales taxes, then income taxes, while abstracting from government services to business firms and to households, which will be brought into the analysis later. Fixed exchange rates will be assumed throughout this discussion.[42]

(A) SALES TAX[43]

Sales taxes are almost universally imposed on the destination basis, exports being exempt and imports being subject to an import compensating tax (see Chapter 8, Section A). Upon formation of a common market this practice will initially be continued. A desire to eliminate border controls will induce consideration of a change to the origin principle with respect to trade within the common market. The destination principle will remain in force with respect to trade between any of the common market countries and the outside world. Following Shibata,[44] we may term this mixed system one that is based on the "restricted origin principle."

This new system will not make for more efficient location of producers within that market. The destination principle assures that producers in all countries will be treated alike in their competition for the trade of consumers in any one country. Production will therefore have been located in the common market country or countries with the lowest cost ex-tax. Adoption of the origin principle for trade among the member countries will not disturb this pattern if the rates of tax are made equal. But if they are not equal, and if exchange rates are fixed, a high-cost but low-sales-tax country will be able to invade the markets of low-cost, high-sales-tax countries, under the origin principle, and high-cost production will replace at least some low-cost production.[45] In practice, however, producers in the high-tax country

41. This theorem with respect to export taxes was formulated by Marion H. Gillim; see her analysis in "The Fiscal Aspects of the Central American Common Market," in Shoup (Ed.), *op. cit.*, vol. 2, pp. 509–512. See also her analysis of export taxes in "Some Fiscal Aspects of the Latin American Free Trade Association," *ibid.*, pp. 538–41.

42. The following analysis draws heavily on Douglas Dosser, "Economic Analysis of Tax Harmonization," in Shoup (Ed.), *op. cit.*, vol. 1, pp. 41–92. See also Douglas Dosser, "Theoretical Considerations for Tax Harmonization," in *Comparison and Harmonization of Public Revenue Systems*, Congrès de Luxembourg, September, 1963 (Saarbrücken: Institut International de Finances Publiques, 1966), pp. 66–92, especially pp. 85–92.

43. See Clara K. Sullivan, "Indirect Taxation and the Goals of the European Economic Community," *ibid.*, vol. 2, *passim*.

44. Shibata, "The Theory of Economic Unions," *ibid.*, vol. 1, pp. 193–94.

45. If exchange rates are flexible and the sales tax is truly general, international trade will not be disturbed if all countries move from the destination principle to the origin principle, or vice versa, provided that the balance of trade is in equilibrium and provided that international flows of services and capital and transfer payments are either zero or balanced before and after the exchange rate is altered. For a review of the literature and a demonstration of this

will protest so vigorously that the origin principle will not be adopted unless the tax rates are made uniform. In summary, sales tax rates can remain disparate among the member countries without impairing allocative efficiency viewed narrowly as a problem in location of production, provided the destination principle is retained, but, if the restricted origin principle is adopted, this type of efficiency will be impaired unless the rates are made uniform.

A broader view of efficiency requires that consuming households in the several member countries be compared and that rates of transformation be compared with rates of substitution in consumption.

If consumers in, say, Germany pay a different rate of sales tax on what they consume than do consumers in, say, France, the condition for optimal exchange has been violated; the consumption patterns of German and French consumers will be such, under these differing rates of tax, that the contents of the market baskets they buy could be rearranged, without altering the contents of the aggregate of the baskets, in a manner that would make some households better off while making none worse off. Such a rearrangement through the functioning of the market is blocked by the fact that the tax rates on the two groups of households differ. Now, if tax rates differ, it is the destination principle that is at fault; the origin principle treats all common market consumers of a particular common market product alike, whatever country they live in (abstracting from transportation costs), and whatever the differences in rates from country to country. The lowest rate is the maximum that can be shifted to consumers. If all tax rates are the same, no problem arises under either principle.

Full Paretian optimality, apart from optimal effort, is optimized production, which requires that the proportional difference, if any, between the marginal rate of transformation, that is, the rate as seen by the producer, ex sales tax, and the marginal rate of substitution in consumption, be equal for any two products. This condition is violated by any sales tax that is not perfectly general and perfectly uniform. To achieve this high level of optimality, the common market countries must levy their sales taxes at a single, uniform rate. It then makes no difference, for optimality within the common market, whether the destination or origin principle is uniformly employed.

Optimality conditions as between the common market countries and the rest of the world are not going to be satisfied in any case, given the continuance of tariffs and the immobility of factors. No generalization as to choice between destination and origin principles seems possible, or as to disparities between uniform common market tax rate (if any) and rates in the rest of the world.

theorem, see Shibata, "The Theory of Economic Unions," in Shoup (Ed.), *op. cit.*, vol. 1, pp. 194–206. If the restricted origin principle is applied, deflection of import and export trade will occur that will transfer real income from the high-tax member country to the low-tax member country. For this theorem, originated by Shibata, see *ibid.*, pp. 206–24. Shibata demonstrates that this difficulty can be overcome by adoption of a common "external tax rate" for the member countries (*ibid.*, pp. 228–38).

Transport costs will normally prevent the low-tax country's producers from capturing the entire market in the high-tax country, under the origin principle. For an analysis of this and related problems, see William M. McNie, "The Origin Principle and Transport Costs," in Shoup (Ed.), *op. cit.*, vol. 1, Chapter 3.

If all countries in the world initially employ destination-principle sales taxes, and if, upon formation of the common market, the member countries change to an origin basis among themselves, after the high-rate countries have lowered their tax rates and the low-tax rate countries have raised theirs, a change in revenue flow occurs. Let H be the initially high-rate country, L the initially low-rate country, and W the rest of the world, outside the H–L common market. Country H now gets some tax revenue from L's consumers (but none from W's) and less from its own consumers, and probably less altogether, because it has lowered its tax rate. Country L gets some revenue from H's consumers (but none from W's) and less from its own consumers, but probably more altogether, because it has raised its tax rate. Country W continues to obtain tax revenue only from its own consumers. These revenue changes must give rise to changes in government expenditures or rates of other taxes, changes that have welfare effects. But no a priori statement can be made as to the direction of change for either H or L. Indeed, it is not even certain that country L, which raises its rate, will get more revenue. On this point, let us consider an extreme case of triangular trade, where W exports only to H, H exports only to L, and L exports only to W. With adoption of the origin principle for, and only for, intra-market trade, H's import tax base is unchanged and it gets an entirely new export tax base, while L is not allowed to tax any of its imports or any of its exports.

The import content of exports necessitates drawbacks in a free trade area if free internal trade is to be achieved, since the duties to be recouped will differ from country to country. Even so, drawbacks may cause misallocation of resources, once the intra-area tariffs have been repealed. A high-cost member country processor of materials from the rest of the world can undersell a low-cost member country in the latter's own market, if the latter country's tariff on those materials is high enough; and the latter country's processors, in turn, can undersell those of the former country everywhere else in the free trade area.[46] The problem, which is linked with that of anti-trade-deflection measures, is in practice most likely to arise with "area" manufactures that contain materials not available in the area and that are imported in intra-area trade tariff-free. In a common market, on the other hand, drawbacks are not needed; any import will have paid the same duty, whatever the importing country. Absence of a drawback, though it affects inter-country distribution of tax revenues, does not affect the competitive position of firms in the several countries of the common market.[47]

If customs duties (not compensating import taxes) on imports from the now member countries were, for any one country, an important source of revenue before they were repealed by the common market or free trade area agreement, and if that country seeks replacement revenue from sales taxation on a destination basis,

46. This theorem was developed by Marion H. Gillim, in "Some Fiscal Aspects of the Latin American Free Trade Association," in Shoup (Ed.), op. cit., vol. 2, pp. 542–45. If member-country A's processors sell in A, they receive no drawback of A's tariff levied on the materials they use, imported from outside the free-trade area. If instead they export, even if only to another member country, they do receive a drawback.

47. See Marion H. Gillim, "The Fiscal Aspects of the Central American Common Market," ibid., pp. 512–13.

producers in the other member countries may find that the value to them of the elimination of tariffs by that country is substantially reduced by the higher prices they must charge there under that country's new sales taxes, even though they compete on even terms with that country's producers.[48]

(B) INCOME TAXES

Income taxes in a common market composed of advanced industrialized economies will already have been made more or less uniform in their impact upon all capital originating in a given country wherever it may flow, or alternatively upon all capital employed in a given country, wherever it may have come from. This kind of coordination will have been reached by the unilateral tax credits and bilateral tax treaties discussed in Sections 1 and 2 above. Any further coordination made necessary, or feasible, by formation of a common market among such countries will be evoked by the greater mobility of capital and capitalists among the member countries, and, to a lesser degree, the greater mobility of labor. The discussion of allocative efficiency given in Section 1 above on tax credits is applicable here and need not be repeated, except to note that the possibility of migration of capitalists themselves is not so remote in a common market as was assumed in Section 1 above.

Thus if Country B in a two-country common market imposes a corporate profits tax and personal income tax on dividends that add up to much less than the corresponding taxes in A, at least a few capitalists in A will move to B, to invest in B. If this migration, made feasible by the atmosphere of the common market, is intensive, it may drive pre-tax returns on investment in B below the pre-tax returns on investment in A, if indeed the pre-tax returns were not already lower in B than in A. Formation of the common market could then be charged with creating inefficiency in allocation of resources.

The importance of uniform taxation of corporate profits among members of an industrialized common market is the greater, the more heterogeneous has been the coordination through tax credits and tax treaties prior to formation of the common market.[49]

Income taxes in a common market composed of undeveloped countries that are eager to attract foreign capital need to be regulated by some understanding among the member countries, lest competitive bidding for foreign capital through tax holidays, extra depreciation allowances, and the like lead to a lower level of income taxation than any one of the countries desires. The common market treaty can provide such an agreement.[50] In this respect it may improve allocation of resources between private and government sectors by preventing distortion through competitive bidding in an imperfect market.

Although income taxes are almost everywhere imposed on an origin basis (this does not mean "source basis"), with no exemption for exports and no compensating

48. Marion H. Gillim, in "Some Fiscal Aspects of the Latin American Free Trade Association," *ibid.*, p. 545. .

49. This remark applies to the EEC.

50. As in the Central American Common Market. See note 58 below.

tax on imports, the reverse procedure needs to be specifically prohibited if a country with a persistently unfavorable balance of payments is not to be tempted to apply the destination principle, hoping that for a while at least it will gain a trade advantage.[51]

(C) GOVERNMENT SERVICES

Some of the free services supplied by government may reduce the cost of doing business (see Chapter 5 above). The product can be sold more cheaply, either at home or abroad. The free service is distributed on the origin basis not on the destination basis. An amount of sales taxation equal to the cost of such service must be levied on the origin basis if optimal allocation is to be achieved. Otherwise, foreign purchasers of the product will be subsidized by domestic consumers of imports, who make up, under the destination principle, for the revenue loss incurred on exports. What is significant now, for optimal allocation of resources among countries, is the net fiscal burden on sales, the sales tax less the subsidy to sales inherent in the free government service to business. It is the net burden that must be put on the destination basis if production is not to be reallocated by the fiscal system to high-cost areas. The rate of tax in a country that supplies free service to business must be higher than, not uniform with, the rate of tax in a country that does not supply such services, if production is to be allocated optimally.[52]

If government services to firms and households are considered apart from the taxes levied to finance them, the allocational effects may be analyzed along much the same lines as are those of taxes in Sections (A) and (B) above,[53] though with less precision because the quantitative aspects of the impact of the free services, to say nothing of the "shifting" possibilities, cannot be formulated so precisely (see Chapter 4, Section E).

Cash subsidies may be treated as negative taxes in their income effect, and to that extent the tax analysis of Sections (A) and (B) may be used, in reverse, but it appears

51. Uruguay exempts the estimated net income from exports but apparently does not impose a compensating "income" tax on imports (Gillim, "Some Fiscal Aspects of the Latin American Free Trade Association," *ibid.*, p. 548). This exemption favors capital-intensive industries. For the contrasting case of Colombia, see *ibid.*, p. 549. Signatories of the GATT (General Agreement on Tariffs and Trade) are prohibited from placing their direct taxes on the destination basis. France, Germany and Japan have on occasion granted profits tax relief on, or proportionate to, exports or increases in exports. See E. Gordon Keith, ed., *Foreign Tax Policies and Economic Growth* (New York: Columbia University Press, 1966), papers by: Ryutaro Komiyo, "Japan," p. 65; Pierre Tabatoni, "France," pp. 296, 316; Karl Häuser, "West Germany," pp. 121–124. Apparently no country has gone so far as to impose a compensating profits tax on the profit element in imported goods.

52. And if the balance of payments is to be in equilibrium. For details on this theorem, together with proof that this sales tax–business service combination is equivalent to an income tax on a source basis, see the original formulation by Hans Möller, "Ursprungs- und Bestimmungslandprinzip," *Finanzarchiv* (June, 1968), 27: 385–458; Maria-Dolores Schulte, "The Economic Theory of the Destination Principle and the Origin Principle," and Carl S. Shoup, "The Theory of Harmonization of Fiscal Systems," in *Comparison and Harmonization of Public Revenue Systems*, Congrès de Luxembourg (Saarbrücken: Institut International de Finances Publiques, 1966), pp. 217–48 and 23–42. See also Andel, *op. cit.*, pp. 346–51.

53. Such an analysis is carried through by Norbert Andel, *op. cit.*, sec. 2, pp. 317–34.

better not to regard pure subsidies as negative taxes generally, for reasons given in Chapter 6 above. In any event, most of the issues treated under taxation and harmonization do not arise under subsidies, since there are no general subsidies in the sense that there are general sales or income taxes. And just as excise taxes are not promising candidates for harmonization, especially those on liquor and tobacco, subsidies to particular industries, including agriculture, may be expected to continue in the several countries of a common market.

Harmonization of welfare payments becomes important only as the common market succeeds in enhancing mobility of labor and results in enhancing the mobility of relief recipients. The contributory welfare payments, along with their taxes, notably old-age pension payments and unemployment compensation that are financed in part by taxes on payrolls or on number of workers, can differ widely within the common market without inducing factor flow, insofar as the higher the pension or payment the lower is the take-home pay of the worker. Great differences in outright relief payments financed from general revenues, on the other hand, might induce substantial flows, not of factors, but of nonproducers, to the country with the highest benefit payments. But language differences, residence requirements in the relief-payments law, and other circumstances will no doubt restrain this flow unless the disparities in payment are very large.

The mobility of labor that the common market is expected to foster can be hindered if social security taxes paid in one country are not carried over into benefits paid in another country to which the worker, aged person, etc., has moved.[54]

(2) Growth[55]

Undeveloped countries that combine into a common market will normally discover that economic growth is already being fostered by a number of fiscal measures, but that the pattern of such measures differs widely among the countries. This heterogeneity will persist while commitments are being honored, but as they expire the opportunity arises for uniformity. As noted on page 647 above, without some sort of uniformity, competition for industry may drive tax rates down and tax exemptions up beyond what any country desires. The competition will be exceptionally severe now that the common market has eliminated tariffs among member countries, so that each country can promise a wider market to foreign capital than before. The agreement reached by the common market countries need not provide absolute uniformity; some of the less developed members may be permitted to offer greater fiscal incentives than the others.[56] But the rules of the game will be clearly defined.

The fiscal incentives are usually reserved for manufacturing concerns, and occa-

54. For a discussion of these and other aspects of welfare payments, see Norbert Andel, "Problems of Harmonization of Social Security Policies in a Common Market," in Shoup (Ed.), *op. cit.*, vol. 1, Chapter 5.

55. This section draws heavily on Marion H. Gillim, "The Fiscal Aspects of the Central American Common Market," and "Some Fiscal Aspects of the Latin American Free Trade Association," in Shoup (Ed.), *op. cit.*, vol. 2, Chapters 13 and 14.

56. E.g., Honduras and Nicaragua in Central America (*ibid.*, p. 499).

sionally are given to specified extractive, timber, fishing, agricultural and service industries, and low-cost housing.[57] Only those manufacturing concerns that are deemed to meet certain general tests may be granted the incentives, and the formation of a common market affords an opportunity to formulate these tests for market-wide application.[58]

Further fiscal advantages may be granted to one-firm industries that are promoted by the common market agreement in order to obtain production on a large enough firm scale to reach low-cost output when the entire market is small.[59]

Market-wide uniformity in granting fiscal incentives puts pressure on the member countries to make their fiscal systems uniform. An income tax incentive will bring business into a country with an income tax but no sales tax, but not into a country with a sales tax but no income tax. To be sure, a sales tax incentive redresses the balance. But in an attempt to make the most of the uniform incentives, especially if each incentive is in some way limited, the countries will probably tend toward a uniform fiscal system.

The incentive techniques employed are common to virtually all countries and need not be listed here. Undeveloped countries differ, however, from developed countries on this score in two respects.[60] First, if the fiscal concession is a reduction or exemption from customs duties, the undeveloped country commonly sustains thereby a significant loss of tax revenue. Second, exemption from export taxes can occur in practice only in the undeveloped countries.[61]

(3) Full Employment and Price Stability[62]

Since an economic union may be presumed to increase the member countries' marginal propensities to import, at least from each other, any stimulative or depressive fiscal or monetary measure taken by any one member country to reduce unemployment or to check a boom within its own borders will thereby be less effective domestically than before the union, since more of that measure's effects will be absorbed by leakage into imports. However, the multiplier effect of any

57. As in Central America. See Gillim, *op. cit.*, p. 488.

58. Thus, in the CACM, "To qualify, manufacturing enterprises must have plants meeting one of the following ends: (1) use modern methods of manufacture, (2) yield a product essential to the production of other products or one needed by consumers, (3) produce a substitute for imports, or (4) increase exports. A plant's contribution to economic development will be judged further by its addition to total product and by its use of Central American materials, resources, and labor" (*ibid.*, pp. 489–90). Another test is that the enterprise be sufficiently labor intensive: "using efficient industrial processes, [and expending] . . . in direct labor costs a sum representing a high proportion of the total cost of production." Professor Gillim calls attention to the often conflicting ends exemplified by this requirement (*ibid.*, p. 492).

59. See Gillim, *op. cit.*, pp. 496–98, on the Regime for Central American Integration Industries.

60. See Gillim, *op. cit.*, pp. 506–512.

61. For the possible effect of economic union upon relative growth rates of member countries, see G. K. Shaw, "European Economic Integration and Stabilization Policy," in Shoup (Ed.), *op. cit.*, vol. 2, pp. 367–79.

62. This section follows G. K. Shaw, *loc. cit.*, pp. 344–439.

disturbance originating domestically will be correspondingly smaller. The medicine is weaker, but so is the infection. But if the disturbance originates in another member country, more of it will be transmitted to the country in question, now that the economic union has increased the marginal propensities to import. And that country's power to check the multiplier effects of the disturbance will, as just noted, have been weakened by that higher marginal propensity.

This destabilizing effect, on any one member country considered separately, of the higher marginal propensity to import that results from an economic union has been termed by Shaw the "integration effect." If one of the member countries is much smaller than another, a disturbance in the latter can have severe effects on the smaller economy, now that it will be exporting more of its disturbance. In general, however, Shaw concludes that the integration effect is probably relatively minor.[63]

Moreover, for the economic union as a whole, integration will tend to increase stability in the face of disturbances originating in the rest of the world, since the marginal propensity to import from the outside world on the part of the member countries as a group will be reduced by integration. When still other aspects of integration are taken into account, the general conclusion reached by Shaw is that integration will enhance the "over-all degree of stability within the community."[64]

But there remains the question whether changes in taxation that have been made in the name of harmonization, chiefly under the allocative efficiency criterion, will strengthen or weaken the ability of fiscal measures to counteract the effects of a disturbance, reduced though those effects may be.

The general answer seems to be that a member country's ability to use its tax system for counter-cycle purposes will have been somewhat weakened, but not by enough to cause much concern. General sales taxes on an origin basis will presumably be levied at a uniform rate throughout the common market, and hence will not be available as a counter-cycle instrument, by way of a rate change, for any one country. This could prove a serious handicap, especially if changes in income tax rates turn out not to be very effective over short periods.[65]

APPENDIX TO CHAPTER TWENTY-FIVE

The formulae suggested by Henry J. Frank ("Measuring State Tax Burdens," *National Tax Journal* [June, 1959], 12: 179–185) and Richard Bird ("A Note on 'Tax Sacrifice' Comparisons," *ibid.* [September, 1964], 17: 303–308) to meet objections raised to the use of a simple ratio of tax revenue to national (or local) income are in effect progressive tax schedules, but ones which for extreme values of income give

63. *Ibid.*, p. 379.
64. *Ibid.*, p. 393.
65. See Chapter 22 above, page 544. Shaw concludes that the limitations on fiscal and monetary policy combined, for any one country, that are imposed by the institutional features of a common market are important enough to warrant "the greatest possible stress upon -measures to improve the degree of automatic stabilization" (*ibid.*, p. 427).

unacceptable results. They have the merit, however, of simplicity, and may prove acceptable within a moderate range of ratios of tax to income.

If Y is aggregate income of the community, T the tax bill, and P the population, the Frank formula for ranking communities by tax sacrifice is $(T/Y)/(Y/P) = TP/Y^2$, and the Bird formula is $[T/(Y-T)]/(Y/P) = TP/(Y^2 - TY)$. If P is taken as 1, the formulae become, for a single individual, T/Y^2 and $T/(Y^2 - TY)$, respectively. If two individuals, 1 and 2, are compared, one of them having an income k times that of the other, tax sacrifice is equal (Frank) when $T_1/Y_1^2 = T_2/(kY_1)^2$, i.e., when $T_2 = k^2 T_1$. If k exceeds Y_1/T_1, then T_2, by this formula, exceeds Y_2. Under the Bird formula, tax sacrifice is equal when $T_1/(Y_1^2 - T_1 Y_1) = T_2/(k^2 Y_1^2 - kT_1 Y_1)$, i.e., when

$$T_2 = (k^2 T_1 Y_1 - kT_1^2)/(Y_1 - T_1) = [k(kY_1 - T_1)/(Y_1 - T_1)]T_1.$$

If k exceeds $Y_1/T_1 + T_1/Y_1 - 1$, then T_2, for equal sacrifice under the Bird formula, must exceed Y_2. For example, if $Y_1 = 5$, $T_1 = 1$, and if k equals $5 + \frac{1}{5} - 1 = 4.2$, so that $Y_2 = 21$, the value of T_2 that gives equal sacrifice (Bird) is itself 21, whereas if k is, say, 4.3, so that $Y_2 = 21.5$, the equal sacrifice formula calls for T_2 to be 22.037. Since $Y_1/T_1 > Y_1/T_1 + T_1/Y_1 - 1$, when $T_1 < Y_1$, the k value at which $T_2 = Y_2$ is slightly smaller under the Bird formula than under the Frank formula.

Index